THE
NEW
REGIME

ALSO BY ISSER WOLOCH

Jacobin Legacy: The Democratic Movement Under the Directory (1970)

(editor) *The Peasantry in the Old Regime: Conditions and Protests*
(1970)

The French Veteran from the Revolution to the Restoration (1979)

Eighteenth-Century Europe: Tradition and Progress, 1715–1789
(1982)

THE
NEW
REGIME

TRANSFORMATIONS OF THE FRENCH
CIVIC ORDER, 1789–1820S

ISSER WOLOCH

W.W. NORTON & COMPANY · NEW YORK · LONDON

The text of this book is composed in 11/13.5 Garamond 156 with
the display set in Trajan
Composition and manufacturing by the Haddon Craftsmen, Inc.
Book design by Chris Welch

Library of Congress Cataloging-in-Publication Data
Woloch, Isser, 1937–
The new regime : transformations of the French civic order,
1789–1820s / Isser Woloch.
p.   cm.
Includes bibliographical references and index.
1. France—Politics and government—Revolution,
1789–1799—Influence.   2. Social change—Political aspects.
3. France—Politics and government—19th century.   I. Title.
DC155.W65   1994
944.04—dc20   93-1917

ISBN 0-393-03591-3

W. W. Norton & Company, Inc.
500 Fifth Avenue, New York, N.Y. 10110

W. W. Norton & Company Ltd.
10 Coptic Street, London WC1A 1PU

1 2 3 4 5 6 7 8 9 0

To
Jean-Paul and Michelle

CONTENTS

LIST OF TABLES, MAPS, AND ILLUSTRATIONS

TABLES

MAPS AND ILLUSTRATIONS

PREFACE

By 1792, French revolutionaries had coined the term *ancien régime* ("old regime") to signify their belief that they had broken with a discredited past. The neologism stigmatized an amalgam of "feudalism," absolutism, and other oppressive realities of the seventeenth and eighteenth centuries: the absence of a constitution, land encumbered by seigneurial claims and exactions, venality of office, hereditary social privilege, provincial particularism, censorship, and religious fanaticism. Yet the most influential book ever to use that term in its title, Alexis de Tocqueville's *The Old Regime and the French Revolution,* implicitly warned that it could be a trap, since it masked the larger continuities in French history that revolutionary enthusiasm ignored. Tocqueville developed a long-durational perspective by positing the gradual movement of French society toward an increasing "equality of condition" long before the Revolution. Most important, he emphasized the growth of a powerful centralized state—a development advanced prodigiously by Louis XIV, embraced with zeal by the Committee of Public Safety, and consummated by Napoleon, always at the expense of public liberty. [1]

To virtually all students of French history Tocqueville's cautionary argument is by now second nature. No one sees the Revolution as marking a comprehensive discontinuity in the fabric of French history. We also recognize that the Revolution was not over when it ostensibly ended with Napoleon's seizure of power. Recent historians have made the case both indirectly and explicitly that the French people did not accept the Revolution as a kind of consensual basis for their nation, a fait accompli, until the Third Republic. [2] But arguments about continuity across the divide of 1789 or about the incompleteness of the French Revolution scarcely negate the notion of an old regime or of its corollary, the creation of a new regime after 1789.

Tocqueville does not help us very much here, since his classic volume has little to say about the Revolution. His novel archival research and his remarkable analytic insights focused almost exclusively on the two hundred years before 1789, despite his larger theme. Moreover the great historical sociologist never got around to writing the intended sequel about the French Revolution and post-revolutionary France, although fragmentary sketches can fuel speculation on how he might have proceeded. To this reader, in any case, Tocqueville's book about the old regime has long stimulated one unintended response: the tantalizing prospect of writing a volume on "The New Regime." True, this term had little currency during the 1790s, since successive cohorts of revolutionaries referred to their enterprise simply as "the Revolution," or later "the Republic," while governments starting with Napoleon's Consulate tried to distance themselves from the Revolution. Still, the revolutionaries had not simply conjured up an old regime to serve their ideological convenience, but had consciously set out to construct a new one. In a manner of speaking, then, my project began as a title in search of a book.

What should such a project entail? What would be the most rewarding thematic paths and the most appropriate chronological boundaries for a study of the new regime? In both respects, a general history or narrative of the French Revolution is obviously ruled out. Clearly the chronological range must go past the revolutionary decade, and the thematic focus must move beyond the realm of political movements or the clash of Revolution and Counter-Revolution.[3] But neither would this be a history of French society. Social stratification, property and income distribution, family structure, and the like would constitute a very different kind of project. To describe the cluster of issues that I set out to study, I fashioned a term of my own, "the civic order." It is meant to encompass the values, policies, and institutions at the juncture of state and civil society—the framework, in other words, for the collective public life of the French people. It would be a gross exaggeration to say that 1789 produced a blank slate for creating an entirely new civic order, but never before in French history had there been such latitude or opportunity for change. No amount of revisionism can drain from this historical moment that sense of possibility and the ensuing need at all levels of society to make choices or to respond to choices made by others. This, then, is the central question of the book: How did the French civic order change after 1789? What civic values animated the new regime, what policies did it adopt, what institutions did it establish, and how did they fare when carried into practice? Finally, since this is as much a matter of process as results, what alternatives in various domains were discarded or foreclosed along the way?

At an early stage I visualized the civic order in an almost physical sense, as embodied by buildings in the urban landscape, whose influence extended, unevenly and ever more faintly, into the countryside. Imagine, for example, approaching a typical French town in 1798 or 1808—the capital of one of the eighty-odd departments that the National Assembly created by redividing the nation's territory. The spires of a cathedral or the largest parish churches would still command the horizon. But as one moved about the town one could readily identify its civic institutions: the departmental administration (later the prefecture); the town hall or *mairie;* the local schools; several new courts or tribunals; the institutions of poor relief such as an *hôpital* or workhouse; a *dépôt* for mustering conscripts. Of course most such functions and institutions existed before 1789. But even where the new regime did not create entirely new civic institutions (and it did create several), it repeatedly refashioned all of them. The palpable image of a civic order in a departmental capital assuredly helped launch my research. Gradually, however, I found myself pushing beyond the towns into the bourgs and villages of the countryside where the civic order had at first seemed much less tangible or visible. The great preoccupation of the new regime, it turned out, was to penetrate the countryside and implant a new civic order in the villages. The center of gravity in my work eventually shifted to the countryside.

Chronology posed another challenge or opportunity. On one level, the new regime quickly gave way to a succession of others. While French society remained relatively stable after the initial revolutionary displacements and upheavals, the French polity lurched from one form of government to another with dismaying frequency: the constitutional monarchy of 1789–92; the Jacobin dictatorship of 1793–94; the thermidorian reaction; the Directory; the Consulate; the Empire; the Bourbon Restoration and onward. Yet beneath these roiled political waters, a new matrix of civic practices and institutions endured to one degree or another. In that sense the new regime was not coterminous with any phase of the Revolution but survived through all its phases and thereafter as a foundation for French public life. At the least, then, one must study the new regime through the Napoleonic experience, which rejected, modified, preserved, or expanded various elements of the Revolution's legacy. But for that very same reason one should not simply cut off the analysis at 1814. The perspective afforded by the Restoration, which in turn sifted what it inherited, allows us to appreciate retrospectively the significance of certain issues, and underscores the continuities beneath the changing political scene. By the same token, however, the succession of governments naturally affected civic policies, institutions, and popular responses. My analysis therefore rests on an implicit dialogue over the question: After 1789, one regime or many? To evoke this dialogue most succinctly, I could have used the distasteful if not appalling locution: the new regime(s). Instead, I feel free to speak of the new regime or the new regimes as the occasion warrants, with confidence that readers will not be disconcerted.

I BEGIN WITH three chapters that set the stage. An introductory chapter sketches the successive transformations of authority in lawmaking and local administration introduced from above after 1789. During the Revolution, however, government involved politics as well as administration. Chapters II and III address the question of political participation, with particular emphasis on the electoral process, a theme which obviously winds down precipitously after 1799. I then move on to less familiar territory and to the heart of the book. Chapters IV and V examine how the state attempted to gain control over the villages, integrate them into a larger national community, and establish a new civic order in rural France: How were villages to be organized and governed? What control did the state exercise over local revenue and expenditure? What new norms did the state establish in functions that it deemed crucial, such as rural policing and the maintenance of local roads, and how realistic were those norms? Two pairs of chapters then address more prominent elements of the civic order: elementary schooling (where the contested influence of Catholicism is considered at length), and poor relief (where the alternatives of public assistance and charity take center stage). The new regime attached great importance to accessible, expedited justice, and Chapters X–XII shift attention to its judicial institutions: new types of magistrates and civil courts; the problematic roles, indeed the very existence, of the legal professions; and in the domain of criminal justice, the great novelty for France of trial by jury. One could go on to other dimensions of the civic order, which for practical reasons, including the endurance of author and reader, I have passed over: Church-State relations, for example; state intervention in relations between labor and capital after the abolition of guilds; or secondary education. But there is one feature of the new civic order that could not possibly be omitted since it ultimately loomed above all others. The final chapter concerns the imposition of military conscription.

With the exception of the first three chapters, the book is based largely on archival sources. Many of these documents are of a particular kind that warrants comment, and not only for specialists and scholars who always need to know about such things. The scope of this study ruled out a resort to the dispersed and voluminous riches of local archives. Instead, I have turned to advantage one characteristic of the French state, old and new—its insatiable thirst for information from the provinces. As I see it, the Archives Nationales in Paris is like the receptacle of a gigantic vacuum cleaner with hoses extended all over France. Vast amounts of material poured into Paris from the departments, which in turn subsumed a huge if chaotic flow of information from towns and villages. Better yet, officials sorted most of this material along thematic as well as geographic lines when it reached the capital. Occasionally the processing in Paris went even further, in which case the scholar today owes a debt to the bureau heads and clerks who prepared queries to their superiors, collated information, and generated endless reports. Likewise he or she is indebted to the ministers themselves when they launched systematic inquests among officials in the departments. Reading in sequence the periodic reports from the Directory's commissioners, Napoleonic prefects, and Restoration prefects from departments all across France on a host of subjects related to the civic order proved to be a particularly high-yield experience. These reports sometimes lapse into formulaic generalities or evasions but just as often offer pointed comments and shrewd observations.

There are of course limitations and even dangers in relying on such sources. Sitting at the center of this spider's web one can be misled by the official mind that is represented in most, though by no means all, of this mass of correspondence, local reports, *comptes-rendus,* circulars, internal government memos, and petitions. Nonetheless the rewards can be handsome, for the images and emphases that emerge from the wide sweep of such documents (for example, an unexpected governmental obsession with the prosaic matter of local roads) could easily be lost in a study from the bottom up of one or even several localities. At the least one avoids the classic dilemma of any local case study, which is how to estimate its typicality or significance. Here the limitation is the opposite one: the impossibility of knowing exactly how various issues worked themselves out in a particular place, with the reassuring depth of detail and nuance that can only come from local study.

At bottom we face the issue of unity and diversity in French history as posed by Fernand Braudel:

> Historians have to be able to see both perspectives simultaneously, and must therefore be wary of one-sided views. . . . Jean-Paul Sartre remarked once in passing that France was "non-unifiable," which is at once true and plainly wrong. France may have found it difficult to be *one,* but could not, and never has been able to resign itself to being *several.* . . . I myself began this book [*The Identity of France,* 1986] by describing the France whose "name is diversity," and did so, I confess, with great pleasure. . . . But it is time to move from the plural to the singular, to cross the divide in search of France one and indivisible, and to seek that unity, if possible, in the realities and forces that lie deepest.[4]

The kinds of sources I have used would seem to favor the theme of unity at the expense of diversity, but that is not entirely the case. While a series of local monographs would no doubt do greatest justice to France's diversity, the view from the center, if it is critical and based on a wide range of evidence, amply evokes that remarkable, refractory diversity and the endless variety in grass-roots responses to impulsions from the center.

THE
NEW
REGIME

I

LAWMAKING AND LOCAL AUTHORITY

S overeignty in France passed from the king to the nation in 1789, and
from that revolutionary premise there could ultimately be no turning
back. In practice, of course, this settled very little. To look only at
constitutions: no country in the Western world has seen a longer parade of
charters than France—some fifteen between 1791 and 1959, by a conservative count. For decades the divisive mobilizations and legacies of the French
Revolution fed this instability. The political and social conflicts unleashed in
1789 had perforce to express themselves in institutions insufficiently tempered to contain them. But this notorious picture of French political instability can be misleading. Beneath the succession of revolutions, counter-revolu-
tions, and coups, the French people inhabited a new civic landscape after
1789. Even if its details changed repeatedly in subsequent years, and even if
some features disappeared quickly, its foundations endured.

The revolutionary civic order rested on a new framework of authority,
two of whose dimensions we examine in this introductory chapter: the new
locus of power established at the top, and the system of local government
in the provinces. Though extremely malleable, these structures provided a
thread of continuity in the fabric of modern French history marking it off
from the old regime. Indeed, the installation of so many regimes after 1789
was facilitated by the existence of these new building blocks, which successive claimants could appropriate on their own terms. This chapter will give

equal attention to the basic elements of the new civic framework and to important modifications between 1789 and the 1820s.

FOUNDING ACTS

Whatever its antecedents, the French Revolution effectively began when the deputies of the Third Estate unilaterally transformed the Estates General into a "National Assembly" on 17 June, 1789, after vainly inviting deputies of the other two estates to join them. True, sustained attacks on absolutism had begun during the fiscal crisis of 1787, and denunciations of privilege had erupted in late 1788 after the crown agreed to convene the Estates General but had left hanging the question of a vote by order or by head. The outpouring of grievances and aspirations during this "pre-revolution," however, did not burst the bounds of traditional authority. Few of the *cahiers* drafted at the king's invitation all over France, and few of the thousands of pamphlets published in those months, had argued for so drastic a rupture with the past.[1] But when the frustrated deputies proclaimed the existence of the National Assembly in June, France truly embarked on a revolutionary course. In their juridical revolution-from-above, the deputies replaced the myth of divine right monarchy with the more complex fiction of popular sovereignty, and immediately appropriated that sovereignty by vesting it in themselves as the legitimate representatives of the people. Moreover, within weeks they further declared themselves to be a "Constituent Assembly" with the power to draft and promulgate France's first written constitution, wresting that prerogative from an astonished monarchy.

This deft operation was scarcely unprecedented, except perhaps in its thoroughness and startling rapidity. The historian Edmund Morgan has analyzed the same process as it unfolded long before in England. In its various struggles with the crown, he suggests, Parliament invoked the residual authority of the people over their government as a mandate to sustain its own power and prerogatives. At the heart of the fiction of popular sovereignty, Morgan observes, lies the enigma of representation in which the whole parliament or legislature looms much larger than the sum of its parts. For what majesty would a legislature have if it was merely a congeries of deputies voicing the narrow interests and desires of their own particular constituents? By what alchemy could the veritable national interest be discerned and sustained—a national interest which kings had formerly claimed both to represent and promote?

From the modest, plausible fiction that a deputy can stand in for a whole community and in turn bind that community by his actions, British statesmen such as Edward Coke and Edmund Burke extrapolated the more demanding fiction that such deputies actually represented the people of the entire nation. Effectively wielding the power to govern the country, the locally chosen representatives claimed that their powers derived from the sovereign people as a whole. As Morgan puts it, the people thus existed as a sovereign force "only in the actions of the Parliament or legislature that claimed to act for them. . . . In the name of *the* people they became all-powerful in government, shedding as much as possible the local, subject character that made them representatives of a particular set of people."[2] This was precisely the revolutionary stance of the French National Assembly in the summer of 1789.

Ironically, the National Assembly owed its ostensibly representative character to the monarchy, which had established the procedures used in 1789 for the selection of deputies to the Estates General. Royal guidelines employed a novel standard of demographic proportionality in determining the number of Third Estate deputies from each electoral district *(bailliage)*, and authorized a primary franchise that, with a few exceptions like Paris, encompassed almost all domiciled adult males inscribed on the tax rolls for even the most negligible amount. At the same time, new voting procedures for the First Estate favored parish priests at the expense of the Church prelates who had traditionally dominated the clergy's affairs. In short, after adamantly resisting the notion of convening the Estates General at all after an hiatus of 175 years, the crown in its hour of extremity unwittingly launched French public life in a democratic direction.[3]

Having transformed themselves into a National Assembly, the representatives at Versailles pondered the "imperative mandates" that ostensibly bound many of them as deputies to the Estates General, and eventually voted to nullify them. After all, each deputy now represented not simply his own *bailliage* but the entire nation. The parochial demands and remonstrances to the king that they carried from their districts were no longer valid, since each deputy must have no concern but the well-being of all the French people. Deputies must henceforth be unencumbered: instructions by the voters who chose them, or the right of retrospective censure or referendum by those voters, had no place in this system. The deputies were the only persons directly involved in the free interchange of the deliberative process through which policies in the national interest could be forged. Thanks especially to the timely theoretical improvisations of Sieyès, the *constituants* thus managed to embrace the Rousseauist spirit of popular sovereignty while liberating themselves from Rousseau's paralyzing strictures against representative institutions. With the concept of popular sovereignty filtered through this rigorous notion of representation, the Assembly firmly established the Revolution's locus of power at the top right from the start.[4]

Yet this appropriation of sovereignty would not have succeeded but for popular mobilization against a monarchy intent on extinguishing the pretensions of the National Assembly. The king had conceded only tactically at the end of June and immediately began deploying military units in the Paris region to restore his authority. On July 14 the Assembly's triumph became irreversible, however, when Paris rose against this impending threat of royal force. While prominent citizens in the capital's sixty electoral districts formed a revolutionary municipality, crowds of armed Parisians successfully besieged royal strongpoints at the Invalides (without bloodshed) and at the Bastille (with fierce fighting and loss of life).

The people of Paris thus claimed a decisive influence on the Revolution from its inception, and the Assembly implicitly acknowledged this when it adopted a tricolor flag for France, melding the traditional white of the Bourbons to the red and blue standard of Paris. Nor was popular mobilization against royal absolutism limited to the capital. During the summer of 1789 municipal revolutions erupted in twenty-six of France's thirty largest cities, as local elites displaced or absorbed royally sanctioned officials with new municipal committees.[5] Meanwhile peasant uprisings against seigneurial châteaux and other targets overwhelmed the monarchy's ability to maintain law and order in the countryside. Faced with such pressures from below, the fledgling Assembly was forced to act rapidly: should it prudently endorse royal repression to restore order, or should it take initiatives to rally the people and strike further at the old order?

The answer came with the celebrated August 4 decree. To appease peasant opinion, the decree boldly proclaimed that "The National Assembly completely abolishes the feudal system." The deputies later backpedaled by preserving most seigneurial dues, subject to an exorbitant form of redemption by peasants. These dues remained legally binding until peasant resistance forced their suppression without compensation in 1792–93. But the August 4 decree categorically condemned such forms of seigneurial power as serfdom, personal servitudes, hunting rights, and seigneurial justice, along with the church tithe, venality of office, fiscal privilege, and regional and corporate privileges. While the Assembly later dissected seigneurialism into legitimate property rights and illegitimate social usurpations, its August 4 decree unequivocally attacked the tissue of formal privileges on which the old regime had been built.[6]

The Declaration of the Rights of Man and Citizen (August 26) then announced the principles of the new regime. This historic proclamation simultaneously affirmed individual liberties and set forth the obligations of citizenship. Although the Assembly rejected the proposal for an accompanying Declaration of Duties, its Declaration of Rights effectively internalized the concept of duty. Rights and duties converged around the concept of obedience to legitimate law. Even in enumerating natural liberties such as freedom of expression or freedom of religious conscience, the text stipulated that these rights were not absolute but could be circumscribed by law. The Declaration also sketched the basic criteria for a legitimate government, which the constitution would eventually amplify: representative government, elections, the separation of powers. While entirely sincere about the fundamental claims of individual liberty, the *constituants* signaled that the writ of the law, emanating from a legitimate government, stood as their supreme civic value. A positive concept of law, they assumed, would bridge the inherent tensions between the individual and the community, between liberty and authority. Under their doctrine of representation, the legislature would of course be the arbiter of that law.[7]

Some revolutionaries of 1789 entertained the improbable hope of making a complete break with a bankrupt past, of substituting the promise of reason for the burden of history. Their repudiation of the past could sound extremely sharp, as the very neologism "old regime" implied, but it can easily be exaggerated. The need to reach an accommodation with the past imposed itself, for example, on the question of the monarchy. Where the Americans in the Constitutional Convention of 1787 had a blank slate on which to design the executive branch of their federal government—allowing them to erect a strong yet limited presidency—the French had little choice but to incorporate their king into the new regime. Almost no one considered republicanism as a practical alternative at this juncture, although some historians see the outcome as republican in everything but name.

While the Assembly utterly denied the monarchy's traditional religious or secular claims to sovereignty, however, it conferred substantial executive powers on Louis XVI nonetheless. After an impassioned debate, it is true, the Assembly rejected an absolute veto for the king (along with an upper legislative house of peers), but it agreed to a suspensive veto by which the king could effectively block legislation for up to four years, and granted him the power to appoint ministers of his choosing without reference to the legislature. Louis XVI may have emerged from this humiliating desanctification as a "citizen-king" deriving his authority from the nation and its constitution, but he was scarcely being marginalized.[8] Hoping to win over the king, the Assembly did little to undermine the reserves of symbolic and moral capital that he still enjoyed. Its sense of compromise, on the contrary, was expressed in the new regime's official slogan: "The Nation, the Law, the King."

When it came to designing the units of government from which the new polity would arise, the Assembly gave itself a freer hand. August 4 had nearly

swept the slate clean by delegitimizing France's skein of corporate, provincial, and seigneurial institutions, whether historic survivals accepted by the
crown or creations of the monarchy itself. To fill the vacuum, action had to
be taken quickly, lest revolutionary activists in the towns, where envy and
fear of Paris often ran high, build an irresistible momentum at the expense
of control from the center. The potential antidote to such centripetal tendencies lay in the new, integrative ideology of national unity and civil equality.
To institute those principles, the Assembly first had to divide the nation's
territory into viable administrative units; define the underlying cells of civic
life; and establish the rules for the elections that would animate the entire
system.

In the National Assembly's vision, local government was to be an amalgam of traditional administrative concerns and a new kind of politics or
citizen participation. The Assembly designed the hierarchy of governmental
structures to promote administrative control from the center and an unprecedented degree of uniformity in French public life, but also to create a
reciprocal relationship between citizens and government through elections
and civic education. During all the permutations between 1789 and the
1820s, however, local officials remained subordinate to national law.
Whether elected or appointed, they never constituted an independent branch
of government and never possessed even a modicum of lawmaking authority. "The electors name public officials in behalf of the nation by virtue of
the power delegated by the constitution," explained the Assembly. "At the
moment they are elected, these officials belong to the nation, are independent
of those who have chosen them, and are responsible only to the law in the
person of their superiors as established by the constitution."[9] Still, for the
constituants, local officials at all levels were supposed to be agents of their
constituents, responsive to local needs as well as the arms and ears of the
national government. But if the framework created in 1789–90 endured, the
original balance between administration and self-government through elections kept shifting, until Napoleon virtually eliminated citizen participation
altogether even if he still paid lip service to the principle, as we shall see.

THE DEPARTMENTS: BUILDING BLOCKS OF THE
NEW REGIME

With the supremacy of legislative authority firmly established at the top in
1789, where would government at other levels find its locus? No preexisting
institutions or jurisdictions were likely to serve that purpose. Compared to

the American Constitutional Convention of 1787, which had to accommodate the interests of the thirteen sovereign states, the French Constituent Assembly could freely subdivide the national territory to create a new political and administrative map. Since Turgot's tenure as comptroller-general in 1774, the monarchy had sought ways to involve large landowners in the routine responsibilities of local government and taxation, but the revolutionary schema owed relatively little to the royal reformers who promoted local consultative bodies. The Assembly's redivision of the territory emphatically lacked continuity with the past.

The "departmentalization" of France flowed from the Assembly's concept of representation. Since each deputy was supposed to represent the entire nation, the Assembly required electoral circumscriptions as free as possible from local parochialism—essentially neutral subdivisions based on equality and proportionality. Such new territorial subdivisions could also replace the inherited tangle of unequal and overlapping royal administrative circumscriptions in the provinces, thereby providing a uniform basis for local government. As Sieyès put it in September 1789: "France is and ought to be a single whole, uniformly subordinate in all its parts to a single legislation and one common [system of] administration."[10] The extreme form of the initial proposal by the Assembly's Constitutional Committee, however, touched off a fierce debate. The Sieyès-Thouret plan presented a shockingly abstract geometric formula for dividing the national territory. It proposed a gridlike pattern of eighty *départements* radiating from the capital, each roughly square in shape and equal in size, and each in turn partitioned into nine *districts* (called communes in the original proposal), with each district to be subdivided into nine *cantons*. Although departments would vary in topography and population, their uniformity of size was intended among other things to provide a common standard of access for all citizens to the departmental and district seats.

Deputies who attached greater value to the provincial traditions of France, or who opposed Jacques-Guillaume Thouret's spatially oriented abstraction, denounced this geometrical plan. "It is not the realm that I wish to have divided," declared Mirabeau, "it is the provinces." Mirabeau wished to respect the natural boundaries of the old provinces, but admitted the need to weaken any undue particularist spirit by carving 120 departments out of those provinces. That many departments would in turn obviate the need to subdivide departments into districts. Mirabeau further argued that population density rather than spatial equality was a more reasonable criterion for administrative subdivision. Others opposed Thouret's plan from their long-standing fear of domination by Paris. Only strong, well-articulated provincial assemblies could effectively stand up to the influence of Paris, they argued, whereas Thouret's plan would dissipate such countervailing influence. Thus Verdet urged that 720 *"grandes communes"* be created that would send delegates to provincial assemblies. But such proposals in the tradition of royal administrative reform did not prevail. Large provincial assemblies with their likely particularist coloration were exactly what the Constitutional Committee wished to preclude. As Thouret countered, "In their great number, their multiplicity, lies the central guarantee for the subordination of each [unit]."[11]

While certain deputies expressed hostility to any survival of provincial identity, Thouret made a tactical concession by claiming that he did not wish to obliterate historic provincial boundaries altogether. Insisting that the departments number around eighty and be roughly equal in size, he backed away from the geometrical rigidity of the original plan and agreed to take into account the traditional contours of the provinces in drawing some of these new circumscriptions. The committee would determine just how many departments a former province should have, but then the deputies from that province could fix their actual boundaries. In the end, Thouret promised due consideration of local topography by those deputies most familiar with it, and in addition agreed that each new department need not have exactly the same number of districts. If the Assembly did not entirely ignore provincial boundaries in designing France's new departments, however, in every practical respect it effaced provincial identity. Symbolically, the Assembly insisted that the names of the new departments be taken from rivers, mountains, or other physical features (such as Seine-et-Marne or Hautes-Alpes) rather than from historic regional designations such as Poitou, Limousin, Dauphiné, or Artois (see Figure I-1).[12]

As embodiments of administrative uniformity and equality, many departments lacked ecological unity of any kind. In the department of the Nord, for example, the historian Georges Lefebvre found six distinctive agrarian regions, not to mention the bifurcation of Flemish-speaking and French-speaking areas; in the Loire department, inhabitants of the lowlands and of the mountains historically regarded each other with antipathy. When armed rebellion exploded in 1793, it did not usually set department against department but tore apart certain departments along ecological as well as political fault lines. In the Sarthe, a patriot eastern region clashed with an anti-revolutionary west; in adjacent Maine-et-Loire, the valley and plains of the Val Saumurois remained in the republican camp while the *bocage* country of the Mauges spawned a militant rebellion.[13] And yet the departments—the most arbitrary and artificial creation of the National Assembly—proved to be perdurable, and survive to the present day.

After fixing the number and boundaries of the departments, the Assembly had next to designate the departmental capitals. In effect, it was more

England Channel

PAS-DE-CALAIS • Lille
Arras • NORD

SOMME
SEINE-INFÉRIEURE • Amiens
Rouen • AISNE
• Beauvais Laon • Mézières
OISE ARDENNES
MANCHE • Caen • EURE SEINE • Châlons-s.-M. • MEUSE MOSELLE
St.Lô CALVADOS Évreux Versailles • SEINE- MARNE Bar-le- • Metz
ORNE Chartres ET- PARIS MARNE Duc Nancy BAS-RHIN
FINISTÈRE St.Brieuc • Alençon OISE Melun AUBE MEURTHE
CÔTES-DU-NORD ILLE- EURE-ET- Chaumont • Strasbourg
Quimper • ET-VILAINE MAYENNE LOIR Troyes VOSGES • Épinal
Rennes Le Mans HAUTE- • Colmar
MORBIHAN Laval Orléans LOIRET Auxerre MARNE HAUT-
Vannes SARTHE Blois YONNE CÔTE-D'OR HAUTE- RHIN
LOIRE- MAINE- • Angers Tours LOIR- CHER NIÈVRE Dijon SAÔNE • Vesoul
INFÉRIEURE ET- ET-CHER Bourges Nevers • Besançon
Nantes LOIRE INDRE- DOUBS
ET-LOIRE Châteauroux • SAÔNE- JURA Lons-
VENDÉE Poitiers INDRE Moulins ET-LOIRE le-Saunier
La-Roche- DEUX- VIENNE Mâcon
sur-Yon SÈVRES • Guéret ALLIER Bourg
Niort CREUSE RHÔNE- AIN
La Rochelle Limoges PUY-DE-DÔME ET-LOIRE Lyon
CHARENTE- CHARENTE HAUTE-VIENNE Clermont-
INFÉRIEURE Angoulême Ferrand
CORRÈZE HAUTE-LOIRE ISÈRE
Périgueux • Tulle CANTAL Le Puy Grenoble
DORDOGNE Aurillac Privas Valence
Bordeaux • HAUTES-ALPES
GIRONDE LOT Mende ARDÈCHE DRÔME Gap •
LOT-ET- Cahors Rodez LOZÈRE BASSES-
GARONNE Agen AVEYRON GARD Digne • ALPES
LANDES TARN Nîmes BOUCHES-
Mont-de-Marsan Albi Montpellier DU- Aix Draguignan
GERS Toulouse • HÉRAULT RHÔNE VAR
Auch HAUTE-
BASSES- • Pau GARONNE Carcassonne
PYRÉNÉES Tarbes Foix AUDE
ARIÈGE Perpignan
HAUTES-
PYRÉNÉES PYRÉNÉES-
ORIENTALES

ATLANTIC OCEAN

Mediterranean Sea

France, Departments 1790

·········· Department boundary
• Department capital

0 40 80 120 160 200 Miles

Bastia
CORSE

FIGURE I-1: *Departmentalization*

than doubling the number of local administrative capitals from the old regime's thirty-six intendancies to eighty-three. About two hundred towns realistically entertained hopes of becoming the *chef-lieu* of a department, and for those that lost out in the competition, selection as a district capital might seem a meager second prize. More modest towns, however, fiercely coveted that honor, and roughly sixteen hundred towns vied for approximately six hundred slots. For most of those losers, designation as a cantonal seat would be scant consolation since at this juncture the canton did not figure heavily in the Assembly's civic agenda. But again, for rural bourgs or villages the prestige was not negligible and the thought that a local rival might be designated instead was hard to abide. The stakes in this process grew as the prerogatives of departmental and district capitals accumulated, since the Assembly was using the new administrative grid in its judicial and ecclesiastical reforms. After the abolition of all existing royal courts, each department was to have a new criminal tribunal (in the great majority of cases located in the *chef-lieu*), while each district capital would have a civil court and each canton a justice of the peace. Similarly, after the Assembly reduced France's 130 dioceses to 83, each departmental *chef-lieu* became the seat of a bishop. It was expected that military, educational, penal, and charitable institutions would eventually cluster in the departmental or district capitals as well.

In laying out the departments the Assembly initially ignored the claims of urban centers, but France's towns soon began a feverish scramble for the administrative and judicial spoils.[14] In the Seine-et-Marne, nine towns initially vied for the honor of becoming the departmental *chef-lieu*. Old local rivalries rekindled—between Vienne and Grenoble in the Isère, Sarlat and Périgueux in the Dordogne, Cahors and Montauban in the Lot, and Marseille and Aix in the Bouches-du-Rhône. Demographic or commercial superiority did not assure a town's designation, and about half the capitals eventually chosen for the new departments had fewer inhabitants or lesser commerce than a rival claimant. Geographic centrality, however, became an asset in lobbying for preferment.

The selection process for department and district seats was highly political, as thousands of towns and bourgs deluged the Assembly with petitions, while many sent deputations to press their case. Approximately five hundred towns went further and circulated petitions in the countryside to support their claims for designation as administrative seats. Rival towns used a variety of strategies: some argued from their historic roles; others, perhaps by default more attuned to revolutionary rhetoric, spoke of equity and their hopes for a better future. In their competition to become the capital of the Aisne department, for example, Soissons made an upbeat case for its well-established commercial connections with the countryside, while Laon looked for sympathy, successfully arguing that with few natural advantages, it desperately needed the resources that designation as the *chef-lieu* would bring.[15] The Assembly absorbed all this pressure and made its decisions, first for the departmental capitals and then for the districts, whose number was also much disputed. Mountainous departments in particular argued for more subdivisions in their rugged terrain. To accommodate the most implacable rivals, the Assembly at one point voted to permit alternation of a departmental capital between towns, but in the end it abandoned that evasive compromise.

A SURFEIT OF COMMUNES?

As the Assembly settled on the department as the largest subdivision of the nation, a parallel debate unfolded over what the lowest unit or cell of civic life should be. Some deputies proposed to recognize as autonomous entities or *communes* not only the nation's towns and bourgs but all existing rural communities as well. Others, including the Constitutional Committee, opposed this prodigality, urging instead that rural communities be grouped into a smaller number of "municipalities" or *grandes communes*. They did not see anything sacred or definitive about the existing civic fragmentation of the countryside, and regarded many rural communities as mere products of circumstances (as a Napoleonic prefect later put it) "created by feudalism, by the ecclesiastical order, or by the caprice of the inhabitants," and therefore unworthy of political autonomy.[16] The first view prevailed, however, and the Assembly officially recognized "each town, bourg, parish, or rural community" as a commune. Specifically, every village with any kind of legal personality under the old regime—whether a parish church or simply elected, coopted, or appointed officials of some sort—entered the new civic order as a commune.

True, in areas of dispersed settlement—in mountainous pasturing regions, in the *bocage* or hedgerow country of the West, and in the open cereal plains *(pays de grande culture)*—tiny hamlets never had an independent identity and did not gain one now. Rural communities in such regions often consisted of a dozen or even several dozen hamlets and isolated farmsteads—like the commune of Anthully (Saône-et-Loire), population 1,189, which comprised thirteen hamlets, or the commune of St. Laurent-en-Gâtine (Indre-et-Loire), with its population of barely 600 scattered in 34 hamlets (see Figures I-2 & 3). But in the areas of agglomerated settlement that constituted about two thirds of the realm, especially in the classic regions of smallholdings *(pays de petite culture)*, the Assembly's policy recognized a plethora of communes—"as

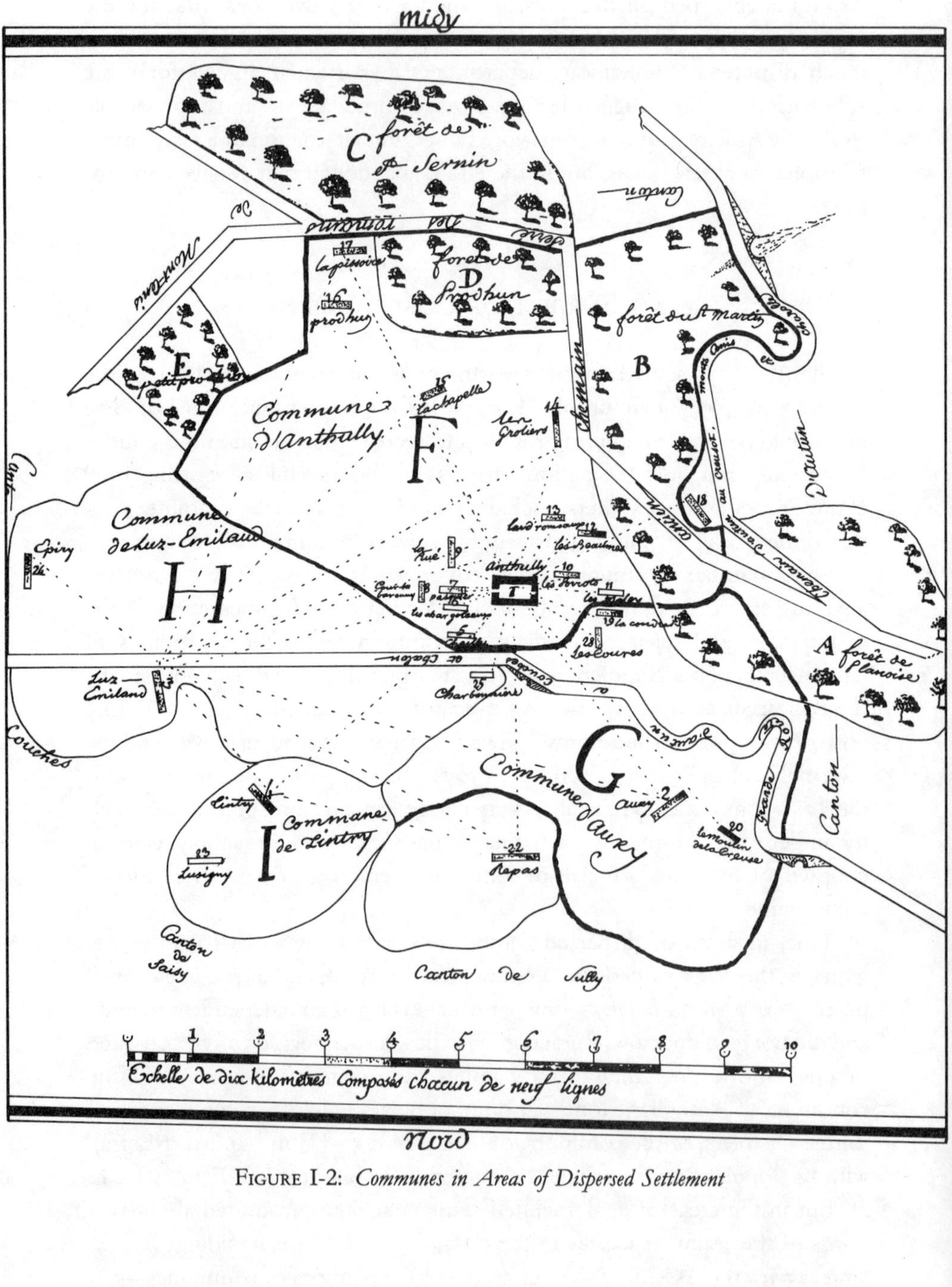

FIGURE I-2: *Communes in Areas of Dispersed Settlement*

FIGURE I-3: *Communes in Areas of Dispersed Settlement*

many municipalities as there were villages." Moreover, all 44,000 communes (except for the four or five largest cities) were to have a similar form of government: an elected "municipal administration" consisting of a mayor, procurator, notables, and general council.[17]

Thus the Assembly established as units of the nation's administrative system a surfeit of rural communes, many extremely sparse in population and resources. The problem is apparent in forty-three departments where the available data allows us to calculate the mean population of rural communes after subtracting urban communes: the median of these averages is 509 and the combined weighted average comes to 499.[18] These averages of course subsume a bottom tier of minuscule communes with fewer than two hundred or even one hundred inhabitants. Here, culled from sources dating from around 1800, are examples from various parts of the country:

Eure: 43 smallest communes averaged 58 inhabitants
Hautes-Pyrénées: 48 smallest communes averaged 72 inhabitants
Seine-Maritime: 68 smallest communes averaged 82 inhabitants
Nord: 114 smallest communes averaged 186 inhabitants
Calvados: 81 communes below 50 population
Haute-Saône: c. 50 communes below 100 population
Moselle: 65 communes below 100 population
Corrèze: 292 communes below 150 population
Haute-Garonne: 131 communes below 200 population
Pas-de-Calais: 161 communes below 200 population[19]

Ignoring such stark facts, the Assembly took the easiest, most liberal, and most popular course by simply accepting the status quo of rural communal identity. It must have felt that it was courting enough recrimination in obliterating the provinces, calling into question the hierarchy and traditional privileges of hundreds of towns, and disappointing the communes that lost out in the selection of departmental, district, and cantonal seats.

It may seem quixotic of the Assembly to have endowed even the smallest of these commune with a full-scale "municipal administration," but in the face of the old regime's endless variety of regional traditions, uniformity had a compelling attraction. After all, every commune in principle faced similar needs, apart from the localized requirements of husbandry or trade: the assessment of property for taxation; upkeep of church, cemetery, and rectory; management of communal property (whether leased out or retained for local use); upkeep of local roads; schooling; policing; home relief for the indigent. Was it not logical, then, to ensure that every community had similar administrative mechanisms to meet those needs?

Before 1789, the weight of seigneurial authority over village affairs had varied considerably by region. Weak but by no means extinct in the Midi, where communal self-government was well entrenched, seigneurial power was most palpable in the North and the Paris Basin. In provinces such as Burgundy, the intendants had recently attempted to shield village government from undue seigneurial interference while extending royal authority further into routine affairs. The degree of oligarchy in village governance had also varied. It is probably safe to generalize that, if they were not designated by the seigneur, village officials (known variously as *syndics, consuls, échevins, jurats, lieutenants,* or *généraux de paroisse*) were usually coopted by current and outgoing officers rather than being elected by the "community of inhabitants." Traditions of village democracy were not entirely moribund, and a general assembly of inhabitants might be convened from time to time to discuss important questions, but vestiges of village democracy had generally waned in the face of oligarchic tendencies. Royal initiatives sometimes accelerated that trend. Thus the intendant in Champagne ordered the formation of a corps of notables in each village to replace the general assembly of inhabitants as the arbiter of communal affairs. [20]

No institutional reforms were likely to alter the social balance of power among the inhabitants of rural communities dramatically, but the changes introduced by the National Assembly were significant nonetheless. The Revolution undercut seigneurial domination of village affairs where it still existed; increased the number of men involved in governing the villages; and, while precluding a return to direct governance by the "community of inhabitants," democratized the process by which local officials were selected. In the Artois region of Northern France before 1789, for example, the local seigneur appointed the head village official, known as the *lieutenant* or *bailli.* In 113 out of 119 Artesian villages studied by J.-P. Jessenne, the *lieutenant* on the eve of the Revolution was none other than the seigneur's principal tenant or *fermier.* The Revolution dramatically broke the grip of the seigneurs and their handpicked men on the reins of village power.

In the elections of 1790 for the new municipalities in Artois, voters chose only 15 percent of the former *lieutenants* as mayors, with another 35 percent receiving seats on municipal councils, but excluded altogether at least 45 percent of the old-regime village heads. Wherever a village had been involved in a conflict with the seigneur, his man was especially likely to be cast aside in the new regime. The *"fermocratie"* of large tenant farmers remained the dominant social group in these villages, but village leaders were now chosen by their peers. Artesian peasants consistently manifested what their historian calls "the will to regulate their collective affairs themselves." [21] Similarly a study of four rural communes in Burgundy suggests that if half the households had little chance of acceding to municipal office, within the social strata that did exercise power, rotation in office now became the norm.[22]

While the Revolution foreclosed the most democratic form of village government by general assemblies, it did vest the power of designation in virtually the entire population of adult male taxpaying inhabitants. That is to say, if the Revolution empowered village oligarchies, they were now popularly mandated rather than purely cooptive, and collective rather than personal. The real seat of authority lay in the general council, consisting at a minimum of nine elected members in even the smallest village: the mayor, procurator, three municipal officers, and four other aldermen called "notables." The mayor and procurator reported to the general council on all important matters. Though he had much responsibility in behalf of the state, the mayor in fact had little formal power. At the local level, the municipal legislation of 1789 worked against one-man rule, promoted rotation in office, and fostered an accountability on the expenditure of public funds that became a bedrock of the new civic order.

Although the Assembly rejected the idea of *"grandes communes"* or conjoined rural municipalities for administrative purposes (a decision later reversed by the thermidorian Convention, as we shall see), it did aggregate citizens beyond their communes for other purposes. Accordingly the Assembly subdivided the districts into about 5,250 cantons, choosing as many bourgs or villages for cantonal seats. (To give a sense of scale: the district of Reims had fifteen cantons, which comprised 132 communes.) The cantons became electoral and judicial circumscriptions.[23] While municipal officials were elected by the direct vote of citizens in their communes, deputies to the legislature, departmental officials, and judges were chosen indirectly by departmental electoral assemblies, to be discussed in the next chapter. In the countryside, citizens did not gather in their own separate communes to choose their electors, but rather in *primary assemblies* at each cantonal seat. Throughout the revolutionary decade the canton thus became the arena for the participation of voters in departmental and national elections. Rural voters also filled one office directly at the cantonal level, the exception being the *juge de paix*. This magistrate replaced royal or seigneurial authority in settling petty civil disputes and minor criminal matters. To assure both their accessibility and popular acceptance, the justices of the peace were to be elected directly by the voters in towns and in rural cantons.

The New Civic Landscape

By annihilating the provincial institutions and urban particularism synony-
mous before 1789 with privilege, the Assembly's administrative revolution
opened the prospect of an integrated nation. Citizens in all parts of France
might now enjoy the same rights, responsibilities, institutions, and public
services. The promise of national uniformity was as central to the revolutionary project as its ideals of liberty and equality. Recent studies of rural society
in this period, however, alert us that peasants were likely to resent the price
that accompanied such promises. True, even peasants who later turned
against the Revolution welcomed the extrusion of seigneurial power over
village life and the advent of communal self-government in 1789–90. In the
villages, however, liberty instinctively meant being left alone, and was not
consistent with greater intrusion by the state. The Assembly clearly hoped
that the new civic order would mitigate the isolation of village life, but for
ordinary people in the countryside isolation could also mean insulation from
scrutiny and demands.[24]

The Assembly's vision of integration and uniformity took root most
readily in cities and towns, where the new regime generated a sense of
empowerment that reached deeply into the ranks of the middle classes,
artisans, and shopkeepers. The *constituants* hoped also that town and country
might now develop closer social ties in the wake of their new civic bonds.
The districts, like Anglo-Saxon counties, were meant to be a nexus of urban
and rural interests, particularly in relation to subsistence provisioning, their
capitals never more than a day's journey from any part of the district. For its
part, a rural canton generally united a market village with its agrarian hinterland, and was supposed to be accessible enough to permit a journey back and
forth for the transaction of public and private business within the same day.
If closer ties and greater state penetration ultimately encouraged urban
domination over the countryside, at the outset the Assembly seemed to
believe that with an electoral system weighted in favor of the demograph-
ically preponderant countryside, a healthy equilibrium would result. That
urban-based radicals came to exercise a kind of tyranny over their fellow
citizens in the villages in 1793–94 should not obscure the original intent of
the *constituants* to integrate town and country on terms favorable to both.

Like the citizens at the time, we must familiarize ourselves with the
elements of the new civic landscape that, except for the communes, were
untested creations of 1789–90, terra incognita to voters and officials alike.
There was much to decipher, with or without the help of the departmental

and district almanacs that soon offered themselves as guidebooks for citizens.[25] The Assembly no doubt visualized the layers of local government as a supple machine to carry out its laws and directives. But even if the departments, districts, and communes entirely lacked legislative initiative, they were something more than mere agents of the central government, local auxiliaries (salaried or unsalaried) of a national bureaucracy that scarcely existed in France. Until shown otherwise, citizens could reasonably believe that departmental, district, and municipal officials were their surrogates as well as the state's. Even if these officials were under the scrutiny of Paris, they were chosen by a local political process to which they were ultimately answerable. While asserting the primacy of national law, the Assembly still left a large gray area for the competing imperatives of centralization and local autonomy.

For all their novelty, the departments on one level simply inherited the administrative tasks formerly supervised by the royal intendants as well as some of the "police" powers of the parlements. Accordingly, the provincial archives of the monarchy as well as the units of its mounted constabulary had to be subdivided and parceled out to the new departments. The allocation and collection of taxes for the state remained the inexorable element of continuity; the most fundamental role of the entire governmental hierarchy was to assure the flow of tax revenue to Paris, both pre-1789 arrears and new taxes levied from 1790 onward. Other traditional functions included maintaining public order; disseminating the laws that came pouring out of Paris; planning local public works; and coordinating inquests on such matters as poverty or subsistence supplies.

New types of demands quickly bulked as large in the departments' work: assuring the integrity of the electoral process; finding sites for the new courts and installing judicial personnel; supervising the inventory and sale of church property nationalized by the state as *biens nationaux;* and overseeing implementation of the civil constitution of the clergy in 1790. Within the narrow latitude permitted them, departmental administrations spelled out the details for executing the Assembly's policies, which were often hastily drafted and ambiguous. Then in most cases the departments turned matters over to the districts for implementation. The departments, in other words, organized tasks assigned to them by Paris, apprised the districts of their duties, and scrutinized the manner in which district administrations carried them out. In theory the districts did little more than implement the laws as delegated or directed by the departments. In practice they of course had considerable discretion, and heated disputes between districts and departments were not long in coming.[26]

Basic decisions, such as the share of each district in the department's tax quota, were made by the *general council* of the department, which consisted of thirty-six members elected by the departmental electoral assembly for two-year terms, with half renewable each year. If they were prudent, the electors balanced the council geographically by choosing men from each district. The general council convened for only a few weeks each year, and selected eight of its members as a permanent and salaried administrative body known as the *departmental directory*. The directorate worked with the department's chief executive agent, the *procurator-syndic*, also chosen by the electoral assembly, who doubled as the department's official liaison with the central government. The districts operated in the same fashion: the district's electors convened separately to choose a twelve-man general council and a procurator-syndic; the district council then designated a salaried four-man directorate from its ranks.

"If the departments were the hinge between Paris and the periphery," writes the historian Alison Patrick, "the districts were the hinge between department and populace." The districts exercised the same supervisory role over their communes that the departments had over them. It was the district's responsibility to allocate tax quotas to each commune, collect information from them, monitor their compliance with laws and directives, and (an exhausting task) scrutinize their local budgets. The district administration became the major point of contact between state and citizens. District officials carried out contentious tasks such as requisitioning food supplies during subsistence crises, installing new constitutional priests in their parishes, and auctioning off *biens nationaux*.

A lack of experience and established routines naturally troubled department and district personnel in the early months: How many clerks should be hired? How many bureaus were needed and how should tasks be allocated? How should information be gathered, collated, or disseminated? By astute improvisation these men usually mastered the sheer novelty of their tasks in short order. Some won local reputations for competence, dedication, or sagacity. With no formal requirements for serving at a lower level of administration before one could be eligible for a higher post, such ascension nonetheless occurred naturally as municipal officials subsequently passed up to the district and district administrators won election to departmental posts. Successive legislatures in turn drew many of their new members from these local administrators, while lateral moves between administrative and judicial offices were also common. Rarely did individuals entrench themselves in a particular post, although the political vicissitudes of the decade make this something of a moot question. From these local political elites a national political class of sorts emerged very quickly, considering the absence of political parties and the number of departmental orbits in which the politically ambitious had to make their way.[27] Until Brumaire, with the exception of the year of the Terror, this new political elite required electoral sanction to govern.

Public accountability was a complementary and less remarked feature of the new regime. Under the Directory, for example, the constitution required each departmental administration to publish an annual accounting or *compte-rendu* of its stewardship. These substantial reports illustrate how quickly the work of administration became routinized around a tradition of scrupulous accountability for every livre of public funds.[28] There is undoubtedly an interesting history to be written of official corruption in the 1790s, particularly concerning disposition of the *biens nationaux,* government contracts, and (on a petty level) the forgery of official papers. But in the overwhelming majority of departments, districts, and communes such acts would surely represent the exceptions rather than the rule of incompetence and corruption that the royalist press might lead one to expect.

MODIFICATIONS, CONTINUITIES, MUTATIONS

AT THE SUMMIT: THE TRAVAILS OF LEGISLATIVE AUTHORITY

Representative government and legislative supremacy stand out as the fulcrum of the revolutionary project. Sorely tested by the turmoil of revolutionary politics, they nonetheless endured through the 1790s, as the French polity lurched through its four successive forms: the constitutional monarchy consolidated in the Constitution of 1791; the democratic republic, symbolized by the unimplemented Jacobin Constitution of June 1793; the revolutionary dictatorship codified under the law of 14 frimaire Year II (4 December 1793); and the directorial republic under the Constitution of the Year III (1795). Even during the Terror—which contrasts in that respect to modern totalitarian regimes—the supremacy of law ostensibly stood as an official value, but the legislature remained the sole source and interpreter of that law.

The nation's routine parliamentary life began when the Legislative Assembly convened in October 1791. In contrast to the National Assembly before it and the National Convention that replaced it—both in effect constitutional conventions free to govern in the interim as they saw fit—the Legislative Assembly was bound by a constitution. Specifically, it had to work with the king, who headed the executive branch, appointed ministers at his pleasure, and held a suspensive veto over legislation that could run up to four years. As a recent study of that body demonstrates, the Legislative Assembly strove consistently to respect the independent exercise of the king's prerogatives, no matter how much grief he caused. The new deputies held faithfully to the letter and spirit of the Constitution of 1791 until the last possible moment, despite the king's uncooperative, disdainful, and ultimately treasonous behavior.[29] In the end the Legislative lasted for only one year, doomed to extinction when the fall of the monarchy in the Parisian insurrection of August 1792 brought down the entire constitutional edifice of 1791.

Like the National Assembly, the Legislative Assembly sat in the Manège (the riding school of the Tuileries Palace), inheriting its inadequate heating, ventilation, lighting, and acoustics. The discomfiting physical continuity, however, was not matched by a continuity in personnel. For the National Assembly had decreed that none of its members could be elected as deputies to the Legislative Assembly. Like its idealistic "Declaration of Peace to the World" in 1790, the self-denying ordinance epitomized the periodic optimism of the Assembly's mood. In any case, no one could accuse the *constituants* of seeking to perpetuate themselves in power. The Legislative Assembly's ranks were therefore filled with new men from local political orbits without the nationally renowned figures who had emerged from the Estates General of 1789. Chosen by the departmental electoral assemblies (rather than by voters in individual constituencies as in the British House of Commons or the U.S. House of Representatives), the deputies were not prone to regional parochialism or sharp urban-rural polarization. But the new representatives did hold a wide range of conflicting political opinions. No stable majority emerged from their ranks. Whether choosing presiding officers or voting on policy, the Legislative Assembly remained unpredictable. In the seven surviving roll-call votes on politically divisive issues, for example, the royalists and moderate Feuillants carried four, while the Jacobins prevailed in three others.[30]

Representative government started with elections, but to function successfully it had to acquire coherent form once the elected deputies convened. With only the uncertain precedents of the National Assembly to guide them, the legislators were free to organize the nation's new parliament as they saw fit. How could business be transacted most efficiently? How could wise laws and decrees be drafted that would win approval? How, in the absence of parties, could any measure of discipline be achieved among the 750 deputies? Following the National Assembly, the new legislature created standing committees to initiate legislation, twenty-two in number with twelve to twenty-four members each designated by the full assembly. But where a small group of strong personalities had dominated the committees of the National Assembly—it is estimated that 33 deputies held 20 percent of the 744 committee seats[31]—the Legislative decided that no member could sit on more than one committee. Nor did any committee have the leverage of the National Assembly's Constitutional Committee or Committee on Reports.

The Legislative nonetheless came to appreciate the need for continuity. It originally intended to renew committee memberships every three months, but when it finally got around to renewing fourteen committees in March 1792, the Assembly reelected all the retiring members of ten.[32] In the end, of course, such organizational details had scant bearing on the fate of the Legislative Assembly. As it stumbled vainly between gestures of accommodation and resistance to the Revolution's opponents, the Legislative lost the initiative to the militants of the capital, and could save neither the king nor itself from the "second revolution." Still, its improvisations constitute a first groping chapter in the parliamentary history of modern France.

Like the deputies to the Legislative Assembly, the members of the Convention were elected by departmental electoral assemblies (see Chapter II) with approximately the same distribution of seats—an arrangement that would carry over into the Directory regime as well. With its radical majority (though one that would soon fragment fratricidally), the Convention quickly regained the authority that the Legislative had lost as "the representatives of the people."[33] With no independent executive to thwart them, the *convention-nels* reasserted legislative supremacy more thoroughly than ever. By the same token, they allowed the principle of the separation of powers to lapse. After the disappearance of the monarchy, the executive branch of government fell directly under the Convention's control. Indeed, in the Year II the Montagnards effaced the very terms "ministry" and "minister" by renaming the organs of the central government "executive commissions." Only direct action by the people—"popular democracy" in the Paris sections and anti-revolutionary rebellion—threatened the Convention's authority, and it ultimately mastered those challenges as well.

The Convention had multiple tasks. Its exceptional role as arbiter of the king's fate it discharged with scrupulous procedures and extensive debate.[34] After unanimously finding Louis Capet guilty of treason, each deputy went to the rostrum to explain for the record his vote on the death penalty, which passed in January 1793 by a razor-thin margin. The Convention's mandate to draft a new constitution, on the other hand, languished until June amidst the more urgent imperatives of serving as a temporary legislature and an emergency war government. Its twenty-one standing committees reflected those priorities. While five dealt with internal organizational matters, sixteen oversaw executive agencies, dealt with inquiries and petitions, and drafted laws on particular subjects.[35] They included the Committee on Legislation, which laid the groundwork for the civil code; the Committee on Public

Instruction, which formulated policy on an array of cultural institutions and campaigns as well as formal schooling; the Finance Committee, which labored on the staggering problems of tax collection, the *assignats,* and the *biens nationaux;* and the Committee of General Security, in effect a political police committee, which supervised the repressive apparatus of the Terror.

As an emergency government, however, the Convention gradually gave precedence to its Committee of Public Safety. After repeated fumbles by its Committee of General Defense in managing the war crisis, the Convention in April 1793 named a smaller and more politically supple group to serve as its steering committee and war cabinet. A few months of finetuning removed the original Dantonists and left Robespierre and his allies to set the tone among the twelve members. By September, the Committee of Public Safety began to exhibit the anticipated energy and resolve. The committee became the heart of the revolutionary government and the Jacobin dictatorship, with responsibility for military strategy, related problems of subsistence supplies, and general political policy. Reports from the armies of the republic, local constituted authorities, revolutionary committees, and the Convention's own representatives-on-mission to the departments all flowed to the green room where the committee met. The Convention even delegated to "the twelve" the power to name members of all other committees. The Convention accepted most of the strategic, repressive, and egalitarian proposals presented by Bertrand Barère or some other spokesman for the committee without extensive debate, even the purge of the popular Danton. The committee's virtually dictatorial powers, however, derived from a monthly ritual in which it reported to the Convention and received a new mandate. What the Convention granted with regularity month after month it could in fact withhold. The Robespierrists were ultimately overthrown in Thermidor not by an armed coup, but by the Convention's sudden decision to oust them. [36]

The entire experience of the Montagnard Convention caused second thoughts among the thermidorians—not about legislative supremacy as such but about the principle of uni-cameralism that the *constituants* had embraced so decisively in 1789. To begin with, the Constitution of the Year III reestablished the separation of powers by creating a five-man Executive Directory—a form of collective responsibility reflecting the lingering fear of dictatorship or monarchy. Though its members were designated by the legislature and had no veto over legislative acts, the Executive Directory was independent in its powers to appoint and remove ministers and departmental commissioners (see below), and to develop diplomatic and military strategy. Then, with the aim of restraining legislative action, of inhibiting the representatives of the people from the precipitous acts that had been legion in 1793–94, the new constitution created a bi-cameral legislature. The Constitution of the Year III took the same number of 750 deputies and divided them into two houses. The Council of Five Hundred *(Conseil des Cinq Cents)* was to initiate legislation, which then had to be approved by the 250-man Council of Elders *(Conseil des Anciens)*. Differences in qualification for the two houses were relatively minor: an "elder" had to be married or widowed, and at least forty years old, as against thirty for the Council of Five Hundred. Otherwise, little distinguished the two bodies. Departmental electoral assemblies chose deputies to both houses for three-year terms, one third to be renewed each year.

The directorial legislature distanced itself from the Convention not only in its bi-cameralism but in its internal organization. Reacting against abuse of power by the Montagnard committees of Public Safety and General Security, the new bodies did not form standing committees of any sort. All business, from the most complex general law to the most parochial decree, was handled by ad hoc committees (or "commissions," as they were called) established expressly to discharge a designated task. Veteran lawmakers with good reputations naturally turned up often on the more important ad hoc commissions, but the mass of deputies was now more actively involved in routine parliamentary business as well. The legislature's procedures cultivated an equality of status for all deputies. It was far less likely that a small group of deputies could dominate the proceedings. By the same token this system assured that vast amounts of time would be consumed on minor matters; it ruled out a streamlined method of managing routine affairs, such as shifting the *chef-lieu* of a canton or authorizing expenditure for local public works. With few procedural impediments to long-winded oration, and with a deputy's right to have his opinion printed as a pamphlet by the Imprimerie Nationale, few could resist presenting and embellishing their views.[37]

The combination of bi-cameralism, a kaleidoscopic system of ad hoc committees, and a relatively unlimited mode of parliamentary debate made the passage of major legislation cumbersome and problematic. Bi-cameralism in France served no specific interest—neither the representation of a particular social status embodied by the British House of Lords, nor the principle of federalism and state's rights enshrined in the United States Senate. Yet it created comparable impediments to the legislative process. Without party discipline or other informal mechanisms of consultation, bi-cameralism magnified the atomization of opinion. Even when debate on a contentious issue finally reached closure in the Council of Five Hundred, its proposal had to go to the Council of Elders, where the debate began all over again. To study each bill the elders set up their own commission, which could recommend passage or rejection. Lacking the power to enact amendments, but zealous of their own role, the elders frequently rejected bills after long debate.

Sometimes their collective opinion simply differed; often they found minor or technical flaws in the Council of Five Hundred's bill, and rejected it in the expectation that the lower house would redraft the legislation accordingly. But of that outcome there was no assurance.

Up to a point these procedures were no doubt salutary. Clearly the Convention's energetic record was marred by actions arising from spontaneous emotional combustion. The Convention legislated too quickly about too many things, sometimes on the spur of the moment and for expedient political reasons. Intent on precluding such precipitous action, the directorials succeeded too well. On some questions the Council of Five Hundred itself could not reach any decision; in other matters consensus between the two houses proved impossible to achieve. The legislature did pass laws to restructure the national debt, revive indirect taxes, revise veterans' benefits, reimplement the republican calendar, and introduce conscription. Protracted debate, however, failed to produce urgently needed legislation on the boundaries of press freedom, regulation of political associations, reorganization of the legal profession, reform of local administration, and the financing of primary schools. Such frequent stalemate on admittedly difficult issues must have frustrated conscientious legislators. For its part, the Executive Directory bombarded the legislature with formal "messages" urging action on such matters and sketching its recommended policy, but it did so in vain. [38]

True, on the most pressing political issues the branches of government did effectively concert under the Directory's leadership. Together they executed two purges of dubious constitutionality against rightists and Neo-Jacobins elected respectively in 1797 (the coup of Fructidor Year V) and 1798 (the coup of Floréal Year VI). Immediately after the first purge, they agreed to revive proscriptions against refractory priests and émigrés. But on more mundane matters the legislature simply would not respond to pressure from the executive. Moreover, the right and the left were too amorphous to be thoroughly purged. Kindred deputies escaped ouster in 1797 and 1798, and subsequently found numerous opportunities to assert their independence. Despite the purges, both houses contained a bewildering spectrum of opinions on almost every significant issue. Thus, political purges and violations of the constitution—the Directory's fruitless balancing act between left and right—punctured the regime's integrity without producing sustained consensus. [39] Ironically, the relatively unfettered parliamentary freedom that survived those purges sapped the regime's coherence even further. The parliament's aura of vacillation and self-indulgence, its record of legislative stalemate, clouded the republic's future. Whatever its virtues or demerits, the Napoleonic system would put an end to that particular problem.

THE ECLIPSE OF LEGISLATIVE POWER

Brumaire changed the locus of authority decisively. On behalf of the nation, the National Assembly had wrested sovereignty from the king and delegated the lawmaking function to itself, bowing to the monarchy's historic role only by endowing the king with a suspensive veto. The Convention later transformed France into a republic and underscored the finality of that change by executing Louis XVI, but it adhered to the National Assembly's concept of sovereignty, representation, and legislative supremacy. Indeed, by resisting *sans-culotte* demands for popular democracy, it reaffirmed that formulation. Under the directorial republic of the Year III the legislature remained the central locus of power, initiating and drafting laws at its discretion, free from any kind of executive veto, and even designating the members of the Executive Directory itself.

By 1799, however, some of the republic's most influential adherents had become disenchanted with the regime's manifest unpopularity and chronic instability. These "revisionists" wished to end the republic's dependence on mercurial annual elections; to recast its unreliable collective executive; and to reform its undisciplined parliamentary system. The revisionists railed at the surviving Neo-Jacobin presence permitted by the republic, but probably feared the threat of a royalist backlash even more. They censured the Directory for its unconstitutional purges, yet recoiled themselves from the residual political freedom that allowed royalists, Neo-Jacobins, or incompetents to win election. They genuflected to the sovereignty of the people, but deplored the prevailing "public spirit" with despair or contempt.[40]

General Bonaparte disdained the republic's political clamor and alleged ineffectiveness as much as anyone. He wished France to be depoliticized, at the summit and across the land. An undisciplined liberty must cede to responsible authority; endless debate must give way to efficient lawmaking. Above all a single, strong hand must command the helm to guide France on a sound course at home and abroad. Since Bonaparte and the revisionist politicians engineered their coup without a blueprint for the future, their maneuvering after Brumaire yielded unanticipated results. All agreed that France's government must not be exposed to continuous electoral renewal, and that it must have firmer executive leadership. Sieyès and his colleagues, meanwhile, were most intent on establishing a senatorial system where an elite group of solons could provide the nation with the laws it so badly needed. In the end, a compromise of sorts resulted.

Bonaparte emerged as the single head of state, a First Consul with a panoply of unprecedented executive powers, both civil and military. Sieyès prevailed in establishing a coopted Senate of sixty members with high prestige and vague responsibility to conserve the constitution, and a bi-cameral legislature that ostensibly retained the power to enact the laws of the land. Every element of initiative, however, lay with the executive. Only the First Consul had the right to draft and introduce legislation. A new institution called the Council of State would assist him in preparing the laws. Staffed by a select group of legal experts and experienced administrators from across the political spectrum, the Council of State removed the formulation of policy from the public limelight and transformed lawmaking into an essentially technocratic affair. The hub of government immediately shifted from the Manège to the room in the Tuileries Palace where Napoleon Bonaparte met with his Council of State. [41]

This arrangement left the new legislature with only the power to debate proposed laws and to vote them up or down. Moreover the Constitution of the Year VIII carried bi-cameralism to an extreme by totally separating those two functions. One house was to debate government proposals, but without a binding vote, and the other was to vote without the right to debate. (The argument that this form of bi-cameralism was more functional than the system of Great Britain or the Directory—where the two houses seemed to duplicate each other—need not be taken seriously. Yet as a reaction against the frustrating parliamentary history of the Directory it was not devoid of sense.) The Tribunate was to receive a proposal from the Council of State, hear three government spokesmen explain its virtues, examine it in committee, and publicly debate it. After taking a non-binding vote, the Tribunate would designate three members to accompany the government's *rapporteurs* to the other house, the *Corps Législatif.* There the six spokesmen addressed the legislators—either echoing each other or disagreeing, as the case may be. Much like a criminal court jury, the legislators would listen to the presentations and then vote in a secret ballot to approve or reject the law. The legislature thus lost all initiative but in theory retained the ultimate say.

Its mandate was problematic, however. For the legislature no longer embodied the principle of representation that supported the entire revolutionary experience. Initially the Senate filled the two houses by appointment rather than election, and subsequent renewals depended on a convoluted process of multiple nominations by departmental electoral colleges and designation by the government. The members lost their relationship not only to their electorates but even to their departments. The one hundred tribunes, ostensibly spokesmen for the people at large, were coopted entirely without reference to their domicile. For the Legislative Corps of three hundred the requirement was merely that there be at least one deputy from each depart-

ment. As in most previous changes of regime, however, continuity of personnel remained substantial. Two hundred and forty of the three hundred
nominees to the Legislative Corps came straight from the directorial legislature, and only twenty-one had never sat in a revolutionary assembly; of the
one hundred tribunes, sixty-nine were members of the directorial legislature,
and another dozen were Parisian intellectuals of note. On the other hand,
virtually no outspoken Neo-Jacobins slipped through the filtering process
into the new parliament, and only twenty out of the four hundred members
had been regicides. [42]

Mute and voting secretly, the members of the Legislative Corps were
essentially faceless. The tribunes on the contrary had high visibility and a
chance to feed whatever public interest in parliamentary politics remained.
Their oratory could make an impact, especially since it was now rationed out
so sparingly. In that respect their very function clashed with Napoleon
Bonaparte's sense that public opposition had no place in his republic. The
people were sick and tired of posturing politicians and ideologues, he believed. It was not enough that the executive now controlled the agenda.
While Napoleon usually tolerated genuine and even exhaustive debate within
the closed meetings of the Council of State, he bridled at the occasional
displays of independence in the Tribunate, and even claimed to see in certain
outspoken tribunes the nucleus of a systematic opposition to his regime. The
most dramatic confrontation came over a bill to establish special tribunals
without juries to try certain crimes against public order. Dissenting tribunes
relentlessly attacked the bill on the basis of liberal principles. But at the end
of the debate the Tribunate's straw poll saw only 41 votes against and 49 for
the bill. Then in the Legislative Corps the government won the deciding vote,
192 to 88. The real losers here were the parliamentary liberals, who incurred
hostility and veiled intimidation from the government. [43]

The First Consul could not abide the seeming humiliation of public
criticism in the Tribunate or the need for an occasional retreat to delay a bill
for further refinement. Opposition in the Tribunate, largely on technical
grounds, did indeed oblige the government to withdraw certain bills temporarily, although it usually resubmitted them without much change a few
months later—among them bills on judicial reform and the first articles of
the Civil Code. But the government almost never lost when it sought a vote
on an important bill in the Legislative Corps. Only on minor matters did the
legislators occasionally balk at the arbitrary or hasty manner of the executive
branch in framing legislation. The government's most definitive defeat in
both houses came over a bill on the maintenance of official archives! [44]

Bonaparte could not curb independent-minded tribunes by leaking
denunciations of their alleged obstructionism or personal ambition. But

when one fifth of the Tribunate was due to be renewed in 1802, the government simply designated the tribunes to be removed, instead of allowing them to be chosen by lot, and replaced them with docile loyalists. Yet even a more compliant Tribunate could question the government's wisdom or show insufficient enthusiasm. According to the historian Irene Collins, the emperor finally eliminated the Tribunate altogether because its orators "failed to secure a satisfactory degree of cooperation from the legislators. Bills again and again received what were to Napoleon sizable opposition votes in the Legislative Corps." Thus a bill empowering the emperor to name the governor of the Bank of France passed by only 186 to 70; a bill authorizing appeals to the Council of State from the *Tribunal de Cassation* was opposed by 60 out of 226 legislators; and 42 out of 252 even voted against the law establishing the Napoleonic University.

In 1807, the Senate obligingly abolished the Tribunate and folded its fifty current members (vacancies not having been filled) into the other house. The Legislative Corps was then reorganized to facilitate preliminary consideration of draft legislation before the voting took place. The legislature now divided into three sections (finance, interior, legislation), each of which chose a seven-member commission to work with the Council of State on proposed bills. Upon concluding its deliberations, the chairman of the relevant commission would report to the Legislative Corps alongside the government's spokesmen. The days of serious public remonstrance were over, but even that did not ensure the unanimous votes Napoleon desired. When the parliament considered the new Code of Criminal Procedure in 1808—including such controversial issues as trial by jury, the power of public prosecutors, and the policing role of rural mayors—its separate votes on the code's nine sections echoed those cited above, producing in one case only 150 ayes against 105 nays. [45]

The Napoleonic regime's most arduous legislative trials indeed came over its five comprehensive legal codes: the Civil Code, the Code of Civil Procedure, the Code of Criminal Procedure, the Penal Code, and the Commercial Code. Each had to be negotiated section by section through the shoals of legislative opinion. [46] Once those pillars were in place, however, the government scarcely consulted the parliament at all and had long since grown accustomed to ruling by executive decree. After a few years of trial and error and an initial flurry of legislation major and minor, in other words, Napoleon presented only the broadest of measures to the legislature, along with a steady stream of routine bills to authorize local public works and communal property transactions. Thus the emperor submitted a vague law creating the Napoleonic University to the parliament, but filled in all the important provisions later by executive decree. As long as Napoleon did not seek to increase the level of direct taxes, approval of the annual budget remained an empty ritual. And in 1805 the emperor shifted the charade of authorization for annual draft levies from the legislature to his even more pliant Senate.

To Napoleon, the atrophy of legislative authority seemed eminently reasonable: "When all is organized in the Empire, it is natural that the work of administration should increase and that of legislation diminish." In 1809, he could observe that the nation's will was embodied in the constituted authorities, which were, in order of precedence, the emperor, the Senate, the Council of State, and the Legislative Corps. Yet the residual authority of the legislature survived. In March 1813, when the desperate military situation required unprecedented levels of revenue, Napoleon sought legislative approval for his scheme to nationalize and sell off communal property in exchange for state annuities. He won this approval handily by a vote of 303 to 26, but not without anxiety. Then in December, hoping to rally the nation to his last stand against the oncoming coalition, Napoleon turned to his parliament for endorsement of his purported peacemaking efforts during the previous months. When a legislative commission produced a sharply critical appraisal of the emperor's diplomacy, the government sought to suppress it, but the legislature voted 223 to 31 to publish its commission's report. On a technicality Napoleon dissolved the legislature the following day, and was quoted as shouting at a group of deputies that he encountered at a reception: "You are not the representatives of the nation; you are deputies of the departments. I alone am the representative of the people. . . . Even if you think me at fault you should not reproach me publicly." [47]

The evolving dictatorship had not entirely obliterated the revolutionary premise, and the latent claims of representation and legislative authority apparently haunted the emperor himself. Indeed, the legislators had the last word a few months later when they joined with the Senate to help effect the restoration of the Bourbons under a constitution assuring a role to an independent legislature. The Charter of 1814, it is true, frustrated liberal sentiment when the king refused to acknowledge that he held his mandate from the people. Its preamble presented the Charter as a unilateral act of the Bourbon monarch, even though a drafting committee of senators and legislators had contributed many clauses in a different spirit. Moreover, borrowing a leaf from Napoleon, Louis XVIII retained the power of legislative initiative. Sidestepping the separation of powers, the Charter declared that "The legislative power is exercised collectively by the King, the Chamber of Peers, and the Chamber of Deputies chosen from the departments." Article 16 stated flatly that "The King proposes the laws," although Article 19 left each house "the right to petition the King to propose a law on any subject and to indicate what they think the law should contain." Yet with its strategy of depicting

Napoleon as a tyrant and itself as moderate, the Bourbon regime accepted open debate in the Chamber of Deputies, and suffered the ensuing political conflicts and stalemates. The Restoration legislature could not compel the king to do its bidding, but it could challenge him when he went against its will.[48] While keeping the upper hand, the Bourbons effectively restored legislative authority alongside their own.

LOCAL AUTHORITY: REVOLUTIONARY IMPROVISATIONS AND REACTIONS

The Assembly's local government model survived the fall of the monarchy in 1792, when special elections to renew departmental and district administrations replaced outspoken royalists, but it could not withstand the demand for revolutionary government in the Year II (1793–94). In the spring of 1793 rival factions in the Convention began to joust over the authority of local officials. The Girondins defended embattled municipalities and departmental directorates in their occasionally bitter clashes with the Convention's representatives-on-mission—deputies sent out in March 1793 to mobilize men and supplies for the war effort. While the Montagnards supported the right of these ambulatory deputies to supersede local authorities, the Girondins argued that drastic encroachments on local autonomy threatened the liberty of French citizens.[49]

The Girondins lost this battle as they lost the wider struggle for dominance in the Convention. After their expulsion on June 2, a majority of departmental administrations protested against the purge, thereby compromising themselves in the eyes of the victorious Montagnards. Stigmatizing these elected officials as "federalists," the Convention shouldered aside the departmental directorates, suppressed their councils altogether, and handed most administrative responsibility directly to the districts. The Montagnard's parliamentary dictatorship temporarily suspended the guarantee of individual liberties as well as the election of local officials. Under the law of 14 frimaire II (4 December 1793)—the charter, so to speak, of the revolutionary government—procurator-syndics of districts and communes now became *national agents,* responsible to the central government, which could remove and replace them at will. Scrutinized by the Committee of Public Safety and the representatives-on-mission, the national agents became the pointmen of revolutionary government. Seconded by clubs and revolutionary committees of *sans-culottes,* they implemented the torrent of emergency decrees to mobilize, requisition, police, and repress.[50] In the countryside these administrative changes might have caused barely a ripple in the tenor of public life, yet in certain villages the revolutionary committees, with their members of humble social status, could still unsettle the power structures and social equilibrium of their communities.[51]

The countryside was assuredly disrupted by urban paramilitary battalions during the brief period of "anarchic terror" between September 1793 (when the Convention, under pressure from the Paris sections, "placed Terror on the order of the day") and December (when the law of 14 frimaire established a measure of control over freewheeling local militants). Under duress in September, the Convention authorized the formation of domestic paramilitary units or *armées révolutionnaires*. Organized by the clubs and municipalities in Paris and about fifty provincial towns, these forces gave unprecedented muscle to urban revolutionaries in their claims against a resistant countryside. Their advocates hoped especially "to bring back abundance" by intimidating peasants into disgorging their grain surpluses. The *armées révolutionnaires* executed arrest warrants or requisition orders issued by duly constituted authorities.

Led by local militants elected by the men who had signed on, the *armées révolutionnaires* deemed themselves "the people armed for the People," ambulatory instruments of the Terror. As they swung through the hinterland on policing or subsistence missions, the battalions fraternized with isolated rural *sans-culottes* and stirred their emotions. But their incursions were even more certain to provoke hatred against urban radicals and outrage at the temerity of their local supporters. Their violent language, intimidating gestures, and "gastronomic pillage" (taking food and drink as their due) assaulted the aura of revolutionary legality that the Terror's sponsors in the Convention wished to preserve.

The paramilitary forces particularly offended rural sensibilities when they promoted "de-christianization" in rural parishes by harassing constitutional priests, profaning churches with acts of blasphemy, or closing down church buildings altogether. The Convention's disapproval of such offensive militancy was predictable. In December, at the first real opportunity, the Committee of Public Safety ordered the *armées révolutionnaires* to disband, except for the 5,000-man Parisian force, whose vital provisioning missions and political clout allowed it to survive until the spring of 1794.[52]

THE BRIEF REVOLUTIONARY government left its mark on the future structures of government, although it might seem as if its improvisations would disappear without a trace. Until they completed a new charter in the fall of 1795, the thermidorians in fact maintained the centralized apparatus created by the

Montagnards, using it of course in a different spirit. Then the Constitution of the Year III (1795) introduced a number of changes. First, it abolished the districts altogether, in part no doubt to exorcize their legacy of dictatorship and terror. Conversely, it restored the departments to their original prominence, but replaced the large elected council and its directorate with a simplified departmental administration of five full-time, salaried members to be chosen by the departmental electoral assembly. Finally, the new constitution revised the nation's civic geography by elevating the cantons to a new kind of administrative responsibility at the expense of rural communes (see Chapter IV).

Yet the thermidorians did not entirely forsake the instruments of the Year II. Within limits, they appreciated the control from the center exercised by the Committee of Public Safety through its "national agents" in the provinces. And so while restoring elected local governments, the thermidorians established a parallel bureaucratic presence alongside them. The Constitution of the Year III authorized the Executive Directory to appoint a salaried *commissaire* to each departmental and cantonal administration. The Directory's commissioners monitored elected local officials to assure that they complied with the laws and decrees of the central government. Cantonal commissioners corresponded with the departmental commissioners, who in turn reported regularly to the Ministry of the Interior about conditions in their departments. They could recommend the suspension or ouster of local officials, and in emergencies could assume their duties.

Local political men rather than non-partisan functionaries, the Directory's departmental commissioners usually owed their nomination to recommendations by members of their department's parliamentary deputation. They were chosen for their experience and likely political reliability. When the political climate changed abruptly, as it did several times, they could be ousted for the same reason. Departmental commissioners who pleased the Directory might be encouraged to stand as candidates for the legislature. Like the "national agents" of the Year II, the Directory's commissioners became the most visible political figures in their departments, political operatives for the incumbent government in Paris. [53]

The decentralized, three-tiered model of 1790 had thus changed substantially by the mid-1790s, but in modified form the practice of elective local government survived. At the departmental capitals the Directory's commissioners usually reflected the political tone prevailing in Paris, but without the power to act directly in ordinary circumstances. Ostensibly the duties of these appointed commissioners were clearly demarcated from those of the elected administrators, but in fact their relations remained uncertain and even adversarial. As for the departmental circumscriptions themselves, apart from shifting a few *chef-lieux* for political reasons,[54] no regime was inclined to tamper with them or reconsider their utility. After Brumaire, however, those perdurable creations would be used in a very different way.

THE ECLIPSE OF LOCAL AUTONOMY

In 1790 the departments, apart from their electoral function, became the vehicle for three distinct projects: uniformity and integration of the realm, administrative efficiency, and local self-government. This last component was now to disappear, though not without some gestures to preserve the principle. The Consulate conflated the roles of the elected departmental administration and the Directory's appointed commissioner, and placed them in the hands of one man known as the prefect—a role that may well have been the common fantasy of those directorial commissioners as they skirmished with elected officials and censured their inertia or political attitudes. Under the landmark local government law of 28 pluviôse VIII (17 February 1800), prefects were appointed and removable by the head of state, initially the First Consul, then the emperor, still later the restored king. Such control by Paris precluded the vagaries of electoral designation and collective administration. Responsibility in each department began and ended with the prefect, seconded by three to six appointed subprefects in newly established arrondissements, comparable to but somewhat fewer than the old districts. Appointed mayors in the communes rounded out the new administrative pyramid.

The Napoleonic system eliminated the ambiguity in local government that the *constituants* had willingly cultivated, where elected officials were simultaneously agents for the central government and for their constituents. The prefects and subprefects were exclusively the government's men. Whereas even the Directory's commissioners had been local citizens, with a minimum of one year's domicile in the department required for appointment, the Consulate consistently named prefects who were not native sons of the departments they were to govern. Like the old royal intendants, such outsiders were supposed to be less susceptible to influence by local cliques or notables. Unlike the Directory's politically committed commissioners, Napoleon's prefects did not have to worry about elections. On the contrary, they understood that they were supposed to depoliticize their departments.[55]

In the original design, however, the prefects were not to be proconsuls armed with absolute power, and citizens were not entirely unrepresented in local government. Notwithstanding his mission to incarnate the authority of the new regime, a prefect's every move had to be reported back to the

Ministry of the Interior for review, and often to the Ministry of Police as well. These ministers were in turn monitored by a Council of State responsible for upholding the rule of law. Prefects often saw their *arrêtés* criticized and occasionally quashed altogether. Formally, the prefect implemented decisions made in Paris. His role was "to assure the execution of orders and the transmission of information."[56]

Moreover, the prefect and his subprefects had auxiliaries to share the burdens of local government. Each department had a *conseil de préfecture,* consisting (along with the prefect himself) of three to five counselors appointed by the government and salaried at 1,200 francs for a decidedly part-time job. As departmental almanacs explained to the citizens, the prefectorial council dealt with "les affaires contentieuses." Problems over individual tax assessments; complaints arising from the disposition of national property, eminent domain, or rights of way; disputes with entrepreneurs undertaking public works all ended up on the prefectorial council's docket. Redress of a citizen's grievance with the state over property, in other words, was not left to one individual or his hired staff, but to a handpicked board of local notables. In the Moselle in 1808, for example, the *conseil de préfecture* considered 830 petitions for a reduction or postponement of property tax assessments, ruling favorably on 586 while rejecting 244; in the Loir-et-Cher in 1809, the prefectorial council was even more accommodating in accepting 495 petitions and rejecting only 74.[57] Occasionally the prefect might send one of his counselors on a fact-finding mission, and a counselor usually stood in for the prefect when he was away from the *chef-lieu.* But in the main the prefectorial council was an administrative arbitration service, a local buffer between the propertied public and the state.

More fundamentally, the creation of a *general council* in each department and arrondissement nominally preserved the principles of consent to local taxes and fiscal accountability. These bodies resembled in size and periodicity the elected departmental and district councils of 1790, but their roles were far more limited. At their inception the members were appointed rather than elected, although they were ostensibly to be renewed periodically by a tortuous and essentially factitious process of local nomination and government selection. The *conseil général du département* numbered sixteen to twenty-four local citizens, depending on the department's population. It helped in the routine task of fiscal allocation, served as a watchdog over the prefect's budget and expenditures, and offered the government its views on administrative problems. To discharge their business the councils convened once a year in a session lasting no more than two weeks.[58]

As its top priority the general council divided the department's quota of direct taxes among the arrondissements, with comparable councils at the arrondissement level allocating those quotas among their communes. Next, just as the *conseil de préfecture* decided on individual requests for tax relief, the general council of the department heard collective appeals for reduced quotas by arrondissements or municipalities. Then it received the prefect's proposal for next year's budget and approved his recommendation for the local tax surcharge *(centimes additionels)*. Finally, the prefect presented his accounts of last year's expenditures for the council's scrutiny and verification. All of this constituted the councils' "administrative functions."

In addition, the councils had what Interior Minister Jean-Antoine Chaptal called a "representative function": to submit their views to Paris on matters affecting the welfare of their department. Since the prefect was an outsider, the Consulate expected these delegations of local notables to provide "details precise enough so that the Government can determine the kind of surveillance, repression, encouragement, and protection that will produce the happiest results in the various localities." Besides using such observations to formulate responses to local problems, however, Chaptal treated these councils as informants in a systematic national policy reassessment for the improvement of public administration. Accordingly, he drafted a uniform agenda for all the councils so that their opinions would yield "results susceptible to being classified in a common, methodical order."[59] At first the minister took this very seriously indeed. After sifting the general councils' views on a wide range of issues in the Years VIII and IX, he published two substantial volumes summarizing their opinions.[60]

The aura of legitimacy and good government that the general councils imparted to the Napoleonic regime at its inception should not be underestimated. They indisputably softened the authoritarian tenor of the prefectorial system, particularly in matters of the purse. At a minimum they resembled the provincial advisory bodies promoted by ministers of Louis XVI such as Turgot and Calonne, who hoped thereby to win the cooperation of local notables without losing the initiative to them. In 1804, a quasi-official newspaper in the Haute-Garonne could greet the approaching convocation of the department's general council with enthusiasm: "This institution is precious, and ought to enhance the popularity of a Government which thus hastens to call forth wisdom and truth from all sides."[61] But Chaptal's decision in the Year X to discontinue publication of their opinions suggested that Paris was losing interest, even as the social composition of the departmental councils was changing in a way that enhanced their prestige. The first councils had been filled by experienced revolutionary administrators. Later, the Napoleonic regime promoted the fusion of new and old elites by coopting members of socially prominent and wealthy families. As general counselors retired or died, their replacements usually came from the wealthiest citizens of the department and from ex-nobles associated with the old regime. [62]

Despite this new social cachet, the functional importance of the *conseils généraux* continued to decline. The pomp and publicity surrounding their annual meetings in the first few years diminished. Prefects began to treat them as a formulaic exercise to be gotten through as quickly as possible. When the general council of the Haute-Garonne ventured some unspecified critical remarks during its session of 1807, the emperor chastised his minister of the interior, who in turn promised that such "ill-considered expressions" would not recur. The minister's blunt circular to all prefects warned that the councils' "representative function" must be strictly confined within pre-scribed limits:

> They are authorized to describe the abuses that strike them, whether in the details of local administrations or in the conduct of the administrators. To indicate the views and the needs of the inhabitants and, in a word, to provide the documents that are necessary to the Government. . . . [But] the laws, the decrees, the system of government, the institutions that generally constitute the public administration, must be for them sacred objects to which . . . they owe respect and passive obedience. [63]

Even the "administrative function" of the councils grew perfunctory in 1810 when prefects gained virtually complete authority over their depart-mental budgets, with the council merely receiving rather than approving the document. [64] It was the Bourbons who salvaged the consultative roles of the general councils. During the Restoration, these notables enjoyed a new respect. Although the Bourbons warned prefects not to entertain any discus-sion of politically sensitive issues, they usually welcomed the advice of the general councils in the areas of agriculture, commerce, public works, educa-tion, and poor relief. [65]

Despite the mitigating elements of the new system, then, prefects enjoyed a sweeping kind of authority, exceeded only by the representatives-on-mission of 1793. Who, then, were these men who assumed such unimagined importance in governing the French people after 1800? General Bonaparte, after all, had scant knowledge of the political or administrative talent availa-ble to fill these key posts. Several collaborators, including the other two Consuls, submitted lists of nominees, but when the First Consul made the final choices he followed the advice of his politician-brother Lucien, briefly his interior minister, in sixty-five cases. Unsurprisingly, the initial nomina-tions fell largely to lawyers and politicians, veterans of revolutionary legisla-tures and local administrations. [66] Nor were they unerring; one third left the

prefectorial corps within three years. As time wore on, Napoleonic appointments exemplified the regime's desire for social fusion. The proportion of
revolutionary politicians and lawyers declined as Napoleon appointed an
increasing number of ex-nobles. This favoritism to aristocrats led some
historians to conclude that after a splendid start the prefectorial corps deteriorated. The most thorough study, however, convincingly argues that this is
a myth.[67]

On the contrary, the most striking trend was the professionalization of
the prefectorial corps. Experienced administrators groomed for the job
gradually replaced the lawyers, politicians, and army officers to whom the
Consulate first turned. By 1810, new prefects typically had served as subprefects or as auditors in the Council of State. Men were being trained for
higher office much like the masters of requests attached to the royal councils
and ministries of the old regime—trained to apply national laws to local
circumstance. Between 1810 and 1813 the government shifted and retired
many prefects, which had the appearance of a purge colored by an aristocratic reaction. More likely this reflected an effort to replace aging prefects
by younger men better qualified for responsibility by way of apprenticeship.
Toward the end of the Empire a bureaucratic career path had emerged. It was
not formal and invariable, but rather a modal pattern: appointment as an
auditor in the Council of State, designation as a subprefect, appointment as
prefect to a low-ranking department, and finally transfer to a major prefecture with a larger population and a higher salary.[68] The growing efficiency of
the prefects was manifest, not least (as we shall see elsewhere) in the crucial
domain of conscription.

The Restoration, however, brought a halt to this emphasis on training.
The Bourbons left intact the centralized, authoritarian machine that Napoleon had constructed, but animated it with new concerns. Having restored
an elected Chamber of Deputies, the Bourbon regime was always looking
over its shoulder at the political climate in the departments. As seven distinct
ministries came and went between 1815 and 1829, the chief minister usually
purged the prefectorial corps to install loyalists attuned to his own political
views. Hence the frequent "massacres" and "waltzes" or transfers of prefects, which eroded the Empire's pattern of apprenticeship and advancement. Since Restoration politics reflected social rivalries, the old-regime
nobility and émigrés now achieved a striking preponderance. At the end of
the Empire only 21 percent of the prefectorial corps (prefects and subprefects) was of noble extraction, compared to 45 percent in 1830. By then
fully 70 percent of the prefects came from noble families of the old regime.
With political patronage all-important, experience and technical qualification

became rarer among the Bourbons' prefects, although their historian believes that they did not lack commendable personal qualities.[69]

WHATEVER THEIR ROUTE to appointment, Restoration prefects presided over increasingly routinized procedures, some inherited from the departmental administrations of the revolutionary decade and others from their Napoleonic predecessors. The departmental prefectures fulfilled the National Assembly's vision of integration and uniformity, of an articulated administrative state. The Assembly's parallel belief in local autonomy, self-government, and participation, however, had been all but discarded with Napoleon's determination to depoliticize this administrative state. Only the general councils preserved the principle of consent at the local level, albeit in an extremely indirect and restricted fashion. (How this process worked itself out at ground level in the villages of France we shall consider in Chapter IV.)

Meanwhile, the supremacy of national law stood as a decisive element of continuity from one regime to another after 1789. The revolutionaries, of course, had a debt here to the old-regime monarchy, which had long governed by explicit ordinances, duly registered by its parlements and cited by royal administrators. But old-regime law had been partial and incomplete, offset by regional particularism and corporate privilege, periodically contested by the parlements themselves, and subject to arbitrary derogations. Above all, old-regime law was formulated in secret and was in effect the property of royal officials, magistrates, and barristers. The revolution not only made law systematic and universal, but made it transparent as well. Whether drafted by the legislature in the 1790s or by the Council of State after 1800, laws received their legitimizing sanction from a publicly visible legislature even during the Empire (although barely), and again under the Restoration. After 1789, executive decrees from Paris as well as local ordinances *(arrêtés)* had to conform to the nation's basic laws. Even laws passed by the regicide Convention of 1793, if they had not been explicitly repealed or superseded, maintained their writ under the Bourbons after 1814. The departments and the communes remained the most tangible outcroppings of the new civic order, but the cumulative volumes of the *Bulletin des Lois* stood at its core.

II

POLITICAL
PARTICIPATION
THE FIRST WAVES

I n the summer of 1789 the National Assembly proclaimed the sovereignty of the French nation and, as we have seen, immediately appropriated effective control of that sovereignty through the doctrine of representation. But in order for this profound revolutionary act to take root and yield a stable civic order, these new fictions of popular sovereignty and representation had in some measure to be credited and supported by French citizens. Although the Assembly asserted its supremacy, it remained in a delicate position, simultaneously empowered and constrained by the mystique of popular sovereignty, anxious to cement popular support even while attempting to channel and limit its force. From inside and outside the Assembly a revolutionary "discourse" articulated the new regime's civic values such as law, liberty, and equality. New rhetoric, symbols, and images initiated a long and complex process of cultural change and resistance.[1] Equally important in anchoring popular sovereignty would be the tangible opportunities for political participation, to which we turn in this chapter.

ELECTIONS AND MORE ELECTIONS

The Declaration of the Rights of Man and Citizen affirmed the notion of popular sovereignty explicitly enough—"The principle of all sovereignty rests essentially in the nation," proclaimed article 3. "No body and no individual may exercise authority which does not emanate from the nation expressly"—but it barely sketched the mechanisms that would institute that sovereignty. The Assembly's founding manifesto merely declared with studied vagueness that "all citizens have the right to take part, in person or by their representatives," in the formation of law and the levying of taxes (articles 6 and 14). It said nothing about the forms of legislative authority, about elections, or about suffrage. As the Assembly gradually filled in the blanks, it translated popular sovereignty into the election not only of parliamentary deputies but of all kinds of officials who, once chosen, were to be insulated in the exercise of their offices until the next election. Rousseau had scorned such delegations of sovereignty, underlining his argument with a swipe at the English: "The people of England regards itself as free: but it is grossly mistaken. It is free only during the election of members of Parliament. As soon as they are elected, slavery overtakes it, and it is nothing. The use it makes of the short moments of liberty it enjoys shows indeed that it deserves to lose them."[2] In France, however, elections were to be so numerous and so frequent that they could hardly be dismissed as cavalierly as the parliamentary elections held every seven years across the Channel.

Elections became a veritable fetish of the new regime. Enfranchised citizens would vote biennially and directly for a mayor, other municipal officers, and a municipal council, whether they lived in a tiny rural commune or a large town. On other occasions citizens would directly elect national guard officers and local magistrates called justices of the peace. In the largest cities such as Paris, Lyon, and Marseille, they participated as well in the assemblies of their neighborhood wards or sections, where they designated sectional officials and committees. Citizens also convened in *primary assemblies* to choose electors who would assemble in turn to fill a host of other elective positions. To choose electors, "all citizens who have the right to vote will meet not in parish or community assemblies [as they had for the elections to the Estates General], but in primary assemblies or by cantons."[3] Voters from rural communes, in other words, had to travel to the seat of their canton, where their votes were aggregated into one pool. (They also elected their justice of the peace at such cantonal assemblies, though not necessarily on the same occasion.) The primary assembly—optimally accommodating 600 potential voters, with a minimum of 450 and a maximum of 900— designated one elector per hundred enfranchised citizens (not actual voters).

Direct elections provided only the minor chord in this electoral fugue. The electors chosen by the primary assemblies operated at two levels. Electors from a particular district chose the district's administrative council and procurator-syndic, discussed in the previous chapter. Electors from the entire department gathered in a departmental *electoral assembly* to choose, not necessarily at the same time, the departmental council and procurator-syndic, the department's judges and public prosecutor, and its legislative deputies. Between early 1790 and mid-1791, voters convened at least four different times, and more frequently if resignations or partial renewals of local offices required it: to elect municipal officers directly; to choose electors who would designate district administrators, departmental officials, and judges; to elect justices of the peace directly; and to choose a new slate of electors for the legislative elections of 1791. In the bourg of Rancon (Haute-Vienne) voters were convoked twelve times between February 1790 and December 1792, five times in 1790 alone. To discharge their multiple responsibilities, electors might in turn have to meet repeatedly, depending on the frequency of vacated positions. The electoral assembly of Paris, for example, convened in November 1792 to renew the capital's numerous tribunals, and finished its work only in June 1793 after 157 sessions.[4]

The electors' duties included the selection of bishops and priests under the Assembly's Civil Constitution of the Clergy. After reducing the number of dioceses by about a third and changing their boundaries to coincide exactly with each of the new departments, the Assembly left it to the departmental electoral assemblies to designate their bishops from the ranks of qualified priests. When a new priest had to be named to fill a vacancy in a parish (and about half the parishes in France became vacant when their curés refused to take the oath of allegiance required by the National Assembly at the end of 1790), then the district electors convened to name a replacement from among the pool of ordained vicars and seminary graduates. This method of electing priests proved to be singularly contentious since it alienated the most concerned parties. The clergy might have welcomed the election of bishops by the priests of a diocese, but generally resented the devolution of this power to the laity, while the congregations of a particular parish were left with no greater control over the recruitment of their own priest than they had under the old regime. When a familiar, popular priest refused to swear the new oath, parishioners often regarded the replacement sent in by the district electors as an unwelcome intruder. In the West, where 85 percent of the curés refused the oath, tensions exploded into a running conflict between district authorities and their rural constituents.[5] Ultimately the crisis of the ecclesiastical oath caused a catastrophic rupture between the Revolution and Catholicism. At its inception, however, this system of choosing clergymen reflected the *constituants'* faith in the self-evident virtue of elections.

The Assembly found the electoral sanction so compelling that the deputies applied it even to the 2,500 disabled and retired veterans residing in the Hôtel des Invalides. This monument of Louis XIV's paternalism had been run in dictatorial fashion by a powerful royal governor, whose administration the veterans denounced in 1789 as harsh and arbitrary. The Assembly's reform plan instituted governance by an administrative council consisting of six municipal delegates from the Paris Commune and thirty *militaires invalides* chosen by direct election of their comrades. The veterans also elected the new chief executive officer, as well as a nine-man "tribunal of conciliation" to handle disciplinary matters. For the Assembly, this change would transform the Hôtel des Invalides from a symbol of royal despotism to a model commonwealth. [6]

In all, an array of civic positions now depended on direct or indirect election: mayors, municipal councils, urban sectionary officials, national guard officers, district administrative councils and syndics, departmental administrative councils and syndics, justices of the peace, civil court judges, departmental criminal court judges, public prosecutors, members of the national *Tribunal de Cassation,* parish priests, bishops, and of course legislative deputies. Subsequently the Convention authorized rank-and-file soldiers to elect their non-commissioned officers. And when the Convention established a national system of public elementary schools in 1794–95, its architects envisioned that parents would elect the teachers, although for the time being a *juri d'instruction* appointed in each district acted as their surrogate. [7]

By the same token, however, the Assembly intended that after voters or electors chose their officials, they would have no power to instruct or sanction those officials. Apart from the general assemblies of urban sections—which operated as direct democracies with running control over their affairs—primary and electoral assemblies were emphatically barred from acting as deliberative bodies during most of the revolutionary decade. As much as the Revolution's electoral system owed to the procedures crafted by the crown for the elections to the Estates General of 1789, the Assembly abandoned completely the traditional deliberative element conserved in that historic electoral consultation. For in 1789 the crown had invited both the parish assemblies of voters and the *bailliage* assemblies of electors to draft grievance petitions, while the latter could in theory bind their deputies with "imperative mandates." This changed completely, as we have seen, after the summer of 1789. The people would exercise their sovereignty by participating frequently and repeatedly in the election of all constituted authorities, but they were not to deliberate on policy questions in their primary or electoral assemblies.

Delimiting popular sovereignty further, the Assembly refused even to submit the new constitution itself to a popular referendum. This barely debated decision remains veiled in obscurity, but seems to have been a matter of political expediency more than principle. Nor does it appear that most demands for a referendum came primarily from radical democrats. To be sure, a few Jacobins broke silence on this matter with the obvious Rousseau-ist argument that "this precious right [to ratify the constitution] is the very essence of sovereignty; the nation cannot lose it or delegate it."[8] One pamphlet stigmatized the Assembly's unwillingness to turn ratification over to the people as "a new papacy of political infallibility." But the strongest call for a referendum came from the right, notably from the *monarchien* deputy Pierre Malouet. It thus seemed to patriot deputies a trap, and they success-fully squelched the idea as "rather counter-revolutionary," implying that it might produce a rejection of the Assembly's monumental labors. Having precluded the charge of perpetuating themselves in office by making them-selves ineligible for election to the new legislature, the *constituants* could accept LeChapelier's contention that citizens were implicitly approving the constitution by their participation in the legislative elections of 1791.[9]

THE FRANCHISE

Before the nation's panoply of elective offices could be filled, the Assembly had to determine suffrage and eligibility qualifications, as well as voting procedures in the primary and electoral assemblies. Prudently avoiding these awkward questions in the Declaration of the Rights of Man, the Assembly had every intention of imposing significant requirements. On the eve of 1789, influential patriots from all three estates had promoted a fusion of elites around a loosely defined core of values: talent, property, social utility. Popular sovereignty created a huge opening to advance that agenda, but also a potential for subverting it. To get back on course, the Assembly now distinguished political rights from the universal rights it had proclaimed that summer. While every French citizen would have equal civil rights, only certain citizens would be qualified to exercise political rights, to be enfran-chised or "active" citizens. The *constituants* justified this resonant distinction by embracing a pre-revolutionary view of voting as a civic function rather than a universal right. As Antoine Barnave put it, voting was "a right that the society dispenses as prescribed by its interest." The national interest dictated that voters must be independent to some degree (lest they be manipulated by the powerful) and must possess "an interest in the public establishment" (lest they act irresponsibly). The Assembly therefore excluded from "active" citizenship those in its view who did not meet these criteria: women, men under twenty-five years of age, domestic servants, convicted felons, and bankrupts, as well as men who did not pay at least a minimal level of direct taxes in the equivalent of three days' local wages—a sum that could vary between 1.5 and 3 livres. The Assembly also required voters to be of settled domicile (with at least a year's residence in their canton), to be inscribed as members of the national guard, to sign a civic register well before the elections, and to take a civic oath when they came to vote. Literacy, however, was not made a qualification for political rights.[10]

Wholesale restrictions on the right to vote did not sail through the Assembly without provoking an outcry. Whatever the Assembly's intentions, dissenters could invoke the vague but seemingly implied promise of political rights for all citizens in the Declaration of the Rights of Man. Petitions and pamphlets arguing for women's suffrage, including a "Declaration of the Rights of Women," forced the Assembly to justify the exclusion of women instead of taking it for granted. But if proponents of women's suffrage drew strength from the sense of unimagined possibility opened by 1789, more conventional attitudes prevailed. The Assembly rebuffed feminist advocates with circular arguments about women's supposed emotionalism, dependent status, and unsuitability for the public sphere. In contrast, religious tests for active citizenship seemed to be ruled out: despite the Catholic clergy's historic opposition, the Assembly quickly extended full political rights to Protestants without serious debate. Deputies from Alsace, however, where most of France's forty thousand Jews resided, echoed the hostility of their constituents and vehemently opposed the enfranchisement of Jews. As members of an alien religion, culture, and society, they argued, these Jews were not really French citizens at all. This adamant intervention immobilized the Assembly, which uneasily postponed its decision, in effect disfranchising the Ashkenazi Jews of the East in the elections of 1790 and 1791 even while permitting smaller, long-assimilated Sephardic Jewish communities of the South to vote. Just before its dissolution, however, the Assembly finally embraced the egalitarian logic of its principles and extended full citizenship rights to all Jews.[11]

In the Assembly's electoral blueprint, the imposition of property qualifications for political rights has drawn the most attention from contemporaries and historians alike. For Sieyès and his colleagues, property or fiscal qualifications for voting (the *cens*) denoted a citizen's stake in society. Initially the Assembly created a three-tiered hierarchy: the threshold of three *journées de travail* in direct tax payment established basic voting rights; a direct tax payment of at least ten *journées de travail* was necessary to be *éligible*—to serve as an elector, local official, or judge; and only those paying at least a *marc d'argent* (approximately 53 livres) in taxes qualified for election to the legislature. This censitary system stirred a tempest of opposition in the radical press and even in the Assembly. Critics like Robespierre denounced the intention to segregate "active" and "passive" citizens—the latter being a contradiction in terms, nothing more than a sanitized euphemism for the taboo word "subject."[12] Some lauded the Parisians who stormed the Bastille as the nation's veritable "active citizens." At the other end, they attacked the *marc d'argent* for negating the Revolution's commitment to free rein for talent; more than one polemic observed that Jean-Jacques Rousseau himself would have been barred from the French legislature by that provision. In its final revisions of the constitution before disbanding in September 1791 (which therefore did not affect the legislative election that had already occurred), the Assembly dropped the discredited *marc d'argent* and left no restriction on eligibility to the legislature. Simultaneously, however, it raised the fiscal qualification for electors. The concept of voting-as-function prevailed over voting-as-right.

Reckoning the practical effect of the Assembly's restrictions on the franchise is no simple matter. The deputies had set the *cens* for active citizenship at a minimal level, and could well have believed that in time the vast majority of citizens would be able to cross that threshold. The historian Patrice Gueniffey plausibly argues that at the primary level, the censitary franchise of 1790 can be viewed as "a prelude to universal [male] suffrage." For the moment, however, it did exclude certain adult males from the most fundamental political right and became a telling point in the radical critique of the Assembly. The National Assembly published a departmental enumeration of "active" citizens in May 1791 totaling 4,299,000 as against an estimated population of 27 million. But was the French population really that large? And in any case what proportion consisted of males above the age of twenty-five? By general agreement among current historians, franchise restrictions relegated about one third of adult males to "passive" citizenship because of their poverty, status as domestics, or itinerancy.[13]

In any case the proportion of active citizens is just the beginning, since stringent registration requirements compounded statutory exclusions from the franchise. The potential number of active citizens, in other words, was greater, perhaps far greater, than the actual number of registered citizens who might vote in any election. In order to vote, citizens had to be motivated enough to document their tax payment, national guard membership, and prior inscription on civic register. A notoriously poor voting profile for Paris, for example, began with its unusually low ratio of active citizens (only 48 percent of adult males), but contracted further at the level of registration. Extrapolations from a few detailed neighborhood records suggest that of the capital's 78,000 *"actifs virtuels"* of 1791, Parisians who had actually fulfilled all registration formalities numbered only 27,000 to 31,000.[14] Late in 1791—after the first departmental and legislative elections had been held—the

Assembly added another requirement that threatened to depress voting rolls even further, although it never actually came into play: citizens qualified to serve as criminal court jurors had to enroll for jury service in special registers maintained in the district capitals. To promote compliance, the Assembly decreed that citizens failing to sign up for jury service would lose their right to vote. In its exalted demands for civic responsibility the Assembly thus linked national guard duty, jury service, and voting, with the right to vote contingent on fulfilling the other more demanding responsibilities, but with the more likely effect that some citizens would shun all three. [15]

It could be argued in any case that the real political nation was defined not by the relatively porous exclusions of the primary franchise but by the qualifications for serving as elector or official. The proportion of *éligibles* relative to the number of active citizens is therefore a fundamental question but an elusive one, which the National Assembly did not attempt to document. Recent research suggests that earlier estimates of 75 percent for the proportion of *éligibles* to active citizens are too high, with the average closer to 60 percent (meaning approximately 40 percent of all adult males). An analysis of the elections of 1790 in the Landes—based on an exhaustively detailed *Tableau* prepared by the department—provides a unique case study of such questions in the first nationwide elections (for departmental administrations) of the new regime. In this relatively undeveloped, decidedly unurbanized department of the Southwest, 23,000 out of 40,000 active citizens were *éligibles,* or 57 percent. The spread in the proportion of *éligibles* to actives among the department's twenty-five cantons, however, ranged from a high of 76 percent in Mont-de-Marsan to a low of 32 percent in Gabarret. At the level of the commune, contrasts are even sharper: in one third of the Landes' communes fewer than half the active citizens qualified as *éligible,* but over 80 percent were *éligible* in one quarter of the communes, thanks in all likelihood to a wider distribution of agricultural property. Finally, the larger towns all had lower percentages of *éligibles* than the average for their surrounding cantons, in part because the level of taxation in 1790 remained lower in towns than in the countryside. [16] All told, the fiscal criterion for eligibility as electors seems to have functioned as a substantial barrier, but with enough variation and exceptions to make generalization problematic.

If we pass from eligibility for designation as an elector to the actual composition of the electors chosen in that first revolutionary election, the distance between the electors and ordinary voters looks much greater. The exhaustive *Tableau Générale* of the Landes records the electors' tax payments, revealing an average of 115 livres, over ten times greater than the qualifying amount for *éligibles.* Indeed, more than two thirds of the electors in the Landes would have met the elevated standard of the *marc d'argent.* Currently this is the only department apart from Paris for which we have such fiscal information, however, so nothing can be said about its typicality. The social composition of the electors, on the other hand, we know to have varied widely by departments as one by now expects in the ethnographic mosaic of France. In the Landes, 72 percent of the 408 electors were rural residents, but the largest occupational group comprised men with legal or judicial background (24 percent), followed by rentiers (24 percent). Only 17 percent were agriculturalists and 15 percent from the arena of commerce. Cultivators dominated in the Breton departments of Finistère (48 percent) and Ille-et-Vilaine (35 percent), while electors with business ties formed the largest group in the Mediterranean Bouches-du-Rhône.[17] The underlying explanations for such regional patterns, if such they were, have yet to become apparent.

A more pertinent question perhaps is the extent to which the same individuals were chosen as electors from year to year. Patrice Gueniffey estimates that 30 to 40 percent of electors were chosen more than once between 1790 to 1792, and that in a given assembly up to half the electors may have served previously. Similarly, public officials held a substantial place in certain assemblies, while conversely (and predictably) assemblies often elected officials from their own ranks, leading Gueniffey to posit "the precocious consolidation of a homogeneous political class" within this matrix of departmental electoral assemblies.[18] As planned, the nation's 43,000 electors wielded real political power. As also intended, their passport to this power was anything but automatic. Voters in the primary assemblies had wide latitude in choosing whom to propel into this nascent political class, this open oligarchy.

THE ELECTORAL PROCESS

One morning in June 1791, 235 citizens in the Alsatian canton of Dannemarie (Haut-Rhin) gathered for their primary assembly to choose electors for the impending legislative elections. Led by provisional officers designated according to age (the oldest and youngest who could read and write), the citizens began by electing the *bureau* that would officiate over the voting: the president (with the power to resolve procedural disputes, to prolong the assembly or to adjourn it); the secretary who kept the indispensable *procès-verbal;* and three *scrutateurs,* alone authorized to fill out ballots for illiterate voters and to keep the tallies as votes were counted at the completion of each round *(scrutin).* Voting always proceeded with a roll call *(appel nominal)* of registered voters who one by one deposited their ballot *(bulletin)* in the urn.

(The law insisted on this laborious *appel nominal* as the best guarantee against electoral fraud, since it matched a name on a register to a specific face before anyone voted.) Election to any position required an absolute majority on the first or second round, with a plurality sufficing on the third and final round.

Election of the *bureau*—requiring separate *scrutins* for president, secretary, and *scrutateurs*—took two full sessions at Dannemarie, stretching across the entire day. This preliminary balloting often gave a foretaste of the political coloration or preferences of the assembly, and voters took it seriously. The monotony of that day's proceedings was relieved only after the president and secretary had been chosen, when the assembled voters swore the required electoral oath: "To maintain the Constitution of the Kingdom with all their power; to be faithful to the nation, to the law, to the King; to choose according to their spirit and conscience those most worthy of public confidence; and to fill with zeal and courage any civil and political function confided to them." Next day 404 voters turned out to cast ballots for the canton's seven electors. Each inscribed seven names in this *scrutin de liste*. By the end of the day the tallies for a host of nominees showed that only two had won the necessary majority. The assembly took two more ballots on the third day, attracting 279 and 260 voters respectively, to fill its quota of seven electors.[19]

Voting in France's primary assemblies thus loomed as an endurance contest. Under the Assembly's detailed guidelines, citizens found themselves enmeshed in an extremely tedious and time-consuming rite in which participation ebbed and flowed, generally tapering off as time wore on. The primary and electoral assemblies created by the French Revolution were awkward hybrids of traditional communal assemblies and a new-style political individualism based on the secret ballot.[20] Moreover, with their departmental legislative delegations, French elections differed dramatically from those in the American states and Great Britain. In the Anglo-Saxon world, eligible citizens elected their legislators by direct vote in single-constituency districts, where candidates actively and publicly sought their support; after such elections, voters could presumably identify their representative. In France, by contrast, each representative served in effect as a deputy-at-large for the entire department. The system severed individual deputies from a particular locality or constituency, and reliance on indirect voting by electors compounded this effect. As debates in several American states suggest, these options represented the most conservative approach available. When the architects of state constitutions in America sought to enhance the influence of local elites to counteract democratic or localist tendencies, they resorted to indirect election (as in Maryland), or opted for upper legislative houses with larger constituencies, at the extreme (in Connecticut and Rhode Island) recruiting the entire upper house by at-large election.[21]

The indirect elections and departmental deputations of the French system meshed comfortably with a moral consensus in 1789 against the active pursuit of office, the insistence on public modesty among political leaders. Searching the newspapers and pamphlets published in Alsace, the historian Roland Marx could find no evidence of the names of potential candidates being offered to the voters before elections. He attributes this singular lack to "the general prejudice of those times against all individual propaganda, considered as one and the same with intrigue." The consequences, he adds, were damaging.[22] Candidacy in France, to the extent that it existed, remained unofficial and subterranean, advanced only by oral means and in private. Although individuals were not expected to campaign for office, their friends and clients might act in concert to advance their cause.

Patrice Gueniffey has studied this system closely and takes an extremely dim view. While a lack of avowed candidates ostensibly maximized the liberty of voters to choose whom they wished, in reality (he argues) it created an excess of choice that in effect nullified the average voter's liberty and rendered his influence nil. While small coteries of voters might know exactly what they wanted to accomplish, most citizens operated in the dark. Most voters or electors—those outside the orbit of clubs or "cabals"—had no obvious way of assessing or even identifying possible candidates in advance of the balloting. In the early *scrutins* many squandered their votes by dispersing them among an impossibly large number of individuals, while others cast incomplete or invalid ballots. Ultimately many voters were obliged to cast their ballots on the third round for the choices of minorities in the preliminary rounds who were unknown to them. Unofficial campaigning most certainly occurred, for what else could explain the large number of first ballot victories in the legislative elections of 1791 (33.6 percent) and 1792 (43.6 percent)? But, with exceptions, such results did not follow from open competition or campaigning by opposing candidates.[23]

Campaigns for invisible candidates remained one of the most dubious elements of the electoral process in revolutionary France. No doubt this enhanced the power of "cabals," of compact groups of voters, to initiate momentum for a majority among the dispersed votes of the unorganized, as Gueniffey argues—although he consistently undervalues the opportunity of all voters to reject known incumbents, surely the most fundamental element of any democracy. But apart from the leverage that it might have given to organized minorities—a leverage scarcely lacking in America or Britain—the Revolution's electoral system deprived French citizens of the engaging rituals of election campaigns, with their carnivalesque acting-out, purgative rhetoric, and momentary opportunities for social role reversal that served in the Anglo-Saxon world to integrate ordinary citizens into a political process over which, in reality, they had little real power. [24]

Scrupulously fair on paper, the procedures of France's protracted assemblies locked voters together at close quarters for days on end and could easily erupt in contention and turmoil. Disputes over the right of individuals to vote, procedural conflicts, stalling tactics, accusations of fraud (denunciations of pre-written ballots, for example, or an excess number of ballots cast), intimidation, and occasional brawls disrupted many primary assemblies. Initially, most such incidents stemmed from antagonisms between citizens of rival communes thrown together into the same canton. But the cantonal circumscriptions generally came to be accepted and apparently did not cause an inherent dysfunction in the electoral system. By 1792, political partisanship rather than local rivalry set off most incidents in the primary assemblies. [25] The imposition of an oath to the regime also gave the new electoral system an inflection that changed over time. At first, it must have seemed an innocuous form of civic pedagogy. But by 1791, when religious and ideological division began to alienate certain groups of citizens, the oath might have deterred the most disaffected from participating altogether. Voter absenteeism, in any case, soon reached dismayingly high levels.

VOTER TURNOUT AND ABSENTEEISM

Evidence for a splendid start but subsequent deterioration of the Revolution's electoral system emerges from several local studies of voting between 1790 and 1792. (The only practical method to assess voter turnout is to use the highest number of citizens recorded as present for any ballot during the course of a primary assembly as against the total number of active citizens in the canton, although this method probably underestimates total participation.) [26] An overview of electoral participation by Melvin Edelstein draws together complete or partial data from twenty-six departments for the primary assemblies of 1790 and nineteen departments for the primary assemblies of 1791. In the relatively harmonious atmosphere of 1790, the novelty of the primary assemblies evidently produced a high level of interest in many departments and brought an impressive turnout of voters in the first nationwide balloting for electors to choose the new departmental administrations. In 1790, the participation rate averaged 48 percent, approximately the median among the departments as well, with two Burgundian departments achieving remarkable turnouts of over 70 percent. The following year, to choose electors for the legislative elections (which some locally oriented voters might have considered less important), turnout fell to an average (and median) of about 23 percent.[27]

Taking seven departments with virtually complete figures for both years, we find the following contrasts in the range of departmental participation rates:

	1790	1791
Aube	73%	40%
Côte d'Or	71%	40%
Marne	64%	32%
Haute-Garonne	55%	23%
Aude	48%	15%
Eure	41%	19%
Seine	16%	13%

Naturally departmental figures mask dramatic local variations. In the Landes, for example, the overall turnout in the election of 1790 was a robust 61 percent, with eight of the department's twenty-five cantons reaching over 70 percent; but in six other cantons, participation fell below 50 percent of active citizens, with a low of 34 percent.[28]

Historians and social scientists have long pondered whether urbanites have generally been more assiduous voters than rural citizens. Judging by the low turnouts in Paris during the first two national elections, they certainly were not, notwithstanding the capital's growing neighborhood activism and mobilizations in 1792. Indeed, allowing for the inevitable exceptions, rural citizens as a rule voted in greater proportions than urban inhabitants in the Revolution's first two national elections. In one study of the 1790 elections, for example, participation proved decidedly stronger in the rural cantons of five districts compared to turnout in their urban centers; only in the Breton district around Vannes did urban voters participate more actively. By 1791 the trends were less clear. Rural participation plummeted in five of the districts, but still exceeded urban rates in three. Similar studies point to the same pattern.[29] Initially, rural communitarian habits may have predisposed peasants to participate in the collective electoral consultations of the primary assemblies even with the novelty of the individual written ballot. In many towns, where all vestiges of democratic civic life had disappeared in the era of absolutism and venal offices, urban elites quickly adapted to the revolutionary electoral system, but artisans, shopkeepers, and journeymen were slower to involve themselves. Later, however, the rural preponderance in voting generally waned while the influence of activist urban minorities accelerated.

Even if most qualified citizens did not turn out for the primary assemblies to choose electors (being indifferent, or too busy, or assuming that their social superiors could handle this task without them), did they perhaps show greater interest in direct balloting for their own municipal officials? In a village, after all, the management of communal property was of immediate interest to every inhabitant. And in a town or bourg, one would be designating a mayor present on the scene and perhaps familiar at least by reputation. Fragmentary evidence suggests that turnout for municipal elections in town and village alike ran higher than voting for electors in the primary assemblies, although how consistently is uncertain. Having combed through a dizzying variety of electoral records, for example, Roland Marx writes confidently of Alsace: "Everywhere and always citizens were more assiduous in municipal elections than in [indirect] legislative elections." Thus in Belfort (Haut-Rhin), 84 percent of the active citizens (9,684 out of a possible 11,552) turned out for the very first revolutionary election of municipal officers in January 1790, whereas the turnout for the legislative primary assemblies of 1791 in Belfort reached only 56 percent. But Marx's second generalization is that in all types of elections, whether municipal balloting or primary assemblies, "electoral participation declined over the years"—not uniformly or linearly, of course, but overall. A study of mayoral elections in nine towns alongside the results of selected primary assemblies suggests the same two points: generally stronger turnout in municipal elections, and falling rates of voter participation in successive elections.[30]

Most of the evidence about voter participation and absenteeism seems to converge around one major generalization. The new regime's electoral system—the centerpiece of its entire political edifice and its indispensable mechanism for reconciling popular sovereignty and the doctrine of representation—began auspiciously at all levels, with rural participation (contrary to conventional wisdom) notably strong. But indifference, disenchantment, or hostility (very different phenomena, to be sure) quickly took their toll. Disturbances and contention in the primary assemblies were not inordinate and can even be read as a sign of vigor and interest. Rather, it was absenteeism starting in 1791 that cast a shadow across the Revolution's single-minded commitment to elections. During the decade to come, there would be localized surges of participation, but the rise in absenteeism after 1790 would never be decisively reversed.

THE REVOLUTIONARY PRESS

If a majority of "active" citizens registered indifference, unawareness, or disenchantment with the new regime by failing to vote after 1790, a growing minority embraced politics as a fact of daily life, even a consuming passion. The Assembly's attempt to channel popular sovereignty into the performance of one civic function proved unrealistic from the start. In the towns, citizens quickly challenged the hermetic structure of electoral representation by forming political clubs, while a vibrant free press breached the insulation of constituted authorities and nurtured an unsettling spectrum of political opinions. Beyond this triad of democratic institutions (elections, clubs, newspapers), an expanding repertory of direct action by men and women, both violent and peaceful, colored the emerging political culture—from food riots and anti-seigneurial château-burnings to such new forms as petitioning, heckling from the galleries, or turning out for political demonstrations. In vain, the *constituants* chased after activists with their foremost weapon, the prerogative to define revolutionary legality. They criminalized seditious speech acts with an overhanging threat of capital punishment;[31] pursued inflammatory journalists even while failing to agree on a press law that fixed the boundary between liberty and license; and tried to limit the role of clubs by prohibiting their "collective" petitions. These fingers in the dike, however, did little to curb the swirl of popular activity.

The arena of political activism expanded as much in response to anti-revolutionary sentiment as to radical agitation. Apart from ideological counter-revolution and the calculated opposition of disaffected nobles, émigrés, or foreign princes, the new regime faced reactive waves of anti-revolutionary hostility. Above all, the Civil Constitution of the Clergy provoked popular protests from parishioners against the "strangers" designated to replace familiar refractory priests. When local authorities responded with high-handed tactics of their own, legality became the first casualty on both sides.[32] Under the stress of such polarization, the Revolution's center of gravity inexorably shifted. The epiphany of revolutionary unity in July 1789 lasted by the most generous estimate little more than a year. With startling rapidity, yesterday's bold spokesman for the Third Estate became today's disaffected conservative, while today's bystander became tomorrow's militant.

The revolutionary press contributed mightily to the viability of the new regime in its early days and to the subsequent fractionalization of opinion. Late in 1788, the crown had sanctioned the free expression of opinion on the forthcoming meeting of the Estates General, unleashing a deluge of over four thousand pamphlets in eight months. It drew the line, however, when deputy-elect Mirabeau and the writer J. P. Brissot separately announced their intention to publish unauthorized newspapers to cover the proceedings of the Estates General. By reporting regularly on its deliberations, they hoped to solidify the forum of public opinion with the permanence of an uncensored periodical press. Though temporarily frustrated by the monarchy's opposition, these pioneers persisted, and along with others of the same mind effectively shouldered aside the tottering royal censorship apparatus.

Other impediments to a free press disappeared as well when the legal privileges and monopolies that had restricted publishing and printing in the old regime lost their writ. The fall of the Bastille accelerated the rise of the revolutionary press, calling forth new journalistic styles to report and explain such rapidly unfolding events.[33] In 1789, 140 new journals appeared in the capital—24 in July and another 20 in August; over 30 of these revolutionary periodicals lasted at least a year, including 20 daily newspapers.[34] In the course of the 1790s, about two thousand newspapers would be launched in the capital; most folded quickly, but others continued until circumstances or repression forced them to close. The more successful publishers quickly moved from selling by individual numbers to sale by subscription. Freed of legal and guild restrictions, requiring relatively low investments of start-up capital, and working with a break-even point of perhaps 400 to 450 copies per issue (with the prospect of handsome profits if 1,000 copies were sold), journalism became a freewheeling competitive vocation.[35]

Revolutionary journalists mixed news and commentary liberally and often indiscriminately, but the greatest commercial rewards flowed to the newspapers that made intelligible the confusing deliberations of the National Assembly, selecting and reordering material from the mass of speeches and decrees. The journals with the largest circulations (nearing or topping 10,000 subscribers from time to time), sober in style and patriotic but moderate in approach, included the relatively bland *Journal de Perlet, Gazette Universel,* and *Journal du Soir,* an evening newspaper with an effective circulation strategy. The didactic *Feuille Villageoise* (at a subscription price of only 9 livres per year) won respect and a circulation said to top 15,000 for its self-assigned mission of enlightening rural citizens in the ways of the Revolution, especially by printing letters from readers.[36] The *Moniteur,* a creation of the old-regime press baron Charles-Joseph Panckoucke, ultimately proved to be the Revolution's most durable newspaper after establishing its image as a journal of record.

Entrepreneurs in the provinces were quick to seize new publishing opportunities as well, even if they lacked the national market potential of

Parisian journalists. Publishers transformed their regional *Affiches* or advertising sheets into political newspapers, published bulletins from deputies or other correspondents in Paris, and founded new journals. The publisher of the *Affiches, Annonces et Avis divers de Toulouse et du Haut-Languedoc,* for example, converted his local literary gazette and advertiser into a *Journal Universel et Affiches de Toulouse et du département de la Haute-Garonne,* expanded its length and frequency, and increased its political content until the literary and scientific articles, local advertisements, and commercial announcements that had been its staple fare before 1789 practically vanished.[37] Lyon, home to two pre-revolutionary periodicals, saw fourteen journals started by the end of 1791; in Bordeaux, with only one newspaper before 1789, sixteen appeared within the next two years; and in Strasbourg, a handful of new German-language journals struggled to win an audience seeking information in a comprehensible idiom.

Encouraged by revolutionary administrations trying to promote a sense of identity in their new departments, printers launched newspapers in departmental capitals that had never supported any local periodical. Some foundered quickly, but others took root. With limited horizons and very small circulations, provincial journalism remained a fragile "cottage industry": only about a third of the six hundred provincial newspapers launched during the revolutionary decade lasted a year or more, and only four passed 1,000 in circulation. But throughout the decade at least one hundred newspapers were being published in the provinces at any given time, the great majority devoted to government and politics.[38] Most provincial newspapers avoided extreme opinions for obvious reasons, but in the larger cities like Lyon, Marseille, and Toulouse, the partisanship of certain journalists helped raise the local political temperature.

One can scarcely imagine the National Assembly enacting its torrent of innovations without widely disseminated newspapers to inform citizens and engage their support. But the enlightened, unified opinion that Brissot and others expected to form around a free press proved to be short-lived. The earnestness of the first revolutionary editors was soon challenged by journalists adept at ridicule and defamation, the literary heritage of underground pamphleteering in the old regime. Civility toward one's political opponents or rivals evaporated in their pages. Radical patriot journalists, describing themselves as sentinels or tribunes of the people, alarmed the public with constant talk of counter-revolutionary plots, and raised the term "traitor" to a cliché of political discourse.

The radical press emanated above all from a cohort of competing journalists associated with the Cordelier Club on the Left Bank. Men who had failed to gain a foothold in the republic of letters before 1789, these writers and

editors identified body and soul with the Revolution. The "Cordelier journals" included the weekly *Révolutions de France et Brabant* of Camille Desmoulins, whose street-corner orations helped spark the July 14 uprising; the
pioneering weekly *Révolutions de Paris,* which began by reporting that epochal
event; the daily *Orateur du Peuple* of Stanislaus Fréron; and the daily *Ami du
Peuple* of Jean-Paul Marat. The radical journalists relentlessly denounced the
machinations of the crown, the derogations of revolutionary notables like
LaFayette and mayor Bailly, and the equivocations of the National Assembly
itself. Distrusting constituted authority of any kind, they considered popular
sovereignty to be more than a convenient fiction, and goaded their readers
to a high pitch of vigilance, suspicion, and activism. The radical journals
propagated a vague and ultimately problematic social vision hinging on a
moral dichotomy between a good, civic-minded, freedom-loving "people"
and an evil "aristocracy" comprising elements of the nobility, the clergy, the
very rich, the lawyers—anyone whose egocentric and avaricious behavior
revealed their lack of commitment to the commonweal. [39]

Marat was by all odds the most notorious and influential of the radical
journalists. Selling at an elevated 48 livres for a year's subscription, the *Ami
du Peuple* had no more than 3,000 or 4,000 subscribers. But Marat's inflammatory style evidently riveted his readers. His tirades and periodic calls for
heads stirred (or more accurately, poisoned) the political atmosphere in Paris.
Half a dozen official prosecutions failed to silence his violently paranoid
voice. The royalist camp took somewhat longer to establish its journalistic
beachhead, but was supporting twenty periodicals by the summer of 1790,
some of which matched the incendiary style of the radical press. The impassioned, rejectionist polemics of abbé Royou's *Ami du Roi* won over 5,000
subscribers in 1791, while the mordant salon-style satires of the *Actes des
Apôtres* mocked every individual and principle dear to the revolutionaries. [40]

After August 10—a violent confrontation long anticipated by the press
and promoted by certain journals on both sides—the capacious freedom of
political journalists came to an abrupt end when the insurrectionary Paris
Commune suppressed the leading royalist journals and arrested several editors and publishers. Right-wing journalists continued to publish in more
muted tones, but the boundaries of press freedom narrowed again after the
purge of the Girondin deputies in June 1793, as the government suppressed
the influential journals associated with their position. When the Convention
instituted a temporary revolutionary dictatorship between September and
December 1793, a handful of newspapers enjoyed official favor, including
the *sans-culottes'* favorite journal, Hébert's populist and heavily subsidized *Père
Duchesne,* and the new organ of the Paris Jacobin Club, the *Journal de la
Montagne.*

Yet even the Terror did not entirely muzzle the press or limit newspapers to reprinting official handouts, as Napoleon would. Aesopian techniques kept contrasting viewpoints in print, although the room for maneuver kept narrowing as the danger of arrest increased.[41] In the end, the Terror claimed two of the most accomplished revolutionary journalists who refused to walk the narrow path established by the Committee of Public Safety. In March 1794, Hébert, suddenly stigmatized as a subversive ultra-revolutionary, went to the guillotine. A month later Camille Desmoulins, the veteran radical journalist and member of the Convention, perished with his comrade Danton after badgering Robespierre to moderate the Terror in a series of pamphlets entitled *Le Vieux Cordelier.*[42] Thermidor, however, liberated journalists of all persuasions, and the outpouring of newspapers across the political spectrum seemed like 1789 all over again.

THE JACOBIN CLUBS

Alongside revolutionary journalism, the spread of political clubs gave the French Revolution its distinctive character. The Revolution's premier club, different from the others, began as a caucus of deputies to the Estates General in Versailles. When the Assembly moved to Paris, this Society of the Friends of the Constitution became known as the Jacobin Club, after the former convent of the Jacobin Order that it used as a meeting hall. While deputies continued to form the core of its membership, the club opened its doors to middle-class Parisian enthusiasts. Clubs elsewhere began independently in local contexts. Members of the fledgling national guard of Marseille, for example, established a club in the nation's third largest city. Like other early clubs, it had roots as well in older urban associations such as reading clubs, confraternities, and Masonic lodges. But the new clubs quickly outgrew such antecedents even where they had been noticeable. Responding directly to the stimulus of the Revolution, the clubs focused exclusively on politics, and their new brand of sociability cut across the parochial social boundaries that often defined the confraternities and Masonic lodges of the eighteenth century.[43] Unlike old-regime associations, the Jacobin clubs usually held their sessions in public. When the revolutionary government made public sessions obligatory for clubs in October 1793, it merely gave legal writ to the clubs' long-standing belief in "transparency."

"Jacobinism," while denoting the ideology of revolutionary leaders like Robespierre, also and perhaps more accurately refers to the grass-roots mobilization in clubs that made politics into a tangible experience, embodying political participation for a socially diverse minority of citizens. On one level the clubs functioned as miniature polities, echoes within civil society of the official world of government. Club members became familiar with procedures that had been practiced only in the rarefied and closed worlds of the elites, if at all: the recourse to elected officers, by-laws, agendas, minutes of meetings, and correspondence secretaries. They framed, debated, and voted on motions, and approved or rejected documents drawn up by committees or other clubs. Citizens from one end of France's regional mosaic to the other stepped into political life through this common form of organizational ritual and associative practice. Could there have been a more effective impetus for political acculturation?[44]

Tracing the history of Jacobinism involves an exercise in quantification to chart the diffusion of clubs across the nation's territory. Keeping in mind that the clubs had no official standing at all in the Revolution's early years, one must regard their spread across urban France as impressive. By the spring of 1791, almost 450 Societies of the Friends of the Constitution were affiliated with the "mother society" in Paris, with at least one in every department. Since the Paris Club decided early on to affiliate with only one club in any town, alternative clubs in places like Bordeaux and Lyon (not to mention "fraternal societies" in Parisian neighborhoods) existed alongside the official Jacobin affiliates, in addition to clubs in small towns that did not seek or could not qualify for affiliation—altogether perhaps an additional five hundred clubs. By the end of 1792 over one thousand five hundred communes had a club.

But the foundation of clubs did not follow a uniform rhythm orchestrated from a central point. Regional variations in the density of clubs belie any notion of a coordinated impulsion from Paris. Outside the departmental and district *chefs-lieux,* the most fertile ground for the early formation of clubs proved to be the "urbanized villages" of Provence. The departments with the highest concentrations of clubs clustered in the Mediterranean Southeast (Vaucluse, Bouches-du-Rhône, Basses-Alpes, Drôme, Var); the Southwest (Gironde and Haute-Garonne); and the North/Northwest (Pas-de-Calais, Seine-Inférieure, Seine-et-Oise). But whereas the Southwest achieved a high density of clubs by 1791, in the North/Northwest, clubs proliferated only in 1793.[45]

The founding of political clubs and the flowering of political journalism after 1789 were not intrinsically symbiotic; but once established, the clubs developed in tandem with revolutionary newspapers and in turn gave the press added extension and influence. Provincial clubs typically scheduled their meetings to coincide with the arrival of the postal courier, and most clubs held public readings of their favorite newspapers. Initially the clubs preferred moderate journals with the latest news and reports on the Assembly, such as the *Moniteur* and the *Feuille Villageoise.* Their favorite newspaper seems to have been the *Annales patriotiques* of Jean-Louis Carra, the "oracle" of provincial Jacobinism who actively cultivated the goodwill of the clubs. Interestingly, however, the clubs shunned extremists; with the rarest exceptions Jacobin societies in the provinces simply would not subscribe to Marat's *Ami du Peuple* or Hébert's *Père Duchesne* until 1793, if at all. [46]

The example and impetus of the Paris Club unquestionably nourished the spread of Jacobin clubs, and affiliation with the "mother club" certainly enhanced the self-image of provincial *sociétaires.* But correspondence with the "mother club" was only the most obvious way in which these local activists attempted to expand their horizons and influence. The Jacobin clubs did not constitute a political machine commanded from Paris, but rather a supple communications network open to input from all directions. [47] Each club typically had its preferred grid of correspondents, including important regional centers like Marseille, Bordeaux, Dijon, or Rouen; a number of medium-sized towns; and smaller clubs in its own hinterland. The circular letters that passed back and forth formed the matrix of Jacobin politics. Crucial initiatives sometimes began in Paris, of course, but frequently one or another provincial society launched a provocative *démarche* and enlisted other clubs, which then relayed the proposal to their own networks. At times of heightened conflict clubs would be weighing alternative recommendations from their "friends and brothers" elsewhere, voting to endorse or reject this petition or that circular letter, perhaps later revisiting the issue and changing their minds.

This is not to deny that at crucial junctures events in Paris drove the Revolution. But it would be entirely misleading to conclude that as Paris went, so went provincial Jacobinism. At moments of crisis, provincial Jacobins usually fell in behind the "mother club," but that outcome was anything but assured. Each time the revolutionary leadership split, the Paris Jacobins staked out their position (usually but not invariably the most radical one), exhorted their "friends and brothers" to follow suit, and held their breath while the provincial clubs sorted out their reactions and chose sides. The first and perhaps decisive crisis came in the summer of 1791 with the king's flight to Varennes. Revolutionary leaders divided sharply on how to handle this betrayal by the king, and the Paris Jacobin Club, under pressure from radicals in the Paris sections, split apart at the seams. Most of the deputies who formed the backbone of its membership walked out and formed a new, avowedly moderate club (the Feuillant Club).

A more radical core led by Robespierre and Jérôme Pétion, feeling decidedly like a besieged minority, stayed on. Against the odds, this rump worked strenuously to rally the network of provincial clubs. Initially, most of the affiliates expressed dismay at the schism and pleaded for a reconciliation. When the schism hardened the provincial clubs delayed choosing sides, but in the end most responded to the shrewdly framed appeals of Robespierre and Pétion, and reaffirmed their ties with the mother club. Having made their commitment, some clubs then reoriented their reading habits, favoring anti-Feuillant newspapers such as those edited by Carra, Brissot, or Gorsas. Conversely, when a journal tilted to the right, the clubs tended to abandon it.[48]

The Jacobin-Feuillant schism took its toll. Some of the weaker clubs disappeared altogether in this dispiriting situation, while the ranks of most remaining clubs thinned as more conservative members dropped out. The Jacobin network did not grow in linear fashion, and achieved new momentum only with the crisis precipitated by the war. But when the insurrection of the Paris sections in August 1792 overthrew the monarchy—once more seeming to pull the rest of the country in its wake—most of the clubs had already turned against the king and had no trouble rallying to the republic.[49]

THE SECOND REVOLUTION

The insurrection of 10 August 1792 drove Louis XVI from his throne, rendered null the Constitution of 1791 that depended on him, caused the flight of most deputies to the Legislative Assembly (which had refused until then to suspend the king), and overthrew the Paris municipal government. Did all this usurp or vindicate popular sovereignty? Shaken legislators who decamped that evening regarded the uprising as an outrage perpetrated by a small minority of Parisians claiming presumptuously to speak for the people of France, a sentiment doubtless shared by the twenty thousand citizens who had signed a petition deploring the harassment of the monarch by a Parisian crowd two months earlier. To the militants of the Paris sections, the provincial clubbists who had finally despaired of the monarchy, and the deputies who remained, this direct action, with its high cost in Parisian lives, constituted an authentic expression of popular sovereignty. For the victors, August 10 seemed a legitimate and timely sequel to the providential uprising of July 14. But, it is important to remember, after mounting their show of force against the king, the emissaries of the sections who formed the insurrectionary Commune seized power only in the municipality, and did not claim to control the national government. Although their action destroyed the constitutional edifice of 1791, they did not prevent a new application of its most fundamental principle—national representation through elections.

After the convulsion of August 10—and the horrific aftershock of the

Paris prison massacres—the elections to the National Convention in September may have seemed like a reassuring return to normalcy. In order to convene a constitutional convention and interim government with little preparation or gestation, the rump of the Legislative Assembly relied on the familiar two-stage electoral process of primary assemblies and departmental electoral assemblies. The availability of this tested mechanism created a bridge of continuity between the failed constitutional monarchy and the republic. At the same time, changes in the franchise gave these elections a democratic aura they had previously lacked. Under pressure of popular opinion in Paris, the legislature jettisoned the censitary franchise with (in deputy Merlin de Douai's disingenuous words) its "monstrous and fatal distinction" between active and passive citizens. [50] Voting finally became a right rather than a social function.

The change was not tantamount to universal male suffrage—transients, domestics, and indigents were still excluded—but it was a major step in that direction. The more so since the Assembly also lowered the voting age from twenty-five to twenty-one, which brought voting into conformity with revolutionary family law that had dropped the age of majority and consent to twenty-one. Besides erasing the dubious category of "passive citizens," the legislature eliminated special qualifications for *éligibles:* any voting citizen could now serve as an elector or hold office. In recognition that electors might be of more modest circumstances, they were now promised an indemnity of 3 livres a day to defray travel and living expenses.

An expanded electorate, however, did not necessarily increase the rate of voter turnout. New voters certainly participated—in one Paris section, 1,462 citizens enrolled in special voting registers opened in August–September 1792, of whom only 871 were previously "active citizens"—but across the nation no dramatic upsurge in voting occurred. Some primary assemblies had large numbers of voters, particularly in urban precincts, but nationally the proportionate level of absenteeism matched the sagging rates of 1791. Voter turnout in September 1792 probably averaged no more than 15 percent. Among the departments that have been studied, participation dropped below 10 percent in the Eure, Oise, Aveyron, and in certain cantons of the Var and the Pas-de-Calais, which saw massive absenteeism in the countryside. The Hérault did better, drawing an estimated 15 to 27 percent of its voters to the assemblies, and the Haute-Saône 25 percent; but voter turnout in the election of 1790 in the Haute-Saône had been 53 percent. [51] Little is known about the extent of intimidation or exclusion of avowed royalists in these primary assemblies, but boycotts by royalists were probably more common than exclusions.

The electoral assemblies of 1792 in turn became the birthplace of the new republic, providing a solid mandate for the deputies they elected to the National Convention. Under circumstances of crisis and confusion—in four frontier departments the war was virtually at their doorstep—the assemblies performed their task efficiently and (with a small number of striking exceptions) freely.

Whatever the defects of the Revolution's electoral system, electors normally had the chance to return or repudiate incumbents. The rump of the Legislative Assembly framed the elections to the Convention by disseminating to the electoral assemblies its official version of recent events. This *Exposition des Motifs* glossed over the Assembly's equivocations, emphasized the king's treasonous behavior, and said little about the role of the insurrectionary Paris Commune. A pamphlet compiled by the Paris Jacobin Club, which its affiliates disseminated to at least half the electoral assemblies, reinforced the effects of this manifesto by celebrating the 250 or so legislators who had "remained faithful to the cause of liberty" in seven crucial roll-call votes, including their losing efforts to counter the treacheries of LaFayette and the court.[52] The Jacobins' *Tableau Comparatif,* however, did not apprise the provinces of the struggles that were tearing apart the left in Paris at that very moment, the feud between the "Brissotins" who were leaving the Jacobin Club under duress, and the future "Robespierrists" who now controlled the club in alliance with the insurrectionary Commune.

The patriot rump of the legislature therefore became the candidates par excellence for these elections, and the electoral assemblies sent a stunning 194 of them (over 80 percent) to the Convention, while repudiating the Legislative Assembly's more numerous conservatives almost to a man. With the great majority elected overwhelmingly on first ballots, seventy-one departments chose at least one current deputy. The electors also reached back to choose eighty-three ex-*constituants* deemed able and reliable patriots. Most of the 750 men elected to the Convention had held only local revolutionary office until now, including 116 departmental officials (a low number, since many of these most visible administrators were suspect as royalists), 94 district officials, 94 municipal officers, and 61 magistrates. In this sense, the political experience of the constitutional monarchy prepared the way for the birth of the republic.[53]

Since the legislature's brief *instruction* left them an unaccustomed level of discretion and even authorized them to deliberate as well as vote, the electoral assemblies of 1792 operated like sovereign bodies. Many passed policy resolutions and, as requested, some discussed and approved a kind of open-ended mandate for their deputies. About a quarter took the opportunity to purge and renew their departmental administrations, although that was not part of their official brief. The assemblies excluded individual electors for the usual variety of reasons—age, defective credentials, and the like—and a small number for their royalist sentiments. But the overwhelming majority of these assemblies acted in scrupulous fashion, free from outside intervention or intimidation. Local Jacobin club affiliates were of course intensely interested in these elections, and several provided after-hours gathering places for the electors. In at least twenty-six departments clubs sent a deputation or address to the electoral assembly, but only in Lot and Finistère did they mount a concerted effort to dominate the elections, and in the latter they failed completely. While most of the future deputies probably belonged to a Jacobin club at the time of their election, the clubs did not propel them into the Convention. [54]

What, then, of manipulation or intimidation within the assemblies that may call into question their fairness or freedom? The most damaging possibility arose where electors proceeded by voice voting rather than secret ballots. Since the *instruction* did not specify the mode of balloting this time, twenty electoral assemblies debated the matter. In the end Paris and eleven others chose to go that route, claiming that it reassured the illiterate, saved a great deal of time, would expose cabals, or simply on the dubious grounds that voice voting was the most appropriate method for a truly free people who had nothing to hide. But voting aloud did not inevitably facilitate intimidation or cabals, and could even function in the opposite spirit, as its advocates contended. Only eight assemblies, most of which used written ballots, can be stigmatized for a climate of intrigue or intimidation, notably the two bastions of Jacobinism, Paris and Marseille (Bouches-du-Rhône), where voice voting prevailed. "Apart from Bouches-du-Rhône and Paris, very unusual assemblies," Alison Patrick concludes, "there seem to be signs of some cabal at work in Finistère, Loiret, Orne, Rhône-et-Loire, Somme, and Seine-et-Oise." [55]

The Paris electoral assembly of 1792 stands in stark contrast not only to most other departments but to its own predecessor in 1791. To be sure, partisanship had already reached intense levels in the capital when, in the wake of the Feuillant-Jacobin schism, the Paris electoral assembly convened in September 1791 (later than other departments) to elect deputies for the new Legislative Assembly. "Barely organized," observed the *Révolutions de Paris,* "the electors are already labeling one another with the epithets of factious or republicans, moderates or monarchists." [56] With a precociousness all their own, the electors of 1791 formed an "electoral club" to evaluate and discuss possible candidates before the balloting. Open to all electors, it was dominated by Brissot and his Jacobin allies, who finally succeeded in propelling Brissot to victory after seven losing ballots in the assembly. Exasperated Feuillant sympathizers withdrew at that point to form their own caucus. Of the 967 electors, 390 ended up in the Feuillant's Club of the Sainte-Chapelle, while 179 remained in the original caucus, the Club of the Evêché, leaving about 400 uncommitted electors holding the balance of power. In the end, two thirds of the assembly's choices for deputy and other offices were moderates agreeable to or recommended by the Sainte-Chapelle caucus.[57]

The rivalry of two groups in a kind of open electoral competition, however, proved to be ephemeral. Next time around, open competition gave way in Paris to a one-sided domination, with the victors of August 10 in full control and adamant about their preferences. In a truculent partisan mood, the capital's primary assemblies generally excluded signers of the mass petition protesting the mistreatment of the king by a Parisian crowd on June 20. Only six electors of 1791 who had joined the moderate Sainte-Chapelle caucus were chosen as electors again in 1792, as against sixty-three who had remained in the Club of the Evêché. On the whole, Parisian voters turned to new men in 1792, for only 188 of the 849 electors from the city had ever served in that capacity before. Younger on average, the new electors included far fewer lawyers and officials than previous cohorts of electors; entrepreneurs, merchants, artisans, and shopkeepers deeply rooted in their neighborhoods now predominated.[58]

The rivalries that would metastasize into the Girondin-Montagnard conflict in the Convention had already congealed in Paris. While Brissot, Condorcet, Pétion, and their comrades enjoyed national popularity as revolutionary leaders, Parisian radicals repudiated them for their equivocations in the weeks before and after August 10. For the moment, the Brissotins (to use that imprecise shorthand) ironically profited in the provinces from circulation of the Jacobin Club's *Tableau Comparatif*, its attack on the right wing of the Legislative Assembly. Political opinion in Paris, however, had become more nuanced and schismatic. When Marat circulated a list of suggested candidates for the Convention, he included none of the future Girondins, in particular omitting Brissot, Condorcet, and Kersaint, who had all won election in the capital the year before.

After deciding to proceed by voice vote, the Paris electoral assembly systematically rejected the men promoted by Brissotin journalists who were commanding impressive majorities elsewhere. Even ex-mayor Pétion could garner no more than 136 votes, although his failure might have been influenced by knowledge that another department had already chosen him. Not that the electoral assembly voted monolithically; opposition to Jacobin and Cordelier Club radicals certainly found expression, as it did in the direct elections for a new mayor that followed later. Thus, if nineteen of the department's twenty-four deputies were elected on the first ballot, only twelve received 65 percent or more of the votes cast. Still, the tide flowed in only one direction. While Marat remained anathema to patriotic provincial opinion (even the Marseille Jacobin Club would not subscribe to his paper), Paris elected thirteen of the men he endorsed, along with the notorious "friend of the people" himself.[59] Those spurned in this electoral juggernaut would reciprocate with an implacable hostility to the Paris Commune and to the department's deputation, particularly the men they stigmatized as the "triumvirs"—Robespierre, Danton, and Marat.

WHILE PARIS RENEWED its political representation more drastically than most other departments, creating a sharp discontinuity between monarchy and republic, the provinces did not fully grasp the role of Parisian militants in overthrowing the monarchy, the national influence they would claim on the basis of that decisive act, or the narrowing definitions of patriotism that now held sway in the capital. This situation laid the seeds for profound tension between Parisian and provincial opinion. Yet it is possible to exaggerate that gap. For if Paris had truly left the rest of the country behind, its self-consciously radical delegation would have been isolated and impotent among its colleagues in the Convention. Some *conventionnels* did in fact support the Brissotin core in its relentless attack on the militancy and pretensions of the Paris Commune, the Paris sections, the Paris Jacobin Club, and the Parisian deputies. Once they had oriented themselves to the scene in the capital, even provincial Jacobin firebrands like Barbaroux from Marseille quickly allied with the emerging Girondin faction in the Convention. But totaling at most 180, that extremely amorphous group of like-minded deputies came nowhere near a majority. An even larger number of about three hundred deputies from all parts of the country gradually cohered around the Jacobin Club and the Parisian delegation—attracted by their revolutionary fervor and dramatic improvisations—to form the Montagnard faction. In fact, more than three fifths of the departments sent three or more deputies to the Convention who would end up identifying with the Mountain.[60]

Rancorous battles between the leading personalities in each faction confused and dismayed provincial Jacobin clubs, the Convention's most active supporters. Each side had its liabilities. After the king's trial in January 1793, Pierre Vergniaud (a deputy from the Gironde) and other advocates of leniency had proposed to submit the king's fate to a popular referendum. Montagnards attacked this impeccably democratic idea as a devious subterfuge to spare the king and as an utterly impolitic invitation to discord and civil strife. They defeated the *appel au peuple* by a vote of 424 to 283, and thereafter repeatedly castigated its supporters for ineptitude if not treasonous designs. On the other side, the Montagnards' association with the arrogant

Paris Commune, with Marat, and (by implication) with the September massacres caused no end of recrimination. Most Jacobin clubs longed for a truce and rained down petitions pleading that "unity will return and the Convention will recover its dignity."

Among clubs willing to choose sides, more initially tilted toward the Girondins and some rebuked Parisian radicalism by breaking off communication with the "mother society." The sacking of Girondin newspaper offices in March by Parisian mobs stoked their resentment. Gradually, however, the balance of opinion among the clubs shifted toward the Mountain, galvanized by such events as the rebellion in the Vendée and the military reversals of early 1793. The Montagnard cause also advanced through the proselytizing activities of deputies sent by the Convention on missions to the departments in March. While the Girondins declined these assignments for fear of depleting their ranks in the Convention's struggles, Montagnards willingly left their benches to carry out war-related tasks in the provinces. Like P. J. Duhem in Lille or C. A. Ysabeau in Pau, these representatives-on-mission extolled the zeal of Parisian militants and tried to wean local clubs away from their Girondin newspapers. [61]

When the defection to the enemy of Dumouriez—the Girondins' favorite general—set off a new round of bitter denunciations in April 1793, Girondins and Montagnards faced a showdown. Most of the clubs despised Marat and sympathized with Girondin attempts to indict him; but on the larger issues of leadership and revolutionary strategy the Girondins were losing the battle of public opinion in the provinces, which they had long since lost in Paris. The influential Jacobin Club of Marseille, for example, matched the Parisians in their campaign against the Girondin deputies, who created "a foyer of counter-revolution in the Convention." No doubt most clubs still yearned for an end to personal vendettas and factional conflict, for a return to revolutionary unity. But most did not sit immobilized by their discomfort. Debating, sifting their information, communicating with other clubs to support one position or another, the Jacobin network remained divided and uncertain but hardly passive. By the end of May 1793, 126 clubs (especially in the West and Southwest) are known to have inclined to the Girondins, while 195 (mainly in the Southeast, Center, and North/Northeast) leaned toward the Montagnards. [62]

The conflict finally came to a head with two nearly simultaneous upheavals. On June 2, the Paris Commune and sections ringed the Convention with five thousand armed national guards, bayonets fixed, and compelled it to suspend twenty-nine "perfidious" Girondin deputies. At just about that time, anti-Jacobins in Marseille, Bordeaux, and Lyon wrested control of their sectional assemblies, ousted Jacobin municipalities, and suppressed the radi-

cal clubs that had briefly dominated and terrorized their cities. After news
came of the purge of the Girondins, these cities then placed themselves in
rebellion against the Convention itself until such time as the Convention
recovered its freedom. [63]

Back in Paris the influential deputy Bertrand Barère had mediated franti-
cally until the last possible moment to placate the rival factions in the
Convention and avoid a purge. Barère now put the best face he could on the
demoralizing recourse to unity by partition on June 2. Once the Convention
had voted to suspend the deputies, he declared, patriots must accept it as a
fait accompli, "yield to circumstances," and go forward. Had provincial
revolutionaries resisted this notion of revolutionary necessity, and turned
against radical Paris and its Montagnard allies, there is no telling what the
outcome might have been. But if officials in over half the departments flirted
briefly with supporting the anti-Jacobin rebels, most quickly abandoned that
course. Armed "federalist" rebellion (as the Convention stigmatized it) was
confined to about half a dozen cities and their hinterlands, mainly in the
South. [64]

THE PLEBISCITE OF 1793 AND AFTER

For a few weeks in the summer of 1793, however, it appeared as if national
unity had disintegrated completely. Revolutionary legality seemed to be
breaking down as insurrection exploded on all sides of the political spectrum:
from counter-revolutionary uprisings in the Vendée to anti-Jacobin revolts
in the great cities of the South to armed demonstrations by Parisian *sans-
culottes* against the Convention itself. It was up to the victorious Montagnards
to put the lid on this anarchic situation. As a top priority they rushed through
the draft of a new constitution, one original purpose of convening a National
Convention in the first place. With "federalist" sentiment rippling through
many departments, the Convention hoped that a new constitution would
rally popular opinion, reinforce the republic's legitimacy, and promote a new
sense of national unity. Since the Montagnard constitution vested the primary assemblies with the power to sanction laws passed by the legislature,
the Convention could scarcely avoid submitting the constitution itself to a
popular referendum. But in keeping with their democratic commitments, the
deputies went further. Besides calling on citizens to accept or reject the
constitution, they invited them to discuss the charter and to propose changes
and amendments, although how such suggestions would be dealt with was
left unstated. Guided by a brief *instruction* and Barère's report to the people
on the constitution, French citizens assembled in their primary assemblies in

July 1793 for a direct exercise of sovereignty. Depending on one's angle of vision, this moment stands as the apogee of democratic experience in the French Revolution or as an orchestrated exercise in political conformity.

Notwithstanding the Revolution's fratricidal conflicts and narrowing political orthodoxy, the 4,800 primary assemblies of July seem to have been open and free. Naturally many began with such unifying rituals as patriotic speeches, fêtes, or parades. But the assemblies enjoyed great latitude. Almost four hundred, for example, chose constitutional priests as their presidents despite the growing rift between the republic and the Catholic Church. And because they were voting on a constitution not yet in force, most assemblies did not require an oath of allegiance that might have deterred certain people from participating. In any case, turnout in the primary assemblies rebounded from the low levels of 1792 to around 30 percent, drawing almost 2 million of approximately 7 million eligible voters.[65] While absenteeism remained high, the referendum generated real enthusiasm as well, an enthusiasm especially palpable where women mobilized and insisted on participating. Women won that right in at least two dozen primary assemblies that took votes by acclamation, and in Laon and Pontoise where roll calls recorded 743 and 320 votes by women. But even where the assemblies rebuffed them, the insistent involvement of women reflects the plebiscite's democratic resonance.[66]

On the other hand the results of the voting might make participation in the plebiscite appear passive or formulaic. The outcome, after all, was entirely one-sided: Over 1,850,000 citizens voted to approve the constitution, while only 12,766 voted no; 4,713 primary assemblies accepted the constitution, while only 38 rejected it, with two thirds of the no votes coming from only three Breton departments (Finistère, Morbihan, and Côtes-du-Nord). But judging simply by results is misleading, since it ignores the unparalleled participatory opportunities of these assemblies. To be sure, most assemblies simply listened to a reading of the constitution (in translation where necessary) and proceeded without discussion to a vote that was often unanimous. But others debated various articles and proposed an array of criticisms and amendments. Indeed, about 140,000 of the yes votes can be classified as conditional.[67] A few assemblies actually made pro-Girondin proposals (such as transferring the capital from Paris, or liberating the arrested deputies), while others took an anti-establishment stance by demanding that the *conventionnels* disqualify themselves for the new legislature. Some expressed support for price control (the Maximum), but others opposed it. Primary assemblies questioned the criteria by which legislative districts would be drawn, and called for a guarantee of state salaries for priests. Altogether, while relatively few assemblies registered criticisms or amendments, and while no single issue drew more than one hundred comments, the profusion and range of these proposals indicate that the referendum encouraged genuine discussion of the constitution.[68] The plebiscite of July 1793 did not simply impose a ritualistic expression of political unity on a passive citizenry.

The most novel element in this participatory drama was the Convention's request that each primary assembly elect a delegate (preferably one who did not already hold public office) to deliver his assembly's *procès-verbal* to the Convention, and to participate in the great festival planned for the capital on the first anniversary of August 10. In a fashion never equaled before or since, over five thousand envoys from the primary assemblies converged on Paris, no doubt with a keen sense of mission and self-importance. From every canton in the nation, these delegates gave a unique extension to the democratic character of the July 1793 referendum, with its manhood suffrage, direct voting, and popular deliberation. Indeed, the presence of these emissaries of the sovereign people gave pause to certain members of the Convention, making them wonder if they had not conjured up a presence that might undermine their own command of the situation. As yet the comportment of these delegates has not been fully explored, but we know that some interacted with Parisian militants and clubs, and that they lobbied the Convention to adopt the mass military levy and "to place terror on the order of the day"—a demand usually ascribed to the Paris sections alone. Their participation in the processions and ceremonies of the August 10 festival in turn belies any notion of a complete Parisian ascendancy over the rest of the nation.[69] Later in August the delegates departed for home, where many probably ended up serving the emerging revolutionary government.

Ironically, these envoys of the primary assemblies—empowered to mark the ratification of a new constitution—contributed to the advent of a revolutionary dictatorship that (as we saw in Chapter I) temporarily set aside the constitution in order to surmount by any means the presumed threats to the republic's survival. For the duration of the emergency the Convention suspended all elections, the most tangible and essential form of political participation. In a kind of Jacobin putting-out system (to use Richard Cobb's inspired phrase), the lines of power and authority now ran from the Committee of Public Safety in Paris down to the districts (whose key officials became "national agents"), and on to local revolutionary committees. Besides crushing and punishing armed rebellion, the apparatus of the Terror intimidated citizens into conforming to the republic's official policies and values. Those who refused joined the victims of personal vendettas and the citizens being persecuted for their past status who filled the republic's overflowing jails. By threatening to punish public dissent, the Terror muted overt political conflict and enforced a factitious uniformity of behavior that could not last. When the Convention itself dismantled the Terror after Thermidor, partisanship reignited with murderous intensity, for there were now so many more scores to settle, so many victims of revolutionary repression seeking retribution.

THE YEAR II of the republic (1793–94), the year of the Terror, thus presents us with a grim paradox: the simultaneous expansion and contraction of democratic space. The negative side is most obvious: the suspension of elections and the increasing centralization of authority; the arrest of tens of thousands of citizens for allegedly subversive acts or opinions; the destructive spasm of "de-christianization," with its church closings and persecution of constitutional priests; the power plays of urban paramilitary forces against peasants with grain surpluses. On the other hand political participation expanded—not only through the landmark constitutional referendum but through the medium of political clubs, now known as popular societies. Encouraged by representatives-on-mission, district agents, and well-established urban clubs, citizens founded numerous new clubs, especially in the rural bourgs of the North and the Center of France.

In the Year II citizens organized more than 3,000 new popular societies, meaning that over 5,300 French communes altogether now had clubs, 13 percent of all communes (see Figure II-1). By the spring of 1794 the density of clubs in certain departments reached remarkable levels. While no department had boasted more than 50 clubs in 1791 or 100 in 1792, in the Year II the Drôme had 268, the Pas-de-Calais 186, the Seine-Inférieure 180, and the Seine-et-Oise 167.[70] The membership of the new clubs also reached more deeply down the social order—into the ranks of artisans, journeymen, small shopkeepers, clerks, and small peasants—than the clubs of the early years. And where once the typical urban club of 1790–92 had been affiliated with the Paris Jacobin Club, the new *sociétés populaires,* like the sectional clubs of Paris in the Year II, stood well beyond the reach of the "mother society" in the capital. Indeed, Robespierre came to distrust this proliferation of clubs, no doubt because it seemed impossible to impose any meaningful influence from the center. In frustration, the Paris Jacobin Club moved in the other direction by refusing affiliation to any club founded after 31 May 1793. For the revolutionary state, however, clubs new or old became "arsenals of public opinion" and necessary "auxiliaries" for providing information to fill local offices. Spurring political participation and introducing revolutionary sociability into the small towns and large villages of France, the popular societies of the Year II altered the political landscape.[71]

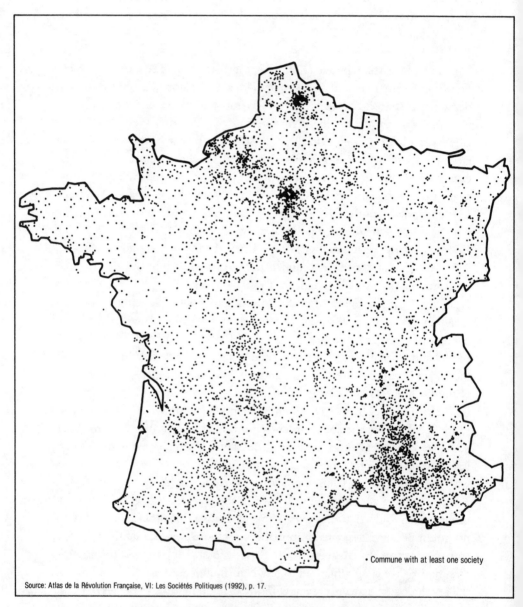

• Commune with at least one society

Source: Atlas de la Révolution Française, VI: Les Sociétés Politiques (1992), p. 17.

FIGURE II-1: *The Proliferation of Political Clubs, 1793–94*

While the geographic and social base of provincial Jacobinism thus expanded, its political base narrowed. Moderates dropped out under the pressure of public purges *(scrutins épuratoires),* while self-censorship promoted conformity and posturing. Richard Cobb, the connoisseur of provincial Jacobinism, has drawn a nuanced portrait of its style and mentality. "From September 1793 to February and March 1794," he writes, "discussions were very lively within the Parisian [sectional clubs] and provincial societies. They discussed everything with great vivacity and often in utter confusion. . . . It was a situation [however] that permitted noisy and militant minority groups to stampede the assembly into voting, for instance, for the closing of churches . . . while a majority had sat by in embarrassed silence or offered a few timid protests that were quickly withdrawn."

The *sans-culottes* emerge under Cobb's scrutiny as extremely gullible toward the ever-changing official version of high politics handed down from Paris, where the popular Hébert or the intrepid Danton suddenly became a treasonous conspirator. On their own ground the *sans-culottes* could be credulous as well, eternally sniffing out counter-revolutionary plots. Quick to take offense at any sign of disrespect for the republic, they were prone to extravagant rhetoric in denouncing their presumed enemies. Their ardor and imprudent verbiage provoked, offended, and threatened traditional social elites— for which the *sans-culottes* would pay dearly after Thermidor. Local subsistence issues most exercised the *sociétés populaires.* About scarcity and hoarding they needed no instruction from Paris. Aggressively communalist, the clubs justified repression against recalcitrant peasants or uncooperative merchants in terms of economic necessity. "When it came to local affairs and local personalities," Cobb concludes, "there were many genuine and passionate debates."[72]

The efflorescence of popular societies in the Year II advanced the political acculturation of the French people both geographically and socially, even as the quality of political life became more shallow, repressive, and lethal. The clubs of the Year II may not have been democratic in the conventional sense of the term, but their composition was assuredly popular and their atmosphere egalitarian. The record they left is a problematic blend of self-reliance and credulity, populist enthusiasm and conformism, egalitarian sentimentality and intolerance. After Thermidor the backlash against the Terror was therefore social, as well as ideological, humanitarian, or political, flavored by bitter resentment over the unnatural hegemony of cobblers and tailors, village carpenters and small peasants who had briefly exercised and sometimes abused a modicum of power. The settling of accounts was especially violent in the "white terror" that swept the Midi and the Rhône Valley, where the federalist rebellion had centered and where Jacobin repression had been exceptionally harsh. For years to come the cycle of recrimination in such communities blurred the boundary between public and private vendettas, and envenomed public life. In this unhappy respect the impact of the revolutionary committees, paramilitary battalions, and popular societies of the Year II long outlasted their temporal duration.[73]

III

POLITICAL PARTICIPATION

THE DENOUEMENT

STARTING OVER?

In the thermidorian postmortem, the "anarchy" and lethal persecutions of the Year II had been spawned by demagogues capitalizing on an excess of democracy. They vowed that it would never happen again. But entangled with their visceral anti-Jacobinism came an abiding commitment to republicanism and a mortal fear of royalists—refractory priests and their "fanatical" supporters, émigrés and their relatives, *chouans* in the West and murder gangs in the South. The thermidorians yearned for an end to revolution and counter-revolution, for the safe harbor of republican normalcy, which they believed to be in sight. The Constitution of 1793, however, would not serve that purpose. Purged of the leading Montagnards, the Convention jettisoned the Jacobin charter, which still lay on the shelf, and designed a republic shorn of its democratic penumbra. The Constitution of the Year III (1795) dropped the guarantee of popular rights such as subsistence or public education; eliminated such democratic practices as direct elections and referenda; and put aside scruples against a relatively strong executive. The underlying principles of popular sovereignty, representation, and elections, however, survived intact.

Indeed, the Convention found one innovation of 1793 impossible to resist. Arguing that force and terror had created "only an appearance of acceptance" in the constitutional plebiscite of 1793, the thermidorians submitted their own constitutional draft to a referendum as well. The plebiscite of fructidor Year III called for a simple yes or no vote, without the symbolic deliberative gestures of the earlier referendum. Again the vote produced a lopsided approval, but where the first plebiscite attracted 1.8 million voters, only 1,057,000 turned out in September 1795, and about 50,000 voted no.[1] Simultaneously the Convention submitted to the voters its "two-thirds decree," a piece of political legerdemain designed to create a smooth transition for the new regime.

Fearful that royalists and other disaffected citizens would swamp the republican center if the entire legislature stood for election at this juncture (as a new constitution seemed to demand), the Convention preempted that threat by enforcing political continuity. Instead of openly facing the voters for reelection or giving way to an entirely new legislature—as the National Assembly had done after completing *its* constitution in 1791—the Convention perpetuated itself in power with the two-thirds decree. Since only one third of the legislature was to be renewed in a given year under the new constitution, the Convention decided that the forthcoming electoral assemblies in the departments should name new deputies to form only one third of the legislature, while the remainder would carry over from the Convention. Or, putting it the other way: "The electoral assemblies may not select fewer than two-thirds of the sitting members of the Convention in forming the [new] legislature." The Convention directed that each electoral assembly first choose its quota of the two thirds (as well as a supplementary list of nominees from the present Convention), and then its quota of new deputies. If, as was likely, the departments' choices overlapped and did not round out the necessary two thirds, the outgoing Convention would sit as a national electoral assembly to decide which of its unreturned members should continue on as deputies for the next year or two. "It is with the ardent desire to spare the people the disasters of a new revolution that we have drawn the courage to propose maintaining two thirds of the Convention," explained the influential moderate Pierre Baudin, without irony. Royalists were of course furious at losing the chance to sweep out the *conventionnels* en masse, but the fact that "royalism, for the first time, suddenly declares itself the ardent defender of the sovereignty [of the people]," impressed Baudin not at all.[2]

As a gesture of good faith, however, the Convention submitted the two-thirds decree to the voters for approval along with the constitution. This part of the hastily organized referendum proved confusing and contentious. Many primary assemblies never addressed the two-thirds decree, either unaware of its existence or believing that the constitution subsumed it; others no doubt expressed disapproval by ignoring it. In the assemblies that did vote, 205,000 citizens approved the measure but 109,000 voted no. Nineteen departments rejected the two-thirds decree, and about a fifth of the no votes came from the Seine department, where ultra-conservative opinion now held sway. While all forty-eight Paris sections accepted the constitution, forty-seven decisively rejected the two-thirds decree—which suggests that votes for the constitution did not necessarily denote support for its republican sponsors.[3]

Thoughtful royalists might have believed that only the Convention's continued existence blocked their road to power; a new constitutional order (whatever its defects) would presumably remove that obstacle, the sooner the better. Stymied by what seemed a last-minute palace coup, Parisian royalists rose in arms against the Convention on 13 vendémiaire Year IV (5 October 1795), but faced an improvised military force, commanded by a young officer named Bonaparte, which easily put down their revolt. Meanwhile the prescribed elections of the Year IV took place. As anticipated, the electoral assemblies returned a cohort of ultra-conservative deputies for the "new third."[4] These representatives took their seats alongside the remaining two thirds of the Convention to constitute the legislature of the Directory regime. The elections of the Year V would obviously be crucial.

In fact the most striking feature of the Directory's political system was its recourse to annual voting. In this improbably ambitious plan, one third of the legislature, one fifth of the departmental administrators, one half of the municipal agents, and comparable numbers of judges were to be renewed each year. Though the Convention's wisdom on this matter seems questionable, its hopes and intentions are clear enough. Partial annual renewal would prevent any group of officials or deputies from entrenching themselves, while yet avoiding abrupt upheavals in the nation's political equilibrium. Perhaps too annual convocations of voters would compensate for the absence of other democratic practices and provide a sense of empowerment to the electorate. But it was asking a great deal of ordinary citizens to convene in their primary assemblies year in and year out. Worse yet, annual electoral assemblies in each department were bound to fan political passions, just when the nation needed a respite. The succession of violent confrontations between 1792 and 1795—the war against royalist and "federalist" rebellions; the terror and de-christianization; the anti-Jacobin reaction—had alienated much of the population, while leaving scattered minorities behind as irreconcilable enemies. The directorial republic existed in a singularly unpromising political atmosphere, weighed down by massive apathy and cynicism on the one hand and fierce, even murderous, partisanship on the other. By continually calling into question the political balance of power, annual elections would never give those vapors a chance to subside.

To reknit the civic fabric of the republic after the "anarchy" of the Year II, the Directory returned to the two-tiered censitary voting system of the National Assembly, but with modifications. French males over twenty-one (instead of the original age of twenty-five) could vote in the primary assemblies if they were domiciled in the canton for a year and paid any direct personal property tax whatsoever or a voluntary poll tax in the amount of three *journées de travail.* With such differences, the potential voting population expanded compared to 1790. In Paris, for example, 78,000 men qualified as active citizens in 1790, while the number of potential voters totaled 121,000 in 1799.[5] About 1.5 million adult males were probably disfranchised nationally under the new requirements, only half as many as the "passive citizens" of 1790. As before, citizens also had to document their membership in the national guard reserves and their prior inscription on a local civic register. New voters after the Year XII would also have to demonstrate an ability to read and write. Citizens now elected approximately 30,000 electors, one for every 200 potential voters instead of the previous 100. But under the Constitution of the Year III, only citizens who owned or rented property valued at between one to two hundred *journées de travail* (depending on where they lived) could be chosen as electors. The censitary barrier was back in place. Retreating further from the bow to popular democracy in 1793, the directorial charter barred primary and electoral assemblies from any deliberation, petition, or deputation.

At the crossroads of 1795 some *conventionnels* hoped to bring constituents and their representatives closer together, aware that the lack of declared candidates and the election of departmental delegations left too great a distance between them. Charles-François Oudot, a surviving Jacobin deputy, proposed a four-stage procedure to give voters in the primary assemblies more tangible influence. First, the primary assemblies would fashion *listes de présentation,* in effect nominations of possible candidates. These would then be tallied and conflated by the departmental electoral assembly into an official *liste de candidats* for that department (comprising twice the number of names for the positions to be filled), "in order to make known to all the citizens of a department the names presented by its various assemblies." This official list of candidates would go back to the primary assemblies for balloting. Finally the departmental electoral assembly would tally the votes from around the department and declare the winners. The Convention's constitutional committee also considered shifting to the direct election of deputies, probably with a mind to diminishing the potentially inordinate influence of urban activists.[6] Finally, however, it decided against such changes and reverted to the system of 1790, except for the introduction of a "candidates list" quite different from the one proposed by Oudot. Starting with the Year V elections, prospective candidates would be invited to inscribe their names on an official list—a frank and dignified way for republicans to behave, claimed the legislators, "preferable to secret lobbying and the obscure maneuvers of intriguing ambition." Each departmental administration was to collate and publish the names, although electors could later vote for citizens not inscribed on these lists of candidates.

The directorial legislature introduced another modification in the Year V, undoubtedly aimed against former Jacobins, called the reduction ballot or the rejection ballot. On the second *scrutin,* electors would cast two ballots simultaneously in two different urns: the first (with as many names as there were positions to be filled) to elect their choices by an absolute majority; the second to eliminate particular individuals from further consideration. On the final round those not excluded by a majority of voters could as usual be elected by a relative plurality of votes. According to its advocates, the reduction ballot allowed a majority to veto in advance someone it detested (i.e., a former terrorist), who might yet receive a relative plurality, thereby qualifying for the third and final ballot where he could win by default, so to speak, without an absolute majority.[7]

These procedural novelties could not have been entirely innocuous since, in a very different political climate the following year, the legislature rescinded both. Deputies assailed the candidates lists and especially the rejection ballot as divisive. The inscription for candidacy, three months before the electoral assemblies, stretched out the electoral process and maximized the likelihood of "lobbying, intrigues, and even possibly the suborning of electors," they argued, besides exposing to sarcasm and insults men whose names were involuntarily placed on the lists by others. As for the reduction ballot, such negative voting "is and cannot be anything but an instrument of faction"; moreover it was unfair to bar someone who might receive enough votes to be lawfully elected. While recommending a return to the procedures of 1790, however, the *rapporteur* admitted that "the mode of balloting is the most difficult political problem."[8] Which is to say that the Directory's electoral system remained seriously flawed, with laborious procedures in both primary and electoral assemblies, low turnouts, and no direct connection between deputies and their constituents. But these familiar deficiencies masked a more fundamental problem: the incompatibility between an electoral system designed in 1790 for individualized voting and non-partisan government, and the realities of intense partisan rancor after the Terror and the thermidorian reaction.

THE ELECTORAL WARS OF THE DIRECTORY

French citizens now inhabited a new political universe. A chasm separated the relatively peaceful, optimistic atmosphere of 1790 from the virulent political climate of the Directory. As the historian Colin Lucas has argued, the stakes were now extremely high for the exposed, committed minorities, the networks of Jacobins and conservatives who had each experienced domination and persecution in turn, and between whom the directorial republicans tried to stand on a shaky, shrinking terrain. To assure their security, to ward off future victimization, each side strove to influence the election of municipalities, departmental administrators, judges, and deputies. In the most troubled regions, such as the area of the Vendée rebellion and *chouannerie* in the West and the former zone of federalism in the Southeast, the threat of assassination often shaped the disposition of local power. More commonly the struggle for influence took place in hotly contested primary and electoral assemblies, then in local administrative bodies or courtrooms, and finally in the ministerial antechambers of Paris—the Directory being the ultimate arbiter of such power conflicts, thanks to the wide constitutional latitude it had to remove local officials. At bottom, as Lucas puts it, "the key to success in local politics lay in the manipulation of higher authorities, above all the Directory itself. . . . The basic technique consisted in demonstrating either the detailed illegality or the general unconstitutionality of the behavior of one's enemies . . . [by means of] petitions, lobbying, misrepresentation, and pettifogging legalism." [9]

Each side in these bitter local rivalries played on the government's professed intention to steer a course between the extremes, which it carried out by alternately tacking to the left and the right. To summarize this story briefly: after purging, disarming, arresting, and occasionally putting on trial Jacobin cadres during the thermidorian reaction, the Convention in its last days swung the other way with a general amnesty after the abortive Parisian rising against the two-thirds decree. The Babeuf plot in 1796, however, propelled the government back toward the right. The Directory turned against former Jacobins, ousting most of those who still held local office and permitting their foes to harass them with impunity. While the Directory continued to pursue armed royalist rebels, royalists willing to work within the system now enjoyed considerable latitude. Prominent right-wing deputies gathered publicly at the Clichy Club in Paris in 1797, while the royalist press came vigorously back to life. Far from homogeneous, the right comprised cautious conservatives and constitutional monarchists as well as militant ultra-royalists, but it shared a sense of common purpose against the prevailing republican consensus: to be rid of the Convention's last vestiges, to welcome back non-juring priests and émigrés, to settle scores with ex-terrorists more aggressively, and to seek peace in Europe through negotiation rather than victory. Under their aegis France would be a very different kind of republic, if it remained a republic at all. [10] But if the Directory adhered to its own constitution, how could it stop this drift from accelerating through the electoral system?

With the temporary reprieve provided by the two-thirds decree, the government at first took an ostrichlike attitude to its predicament. Instead of adapting to the partisan realities bequeathed by the Revolution, the Directory tried to read royalists and Jacobins out of the republic's political culture. Clinging to a nostalgically individualistic view of politics, the government would not countenance organizations on the local or national level that actually reflected the current spectrum of political opinions. At the summit, the legislature symbolized its attitude by insisting that deputies rotate their seating positions monthly by lot, to preclude like-minded deputies from caucusing in one part of their hall. Any organized oppositional movement the Directory stigmatized as a "faction," subversive to the republic. Moreover the Directory regarded electors as public functionaries and wished them to take a loyalty oath. This touched off a heated debate in a deeply divided legislature, which declined to impose a formal oath because it would violate religious freedom. In the end, however, the legislature rebuffed arguments that declarations of fidelity were both futile and superfluous in an established republic, and demanded of all electors a "promise," albeit one that did not carry a punishment for refusal. Electors were to declare their attachment to the constitution (a plausible requirement, perhaps) but also their engagement to defend it "against the attacks of royalism and anarchy" (impossibly vague). [11]

A detail in the legislature's *Instruction* for the Year V elections signifies its rigid attitude toward political life. To curb "confusion, indecency, and scandals" in the elections, and to "weaken the influence of passions and of parties"—these parties being, of course, "les ennemis de la Révolution" (the royalists) and "les partisans de l'anarchie" (the Jacobins)—it forbade "any sign of disapproval or approbation" in the primary assemblies, and instructed the presidents to "prevent any groups or private conferences from forming inside the hall," thus extending the prohibition against parliamentary caucuses to the primary assemblies. [12] The engagement of the electorate, the rituals of involvement that seemed to work so well in America were denied to French citizens, then, not only by the basic framework of their electoral system—indirect elections, protracted balloting, the absence of open campaigning—but even in regulations governing the demeanor of citizens turning out to vote. Attempting to wring out every manifestation of commitment, enthusiasm, and ad hoc organization in the primary and electoral assemblies, the government promoted an idealized but desiccated style of electoral deliberation.

Such strictures, however, could scarcely stop the tides of opinion from finding expression one way or another. While absenteeism still ran high, partisan conflict promoted a surge in voter turnout for the elections of the Year V (1797) in certain departments such as the Haute-Garonne, and confrontational incidents in the primary assemblies multiplied.[13] Reaffirming the prevailing mood of balloting for the "new third" in the Year IV, the electoral assemblies gave a resounding victory to the right, with only 14 of 97 electoral assemblies showing any trace of republican loyalties in their choices. The electors returned only 11 of the 216 retiring *conventionnels,* rejected former Jacobins almost completely, repudiated most directorial republicans as well, and sought instead men free of any association with the current government. The overwhelming majority of the new deputies of the Year V had no prior legislative experience, and about 180 were probably royalists of one kind or another; in Paris the electors rejected even ex-Feuillants as insufficiently conservative.[14] After this infusion of new men, the legislature revoked all laws against the refractory clergy, and began to debate several policies that would have broken the thermidorian consensus. Similarly most departmental administrators and judges elected in the Year V displayed an uncooperative, if not royalist, attitude in the way they conducted their business.

Faced with this uncertain situation, the five-man Executive Directory finally split apart. Two directors were willing to abide by the results of the elections, hopeful that reaction would stop short of a royalist restoration. The three others were less sanguine. With their resolve stiffened by several generals, including Bonaparte, they mounted a coup d'état. Arresting prominent critics (among them fifty-three deputies) and closing over thirty royalist newspapers, they conspired with a rump of the legislature to annul retrospectively the elections in 49 departments, thereby purging 179 new deputies as well as hundreds of departmental administrators and judges. Greeted as a deliverance by Neo-Jacobins (for whom it assuredly was) and, ostensibly, by most moderate republicans, the coup of 18 fructidor Year V purchased another reprieve for the republic, but at the exorbitant cost of nullifying its own electoral foundation.[15]

WHAT BEGAN AS an improvised response to threatening political trends—the two-thirds decree of the Year IV—now hardened into a calculated strategy of manipulation to maintain the nation's political equilibrium at a steady state. With the royalists in disarray, the brunt of this strategy was destined to fall next on the Neo-Jacobins. After Fructidor the Directory allowed the democrats (as they regarded themselves) to regroup, but it did not intend to forfeit power to this other purported extreme. The directorials clung to their elusive centrist position, and excluded in advance the possibility of challenge through future elections. At any show of independence and political clout, the government was prepared to come down hard on the Neo-Jacobins, if need be by another purge. In short, from the very beginning of the Directory regime, and more emphatically with the Fructidor coup, electoral victory would be no guarantee of political power. When the constitution plausibly directed the legislature to certify the results of the electoral assemblies, it could hardly have anticipated the willful abuse of that prerogative by which the legislature could simply annul the choices of the electorate.

Unfortunately an opening for this kind of intervention—though the Directory scarcely required one—was being provided by some of the electors themselves. Early in the Revolution when procedural conflicts, charges of fraud, or acts of intimidation disrupted primary assemblies, voters occasionally withdrew to convene separately in order to send their own slate of electors to the departmental electoral assembly. The latter's first substantive task was precisely to rule on irregularities in the primary assemblies and to verify the credentials of electors. In an unforeseen twist in the Year IV, however, the electoral assembly of the Lot department itself split into two rival bodies. "The schism has produced what one could call a monstrosity in the political order," observed a legislative committee, "a double parliamentary deputation, a double departmental administration. . . ." The schism occurred on the assembly's third day, just after it had approved a final report on credentials. The dissenters objected to the irregularity of certain *procès-verbaux* which had failed to mention "if the number of electors corresponds [proportionately] to the lists of those entitled to vote in each canton." Having lost that skirmish, "a large group of electors retired"; eventually 119 organized themselves into an alternative electoral assembly and proceeded to choose their own slate of deputies and departmental administrators.

The legislature, ultimate arbitrator of this dispute, faced a dilemma. The second assembly of *scissionnaires* clearly comprised a minority of electors, yet had followed all the legal forms, while the original, larger body was vulnerable to censure "because it neglected the forms prescribed by the constitution, offers no guarantee of the legitimacy of its credentials, [and creates the suspicion] of having arbitrarily increased the number of electors." (In the absence of up-to-date local lists of voters, population figures suggested that the department was entitled to 300-odd electors, but 420 had shown up.) The Council of Five Hundred's committee recommended that both assemblies be declared invalid, but the legislature voted instead to seat the deputies chosen by the original, majority assembly.[16]

Was this schism in the Lot merely an aberration or did the electoral system face a potentially systemic dysfunction? In the Year V, the same department provided a depressing answer. From the start the electoral assembly in the Lot was tumultuous. The electors barely managed to elect their *bureau,* since the first two *scrutins* were declared null when the urns yielded 384 ballots from 382 electors. One elector then "hurled insults, threats, and provocations . . . and was expelled." Committees to verify credentials finally seated 312 of the 382 individuals who had presented themselves, and the assembly proceeded to elect two deputies. At that point 214 electors walked out (including some of those barred in the verification of credentials) and organized a rival assembly. The *rapporteur* of the legislative committee scrutinizing the affair urged the Council of Five Hundred to recognize this larger group of *scissionnaires.* But in a raucous session of the Council of Elders, dissenting deputies countered that this would be a prescription for disaster. Why, asked one remaining Jacobin deputy, would an actual majority walk out in the first place? What was going on? Instead of recognizing the *scissionnaires,* he argued, the legislature should "repress the scandal of these schisms carried out at the capricious instance of *meneurs.* Let us put an end to the complaints and uncertainties which can render the national representation problematic in the future." His colleague Jean-Antoine Marbot took up the attack: "Do you believe that there is sufficient motive to justify a schism if five or six people in an electoral assembly are mistreated—even beaten, if you will; or if there are [harsh] words and threats?" This attempt to quash the practice of electoral schisms more or less at its inception proved unavailing; despite all logic both houses finally voted to seat the *scissionnaires* of the Lot. [17]

Only two other electoral schisms occurred in the Year V—one in a newly annexed Belgian department, and one in the Landes, where a republican minority withdrew from the regular electoral assembly and offered a rival slate of deputies that the legislature reasonably annulled without debate. [18] The following year, however, schisms became epidemic in the electoral assemblies, precisely because the Directory itself promoted them as a tactic of last resort in its campaign to steer that year's elections against the threat of Neo-Jacobinism.

The Fructidor coup had briefly lifted the blanket of official hostility that barred most Neo-Jacobins from public life. Liberated from persecution by adversaries in local administrations, and spared from the relentless attacks of the royalist press, the Neo-Jacobins were now free to regroup around the triad of democratic institutions born in 1789—clubs, political newspapers, and elections. In the towns where their cadres had not been decimated or entirely cowed, they formed new clubs called "constitutional circles" to signify their adherence to republican legality. Despite lingering sentimental attachment to the Constitution of 1793, they embraced the Constitution of the Year III, and ironically became its steadfast defenders. Scattered groups of Neo-Jacobins achieved a sense of commonality and mutual support through the *Journal des hommes libres,* a durable and commercially successful newspaper that served as a porte-parole and clearinghouse of information and opinion. These clubs were a pale shadow of the old Jacobin network in numbers, size, and local influence. Manifestations of a weak but dogged republican opposition, the constitutional circles of the Year VI rekindled a faint and domesticated echo of the *sans-culotte* spirit. Like their predecessors, the new clubs badgered unresponsive local officials; petitioned on national issues such as tax policy or a veterans' bonus; and cultivated "public spirit" and republican *civisme* with symbolic gestures.[19]

Above all the constitutional circles positioned themselves for the annual elections. First, they launched a petition campaign to reform electoral procedures at the margins. Within the framework of the constitution they sought to interpret the laws as permissively as possible to facilitate the right to vote for potential supporters. The Neo-Jacobins advocated a kind of open registration to enfranchise citizens who had been deterred by the "inexactitude or malevolence" of officials in the Year V from signing civic registers or paying a voluntary poll tax months earlier to qualify in lieu of regular tax payments. They also proposed that indigent fathers of soldiers be permitted to vote, and that the official value of the *journée de travail* be set at the lowest possible level so as to lower the threshold of eligibility for electors.

This push to democratize electoral participation also had a darker side. For the Neo-Jacobins were no advocates of an even-handed pluralism. The exclusion of sworn enemies still ranked high on their agenda. Having been harassed and intimidated by royalist sympathizers in the Year V, they now petitioned to disenfranchise the leaders of that camp (in addition to the ex-nobles and émigrés already excluded): namely, the nominees purged in Fructidor as well as the electors who had chosen them. The Directory rebuffed all of these demands. Apart from the repeal of the reduction ballot, which Neo-Jacobins believed had been used against them unfairly the previous year, the campaign for electoral reform made no headway. But it reveals how seriously the Neo-Jacobins took the rules of the game. The vast open space of contested definitions of popular sovereignty in 1792 or 1793 had given way to the mildly elastic contours of an existing constitutional legalism.[20]

With an insight into elections gained from several years of experience, the democrats tried to nudge the system in new directions. As they organized for the primary assemblies in their towns, the constitutional circles regaled potential supporters with banquets and rallies (which conservatives viewed as attempts to corrupt, suborn, or intimidate voters), and fashioned slates of candidates for electors and municipal offices. In Moulins (Allier), the constitutional circle issued a broadside proclaiming its intention to break the traditional reticence about candidates. The members of the club intended to cast their votes for the same patriots:

> Yes, for the same names! Because if they divide their votes they will lose the majority. . . . We recognize the citizens worthy of our confidence. But to respond to the desire of our fellow citizens [outside the club] we will indicate here those we are planning to name to the *bureaux,* as electors, as municipal administrators, and as justices of the peace.

In at least fifty towns the Neo-Jacobins mounted comparable campaigns. Local Jacobin newspapers in about a dozen towns facilitated the next step— coordinating the efforts of like-minded electors chosen in various primary assemblies. In Moulins, the club prepared to welcome electors from other communes in the Allier, to house and feed them if necessary. "The patriots will hasten to show you to suitable lodgings or will offer you their own homes," explained their local newspaper. "During the sessions of the electoral assembly you will join us at the permanent banquets to be provided by citoyenne Grobon." [21]

The Directory viewed this pre-election activity with irritation, dismay, and eventually with a twinge of panic. On the eve of the elections, after several months of grudging toleration, the government deployed its time-tested repressive measures. Invoking the elastic emergency police powers granted by the constitution, the Directory dismissed certain Jacobin-leaning officials and local administrators, closed most of the Parisian and provincial Neo-Jacobin newspapers provisionally, and shut down over two dozen of their more successful clubs. While warning citizens against voting for "anarchists," and threatening severe responses if they did so anyway, the government quietly promoted the election of its loyal operatives since its ideology prevented it from campaigning openly for such men. In many departments with a moderate climate of opinion these tactics sufficed to produce the desired results, leaving the Neo-Jacobins as a distinct but powerless minority. In about a quarter of the departments, however, they dominated the electoral assemblies and elected dozens of "proven patriots," men who had served the revolutionary government in 1793. In sixteen of the departments where the Directory's supporters found themselves in a minority, the directorials walked out of the electoral assemblies and created their own rival bodies. These schisms gave the government an excuse to scrutinize the results of all the elections and to filter out those it found distasteful. [22]

By now the Directory employed a grotesque interpretation of the theory of representation to rationalize such intervention. Just as deputies represent the entire nation, declared the government's spokesman, the electors who choose them represent the nation and not merely a particular department. In discharging this responsibility, electors must exercise "la volonté raisonnablement présumé de la Nation"—a performance that only the legislature could judge. If electors chose notorious undesirables (meaning, that year, notorious Jacobins), "it is indubitable that, by a choice so scandalous, the electoral assembly has directly contravened its mandate." It was therefore the legislature's duty to rectify the results![23]

This time the government did not wait until three months after the new deputies had taken their seats, as it had in the Year V. Armed with this factitious mandate to screen the electoral results, the government executed its purge before the start of the new legislative session, in what came to be known as the coup d'état of 22 floréal VI (11 May 1798). Working with the Directory, the legislature validated the slates of the minority *scissionnaires* in nine departments (including the Seine and the Allier), thereby annulling the choices of Neo-Jacobin majorities in the regular assemblies. Anti-Jacobin schisms in other departments were too paltry, irregular, or tainted by royalism to permit this preferred scenario, but the government simply annulled all the elections in seven other Jacobin-dominated departments (three with schisms and four without). Finally, in thirteen departments the legislature purged individual deputies selectively, while allowing others to take their seats. In all the government "floréalized" some or all of the deputies elected in 29 departments, purging a total of 127 deputies-elect along with scores of departmental administrators and judges.[24]

BY THE YEAR VII the Directory's repeated interventions had disfigured the republic's political life: closing clubs and newspapers on the right and the left; removing countless locally elected officials; provoking schisms in the electoral assemblies; and purging newly elected deputies after two successive elections. Strong enough to throw oppositional elements off balance, these blows did not suffice to impose consensus or stability. Meanwhile the Directory's other actions heightened the level of discontent. After Fructidor, the Directory squandered its meager political capital in a campaign against Catholic traditionalism. Determined to limit the public display of religious faith, it banned the ringing of church bells. To promote a secular framework for everyday life, the Directory attempted to impose the republican calendar with its ten-day weeks, making the *décadi* the official day of rest and Sunday (the *ci-devant Dimanche*) an ordinary working day for clergy and laity alike. All of this stirred up endless contention, set Paris and its departmental commissioners against pragmatic local officials, and alienated millions of French citizens.[25] On top of that, dire financial straits led the legislature to reinstitute unpopular excise and consumption taxes, while the resumption of war brought the introduction of military conscription. Meanwhile insubordinate generals in the field strained civil-military relations; war contractors came under fire for corrupt profiteering; and anti-republican brigandage in the countryside raged with seeming impunity.

In this demoralizing atmosphere the elections of the Year VII took place on schedule. After three interventions to maintain the political equilibrium, the Directory was not prepared to relinquish its grip. Should elections promote the extremes, predicted one loyal newspaper, "the Executive Directory, which likes the royalists no better than the anarchists, will know how to put things in order."[26] Once again the Directory quietly encouraged the parliamentary candidacy of its loyal servitors; but of 187 candidates so identified, only 66 were elected as deputies.[27] Twenty-six electoral schisms also occurred that year. But this time the legislature balked at seating minority delegations or annulling distasteful results, although it had the self-delegated power to do so. In virtually every dispute the councils certified the slates of the majority assemblies, meaning that many new men, including Jacobin sympathizers, moved up the electoral ladder.

The Directory's heavy-handed, inept leadership had in fact won the five executives enemies on all sides, even among moderate republican stalwarts. Once the new cohort of deputies took its seats, a coalition of angry legislators executed a power play of their own, the so-called coup of 30 prairial VII (18 June 1799). Instead of replacing the one member of the Directory due to step down, they replaced four of the five directors under various pretexts; and instead of thanking them for their services, the angry deputies heaped charges of tyranny and threats of retribution on their departing heads. Although preoccupied with the immediate problems of the war crisis, a new steering committee in the Council of Five Hundred moved to protect the integrity of future elections by precluding electoral assembly schisms, those "auxiliaries of intrigue and tyranny." Two years after a few deputies had vainly tried to squelch this corrosive practice at its inception, the committee recommended that "every minority [break-away] fraction of an electoral assembly shall be considered an illegal assembly, and individuals who provoke schisms . . . shall be considered as instigators of a seditious crowd."[28]

THE NAPOLEONIC ELECTORAL CHARADE

Just when it seemed that a more normalized period in the republic's political life might be starting, however, key figures in the government were plotting its demise. Dissatisfied with the structural flaws in the Directory regime, impatient with the annual electoral wars and the ensuing purges, they had wearied of the whole effort. Led by Sieyès (appointed to the Directory after Prairial), these "revisionists" turned against their momentary Neo-Jacobin collaborators, enlisted the aid of several generals, and carried out the Brumaire coup. Having discussed the structure of authority that emerged from that coup in the previous chapter, it remains to consider how the Brumaire conspirators reconciled their intention to depoliticize the civic order with the principle of popular sovereignty. In brief, citizens would henceforth participate only by bestowing symbolic displays of "confidence from below" on a coopted "authority from above." To insulate the governing elite against challenges from below, the Brumairians severed the expression of popular sovereignty from any outlet in meaningful elections.

Which is not to say that the Napoleonic regime simply imposed itself by military force. On the contrary, with the precedents of 1793 and 1795 in mind, the Consulate sought popular approval and legitimation in a constitutional referendum—which the French people presumably understood to be a plebiscite on General Bonaparte rather than on the details of his new constitution. The official outcome indicated that a record 3 million citizens turned out to vote yes, alongside a minuscule 1,562 voting no. Behind the scenes, however, a nervous government did not anticipate such wide acceptance, particularly after early balloting in the capital revealed massive absenteeism. In fact, the historian Claude Langlois has shown that the government blatantly falsified the results of the plebiscite. In reality only 1.6 million citizens came out to vote, fewer than the 1.8 million in 1793. An institutional vacuum permitted this falsification, since results from each canton came directly to Paris where the tallying took place in four separate bureaus. The government released final figures without breaking them down, leaving no way to verify the results independently. The Interior Ministry apparently added 900,000 to the total civilian vote, and created 500,000 military votes out of thin air, since most military units were not actually polled.[29] Only in 1802, with the plebiscite of the Year X on the Life Consulate, did the wait-and-see attitude of earlier abstainers give way to commitment. Bonaparte's military and political achievements as First Consul did indeed draw a record turnout that year, producing 3.6 million bona fide yes votes.[30]

Atop its plebiscitary foundation, the Napoleonic regime jerry-built a false facade of balloting procedures, assemblies, and electoral colleges, whose details changed several times (particularly between 1800 and 1802) without ever yielding anything like veritable elections. In practice, members of the legislature and the Senate as well as all local officials were designated by Paris. But an elaborate electoral charade disguised the regime's blatantly cooptive

THE NEW REGIME

character. In 1802, for example, citizens were convoked to help choose departmental electoral colleges, empowered to create lists of potential nominees that the government in Paris could use in making appointments to the legislature. Once these permanent electoral colleges were organized, citizens had nothing left to do until such time as one third of their canton's seats in the college became vacant. While justices of the peace had been the sole public officials to be elected directly under the Consulate (see Chapter X), a revision in 1802 removed that last exception, which had evidently rankled the First Consul. Thereafter cantonal assemblies convened at rare intervals (once every five years after 1806), not to elect anyone but simply to propose increasingly lengthy lists of names from which the government could name justices of the peace and members of urban municipal councils when vacancies arose. Without running much risk, the regime could therefore reinstate universal male suffrage, provide every citizen with a *carte civique,* and even arrange for voting in plebiscites to take place by individual balloting in every commune.[31]

One prefect aptly described the net effect of the ensuing depoliticization in 1802: "The Seine-Inférieure has an excellent public spirit, because there reigns a great political immobility and a great movement to domestic affairs. When a people has made a good and serious delegation of public powers, it can do no better than to occupy itself with everything else."[32] The Napoleonic electoral charade in fact had little to do with popular sovereignty and representation, and everything to do with enlisting locally prominent men into the regime's network of informal patronage and symbolic status. The president of each departmental electoral college became a veritable dignitary of the regime, with ceremonial precedence *(préséance)* over prefects and subprefects. At a less exalted level, the presidents of the cantonal assemblies were designated by the government for ten-year terms after 1802, and were deemed to be useful cogs in the unofficial structure of notability.[33]

The details of electoral institutions received inordinate attention from the government, scarcely commensurate with their ostensible function, let alone their actual role. Where the Directory had stipulated that no elector of the Year VI could be named as an elector the following year, for example, Napoleon wanted membership in his electoral colleges to be lifetime appointments, drawn from the six hundred largest taxpayers in each department, who would serve in effect as cheerleaders for the regime. Members of the electoral colleges were to make their loyalty oath in writing, with a copy to be deposited in the archives of the prefecture! On the rare occasions when the cantonal assemblies or electoral colleges convened, the presidents were enjoined to wear a standardized form of ordinary dress, a kind of civilian uniform including a "chapeau français à plumet noir" and a white vest.

Should he be absent from a session, an elector was required to "justify" that dereliction.[34]

It is instructive to observe, however, that the ghost of political participation haunted the regime down to its last days. Any participatory process, after all, no matter how nominal or symbolic, could get out of hand. Fearful that public spirit would falter behind the collapsing military front in 1813, the Interior Ministry was especially nervous about the cantonal assemblies due to convene in one fifth of the departments that year. A resurgence of "intrigue" in these assemblies might revive disruptive political conflicts from the past. The minister requested his prefects to monitor those assemblies and report confidentially to him. Although one can understand his apprehensions, these reports indicated little intrigue, contention, or ambition. On the contrary, insouciance, reluctance to participate, and bare quorums were the rule. "The most profound and the most general indifference for political assemblies" marked the convocations in the Sarthe and almost everywhere else. Cantonal presidents worked strenuously to bring out voters ("It was almost necessary to employ violence in order to obtain a certain number of voters," reported one prefect), but turnout averaged only about 10 percent, ranging between one seventh to one fifteenth of eligible citizens.[35] The citizens who voted may have belonged to all classes, as the prefect of Indre-et-Loire believed, but very few did so. The prefect of the Jura made the most telling observation: "This right once so prized is now exercised with indifference. . . . [But] perhaps one good has resulted. The respectable men *(honnêtes gens)* who sense the importance of making choices with care . . . easily find themselves in the majority."[36]

Under the Restoration one segment of the *honnêtes gens* would enjoy exclusive rights to political participation. The Bourbons reestablished representation and voting, but adopted an extreme version of the National Assembly's censitary franchise by conferring the right to vote only on citizens paying at least 300 livres a year in property taxes, which favored the landed nobility and enfranchised a plutocracy of about 100,000 citizens in all of France. Eligibility to serve in the legislature was set at the higher threshold of 1,000 livres in property taxes, creating a pool of about 16,000 *éligibles,* and yielding a Chamber of Deputies in 1816 and again in 1821 over half of whose members came from the nobility. Yet the Bourbons had restored the principle of representation after an hiatus of fifteen years, and once reestablished it would be relatively easy to change the franchise or eligibility requirements—which is precisely what the July Monarchy did after the Revolution of 1830, when it lowered the *cens* for voting and eligibility to 200 and 500 livres respectively.[37]

Both the Empire and the Restoration created political systems equally remote from that of the National Assembly, but each assimilated convenient elements of that system. The Napoleonic regime maintained the fiction of popular suffrage with its plebiscites and factitious cantonal elections; the Restoration resurrected a veritable if narrowly elected Chamber of Deputies. In these stunted and disembodied forms the principles of popular sovereignty and representation survived into the nineteenth century, alongside the potent memories of 1789 and 1793.

IV

INTEGRATING THE
VILLAGES

A s they rethought their republic after Robespierre's fall, the thermidorians returned to the original revolutionary project of administrative rationalization and national uniformity. In a country overwhelmingly rural and agrarian, with a population dispersed in over forty thousand communes, how could the villages be integrated into a normative fabric of civic life? The Montagnards had experimented and innovated in many areas but had not touched the National Assembly's basic plan for local government. While they shouldered aside the departmental administrations and turned the districts into the fulcrum of revolutionary government, the Montagnards left existing municipalities in place "so as not to deprive their citizens of the consolation of administering themselves fraternally,"[1] although in reality revolutionary committees and the agents of deputies-on-mission often superseded elected municipal officials. After the Mountain's fall, the thermidorians reconsidered the vexing problem of civic fragmentation in the countryside. The debate in the Year III simply recapitulated the arguments of late 1789 on what the lowest units or cells of the body politic should be, but the outcome this time was different.[2]

Now the Convention reversed the National Assembly's decision to confer political autonomy on every village with any kind of legal personality and instead moved to conjoin rural villages into larger administrative units. Each village might still be a veritable "rural community" linked by economic and sentimental ties, as the historian Marc Bloch has persuasively demonstrated,[3]

but it need not have political autonomy in the republic. When the thermidorians abolished the original middle tier of administration by suppressing the
districts—tainted as instruments of revolutionary government and terror—
they could more easily embrace the previously spurned idea of creating
so-called *grandes communes* in the countryside. Nor would they have to fashion
these new units out of thin air, since a convenient jurisdiction already existed
that could be adapted to this new purpose. Thus, under the Constitution of
the Year III, while towns with over five thousand inhabitants continued to
elect independent municipalities, rural communes were grouped around their
cantonal seats to form *"cantonal municipalities,"* which now constituted the
lowest tier of local government and administration. A new civic experiment
began.

THE WIDER WORLD OF THE CANTONS

Territorial units ordinarily comprising between six to twelve communes,
cantons had existed since 1790 as the circumscription for the primary assembly that named electors, and as the bailiwick for a justice of the peace. In the
Directory regime the 5,400 cantons now became the locus of administration
in the countryside as well. They would replace "The 44,000 [communal]
municipalities . . . that immensity of administrations all acting at the same
time, too often in contrary directions, and almost always without subordination."[4] Although villages retained their identity as independent entities called
communes, they lost most of their governmental roles. Rural communes virtually disappeared from the official administrative hierarchy.

The cantonal municipality, known as the *administration municipale,* was in
its way an ingenious contrivance. During their primary assembly the canton's
voters, after choosing their justice of the peace, now elected a president to
head their municipality. Subsequently voters in each commune, who had
elected their mayor and municipal council under the Constitution of 1791,
designated instead one person for a two-year term as their *agent municipal* and
another as his deputy *(adjoint).* The *agent* represented his commune in the
periodic meetings of the municipal administration at the canton's seat. That
is, the canton president and the *agents* from the individual communes together constituted the *administration municipale* of the canton, which in turn
hired a secretary paid from local funds.[5]

Drawing inspiration from the experience of the Year II, the architects of
this system added an official appointed by Paris to represent the national state
in each canton. Like the commissioners of the Executive Directory attached
to each departmental administration and court, the cantonal commissioners

were paid by Paris (though at the far more modest rate of 300 livres a year), in contrast to the locally elected president and *agents* who remained unpaid. In theory the cantonal commissioner did not have the power to initiate anything, although no meeting of the municipality could take place or any act be passed without his presence. Ostensibly he was there to monitor the administration's compliance with laws and decrees coming down from Paris and with the *arrêtés* of the departmental administration. In reality he advised, goaded, and shared the work of the municipality's part-time amateurs, and in extreme cases did much of it himself. Most important, the commissioners became the eyes and ears of the government, reporting to their immediate superiors, the departmental commissioners, who distilled their information and passed it along to the Ministry of Interior in a strictly defined chain of command. For the first time in French history, these cantonal commissioners brought a quasi-bureaucratic presence to the grass roots.

Under this new system, the *agent municipal* had minimal responsibilities. Within the precincts of his commune, he was to maintain the registers of births, deaths, and marriages (the *état civil,* of which more later); to serve as a kind of police officer linked to the justice of the peace; and to participate in the allocation of the commune's share of property taxes among its citizens. Tax rolls, requisitions, budgets, and reports, however, were fashioned collectively at the cantonal level. Cantons also became the repositories of the law. The *Bulletin des Lois*—that ultimate artifact of state building and centralization—no longer went out to each commune but only to the *chef-lieu de canton,* which was required to maintain three subscriptions: for the president, the cantonal commissioner, and the secretary.[6] Except for the *état civil,* all archives were also to be regrouped at the *chef-lieu.* Under the Constitution of 1795 each cantonal seat was supposed to maintain an elementary school while other communes need not. When the *fête décadaire* became obligatory in 1798, official observance was required only in the cantonal seat and not in each commune. Similarly civil marriage ceremonies were to be performed henceforth by the cantonal president at the *fête décadaire* rather than by the *agent* in each commune. All told, the canton figured very heavily in the Directory's civic agenda.

Unlike the former mayor, the *agent municipal* was not obliged to correspond with superior authorities, nor was he responsible for the budget and expenditures of his commune. He merely supplied information to his colleagues on the cantonal municipality. All decisions, correspondence, and accounting were handled collectively at its meetings. Instead of anywhere from 200 to 950 separate sets of instructions, reports, budgets, and accounts per department, formal administration now required only 30 to 90. Moreover the system was stronger than its weakest links, for it could tolerate a number

of incompetent or absentee *agents* while the abler ones shouldered the paperwork with the president and secretary.

According to the few local studies we have, however, the disengagement
of rural citizens from this experiment made it difficult to launch the cantonal
administrations. Perhaps because they resented this dilution of communal
autonomy and local self-government, villagers showed little interest in choosing their *agent municipal,* and even less in electing a cantonal president. And
when a quorum of voters finally acted, their nominees often declined the
dubious honor. Reluctant to haul themselves periodically to the cantonal
seat, tired of revolutionary politics or hostile to the republic, and (especially
in the West) fearful of anti-republican violence, many declined or immediately resigned after pleading inability, infirmities, or the need to tend to their
own affairs. When local voters could not designate an *agent,* those already
serving or the departmental administration (in behalf of the Directory) were
authorized to do it for them, but their designees could decline as well. An
expense allowance might have increased the acceptance rate, since these
unpaid posts required an outlay of cash for food and drink on meeting days,
but that simple inducement was never offered.[7]

Though it took as long as a year in certain departments, enough agents
were eventually recruited to get the cantonal administrations functioning.
Their ability was usually minimal, however, and their participation grudging;
if threatened with dismissal by the department for indifference and lassitude,
they were likely to depart with a smile. "Almost all the *agents* lack capacity and
talent; they do not bother to read the laws. Indifference *(insouciance)* is at its
height," complained one departmental commissioner. "If the department
orders rigorous measures, they produce resignations," warned another. Unfortunately the government repeatedly called on the *agents* to implement
unpopular and distasteful measures of several kinds, even if they seemed mild
by the standards of the Terror. Immediately they were obliged to allocate the
forced loan of 1796, detested by everyone except the Neo-Jacobins. Even a
massive purge of *agents municipaux* after Fructidor—302 out of 576 *agents*
ousted in 43 cantons studied in the Pas-de-Calais, for example[8]—did not
alter the basic equation. For the new designees, if they did not resign
immediately, were soon dragging their feet over other unpopular policies
such as implementing the military draft of 1798–99. Above all, the Directory
sorely tried their goodwill by its demands in 1798–99 to enforce the republican calendar with its ten-day weeks. While officials in the departmental
capitals found ways to appease their masters on this issue, most *agents*
municipaux on the front lines were neither able nor willing to coerce their
constituents into observing the *décadi* as a day of rest instead of the *"ci-devant*
Dimanche."[9]

Relentless pressure over the republican calendar and other matters caused mutual disenchantment between the government and its cantonal commissioners as well. In return for their modest salary (a third or less of what the cantonal secretary earned), the commissioners were supposed to maintain "a regular, constant, and habitual correspondence" with the departmental commissioner. No such thing could have been expected from unsalaried and often barely literate mayors or *agents* in each village. But even on the cantonal level it proved endlessly difficult to achieve the desired standard of reporting, although the government depended on these reports if it was to know what was happening in the countryside. The purges of obscure cantonal presidents and *agents* after Fructidor, for example, could be based only on information from the cantonal commissioners. Initially the government demanded a weekly report *(compte décadaire),* but the results were unsatisfactory: "silences, inexactitude, pusillanimous wariness," complained the commissioner to the Jura. In June 1798 the Directory agreed to settle for one report per month from cantonal commissioners.[10] But even elaborate model forms provided by some departmental commissioners did not necessarily help, since it was just as easy to be perfunctory or dilatory with them as without.[11]

Ostensibly the cantonal commissioners were the lowest echelon of the national government's functionaries. They were chosen by the Directory upon recommendations from the department's legislative deputation and central administration. But unlike the departmental commissioners, who belonged to the Revolution's national political elite, most were local men without significant experience or ambition who were likely to respond as much to local interests or inertia as to pressure from above. Most were petit-bourgeois, minimally familiar with the world of public affairs and the art of the pen (modest country lawyers, notaries, low-level public employees, and the odd constitutional priest), along with a scattering of rural proprietors, cultivators, tradesmen, and artisans. The Directory was of course free to recruit its commissioners from the towns, but few capable men would accept underpaid postings to small rural bourgs. When a former deputy to the Convention like Mauduyt or Fayau turns up on the roster of commissioners in the Seine-et-Marne, one can be reasonably certain that the Directory appointed him to an urban municipality.[12]

During the near anarchy and anti-republican violence that engulfed certain departments in 1796, it was understandable that these commissioners were "paralyzed by the [white] terror and persecutions." But even after the violence abated, most could not energize their administrations or convey information effectively. (The fact that their pay fell chronically in arrears did not help.)[13] "The commissioners attached to the municipal administrations," complained one departmental commissioner, "are isolated and without force." In the eyes of some observers, the old districts regained their attraction as reasonable outposts for the state's bureaucracy. As a correspondent of Director Merlin de Douai wrote from Vienne: "I again propose suspending the cantonal commissioners, almost all imbeciles, and turning over their functions to the commissioners in the former district capitals, who are generally better educated and more detached from individual passions." It appeared as if the thermidorians had overreached themselves. [14]

Experience seemed to be revealing fatal flaws in the concept of cantonal municipalities. Peasants who craved veritable local autonomy resented the removal of authority to the cantonal seat, and many registered their disenchantment by refusing to vote or to serve. The bureaucratic capacity or impetus of the salaried commissioners was proving questionable. Moreover when subsistence problems arose, the regime might be incapacitated by the fact that cantonal boundaries fragmented historic provisioning networks whereas the districts had reinforced them. Yet it would be hasty to write the cantons off as artificial creations doomed to fail. From an ecological and social perspective, the cantonal municipalities offered a promising basis on which to aggregate citizens and nurture civic life in the countryside while leaving each commune its residual autonomy. In the first place, most cantonal seats had periodic markets that attracted peasants from surrounding villages. In addition to their justice of the peace and primary school, many had a local notary and a local registry bureau as well. While citizens of relatively undeveloped and autarchic villages might entertain deep resentment of market villages, the cantonal seat was still far closer and less forbidding than the old district capitals. The canton's *chef-lieu* was likely to be a locus of rural life already—like Bonnières-sur-Seine (population c. 700), where "for as long as anyone can remember people from the neighboring communes have been coming daily to sell their goods in our bourg." [15] Small, isolated villages did not after all constitute self-contained worlds. Peasants and rural artisans required wider communities for marriage, hiring, credit, purchasing, and selling—communities likely to form around market villages or bourgs.

The anthropologist William Skinner has charted such communities in traditional China, which he calls "standard marketing areas." Chinese market villages served an average of eighteen smaller villages with total populations of around 7,000; [16] the average population of a French rural canton was slightly over 6,000. In China, of course, the state made no attempt to build a formal administrative structure at this level. Chinese administration more or less stopped at the *hsein*—the geographic and demographic equivalent of a French department. Beyond the government seat or *yamen* in the *hsein* capital, the dynasty relied on the Confucian scholar-gentry to serve as informal intermediaries among networks of village headmen or lineage elders. From the beginning, in contrast, France's revolutionaries set out to create formal and uniform administrative mechanisms in the most basic units or cells of their nation. When the thermidorians reconsidered the original decentralized, three-tiered plan in 1795, they backed up one step by withdrawing almost all administrative responsibility from rural communes. Yet at the same time they extended government bureaucracy further down than ever by organizing cantonal municipalities in the equivalent of "standard marketing areas," and by stationing a paid commissioner of the Directory in each one. Finding some five thousand presidents and commissioners for these rural posts may have stretched the nation's administrative capital too thin, but it seemed preferable to relying on forty thousand unpaid mayors. Given time, cantonal government might have reduced the isolation of individual rural communes by building on the existing relationships of their citizens with market villages, although in a region like the southern Massif Central the intense hostility of small "village diasporas" to those favored bourgs made this outcome unlikely.[17]

ONE TYPE OF evidence for the potential viability of the cantons comes in a paradoxically negative form, in petitions from rural communes to be included in a different canton *(distraction),* and in petitions by an *administration municipale* or some of its members to transfer the canton's *chef-lieu* from one commune to another. Virtually all such petitions claimed that the original circumscriptions drawn by the National Assembly in 1790 were faulty. But the petitions usually provide a counter-image of a soundly designed canton— presumably the situation in the large majority of places that did not find it necessary to mount such demands.

The petitions for *distraction* complained of the distance and inaccessibility of the *chef-lieu* in contrast to that of the neighboring canton in which they wished to be included. As the inhabitants of Salès (Haute-Garonne) explained, "everything calls us to Carbonne, which is our common center. All our affairs bring us to that place, whether for the market or by virtue of its riverain commerce . . . whereas nature has placed often insurmountable obstacles in the way of going to Rieux." Similarly the citizens of Lentile (Aube) wanted to be placed in the canton of Chavagnes, "the site of fairs and markets with which relations are frequent and even daily. It has a registry bureau; and finally it is a commercial kind of place with resources that do not exist elsewhere."[18] In requesting the transfer of their communes into nearby Montflanquin canton instead of Montfiguer, the inhabitants of three villages

in Lot-et-Garonne depicted an almost ideal cantonal seat where, among
other things, they could make their quarterly tax payments while taking care
of other business:

> They have their relations and their affairs at Montflanquin. There they
> find frequent markets and fairs for the sale of their produce and livestock;
> merchants and artisans who provide necessary goods; workers to repair
> their broken implements; doctors to treat their illnesses; lawyers and
> notaries to assist them in their civil transactions. . . . In a word, the
> communes in question can be considered so to speak as faubourgs of
> Montflanquin.[19]

The elements determining a canton's social or ecological viability are
apparent too in the more numerous demands for transfer of the *chef-lieu*
within a canton. These petitions note the haste of the National Assembly in
drawing cantonal circumscriptions in 1790, its occasional ignorance of local
topography, and the apparent influence of special-interest pleading. That is
not to say that even with sufficient time and knowledge the task would have
been simple. Should the centrality of a cantonal seat, for example, be reckoned relative to the number of communes it served or to those with the most
inhabitants? What if it was comfortably accessible for seven or eight villages
but excessively remote from one or two? (While the great majority of villages
clustered in reasonable proximity to each other, the veritable isolation of
some threatened to contravene the constitutional principle that no commune
should be more than a *myriamètre* away from the *chef-lieu*.) Nor was mere
distance necessarily a useful guide, since topography could alter its meaning:
Did a swollen river surge through the canton? Was the *chef-lieu* situated in
mountainous terrain? What were the roads like leading into it? Other considerations could loom equally large: Did the *chef-lieu* have facilities for meetings
and archives, and amenities like an inn for the *agents* and for voters in the
annual primary assemblies? Was it a patriotic place or a bastion of counter-
revolution? Petitions for a shift of the *chef-lieu*—for a reconfiguration of the
canton—suggest that choosing the *chef-lieu* could be a difficult zero-sum game
(see Figures IV-1 and IV-2), but they also present a counter-image of a
properly ordered canton.[20]

In 1790, the choice of the cantonal *chef-lieu* was a matter of local pride and
traditional rivalries but scarcely of great moment in the life of the rural
community. But now that administration and taxation had devolved on the
canton, favoritism or ignorance by the National Assembly in 1790 in establishing an inaccessible cantonal seat had grave results. As the citizens of Ufaix
(Hautes-Alpes) put it: "[after 1796] communal charges were not distributed

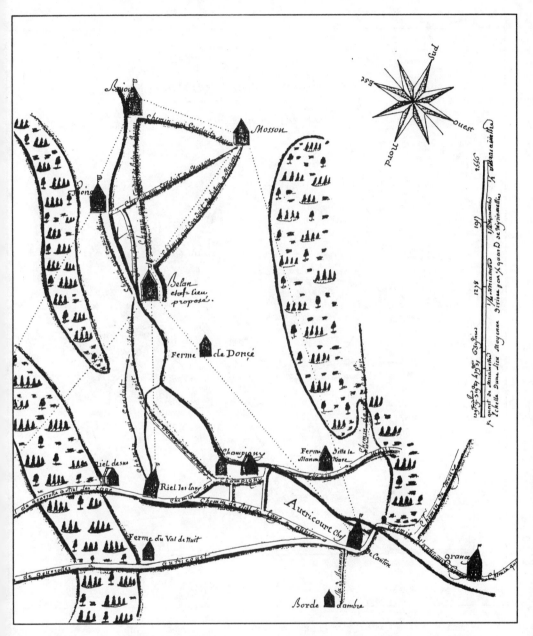

FIGURE IV-1: *Conflicts over Fixing the Seat of a Rural Canton.* Should the *chef-lieu* of this canton in the Côte d'Or be moved from Autricourt to Belan? Autricourt's partisans claimed that three-fifths of the canton's residents were better served by its location and that the commune had "a commodious locale" for sessions of the cantonal administration. Nonetheless the department shifted the seat to the more centrally located Belan, arguing that Autricourt lay at the canton's extremity, as this map demonstrates.

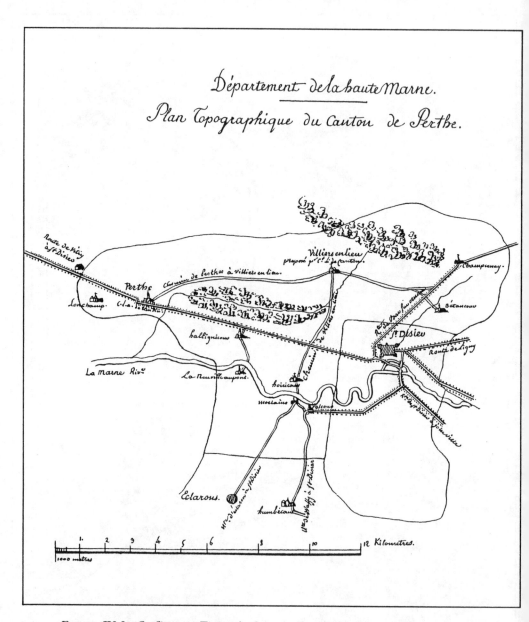

FIGURE IV-2: *Conflicts over Fixing the Seat of a Rural Canton.* Complaints over the distance to Perthe from the two most easterly communes in this canton in the Haute-Marne prompted the department to shift the *chef-lieu* from its original location. Villiers, the most populous commune in the canton, possessed a fine *maison commune,* but the canton's officials insisted that access to Hoiricourt was easier for most citizens. As for a meeting place, "the voluntary offer by a citizen promises the municipal administration the enjoyment of an adequate locale."

with that equality that alone makes them bearable, and the burden fell on those who were not heard." A few errors were blatant and easily rectified. The "vicious organization" of the cantons of Seranon and Mujoulx in the Var, for example, had the citizens of the six northern communes in Seranon up in arms. The legislature eventually performed the necessary surgery by reorganizing a canton centered in Gars. It was also hard to understand how Fontenay (Meurthe) had ever been designated as a cantonal seat, but under the new system it was insupportable. With a population of about two hundred, it had no locale for the authorities or for convening the primary assemblies and no facilities for lodging or feeding them. Gonderville, to the contrary, had about one thousand inhabitants, was in the center of the canton on the main road from Paris to Strasbourg, and had buildings for the administration's meetings and the primary assemblies. In 1796, the departmental administration authorized the provisional transfer of the *chef-lieu* to Gonderville, and the legislature finally ratified that decision in 1798.[21]

Distance, topography, and inconvenience were the most likely causes of protests. The cantonal municipality of Candes (Indre-et-Loire) wished to move the *chef-lieu* to Lerne because "the extreme remoteness of Candes puts off the inhabitants of the other five communes so much that their primary assemblies are too often incomplete and the sessions of the administration lose prodigiously of their majesty and utility." Citizens of five communes in the canton of Monsauche (Nièvre) petitioned to move the *chef-lieu* from its current site, surrounded by swampy roads, torrential rivers, and heavy snows, just as six of the seven communes in the canton of Gault (Loir-et-Cher) demanded the transfer of the *chef-lieu* to more centrally located Arville "because the refusal of the *agents* to travel to Gault obstructs the administrative service."[22]

Lack of facilities sometimes outweighed topography in prompting municipalities or villagers to demand a new *chef-lieu*. The hapless *agents* in the canton of St. Just (Aveyron) wanted to relocate to St. Martial, a central and commodious bourg with "a town hall that is offered free of charge," whereas at St. Just, "there is no locale for our sessions other than the tumult of a cabaret." The administration of Allene (Lozère) likewise "had to meet amidst the hubbub of a tavern, without an archive for the laws and administrative papers, which are as dispersed as its members. . . . Deliberations are made in haste and without adequate information." They would do better, they believed, in Bleymard, with a building "suitable for holding all meetings and as a repository for the laws and papers."[23] Yet another motive for changing the *chef-lieu* was its political environment. The departmental administration of the Manche provisionally transferred the cantonal seat from St. Poix to Coulouvray because the newly elected *agents* refused to be sworn in at St.

Poix, "where their safety was compromised since the renewal of *chouannerie* [brigandage] in that area." A legislative report concluded that Biez (Pas-de-Calais) was more centrally located, endowed with better facilities, and more patriotic than Fressin, a royalist commune where republicans felt threatened.[24]

In disputed cases fate did not always combine central location, adequate facilities, and a patriotic ambience so neatly. Metz-en-Couture (Pas-de-Calais), for example, was at the extremity of its canton, had a population of only 1,100, and obliged the municipality to meet in a private dwelling, according to its detractors, whereas D'Hermy was centrally located, had 1,700 inhabitants, and an unsold former rectory for meetings. The partisans of Metz-en-Couture replied that it could rent or purchase a locale; that the bourg was more convenient for two thirds of the canton's citizens; and that a raging stream stood between them and D'Hermy. In the department's view, however, 4,880 inhabitants would be best served by D'Hermy versus 3,140 by Metz-en-Couture, and a bridge was being built over the stream in question. The citizens of Metz-en-Couture did not accept the department's decision and protested to the minister of the interior that their bourg was a place where people conducted business and could find lodging, while D'Hermy was a strictly agricultural place and one to which republicans "had been obliged to come armed to the sessions before 18 fructidor."[25] This case and about two dozen similar ones were the exceptions, the difficult situations that made the configuration of cantons an almost intractable problem.[26] More commonly the pieces came together and cantons could be superimposed onto existing patterns of interaction among rural communes without such contention.

IN THE INTERIOR Ministry's view, however, after two years the anticipated advantages of cantonal municipalities had not materialized. In a circular of 27 November 1797 it proposed to reduce the number of cantons substantially and called upon the departmental administrations to devise new and larger circumscriptions:

> Undoubtedly none of you have failed to sense how much the multiplicity of cantons has weakened the impetus coming from the central point of the department by dividing it excessively; how much the large number of cogs *(rouages)* undermines the selection process, the uniformity of measures, the activeness of correspondence, the rapidity of execution; finally how much that superfluity of municipal administrations causes useless expenses.[27]

As a corollary to reducing the number of cantons, the ministry also asked the departments rather offhandedly to prepare lists of small communes that might be merged with others—in reality a far more fundamental and difficult operation, as we shall see presently.

Encouraged by the generally enthusiastic responses it received from thirty-four departments as of August 1798, the ministry pushed ahead. Since the 1,886 cantons in those departments might be reduced to 1,081, it expected that a total of about 1,750 cantons could be suppressed. The ministry anticipated the arguments that this project would face in the legislature, which had tabled the question a few months earlier on the grounds that discussion of so delicate a matter would be ill advised on the eve of the primary assemblies. Article 50 of the Constitution read: "The cantons are to retain their present circumscriptions. Nonetheless their boundaries can be modified and corrected by the Legislature; but in that case no commune can be more than a *myriamètre* distant from the canton's seat." In the ministry's view, this did not lock in the number of cantons. The wording *(les cantons conservent leurs circonscriptions actuelles)* "had no other purpose than to avoid inserting into the constitution a lengthy nomenclature." Constitutional scruples need not prevent a drastic reform. The inevitable protests by individual cantons marked for suppression the ministry dismissed in advance as "petty rivalries" that should not deter legislators. [28]

As the "astonished" and "saddened" inhabitants or officials of cantons slated for elimination by their departments indeed protested (see Figure IV-3), [29] the project moved through the Council of Five Hundred. Debate on the bill began on 22 November 1798 and revealed a host of reservations about the plan in addition to the anticipated constitutional objections that the Directory considered specious. According to J.-P. Duplantier, the biggest problem in cantonal administration was getting a quorum of *agents,* with the result that municipalities often went two or three months without being able to deliberate properly. "That inaction which is attributed to the multiplicity of cantons is due on the contrary to their excessive size. In augmenting their territory you will therefore exacerbate the problem." In defending the current size and distribution of the cantons, Duplantier argued that a massive redeployment of primary assemblies and municipal administrations would force a useless change in "the habits and interactions of the citizens." Moreover citizens already found trips to the *chef-lieu* for a *fête décadaire* or a marriage ceremony long enough; the new plan would necessitate far more arduous treks. Pierre Delbrel, accepting the basic premise of cantonal administration, believed that the closer a cantonal seat was to its citizens, the more willingly they would support its expenses. "I am convinced," he added, "that the multiplicity of *rouages* works, up to a certain point, for the maintenance of

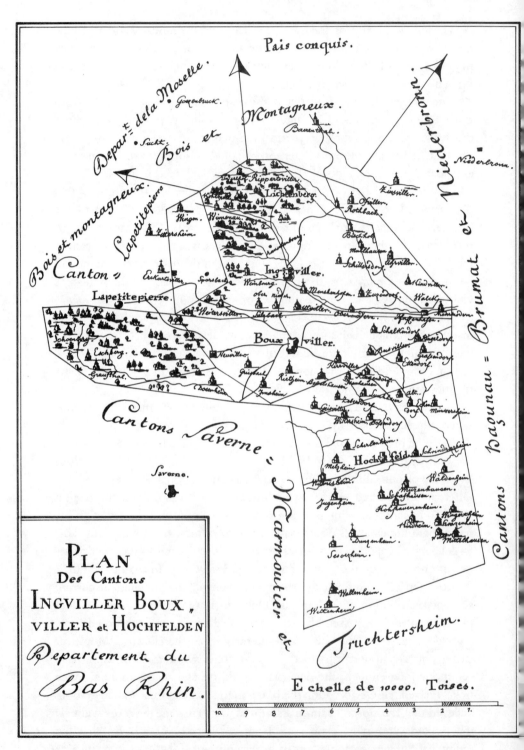

FIGURE IV-3: *A Canton Pleads for Its Viability, 1799*

public liberty by making it possible for a larger number of citizens to participate in governmental activity. . . . A municipal administration whose sessions are public is a kind of school, a source of emulation for the inhabitants of the countryside." [30]

Defenders of the Directory's reduction project focused not on the citizens' relations to the canton but on administrative and financial problems— "the costly nullity . . . the inexecution of the laws . . . the despair of the superior administrations" caused by the present arrangements. J.-B. Bara contended that the success or failure of the system really depended on the capacity of the commissioners. The Directory simply could not find enough competent men; it preferred to rely on a smaller number and pay them better. Indeed, in the budget for the Year VII the salaries of the cantonal commissioners had been doubled in the expectation that their number would be substantially reduced. The other expenses of cantonal administration such as the salaries of secretaries, postal couriers, supplies, and maintenance—which he estimated to average 1,400 lives a year—could be significantly reduced by abolishing a third of the cantons. This would have the salutary effect of diminishing the local surtaxes earmarked for the expenses of the cantons. [31] These arguments proved unavailing, however. After two days of debate the Council of Five Hundred tabled the project and thereby continued the status quo.

NAPOLEON'S MAYORS

Brumaire overturned that status quo completely. The Consulate's local government act of February 1800 jettisoned the cantons (except as judicial and electoral circumscriptions) and reverted to a three-tiered system parallel to the original concept of 1790. Instead of authorizing elections for departmental, district, and communal administrations, however, the Consulate appointed prefects, subprefects, and mayors. Under this model—which endured with minor changes and brief exceptions down to the Third

FIGURE IV-3: *A Canton Pleads for Its Viability, 1799.* When, in response to the Directory's campaign to reduce the number of cantons, the department of Bas-Rhin proposed to eliminate the canton of Ingviller, its administration responded with a beautifully illustrated plea for its ecological and social viability. Suppressing the neighboring canton of Bouxviller instead, it argued, would cause less inconvenience since an expanded canton centered on Ingviller would offer easy access to the *chef-lieu* from all its communes. "Nature itself seems to have designed [this canton] by ringing it on almost all sides with tall mountains."

Republic—communes again became the lowest unit of active administration, the base point in the chain of responsibility and official communication. In that sense the state moved closer to the grass roots. Symbolizing this, the government again redirected the *Bulletin des Lois*. Under the Directory, subscriptions had been maintained only at the cantonal seat; now every mayor had to pay for a subscription out of his communal budget. (The three sets of back issues in each canton were distributed to the mayors of its three most populous communes.) [32] At the same time, when the government suppressed the cantonal municipalities and reestablished a mayor in each commune, it was pulling the state bureaucracy back to the level of the district (now called the *arrondissement* or subprefecture, with three to six per department)—a retreat from the Directory's insertion of salaried functionaries into large villages and bourgs.

The fact that rural mayors were appointed by the prefect rather than elected could certainly entail a significant loss of communal power, but the ground had been well prepared with the frequent purges of *agents municipaux* and their replacement by appointees of the Directory's commissioners or departmental administrations. The prefects in any case had every reason to name men who would be respected in their communes, and if they lost sight of that they might be reminded by their own superior. During the Restoration, the minister of the interior urged prefects in the Yonne and Calvados, in quite extraordinary language, "to give preference for those positions to men who would have a chance of being carried if election was put back in the hands of the citizens. . . . Make your choices fall as much as possible on those whom popular suffrage would designate." [33]

A free field of action did not suffice to recruit a cohort of loyal, attentive, and reliable mayors in rural France. Few citizens eagerly sought this unpaid and potentially onerous position. The prefect of the Côte d'Or claimed in October 1800 that he had to make "four or five thousand nominations to organize seven hundred appointments." Wealthy and educated men often shunned the post, perhaps preferring one that paid or that carried less responsibility. The scarcity of apt individuals and the reluctance of others meant that most village mayors were peasants or proprietors of middling or even modest social condition. The prefect of Vienne complained that many of his mayors were "small cultivators who need all their time to procure subsistence for their families," while his colleague in the Moselle reported on the difficulty in finding rural mayors "who are independent by virtue of their wealth and who can devote part of their time to administration. In appointing on the contrary working peasants *(manoeuvres)* or artisans it is to be feared that their dependence on others will render them too complaisant." His problem was compounded by the desirability of finding men in this German-speaking region with at least a modicum of French.[34]

A recent statistical study of France's mayors from 1800 to the present has given us a degree of precision on such questions without substantially challenging the litany of prefectorial complaint. Based on a sample of thirteen arrondissements in different regions, the study surveys 1,234 communes of which 46 percent were under 500 population and 30 percent between 500 and 999. For the Empire and Restoration, in the two sample years of 1811 and 1824, mayors in these villages and rural bourgs were almost all commoners rather than ex-nobles or nobles, though the latter presided in about 10 percent of the small towns. Nor did the mayors come from the ranks of the very rich. About 50 percent can be classified as middling (with incomes between 1,000F and 9,999F) and another 30 percent belonged to the popular strata (incomes below 1,000F). Fewer than 10 percent of the mayors, generally in the cities, were truly rich. By occupation, over 40 percent were peasants *(cultivateurs)*—with a higher percentage in the *pays de petite culture* of widespread peasant holdings; another 25 percent were rural property owners who did not work the fields *(propriétaires* and rentiers)—most commonly heading bourgs between 1,000 and 2,000 inhabitants. Trailing far behind were men from the liberal professions.[35] We may conclude that under the Empire and Restoration the modal type of village mayor was a fifty-year old landowning peasant with relatively modest income.

What cannot be determined by statistical analysis is the competence, diligence, or moral authority of these men. By definition the mayor could read and write, but (in the view of many prefects) just barely. He was in no way dependent on his post and if leaned on unduly would simply resign. In the statistical study of the mayors in two sample cohorts of 1811 and 1824, most died in office or retired, but an average of 25 percent ended their tenure abruptly by resignation and another 13 percent were dismissed.[36] If the prefect of Bouches-du-Rhône explained in 1803 that he was replacing the numerous corrupt or ignorant mayors in his department gradually so as to avoid the jolt of "an almost general renewal," other prefects felt compelled to purge their mayors wholesale: in the Eure, the prefect replaced one fourth of his mayors in 1807, the majority because they were "incapable, inept, null," while the prefect of the Bas-Rhin replaced 185 mayors in 1808.[37] Nonetheless the average tenure nationally was probably fifteen years. The lack of any alternative in many communes no doubt goes a long way to explain this longevity. As the prefect of Dordogne lamented, "my embarrassment has reached its height with the death of a few mayors who are the only ones in their communes that know how to read, and by the resignation of several others." Occasionally the system broke down completely, as in Montailles (Drôme), population 399. When the *adjoint* resigned and soon thereafter the mayor died, the justice of the peace informed the prefect that there was not "a single person capable of serving as mayor." The prefect temporarily put the mayor of neighboring Albon in charge, hoping eventually to merge the two communes. [38]

ON PAPER, AT least, the government expected a great deal from its mayors, who were appointed directly by the prefects in communes under 5,000 population. Mayors played two not always compatible roles, just as they had in 1790. Though unpaid amateurs, they were "elements of the general administration of the state" on whose cooperation "the superior authorities," the veritable functionaries in the prefecture, depended. Simultaneously they spoke for their fellow citizens and, along with the *conseil municipal* (of which more directly), they were "direct administrators of their commune." The mayor was always on call for the "superior authorities" as well as for local responsibilities. In the exalted image of one prefect, his 730 mayors were much like the *bon curés* of the old regime, although as family men they were not given to exaggerated piety and were therefore superior! [39]

The mayor's fundamental obligation remained the maintenance of the *état civil,* the registry of births, deaths, and marriages. In conjunction with this he officiated at civil marriage ceremonies—a function which had been assigned to the cantonal presidents under the Directory. Secondly, the mayor was supposed to publicize laws and decrees, preferably by reading aloud selections from the *Bulletin des Lois* and explaining them "paternally" to his constituents. [40] Expenditure on the stamped paper for the *état civil* and on a subscription to the *Bulletin des Lois* stood as the rock-bottom elements of every communal budget. These two items were the most tangible artifacts of the new civic order in rural France.

Along with his deputy *(adjoint)* the rural mayor was informally an officer of the judicial police responsible for initiating prosecutions before the justice of the peace. The mayor was also enjoined to nominate a *garde champêtre* for certain police duties in his commune, of which more later. In a well-run commune, the mayor issued a variety of certificates and *procès-verbaux* for his constituents, though if the commune could afford to employ one, his clerk would do most of the paperwork. The *Journal du Département de l'Oise* printed model forms to help mayors deal with such things as petty crimes; alignments of property; passports and certificates of residence (extremely important documents as conscription became a way of life); marriage and divorce certificates; gun permits *(port d'armes);* inspection of inns and communal ovens; regulation of weights and measures; and reporting of serious accidents or the discovery of a corpse. [41] Mayors were expected to aid the tax collectors and to supervise maintenance of local roads, and above all they became cogs in the regime's highest priority, the conscription machine. Beyond these obligations mayors could exert moral authority in several directions. With the installation of the new mayors, the prefect of the Oise optimistically declared, "charitable activity will reappear in the countryside." He also urged his mayors to support primary education, public recreation, and the upkeep of public facilities. [42]

It was one thing for the government to require such labor and punctilious recordkeeping, such "paternalism" and public service. But it was quite another to assure them or even to find out what was actually going on in the villages. Mayors were asked to play a quasi-bureaucratic role without being paid or even rewarded intangibly with significant status. Loaded with responsibilities, they had little power of any kind over the purse strings. And unlike his immediate predecessor, the *agent municipal,* the mayor was on his own, lacking anyone within easy reach to explain things or back him up. Vulnerable to pressure and intimidation by his constituents (or to the temptation of tyrannizing over them if such was his personality), his actions or omissions were ever subject to censure and badgering by the prefecture.

The most common, well-nigh universal, charge against the rural mayors was *insouciance.* Not so much doing wrong, as one prefect put it, but doing nothing. Letters and circulars would go unanswered, decrees unenforced, vital information unsupplied. "Experience has long convinced me," wrote the prefect of Pas-de-Calais, "that the decrees, circulars, and instructions which I address to the rural mayors too often go without answer or implementation. These separate sheets of paper sometimes are not even read, and instead of saving them, some of these indifferent officials use them to light the pipes which they are forever smoking." (His decidedly ambitious response was to put out at the prefecture's expense a weekly printed newsletter to win the mayors' attention for his communications.) [43] Accomplishing anything at the communal level was the most tedious and thankless part of the prefect's job. As Napoleon's prefect in the Dordogne complained, "my bureaus and those of the subprefects exhaust themselves with correspondence that is as voluminous as it is fruitless." Years of research would probably not improve on the judgment of an official in the Interior Ministry shortly after the Restoration: "Out of 500 mayors to whom a prefect writes on any kind of measure at all, 200 execute it, 150 answer that they are executing it without actually doing so, and 150 do not respond at all." [44]

Nothing could be taken for granted. Even as registrars for the *état civil* the mayors were not always reliable, though they were provided with models and

pages of stamped paper, numbered and endorsed by the president of each
local tribunal, to whom the mayor sent a duplicate set of registers annually.
No fewer than seventy-two *conseils généraux* meeting in 1801 deplored the
poor condition of these registers, and fifty-seven suggested confiding them
to a salaried person such as a teacher, notary, or clerk.[45] Like many of his
colleagues, the prefect in the Landes reproached his mayors about the
"almost illegible entries," confusion of dates, lack of witnesses' signatures,
and "grave omissions" of important information in their registers. Some
prefects countered by providing pre-printed forms on stamped paper, but for
reasons that remain unclear they were evidently instructed to discontinue that
practice. In any case the *insouciance* of mayors in assuring that citizens accurately reported births, deaths, and marriages, and the unreliable way in which
they maintained the records, remained a constant source of concern, not least
because the *état civil* was the starting point for conscription and hence for
fraudulent efforts at draft evasion.[46]

In 1806, the prefect of the Loiret informed the Interior Ministry that
something was amiss. The population records for his department revealed an
unaccountable fall in the number of births from 10,459 in the Year X to
8,757 in the Year XI, which happened to coincide with the reestablishment
of the Church under the Concordat. "Does it not appear," he speculated,
"that from that moment on, people in the countryside neglected to declare
births to the municipalities and that a baptism and the note made of it by the
priests appeared to suffice for many ignorant persons?" A concerned ministry circularized all prefects in the belief that parents might be neglecting to
register their children's births, either to help them avoid conscription in the
future or from simple disregard for the law. When prefects as requested
compared the mayors' official registers with samples of parish records, most
did not in fact find major discrepancies, but they continued to worry.[47]

IN CERTAIN AREAS of local government the municipal council of each commune came into play alongside the mayor. Consisting of ten citizens in
communes under 2,500 population (if that many could be recruited), twenty
in those between 2,500 and 5,000, and thirty in towns, the *conseil municipal* was
initially appointed by the prefect. After 1802, vacancies on the urban councils
were ostensibly filled from lists of nominations made by the cantonal assemblies; the term for all municipal counselors was twenty years, half to be
renewed every ten years. These municipal councils stand as the counterparts
of the appointed advisory councils in each department and arrondissement,
through which the Napoleonic regime made its gesture of consulting with
local notables. But membership on a rural municipal council had no cachet

of *notabilité* whatsoever. Though its members had a small voice in setting local budgets, the inconvenience of service could easily offset the attraction. The Bourbons, more explicitly mindful of large property holders, added the ten largest taxpayers in each rural commune as statutory adjuncts of the *conseil municipal,* although many were likely to be *forains,* men who actually resided elsewhere.

The municipal councils had a strictly limited field of activity. They met but once a year for two weeks at most and could only recommend a course of action rather than decide it; anything they voted could be annulled by the prefecture. Fulfilling the Revolution's granite principles of fiscal accountability and participation by citizens in the assessment of taxes, the *conseil municipal* scrutinized the master tax roll and could file appeals on the commune's assessment. Outside the mayor's presence it audited his accounts and indicated any irregularities before forwarding them to the subprefect. The council allocated communal wood rations *(affouages)* and pasturage among the citizens, and could request the government to authorize a loan, *octroi,* lease of communal property, or (in one or two specified situations to be discussed below) a local property tax surcharge.[48]

The shortage of apt personnel for these councils was palpable, although literacy was not required. Prefects wanted public-spirited recommendations from the councils but claimed rarely to get them. Instead they complained of shirking by members more intent on working their plows or tending their sheep; of councils entirely under the thumb of mayors or of councils that would not agree to anything a mayor recommended.[49] Local factionalism was doubtless impenetrable to the prefecture but its results could be obvious enough. And adding wealthy *forains* to the councils under the Restoration exacerbated such problems, if they were unwilling to pay for services or improvements even when mandated by law. As a mayor in the Yonne complained, his council "is always afraid that the ten largest taxpayers, all non-residents, will refuse to vote [that] expenditure."[50] But we shall see in the next chapter that if miserliness caused serious problems, the lack of real autonomy and of resources weighed just as oppressively on the local civic order.

MERGING THE COMMUNES: AN ILLUSORY SOLUTION

Between the spurned innovation of cantonal municipalities and the manifest difficulty of dealing with forty thousand communes and their mayors, the Consulate grasped at one other option. The most persistent response of Napoleonic officials to the problems of civic fragmentation, inertia, and administrative incapacity in the countryside was the notion of amalgamating small communes into larger, more viable ones. Calls for the *réunion des communes* resounded as a leitmotif in prefectorial and notable opinion. At the annual meetings of the *conseils généraux* in 1801, at least forty-two endorsed the idea.[51] Next year, when the Interior Ministry surveyed departmental views on local problems, prefects across the land responded that the number of communes should be reduced by mergers. "Reducing the machinery of administration" would make it easier to find competent mayors, expedite government business, and assure a more reliable maintenance of the *état civil.* Mergers of rural communes would also lower communal expenses since two or more villages could share such recurrent obligations as a subscription to the *Bulletin des Lois,* secretarial and overhead costs, and postal couriers. Conversely their revenues could be stretched further to defray outlays for road maintenance or subsidies to a schoolmaster.[52] Certain prefects became zealous advocates of this policy. "I entreat you, Citizen Minister," wrote the prefect of the Drôme, "to recognize that under our present administrative organization nothing useful, nothing good, nothing complete or durable can be accomplished without the amalgamation of communes." A former general serving as prefect in Indre-et-Loire maintained that "the merger of communes ought to do more good for the Republic than ten battles won."[53]

The Directory had already called for the amalgamation of small communes in 1798 but gave top priority to reducing the number of cantonal administrations. Only a handful of *réunions* were consummated after an exhaustive process of legislative review. Cantonal administrations generally initiated those mergers when it proved impossible to find an *agent municipal* from the commune in question. Normally the departmental administration consulted "a general assembly of the inhabitants," and then the proposed amalgamation had to be approved in turn by the department, the Interior Ministry, an ad hoc legislative commission, and both houses of the legislature.[54]

After Brumaire—with the new prefectorial system in place, the cantonal municipalities abolished, the administrative identity of each commune reestablished, and mayors and municipal councils appointed—the problem of the rural communes demanded attention. Interior Minister Lucien Bonaparte quickly went on the offensive. Maintaining that a piecemeal, case-by-case approach "multiplies the work infinitely," he called for "a general measure . . . covering all the amalgamations that are recognized as indispensable." He told prefects to consult with their subprefects and draw up comprehensive lists of proposed amalgamations as soon as possible, noting the distances between the communes in question and the "reasons of necessity and convenience that should determine the *réunion.*" Few prefects had a chance to respond before Napoleon eased his brother out of the ministry in November 1800, but his successor Chaptal reiterated this directive.[55]

An apparent consensus on the need for mergers, however, did not include agreement on the criteria to be used. Some departmental councils and prefects wished simply to absorb the poorest and most minuscule villages by merger—hamlets with fewer than fifty households, for example, or one hundred taxpayers (Basses-Alpes, Jura, Haut-Rhin). The general council of Ariège proposed to *exclude* any commune of over 500 population from amalgamation, while the council of Haute-Garonne targeted communes of under 400 inhabitants for *réunion*. Others advocated minimum levels of population for all the nation's communes: the council of Loire-Inférieure proposed a threshold of 1,000, Ardèche 1,200, Calvados 1,500. The prefect of Vienne suggested that the standard criteria for communal autonomy should be "a radius of at least two *myriamètres,* a population of 2,000 or more, and a quota of at least 4,000F in taxes."[56]

Notwithstanding widespread support among local notables, the ministry soon backed off from its ambitious initiative. To begin with, a reorganization of communes had to be delayed until completion of a project to reduce the number and enlarge the size of the cantonal circumscriptions for the justices of the peace (see Chapter X). (It would hardly do to create an amalgamated commune in which one section lay within the jurisdiction of one justice of the peace and another within a different one.) More important, by early 1801 the Council of State had raised doubts about the propriety and even the legality of the proposed "general measures"—amalgamation by fiat from above.[57]

A prolonged and enervating period of official ambivalence ensued. Paris no longer issued calls for the amalgamation of rural communes, but individual prefects continued to fashion "general projects" for their departments in the hope that they would ultimately win approval in the capital. No prefect could be confident about the rules of the game. Paris usually responded by stalling and counseling caution; in November 1802, for example, the ministry told the prefect of Haute-Saône that he could indeed prepare a general project for *réunions* in his department but that he should not publicize it, since the proposal might not prove feasible yet would demoralize officials who presently administered the communes. On other occasions the ministry called prefects to task for exceeding their authority and simply quashed their laborious preparations for extensive *réunions.*[58]

The ultimate stumbling block proved to be the question of consent. Prefects, subprefects, and departmental advisory councils could marshall the will and gather the information for a "general project" of amalgamation as long as the *conseil municipal* of each commune did not have to approve. An embarrassing incident in the Haute-Garonne underscored the government's predicament. In April 1802 the prefect explained that a "lack of persons to fill municipal functions" compelled him to merge thirty-eight small communes into twenty-six larger ones in a "provisional arrangement," pending approval of a more comprehensive general project of *réunions*. The interior minister initially gave this *arrêté* his blessing, but he was chagrined when a petition from the village of Mirepoix protested its merger into the commune of Villemur. Twenty-nine inhabitants, including the former mayor, insisted that faulty information had led to this unjust directive. Their commune, with a population of 460 and 184F of annual revenue, they claimed, was over a mile and a half from Villemur, and there was absolutely no need to obliterate its autonomy. The minister ordered the prefect to remove Mirepoix from the list of mergers, and to proceed with the others only after double-checking all information and ascertaining the "absolute" need for any mergers. In his response, the prefect admitted that "a large number of other mayors have protested against this measure."[59]

Over the years prefects complained that such plans would stall if they depended on consent. "One will hope in vain for a mutual consent on the part of the small communes," warned a later prefect of Haute-Garonne in typically condescending rhetoric, "either because they will fear being dominated by the larger ones and administered by their principal inhabitants, or because they give in to the prompting of a few intriguers who know full well that their maneuvers would be futile under an enlightened municipality." His colleague in Indre-et-Loire, who prepared one of the most painstaking "general projects" of amalgamation, urged the ministry to resist the complaints of the communes who would lose their autonomy, in light of the "urgent necessity" for such mergers. The prefect of Seine-Inférieure likewise insisted that "it is necessary under the circumstances to act without recourse to the wishes of the municipal councils."[60]

Others, however, were more circumspect about the issue of consent, recognizing, as one official later put it, that "the magic word *commune* still retains its ancient and fatal acceptance." In the words of a provincial newspaper, "Every commune wishes to have its own mayor and magistrates, to have them in its midst. And it would regard with a jealous eye anything that carried off its municipal privileges. . . . One should bring the people as close as possible to its magistrates." Some prefects who favored the *réunion des communes* acknowledged in the same breath the legitimate misgivings and parish-pump pride of rural citizens. "Small communes attach the greatest value to their existence and do not wish to hear about their amalgamation," warned the prefect of the Yonne. Forced mergers were bound "to revive or even create [parochial] rivalries."[61] Villagers might also be dismayed to see the registers of the *état civil* transferred to a neighboring commune. While the state's highest priority was to ensure complete, accurate, and legible registration of all births, deaths, and marriages, citizens desired maximum convenience in fulfilling these tiresome obligations. Accuracy might dictate control by a more competent hand in a neighboring commune; convenience meant easy access in one's own village. One official in the ministry went so far as to claim that the *réunion des communes* will be "the indubitable cause of death for many infants," since newborns might be exposed during long treks to the new communal *chef-lieu;* at the least, lack of proximity to the mayors would promote indifference about declaring births or deaths at all. [62]

Concern over the dilution of communal property rights aroused even stronger popular opposition to mergers. The prefect of the Doubs had good reasons to push for *réunions* among the 586 rural communes, with an average population of 180, accounting for two thirds of his department's inhabitants. But he sympathized with their fear that amalgamated communes might encroach on the intricate pattern of common lands, pastures, and woods. "That uncertainty over the results of the mergers frightens even those whose interests seem least opposed to them." In the Moselle, the prefect had difficulty convincing villagers that mergers would not bring "confusion in communal allotments or wood rations *(affouages),* rights of pasturage and vacant pasture," though he assured them that such usages would not be affected. [63]

Even among the bland advocates of *réunions* in the *conseils généraux* of 1800 and 1801, a few dissenters intimated that problems could result. In the Deux-Sèvres, "the demand that has been made for the amalgamation of communes has provoked numerous objections . . . [it is] a seed of discord"; in the Somme, "several communes already merged are protesting." The prefect of the Côte d'Or observed that several communes which had already been amalgamated "are always involved in disputes; it is claimed that the magistrates are more favorably disposed toward the commune they inhabit, neglecting the interests of the other one. . . . I have on my desk requests from merged communes demanding their disunion." With unusual moderation the general council of the Gard urged that "no commune be merged with another unless it has asked to be." [64]

The Council of State's intervention in 1801, evidently responsive to such sentiments, derailed an administrative juggernaut from above. Thereafter the Interior Ministry required consultation with each commune and a case-by-case approach instead of "general projects": "In considering the territory of the communes and their political existence as a kind of sacred property," it vaguely directed, "innovations are to be permitted only after consent or formalities which will be very difficult to fulfill." When a prefect asked for permission to draft a general project, the ministry usually although not invariably advised him to defer it; projects executed without prior authorization the ministry rejected or annulled. Meanwhile, for individual *réunions,* every proposed decree had to include the views of each municipal council and the opinion of the subprefect before the minister would submit it "to the decision of his Majesty in his Council of State."[65]

Certain prefects—either unclear about this policy or hoping that it would change—continued nonetheless to draft "general projects" for amalgamation without winning approval from the communes or even consulting them at all. Their daily frustrations in dealing with the villages, and the centralizing ethos of the regime they served, seemed to sanction this course even if official policy for the moment did not. For never, it must be emphasized, did the ministry translate official unwillingness to approve "general projects" of amalgamation into an explicit, preemptive order that prefects refrain from preparing them. These abortive projects thus reflect a knowledge of local conditions and topography but not of the inhabitants' feelings. In chronological order Table IV.1 summarizes nine such elaborate projects—never, it must be repeated, actually implemented—with the total number of the department's communes from a listing of 1794 given in brackets as a reference point.[66]

As justifications for these *réunions,* prefects cited "feeble population," inadequate communal revenues ("the insufficiency of resources for even the most indispensable requirements"), lack of apt personnel ("there are scarcely three people who know how to write in those two communes"), and economies in expenditure. The meticulous list for the Indre-et-Loire emphasized the upkeep of roads and bridges. Though Veigné (population 947) objected to amalgamation, "its revenues cannot suffice to maintain its roads and a costly bridge over the Indre which is in very bad condition." The amalgamation of four communes (populations 378, 511, 912, and 802) was justified because "Poor and very close to each other, they can only meet their expenses by a merger which will eliminate the costs of three administrations. Their bridges and roads cannot be maintained without revenues. And if they are not maintained the area will be left without communications, without culture, without commerce." Prefects sometimes cited the proximity of neighboring communes as a justification for their merger, but substantial distance did not always deter them. Generally two kilometers was the maximum distance between amalgamated communes, or, in terms of time, an hour. But in the Drôme, fifty villages were one hour or more from the center of the project's amalgamated communes.[67]

Table IV-1
Prefectorial Proposals for the Merger of Rural Communes

Calvados [906] (March 1800):   880 communes reduced to 481 (suppressing 399).

Haute-Saône [642] (August 1801):   115 communes amalgamated into 55 (suppressing 60, almost all with less than 100 population).

Indre-et-Loire [315] (March 1802):   310 communes amalgamated into 128 (suppressing 182). All but 12 of the proposed new communes would have over 1,000 inhabitants.

Drôme [361] (March 1803):   300 communes amalgamated into 106 (suppressing 194; of these 27 had fewer than 100 inhabitants, but 20 had over 500).

Dordogne [634] (June 1803):   185 *réunions,* reducing 644 communes to 397 (suppressing 247).

Nièvre [351] (January 1804):   246 communes amalgamated into 102 (suppressing 144).

Pas-de-Calais [948] (March 1804):   929 communes reduced to 548 (suppressing 381, of which 161 had less than 200 population).

Mayenne [290] (May 1806):   285 communes reduced to 205 (suppressing 80).

Moselle [890] (November 1807):   523 amalgamated into 228 (suppressing 295).

Sources: See note 66.

OTHER DEPARTMENTAL INITIATIVES paled next to the willfulness of the Aveyron's prefect. One of the first to respond to ministerial prompting after Brumaire, François de Sainthorent effected a drastic "provisional" consolidation of the department's nearly 600 communes into 184 entities that he called *mairies.* In 1801, the prefect and his departmental advisory council reiterated this policy and considered reducing the number of *mairies* further, to 153. The prefect presumably submitted the project to Paris, but the ministry later claimed that it never received it and most certainly never approved it. When circumscriptions for the justices of the peace were revised the following year, for example, Paris assumed that the Aveyron had 571 communes; when it learned that the prefect had consolidated them into one third that number, it denounced his action as illegal.[68] But orders to rescind the changes were issued "in vain"; the prefecture either never received them or chose to ignore them. The amalgamations stood until 1808, when Paris again tried to bring the distant department into line. The ministry ordered a new prefect to submit a new project for communal organization in the Aveyron after consulting each amalgamated *conseil municipal.* This laborious inquest resulted in a compromise of sorts, a proposal to dissolve the extra-legal *mairies* and to regroup the department's 571 former communes into 346 new ones.[69]

The new prefect's inquest also produced a unique referendum on this question. Members of the almost two hundred *conseils municipaux* of Saintho-rent's *mairies* were polled, and the minutes of their deliberations have been preserved. They immediately belie any simple assumptions, such as the belief of one subprefect in the Aveyron that every small village wanted its own municipality, "a rank in society."[70] Some municipal councils were content to maintain their *réunion,* while others wished to break up the amalgamated commune into its former constituent parts; often the council was divided. In resolving this olio of conflicting views, the prefect followed no obvious rule of thumb. Consent was certainly not the crucial consideration, but neither was the advice of his subprefects, which he sometimes ignored.

Practical considerations rather than local vanity seemed uppermost as citizens gave their views at these unprecedented meetings. In the *mairie* of Villevayre, the council wanted its three former communes to regain their independence: "It has been most wearisome for the inhabitants of Maze-rolles and LeSalvetat to take themselves to the mayor's domicile in Villevayre in order to register the acts of birth, marriage, and death . . . usually having to bring the witnesses from their communes with them." In addition, they claimed, the mayor had trouble providing accurate information about the three communes; conversely citizens were available to serve as mayors in all three places. But the council in Rieupeyroux, which also consisted of three former communes, unanimously wished to maintain the *réunion* despite the subprefect's opinion that its two smaller villages could form a viable commune on their own.

Appointees to a council from constituent villages frequently disagreed. The *mairie* of Valhourlhes, for example, consisted of four communes with a total population of 1,700. Contrary to what one might suppose, the three members from the *chef-lieu* wished to break up the amalgamated *mairie* in favor of three separate communes: their own; Memer (a commercial kind of place located on the main road); and one uniting St. Grat and Calcomier. "Coupling other communes to Valhourlhes means an additional burden for its administrators." Its own population (760) and territory could easily sustain independent status. The central commune, in other words, was not always enthusiastic about an amalgamation even though its "rank" was enhanced. But several other counselors took a different view. The sole representative from St. Grat, the three members from Calcomier, and one member from

Memer preferred that all four communes remain united around the centrally located *chef-lieu,* while a second Memerian wished to regain communal independence.[71] The waters were muddied further when inhabitants of a commune bypassed the municipal council and petitioned the prefect directly in favor of autonomy. Citizens "fatigued by this merger" particularly resented trekking elsewhere for registering births, deaths, or marriages, and believed that "policing would be more active" in an independent commune.[72] Altogether the Aveyron inquest underscored how wise the government was to proceed cautiously case by case in this matter.

SELF-INTEREST, PERSUASION, or both did produce amalgamations of small villages in a number of departments during the Empire, but generally only when the villagers agreed. The individual acts of *réunion* effected during the Napoleonic years were the easy ones, so to speak, and did not resolve the underlying problem. A local historian has noted, for example, that departmental almanacs in the Eure recorded 884 communes in 1790, 842 in 1802, but only 806 by 1812. Had he carried his research further, he would have found the Restoration prefect still fulminating over the multiplicity of communes and the travails of local administration in that Normand department. This official believed that of his approximately 800 communes, 200 had either fewer than 150 inhabitants, 100F of communal revenues, or 150 hectares of territory—precisely the grounds for *réunions,* in his view. But, he complained, "the formalities required for obtaining *réunions* present such difficulties that despite all my zeal . . . I have been able to bring about the merger of only two communes in all of 1818." In the Hérault, the task was likewise "long and wearisome . . . and not a single commune is in accord."[73]

Some officials lost their will altogether. After his tour of the department in 1817, the prefect of the Moselle noted the disadvantages of the *réunions* effected by his predecessors, especially "the offending of diverse interests in the merged communes" over such issues as communal rights and the composition of the municipal council. In the Seine-Inférieure, the departmental advisory council acknowledged in 1820 that "the habitudes of a village, its rivalries, the differences in industry or other reasons render almost unworkable the amalgamation of communes which, at first glance, appeared the simplest to carry out. . . . But when two communes themselves ask for their merger, then there is no reason to hesitate."[74]

Restoration prefects who wished to press forward found the formalities as laborious and the advice from Paris as ambivalent as ever. True, the Bourbon regime seemed to give them more latitude than had the Empire. Still insisting on a case-by-case approach and on consultation with each *conseil municipal,* the government did not require the latter's actual consent. Thus the interior minister encouraged the prefect of Haute-Garonne to proceed with *réunions* in his department: "You fear that the opposition of certain municipal councils will be an obstacle to the execution of the measure. Those councils must be consulted," he agreed, "but their opinion need not be followed." The prefect must simply explain why their objections were unfounded, "vain pretensions." He gave similar instructions to the prefect of Calvados: while you cannot avoid the unpleasantness of "participation" by the municipal councils, you are not bound by their opinions and can ignore their opposition if you deem it unmerited. Yet the minister urged moderation. "A commune is not an arbitrary division established by the administration," he observed. "It has an existence in and of itself. And a merger that makes it disappear is an event of great enough importance that it should at least be consulted."[75]

Under such guidelines only a few prefects went full ahead. In the years 1821–25, for which the records are complete, ten departments had ten or more *réunions,* suggesting a serious effort by their prefects. The most dogged campaigns occurred in the Jura and the Gers, two departments brimming with over 700 communes each in 1794. In the Jura, the prefect consummated 95 *réunions* involving 222 communes, in which 127 were absorbed. In the Gers, 271 communes were amalgamated into 117, with 154 villages losing their autonomy.[76] One of the subprefects in that department explicitly stated that this feat had been accomplished despite the views of the villagers: "None [of these *réunions*] would have occurred if we had been required to halt before the futile considerations put forward by each of the municipal councils, since almost all voted against the mergers submitted for their deliberation."[77]

Mergers usually obliterated the civic identities of the smaller communes. Only occasionally did an amalgamated commune adopt a new hyphenated name, such as Boule d'Amont-Serrabonne (Pyrénées-Orientales), symbolically preserving the historic identity of the village that had been absorbed. In the Dordogne, it is true, most of the eighteen amalgamated communes emerged with such hyphenated names; one, Excideuil-St.Martin-Paroche, incorporated all three of its constituent villages. But these were the exceptions. Most commonly the largest commune emerged as the communal center and the new commune became known by the name of that village or bourg. In the Gers, only 24 of the 117 enlarged communes took on a new hyphenated name, and in the Jura not a single one.[78]

ALL TOLD, ADMINISTRATIVE penetration of the countryside took a giant leap forward with the Revolution and then stalled. Successive regimes advanced two solutions to neutralize the surfeit of communes inherited from the

National Assembly's policy of 1789, but neither succeeded. The cantonal municipalities of the Directory attempted to create a civic community parallel to the wider socioeconomic universe that most peasants already inhabited. But the men of Brumaire discarded the cantonal municipalities before the case for or against them had really been proven. True, the Directory itself had grown impatient with them already, considering the cantons too numerous and unresponsive, too dependent on local elections, and too costly in overhead, but it never repudiated the underlying concept. As the Napoleonic regime dropped the idea of cantonal administration, it intended to govern the countryside with a streamlined hierarchy of appointed officials whose tasks would be facilitated by the *réunion des communes.* That essential element of the plan, however, proved unachievable. Even if Napoleonic and Restoration prefects eventually managed to amalgamate 10 percent of the least viable communes, they did not carry the process far enough to make a significant difference. Laborious formalities, the need for consent or at least consultation, and insistence on a case-by-case approach blocked the "general projects" prepared after Brumaire. Official scruples and ambivalence, driven by local sensitivity and resistance, thwarted the drive for mergers in all but a handful of departments.

As official hopes for a massive *réunion des communes* faded during the Empire, the old cantonal municipalities predictably took on a more favorable allure. Numerous calls for the creation of *grandes mairies* and the like during the Empire and Restoration—cantons by any other name—suggest that the Brumairians may have thrown away a potentially useful approach.[79] In the event, the prefects of the nineteenth century had to deal with a plethora of rural communes. Over these villages prefects held great leverage, but their sheer number diluted that leverage substantially.

V

STATE
INTERVENTION IN
VILLAGE LIFE
BUDGETS, POLICING, AND ROADS

During a debate on local administration in 1829 the deputy A. Delaborde bitterly denounced the "spirit of centralization" that had robbed France's communes of all autonomy under the Empire and Restoration. Expressing a common sentiment among the liberal opposition, Delaborde attributed to the Napoleonic regime a perennial feature of French fiscality which the emperor had only exacerbated.

> Every year the communes were burdened with new charges that ate up in advance all the resources which they could have generated through the improvement of their activity. But that was not all. They were prevented from profiting from any of their particular resources on the pretext that such expenditures might be detrimental to the collection of the State's taxes. The central administration thus established itself as the unique possessor, the sole exploiter of all work. By means of the most complicated procedures and the most puerile obstacles, it deflected the requests [for local revenue] that it could not simply refuse or turn to the treasury's advantage. [1]

Delaborde unmasked the preeminent consideration in national policy on local administration since the seventeenth century. The state protected the flow of tax revenues into its own coffers by limiting the right of localities to tax themselves or to dispose of communal property and by controlling local expenditures, even while leaving as many expenses as possible to those same local budgets. By these tactics the old-regime monarchy insulated the pool of wealth from which it extracted its income. Holding down local taxation and expenditure helped to maintain the flow of tax revenues to Paris. Nor did the monarchy compensate for its monopolistic control of taxation by delivering services to provinces, towns, or villages. Except for the construction of national highways and the care of foundlings, public services accounted for a minuscule portion of royal expenditures in the old regime.[2] Schooling, poor relief, and most local improvements were left to find their own level, supported perhaps to some extent by the Church (which had its own sources of revenue), or by towns and villages themselves as best they could manage.

In one sense this situation changed significantly after 1789, as the revolutionary state took on new responsibilities and showered departments and communes across France with growing lists of mandated obligations. Yet the traditional priorities of national fiscality endured. The state retained its grip over local finances, while revenues allocated by the state to the localities rarely sufficed to fund the requisite services. In combination, the state's mandates and fiscal constraints placed villages and towns alike in a dubious position.

LOCAL FINANCES: THE TUTELAGE OF THE STATE

As the collection of ordinary tax revenues temporarily fell into disarray after 1792, the Convention sustained its revolutionary government by the sale of church and émigré property, by price controls and requisitions, and by an unrestrained output of paper money. After Thermidor—one of the bleakest economic periods within memory—the government financed itself for a while with forced loans of unparalleled contentiousness, and with new paper money of even less value than the retired *assignats*. Finally in 1797 the Directory administered the harsh medicine that seemed indicated: a socially wrenching return to hard currency and a conversion of the national debt which, in effect, wrote down its value by two thirds.

As monetary and fiscal normalcy returned, ordinary routines of tax assessment and collection resumed. The government assigned each department a lump-sum quota as its share of direct personal and property taxes. Departmental administrations in turn allocated quotas to each canton; scrutinized the assessment rolls produced by local people called *répartiteurs* in each commune (a laborious task and one susceptible to favoritism in the absence of a uniform land survey or *cadastre*); and ruled on petitions for a reduction in assessments. Departmental and cantonal commissioners were enlisted as "agents for direct taxation," responsible for collating the paperwork and certifying the official rolls. The money was collected in each department by private individuals called *percepteurs,* who won their franchise by submitting bids. The Consulate eventually replaced this makeshift arrangement with a professionalized agency of bonded collectors, but it sufficed for the moment. Delinquents were brought to heel by pressure from collectors and local officials, especially by the prospect of feeding and lodging *garnisaires* who could be ordered into their homes. But officials rarely had to invoke that sanction. [3]

The collection of direct taxes stood as the Directory's highest domestic priority, and its watchword seemed to be expediency or convenience rather than equity. Estimates of landed wealth remained notoriously imprecise and fixed to the detriment of certain regions. Some departments bore an unconscionably high quota of the land tax *(contribution foncière),* obliging their citizens to pay as much as double the assessment of someone in another department with the same kind of landholding. The modalities for assessing personal property taxes *(contribution mobilière, personnelle et somptuaire)* were even more questionable and provoked widespread discontent until 1799, when the government modified the components and sharply lowered the rates. [4]

For all the inequities and taxpayer resentment, however, the departmental administrations and the Directory's commissioners generally viewed the collection of direct taxes as a relatively bright spot in their stewardship. In the Haut-Rhin, for example, out of about 25 million livres in direct taxes due between 1791 and the Year V, all but 1 million had been recovered. Tax payment "goes just about as well as one can wish," the commissioner to the Orne reported; "the inflow of taxes has surpassed my hopes," echoed his colleague in the Corrèze. Although their tax quota severely overburdened the citizens of his department, wrote the commissioner to the Gers, "astonishingly enough they pay it to the letter." He shrewdly observed that Frenchmen had long since been inured to this under the monarchy, when citizens "were unsparingly coerced into paying their taxes with a punctuality in which the intendants took pride. They still retain that impulse . . . to pay their taxes with dispatch." [5]

With direct taxes flowing into the treasury, the directorial legislature revised the ground rules for local finance. It divided the expenses of local administration into three categories whose relative weight may be gauged from the example of the Mayenne department in the Year V: local expenses assumed by the national treasury, 240,000 francs; those charged to departmental funds, 173,000 francs; and those payable by the municipalities (cantons and towns), 116,000 francs. The national government paid directly for its commissioners, major public works, prisons, criminal justice, the gend-armerie, and hospices (whose endowments had been nationalized in the Year II but whose upkeep would soon revert to the localities). Departmental funds covered the costs of the departmental administration in the *chef-lieu,* civil courts, the justices of the peace, the departmental secondary school (*école centrale*), public buildings, and certain costs related to tax collection. Cantons (and after Brumaire, communes) were responsible for other expenses.[6]

Departmental revenue came almost exclusively from a surtax of 15 centimes per franc on the land tax payable by its citizens. To meet cantonal and communal expenses, municipalities drew upon a surtax of 25 centimes per franc on the personal property tax payable by their inhabitants. The *percepteurs* collected both surtaxes, and the treasury's departmental receivers disbursed the funds. Later, when the government more or less amalgamated these two kinds of direct taxes, it merged the surtaxes as well. Known as the *centimes additionels,* the surtax totaled an average of 20 centimes per franc of direct taxes paid during the Napoleonic era: 5 centimes for the commune, 10 centimes for the department, and 5 centimes to cover defaults (*non-valeurs*) and contingencies. The actual amounts coming to the localities, however, fell short of this ostensible 20 percent. Figures from the Isère for the Years VII through XIII indicate that the department's citizens paid an average of 2,701,000 francs annually in land and personal property taxes, but their surtaxes produced only 324,000 in *centimes additionels* for departmental and communal budgets.[7]

Most important, in a direct throwback to old-regime "tutelage" over local finances, a law of March 1797 prohibited communes from levying direct surtaxes on themselves beyond the nationally authorized *centimes additionels.*[8] This principle remained the law of the land, though one much disputed and qualified eventually in one or two respects. Towns, bourgs, or villages possessing communal property such as woodland, pasturage, or buildings that could be leased out for income (as opposed to land used by the inhabitants themselves for grazing or fuel) obviously had a second source of revenue for communal budgets. Beyond that there was little they could do, since they were barred from levying direct taxes on their inhabitants. Charges for market stalls and similar user fees in towns and market villages might bring in a bit of revenue, but police fines yielded only minuscule sums by the time they reached municipal coffers.

To help meet uniquely urban expenses, such as a town hall, paving, streetlights, and hospitals, towns had one source of revenue not available to the villages. Indeed, Napoleon virtually compelled the towns to reinstitute the hated municipal excise taxes (*octrois*) of the old regime on alcoholic beverages, livestock, and other consumption items entering their portals, in part to skim off some of their yield for the state. Cities raised the bulk of their revenue by this unpopular means.[9] But for those rural bourgs and villages without income from communal property or the possibility of establishing an *octroi,* the *centimes additionels* provided the only revenue. Napoleonic legislation permitted a commune to request a rate lower than the national maximum for the *centimes* surtax if revenues from its communal property sufficed, but the ordinary rate could not go higher regardless of the commune's needs.[10]

Prefects and departmental notables under the Consulate complained almost unanimously about inadequate local revenue. In their first annual meetings in 1800, at least seventy-eight departmental advisory councils protested over the insufficiency of the *centimes additionels* for their communes. When the minister of the interior canvassed prefects about local administration two years later, their complaints about deficient local finances matched their calls for the merger of communes. (Almost alone, the prefect of the Loire suggested that squandered money or corruption was the problem, as in communes "where they don't write two lines all year" yet spend 300 francs on pen and paper.) The prefect of Ardèche argued that the power of deciding for themselves on the amount of *centimes additionels* could safely be granted to the communes, since the principal taxpayers usually sat on the municipal council and were not likely to tax themselves for "useless expenses." The prefects of the Cantal, Eure, and Drôme likewise believed it a mistake "to refuse a commune the right to tax itself in order to meet its necessary expenses" below a sum like 500 francs. From the Gironde, Sarthe, Hautes-Alpes, and elsewhere, prefects urged that they, at least, should be empowered to authorize individual communal surtaxes when justified. But the government would not loosen the reins. As the minister replied to one prefect, the legislature was free to augment the national rate of *centimes additionels* if truly necessary.[11]

In 1811, the prefect of Hautes-Alpes summarized the effects of this impasse. "The revenues of the communes are nil in three fifths of the department, and they are not even permitted to create resources for themselves. That is the great plague of the administration. . . . The communes are deprived of even the most indispensable resources." This penury, he concluded, paralyzed efforts to deal with the most routine expenses, let alone do anything useful.[12]

TO DEVELOP HIS point, one must pass from the question of revenue to expenditure. No doubt the constraint on local taxation helped assure the flow of direct taxes into the national treasury. Nor did peasants have the slightest desire to see their local surtax rise. But this lid forced the communes into contortions to meet the very obligations that the new regime imposed in the name of national integration and progress. It precluded the communes from creating the infrastructure or social overhead capital that the French state itself now espoused.

Under the Empire and into the Restoration about half a dozen expenses were absolutely incumbent for every commune. We have already discussed the sine qua non of communal identity—the registers for the *état civil* and a subscription to the *Bulletin des Lois.* A lodging indemnity for parish priests who did not have a rectory; payment of a courier *(poste-piéton)* who fetched the commune's mail from the nearest post office; certain fees incidental to the tax collection process; payment of the property tax on communal property (if any); and purchase of paper, ink, and the like for the mayor—these expenses had to be met. The smallest or poorest communes could barely manage even these minimal outlays. The prefect of Haute-Garonne, for example, reckoned the cost of such mandated communal responsibilities to be around a minimum of 240 francs, but believed that "there are 86 communes whose revenues are below 50F, 123 below 100F, and 172 below 200F. . . . In several communes the paper for the *état civil,* the *Bulletin des Lois,* and the salary of the courier absorb the entire sum of their 5 *centimes additionels.* "[13]

Beyond the most basic outlays, however, we enter a gray area. In law, communes had to meet additional "fixed expenses," but in practice they could avoid them. (See Table V-1, Three Communal Budgets in the Calvados, 1810.) [14] The state, for example, insisted that every rural commune hire a constable or *garde champêtre* after 1795, and that each commune repair and maintain its local roads or *chemins vicinaux.* Yet, as we shall see, it had no way of assuring that communes complied. Likewise, successive regimes urged villages to hire a schoolmaster or to subsidize one in conjunction with neighboring communes, but did not compel them to do so. Policing, communications, and schooling, the core of the civic order in rural France, will be discussed individually in due course. But it is important to keep them in mind from the outset. When the prefect of Hautes-Alpes lamented that lack of revenue made it impossible "to do anything useful," he was doubtless referring to the provision of such services. Paradoxically, then, the heavy hand of the state not only stunted the growth of local civic responsibility, but made it difficult for many communes to meet the state's own standards for enhancing their material and social environments.

Limitations on the right of communes to set local surtaxes were matched by prefectorial control over their expenditures and disposition of their communal property. Prefects actively scrutinized communal budgets and had the

Table V-1

Three Communal Budgets in the Calvados, 1810

REVENUE	*St. Hippolite*	*St. Martin*	*St. Honorine*
Centimes additionels	101	125	177
Rental of cemetery	7	2	24
Levy for *garde champêtre*	40	96	136
Balance from 1808	106	104	143
Total	254	327	480

EXPENSES			
Land tax for communal property	—	—	6
Subscription to *Bulletin des Lois*	6	6	6
Registers for *état civil*	12	19	18
Mayor's administrative expenses	25	40	40
Rental of *maison commune*	—	—	—
Schoolmaster's lodging indemnity	—	25	25
Salary for clerk	—	—	—
Salary for *garde champêtre*	35	85	120
Lodging indemnity for priest without rectory	50	70	—
Postal courier	5	13	7
Reserve company	5	6	10
Commissions to collectors and miscellaneous	6	11	19
Expenses common to several communes	6	14	—
"Variable Expenses" *(Travaux)* requiring special authorization	109	97	—
Total	259	386	251

Source: A.N. F^3 II Calvados 1.

power "to modify, rectify, and annul the acts and deliberations of the mayors and municipal councils." [15] The French state maintained a Burkean rationalization for this tutelage, as it was called. "You must never forget that the communes are merely usufructuaries of the wealth and property in their possession," the Interior Ministry reminded its prefects in 1821. "The administrators charged with managing them owe an accounting to those who come after them. . . . Guardianship essentially belongs to the [national] government." By scrutinizing communal budgets, by flushing out hidden resources, corruption, or waste, Napoleonic and Restoration prefects would provide "a guarantee against local administrators who might abuse their influence." [16] Like the old-regime monarchy, the new regime would protect communes from their own mistaken notions. Prefects could especially prevent communes from heedlessly alienating their collective property to meet some emergency. [17] They could press communes to liquidate previous loans gradually and avoid new ones. They could insist that communes keep down expenditures and build up reserve funds.

To be sure, many communal initiatives won the necessary sequence of approvals by prefect, minister, Council of State, and legislature. Rural communes could still sell bits of communal land to individuals wishing to build houses. During the Consulate hundreds of communes were authorized to sell, exchange, or lease out communal property to raise funds for repairing their church or rectory, now that the Concordat had restored religious worship. Less frequently, communes won approval for such transactions to pay for public improvements: closing a cemetery, building drainage, repairing a bridge, wall, or fountain, or purchasing an appropriate building to house public authorities—like the town of Givors, which the legislature authorized "to sell a building belonging to that commune in order to employ the money to repair a road and construct a vault over a ditch." [18]

Yet a sad story related by Delaborde in his 1829 pamphlet suggests how heavy-handed the state's "tutelage" over communal property could be. As the mayor of Méréville, a bourg of 1,500 inhabitants in the Seine-et-Oise, Delaborde's top priority in 1801 was to rebuild the church, which had deteriorated to the point of collapse during the Revolution. As a first step he wished to sell off the residue of stone and timber. By the time he obtained the government's permission two years later, however, the wood had rotted. Next the mayor commissioned detailed plans and estimates for the reconstruction totaling 40,000 francs and submitted them for approval to the government along with a request to levy a special surtax over four years. Eventually the plans were approved, but the levy was vetoed as illegal and "a dangerous innovation that can harm the collection of state revenues." What resources did the commune possess, asked the government, which might be used to offset the costs? The answer at first glance was none, since communal income barely sufficed to maintain the market square and the bourg's paved road. Then someone made a proposal which the municipal council ultimately approved after much agonizing. "The bourg possessed a mall shaded by beautiful poplars; it was the sole promenade, the sole rendez-vous for the inhabitants on holidays or in the evening after work. What sadness to see them cut down. . . . But finally it was decided to offer them up." In the face of such sacrifice they trusted that the government would at last expedite its approval and agree to help them out.

For over a year the matter was shunted between the forestry bureau (whose agents inspected the trees), the Finance Ministry to whom the forest-ers reported, and the Interior Ministry. Finally the commune received per-mission to sell the trees. But since the sale produced only one quarter of the church's reconstruction cost, and since the government had yet to decide how the remainder should be funded, the proceeds had to be deposited in the state's *caisse d'amortissement* while everyone waited.

> What happened next? Something unbelievable, something which would be laughable were it not hateful. The money was dissipated in 1813 along with similar deposits in that *caisse*. And even today it is impossible to recover or even hope to recover a single sou. Thus, the only result obtained by one of the largest rural communes in France, after eighteen years of solicitations and *démarches* in behalf of this important object, has been to add the loss of its promenade—the ornament of its identity—to the loss of its religious edifice.[19]

The tutelage of Paris over communal property reached a brutal crescendo of arbitrary action toward the end of the Empire. Desperate to raise cash for his all-out mobilization, Napoleon in March 1813 ordered the communes to transfer to the state all "rural properties, buildings, and factories" that they owned and leased out for revenue. (*Biens communaux proprement dit*—property used collectively by the citizens themselves for pasturage and the like—was excluded from this seizure.) The government immediately began to sell off the property, and promised to indemnify the communes with annuities drawn on the *caisse d'amortissement*. From a short-term financial perspective it was a brilliant stroke. Covetous citizens with capital eagerly bid up some of this real estate to thirty or forty times the value of current leases. But this permanent alienation of communal property went against a century and a half of royal efforts to prevent communes themselves from taking just such action individually for their own benefit!

This coup, this "spoliation cloaked in legal forms," enraged French citizens. Rumors spread that "after selling the leased properties the government will help itself to those that are not being leased. The peasants threaten in advance, so to speak, not to let the purchasers enjoy any peace." In some departments, popular reactions troubled officials even more than difficulties with conscription.[20] Nonetheless the government sold off most of this property, even if buyers could not be found for every item, and reaped its bonanza. In the populous department of the Nord as many as 366 communes had properties confiscated, and even in departments with relatively negligible resources the sums involved were significant. To make matters worse, the government deducted substantial sums from the promised annuities for repairs, depreciation, taxes, and other charges (see Table V-2).[21]

Nor did the Restoration halt this operation. Although the returning Bourbons regarded the seizure of communal property as unjust and distasteful, they evidently found the flow of cash too tempting in view of the reparations that France owed the allies. The Bourbon regime did not revoke the law of March 1813 until April 1816, after which any property not yet sold reverted to the communes. In 1818 the prefect of the Eure closed the books on this affair by observing that "the results are too distressing to the communes for one to dwell on the details."[22]

AFTER LIQUIDATING THIS deplorable Napoleonic legacy, the Restoration's benchmark law of May 1818 inched away from the stranglehold over local finances of the 1797 law without, however, granting veritable autonomy to the communes. As mentioned earlier, after 1814 the commune's ten largest

Table V-2

Sales of Nationalized Biens Communaux, *1813–15*

	Nord	Nièvre	Eure
Value of sales consummated	5,362,000F	177,100F	373,900F
Value of unsold properties	(2,560,000F)	(27,600F)	(33,700F)
Annual lease values	460,000F	9,400F	17,100F
Deductions	−176,000F	−3,600F	−7,200F
Net annual income to communes	284,000F	5,800F	9,900F

Sources: See note 21.

taxpayers, often absentee landowners, had to be convened along with the regular members of the municipal council to approve the mayor's proposed annual budget. (If some non-residents did not turn up, it was necessary to go further down the list of taxpayers to fill a quorum of two thirds.) When a shortfall in revenue from communal property and *centimes additionels* made it impossible to meet necessary expenses, the municipal council could request an emergency or "extraordinary" tax surcharge to make up the difference. (Prefects evidently felt free to make such requests themselves if a penurious municipal council neglected to do so. When the largest taxpayers of Frohmuhl refused without explanation to vote for an extraordinary levy to fill the commune's deficit in 1821, the prefect of Bas-Rhin "did not hesitate to add that commune to the List on my own authority so that the tax can be established. . . . Otherwise that blind recalcitrance would compromise and paralyze the action of the administration.")[23]

Each prefect consolidated all the requests that won his approval and forwarded the list to Paris, where the Interior Ministry submitted it to the legislature's vote as part of the national budget. This was a monumental administrative labor. In the Yonne, for example, 332 out of 481 communes faced deficits in 1820; nationally an average of about 15,000 communes applied for extraordinary levies each year between 1818 and 1830. Prefects continued to urge that they should have the final word for any sum under some modest threshold in order to avoid this exhausting procedure. But Paris insisted that each communal levy must win legislative and royal sanction annually.[24]

In 1819, with the national rate of *centimes additionels* for the communes at its customary level of 5 centimes per franc of direct taxes, the minister reported that the addition of these "extraordinary impositions" brought the incidence of communal surtaxes to an average of 11 centimes per franc, and he instructed prefects never to allow a total of more than 20 centimes in any commune.[25] The annual budget report to the king on communal levies thus had two sections. "Ordinary services" (recurrent and routine expenses) typically showed an aggregate deficit of 600,000 to 700,000 francs, no doubt entirely of rural provenance, which had to be made up by "extraordinary levies." But the bulk of the "extraordinary levies" (whose total averaged around 4.5 million francs annually) covered "extraordinary services" such as repair of church buildings; "acquisitions, constructions and works of common utility" (primarily urban); debts and expenses of law suits; and local bridge and road repair. (Poor relief figured negligibly in these budgets, but during the subsistence crisis touched off by crop failures in 1817, 3 million francs were raised for "extraordinary" local relief and grain purchases.) Over the years the two components of local taxation—the standard return from the *centimes additionels* and the aggregate of "extraordinary levies"—remained more or less even. [26]

It was a charade of sorts, and an extremely laborious one, but these procedures effectively preserved the state's "tutelage" over the communes. The government religiously avoided the obvious expedient of raising the national rate of *centimes additionels.* It was established policy to keep this rate—the last straw of the direct tax burden—as low as possible, especially since self-sufficient communes did not need an increase. The simplest alternative of all, giving each commune the power to set its own local tax rate in order to pay for mandated expenses and local initiatives, remained a heresy in official circles. Apart from the traditional fiscal priority of insulating state revenues, successive regimes distrusted the capacity of the mayors and municipal councils to deal with such matters honestly or efficiently on their own. The appointment rather than election of these officials (much criticized by the liberals) was less crucial for the state's control than the veto that the prefects and interior minister held over the flow of local revenues and expenditures. [27] Thus was the old-regime legacy of governmental "tutelage" over the communes renewed by the Directory, carried to an extreme by Napoleon, and perpetuated under the Restoration.

What, then, of the local services and infrastructure that the revolutionaries hoped to develop for the well-being of French citizens? National policy objectives, fiscal imperatives, and local attitudes did not mesh smoothly. We must now see how they worked themselves out in several areas: rural policing, road maintenance, and (in subsequent chapters) primary schooling and poor relief.

POLICING THE VILLAGES

The clashing imperatives of private property rights and collective land usages in rural France posed a frustrating conundrum for the revolutionaries. Such traditional practices as communal gleaning, grazing on the harvested stubble (vacant pasture), and free access to common pasturage proved so tenacious that progressives who hoped to bar them altogether never carried the day. Drafting a "rural code" to settle such matters uniformly became, as one historian has put it, an impossible project. The preliminary rural code of 1791 left such issues hanging, and even at the zenith of imperial centralization, regional diversity and custom had the last word. An exhaustive project drafted between 1812 and 1814 condemned those collective usages as retrograde and slated them for oblivion, yet in the next breath set out procedures for local exemptions that undercut the major premise. Buried in the upheaval of 1814, the draft, in any case, was never enacted.[28]

Within the limits of such indecision or pragmatism, successive regimes after 1789 did what they could to bring order to the countryside. The National Assembly took a first step in 1791 with a code spelling out various rural misdemeanors. As their chief weapon against these *délits ruraux,* the deputies authorized rural communes to employ a constable or *garde champêtre* "to secure property and conserve the crops." Appointed by the municipal council, which also determined his salary, and supervised by the mayor, the guard was to deter violations and report perpetrators to the justice of the peace. The Assembly's approach was impeccably liberal and strictly voluntary. Communes could employ these guards but they were not required to; if it suited them, "several communes may choose and pay the same *garde champêtre.*"[29] In reality, the first law on rural police did little more than formalize the status of crop watchers in local communities that customarily employed them. It made their presence normative but not obligatory.

During the subsistence crisis of 1795 complaints about theft of crops and plundering of property in the countryside deluged the Convention's agriculture committee. *Police rurale* became an urgent concern and the *garde champêtre* appeared to be an answer. Until now, the committee observed, "this institution—neglected in most municipalities, poorly paid, often confided to corrupt hands and accomplices of brigandage—has not been an effective deterrent to theft and depredations. . . . It is necessary that an honest salary place them beyond the reach of temptation and that the responsibility for their conduct be better assured."[30] Stating the problem accurately enough, the committee's proposal (immediately enacted into law) presumed to solve it by *requiring* every rural commune to hire a *garde champêtre.* No longer to be a matter of local custom or discretion, the *garde champêtre* was incorporated into the drive for uniformity, for national standards of local government.

In the same spirit, the Convention involved the district administrations: while municipal councils still nominated the guards, the district directorates would formally install them and would also set their salaries "on the advice of the municipalities." Without any practical mechanisms of enforcement or financing, however, the new law expressed little more than wishful thinking, symbolized by its stipulation that an inscription be placed at the main gateway to every commune exhorting: "Citizens, respect the properties and output of others; they are the fruits of his labor and industry."[31] Moreover, having tied this newly mandated post to action and scrutiny by the districts, the Convention undermined its viability five months later when the Constitution of the Year III abolished the districts altogether. Jurisdiction over the *gardes champêtres* fell uncertainly to the new cantonal and departmental administrations.

By this time perplexing questions about the *gardes champêtres* that would persist for years had accumulated. What, in fact, could the guards accomplish? Watching over the crops would be challenge enough. Periods of scarcity always put the grain harvest at risk, while orchards were always vulnerable. (In the Aveyron, a prefect later warned, "Fruits especially are the object of so much pillage that a large number of proprietors have renounced the planting of fruit trees.")[32] Guards in well-policed communes were supposed to regulate the movement of animals as well, but was this a reasonable expectation? Inadequate pasturage and forage for livestock remained a great deficiency of French agriculture and one reason why peasants clung to timeworn practices. Newly harvested land, private meadows, even fields with growing crops might be invaded by hungry farm animals. To reach pasturage for their livestock, peasants might smash through hedges and trample over drainage ditches, especially under cover of darkness. "Livestock sent to graze on the stubble trample through enclosed properties or orchards," complained the prefect of Deux-Sèvres, "and the *gardes champêtres* do nothing about it." And could the guards protect water supplies against pollution or stop the dumping of waste and other encroachments on public thoroughfares?[33]

Finally, could they enforce the increasingly stringent laws on hunting? The abolition of "feudalism" in August 1789 gave all citizens the right to hunt, once an exclusive and destructive privilege of the seigneurial class. With pent-up zest peasants immediately set to slaughtering the game around their villages, enjoying the recreational and material rewards of hunting as well as their new status. The rural code of 1791 ostensibly limited hunting rights to one's own property, but "the passion of the hunt" respected no boundaries as hunters and their dogs chased game onto other people's land without scruple.[34] This apparent clash between liberty and license distressed local notables and officials. In law, at least, the Napoleonic regime resolved the dispute in favor of property. Local prefectorial decrees restricted hunting rights to property owners and taxpayers, and in 1810 the government established an annual fee of 30 francs for a firearms license *(port d'armes)*.[35] But even substantial property owners did not necessarily accept the legitimacy of such regulation. Sales of firearms licenses in most departments numbered only in the low to mid-hundreds, and infractions of the hunting laws continued unabated.[36] Could the *gardes champêtres* really be expected to uphold them?

These questions can be put in a different way: Were the *gardes champêtres* meant to protect rural property against vagrants and outsiders or also from the depredations of undisciplined villagers who did as they pleased? A local man nominated by the *agent municipal* (after 1795) or the Napoleonic mayor (after 1799), the *garde champêtre* might be a pawn of his patron, easily intimidated by the commune's wealthy inhabitants into ignoring their infractions. "They clamp down only on the unfortunate while the large cultivators can devastate the crops with impunity," claimed the prefect of Côte d'Or; "they are obliged to spare the rich who give them employment." [37]

To ask what kind of person the *garde champêtre* was likely to be is to address the question of his salary. Under the Directory and Consulate, funds for the guards could be drawn by the communes from ordinary revenues, fines (which rarely amounted to anything), or voluntary contributions. The numerous communes with insufficient *centimes additionels* had no way to fund the guards unless peasants were convinced of their utility and willing to subscribe voluntarily, as many villages had under the old regime. But in certain agrarian regions—notably some areas of small peasant holdings (*pays de petite culture*), the hedgerow or *bocage* country of the West, and areas of viticulture—no such tradition existed, and peasants generally did not feel the need to pay for this service at all. For lack of resources or will, the salaries offered by most communes to the guards were usually derisory and therefore attracted no takers at all or were taken and forgotten. [38]

Local discretion over salary effectively nullified the attempt in 1795 to strengthen the post by making it mandatory. The Indre department's seventy-six *gardes champêtres* in 1802, for example, earned annual salaries averaging only 81 francs. [39] Such low and often uncollectible pay would attract only part-timers who concentrated on their own affairs, or disreputable incompetents, constables who ignored infractions out of prudence or took bribes to forget them. In the eyes of many officials, a *garde champêtre* was as likely to be a poacher as to catch one. Indeed, with their reputation for illegal hunting, the guards were prohibited from carrying firearms! [40]

Despite continuing complaint from all corners of France that the *gardes champêtres* were underpaid, unreliable, and easily corrupted; and despite evidence that thousands of communes considered them unnecessary and did not employ one at all, no government revoked the law of 1795 making a guard mandatory in every rural commune. For all his equivocal and even pathetic characteristics, the *garde champêtre* became and remained a central figure in the official vision of the rural civic order.

Napoleon Bonaparte took a brief personal interest in this beleaguered institution. Less than a month after Brumaire, he urged that "the current *gardes champêtres* whose time is claimed by agriculture" be replaced by military veterans accustomed to discipline. Other officials frequently discussed this notion as an antidote to the deplorable quality of the incumbents. But a decree for the preferential hiring of veterans the following year could not be successfully implemented. For one thing, the War Ministry never managed to produce or disseminate the lists needed to identify and place qualified veterans. Still, the implication had been established that, unlike mayors, the *garde champêtre* need not be considered strictly as a local man.[41] Recruitment could operate from a larger and more promising pool of manpower. For that very reason, a few officials criticized the idea because they envisaged the *garde champêtre* precisely as a person with local roots. In a handful of prefectures an older voluntaristic notion lingered on, a preference that the function of guard be filled in rotation by "each inhabitant in his turn."[42] But that nostalgic approach found no favor in Paris. What seemed as a reasonable obligation to some might appear as an arbitrary *corvée* to others, and there would be no easy way to enforce it against unwilling peasants.

In 1805, the government attempted to place the payment of the *gardes champêtres* on a more solid footing by authorizing special communal levies to pay the guards' salaries. A feature of the original law of 1791, communal levies had been ruled out in 1797 under the Directory's law on local finance which, as we have seen, denied communes the power to tax their inhabitants beyond the rate of the national surtax. Now, if the guard's salary could not be covered by regular communal revenues or voluntary subscriptions, the municipal council could propose a local surtax, "an assessment on the proprietors or farmers of unenclosed properties proportionate to their land tax" (see Figure V-1).[43] Here was a unique exception to the iron constraints on local fiscal initiative. For this purpose alone—evidently a high priority in the regime's thinking—a municipal council (subject to prefectorial approval) could tax the village's landowners and cultivators beyond the ordinary *centimes additionels.* This decree liberated village councils that wished to hire a competent guard at an adequate salary but could not muster a voluntary contribution roll. It had scant impact, however, on recalcitrant communes. When the peasants of a municipal council did not care about a guard at all or wished to avoid any financial burden in employing one, they could comply with the law simply by continuing to offer their guards a derisory salary of 25 or 50 francs.

Sidestepping that problem for the moment, the regime revealed its ambitions for this humble post in another way. A decree of 1806 took up an idea touted, among others, by Gouvion Saint-Cyr during a fact-finding mission for Bonaparte to Normandy in 1803. Besides repeating that *gardes champêtres* should be recruited from military veterans, he proposed that they "be organized in a way that they can be under the surveillance of officers of the gendarmerie and can serve as auxiliaries to that armed force. . . . [Then the *garde champêtre* could become] a kind of police agent . . . who is concerned with public safety and serves everywhere as the Magistrate's eye."[44] The decree of 1806 directed all guards to register with the company of the

GARDES CHAMPÊTRES.

ARRONDISSEMENT
DE

CANTON
DE JUSTICE DE PAIX
de

ANNÉE

COMMUNE
DE

~~~~~~~~

*La Contribution que sup-
portent les terrains non clos,
s'élève à.........*

*La somme à répartir est
de.............*

*Le taux de la répartition
est de   pour franc.*

RÔLE de Répartition des Sommes qui doivent être payées en l'an   , par tous les Propriétaires, Possesseurs et Usufruitiers de *Terreins non clos* (Décret du 23 fructidor an 13), situés dans la Commune de   pour parvenir à l'acquit du traitement du Garde champêtre, et des autres Dépenses relatives à cet objet.

Ladite répartition, faite au marc le franc, de la Contribution foncière que paye chaque Propriétaire, Possesseur et Usufruitier, par nous Maire   et Membres du Conseil municipal de ladite Commune.

SOMMES à Répartir.

1.º Traitement du Garde champêtre.................

2.º Portion du traitement du Brigadier du Canton....

3.º Frais de confection de Rôle. ....

4.º Frais d'Impression et Papier...................

5.º Frais d'Habillement et d'Armement..............

6.º Réimposition pour couvrir les non-valeurs.......

TOTAL.. ....

7.º Frais de Perception , à raison de 5 cent. pour franc..

TOTAL GÉNÉRAL.. ....

FIGURE V-1: *Official Form for a Communal Surtax to pay a* Garde Champêtre *in the Seine-et-Oise, 1805*

gendarmerie (mounted state constabulary) stationed in their canton. The officers could then keep an eye on the guards and evaluate their performance from time to time for the subprefect. With authorization from the prefect the gendarmerie could also "requisition" the *gardes champêtres* for special campaigns against brigands, vagabonds, or *insoumis* (military deserters and draft evaders).

Under this policy, the guards were assigned "two distinct objectives," noted the prefect of Isère: "the preservation of crops and rural properties, and the maintenance of public order." But the prefect of the Nord shrewdly observed that the two roles could conflict: "The guards are subject to being taken away from their natural surveillance at the most crucial moments."[45] Originally responsible for purely agrarian policing duties, the *gardes champêtres* were being enlisted as instruments in the state's penetration of the countryside—no doubt a disconcerting prospect to villagers who did not relish auxiliaries of the gendarmerie poking into their affairs, especially if they had to pay for the privilege with special tax levies.

THE IMPERIAL REGIME, however, intended to establish *gardes champêtres* everywhere and take them in hand. In August 1812 the minister of the interior proposed a drastic innovation already hinted at in experiments by two or three prefects. The guards could be officially incorporated as a lower tier of the gendarmerie. The 1806 decree making them informal auxiliaries was merely a tentative and largely symbolic step compared to this proposal for the formal *embrigadement* of the guards. What did his prefects think of the idea, asked the minister. The prefects responded candidly and with real passion. A few objected strongly, seeing this scheme to nationalize a local institution as unnecessary, impractical, and even undesirable. Several praised the idea but pointed to potential financial hurdles or jurisdictional tangles that made them wary. The majority of prefects, however, cheered the proposal's modernizing vision, its promise of "a uniform and permanent organization." It is as if the imperial regime had suddenly unveiled its veritable centralizing ethos, its will to power.[46]

For a start, the prefects poured out their frustration with the current situation. Underpaid, barely supervised, and dependent on local patrons, most *gardes champêtres* were part-timers and incompetents more likely to countenance or consort with lawbreakers than to pursue them. Unreliable even as crop watchers, they were feeble reeds in the state's struggle against vagabonds, poachers, and deserters. "Their isolation renders their service absolutely nil in respect to policing," declared the prefect of the Somme. Most prefects jumped at the prospect of transforming these slackers into veritable *fonctionnaires.* They endorsed the idea of permanent tenure *(nomina-tion à vie)* to end the dependence of guards on the local notables; "uniform and ample salaries"; and even pension rights in retirement—all of which would promote "emulation" among the guards and render them more resist-ant to local pressures. As functionaries, the morale of the guards would improve. They would gain "moral force, confidence in themselves, and consideration in the eyes of others," all sorely lacking at present. [47]

With *embrigadement,* officers of the gendarmerie could actively scrutinize the guards and convene them periodically at the cantonal seat to report and take instruction. They might require the guards to keep a journal, which would help them learn how to fill out forms properly. Under authorization from the prefect, the gendarmerie could readily mobilize the *gardes champêtres* for special missions. Some prefects therefore felt that the guards should be permitted to carry firearms, and some even argued that they should wear uniforms, though others regarded this as a needless expense. As function-aries, the *gardes champêtres* had to be kept "above neediness" with reasonable pay. Vagaries in funding therefore had to be eliminated; in the past, local discretion in setting salaries rendered the entire institution "too precarious and excluded that uniformity." One possibility was to establish a common fund in each arrondissement to level out disparities between wealthy and poor communes. But the simplest way and the one endorsed by most prefects was to mandate a fixed annual salary such as 300 or 350F, leaving each commune to pay the bill as best it could. One prefect went so far as to argue that "the *gardes champêtres* should not be attached exclusively to the territory of one commune but to the entire circumscription assigned to the brigade of gendarmes." [48] But he had probably missed the point. In his own commune, with *embrigadement,* a standardized salary, and the accouterments of a *fonctionnaire,* the *garde champêtre* would bring the state to the very portals of every village in France.

The ministry eventually dropped its proposal for *embrigadement* and we do not know precisely why. In all probability it was simply a question of timing. Early 1813, when the Empire's military position began to unravel, was hardly the moment to implement an ambitious domestic plan floated in a more favorable environment months earlier. But even if the times had been tran-quil, disagreements and objections by prefects over specific details must have dampened the ministry's enthusiasm. The bland summary that sixty-two prefects favored the plan and eighteen opposed it was slightly misleading. Besides forming a catalogue of every shortcoming in the institution as it stood, their responses indicated that a minority of prefects still respected local sensibilities even while a majority would trample them in behalf of the centralizing vision. [49] In any case, the ministry quietly dropped the matter.

That left the situation in the early years of the Restoration more or less where it had been. After a brief hiatus during which communes could and did dispense with their guards, the Bourbon regime reinstated "the formal and imperative obligation" of 1795 that communes must hire a *garde champêtre;* if necessary, "the superior authorities should constrain the communes to provide themselves with *gardes champêtres.*"[50] The procedure for authorizing a local surtax to pay a guard's salary—which now required not only prefectorial and ministerial approval but legislative sanction as well—at first created a daunting morass of red tape, but was gradually simplified until it became routine.[51] Problems remained, however. Municipal councils still set the salaries, with all the equivocation that this permitted. And the law specifically exempted owners of enclosed properties from any surtax, but that term was imprecise. The Council of State ruled at one point that it meant only fields surrounded by walls rather than hedges, but that still left room for argument. In the Jura in 1819 the prefect faced "a multitude of claims from citizens who had not been left off the special rolls because the enclosure of their property was questioned." The need for the mayor, municipal council, and subprefect to agree on a nomination formed another obstacle. The municipal council in particular could use this prerogative to stall the appointment of a guard altogether. No manifest way existed to get around this, although prefects usually found the leverage to force the issue eventually.[52]

In this long saga, the law of 1795 requiring all rural communes to hire a *garde champêtre* formed a real turning point. Initially symbolic and unenforceable, the law availed little at first in the thousands of communes unwilling or unable to pay adequate salaries for competent men. Yet every regime embraced this policy, and slowly but relentlessly cajoled and pressured the communes into compliance. The Empire proposed to go further. After coopting the guards as informal auxiliaries of the gendarmerie in their struggle against *insoumission* and vagabonds, the regime proposed to convert these underpaid and disreputable figures into state functionaries "brigaded" under the gendarmerie. When the ministry shelved this extraordinary plan in 1813, however, the *garde champêtre* remained a simple employee of the commune who was not really at the disposition of the state or under its surveillance. In his more modest local roles, however, the *garde champêtre* became a fixture of the civic order in the countryside. Even if he cut a dubious figure, the government deemed his presence so important that it permitted communes to tax their landowners and cultivators to cover his salary. By the 1820s this salary figured as a routine element of communal budgets. Though still minimal and lax as often as not, rural policing was becoming a reality across France.

COMMUNICATIONS: MAINTAINING LOCAL ROADS

In the eighteenth century the Bureau of Roads and Bridges *(Ponts et Chaussées)*, that harbinger of technocratic administration, had charge of the royal high-ways—a network of national and preeminently military roads. These state engineers continued to maintain the main highways or *routes nationales,* as they were now called, under the new regime. Over the largest segments of the nation's communications, the secondary or departmental roads, however, the *Ponts et Chaussées* had only indirect responsibility, and over purely local roads scarcely any at all. Local roads were known as *chemins vicinaux,* something of a misnomer. True, they included all the paths that gave villagers access to their fields and to each other. But a large proportion of the *chemins vicinaux* could not be considered entirely or purely local, for they also linked rural communities to the outside world. These roads connected neighboring com-munes to each other and in the more fortunate villages joined up with secondary roads *(routes départementales).* The *chemins vicinaux* formed a finely meshed if utterly haphazard communications grid across the countryside.[53]

Under the old regime, maintenance of the *chemins vicinaux* depended on the uncertain structures of local authority. Seigneurs and the judges they employed usually had primary responsibility. They were supposed to inspect local roads in their bailiwick and order repairs, to be supervised by the seigneur's agent using peasant labor. The abolition of seigneurialism in 1789 left the new communes on their own for the upkeep of *chemins vicinaux.*[54] But the revolutionary stigma against forced labor or *corvées* as violations of liberty undermined their ability carry out such work. By all accounts, the ensuing decade brought complete neglect of these roads in the absence of traditional constraints. To those taking a broad view of France's future, this was cause for alarm. Seventy-three departmental advisory councils complained in 1801 that most *chemins vicinaux* became impassable in inclement weather as a result of neglect; several warned that "all communication is on the verge of being interrupted." Wagons could not traverse the deep holes and ruts; roads washed away altogether because the drainage ditches that ran parallel had filled with debris, weeds, or bushes. Meanwhile peasants usurped local paths for private purposes such as planting an additional row of crops or establish-ing compost piles. In the fertile plains of the Isère, proprietors of land abutting the *chemins vicinaux* "have filled up the drainage ditches and have compressed the roads in such a way that almost everywhere wagons are unable to pass each other when they meet up." Water left to accumulate "hollows out the roads and damages them beyond hope of repair." Such abuse degraded not only paths between fields but the roads between communes. [55]

Who was responsible for undoing these usurpations and repairing local roads? Prefects, backed by departmental *notables,* believed that they should have the authority to plan, authorize, coordinate, and if necessary impose sanctions to effect repairs. They did not consider the *chemins vicinaux* to be of purely local concern, although the earliest revolutionary legislation had so classified them, along with village fountains and the like. But these roads actually served anyone and everyone who might be passing from one point to another across a particular locality. "With each commune responsible for the roads that traverse it," observed the prefect of Calvados, "they are repaired without any coordination . . . with the result that after a length of well-maintained road a traveler comes to an absolutely impassable stretch." Moreover, as the prefect of the Moselle noted, if location alone determined responsibility, small or impoverished communes could be crushed by the burden. [56]

Road maintenance seemed too important to leave to the communes. "If to save on the costs one prefers to rely on the mayors, the objective will be lost," argued the prefect of the Doubs. "Those officials are capable of neither firmness nor oversight." The prefect of Ardennes held the same view: "We know that local considerations to which rural mayors and municipal councils easily succumb preclude us from charging them directly with the execution of any measure relating to the repair of chemins vicinaux." *Insouciance,* the endemic malady of rural mayors, seemed to be rampant in this matter. "Whether from indifference or from fear of affronting the interests of the inhabitants who have usurped part of those roadways, almost the totality of mayors have neglected to concern themselves," complained the prefects of Haute-Marne and Jura. Some officials and departmental councils called for a system of common treasuries for each subprefecture *(caisses d'arrondissement)* to level out disparities in local resources and obligations, and advocated the appointment of special inspectors or commissioners on the arrondissement level to supervise the repairs. [57]

This was a logical but largely futile wish. Departments did occasionally employ inspectors to check such work but had no resources for a permanent bureaucratic presence of this sort. When the prefect of the Nièvre hired a *commissaire-conducteur des chemins vicinaux* at a salary of 1,000 francs, and assessed the larger communes for the costs, the minister of the interior rebuked him and other prefects who had done the same: "I cannot approve this measure and I invite you to revoke the decrees by which you have made appointments of this kind." [58]

In the final analysis, the actual work depended on local labor and equipment and thus on local cooperation. If modernizers dreamed of removing road repair from the vagaries of communal penuriousness and self-absorption, common sense suggested that the burden still had to fall on local shoulders. The rural legislation of 1791 had indeed placed it squarely there, and even in the Year II, when the Convention extended the reach of the state in unprecedented fashion—declaring that "all public works will be carried out at the Republic's expense by the Treasury"—it excepted the *chemins vicinaux,* which were still to be maintained "at the expense of the inhabitants *(administrés)."*[59] Despite repeated calls to preempt responsibility at a higher level, this remained the most obvious way to maintain local roads.

Higher authorities did of course have a role to play under any system. Departmental administrators and their Napoleonic successors were supposed to investigate the state of the *chemins vicinaux* and establish the equivalent of a census or *cadastre* (decree of 23 messidor V). They were expected to remind mayors and municipal councils of their obligations, to exhort and badger them into doing what necessity required. But if they exceeded this authority and tried to take direct command of local road repair, the ministry challenged them. In its annual report in 1801, for example, the general council of the Aube complained of their prefect's frustration. His master plan for the *chemins vicinaux,* "a decree full of wisdom," had allocated tasks to various communes. But "an order from the Minister suddenly descended, without explanation, prohibiting this action."[60]

How, then, were villagers to proceed? The preliminary rural code of 1791 had authorized municipal councils short of funds to levy a surtax for the purpose just as they could to hire a garde champêtre. But for more basic reasons, as we have seen, the law of 1797 on local finances revoked those options. For more than two years after Brumaire, uncertainty prevailed. The departmental advisory councils divided almost evenly over how local road repair should actually be organized. Twenty-one advocated authorizing a special local tax, "the right of the communes to tax themselves [for this] in proportion to their needs"—an approach likely to place a good part of the burden on absentee landowners, and also to create employment for indigent laborers in the vicinity. But twenty other councils endorsed the use of local *corvées.*[61]

The Consulate ostensibly settled the matter in a decree on local finance of 4 thermidor X (23 July 1802). One article restated the principle of 1797 that "the municipal councils may not request or obtain any extraordinary levy for the communes," ruling out special surtaxes for financing the upkeep of *chemins vicinaux.* The next article's rather fuzzy language authorized the alternative: "The *chemins vicinaux* will be the responsibility of the communes. The municipal councils will express their views on the method they judge most appropriate to provide for the repairs. To that end they will propose their preferred way for arranging a *prestation en nature.*" Upon the vote of a municipal council, local roads would be repaired by the labor of the villagers, organized by their mayor. The *prestation en nature,* as the prefect of the Yonne put it, "means reestablishing the *corvée* . . . considering that all citizens without exception will be called to work . . . and will be free to discharge their task either in person or in cash according to the local price of labor." The decree of July 1802, he believed, at last permitted "those coercive means which are indispensable . . . [since] the inhabitants can now be constrained to contribute to the work."[62]

Yet it was not at all clear how the communes would frame and enforce their demands. The prefect in Charente-Inférieure called for a uniform standard: "a general administrative regulation *(règlement)* that obliges the inhabitants of each commune to contribute two days a year," with sanctions to be enforced on delinquents by means of requisition. "No one should be permitted to meet their obligation with money," argued the prefect of the Indre; "someone who can't work should have himself represented by a laborer." All well and good, but what if he did not! His colleague in Ariège was more thorough. "Each individual should be constrained to work or to send a worker in his place. The mayor should be authorized to replace anyone who refuses, at the latter's expense." Few officials shared the prefect of the Haute-Marne's concern that a *prestation en nature* might not allocate the burden fairly: "One should not require free labor from someone who is obliged to work every day for his family's subsistence," he objected. Such nuances were left to the discretion of the municipal councils. The *prestation en nature* generally offered a choice between performing the labor personally or paying the equivalent value in cash.[63]

The decree of 1802 directed communes to assume this responsibility, but what if they did not? How could a prefect compel a municipal council to act if it regarded the government's demand as illegitimate, "a trace of the old *corvée,*" and refused to accept it? What could a prefect do when the municipal councils, "those stumbling blocks on which the most sage and useful projects break apart, almost always refuse their consent out of secret motives of hatred or jealousy"? And how could recalcitrant individuals be brought to heel when their municipal council did authorize a *prestation?* Resentment against *corvées* that violated individual liberty; unwillingness to spend one's time and energy on work without any immediate return; the temptation to usurp public space for private gain—these factors remained the underlying obstacles to local road maintenance. In the most inward-looking or penurious places the situation no doubt approximated missionary Arthur Smith's view of rural China a century later, where a raised local road seemed to him "a triple impossibility. The person whose land must be disturbed would not suffer it; no one would lift a finger to do the work . . . and no one would furnish any of the materials which would be necessary to render the road permanent." [64]

But this was not an appropriate description for all of France. French peasants could be prodded into accepting work on the *chemins vicinaux* as a civic obligation. Without communal revenues or bureaucratic control, everything depended on local initiative and goodwill. Forceful mayors did lead their communities into action, organizing work parties, securing the necessary draft animals and carts, gathering wagonloads of gravel, perhaps even raising subsidies for the village's poorest laborers. "Good examples are spreading," wrote the prefect of the Indre. "At Auteuil, Rigaut, the mayor and a cultivator, has set the example," reported the local gazette in the Oise. "All his horses and all his workers *(son monde)* toiled without let-up; he directed the work himself, and his activity produced the best effect." Citizens of Buicourt in the same department collected and spread 220 wagonloads of gravel in the most defective places under the mayor's supervision. "Only citizen Adrien Eve did not respond to the general appeal." [65]

If a lone holdout could be scorned, however, several uncooperative villagers might well undermine a community's will to do the job. In parts of the Côte d'Or, reported the prefect, "some recalcitrants have impeded the goodwill of those who responded to the mayors' invitations." Similarly the prefect of the Sarthe complained that "since there exist no legal means of constraint . . . I have seen my authority fail in several communes against the opposition of private interests." [66] But the interior minister would not permit serious sanctions against the Adrien Eves of France. Judicial enforcement was ruled out entirely. "The tribunals cannot be invoked against the recalcitrants because they can order only what the laws have commanded"; these *prestations* were purely local ordinances that did not have such writ. Nor did the minister sustain prefects who threatened shirkers with administrative fines. In Calvados, for example, the prefect decreed that "inhabitants who refuse to turn out for the work without a legitimate excuse will be required to pay into the hands of the collector twice the value of the labor or the animals that they were supposed to furnish." The minister vetoed this decree and told the prefect "that he did not have the right to establish this kind of fine." Nor did Paris permit municipal councils to withhold communal fuel allotments *(affouages)* from citizens who balked at the *corvée. Affouages* constituted a distinct entitlement that could not be used as a sanction in an extraneous matter. [67]

Still, progress occurred, and not only in departments like Indre-et-Loire, where adequate revenue from *centimes additionels* or *biens communaux* could subsidize road repair without resort to *corvées*. The inhabitants of Bas-Rhin, for example, showed "zeal and devotion" in repairing their local roads. Prodded by an aggressive prefect, two thirds of the communes in the Hautes-Pyrénées were said to have gotten their *chemins vicinaux* into good shape by 1805. Communes using the *prestation en nature* in the Château-Chinon arrondissement of the Nièvre reportedly inspired each other with zeal after 1804: "With that spirit of an enlightened devotion, communications which were almost entirely severed all over have been reopened and reestablished." In the Gard during 1812, 153 communes without sufficient communal revenues organized and executed a *prestation en nature*. [68]

THE RESTORATION'S STRINGENT approach to local taxation, however, made it more difficult than ever to sustain such momentum. The interior minister acknowledged in 1817 that "in effect the recovery of the *prestation en nature* is not authorized by any of the recent laws on finances." [69] The Chamber of Deputies took up the subject in 1818 but could not agree on a new policy. As the prefect of the Eure observed, "nothing seems more difficult than drafting sound legislation on the *chemins vicinaux*." Before 1824 any initiative by a commune to organize road repair work, for which ordinary revenue did not suffice, had to be treated as a voluntary subscription or as a transaction funded by an "extraordinary levy" that had to clear all the procedural obstacles discussed earlier.

The state left itself with little recourse against inertia or local evasion of responsibility. Restoration prefects complained that municipal councils showed little readiness to solicit authorization from the crown to levy a surtax. The addition of the ten largest taxpayers to each council exacerbated the problem, added the prefect of Vienne, "since they almost always block the impulsion to request a special levy." At the same time these officials condemned "the insufficiency of the *prestation volontaire* which is susceptible to all the effects of caprice," and their lack of "coercive means to overcome resistance." The *prestation en nature,* declared the general council of Ille-et-Vilaine, "becomes illusory if, as your excellency states in his circular, there exists no legal means of compelling the citizen who refuses to acquit himself in person or with a cash payment." Local road repair ground to a halt as only five communes in the department executed a *prestation en nature* in 1819. [70]

Meanwhile criticism of the *prestation en nature* abounded in public statements by proponents of the centralizing vision. Baron Ramond told the Council of Agriculture in Paris that the *corvée* was "the way to accomplish the least amount of work and the worst kind of work," unless it was merely "a pretext for the establishment—legal or not—of a veritable cash assessment."

Whatever success occurred in maintaining local roads, he added, came from the personal influence of the prefects "and the opportune use of arbitrary methods." Ramond's essay encapsulated the stance of the modernizers in each successive regime. He deplored "the bizarre idea of carving up our internal communications into as many strips as there are communes. . . . It entirely subordinates the public interest to private interest. Wherever there is a public interest there ought to be a public authority to protect it, and that authority should be superior to the interests which resist it."[71]

This coherent but extreme view was echoed by Monsieur Levavasseur in the Agricultural Council of the Oise, a department with over seven hundred communes. "The chief vice is the initiative left to the communes for all the measures that are to be taken," he declared. Such fragmentation was bound to produce inertia. "It is necessary to invest the superior administrative authority with a force of action . . . and to rely on a means of subvention at once less onerous and more effective." Yet Levavasseur was forced to concede that at present the *prestation en nature* remained the most practical method for getting the job done, given the absolute undesirability of raising local property taxes, and the impossibility of establishing tolls on back-roads.[72]

After six years of indecision the Chamber of Deputies finally passed a law settling matters for the next decade but falling short of the modernizers' hopes. The law of 28 July 1824 empowered communes with insufficient ordinary revenues to tap each head of household on the tax rolls (proprietor and farmer alike) for "a *prestation* not to exceed two days of labor or the equivalent value in cash" for each adult male in his household (including children and domestics), and for the use of his carts and draft animals. The legislature evidently respected the feeling, as a prefect in the Puy-de-Dôme had put it, that "peasant proprietors are more disposed to cooperate with their arms than their purses for the execution of the work."[73] If the *prestation* did not suffice to get the job done, the municipal council could request a tax surcharge in its budget, to be collected from every taxpayer for up to 5 additional centimes per franc on the principal of his direct taxes. Collection procedures for both the *prestation* and the tax surcharge "will follow those for recovering direct taxes." Thus this law finally established routine sanctions for enforcing a commune's demands. Responsibility, however, remained in local hands; there would be no *caisse d'arrondissement.* Prefects of course had to countersign the local ordinances but the municipal councils made the actual decisions and the mayors supervised the work. Prefects still had no easy way to force mayors and councils to act with the dispatch or on the scale they deemed necessary.[74]

The traditional, uncoordinated *corvée* remained the prevailing method by which less prosperous communes maintained their local roads. It had proved impossible to bureaucratize the upkeep of the *chemins vicinaux*. Financially and administratively the state had yet to find a practical way to preempt local responsibility. Communications in the interior of the country, like rural policing, still depended on the individual wills of forty thousand communities. Yet the new regime had made an impact. Communities could stall and resist, but prefects (under the decree of 1802 and the law of 1824) kept up the pressure until they acted in at least some fashion. Usurpation of local paths for private gain and the degradation of *chemins vicinaux* undoubtedly diminished. The gains, however, remained uneven and fragile. Any relaxation of prefectorial pressure might result in communal neglect and thus in impassable roads and a rupture of communications. At best, moreover, communal *prestations* refurbished primitive roads created haphazardly in the past. They offered no possibility of transforming these rudimentary arteries into a rationalized, permanent network—a goal much discussed after 1800 but destined to be realized only under the Third Republic.[75]

THE FRENCH REVOLUTION of 1789 brought a sense of liberation to the countryside above all because it pledged to abolish feudalism and privilege. Peasants immediately grasped and celebrated this promise by exercising their new right to hunt with abandon. Later that year the National Assembly's plan to confer powers of self-government on every *commune* must have reinforced this sense of liberation with its prospect of local autonomy. Unfortunately, many disappointments were to come. The Assembly, as we have seen, did not in fact abolish "feudalism," since it later legitimized many seigneurial dues as property rights, subject to a redemption whose burdensome terms made that option unlikely. Even more dramatically, the Assembly's religious policy soon produced a catastrophic confrontation between religious traditionalists and ardent supporters of the regime. Issues of governance lacked the explosiveness of those agrarian and religious conflicts. But in the long term they helped define the evolving relationship of the French state to the provinces, in particular the possibility of national integration, of establishing a uniform civic order in the countryside.

The control of the state over villages finances is one of the great lines of continuity from the old regime to new, although the original formulations of 1790–91 initially loosened the state's grip. With the Directory's law on finances of 1797, the new regime reasserted that tutelage as explicitly and systematically as ever, even while maintaining a framework of local self-government. The Empire, however, reduced local autonomy to a bare minimum, while pushing government tutelage to new and even frenzied extremes. Napoleon's seizure of the *biens communaux* in 1813 constituted an utterly unrestrained use of state power, undoubtedly one of the most blatant instances of fiscal tyranny in the history of the French state.

State control over local revenue and expenditure did not inherently conflict with the revolutionary program of national integration and uniformity, but in practice the two imperatives coexisted uneasily. By focusing on the prosaic issues of rural policing and road maintenance, we can see the thrust and the limitations of the Revolution's integrating vision as it reached into the countryside, into *la France profonde.* It is instructive to observe that no regime backed away from the largely symbolic law of 1795 requiring every rural commune to hire a *garde champêtre,* despite the evidence that thousands of communes were unwilling or unable to do so. More revealing still is the ministerial proposal of 1812 to "brigade" the *gardes champêtres* under the surveillance of the gendarmerie, to make these part-time, underpaid slackers into low-level state functionaries. Similarly voices in the new regimes kept hoping somehow to preempt the maintenance of local roads from communal initiative or inertia, since *chemins vicinaux* were more than purely local means of communication. In neither case did the most ambitious plans take hold. The guards were not brigaded and the prefectures did not take charge of road maintenance; the state continued to rely on the uncertain will and cooperation of forty thousand communes. But within those traditional and not implausible limits, the state pushed as hard as it could for incremental advances, which by the 1820s amounted to a modest but visible transformation.

For most prefects, the *garde champêtre* and the repair of *chemins vicinaux* constituted recurrent frustrations in their dealings with the communes, an endless struggle for results in a gray area where constraint and coercion did not avail. It was here above all that the state eased its resistance to increased local taxation, and in the end encouraged communes to tax themselves if necessary (under the watchful eye, to be sure, of prefect, minister, and legislature) in order to carry out these two civic obligations. By the 1820s the salary for the *garde champêtre* and the *prestation en nature* (or, if necessary, the special surtax) for road maintenance figured as routine elements of communal budgets. Even if minimal and makeshift for the most part, rural policing and local road maintenance became increasingly common in rural France. Periodic repair of *chemins vicinaux*—like patrols by the *gardes champêtres*—entered the normative fabric of rural civic life. But could the same be said for primary schooling or poor relief?

VI

PRIMARY
EDUCATION
CREATING PUBLIC SCHOOLS

Schooling in the Old Regime

Without any impetus from the absolutist state, whose educational concerns centered on the *collèges* or secondary schools, primary education had become an established tradition in many regions of France well before the Revolution. While Protestantism made more explicit demands for literacy among its adherents, the French Catholic Church also believed that the spread of literacy would serve its cause in the battle against heresy. As schoolmasters provided religious instruction and practice in catechism, they also socialized children into the moral precepts and decorum that went with a Catholic way of life. Elementary schooling was certainly not intended to transform society or lift the mass of people out of the situations into which they were born. On the contrary it was supposed to reproduce the local social order, while seconding the family in promoting piety and decent behavior among the young. If elementary education also allowed unusually talented children from modest circumstances to move ahead in the world, so much the better. The fundamentally conservative religious, moral, and social aims of primary schooling did not rule out the occasional instance of social promotion. [1]

The elementary schools *(petites écoles)* of the old regime taught reading first, and writing separately and later. Writing involved distinctive kinds of discipline and classroom materials that parents did not always desire, besides which teachers charged higher tuition for writing and arithmetic than for reading. Many children, especially girls, therefore left school without the ability to write. In almost all schools save those run by the Christian Brothers order, teachers used the "individual method." Children of all ages and varying levels of skill sat together in one classroom, bringing whatever books they happened to own. Teachers worked individually with each child; children recited for the teacher rather than the rest of the class. In a class of average size, say thirty students, each child could scarcely receive more than ten minutes of attention during the school day. Once they had finished their own assignments, children were usually left at loose ends, and progress for everyone was painfully slow.

Though widespread in many provinces, schooling and literacy were far from commonplace in old-regime France. Nationally, on the eve of the Revolution, only 27 percent of the brides and about 47 percent of the grooms could sign their names in the parish registers on the occasion of their marriage, reflecting (by consensus among historians who have studied this question) an ability to read though not necessarily to write—a total literacy rate in the 1780s of 37 percent. These averages subsume a stark division between an advanced North-Northeast of the country and a relatively backward South. Astride that pattern lay a triangular zone, with its base along the Atlantic and its point in the Massif Central (including much of Brittany and the Southwest), which showed the most abysmal literacy rates and the least propensity to progress in the eighteenth century (See Figure VI-1). Rural literacy rates, meanwhile, generally lagged significantly behind those of the towns with their large contingents of artisans for whom literacy was either materially necessary or culturally desirable. And in the more backward rural areas a chasm separated literate peasant proprietors or farmers from illiterate day laborers, though the wives of the former might still be illiterate—the male/female gap being the most striking of all.[2]

What influenced a community's propensity to provide schooling to its young? More prosperous agrarian economies actively integrated into markets were likely to be favorable. Larger rural communities, especially those with agglomerated settlement patterns, were usually more hospitable to schooling than thinly settled and widely dispersed hamlets. Perhaps the most fundamental variable, however, was the collective wealth of the community itself. Villages that owned and leased out significant communal property *(biens communaux)*, such as grazing land or forests, could more readily underwrite the costs of schooling. The prevalence of schooling also reflected the degree of the Church's interest as well as the availability of schoolmasters. Where the Protestant Reformation had made no impact at all, or where local bishops displayed no interest in the issue over long periods of time, schooling was more likely to be deficient.

A village usually hired a schoolmaster in conjunction with the parish priest. The teacher might be engaged by the curé himself, by the parents, or

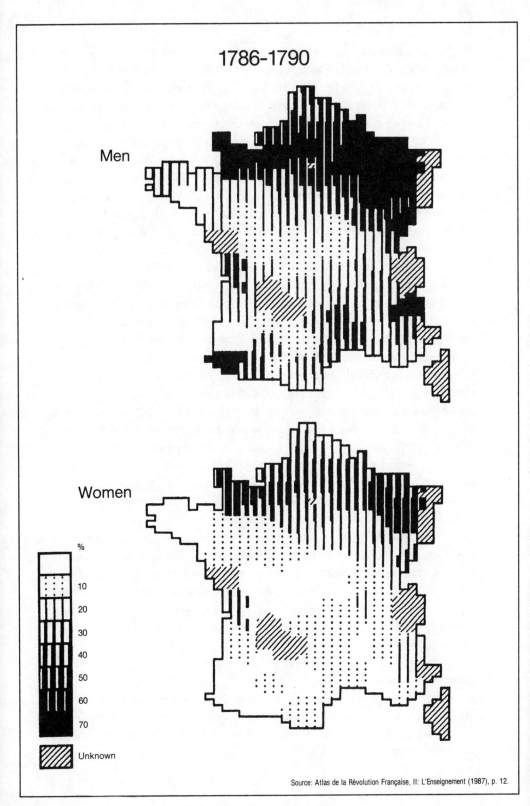

1786-1790

Men

Women

%
10
20
30
40
50
60
70

Unknown

Source: Atlas de la Révolution Française, II: L'Enseignement (1987), p. 12.

FIGURE VI-1: *Male and Female Literacy Rates, c. 1786*

by the village leaders. In any case the *petites écoles* straddled community and church, since the schoolmaster often served as the priest's auxiliary—his sacristan, chorister, and possibly his factotum. Bishops had the authority to scrutinize the schools in their diocese, but as a rule were not directly involved in recruitment or supervision. Towns with charitable foundations for elementary education naturally had the advantage in attracting the few trained teachers available, such as the members of the Christian Brothers teaching order or comparable female orders.[3] In the countryside, where such foundations were extremely rare, the individual parents, the village, or some combination of the two paid the schoolmaster, while the curé usually took responsibility for day-to-day supervision of the school. At bottom, then, the community remained the ultimate authority in this matter, as evidenced by the numerous villages without any school at all.

Villages were generally parsimonious in using their resources. If they did not possess substantial *biens communaux* generating income, they were unlikely to tax themselves to pay for a schoolmaster but instead placed the burden entirely on the families using the school. Parents usually paid the tuition or *rétribution scolaire* by monthly installments in cash or in kind. But even a modest tuition might deter impoverished parents from combining to hire a master or enrolling their children, apart from any feeling they might have about the value of schooling to begin with. If enough parents in the village were unwilling or unable to pay, there would be no school. And even if one existed, parents might pull their children out during any period of family adversity. On the other hand if parents were paying tuition, they were likely to ensure that their children actually attended and applied themselves to their work. Schooling, in other words, seems to have been demand-driven, the product of a community's character and consensus.

Intimately connected to the fabric of family, church, and village life, schooling was not considered an absolute or intrinsic good, but simply reinforced prevailing religious and community values. When a region or *pays* achieved a critical mass of literacy, interest in schooling generally became more widespread and gradually reached lower down the social scale. But whether stable or spreading, elementary education was valued in its familiar forms. Though some urban parents were demanding consumers of education, most rural parents apparently did not expect much from their schoolmasters and mistresses. On the eve of the Revolution, in any case, no groundswell of popular discontent arose on the question of primary schooling, and only 1 to 3 percent of parish *cahiers* spoke of it at all. In elite circles most discussion of education concerned its higher levels, and the general *cahiers* had relatively little to say about primary education either. There was every reason in 1789 to suppose that clerical supervision would continue while elementary schooling remained a purely local matter.[4]

THE IDEA OF UNIVERSAL PUBLIC EDUCATION

The Revolution quickly overturned such assumptions. By 1791 influential deputies inscribed primary education on the Revolution's long-term agenda, and by 1793 others catapulted it to a central position in republican ideology. The destruction of the Church's corporate autonomy and traditional roles created something of a vacuum. As the parish clergy became employees of the state under the Civil Constitution of the Clergy of 1790 and the refractory or non-juring clergy its enemies, responsibility for education at all levels came into question. This was not to say that primary schooling would necessarily become secularized, or that Catholicism would be driven from the classroom. It meant that in this domain, as in the matter of poor relief, the state might readily become the arbiter of policy as against the Church or local society.

But more was involved than filling a vacuum. Education quickly assumed an unparalleled ideological and instrumental importance. The revolutionaries came to regard universal primary schooling as the hallmark of a progressive nation and as a key to the future prospects of the French people. And how could it be otherwise if, as they believed, 1789 had produced a sharp break in the continuity of French history—a rupture in beliefs and institutions superimposed for the time being on a hesitant, traditional society that had to be led forward into a new era?[5] Revolutionaries of course expected primary schools to impart skills such as literacy and numeracy *(instruction),* but also to inculcate morality and citizenship *(éducation).* Primary schools for the young, in tandem with new symbols, images, and public festivals for all citizens, constituted a revolutionary "pedagogy" that would gradually wean the French people from its ignorance and prejudices, and inculcate new civic values. The revolutionary passion for national integration, for spreading norms and institutions uniformly across France, also shaped discussion of education, as well it might considering the disparities in literacy previously mentioned between regions, social groups, town and country, male and female.

Shortly before the National Assembly dissolved itself at the end of September 1791, Talleyrand presented the first major legislative proposal to refashion the entire structure of French education. Though by no means the centerpiece of his plan, elementary schools constituted the base of an institutional pyramid whose secondary schools, universities, and research institutes would serve different purposes and through which youths of appropriate qualification might ascend. The Legislative Assembly of 1791–92 did not find the time to take up either Talleyrand's plan or a remarkable project formulated by Condorcet, but education figured repeatedly on the agenda of the National Convention. Its education committee, whose leadership kept changing with the political winds, introduced several plans for a comprehensive national system of education. The rancorous factionalism of revolutionary politics at this time, however, compounded honest disagreements over principle. Each initiative set off harsh controversy, especially over the elite institutions at the top of the hierarchy, and on the degree of state control over the whole edifice—institutions and controls which in the eyes of some deputies were likely to produce a new species of privilege and even a new "sacerdotal caste." As a result, comprehensive proposals rarely came to a vote and in the end the Convention failed to approve any.[6]

In its own way each master plan from Talleyrand's onward made universal primary schooling normative, proposed to bring it under some degree of state supervision, and assigned it a new civic mission. Starting with Condorcet's project, most also proposed to secularize elementary education. The plans of 1791–93 all assumed that access to primary schooling should be widened, that schools ought to be established on some uniform basis, and that the state should underwrite the costs—though they never specified how this was to be carried out. Even before the advent of the republic in 1792, universal primary schooling became a commonplace, consensual goal. The Jacobin Convention subsequently enshrined the idea in its new Declaration of the Rights of Man of 1793 along with the right to public assistance: "Education is the need of everyone," it stated, thus resolving a question that had perplexed Enlightenment thinkers like Voltaire. "Society must do everything in its power to favor the progress of public reason and to put education within the reach of all citizens."

In this sense elementary schooling, necessary for everyone, stood apart from the hierarchy of more advanced educational institutions. The Convention could in fact act on it independently rather than as part of a master plan, and the egalitarian atmosphere in Paris now placed a premium on doing so. In May 1793 the Committee of Public Safety pledged that in the future the republic would establish a free primary school in every community of more than six hundred inhabitants. Several representatives-on-mission in the provinces implemented comparable measures on their own authority. The ex-priest and secondary school teacher Joseph Lakanal, for example, had been sent to the Dordogne to requisition horses for the army. In collaboration with the Jacobin Club of Bergerac, he paused to levy a special tax on the rich in order to establish four free primary schools in the town. Each was to employ a male and a female teacher at annual salaries of 1,200 livres, to be chosen (preferably from among married citizens) by a committee of local officials and club members. Bergerac's revolutionary authorities promptly carried out Lakanal's instructions and these secular schools began to operate. [7]

Repeated assertions that the fate of the republic depended on regenerating the people through education; statements of intention to establish schools everywhere; and ad hoc local efforts, however, did not add up to a real policy. How could universal, free primary education actually be brought into being? An answer was delayed while the Convention took up a bizarre proposal introduced in behalf of the recently assassinated Jacobin deputy Michel LePeletier. The LePeletier plan took off from the respectable Jacobin premise that citizens ought to experience a common education (*éducation commune*), for only by such contact could equality and fraternity develop among children of diverse social backgrounds. A more problematic assumption of this scheme held that children belonged to the nation as well as their families. As Danton melodramatically declared, "I too am a father, but my son does not belong to me, he belongs to the Republic."

Elementary education, in other words, was too vital for the commonweal to be left to the discretion and circumstances of families. LePeletier therefore proposed to create state boarding schools (*maisons d'égalité*) where children between the ages of five and twelve could experience veritable equality in food, clothing, lodging, work, play, and learning. Robespierre and the Jacobin Club publicly endorsed the plan, as homage to the Montagnard martyr. Despite pointed criticisms of its "chimerical" qualities, the Convention, in an act of momentary political expediency, adopted a modified version of the proposal on 13 August 1793, decreeing that such state boarding schools would be offered as an option without being obligatory. The willingness to endorse this Spartan fantasy even momentarily may have been an ominous portent of the Jacobin mentality, but it had no practical impact on the issue of primary schooling. On the very next day the Convention "suspended" application of its decree, and it was never heard of again. [8]

No sooner were the *maisons d'égalité* of the LePeletier plan forgotten than the Convention made another false start in October 1793 at the height of the de-christianizing frenzy. Voting again in principle to have salaried public school teachers in virtually every commune, the Convention excluded all ex-religious personnel from the bounties of this system, while seeming to deny such individuals the right to operate schools independently. The deputies soon thought better of that rash decision. The anti-religious animus of October appeared impolitic a few weeks later, as the Convention reaffirmed religious liberty and tried to curb zealous de-christianizers in the Paris Com-

mune and the provinces. It now seemed sensible to extend an olive branch
to old-regime teaching personnel such as ex-teaching sisters, schoolmasters
who had doubled as sacristans, or ex-priests who had turned to teaching as
an alternative career.

Prodded by the Committee of Public Safety, the Convention made a
volte-face and on 19 December 1793 adopted the Bouquier Law, the first to
provide an actual formula for free primary schooling. A deceptively simple
but oddly ambivalent approach, Gabriel Bouquier's plan seemed to incorporate a liberal anti-statist viewpoint on the one hand and a strong dose of
Jacobin egalitarianism on the other. At first glance it seemed to accommodate familiar local patterns of primary schooling. Indeed, the Bouquier Law
did not create a veritable system of public schooling at all. Rather, it committed the state to paying the tuition *(rétribution scolaire)* of each student at a
standard rate. Schooling would also be "free" for parents in the latitude they
would have for finding teachers that suited them. All teachers were required
to come under the umbrella of this plan, but their hiring did not depend on
any official body. They simply had to secure a *certificat de civisme* and announce
their intention to open a school. What they did in the classroom was between
them and the parents, since they would not be subject to special surveillance.
In theory the plan accommodated ex-priests or nuns as well as ardent
sans-culottes eager to spread the revolutionary gospel in the classroom.

In reality this talk of maximal freedom was disingenuous. While teachers
would not be officially screened for their skill, or enmeshed in a public
bureaucracy, they could teach only after acquiring a *certificat de civisme* from
their local municipality or revolutionary committee. True, every other public
or quasi-public functionary required this bill of civic good health in 1793, but
traditional Catholic teachers might shrink from seeking it, either out of
principle or prudence. The freedom of parents was limited in another respect
as well. Though manifestly lacking any ability to enforce this, the law *obliged*
parents to send their offspring to school. As Danton put it, "In the Republic
no one is free to be ignorant." The Bouquier Law was the first and only
decree of the revolutionary era that in theory took this decision entirely out
of parents' hands. [9]

The Convention implemented this "democratic law" immediately, and
four months later queried the districts about its progress. The responses were
dismaying. In the 400-odd districts providing specific information, officials
estimated that there should have been about 23,000 schools. But only 6,831
were said to be operating, the majority concentrated in about 50 districts.
Elsewhere, the "absolute famine of teachers" effectively nullified the law's
prospects. Numerous old-regime teachers evidently balked at working for
the republic or were unable to acquire a *certificat de civisme* even if they wished

to. Forgoing state tuition payments, many resisters probably continued to teach clandestinely without inscribing themselves as *instituteurs publics*. At the same time cooperative teachers were demoralized by the "meagerness and instability of their pay," which depended on enrollment. Though the Convention subsequently voted a floor of 500 livres for each *instituteur public* irrespective of enrollment, teachers considered that sum insufficient. But to achieve adequate enrollment and remuneration, teachers were dependent on the volition of parents, many of whom did not trust the revolutionary government at this juncture. Moreover, when rural parents held their children back from school during busy agricultural seasons, the monthly *rétribution* paid by the state would decline proportionately. In towns that had several schools, on the other hand, teachers complained of a demoralizing competition for students and a resultant insecurity.[10]

THE LAKANAL LAW

In the wake of Thermidor, most Montagnard policies came under attack. Whether in good faith or demagogically, deputies denounced the Bouquier Law as an emanation of Robespierrist terrorism. Because it established no standards of qualification for teachers, some also assailed the law as a sanction for revolutionary "vandalism" and ignorance. Now the advocates of a more structured and ambitious program seized the initiative. Instead of tinkering with the Bouquier Law, the education committee drafted an entirely new proposal, or more accurately resurrected parts of an earlier plan fathered by Sieyès, Daunou, and Lakanal. Lakanal's plan gave a different kind of inflection to the principle of universal, free primary schooling. It would place primary education more firmly under government supervision, raise the status of teachers, liberate them from a dependence on the vagaries of enrollment, and expand the program of study beyond the 3Rs as Condorcet had once proposed. At the same time it would restore the freedom of parents to choose private schools or no schooling at all. Offering a new and comprehensive approach to primary education, the Lakanal Law aimed very high while accepting a number of practical limitations. And instead of acting impulsively, the Convention for the first time gave extended consideration to a detailed proposal on education—with ample debate, modification by amendment, final approval, and, above all, serious implementation.[11]

The Lakanal Law of 27 brumaire Year III (17 November 1794) committed the republic to providing a primary school with a schoolmaster *(instituteur)* and schoolmistress *(institutrice)* in every commune with one thousand or more inhabitants. Smaller villages were to be amalgamated into arrondissements at roughly the same population threshold by the district administrations. The teachers were to be known as *instituteurs nationales* and were considered as public functionaries. They were enjoined to teach a curriculum of reading, writing, arithmetic, the Declaration of the Rights of Man, the Constitution, republican morality, the principles of the French language, elements of geography, the history "of free peoples," and notions about natural phenomena. To promote social virtue and respect for manual labor, teachers were to take their students on visits to hospitals and workshops, and arrange for them to help elderly people in their chores. Students were also to be given exercise and physical education. Religion did not figure in this program.[12]

Teachers were to receive an annual salary from the national government: 1,200 livres for the men and 1,000 for the women, with supplements of 300 and 200 livres respectively for teachers in cities of 20,000 or more population. Upon retirement they were promised a state pension. Apart from these salaries, however, *instituteurs publics* could not accept supplementary payments from parents for tutoring or boarding their children. Whether they could lawfully engage in a secondary occupation was unclear.

To pay this kind of annual salary to a humble elementary school teacher in the countryside was an extremely controversial undertaking. Such generosity might end up subsidizing with public revenues negligent teachers or those with scant responsibilities. But Lakanal insisted that only in this way could competent teachers be attracted to rural schools, where the salary might indeed seem appreciable: "Only in this way can I foresee equality in education." Teachers were to be examined and certified in a *concours* or competition by a three-man *juri d'instruction* appointed by each district administration, but only for the time being. Ultimately this responsibility of selecting teachers would revert to the parents. The *juris* were merely temporary surrogates. In any case the districts were to supervise the whole process, maintain surveillance over the schools, and sign monthly pay vouchers for the district receiver.

Lakanal made his ostensibly secular public schools more palatable to conservatives by explicitly permitting individuals to establish private schools outside the system. Despite impassioned arguments by several remaining Montagnard deputies that this destroyed any hope of *éducation commune* for the nation's children, the Convention sanctioned private schools—or *enseignement libre,* as it was called—alongside *instruction publique.* Gilbert Romme then demanded that private schools must at least be subject to strict surveillance and standards set by public authorities. Lakanal himself was persuaded, seeing this as a compromise between the collective interests of the republic and the right of parents to raise their children as they saw fit. But the thermidorian majority, adamant about shielding traditional religious teachers, refused to place any constraint on private schools. In the same libertarian spirit the Convention abandoned the pretense of the Bouquier Law that parents must send their children to school. Nor did the new law insist that French be the exclusive language of instruction in areas where the populace spoke German, Breton, Flemish, or local dialects. While adhering to the notion that *instruction publique* should promote the use of French as against bilingualism or the use of patois, the law conceded that local languages could be used as an "auxiliary medium" of instruction, and in effect abandoned the battle to impose French in regions such as Alsace or Brittany. [13]

The Lakanal Law might easily appear as simply one variation in a succession of plans, reports, and laws that ultimately came to nought. But that would be to misjudge its significance. In the first place, it commands attention on its merits, as an artful compromise between clashing imperatives. Though thermidorian in provenance, it retained the Jacobin spirit of state-sponsored egalitarianism, and drew on the structures of revolutionary authority to prod local communities into action. No revolutionary law could conjure away the structural and cultural obstacles to universal public education—which we will re-encounter in due course—but the Lakanal Law was a reasoned attempt to confront them. Secondly, implemented with considerable energy, the law guided the only sustained attempt to create and finance a national system of primary schooling, until the far more modest initiatives of Guizot in the 1830s. Its ultimate failure stemmed more from an entirely unforeseen conjunction of circumstances, as we shall see, than from its intrinsic shortcomings. In any discussion of primary education before, during, and after the Revolution, the Lakanal Law ought to be a benchmark of comparison.

THE DEMAND FOR SCHOOLING

Assuming the responsibility for paying teachers, the republic did not wish to squander public funds on an excessive number of schools, but it also had to consider the practical needs of varied communities. Lakanal had acknowledged that the smallest communes would generally not have their own schools under his plan, and he defended amalgamated school districts lest "the schools become communal rather than national, which is less favorable to unity." Nonetheless, the law provided for exceptions to the population threshold "in localities where the population is too dispersed . . . upon the documented request of the district administration and a decree of the national legislature." In principle, then, the new law was quite rigid compared to the Bouquier Law, yet this clause allowed the government to give back to small villages what it seemed to be taking away.[14]

The Executive Commission on Public Instruction (a division of the former Interior Ministry) warned the districts "neither to make the schools too scarce nor to multiply them excessively." Since it was promoting a substantial curriculum, the government reasonably wanted schools large enough "so that the number of students can contribute to forming and maintaining a useful emulation." By the same token, the state did not wish to pay a substantial annual salary to teachers in a community so small that he and she were not effectively occupied. The Convention had additional reason to require substantial arrondissements for its primary schools since it faced a shortage of teachers. On 25 nivôse III (14 January 1795) it raised the recommended population threshold to one school per 1,500 inhabitants.[15] Some districts accordingly readjusted the arrondissements they had drawn for rural schools and reduced the number of schools in their towns. The district of Château-Thierry (Aisne) cut the number of prescribed schools from 53 to 32; Cerilly (Allier) from 32 to 18; Sens (Yonne) from 47 to 36; Dijon (Côte d'Or) from 70 to 56.[16]

This of course made it even harder for small communes to demand their own schools instead of being amalgamated into an arrondissement of three or four villages. Nonetheless, such demands came frequently and persuasively. To be sure, a great many French citizens still had no interest in schooling, free or otherwise.[17] But *instruction publique* was not merely an enthusiasm of republican legislators insulated from reality in the capital. Its allure echoed far and wide, most obviously among the embattled minorities of urban Jacobinism but also in the countryside. The implementation of the Lakanal Law bestirred not only the host of individuals officially involved— district directorates, national agents, *juris d'instruction*—but the inhabitants of countless villages.

Numerous communes petitioned the districts to be treated as exceptions to the threshold of 1,000 or 1,500. On their own authority, certain districts granted individual requests: Soissons authorized a school for a village with 595 inhabitants, Lure granted a public school to a commune of 490 population, and Chaumont approved schools for communes of 498 and 527.[18] With its widely dispersed patterns of settlement, the district of Provins (Seine-et-Marne) proved exceptionally accommodating. It admitted that out of forty-five rural arrondissements, twenty-four did not conform strictly to the law's guideline, "so as to make these establishments truly useful by placing the students in greater proximity to the teachers." The district of Albi (Tarn) likewise bent the rules, feeling "the necessity to reduce the number of primary schools in populous localities in order to preserve our latitude to establish several additional schools in places where the population is dispersed." In St. Girons (Ariège), the district authorized fifteen schools in villages with populations below 1,000, "considering that the inhabitants of places that cannot in any way be amalgamated with others should not be deprived of education."[19] Certain district directorates of course preferred the virtues of amalgamated schools and were reluctant to make such exceptions, while others simply threw up their hands over the "particularism" and narrow "self-interest" of communes that insisted on being the seat of the amalgamated arrondissement or on having their own school: In Sarlat (Dordogne), the requests from isolated communes offered "so many practical difficulties that the administration cannot agree to make any recommendations."[20]

If the rural communes were putting self-interest first, it was an enlightened self-interest of a most compelling kind. The dispersal of population and the small size of communes inherently dragged against national uniformity and administrative efficiency, as we have seen, but they were especially poignant in the matter of schooling. "The amalgamation of communes that are too far from the arrondissement's school provokes a general dissatisfaction in the rural communes," explained the district of St. Quentin (Aisne). "What father would consent to expose his children to perishing of the cold on impassable roads?" The petitions by small communes for their own *écoles primaires* evoke a rural topography of isolated communities separated from each other by rugged terrain, mountains, ravines, marshes, unfordable rivers, torrential streams, or forbidding forests. Even when primitive *chemins vicinaux* connected these communities, they usually became altogether impassable in the rain. A trip that may have been feasible for children in mild weather was simply unacceptable during winter—precisely the optimum season for schooling in communities where children worked in the fields during the busy summers.[21]

In petitions to the Convention such as the "Protest by the inhabitants of the commune of Oriemont [Seine-et-Oise]," rural citizens complained that the new law would benefit only larger communes with concentrated populations. They estimated that in two thirds of France, three or four communes would have to be amalgamated, meaning in effect that "of every three communes there will only be one that can benefit from the nation's beneficence." Boutigny (Seine-et-Marne), with a population of only 741 but with 130 children of school age, for example, was to be amalgamated with St. Fiacre, a considerable distance away. Its inhabitants therefore protested that "two thirds of the commune's children will be deprived of the education that the nation has promised to everyone, except insofar as the parents are forced to pay for a private teacher." Citizens in small villages such as Corcelle (Ain) or Etaulle (Charente-Inférieure) now felt entitled to "a teacher salaried by the Republic." They requested schools of their own "in the name of equality and an education based on true republicanism." Like the citizens of eight rural communities in the Landes, they worried that "small communes will no longer have teachers unless the communes are willing to pay them themselves." As the national agent in Montmédy (Meuse) observed, the inhabitants of excluded communes "already know full well that they all contribute to the salaries of these teachers by paying their taxes."[22]

Trading the flexibility of the Bouquier Law (payment by the state per student) for a fixed salary designed to make the teachers more independent and secure, Lakanal hoped precisely to favor rural communities by assuring attractive remuneration for their teachers. The resultant formula was clearly too rigid, and underestimated the legitimate resistance to amalgamated rural schools. Judging from the lobbying by the communes and the sympathetic reaction of many district officials, however, the substantial demand for free schooling in small rural communes could be met by multiple exemptions and by fine-tuning other provisions of the law. Time would presumably tell. Meanwhile, villagers proposed ad hoc arrangements to draw on the "bienfaisance nationale" in ways that suited their needs. Some offered to share the 1,200 livre stipend among teachers in two or three communes and to supplement it with small contributions by the parents. The district of Château-Thierry (Aisne) petitioned the Convention in behalf of its smaller communes, which wanted "the option of naming a *sous-maître* at the commune's expense . . . to bring the children over the age of six to the arrondissement's primary school on the first, third, fifth, seventh, and ninth of each *décade* in order to partake of *instruction publique.*" In St. Pol (Pas-de-Calais), with its numerous small villages, district officials believed that "strictly followed, the letter of the law will kill its spirit . . . and introduce inequality." They proposed that a district be permitted to collect the full sum due it under the law on the basis of total population, and distribute it to as many teachers as it wished to employ—in proportion to the population of each school's commune and the number of its pupils—on a sliding pay scale of 600 to 1,200 livres.[23]

The most common proposal for circumventing the population threshold of the Lakanal Law turned on the schoolmistresses. The Convention had accepted the conventional wisdom about separating the sexes in schoolrooms: each primary school was to have two sections, one for boys and one for girls. Alongside the *instituteur,* each school was to have an *institutrice* for the girls. In its way this projected a remarkable initiative for separate but essentially equal schooling, which would diverge only toward the end when girls were to be taught domestic skills such as knitting and sewing. Potentially it also opened up a substantial employment opportunity for females. Unfortunately, the current paucity of candidates for these positions and the deficient qualifications of those who did present themselves quickly became evident.

Even after ignoring the nominal requirements and accepting female candidates with only the most rudimentary skills and illegible handwriting, the vast majority of *juris* still expressed utter frustration. Of the eleven *institutrices* who applied, reported the *juri* in Dijon, only one was really qualified, while "the other ten need instruction themselves."[24] With rare exceptions, districts had little choice but to certify three or four times as many men as women, and prospects for the republican girls' schools looked very bleak indeed.[25] In the long term this commitment might have availed as a new generation of young women acquired basic skills, had their own children, and then sought the posts. But for the present, the Lakanal Law was headed for certain failure in providing separate but equal schooling for girls.

This setback, however, could be turned to different kind of advantage. The money already pledged by the state for the salary of so many nonexistent *institutrices* could be diverted to hire additional *instituteurs* for smaller rural communes—provided that the Convention reconsidered its stand on single-sex education. Just how universal that practice had been is open to question. Letters from some provincial officials suggested that it was a chimerical notion that had never been followed. *Institutrices* were "imaginary beings" in his region, observed the national agent in Compiègne (Oise); "separate instruction is not at all practical," and had never existed. In the district of Vézelise (Meurthe), where only two *institutrices* had been certified as against thirty male teachers, officials hoped to provide for the education of girls by admitting them to the boys' classrooms—as they had been previously—perhaps augmenting the salaries of the teachers.[26] But others saw a chance to increase the total number of schools in their districts, like the administrators of Chartres (Eure-et-Loire), who hoped to establish the seventy schools they wanted instead of the prescribed forty "by using the funds earmarked for the positions of *institutrices* that remain vacant, since very few candidates have presented themselves."[27]

Five deputies sent on mission by the Convention to monitor implementation of the Lakanal Law each encountered similar views. L.-A. Jard-Panvillier reported that *juris* and district directorates had urged him "to replace the [non-existent] *institutrices* by the same number of *instituteurs* who, in such cases, would teach children of both sexes . . . thereby multiplying the number of teachers without increasing the cost to the public treasury." His colleague J.-C. Bailleul sympathized with requests to divide rural schools by age rather than sex. Women could teach all the younger children, making it easier to find apt *institutrices* who need only know how to read, and incidentally

assuring that girls received a better education later on in company with the
boys. The deputies could not authorize such practices in direct contravention
of the law, but the Convention might still have revised the law as such
demands for flexibility mounted.[28]

THE SUPPLY OF TEACHERS

With or without such changes, the demand for schools under the Lakanal
Law far exceeded the supply of qualified *instituteurs*. While more plentiful
than female applicants, male candidates were still in short supply in most
districts and their qualifications woefully inadequate. In theory, *instituteurs*
would be teaching penmanship, spelling, grammar, and arithmetic as well as
a smattering of history, geography, science, and republican morality—evidently a very tall order for the schoolmasters of the old regime who formed
the bulk of the present pool. Among the forty candidates examined in Adour
(Hautes-Pyrénées), the *juri* could not find "a single one who mustered even
half the knowledge required by this law." *Juris* in Montflanquin (Meuse) and
l'Aigle (Orne) expressed the same chagrin at certifying teachers "who can
scarcely read correctly and know neither spelling nor grammar. Naming them
as *instituteurs,* it seems to us, will not fulfill the aim of the law and will burden
the government with paying unmerited salaries." The meticulous *juri* of
Dijon's district concluded that not a single candidate in the *concours* for rural
schools had the requisite general qualifications, while only eleven out of
forty-five could read and write reasonably well.[29] Notes left by the *juri*
d'instruction of St. Pol (Pas-de-Calais) on the candidates illustrate its quandary:
Reading: 65% good, 25% passable, 10% poor; Writing: 28% good, 37%
passable, 35% poor; Spelling: 37% good, 24% passable, 39% poor. In arithmetic, 74 percent knew the four basic rules, but 18 percent could do no more
than add and subtract, and only two candidates had any knowledge of
geometry.[30]

The *juris* got around their dilemma by certifying deficient candidates
"provisionally," though usually in the belief that most were "too elderly to
hope for any improvement." Younger teachers—whose zeal presently exceeded their knowledge—might be redeemable if they could be given some
training.[31] Even if they could not maintain standards of ability, however, the
earnest members of these *juris—pères de famille* themselves, as the law required—could at least uphold moral standards by weeding out notorious
drunkards and miscreants.[32]

A few officials referred to the new Normal School in Paris as a resource
holding out some hope for the future, but that experiment was about to

collapse. In November 1794, the Convention had established the *Ecole Normale* in the capital to provide a crash course in "the art of teaching various fields of human knowledge" for candidates nominated by each district in the republic. After their course, the men were supposed to return home and establish training institutes of their own to produce a new generation of local *instituteurs*. The Executive Commission on Public Instruction staffed the *Ecole Normale* with eminent scholars and scientists such as the mathematician Lagrange, the chemist Berthollet, the historian Volney, and the literary critic LaHarpe. Unfortunately, their lectures were far above the heads of their students and had nothing to do with the art of primary education. After a few months the Convention took note of the total disarray that ensued and in May 1795 abruptly shut down the school and sent its 1,200 student-teachers back home.[33] No training schools were subsequently established in the provinces, though some of these men did become *instituteurs* themselves. Months later they were still waiting in vain for the follow-up materials they had been promised. The eminently sensible idea of training new personnel for a new public-sector career had aborted.[34]

Meanwhile military mobilization had claimed an entire cohort of young men for the army, leaving civil society bereft of potential new recruits for public school teaching. *Juris* and local officials therefore petitioned for the right to appoint certain soldiers who would manifestly be more useful to them than to the army. In St. Priest-des-Champs (Puy-de-Dôme), the municipality claimed that the only appropriate candidate for its primary school was a young man who "was among the first of this commune to come to the defense of his country [as a volunteer]. But his physical strength could never equal his zeal," and he returned from the front three times with infirmities. The commune asked that he now be given an unconditional discharge instead of the temporary furlough he carried. The *juri* of Rodez (Aveyron), which faced a dearth of apt candidates, requested the same indulgence:

Among those who rushed to join the army for the defense of liberty, there are three in our district who were impelled more by their zeal than by their physical strength. By reason of their morality and their learning they would serve the republic more effectively in the career of public school teaching than in the armies.

Pierre-Louis Ginguené, head of the Executive Commission on Public Instruction, estimated that *juris d'instruction* were seeking discharges for about six hundred soldiers with "very weak physical conditions"—a minuscule number from the perspective of the war effort.[35] Like the *Ecole Normale*, a reasonable collaboration between the manpower bureau of the War Ministry and the Executive Commission might have helped meet the demands of public instruction, but it never occurred.

Local officials implementing the Lakanal Law faced a host of problems all told: pressure for the establishment of additional schools in small rural communes; practical obstacles to separating boys and girls in the classroom because of the dearth of *institutrices;* a shortage of male teachers and the poor qualifications of most candidates; competition with the army for the services of younger men; and bitter local controversies over the disposition of nationalized rectories that were supposed to be made available to the republic's teachers. To some degree these problems were offset by the dedication of many local officials; by the occasional success of a district in establishing a substantial complement of schools; and by the eagerness of communes to link themselves to an incipient system of *instruction publique.* There were grounds for disappointment, for frustration, for substantially lower expectations, but not for despair.

The Lakanal Law ultimately foundered because of the unanticipated economic disaster that beset France in 1795, after the thermidorians abandoned price controls and unleashed runaway inflation. The ensuing collapse of the *assignat*'s value hit hardest at rentiers, urban workers, and public employees dependent entirely on paper money. Poor harvests and harsh weather that year compounded the agony. The combination of rampant inflation and shortages of grain caused a social disaster and eventually touched off a popular uprising in Paris that spring, which in turn hardened the conservative mood of thermidorian legislators. Meanwhile the great strongpoint of the Lakanal Law, the fixed salary of 1,200 livres for *instituteurs publics,* became derisory. Indeed, it turned into a liability since it was to be the teachers' sole form of remuneration.

The precipitous devaluation of this salary soon dominated the reports reaching the Convention and the Executive Commission. The *juri* of Bergues (Nord) bewailed "the excessive price of foodstuffs which makes a salary that in ordinary times would call forth a favorable response now seem mediocre." Worse yet, teachers already appointed were resigning. In Ambert (Puy-de-Dôme), the *juri* warned the Convention that "the teachers—not finding in the salary accorded to them by the law an income sufficient to procure even half the grain necessary for their consumption—are abandoning their schools to give themselves over to any other occupation. Every day we receive new resignations." Even in districts like Brive that had certified a large roster of teachers, the once attractive salary now yielded less than half a year's subsistence by the spring of 1795, and many *instituteurs* handed in their resignations.[36]

The situation deteriorated with each passing week. By the beginning of the new year (September 1795), the Executive Commission reported to the Convention that "a general cry has gone up over the frightful distress of the teachers. Lacking even the absolute necessities, most are languishing in the horrors of deprivation."[37] Insult was added to mortal injury by the Convention's disregard of their plight. In January, the Convention had authorized supplements to the pay of public functionaries to compensate for the depreciation of the *assignat:* employees who earned 100 livres a month, for example (the salary of a rural teacher), would receive an additional monthly "indemnity" of 80 livres, though the money was fast losing its value anyway. *Instituteurs,* however, found that they had not been included as recipients of this meager supplement. "We cannot believe," wrote two incredulous *instituteurs* from Bourg-l'Egalité, "that we have been included on the list of public functionaries only to exercise our duties and not to receive the indemnity." But such was the case.[38]

The *instituteurs* most likely to endure were those who had already taken possession of former rectories not previously sold off as *biens nationaux,* which the Lakanal Law had pledged to them. This perquisite proved especially useful if the rectory had a vegetable garden. *Instituteurs* might also persevere in the hope that arrears in their salaries would eventually be paid in money of some value.[39] Those who faced starvation while they waited had no choice but to abandon their positions, either to carry on as private teachers paid in kind by parents or to find subsistence in other work.

The Retreat from Public Schooling

Purged by now of most Montagnards, and in a sour mood of austerity and social conservatism, the Convention prepared a new constitution to replace the still-born Jacobin Constitution of 1793. How should education be treated? Should they incorporate the basic commitment of the Lakanal Law, ride out the storm of hyperinflation, and try again in better times? Or abandon the effort in the wake of its failures? With little patience for sentimental egalitarianism or missionary zeal, the deputies' new attitude prompted a decisive shift of emphasis. Beating a strategic retreat in primary education, the outgoing Convention focused its resources on the more tractable question of republican secondary schools.

A report from the Executive Commission on Public Instruction in the Convention's final month did nothing to ward off the blow. Lakanal's plan was simply too ambitious, concluded its *rapporteur,* Ginguené. *Instituteurs* capable of teaching the prescribed curriculum could scarcely be found; many former schoolmasters of religious background had boycotted the system; and those who did come forward found that the rise in the cost of subsistence "rendered their salary virtually nil." The promise of lodging and a garden remained attractive but could rarely be delivered. Ginguené recommended that the republic abandon the idea of paying salaries to teachers, "leaving them the right to draw a salary from the parents who have the means of paying for their children's education—a tuition which will always be very low in the countryside." He deemed this modest approach adequate since he did not believe that public schools "can all of a sudden become superior to the *petites écoles* [of the old regime] that they are supposed to replace." In effect the Commission argued that the traditional haphazard pattern of schooling sufficed: "It would certainly be accomplishing a lot if such general instruction multiplied the number of individuals who know how to read and write, however poorly and without spelling. And that is the goal to which we must limit ourselves, at least in the countryside."[40]

Following this minimalist prescription, the new Constitution of 1795 promised merely that "there will be [public] primary schools in the Republic," and limited the state's role to providing only "the cost of lodging for the teachers appointed to those schools." It also guaranteed the right of citizens to form private educational establishments. In its penultimate session of 3 brumaire IV (25 October 1795), the Convention adopted a law drafted by the former Oratorian and educator P. C. F. Daunou (who had been purged from the Convention as a Girondin sympathizer two years earlier), laying out the republic's future system of *instruction publique* in detail. Its centerpiece was a new kind of secondary school for boys over the age of twelve, with one of these *écoles centrales* to be established in each department. These institutions formed a separate track with no specific connection to the nation's primary schools. On elementary education the Daunou Law promised a public school in each canton, but little more: "In each canton of the Republic one or more primary schools will be established, whose arrondissements will be determined by the departmental administrations." (The districts, it will be recalled, were abolished at this point, with their authority devolving upward toward the departments and downward to the new cantonal administrations.)

In this limited number of public schools the prescribed curriculum would be minimal as well: "reading, writing, arithmetic, and the elements of republican morality." *Instituteurs* were to be paid by tuition from their students' parents in amounts set by each department; cantonal administrations could exempt up to a quarter of the students in each school from this tuition "for reasons of indigence." In Daunou's original proposal, the education of girls would have been left entirely "to the domestic care of parents and to private educational establishments." This was too much for Lakanal, who denounced such a blatant exclusion of half the nation's children from the

opportunity for *instruction publique.* The Convention finally stipulated that
each public school could be divided into two sections, with a male and a
female teacher.[41]

The Daunou Law—which lasted well into the Napoleonic era—abandoned the principle of universal and free primary education. It also left the
instituteurs publics on their own (save for free lodging or an indemnity), with
no salary from the state and no distinctive status to go along with their titles.
As some teachers in Moissac (Lot) later complained, not only were they
reduced to indigence, but "they enjoy no prerogative whatsoever in society,
no dignity, no distinctions. They live amid contempt."[42] Yet if the logic of
Daunou and Ginguené was simply to return primary education to the traditional local marketplace, neither the thermidorian Convention nor the Directory regime were prepared to go that far. They thus left standing a kind of
shell—a thin network of ostensibly state-sponsored schools. For the moment these school were not free of tuition and their teachers did not draw
public salaries. For the time being, too, the libertarian spirit of the Daunou
Law left private schools entirely free from any kind of surveillance or
regulation—free to rival and overwhelm these public schools. But in the
hearts of many republicans, universal and free public schools remained an
integral feature of a proper civic order. The inordinate expectations invested
in that ideal had receded, but the issue was far from settled.

As a start, the new departmental and cantonal administrations went
through the motions of complying with the Daunou Law. Cantonal officials
drew up new lists of potential school districts for town and country, probably
averaging about half the number projected under the Lakanal Law.[43] They
were of course likely to be most energetic in areas that already had strong
traditions of schooling in the old regime—whereas the Lakanal Law had
presumed to treat all regions similarly, precisely to overcome such inequalities. Meanwhile the departments named *juris d'instruction* similar and often
identical to those of the Year III, which interviewed and nominated *instituteurs publics,* subject to approval by the department and appointment by
a cantonal administration.

Futile as it may have seemed, the departments issued decrees on the
questions that they were empowered to decide such as tuition fees. The
department of the Allier, for example, prudently set the *rétribution scolaire* at
10 *livres* of grain per student per month in 1796; only by the following year
did it seem safe to fix the amount in cash. The Haute-Saône department
mandated 15 sous per month for reading, but up to 30 sous for students
learning writing and arithmetic; rates were to be slightly lower in communes
of fewer than 2,000 inhabitants and for *institutrices.* In the Cher, the fees were
40 sous per month in Bourges, 30 sous in other towns, and 20 sous in rural

schools. Cantons in the Loir-et-Cher could set their own rates, which tended toward 10 sous per month for reading and 20 for reading and writing. The departments also set the annual indemnities for lodging (the 90 livres in Aveyron being somewhat on the low side); but finding the money was another matter, and payments were almost always in arrears. [44]

Departmental administrations also regulated the schedules of their public schools. Urban schools in the Cher had two sessions, at 8–11 A.M. and 2–5 P.M. In the country, there was to be only one session, whose duration would be decided by cantonal authorities. The Oise set a similar schedule for its schools for half the year, but pragmatically reduced the hours during the winter months to 9–11 and 2–4. (As the historian Jean Vassort points out, country schools that held two daily sessions made it easier for rural children to attend at least one.) Separation of the sexes continued to be a vexing issue. The Haute-Saône called for separate classes in its public schools, but stipulated that "where there are no *institutrices,* the *instituteur* will hold the morning session for girls and the afternoon session for boys." The Oise was more rigid: teachers were prohibited from teaching pupils of the opposite sex. Most departments probably tried to look the other way on this matter. In Seine-Inférieure, Seine-et-Marne, Charente, and Gers, the great majority of schools were mixed, albeit with at least twice as many boys as girls. Nor was there consensus on when children should start school. The Eure-et-Loire and the Oise departments made them eligible at age six, but the Haute-Saône only at seven. [45]

These local decrees—though addressed to a small and dwindling number of *instituteurs publics*—doubtless had a totemic significance; they showed the republic's flag. They maintained the notion that departments should create a set of uniform standards for primary education even while accommodating local considerations, such as differences between town and country. But such rational planning and uniformity, important from a long-range perspective, did little to raise the actual quality of public instruction or to aid the *instituteurs publics* in competing with private teachers.

COMPETITION

In theory, public schools were supposed to be secular or religiously neutral. As the Directory's commissioner to the Seine put it (in words that Americans will find extremely resonant), "it is necessary to erect a wall of separation between education and religion." To the secular-minded or Voltairean wing of republicanism, it seemed reasonable that "republican education can be in accord with religious ideas, in the sense that it does not adhere to any specific faith."[46] But the public schools were merely one alternative in the free marketplace authorized by the Lakanal and Daunou laws. Most parents did not find religious neutrality a selling point when it came to schooling. Without necessarily being anti-republican, they simply preferred the familiar Catholic style of schooling.

Even the free public schools of the Lakanal Law had been swamped by that preference. Under intense community pressure, most *instituteurs publics* willingly or reluctantly capitulated to the parents' "imperious demands for instruction in religious doctrines and practices," even as they collected their salary from the republic in 1795. "The teachers do not dare use republican books," reported an official in Sancerre (Cher) to Lakanal. "The fathers have obliged them to use religious works." Conversely the *juri d'instruction* in Blois (Loir-et-Cher) informed the Convention that distributing republican class-room materials had backfired: "The private schools are frequented and the public schools are deserted because the teachers in the former still limit themselves exclusively to the long-familiar books."[47] Bailleul, one of five deputies on mission to implement the Lakanal Law, regretfully came to the same conclusion. The private teachers were thriving because they "give children the traditional education and inculcate religious principles. . . . Public school teachers fear seeing their classrooms deserted if they are deprived of the same option."

To make matters worse, some refractory priests and former nuns attempted to delegitimize the *instituteurs publics*. From Troyes, the deputy C.-F. Dupuis confirmed that "fanatical priests and royalists . . . are agitating with incredible activity to disparage the new education. I have seen places where former nuns drawing state pensions have established their own schools where they command a good price; to augment the number of students they villify the republican schools, which they call *les écoles du Diable.*" He therefore authorized *instituteurs publics* to use traditional Catholic materials in their classrooms, for if he barred them, "the parents will take fright and be furnished with a specious pretext for decrying republican education."[48]

During the first two years of the Directory public schooling languished under the benign neglect of the Daunou Law and the competition of the private teachers. The complaint by a frustrated young *instituteur public* in St. Esprit (Landes) conveyed the lack of standing that his position carried despite his official title. In May 1797, he wrote to the minister of the interior to ask

whether an individual has the right to run a private school where there are already *instituteurs* recognized by the law, or whether his function ought to be limited to teaching in private homes? . . . Experiencing daily the effects of the sarcasms of a teacher who will teach at any price in order to procure a greater number of students, my reputation is damaged, public confidence is swayed, and the indigent are deprived of the advantage of a law that entitles them to be taught free of charge in my school. What a contrast! The private teacher by his insidious maneuvers will have a large number of students to the detriment of the legitimate *instituteur*. [49]

We do not have the minister's reply, but he obviously had to tell the disillusioned young man that nothing could be done.

The anti-royalist Fructidor coup (September 1797) promised renewed initiatives in education, but as the Directory's departmental commissioners candidly assessed the situation, the challenge of forming republicans in the classroom appeared daunting. These emissaries of the central government could only lament the poor quality and dubious republicanism of most *instituteurs publics,* even while deploring the ascendancy of the private schools. Moreover they had to admit that when *instituteurs publics* did try to create a republican atmosphere in their classrooms, the parents might pull their children out.

Unquestionably private teachers dominated the educational marketplace in the years of the Directory both numerically and by the pressure they exerted on the public schools. Out of eleven departments surveyed in one study, private teachers outnumbered *instituteurs publics* in nine; in seven of these, the latter constituted only one quarter of the total. In other departments such as the Sarthe and the Aude, the two types were more or less on a par numerically, but in Lot-et-Garonne, 121 men and 23 women were teaching in the public schools as opposed to 185 men and 76 women in the private sector, while the Breton department of Côtes-du-Nord reported a grand total of only twelve *instituteurs publics,* though "there are few cantons or communes that do not have their [private] teachers." [50]

Competition between the two types of schools unfolded in various ways depending on local circumstances. In certain towns, both types of schools were well established, although the public schools drew a smaller and poorer clientele than the private schools. Occasionally reports speak of brawling among students of the two camps. A petition from Riom (Puy-de-Dôme), for example, complained of "seeing our youngest children divided. . . . We see them attacking each other and fighting all out. . . . These excesses are the work of the despicable teachers salaried by our enemies." This was of course the antithesis of what an *éducation commune* was supposed to encourage, and such petitions concluded with a plea to give the public schools exclusive dominion. [51]

Frequently, however, the two types of schoolteachers were scarcely distinguishable at all. The depleted ranks of *instituteurs publics,* after all, were still filled with former old-regime schoolmasters or ex-priests who could thereby retain the rectories they had formerly inhabited.[52] No wonder, then, that many of the Directory's commissioners deplored the quality of these *instituteurs* no less than the private teachers. "The great majority of the [public] primary schools have merely changed in name," reported the commissioner to Haut-Rhin in 1798. "They are former village schoolmasters who are less educated than superstitious." In the Oise, too, "the primary schools are still what they were in the old regime. The *juris d'instruction* have certified all the former *clercs-laics;* the teacher who is not also a sacristan in the church does not have a single student." Things were no better in the Jura, where "public instruction is absolutely nil. The primary schools are of no value, and offer no success at all. The teachers are either men without talent and enlightenment or ministers of religion attached to their old routines and prejudices." Even if students did attend the public schools, claimed the commissioner to the Vosges, they would find themselves placed between superstition and ignorance, since most of the teachers were ex-priests or old-regime schoolmasters. As a republican newspaper in the Yonne concluded, "enter those schools . . . and you will doubt the existence of the Republic."[53]

The line between public and private teaching was actually quite permeable. When local authorities scrutinized the teachers in their cantons, they sometimes found evidence of religious teaching in public schools and indications of minimal republicanism among certain private teachers. Even the zealous officials in Lot-et-Garonne, who relentlessly denounced anti-republican teachers in their department, conceded that there were *instituteurs privés* "equally learned and republicans." Detailed studies of the Bas-Rhin and of the Vendômois likewise conclude that after Fructidor, both kinds of teachers were caught in a squeeze between republican administrators and religious parents, and that many tried to navigate prudently between them. In effect, "a hybrid system established itself in which there was no real gulf between the two types of schools."[54]

Still, the burden of this competition clearly weighed against the long-term prospects of survival, let alone resurgence, for the official schools. Useful to parents interested in literacy and religion, this kind of one-sided competition held out little hope for the republican agenda of civic education, religious neutrality, and national uniformity. In the Doubs, the Directory's commissioner maintained, "the option accorded to parents to choose private teachers for their children has made the republican schools detested." The departmental administration of the Pas-de-Calais pointed out that in some communes without public schools, "the private school teachers are afraid of losing their pupils and hurting their own interests if they allow themselves to be named as *instituteurs publics,* despite the indemnity [for lodging] that goes along with those posts." In many communities, urban and rural, a commitment to the government's secular and civic objectives put the *instituteur public* at risk: "They are under the obligation to flatter the parents' prejudices" (Ardennes); "in order to obtain students they are reduced to lending themselves to all the fanatical and superstitious ideas of the parents" (Isère); "the more they submit to the government, the less they are followed" (Lot-et-Garonne). [55]

IT IS POSSIBLE that veritable neutrality by the state on religious matters might have made the prospect of *instruction publique* more palatable. As a former nun who ran a private girls school in the Gers explained, she would teach republican morality as long as it was not incompatible with her religious principles. Condorcet, the first to propose a strictly secular orientation for primary schools, had argued for genuine neutrality in the classroom and had presciently warned against introducing natural religion in place of Christianity. [56] But other republicans seemed to feel with Rousseau that general moral principles had to be grounded in a spiritual consciousness. Moreover they believed that if schooling lacked spiritual content, the children would easily fall prey to traditional "fanaticism." Republican morality and civic culture, in other words, had to be sacralized. Instead of reflecting Condorcet's rigorous concept of religious neutrality, the books that republican officials wished to introduce into classrooms promoted a deism with manifestly anti-Catholic overtones.

LaChabeaussière's *Catéchisme français, ou principes de morale républicaine à l'usage des écoles primaires* (Year III) was the most widely disseminated republican textbook. (A playwright before the Revolution and an employee in the Interior Ministry, LaChabeaussière was incarcerated during the Terror for Girondin sympathies; no doubt to ward off demoralization, he wrote his catechism in prison.) The text gained currency in 1794–95 even before it won first prize in a competition for new school manuals launched by the Convention in January 1794 and concluded, after various delays, more than two years later. At that point the government reprinted the pamphlet and it appeared in at least eight editions by 1800.

Along with a dozen or so others published between 1792 and 1797, LaChabeaussière's catechism preached an aggressive deism, equally opposed to atheism and organized Christianity. It recognized the existence of God as creator personified in nature but not acting directly on human society. Positing the immortality of the soul, the republican catechism (in utilitarian fashion) implicitly left its fate dependent on a person's good or evil behavior rather than Christian faith or works. In rhymed quatrains, LaChabeaussière asked such questions as:

—What is the soul?

I know nothing about it; I know that I feel, that I think. . . . That there is in me a being that leaps beyond myself. But I do not know whither I am going, nor whence I come.

—What is God?

I do not know what he is, but I see his work. Everything announces his greatness to my astonished eyes. . . . I believe myself too limited to form an image of him. [57]

Most of these republican catechisms and classroom manuals equated Catholicism with "fanaticism" and linked it with tyranny. Some held up for admiration the trinity of revolutionary martyrs (Marat, Chalier, Lepeletier) or honored the "founders of liberty" such as Brutus and Rousseau. Henriquez's *Epître et évangile du républicain . . . à l'usage des jeunes sans-culottes* (Year II)— winner of third prize in the Convention's competition—enlisted into those ranks a very human Jesus, "the *sans-culotte* of Judea." [58] No wonder that private teachers would not use such materials, and that *instituteurs publics* might find their classrooms deserted if they did.

When departmental administrations compelled their *instituteurs publics* to use republican textbooks exclusively after the anti-royalist Fructidor coup of 1797, many parents balked. "Upon your order," wrote one *instituteur* to the department of Loir-et-Cher, "I inquired of several fathers and mothers of my pupils about changing the books; they all responded, If that's the way it is, we find our children learned enough, and are withdrawing them immediately. . . . Consequently, I give you my resignation." The commissioner to the Cher believed that "the department's decree prohibiting books spawned by Roman [Catholic] mythology in the *écoles primaires* has caused the *instituteurs* everywhere to lose a third of their students." Even in the Seine-Inférieure, which had notable success in establishing public schools, the post-Fructidor push for secularism backfired: "Whether because of crafty sacerdotal advice or the obstinacy of the parents, the primary schools—especially in the countryside—have become almost deserted since the *instituteurs* were required to use the new elementary textbooks and were prohibited from giving the unintelligible lessons of the catechism." According to Masson, an *instituteur* in Armeau (Yonne), "The parents simply do not wish to send their children to the school because of the new books." Where once he had eighty students, he was now down to eleven. [59]

CURBING THE PRIVATE SCHOOLS

Despite this cascade of negative information, the governing republicans after Fructidor were determined to reverse Daunou's policy of benign neglect and to establish the primacy of *instruction publique*. Political discourse resounded with lofty references to "republican institutions," but this meant little more than imposing the revolutionary calendar with its ten-day weeks, and founding or resuscitating public schools.[60] The Ministry of the Interior summarized the challenge: "deprived of all assistance, republican teachers cannot endure the competition of the private teachers who are favored by all the prejudices of superstition."[61] More was at stake here than the desire to bring literacy to the masses, though this was important since the Constitution of 1795 stipulated that citizens could qualify to vote after 1804 only if they could read and write. Beyond that, however, the regime hoped to diminish the influence of religion in the civic order. From that perspective, religious schooling promoted "ignorance" even as it advanced literacy. Though the public schools were nearly as bad at this juncture, if they could be insulated from the rivalry of private teachers and given some material assistance, the government believed that they would gradually improve. Properly supported, public schools could eventually produce citizens who were not only literate but who were free from prejudice and superstition.

It was no doubt tantalizing to contemplate an outright ban on private schools that would eventually oblige parents to accept the offering of public schools. The ex-*conventionnel* Jean Quirot, now commissioner to the Doubs, indulged this fantasy momentarily by musing that "parents should not be left the option of sending their children to private schools." But he knew that this was patently unconstitutional, and quickly added, "at any rate it is necessary to restrict that option."[62] In 1794, Lakanal had advocated local government surveillance of private schools in his proposed law. The thermidorian Convention rejected what it took to be an infringement of liberty, however, and the Daunou Law in turn made no provision for official surveillance of private schools. Now, in the wake of the Fructidor coup, the Directory threw aside all scruples about the freedom pledged to *"écoles libres"* under article 300 of the constitution, arguing that elementary school teaching of any kind was a profession subject to regulation by the state under article 356. The welfare of the nation and of the students demanded that private schools be placed under an umbrella of state supervision alongside public schools, thereby creating "a uniform and truly national education plan."

The Directory repeatedly urged the legislature to pass a law that would create "a system of certification for the position of *instituteurs,* even private ones. It must establish an examination of the *civisme,* morality, and talent of the candidates, and rules to which they are subject. Finally it must stipulate the procedures to be followed for dismissal."[63] A bill to this end, reported out of committee in the Council of Five Hundred by Luminais in January 1798, failed to win approval, and in November Dulaure submitted a new proposal. Though differing in detail, both sought "to hold private schools to such severe regulation that neither teachers nor students can escape from the grip of republican principles." The bills specified procedures by which private teachers must seek public certification; obliged them to take the civic oath professing hatred of royalty and anarchy; required that only officially approved books be used by all teachers; and enjoined private teachers to inculcate republicanism in their classrooms. This package seemed so draconian, however, that lingering scruples over religious liberty kept legislators debating it and postponing any decision.[64]

While waiting for the legislature to act, the Directory took what initiative it could on its own authority. In an important decree of 17 pluviôse VI (5 February 1798), it ordered municipal administrations to pay unannounced monthly visits to private schools in their canton. They were to see whether the teachers used republican texts, especially the constitution; whether they observed the *décadi* as a day of rest (though at that point only public employees were obliged by law to do so); and whether they used the term *citoyen* in the classroom. After visiting the classrooms of private teachers, local authorities could shut wayward schools provisionally and recommend to their departmental administration that they be closed permanently. Six months later, in a new law mandating the *décadi* as a public day of rest for everyone, the legislature required public and private teachers alike not only to close on the fifth and tenth days but to hold classes on all other days, including former Sundays, the *ci-devant Dimanche.* In addition, teachers were to conduct their students to the local *fête décadaire.* At least there, the government presumably believed, *éducation commune* would occur.

Anti-clerical officials eagerly seized this mandate to harass private teachers. In several departments they required teachers (quite illegally) to take the civic oath, which some refused on the grounds of conscience. The new demand that teachers escort their pupils to the republican *fêtes* could be used as an acid test that "unmasked" opponents of the republic and led to the closing of their schools.[65] Private teachers found these demands objectionable, but many tried to accommodate themselves as best they could. The most hostile—the veritable enemies of the republic—would not equivocate. When officials visited their schools, confrontations erupted and forced closings followed. In Tonniens and Agen in the Lot-et-Garonne, for example, municipal authorities shut down the schools of obstinate former nuns who refused to use the text of the constitution in their lessons. When the authorities in St. Leger des Aubées (Eure-et-Loir) visited the school of the priest Raboudin, he did not flinch from admitting that he was teaching the principles of his religion and that he did not have a copy of the constitution. Nor did the teacher in a rural school in the Vosges appease the cantonal inspection team. Instead he denounced them as a *queue de Robespierre,* and declared that his school "had orders from authorities much greater than ours."[66]

Even less belligerent teachers found themselves entangled with unsympathetic officials. Feigning cooperation did not always suffice. The municipal delegation in Aix (Bouches-du-Rhône) believed that displays of the constitution in private school classrooms were for show, "only to save appearances," and the same was true of closing on the *décadi.* It was Sundays and religion that really mattered in such schools. In Vendôme (Loir-et-Cher), one teacher produced a republican catechism but admitted under questioning that he actually taught the Bible instead to satisfy the parents. Another displayed his copy of the constitution, and expressed amazement when officials found that it contained instructions for communion and confession in the back![67]

Naturally this surveillance varied greatly from place to place. While the Directory's departmental commissioners exhorted them repeatedly to act, many cantonal officials sidestepped the prospect of clashing with their constituents and possibly interrupting the education of their children.[68] Moreover, executing a local decree closing a school proved to be extremely difficult if the teacher resisted. To cite but one example, the municipality of St. Jean-des-Baisans (Manche) complained that when it turned to the *tribunal correctionnel* to enforce such decrees in the canton, the commissioner to that court returned the papers, stating that he knew of "no repressive law against that type of offense." The minister of the interior pointed out that the matter was clearly covered by article 243 of the constitution making "rebellion against the execution of either judgments or acts emanating from the constituted authorities" a criminal offense. The department replied that it was perfectly aware of this; "what we still do not know is if there exists a penal law that is applicable. That is the point on which you must enlighten us." The exasperated minister responded only that "this question seems absolutely beside the point to me. . . . Guilty teachers should be brought before the courts. Once that step has been taken, it is up to the judges to apply the law if it exists, or to address themselves to the Minister of Justice."[69] Such vagueness assured that the impasse would continue. Meanwhile, banned teachers without the nerve for outright defiance could resist by going underground: "traveling to the houses under the cloak of neighborliness and friendship," as the commissioner to Seine-Inférieure put it, "and offering clandestine lessons in *incivisme* and superstition."[70]

Local surveillance and selective repression did throw private teachers on the defensive and put hundreds of the most hostile temporarily out of business. But the application and impact of this policy was bound to be extremely uneven. In any case, the regime could not rescue or enthrone *instruction publique* through such negative tactics alone.

IN THE TWILIGHT OF REPUBLICANISM

A consensus seemed to exist among republican moderates and Neo-Jacobins for a new commitment to assure the livelihood of *instituteurs publics.* "We must replace the tuition that students are obliged to pay with a fixed salary," argued the commissioner to Pas-de-Calais. "It is indispensable to assure a salary," agreed his colleagues in the Ardennes, the Ain, the Allier, the Aude, and elsewhere. The logic of this position seemed irrefutable. Only if the job provided an assured subsistence and did not depend on the number of students attending at any given time could it attract worthy candidates. Yet such a course carried risks. Interfering with the free marketplace and guaranteeing the livelihood of *instituteurs publics* could end up subsidizing mediocre or unpopular teachers. But leaving them in their present state of abandon would doom any hope for republican schooling. It would leave the republic powerless to spread literacy where it did not yet exist or to promote its civic agenda among the young everywhere.[71]

The current predicament of the *instituteur public* had become ludicrous. Though he received nothing from the government except lodging or a small but rarely paid indemnity, the teacher was bound to the tuition schedule set by the department. He was thus vulnerable to underbidding by private teachers trying to drive him out of business, yet lacked the freedom of private teachers to charge higher fees to wealthier parents. In addition, he was supposed to accept indigent students who paid no fees at all, and for whom his commune or canton provided no reimbursement. Indeed, according to most contemporary testimony, the public schools served largely as schools for the poor. If not altogether indigent, students' families often dwelt on the border between poverty and indigence. As Dupont, an *instituteur* in the town of St. Omer (Pas-de-Calais), complained, his students nominally payed 15 or 20 sous a month, but after three or four months these "children of the poor" usually changed schools, leaving their fees unpaid.[72] Conversely, most poor students did not actually benefit from the Daunou Law since its vague provision for tuition exemption was unenforceable or, in the absence of any public school, inoperable. "In certain areas only the rich have teachers for their children," concluded the commissioner to Basses-Pyrénées. "Education has become exclusive." From the Neo-Jacobins of the faubourg Saint-Antoine and the citizens in a small bourg of the Nièvre came the same complaint: "By what misfortune has the numerous class of citizens for whom the Revolution was especially made been deprived of an advantage enjoyed by the rich?"[73]

Both the Bouquier and Lakanal laws had made primary education free, with the bill to be paid by the national treasury. Most republicans seeking to break out of the current impasse considered that policy impractically ambitious but by no means the only alternative to pay-as-you-go tuition. If national public financing was no longer possible, how, then, should the costs of schooling be met? To the commissioners in the Côte d'Or and in the Vosges the answer was simple: Schooling should be paid for by the local taxpayers in proportion to their wealth, and should be free to all families. Others thought that all parents of school-aged children should be taxed, whether or not they chose to send their children to the public schools. This kind of school tax would differ from tuition in two ways: *all* parents would share the burden; and their actual rate would vary proportionately to their general tax liability. In one well-publicized proposal, parents would be divided into four categories depending on their wealth and would pay annually 20, 10, 5 livres, or nothing. This approach would create an incentive for parents to send their children to public schools so as to avoid paying twice over for private teachers. Those boycotting the public schools would either be cajoled into them by pecuniary self-interest or would at least become their financial benefactors. And with a communal school tax rather than tuition payments, teachers would not have to worry about collecting the money themselves from evasive parents.[74]

It was now up to an overburdened legislature to convert this widespread demand by government officials for free public education into law.[75] Starting in November 1798, a small group of deputies joined forces to place educational issues at the forefront of the legislative agenda. Each prepared a report on one facet of the problem: primary schools, "reinforced" or advanced primary schools, reform of the *écoles centrales,* institutions to replace the defunct universities, medical education, and the arts. Roger Martin, a former physics professor from Toulouse, coordinated their effort and presented a preliminary overview, urging that these subjects be considered in relation to each other as a kind of logical progression, a single democratic track.[76] But as Condorcet and others had learned in the past, it was difficult to deal with various levels of education in the aggregate. Since primary schooling again seemed so vital to the republican cause, it merited priority attention. As the ex-army officer and former departmental administrator J.-M. Hertault-Lamerville—the reformers' spokesman on primary education—put it: over each public elementary school an inscription should read, *"Ici est la République."*

For the basis on which to establish these schools, Hertault avoided the "geometrical spirit" of the Lakanal Law. He believed that only if schools were spread far and wide in the countryside might parents send their children. Schools should be established in each cantonal seat, "and then in the other communes which, by their size, their population, or their location merit that placement"; whenever feasible, these additional schools "can be established in all the communes that make the request." Teachers would no longer be left entirely to the vagaries of the marketplace: "an assured salary ought to compensate the teachers, and all Frenchmen ought to contribute to that salary." The salaries, to be graduated according to the size of the school district, would consist of (1) "a fixed stipend levied as a proportionate surtax on direct taxes"—paid, that is, by the taxpayers of the communes; and (2) "a small *rétribution* proportionate to wealth," paid in advance by all parents of school-aged boys (or girls, in the case of *institutrices*), whether or not their children enrolled in a public school.

This would encourage all parents to use the public school, and would provide free instruction for the poor without the uncertain and stigmatizing device of the Daunou Law. After the initial discussion of his proposal, Hertault suggested specific levels for this compensation: a lodging indemnity of 100 to 400 francs and a stipend in an equal amount, to be collected from local citizens by a surcharge on their tax assessments; and a *rétribution individuelle* ranging between 25 centimes and 1 franc a month, in four gradations depending on the parents' tax assessment, also collected by the *percepteurs de la commune.* Parents who payed 3 francs or less in taxes would be exempt from this *rétribution* altogether, while parents who did not send their children to the public school would pay the maximum amount as a kind of penalty.[77]

The proposal's apparent complexity actually reflected its flexible practicality. There was of course disagreement over details, such as the range of the stipends or the amount of the *rétribution.* But the bill's proponents faced more than demands for finetuning. Fundamental discord still blocked a legislative consensus. The partisans of demand-driven private schooling *(enseignement libre)*—who opposed any serious undertaking by the state in this domain—kept a low profile in the debate but were amply represented by the influential Antoine Boulay de la Meurthe, a leading critic of the Directory's repressive polices on the revolutionary calendar and the Church. At the same time, the most determined opponents of private education and partisans of *éducation commune* found Hertault's plan insufficiently draconian. (Basing his case on the location of a comma in article 300 of the constitution, for example, Duplantier made the preposterous claim that the constitution did not guarantee *enseignement libre* for elementary schools but only for secondary schools. Hertault replied that Duplantier was simply finding what he wished to find, and that no such interpretation could be supported. "I am astonished," he added unhappily, "to find myself defending the private schools!")[78]

Other deputies believed that the plan did not go far enough in meeting rural needs. "All communes being equal in the eyes of the law," argued Pierre D'André, a specific formula should assure a uniform standard of entitlement "on the combined basis of the population and the distance of the communes"; the placement of schools should not depend simply on the request of the commune or canton. With a touch of ingenuity, D'André suggested that perhaps a public school should be established in every commune that had demonstrated its ability to support a school by employing a private teacher.[79] Other contentious issues included the problem of teaching girls in the absence of qualified *institutrices,* and whether priests or ex-religious personnel should be excluded from public school teaching. Finally, Hertault's proposal that certain urban schools be "reinforced" with a more ambitious curriculum so that they could bridge the current gulf between primary schools and the *écoles centrales* turned certain deputies against the plan. Echoing the Parisian intellectuals of the "idéologue" circle, they attacked this model of a one-track educational system in favor of a more traditional elitist view.[80]

Hertault and Martin responded to their critics, refined their proposals, and kept them before the legislature. Together, they offered a new approach to *instruction publique:* primary schools financed by communal surtaxes and special school fees from all parents able to pay, regardless of whether they used these schools or not; strict surveillance of the private schools, which were expected to conform to the civic guidelines already laid down by the Directory; and annual examinations for all children, regardless of which type of school they attended, supervised by departmental *juris d'instruction.*[81] But time ran out before any compromise between *instruction publique* and private teaching could be achieved.

In the summer of 1799 a military and political crisis touched off by the war of the Second Coalition overwhelmed the legislature. Debates on such matters as education had to be suspended. Before they could resume, the fractious legislature of the Directory regime had disappeared in the Brumaire coup. A passionate republican commitment to free public schools—forged in the ideological zeal of 1793 but tempered in subsequent experience—came to a dead end. The laissez-faire approach of Boulay de la Meurthe, Daunou, and the *idéologue* Ginguené prevailed, and with it the ascendancy of religiously oriented, tuition-based primary schooling. Yet even the Napoleonic regime was not ready to abandon the concept of *instruction publique* altogether. State involvement would continue in some fashion; but to what ends and by what means?

PRIMARY
EDUCATION
RETREAT AND CONSOLIDATION

THE ECLIPSE OF THE PUBLIC SCHOOLS

Bonaparte's coup abruptly terminated the legislative debate on *instruction publique.* Of course Brumaire could have cleared the way for executive action in this area as it did in so many others, but primary education held the lowest of priorities on the First Consul's agenda. Despite interventions by the scientists J.-A. Chaptal and Antoine Fourcroy in the Council of State, Napoleon opted for a minimalist policy that perpetuated the benign neglect of the Daunou Law into the Empire. The regime's education law of 11 floréal X (1 May 1802) focused on secondary education. Scrapping the much-criticized *écoles centrales,* it reconstituted some as state-run residential *lycées* and downgraded others to the status of simple *collèges,* while classifying private secondary schools into comparable categories and establishing surveillance over them. On elementary schooling, the new law brought no change or improvement of any consequence. Leaving the *écoles primaires* entirely to local initiative, it mandated no public salary for teachers. Mayors and municipal councils would designate *instituteurs publics* and set the fee schedule for children who attended their schools, with exemptions possible for up to one fifth of the students on the grounds of indigence. Communes were to house their teacher or pay him a lodging indemnity.[1]

Advocates of this minimalist policy in the legislature completely reversed the assumptions advanced by Hertault-Lamerville, Roger Martin, and their colleagues in 1799. The *idéologue* Destutt de Tracy, reviving an argument from one current of Enlightenment thought, attacked the very concept of universal primary education: schooling was not necessary for everyone and should merely be available to those who wanted it for their children. Where supporters of public education previously talked of compensating for the "penury or avarice" of parents who held their children back from schooling, Napoleon's spokesmen insisted that primary education concerned parents, not society. Indeed, for girls it was to remain strictly a family affair, since the new law made no provision whatsoever for *institutrices publiques*. Jard-Panvillier also dismissed the notion of paying a fixed salary to teachers, which reformers had considered essential in 1799. Not only did fixed salaries for teachers with varying numbers of students violate the principle of equality, he speciously argued, but they discouraged emulation and rewarded laziness.[2]

On the plus side, however, surviving public schools no longer carried the ideological burden of republican secularism. As the *décadi* fell into abeyance, public and private schoolteachers alike could observe Sunday as the day of rest, free from the obligation of bringing their pupils to the *fêtes décadaires*. The stigma of impiety now lifted from the *instituteurs publics,* since the government no longer pressed them to create a secular atmosphere in the classroom. They could use religious texts, serve as sacristans to the clergy, and conform to the "prejudices" of the parents without incurring official harassment. When the signing of the Concordat in 1802 required that all unsold rectories revert to the clergy, on the other hand, the *instituteurs publics* lost the one substantial benefit they sometimes enjoyed. Though the establishment of schools in a "specialized and public place" ostensibly remained a goal of state policy, the loss of the rectories undercut that trend.[3]

An indemnity for lodging thus remained the very last prop of *instruction publique,* and upon that expenditure prefects focused their attention. Yet their range of action remained extremely limited. As we have seen in Chapter IV, communes that did not have adequate communal revenues were not permitted to assess their inhabitants for such expenses. As the prefect of the Meurthe explained to the mayors of his department, "a roll for a proportional surtax cannot be approved and rolls already prepared cannot be executed . . . [because] the law of 9 germinal Year V prohibits the communes from taxing themselves without prior authorization by a law enacted expressly for the purpose."[4] The thousands of rural communes that lacked income from communal property could pay for lodging an *instituteur* only by a voluntary levy, which was unenforceable against recalcitrant residents. Hertault-Lamerville's proposal of 1799 would of course have changed all that, but the issue was now moot. Primary schools depended almost exclusively on tuition fees, and when parents reneged on their *rétribution,* teachers had virtually no recourse. (The government rejected out of hand the notion that school fees be collected by the tax collector subject to the same sanctions. It did not wish to complicate or jeopardize the flow of tax revenue in any way.)

Voluntary contributions no doubt went far in places with well-established traditions of schooling, but were less than ideal. As the subprefect of Tonnerre (Yonne) observed, the subsistence of teachers in his area was assured only by "individual gifts of grain, wine, wood, etc. . . . But those who are obliged to solicit these precarious resources are held in a state of abject dependence prejudicial to the progress of education."[5] Only in communities that had the will and the resources to pay a decent lodging indemnity were teachers likely to retain the title of *instituteur public.* In the Moselle, for example, the prefect reported in December 1803 that 369 out of 931 communes had public schools, while the mayor of Metz estimated that 550 pupils attended the city's public *écoles primaires,* 600 were in private schools, and 600 received no education. In Lot-et-Garonne, on the other hand, only 94 of 425 communes had public schools, and most Breton departments had scarcely any.[6]

Why, we might wonder, did the state bother to retain the concept of *instruction publique* at all when the line separating public from private had lost almost all meaning? One answer was the nominal provision for indigent students in public schools. Another was the expectation that public schools would teach the new decimal and metric systems, though most of the elderly teachers were incapable of doing so. In the correspondence of Fourcroy, counselor of state responsible for education, this was the one note which seemed to give any substance to the concept of *instruction publique.*[7] More fundamentally the Napoleonic state may have clung to the notion of *instruction publique* as the basis for asserting such control over primary education as might seem desirable in the future. This is apparent in the reaction of the prefect of the Jura to an initiative in the town of Poligny. With twenty-one private teachers in the town, the municipal council voted to abolish the two public schools and to invite the private teachers to admit indigent children to their schools, with the town offering to pay each teacher "an indemnity proportional to the number of their indigent students." On the one hand this would have given poor parents more choice in the matter, but on the other private teachers were not obliged to accept their children. In any case the prefect opposed this change. It went against the law of floréal Year X, he claimed unconvincingly, besides which the official *écoles primaires* were subject to more control.[8]

How such control might actually be used remained unclear for the moment, but over the private sector there was assuredly even less. As the prefect of Bouches-du-Rhône informed the mayor of Marseille, "the founding of private educational establishments constitutes a free profession *(profession libre)* subject only to surveillance by local authority but not to its authorization." The problem of maintaining an orderly marketplace persisted. Like many of his colleagues, the prefect of Eure-et-Loir complained to Fourcroy that the "unlimited liberty" enjoyed by the private schools undermined the public schools. Shouldn't local authorities, he asked, "have the right to prevent a competition that could redound to the disadvantage of the primary school established by virtue of the law, taking away its pupils and reducing it to the free instruction which it owes to the children of the indigent class?" Fourcroy naturally agreed; but after consulting with the minister of the interior, he was obliged to respond in the negative. "Since the law did not forbid [this competition], the administration is not authorized to prohibit it."

Acting on the request of municipalities, prefects vainly sought coercive authority against private teachers, only to be reminded that they simply did not have it. In the Calvados, where private teachers were underbidding the *instituteurs publics* whose fees were fixed by the municipalities, the prefect intervened against such practices, but the minister of the interior annulled his decree. The prefect of the Drôme was also powerless to protect the *écoles primaires* from the competition of private teachers, who treated education, he alleged, as "a domain to be exploited . . . and who bring customers to their shop by charging lower fees than the ones established by the municipal councils."[9]

Meanwhile the education of girls had fallen into a limbo. Responding to a request from Fourcroy for information about female teachers and students in his department, the prefect of the Nord understandably responded with "astonishment" because "the law of 11 floréal X makes no mention of primary schools for girls. Accordingly I believed that the government did not wish the administration to exercise surveillance over *institutrices.*" Technically he was correct, for the law of 1802 made no reference whatsoever to *institutrices publiques.* That did not mean, however, that the *écoles primaires* actually excluded girls. Contrary to official insistence on segregating the sexes, girls received instruction in mixed classrooms. In the Aube, for example, the prefect counted 357 public schools in 1808 "where the two sexes gather together," staffed by 358 *instituteurs* and 37 *institutrices.* (With a precision that might make one a bit skeptical, he specified that 13,027 boys and 11,058 girls attended these schools.) Yet this was not necessarily a typical situation, since integrating or segregating the sexes remained endlessly contentious. The prefect of the Oise and the mayor of Marseille, among others, reported that mixed schools were common, but the prefects of Ille-et-Vilaine in Brittany and Hérault in the Midi issued local ordinances requiring single-sex classrooms in both public and private schools.[10]

THE NAPOLEONIC UNIVERSITY

Seemingly indifferent to primary schooling, Napoleon was keenly interested in advanced education for the future engineers and administrators of his Empire. All teachers in secondary and higher education ought to be under state control, he reasoned, in order to promote uniformity, uphold standards, and assure their political loyalty. He wished to incorporate them into "a body exclusively charged with teaching," to be known as the Imperial University—a non-ecclesiastical teaching order encompassing both public and private institutions. After prolonged discussion in the Council of State, the legislature endorsed the concept in 1806, and the executive implemented it in an imperial decree of March 1808. A Grand Master headed this new educational bureaucracy that would monitor all teaching personnel, with the country divided into twenty-six educational districts or *"académies,"* each with a rector, an advisory council, and a staff of field inspectors. Here at last was the central authority that certain revolutionary legislators had advocated since the Talleyrand report of 1791.[11]

Elementary education came under the University's umbrella almost by default or through the back door. With the exception of the small and highly regarded Christian Brothers teaching order, primary school teachers were not members of the University, part of its official personnel. Accordingly they gained no material benefits, status, or security, though neither did they have to pay for their diplomas, take an oath, or turn over the annual per-student fees that teachers in the superior branches owed to the University. On paper, at least, private and public primary schools did come under the surveillance of the rectors and their inspectors. All elementary teachers were supposed to register with the University and obtain a provisional diploma; in the absence of such authorization, their schools were illegal and could be closed down.[12]

Since no national standard for examining these teachers existed as yet, and since expectations were so low to begin with, University authorities generally refused this diploma only on the grounds of immorality and offensive behavior.[13] The vast majority of public and private *instituteurs* already in place received their provisional diplomas if they bothered to apply for them at all. At the same time, elementary schools were now explicitly limited to teaching the 3Rs; if their curriculum went any further, they were to be classified as lower secondary schools, subject to the more rigorous certification procedures and fee payments for such institutions.

The University formalized common practice since the Concordat by enjoining public and private elementary schools to teach "the precepts of the

Catholic religion." Though Protestant schools were tacitly excused from this requirement, the wording had been carefully chosen—instead of the more neutral "precepts of the Christian religion"—to mark an explicit alliance between the state and the Catholic Church. With the Catholic traditionalist Fontanes appointed as the first Grand Master, instead of the pliant but less committed Fourcroy, the University quickly cemented this alliance. Prefects were relieved altogether of responsibility for monitoring *instruction publique,* while the bishops were asked to collect information on all teachers from the curés in their dioceses and pass it along to the University's rectors. As the Grand Master pointed out to the bishops, his inspectors could not personally monitor thousands of rural schoolteachers.

In 1811, when Napoleon fell out with the Pope, his minister of the interior insisted that prefects should recover the right of surveillance over primary schools. This left University officials, bishops, and prefects in an uncertain jurisdictional tangle, but it was actually of little consequence. Virtually all primary education now had a religious coloration; the material and professional condition of teachers remained as precarious as ever; and the recruitment of teachers continued to be localized and haphazard. (The law of 1802 had mandated a normal or teacher-training school in each department. But the only one actually functioning was in Strasbourg, with its acute need for French-speaking teachers.) As the historian Maurice Gontard concludes, primary education had reverted almost completely to its condition under the old regime.

Still, the state remained a player in the game as it had not been before 1792, and it now had a specialized educational inspectorate in place for the first time. The University's action at ground level seems most apparent when its officials closed unauthorized schools or barred objectionable teachers. To be sure, they rarely used this power since primary education held the lowest priority and the University's inspectors expected so little from the benighted *instituteurs.* But the University bureaucracy did occasionally bestir itself when goaded by appeals from mayors, curés, subprefects, embattled parents, or rival teachers. Moreover, the University now stood between communities and their *instituteurs publics.* After 1808, municipal councils could only propose candidates for the rector's approval; more important, they lost the power to dismiss an unsatisfactory teacher, and now had to request an inquiry by the University and a formal order from the Grand Master. Between April 1812 and April 1813, the university issued at least forty *ordonnances de clôture* (see Figure VII-I), while its inspectors uncovered and closed another fifty or so clandestine schools, mostly in the vicinity of Paris.[14]

Fornication, debauching the women of the community, gross negligence of duty, "indecency and drunkenness" were the most common charges

UNIVERSITÉ IMPÉRIALE.

ORDONNANCE
Pour la clôture d'une
école non autorisée,

Au nom de NAPOLÉON, Empereur des Français, Roi d'Italie, Protecteur de la Confédération du Rhin, etc.;

En vertu des articles 54 et suivans du décret impérial du 15 novembre 1811,

Nous Sénateur, Grand-Maître de l'Université impériale,

Vu le rapport *de M. le Recteur de l'acad.ᵉ de Nismes,* sur l'école tenue par le sieur *Roux (Boseph Saintin Donatien) Instituteur* *à Carpentras* canton de _____ département de *Vaucluse* académie de *Nismes*

Avons ordonné et ordonnons qu'attendu le défaut d'autorisation de notre part, l'école indûment tenue par le sieur *Roux* soit et demeure fermée.

Expédition en forme de la présente Ordonnance sera sur-le-champ transmise à M. le Procureur impérial près le tribunal du domicile du sieur *Roux*, pour qu'il la fasse exécuter dans les vingt-quatre heures, à sa diligence, conformément à l'article 58 dudit décret.

M. le Recteur de l'académie de *Nismes* est chargé de l'exécution des présentes.

Donné à Paris, au chef-lieu et sous le sceau de l'Université impériale, le *24 Novembre* 1812

LE GRAND MAÎTRE,
Signé Fontanes

LE CHANCELIER,
Signé Villaret

Par son Excellence le Grand-Maître,
Le Conseiller Secrétaire-général,
Signé Arnault.

Pour Expédition conforme:
Le Conseiller-Secretaire-Général

Figure VII-1: *Official Form for the Closing of an Unauthorized Primary School, 1812*

against teachers whom the University barred from the classroom.[15] The curé sometimes instigated these proceedings, but village notables and parents did not always accept his opinion. A teacher named Landrin, for example, explained that he had previously lost a post upon the intervention of a curé who was later transferred, "to the general elation of the inhabitants," while those same citizens drafted a petition with 147 signatures in support of Landrin.[16]

On rare occasions, priest and mayor clashed. In Villeneuve (Charente-Inférieure), for example, the curé denounced a teacher named Marcou for immorality and misconduct. The subprefect duly informed the rector of the academy, who temporarily suspended Marcou. But the citizens of the commune led by the mayor petitioned to retain this "well-liked and esteemed" teacher. When the academy's inspector looked into it, he concluded that most parents found Marcou's "rusticity and grossness" agreeable. The *instituteur* had indeed been guilty of serious misconduct when he introduced some obscene material into a class. But the priest who denounced him was unpopular, disliked especially for his "inflexible rigor," while "an almost general groundswell of public opinion" supported the teacher. The inspector recommended that suspension not be followed by permanent dismissal.[17]

Rivalries between *instituteurs* in small communities also found their way into the University's purview. When newcomers attempted to establish themselves, the University had the right to decide whether a community could support a new teacher, and if not, who should be favored. The challenger was generally younger, more energetic, and better educated than the current *instituteur*. In Montlieu (Charente-Inférieure), for example, the rector of the regional academy had authorized a certain Dutreuil to open a second school in the bourg. This provoked a protest from the long-established *instituteur*, who claimed that he was being ruined. The subprefect confirmed that Montlieu could not adequately support two teachers, and the rector therefore proposed that Dutreuil relocate to one of three possible alternative communes in the region. It was now Dutreuil's turn to protest, "no doubt finding it to his advantage not to leave Montlieu where he already has a good number of students, to the detriment of his colleague." The mayor and the curé both supported the new teacher, attesting that Dutreuil "has more talent than the old *instituteur*, and . . . his handwriting is better." But the rector maintained the incumbent's monopoly in words that reveal how little the University thought of primary education: "it is only a question here of a country school that can be run by a person who simply knows how to read, write and count"; he would not destroy the incumbent's position "just because another teacher has a little more talent."[18]

Under Fontanes, the University tried to enforce the segregation of the sexes. Even if girls' schools were outside his jurisdiction, the Grand Master made it clear that the mixing of boys and girls in any classroom "is an abuse that cannot be tolerated." By the same token women were not authorized to teach boys. True, in isolated and impoverished rural areas, such as those served by the academies of Nîmes and Limoges, women were sometimes the only available teachers and were informally tolerated. But where they could, University officials opposed the practice.[19] Their official obsession with the role of women mirrored the campaign against informal female medical practitioners. It certainly went against more flexible local attitudes. School-masters with wives who could also teach now found it more difficult to maximize their effectiveness by arranging their duties flexibly. And entre-preneurial widows were hindered from establishing profitable classes for boys, even in conjunction with male teachers.

Such was the case of Madame Juin, who ran a cheerful, well-appointed school for nineteen girls and thirty-one boys (including her son) in Paris. When first confronted by the University inspector, she agreed to remove the boys' section of her school to a separate building and to hire a new teacher in place of the *répetiteur* who had previously worked with the boys and who she admitted "was not capable of directing a school for boys all by himself." But she did not receive authorization to run a boys' school under any circumstances and was forced to close it a few weeks later. To make this perfectly clear, officials personally escorted the boys from their new class-room and locked the door behind them.[20]

Bringing order to the educational marketplace and promoting more ef-fective schools were not always compatible aims. The Napoleonic University may have wished to do both, but was not really mandated or equipped to accomplish either. Thanks to the emperor's lack of concern, the state intro-duced no incentives to make primary school teaching an attractive vocation. It made no effort to overcome the "penury or avarice" of grudging parents, or to bring schooling to areas historically deficient. Local demand remained the dominant factor in primary schooling. On the positive side, however, the Napoleonic regime liquidated the anti-Catholicism that had compromised the republic's commitment to public schooling, and it passed on to the Restoration a new educational bureaucracy with a potential to promote higher standards of performance. Thus, in minimal fashion, did the notion of *instruction publique* survive a regime thoroughly uninterested in its potential.

EDUCATION AND RELIGION UNDER THE RESTORATION

Far more than Napoleon, the architects of the Bourbon Restoration shared the revolutionaries' belief in universal popular education. "The day that the Charter was granted," declared Royer-Collard, the chief educational policy-maker in 1815, "universal instruction was promised because it was neces-sary." While unapologetically advocating a two-track educational system, such men rejected the contention that the common people might not require schooling. Their rationale for popular education blended religious tradition-alism and political conservatism with social utilitarianism. Primary schooling "has as its essential object the knowledge of our duties toward God, toward *la Patrie,* the King, our parents, and our fellow men," according to Auguste Rendu, a leading functionary in the education bureaucracy, whose devout Catholicism meshed comfortably with unstinting efforts in behalf of primary education. [21]

But how should such schooling be promoted? The Restoration brought a moment of genuine choice in this matter. The regime could easily have succumbed to clerical pressure for direct control of education, to the claim that primary schooling belonged to the Church's pastoral function. An extreme animus against the centralized Napoleonic University would have made this claim all the more popular among conservatives. As they offered their opinions to Paris at the annual meetings of the general councils of the departments, many *notables* attacked state regulation of secondary education and its compulsory fees to the University as an "odious tax" that financed "a costly general staff in Paris." Royalist *notables* would have been delighted to see the end of this expensive, tyrannical institution, which had been charged with overseeing primary schools as well. [22] Several departmental councils espoused a reactionary fantasy on primary education. Stigmatizing most current schoolmasters as "speculators" and "mercenaries," they hoped that schools could be placed in the hands of religious congregations. The council of the Cher wanted only teachers motivated by "a solid piety, stran-gers to the advantages of fortune, the prestige of ambition, and the vanities of erudition." "Only the celibate state is generally appropriate . . . for *instituteurs,*" declared the council of the Finistère. At the least these councils wanted even more religion in the classroom: "in order to be moral," asserted the council of the Vaucluse, "education must be religious." [23]

On this last point, Rendu, Royer-Collard, and other Restoration officials completely agreed. While unwilling to abolish the University or to turn over primary education exclusively to the bishops, they worked for thoroughly

Catholic *instruction publique,* controlled and supervised by an alliance of Church and State. The landmark ordinance of 29 February 1816 established the basis for this collaboration, while creating new mechanisms to stimulate and oversee primary schooling. Officially, at least, the benign neglect of the Empire came to an end. Not since the Lakanal Law of 1794 had public policy toward primary education turned so positive. Yet an array of structural problems remained, compounded by weaknesses in the new arrangements.

The royal ordinance reinforced the power of the University over the accreditation of teachers. All current and prospective primary schoolteachers were required to come before a University inspector or his agent, usually the principal of the nearest *collège.* After presenting good-conduct certificates signed by their curé and mayor, candidates were examined for a license or *brevet de capacité.* For minimal competence in the 3Rs they received a third-degree certificate (see Figure VII-2); mastery of spelling and arithmetic as well earned a second-degree *brevet;* the exceedingly rare individual who demonstrated proficiency in such things as grammar and geometry could claim a first-degree certificate. Besides licensing individuals to teach, the University alone could authorize teachers to open a school. Only upon approval of the regional rector could an elementary school of any kind operate lawfully. Likewise revocation of a *brevet* or an authorization became the exclusive prerogative of the University bureaucracy.

Between the University and the teacher, however, the ordinance of 1816 interposed both the clergy and the local *notables.* The curé and the mayor, designated as "special surveillants" of schoolmasters in their commune, could not only block an individual's chance to teach by withholding a good-conduct certificate, but they were the only people in a position to exercise direct and constant scrutiny over what went on in the classroom. In effect, then, they shared with the municipal councils the power to nominate *instituteurs publics,* leaving the latter responsibility for financial arrangements with the teachers. Lest the system be entirely at the mercy of local interests and personalities, however, the ordinance created a new body, somewhat reminiscent of the *juris d'instruction* of the Year III but actually modeled on the Dutch system, which University inspector Georges Cuvier had extolled in a widely discussed report to his superiors in 1812.

In each canton, an unsalaried school committee would "oversee and encourage primary education." The senior priest in the canton and the justice of the peace were statutory members of these committees, with the former automatically serving as chairman. In addition, the rector was to nominate three or four local *notables,* upon recommendation of the subprefect. (In the Academy of Besançon, the cantonal committees comprised "a large number of ecclesiastics, former chevaliers de Saint Louis, and proprietors known for

Académie de Toulouse.

INSTRUCTION PRIMAIRE.

BREVET DE CAPACITÉ
Pour l'Enseignement primaire.

Troisième Degré.

NOUS RECTEUR de l'Académie de Toulouse, Chevalier de l'Ordre Royal et Militaire de St.-Louis, Sur le rapport qui nous a été fait par M.

chargé de l'examen des individus qui se destinent à l'Enseignement primaire, portant que le Sieur

né à

le   a été examiné sur la Lecture, l'Écriture, le Calcul, ainsi que sur les procédés de leur Enseignement,

Et qu'il a fait preuve de la capacité requise pour exercer les fonctions d'Instituteur primaire du troisième degré.

Après nous être assurés qu'il possède une connoissance suffisante des Préceptes et des Dogmes de la Religion ; Vu les Certificats de bonnes vie et mœurs produits par ledit Sieur

lui avons accordé le présent Brevet qui lui est nécessaire pour pouvoir être appelé auxdites fonctions, aux termes de l'article 11 de l'Ordonnance du Roi, du 29 février 1816.

Délivré à Toulouse, le

Le Recteur,

Par M. le Recteur :

Le Secrétaire Général de l'Académie,

FIGURE VII-2: *Official Form for a Third-class Teaching License, 1816*

their attachment to the King," according to the rector.) [24] These cantonal committees were to mediate between a distant University bureaucracy and the curés and mayors at ground level, settling disputes among them, lobbying in the communes for support of schooling, monitoring the progress being made and reporting on obstacles to that progress. Specifically, the committees formally presented to the rectors requests for authorization to open schools (see Figure VII-3).

During the ascendancy of the Ultra-royalists in the 1820s, however, the balance between Church and State tilted completely in favor of the clergy. Symbolically, abbé Frayssinous, Grand Master of the University since 1822, was appointed in 1824 as head of a new Ministry of Religious Affairs and Public Instruction, which all but swallowed up the University. A new ordinance on primary education in that year left certification of pedagogical capacity to the University but effectively placed surveillance, authorization to open schools, and revocations in the hands of the bishops. The impact of this shift was even more dramatic in secondary education, but in both cases this interlude proved to be short-lived. In 1828 the government restored the system of 1816, except that it replaced the multitude of cantonal committees with new *comités d'arrondissement,* only three to six per department. [25]

It is readily apparent that this cumbersome set of arrangements depended on the dedication, goodwill, and energy of tens of thousands of individuals, most of whom had little interest and less expertise in primary education. In this intricate web of jurisdictions, curé, bishop, mayor, municipal council, cantonal or arrondissement committee, University inspector, and rector each had responsibility without ultimate power. None could take the initiative to open a school in a particular place and see it through to fruition on their own, and only the commune could produce financial support for the *instituteurs.* The ordinance of 1816 enjoined every commune to assure "that the children who live there receive primary instruction and that indigent children receive it free of charge." But the communes received no new entitlements or powers to tax their citizens that would enable them to discharge this obligation. Nor were there any sanctions against communes that did not.

Each element of the system could frustrate the other, and no one was strictly accountable to anyone else. The rectors could do nothing about curés who refused to report on what was going on in their commune or about cantonal committees that did not bother to meet or to correspond with the University. Though they seemed to have considerable influence over the schools in their communes, curés resented procedures that diluted their traditional power to dominate and browbeat country schoolmasters, many of whom still depended on ancillary income from serving as choristers and sacristans for the local church. By the same token certain mayors zealously

ACADÉMIE
de
TOULOUSE.

INSTRUCTION
PRIMAIRE.

Département
de

Arrondissement
de

Canton
de

COMMUNE
de

N. B. **Aucun Instituteur ne pourra faire usage de la présente autorisation avant de l'avoir fait agréer par le Préfet de son Département.**

AUTORISATION SPÉCIALE

POUR ENSEIGNER DANS UN LIEU DÉTERMINÉ,

Conformément à l'article 13 de l'Ordonnance du Roi, du 29 Février 1816.

NOUS MARIE-JOSEPH-LOUIS DE FERRAND-PUGINIER, Chevalier de l'Ordre Royal et Militaire de St.-Louis, Recteur de l'Académie de Toulouse ;

Vu l'article 13 de l'Ordonnance du Roi, du 29 Février 1816 ;

Vu les articles 20, 21, 22, 23 et 24 de ladite Ordonnance ;

Vu le Brevet de capacité du degré, accordé au Sieur le sous le N.°

Vu la demande faite par le Comité Cantonnal de Arrondissement de Département de

Vu les preuves données par ledit Sieur au Comité Cantonnal, de sa bonne conduite depuis qu'il a obtenu ledit Brevet de capacité ;

Autorisons ledit Sieur à exercer les fonctions d'Instituteur primaire du degré, dans la Commune de à la charge par lui de se conformer aux dispositions de l'Ordonnance Royale précitée.

Délivré à Toulouse, le

LE RECTEUR,

Par M. le Recteur:

Le Secrétaire général de l'Académie,

FIGURE VII-3 *Official Form for Permission to Open a School, 1816*

defended their prerogative when the schoolmaster also served as secretary at the *mairie.*

After an initial flush of enthusiasm, most rectors grew disastisfied with the cantonal committees. The curé chairmen often failed to convene their committees, either out of indifference to their responsibilities or an avidity to monopolize their functions. "Here the committees do not meet because the curé wishes to run everything by himself; there the curés resign because the committees oppose them," complained the rectors in Limoges and in Angers. In any case, the committees had no material means of actually establishing schools: "they see themselves as having only the right to identify abuses, without having the faculty to introduce a remedy." Lay committee members did not win much praise either. Many *notables* did not live in the cantonal seat, and could not be bothered attending meetings which brought them no remuneration or honor but only a steady diet of petty squabbles and frustrations.[26]

Several rectors, particularly in Western France, suspected that a disdain for the idea of popular education itself—condescension about educating the common people—helped explain the lethargy of certain cantonal committees. "Rich proprietors, even administrators are not afraid to state that it is more dangerous than useful to propagate instruction; that we owe a large part of the misfortunes of the Revolution to [popular education], and that peasants who know how to read and write soon abandon the cultivation of the fields in order to follow an occupation that is less useful to society."[27] Such sentiments, however, were no longer respectable in Parisian corridors of power, in the press, or among officials of the University.

Meanwhile, even if some of the most marginal teachers still evaded the required procedures and continued to operate clandestinely, the great majority of *instituteurs* eventually presented themselves to the University's officials. The government reported at the end of 1817 that between fifty to two hundred teachers in each of the University's twenty-six academies or districts had been denied *brevets.* In most cases they were barred from teaching not because of "manifest incapacity," but for their "anti-religious and antisocial principles" (Cahors); "for entirely lacking the required religious, moral, and monarchical principles" (Rouen).[28] Though some rectors claimed to be indulgent in this matter, their agents at the least insisted on repentance and promises of good behavior. "I have accepted the professions of repentance of some obscure and unfortunate *instituteurs,* who merited reproach for their opinions or rather for their political liaisons during the upheavals of the Revolution," reported the rector of Limoges. In the Academy of Rouen, "a considerable number of *instituteurs* seem to have been rejected by the cantonal committees because of their previous conduct," but some were permitted to return under a provisional authorization until they could demonstrate that their "conversion" was genuine.[29]

These parish-pump Voltaires or Jacobins, whose Catholicism seemed wanting or who had identified with the Revolution, remain a mystery. Were they immoral, disruptive, and useless, as their critics imply, or were they dedicated and effective teachers? We simply do not know. In either case the Restoration either barred such revolutionary *instituteurs* (if we might loosely call them that) or coerced them into repenting their past behavior. The rector at Aix believed that after this purge not a single *instituteur* teaching in the precincts of his academy "is dangerous because of his principles, conduct, or opinions," while in the Montpellier Academy "virtually the entirety of the *instituteurs*" demonstrated their religious and monarchical sentiments. For the rector in Grenoble, the purge was "the most tangible benefit produced by the new order."[30]

The competence of the licensed teachers, on the other hand, remained manifestly deficient. Since the Empire had done nothing to train new teachers, the ranks were still filled with the barely literate schoolmasters practicing the old regime's method of individual recitation. The proportion of teachers who earned respectable first- or second-degree *brevets* in the initial rounds of certification ranged from a dismal low of 5 percent in the Academy of Limoges (13 out of 265 candidates) and 7 percent in Strasbourg (52 out of 714—doubtless so low because many German-speakers could not use French), to 10 percent in Cahors (49 out of 540), 16 percent in Amiens (380 out of 2,378), 20 percent in Besançon (196 out of 974), an estimated one quarter in the Paris Academy, and a commendable one third in the Rouen Academy.

Examiners practically gave away third-degree *brevets* out of pity or sheer necessity, after the most perfunctory scrutiny. The situation in the Besançon Academy was probably typical: more than half the teachers given third-degree *brevets* were "old men, complete strangers to any concept of method and incapable of acquiring new notions."[31] But everyone hoped that the enhanced status of a second-degree *brevet* would prompt at least some teachers to upgrade their skills and strive for the more prestigious certificate. As the years went by, rectors discouraged the granting of new third-degree *brevets,* and the proportion of second-degree certifications increased. The Guizot inquiry of 1831 indicated that in departments such as Haute-Marne and Côte d'Or, the proportion exceeded 40 percent. After 1818, the government tried to entice young men into this career by offering exemptions from military service to any licensed *instituteur* who contracted to teach for at least ten years. Then in 1828 it finally pushed to open normal schools. Five years later forty-seven had been established, making it easier for Guizot to insist in 1833 that every department maintain one.[32]

Regardless of their qualifications, the schoolmasters of the Restoration carried out the religious mission of *instruction publique.* The public schools functioned as nurseries of Catholicism and monarchism just as they had once been called on to propagate republicanism. The rectors (many clerics themselves) issued regulations for their primary schools that could not have differed much if they had been written by the bishops. Classes began and ended with appropriate prayers, and Saturday was devoted to practice in catechism lessons for the following day. The *instituteurs* were enjoined to accompany their pupils to catechism on Sunday, and then to mass and vespers, just as they had been expected to lead their students to the *fête décadaire* in 1798. Teachers were also to ensure that their pupils went to confession; to inculcate respect for divine as well as civil authority; and to promote "the exact observance of God's commandments and the Church's." The rector of Montpellier believed that "religious instruction is attended to even in the worst schools," and that most teachers required a *billet de confession* from their students.[33] The religious liberty of Protestants in Alsace and elsewhere, however, was protected by their participation in a dual system. Substantial Protestant communities had their own cantonal committees and their own confessional schools, which were usually off-limits to Catholic children.[34] Only principled non-believers might be offended by the Restoration's concept of *instruction publique.*

A New Pedagogy?

Ironically, while *instruction publique* under the Bourbons served the Catholic religion, the Restoration opened the door to a new method of teaching which challenged tradition and appealed to liberals. When Napoleon's fall permitted free communication with Britain, Frenchmen learned of a pedagogical innovation across the Channel called the Lancastrian or monitorial method. Officials and philanthropists interested in popular education quickly seized on it almost as a panacea. Like other voguish but flawed behavioral doctrines, Lancastrian pedagogy now seems a curious practice. Its appeal obviously lay in the alternative it offered to a much-despised traditional pedagogy, and to the prospect it held out of educating large numbers of children (at least in the towns) without depending on the current stock of incompetent schoolmasters. It must have seemed the counterpart in education to the mechanized factory system in textile manufacturing—the solution to a set of bottlenecks that held back productivity. Indeed, the greater puzzle is how the traditional "individual method" held sway for so long unchallenged.

The Anglican Dr. Andrew Bell and the Quaker Joseph Lancaster had independently pioneered the new method in the 1790s, and the rivalry of their supporters spread their doctrines more widely than either might have achieved on his own. In the monitorial system, which the French called the *mutual method*, one teacher supervised the education of up to two hundred children in one large classroom. By dividing the students into several groups based on their level of skill, the children in each group could be taught simultaneously at an accelerated pace. How could one teacher accomplish this? In fact he could not. Identifying the best students at each skill level, he selected assistants or "monitors" to lead the groups.

The teacher's most important contribution came before the school day officially began, when he tutored and examined the monitors and explained the lessons they were to follow. "The instruction of children by themselves, there is the principle of our method," wrote a French proponent. Unlike the individual method, the monitorial method also integrated the study of reading and writing. Carefully planning the pace of each group and synchronizing their recitations, the teacher in effect became the foreman of a factory. Equally important, the mutual method embodied the principle of emulation. Advancement for each student within the system would be evident and objective, whether in passing up to a higher group or in the honor of being chosen as a monitor, which might bring a small monetary recompense as well. Here was an element of motivation entirely lacking in the individual method. [35]

No wonder that influential French liberals who visited such schools or read about them in 1814–15 became enthusiastic missionaries for the mutual method on both financial and pedagogical grounds. One well-trained and well-supported teacher, they believed, could do more good in a town than a dozen traditional *instituteurs* employing the individual method. Taking advantage of the Restoration's encouragement for private philanthropic associations, they formed the Society for Elementary Instruction. Under the leadership of such men as Baron Gérando—a Napoleonic counselor of state and a noted philanthropist—the society enrolled over five hundred subscribers by the end of 1815, having lived down the official patronage of Carnot during the Hundred Days. The society campaigned to win over Restoration *notables* to the new pedagogy; raised money for demonstration projects or "normal courses" to train teachers in the new method; and acquired buildings for the new schools. With a classroom secured and an energetic teacher engaged, the results would speak for themselves. The society also encouraged the formation of local affiliates in the provinces (forty-two existed by the end of 1818);

sponsored a periodical, the *Journal d'éducation;* published manuals for teachers such as Noyon's concise *Manuel pratique ou précis de la méthode d'enseignement mutuel;* produced textbooks for the classroom; and encouraged the use of slates and arithmetic charts.

Interior Minister L'Ainé and most University rectors saw the mutual method as a great hope for the future, but they could do little to assure its fortunes: "In this too the rectors lack money and authority," complained the head of the Grenoble Academy. Most Restoration prefects were enthusiastic about the new method as well, but they too had a limited field of action. At most they could serve as advocates, offer moral support, and perhaps secure funds for a demonstration project. Given the decentralization of authority and financial resources in primary education, local *notables* and municipal councils would determine the future of mutual schooling. At their annual meetings in 1816 several general councils of the departments expressed interest in the new-fangled pedagogy. The council of Lot-et-Garonne asked the local learned society to investigate Lancastrian methods, while the Ardennes council voted a 3,000F subsidy for a demonstration school in Sedan, on the understanding that the town would take up the expense after the first year. At the same time, the *notables* showed even greater enthusiasm for encouraging the Christian Brothers to establish schools in their areas.[36]

The highly esteemed Christian Brothers teaching order had been deeply implanted in urban France on the eve of the Revolution, with 800 brothers in 116 houses. Their disciplined, tuition-free schools, generally staffed by three brothers, were unique in dividing the children into distinct classes and teaching them by the "simultaneous method." Suppressed in 1792, the order was allowed back by Napoleon on a limited basis with a special status in the University that protected its autonomy. The Empire was not especially enthusiastic about this or any other autonomous Catholic order, however, and kept it on a short leash. The Restoration changed the situation overnight. A clamor went up from towns across France for the services of the Frères. The number of houses tripled between 1815 and 1822, from 58 (with 310 brothers) to 168 (with 730 brothers). By 1830 the order had over 1,400 members operating about 380 schools.[37]

L'Ainé and his prefects initially hoped that the Frères would simply adopt the mutual method. Not only might this enhance their own teaching, but their approval would make the mutual method more acceptable to conservative opinion. A few departmental and arrondissement councils entertained the same hopes in 1816. The *conseil d'arrondissement* in Bordeaux, for example, asked the department for a subsidy "to send one of its Christian Brothers to Paris for instruction in the so-called Lancastrian method."[38] In fact this proposition would soon appear ludicrous. For the Christian brothers had no intention of altering their time-tested methods. Nor were clashing pedagogical claims—that the Frères' method was not fast enough, or that the monitorial method was rigid and superficial—the heart of the issue. The two camps were rivals in a conflict that was pedagogical in form but political in substance.[39]

Proponents of the mutual method understood quickly enough that a peaceful accord between the two movements was impossible. Instead, they tried to promote a healthy competition that would accelerate the spread of popular education. "We must maintain emulation by favoring both methods without distinction," declared the prefect of Ille-et-Vilaine. Municipal councils in Lille, Amiens, and Montpellier voted subventions for both types of schools, and about thirty departmental general councils expressed some support for the mutual method although twice as many endorsed the Frères. By 1821, however, support for mutual schooling had completely evaporated and the view of the council in Loire-Inférieure became typical: "instead of those Lancastrian schools that one is seeking to introduce into France by every means . . . we can reestablish the primary education that our children receive from the Christian Brothers."[40]

Why the ultimate rejection of mutual schooling? After all, the Society for Elementary Instruction was by no means secular in orientation. Its Protestant and Catholic members agreed that mutual schools must promote religion. The school day would open and close with prayers and teachers would lead their students to Sunday services; in Catholic schools the catechism would be taught. But to Catholic traditionalists this was mere window dressing. The clergy did not control the recruitment of teachers or oversee what went on in mutual schools, where religious instruction seemed purely rote, nothing more than an exercise in reading that did not adequately inculcate the nexus of Catholic religious and moral values. Conservatives soon stigmatized mutual schools as liberal institutions with an insufficiently religious atmosphere whose independence from clerical authority was suspect. As one deputy to the Chamber alleged: "there is not an enemy of religion and of the monarchy who is not a friend of mutual education."[41] By 1819 the great majority of departmental general councils had turned against the mutual method and adamantly refused any subsidies or other encouragements despite lingering appeals from prefects.[42] At the grass roots, clerics lobbied municipal councils to withold subsidies, delayed formal authorizations to open schools, and tried to turn parents against the schools. Some resorted to outright harassment, like the curé in Liancourt (Oise) who would not admit the students of the local mutual school to their first communion.[43]

For conservative *notables* and clerics, the Christian Brothers formed the best antidote to mutual schooling in urban France, although the demand for the order's services far outran its manpower. Not only were their schools impeccably religious and their teachers well trained and dedicated, but the classes were tuition-free. Though ostensibly a charitable foundation ministering to the urban poor, the order's schools therefore appealed to wealthier families as well. In Amiens, the rector reported, two Christian Brothers' schools offered free instruction to 320 students in the town, "but their choice does not always fall on the indigent." The same was true in Montpellier, where the rector wished that "the local authority did not grant rich or comfortable families the favor of admitting their children to those schools until they have taken in the poor children. Otherwise a great number of the latter are deprived of education or reduced to seeking in tuition-paying schools the attentions that are due them gratis from the Frères."[44]

This apparent derogation from the Christian Brothers' mission to the needy, however, did not seem to trouble the conservative *notables* whose opinion counted in Restoration society. Conversely, while the original mutual schools, backed by philanthropic contributions and local subventions, had been largely tuition-free, the schools formed as the movement spread were obliged to charge tuition. In part for this reason, in approximately seventy towns where the Frères competed directly with mutual schools, they invariably did better. In Marseille, for example, the six mutual schools had only 370 students while seven Christian Brothers schools enrolled over 1,400 children.[45]

The spread of mutual schools proved spectacular but ephemeral. Between 1818 and the end of 1821, the number of schools jumped from 369 to over 1,500. The biggest gains came in the North and East, in such departments as the Seine, the Oise, the Somme, the Pas-de-Calais, and the Haut-Rhin; but the movement also extended to such departments as the Dordogne, Gironde, Gard, and Hérault. Before long, however, the "deaf and violent" hostility of conservative *notables* and clergy took its toll. Public and private patronage of mutual schools dried up, parents conformed and turned their backs on the schools, and teachers resigned. As the historian of mutual schooling, Raymond Tronchot, puts it, at meetings of the society after 1822, members read no more "victory bulletins" from the rostrum. Tronchot believes that by 1824 only 257 mutual schools survived the onslaught, including 42 in the department of the Seine. "The number of mutual schools is diminishing every year," reported the rector of the Montpellier Academy as early as 1822. "The large schools in Montpellier and Rodez are about to be closed for want of subsidies." In 1828, Baron Gérando sadly observed that "in the department of the Haut-Rhin, where the mutual methods were perfected and widely adopted, the schools have disappeared and the association which presided over them has dissolved itself."[46]

Despite this rout of mutual schooling, the few years of rivalry between Lancastrians and Christian Brothers eroded official tolerance for the individual method of teaching. Although differing in organization and pedagogical style, each camp used a variant of the simultaneous recitation method, and each taught reading and writing more effectively. Both systems therefore made the individual method appear indefensibly retrograde. In many regions this brought a pedagogical breakthrough. [47] Even in adversity, observed the rector at Montpellier, the mutual school movement has been influential "in destroying forever the individual method." As his colleague at Besançon put it in 1821, "the greatest benefit of mutual education has been its contribution to generalizing the method of simultaneous teaching"—the method now used by the large majority of teachers in his academy. The same was true in the Academy of Strasbourg, where "the individual method . . . is practiced only by the very oldest teachers, whose number is diminishing." The rector at Nancy reported in 1821 that in many cantons, "the absurd routine of the individual method . . . has been banished," even if half the schools in the academy were "still bound by that fetter." Support by the cantonal school committees was crucial. Several days before the start of the school year, "the teachers were summoned to the cantonal seat. The president presented a lesson to them using the simultaneous method and they were enjoined, upon pain of suspension or even revocation by reason of incapacity, to adhere to that mode which is so easily mastered." [48]

Old Problems

As this cumulative progress in pedagogical methods began, the number of communes with schools increased from about 17,000 in 1816 to 24,000 in 1821, along with a rise of about 250,000 in the number of boys attending school (an estimated 1,120,000 out of a potential 2,900,000 school-age males). [49] But this incremental advance left most structural obstacles to improved popular education intact: the unwillingness or inability of impoverished rural communes to establish schools; the reluctance of hardpressed families to send their children to school, especially during the long agricultural season; the low status, inadequate income, and dubious competence of most schoolmasters; the problems of financing education for indigent children; the lack of housing for schools and schoolmasters.

If, as it seems, many parents still did not care about sending their children to school, we might ponder what the availability of a free, well-run school in or near their commune might have done to this outlook. Perhaps a more complex parental attitude actually prevailed: a desire for education offset by an even stronger feeling against paying any additional taxes or fees. Or, for those who could afford it, a willingness to pay tuition but at the lowest possible rate and for the shortest period of time. Still, such attitudes would have left the prospects of potential schoolmasters extremely bleak. The same circle of mediocrity that had bedeviled advocates of universal education since 1792 continued to operate during the Restoration. The inadequate supply of teachers and the grudging demand of parents (their "penury or avarice") reinforced each other as long as the state did not attempt to alter the equation by providing an adequate stipend for *instituteurs* through a fixed state salary (as in the Lakanal Law of 1794) or an obligatory local school surtax (as in the proposal by Hertault-Lamerville in 1799).

In areas where parents had a choice of schools, claimed the rectors at Limoges and Montpellier, "too often the worst schools have the most students because of their cheap fees." The rector at Cahors pointed to another effect of a grudging attitude toward tuition: "To save a small sum, the parents pay only the minimum tuition and their children always remain limited to reading."[50] Unwilling or unable to pay an adequate tuition, parents clung to old, makeshift ways of remunerating teachers. Without guarantees or the sanction of law, tuition payments in impoverished communities remained uncertain—"those humiliating fees which the schoolmaster collects from house to house and which are more like alms than a functionary's salary," as the rector at Amiens described it. In the Academy of Clermont— serving one of France's poorest regions—payments in a year of bad harvests like 1817 amounted in some communes to little more than "a few potatoes, a bit of milk, and some pieces of bread which those unfortunate families draw out of their own nourishment." Arrangements in the South were equally makeshift, especially in departments bereft of locales for housing schools or *instituteurs*. "In general, teachers in the Basses-Pyrénées are lodged and fed alternately by the families"; in Hautes-Pyrénées, "the teachers are mostly paid with grain, but then they are given neither room nor board by individuals."[51]

When parents could or would not provide an adequate living for a full-time teacher, the void might be filled in some other manner, with questionable results. In the Ardèche, "there are a great many *instituteurs* if one can use that term for men who teach reading and writing for a few months of the year in addition to pursuing another métier"; their remuneration was so meager that they did not bother to secure authorization from the University. The rectors of Rouen and of Paris reported that in the countryside many *instituteurs* with third-degree *brevets* "consider their schools as only an auxiliary occupation." In the Academy of Cahors, the situation seemed even more precarious. With few rural communes able to provide a locale for a permanent schoolmaster, "they must negotiate with the first ambulatory master who presents himself for three or four winter months, or else have one of their own inhabitants teach the children." [52]

In areas of Brittany and the Massif Central, parents employed female teachers for the same reasons. Both the rector and the prefect in Rennes reported that "in the countryside they prefer to send their children to unmarried women who are called *bonnes soeurs* and who . . . are satisfied with a very small fee." In the Lozère, regular schools could be found only in the cantonal seats; "in the villages there are women who give some lessons in reading and catechism during the winter." Priests in the Limoges Academy also allowed nuns and other females to teach the boys until the age of ten or twelve. And even in the Academy of Strasbourg, with its numerous and well attended public schools, local officials tolerated an extra-legal secondary market of female teachers in small communes. [53] All of these practices reinforced the propensity of parents to regard schooling as a secondary concern for their children, appropriate at most only in the idle winter months. [54]

A great deal seemed to converge around the problem of tuition. Bourbon officials maintained that under the Napoleonic University, despite vague provisions of the law, "indigent children were deprived of education almost everywhere." Yet as organized under the Restoration, *instruction publique* could not assure free education for the rural poor either. To hardpressed peasants or working families the standard levels of tuition seemed excessive and created an incentive to find cut-rate alternatives or to omit schooling altogether. Conversely, the quality of instruction in the countryside was bound to be mediocre as long as teachers depended on the meager and problematic income from tuition. The moment that the Bourbons ostensibly made primary education a high priority, prefects, cantonal school committees, and rectors called for a law authorizing local surtaxes to fund teacher salaries. The poorer rural communes, meanwhile, refused to vote such subsidies voluntarily. "The majority of communes," reported the prefect of Vienne, "not having the resources available, are unwilling to consent to any special imposition." [55] Confronted by this dilemma, the Bourbon regime reacted as the Directory and Empire had before, with a profound unwillingness to mandate departmental or communal surtaxes that might impinge on the flow of national tax revenues. The pleas of prefects and educational professionals did not dent this resistance until the Guizot Law in 1832. Long before that, however, the need had become obvious and the ground had been prepared. [56]

CONCLUSION: FOUR DECADES OF *INSTRUCTION PUBLIQUE*

In their masterful study, *Lire et Ecrire: l'alphabétisation des français de Calvin à Jules Ferry,* François Furet and Jacques Ozouf demonstrate statistically that schooling and literacy were products of social development on whose rhythms the Revolution and successive regimes seemed to have little impact. The First Republic, they found, neither advanced popular education nor ruined it. Conversely by the time the Ferry Laws of the Third Republic created a free, obligatory, and laic school system in the 1880s, males had already achieved literacy rates of almost 85 percent and girls were catching up rapidly. Far from being the basis on which France achieved universal schooling and literacy, then, the Ferry Laws simply ratified and consolidated the localized advances of the nineteenth century. As they trace the broad outlines of literacy and schooling in France across three centuries, the originality of Furet and Ozouf lies in their emphasis on the central role of social demand. "The school is a product of local societies before being an element of their transformation," they conclude. The nature of a community, its level of social development, its individual and collective sources of wealth determined whether or not that community offered primary schooling to its young, regardless of the regime or its policy.[57]

The Revolution's documented lack of impact on literacy does not mean, however, that its shelf of abortive plans and extravagant visions remains the only legacy worth studying. As reflections of the evolving revolutionary mentality, such projects as Talleyrand's, Condorcet's, or LePeletier's—"those great mobilizing dreams of the Revolution"—have indeed been dissected time and again.[58] Here I have steered between that corpus of texts and the long-term outcome demonstrated by Furet and Ozouf. I have emphasized instead how the Revolution created and attempted to implement the notion of public schooling, *instruction publique.* That this did not in itself accelerate the spread of literacy reflects the dilemmas and hesitations in this commitment, above all the fact that it was never really put to the test by being adequately funded for any sustained period of time. Nonetheless, after 1793 the state undertook to promote and improve primary education—it began a campaign of state penetration that left its mark on the new civic order despite equivocations and periodic retreats.

The state's potential role in education was of course much discussed during the Enlightenment, and in the domain of secondary education the monarchy occasionally intervened aggressively. But on the question of popu-

lar education, in contrast to absolutist Austria and Prussia where the state had
begun to take the initiative, eighteenth-century discourse in France did not
advance much beyond a stirring of concern.[59] Before 1789 the French
monarchy had not been galvanized into action, nor did the pre-revolutionary
cahiers attach much urgency to the issue. The revolutionaries, however, soon
began to denounce the deficiencies of popular education under the old
regime insistently. Nor was this simply a by-product of republican anti-
clericalism. Officials continued to decry the poor quality and haphazardness
of traditional primary schooling across the whole period 1792–1830 until the
criticism reached a crescendo in Guizot's inquiry of 1831. Naturally there
were exceptions. *Idéologues* such as Ginguené and Destutt de Tracy seemed
quite content to let local demand for schooling find its own level. Certain
legislative defenders of religious liberty under the republic (whether from
liberal principles or conservative politics) insisted on the right of parents to
seek traditional private schooling for their children, whatever its character.
The most significant exception was of course Napoleon Bonaparte, for
whom popular education held a puzzlingly low priority. For the most part,
however, prominent figures in each successive regime bemoaned the existing
state of popular education.

The opinions of Catholic University rectors under the Restoration rivaled
the scathing comments of the Directory's Voltairean departmental commissioners or Napoleon's prefects. They especially denounced the apparent
complacency of parents and local communities toward barely literate schoolmasters or part-time, marginal teachers. Across the period they deemed the
"penury or avarice" of the parents to be the cause of this dismal situation,
or at least half the problem. The vagaries of the social demand factor that
Furet and Ozouf portray as the crucial variable, in other words, responsible
contemporaries deplored. Since the state could do little directly to affect
parental attitudes, its efforts focused on founding schools, housing schoolmasters, and on the pay, status, and qualifications of teachers, where systematic intervention might accelerate the spread of schooling, increase its appeal,
and eventually improve its quality.

Such visions of progress did not require a mythic break with the past or
a fanatical regenerative fervor of the kind often ascribed to Jacobins. Prussian
reformers, comfortable with their religion and their monarchical regime, had
reached much the same conclusions in the 1790s without such impetus. They
too deplored the "ignorance and superstition" that made rural families be-
grudging or complacent patrons of education for their young, and they
bemoaned the abysmal quality of available teachers, most of them marginal
types doubling as sextons for their pastors. Miserably paid, dependent on the

whims of parents, often victimized by the pettiness of communal life, traditional Prussian schoolteachers like their French counterparts utterly lacked
status or security.[60]

Prussian reformers produced a sheaf of projects to break the vicious circle
of indifferent parental demand and unqualified teachers by state intervention:
compelling parents to subsidize schooling through local levies collected by
the local tax collector rather than the teacher himself (like Hertault-Lamerville's plan), and training teachers for service, a cause notably advanced
during Humboldt's brief ministry after 1806. State penetration thus converged around the status and pay of the schoolmaster, for whom Prussian
reformers had even greater aspirations than their French counterparts. Instead of remaining products and auxiliaries of local society, primary teachers
were to constitute the bottom tier of public service, and a branch, however
distinct and lowly, of the intellectual professions. If a modest security could
be guaranteed, teachers would know that they did not have to depend on the
caprice of parental generosity.[61]

The thrust of *instruction publique* in France paralleled the agenda of the
Prussian reformers, notwithstanding the republic's secularizing moral vision.
That complication, however, assuredly caused problems. An outburst of
regenerative fervor, for example, led the Convention to endorse, if only
momentarily, an idea as preposterous as the LePeletier Plan or, more seriously, led the Directory into its coercive and counterproductive assault on
private Catholic schoolteachers in 1798. The great moment of lucidity and
effective commitment came with the Lakanal Law of 1794, an artful compromise of conflicting imperatives. At last *instruction publique* began to take shape
as district officials established rural school districts, often bending the law's
guidelines to accommodate the demands of smaller communes, and as *juris
d'instruction* engaged thousands of state-salaried teachers notwithstanding
their deficient skills. The essence of the revolutionary project as consummated in the Lakanal Law lay not in secularization but in the concept of
instruction publique—in making schooling normative and a kind of public
service; in founding schools as widely as possible; and in the long run, with
a new generation of teachers, in raising their quality. The prescribed content
of public schools was meant to be secular, but Lakanal and his fellow
deputies quickly recognized that parental preferences for religious instruction
had to be respected. Officials implementing the new law reluctantly permitted their state-salaried teachers to use Catholic textbooks as long as they also
taught "elements of republican morality."

The Lakanal Law—a determined assault on the supply side of the problem—collapsed within a year or so because of the hyperinflation discussed
above. In its aftermath, indecisiveness reigned. Ironically, the Daunou

Law—the supposed product of tough-minded realism—discarded virtually every element of the Lakanal Law that might have given *instruction publique* substance or impetus, but did nothing to erase its potentially divisive secular commitment. The skeletal public schools of the Directory therefore faced the competition of Catholic private schools with a crippling liability and few assets. As the neglect of 1796 gave way to the Directory's futile campaign against those private schools in 1798–99, republicans argued about how to reinvigorate *instruction publique* while looking over their shoulders at the popular preference for religion in the classroom.

Brumaire abruptly terminated that debate, and Napoleon resolved the conundrum by simply returning to a policy of benign neglect, with free rein for "social demand" and religion. In the ironic ways of history, this definitive defeat of the secularizers was probably a necessary step if *instruction publique* was to go forward. Meanwhile, with a very limited mandate, inspectors of the new Imperial University staked out a minimalist regulatory role for the state in the domain of primary education, although their real interests, in keeping with Napoleon's priorities, lay elsewhere.

The Restoration took up the cause of popular education in earnest, and among other things its officials helped discredit the retrograde individual method of instruction. Fearful of straining an insufficient local tax base any further, however, the Bourbon regime refused to translate the normative demands of its landmark ordinance of 1816 ("Every commune will assure schooling . . .") into positive commands. Hertault-Lamerville's detailed and passionate advocacy in 1799 remained the closest that France came to an obligatory local school tax as the basis for *instruction publique* until Guizot tentatively embraced it in 1832, but without the element of progressivity that Hertault had emphasized. *Instruction publique* also meant that public authority should in some fashion certify teachers, whether through local *juris d'instruction* or the *brevets* of the University, and that the state should train new teachers, as in the Ecole Normale in Paris of 1795 and the normal schools founded in the last years of the Restoration.

The revolutionary government of 1793–94 created a concept of *instruction publique* that all subsequent regimes took up in some fashion, but the original formulation had an egalitarian impetus (in addition to its secularizing bias) that did not survive the fall of the republic. By eliminating tuition and putting teachers on salary, Lakanal not only hoped to solve the problem of schooling for the indigent but also offered an incentive to tight-fisted parents who were not indigent. Hertault-Lamerville's plan of 1799 would have accomplished the same things in a different way through a progressive local school tax. Other formulations ostensibly provided for the subvention of indigent students, but in a far less systematic and effective fashion. The approach first set forth in the Daunou Law of 1795 and operative thereafter—that each municipality should designate a proportion of its needy children for free schooling—proved impractical and entirely unreliable.

As it promoted literacy, *instruction publique* might exclude or enthrone religious instruction; it might inculcate republicanism, loyalty to the emperor, or fealty to the Bourbons. Either way, thanks to the National Convention, primary schooling became normative for the entire nation, and all subsequent regimes at the least attempted to prod local communities and scrutinize their efforts. Furet and Ozouf have shown that social demand posed insuperable limitations on any such undertaking by the state at that point of historical development. And with the exception of the Jacobins' Bouquier Law, which vainly proclaimed that parents *must* send their children to school, the new regimes implicitly recognized those limitations. To their credit, however, they did not simply surrender before them. While the spasmodically coercive, secularizing impulses of the Convention and the Directory left divisive recrimination in their wake, their more constructive efforts created a positive legacy as well. Under the banner of *instruction publique,* in fitful and hesitant fashion, the new regimes promoted incremental advances in the most important public service of all.

THE RISE AND FALL
OF REVOLUTIONARY
BIENFAISANCE

Insufficient land, low agricultural productivity, inadequate industrial employment—these and other structural weaknesses in the economy ensured that most French families in the eighteenth century were poor. We
have seen the civic impact of that fact many times over: in the inadequate
local tax base, in the penuriousness of villagers in regard to schooling their
children or hiring a *garde champêtre*. The social consequences were starker. In
the unforgiving mountainous regions, for example, many peasant proprietors
could not feed their families from their marginal acreage without descending
into the lowlands to earn supplemental income as migrant laborers in distant
grape or grain harvests. Textile manufacturing—in the eyes of progressive
thinkers an answer to insufficient agrarian income—absorbed countless
hands in spinning and weaving, but its endemic cyclical slumps periodically
eliminated such employment. And if the cities held out the allure of new
opportunities, their "economy of the makeshift" could not really accommodate all the unskilled emigrants from the countryside who flocked through
their gates. Only so many porters, cleaners, used-clothes peddlers, food
hawkers, or laborers could make their living on urban streets. Nor could the
semi-skilled crafts like shoemaking or tailoring absorb an endless number of
competitors who depressed the conditions of those trades into "sweated
industries" where the least skilled or well connected could barely survive.

Poor families survived by the expedients of an intricate family economy,
with husband, wife, and older children each helping to assure the family's

subsistence and meet its obligations. Despite the deprivation and endless difficulties in coping, they kept a roof over their heads, clothes on their backs, and bread and soup on the table. But if the fragile family economy collapsed, a poor household would sink into a state of indigence where even those minimal necessities might be lacking. Families could be pushed across that frightful line by external circumstances—a regional crop failure or trade depression—or by personal disaster: the death of a spouse, loss of a job, incapacitating illness or accident, even the birth of another child. When one crossed the line into indigence, when ordinary routines collapsed and daily subsistence could not be assured, society had in one way or another to fill the void. In the old regime this meant an uncertain combination of alms, religious or municipal charities, and sporadic royal initiatives to pick up some of the pieces.[1]

THE INDIGENT IN THE OLD REGIME

Contemporaries perceived the indigent in specific guises. Most compelling, most dependent of all, were infants abandoned by their parents. Illegitimate foundlings, left anonymously by their mothers (often servant girls fearful of losing their jobs), were problem enough to deal with. But working parents who simply could not sustain another child might also abandon their infants. Charity hospitals took in both types of babies and arranged for wetnursing, but did not give their wards much of a chance; death carried off over 50 percent of the foundlings in their first year, compared to a normal mortality rate of about 30 percent for that age group.[2] At the other end of the spectrum stood the aged indigents who could no longer care for themselves, along with the disabled of all ages—the crippled, maimed, blind, and feeble-minded. The fate of these timeless "deserving poor" varied. Those with fixed abode and strong parish affiliation could hope for institutional refuge or aid through established channels of parochial charity. People less rooted in a parish could not lay claim to such charity and were likely to end up as beggars.

The beggars who so offended enlightened citizens in the eighteenth century, however (Catholic traditionalists evidently being more tolerant), did not emerge exclusively from the ranks of the aged or disabled. Only 15 percent of the beggars arrested in eighteenth-century Paris, for example, were severely ill or infirm, and about 65 percent were under the age of fifty.[3] It was precisely such able-bodied beggars who posed the most difficult challenge to society, then as now. How many able-bodied beggars were helpless victims of the economy, at a loss for work, reduced to destitution, and forced to beg in order to survive? And how many were doing so by choice, preferring the freedom of life on the road or the rewards of high-pressure begging, persons "purposely idle and lazy by inclination"—like the twenty-two-year-old vagrant René Françoise, alias Namur, arrested in Normandy in 1776 as a suspected brigand, who denied that capital charge but admitted that he did beg and indeed "had to play the part of a mute in order to get handouts from peasants; without doing that no one would give him a thing, [due to his] being strong and capable of earning a living."

Feared and detested, the rural vagrant cozened peasants to provide food and shelter, and sometimes threatened crops and property if they did not oblige. Yet who could confidently draw the line between such rogues and the migratory workers on the same backroads seeking out a harvest, plying an itinerant trade, or offering their muscle to chop wood or dig ditches? For even the person honestly seeking work on the road might be forced to beg until he or she actually found it. The economy required itinerant harvesters and a mobile labor force, but how could one tell such sympathetic *pauvres passants* from the *mendiant vagabonde,* the one who deserved help as opposed to the social parasite?[4]

Before the Revolution, parishes and towns offered poor relief but, as in the case of primary education, there was no consistency in the way clergy and local elites discharged their responsibilities, and their arrangements never meshed into any kind of wider system. The oldest and most common institution was the urban charity hospital, usually called the *Hôtel Dieu,* where the poor went when they fell seriously ill, to be cared for by the nursing sisters and staff doctors. Some cities also supported smaller hospices for the elderly who could not care for themselves, usually more inviting than the dank and overcrowded *Hôtel Dieu.* In the seventeenth century urban philanthropists, spurred on by religious activists, established another kind of institution in their cities reflective of new thinking about charity and indigence. Called by the generic term *hôpital général* (and not to be confused with a medical hospital), they confined the poor in order to impose disciplined routines, religious supervision, and, if appropriate, work. Benefactors and administrators believed that poor relief should be more purposeful, and not simply a transaction by which the wealthy sought to save their own souls, or merely took pity but not responsibility for the poor.[5]

Founded under private or municipal auspices and administered by urban elites (sometimes but not always in conjunction with the clergy), these *hôpitaux généraux* absorbed the lion's share of charitable benefactions. The monarchy encouraged them—indeed, on paper, ordered all cities to establish one—but provided no funds or oversight. Starting in the 1680s, however, the government issued periodic ordinances directing the *hôpitaux généraux* to conduct round-ups or *renfermements:* to sweep up the beggars in their vicinity and then provide them with work and a harsh regimen that would change their idle ways. By 1724, when the monarchy began its most sustained pressure on the *hôpitaux généraux* to confine beggars, these custodial dumping grounds were being asked to do far too much.[6] Refuges for the desperate and woebegone, they threw together people who had nothing in common— the crippled, aged, and insane who needed peace; orphans and other children who needed instruction (often the largest single group in an institution); and deviants like prostitutes and beggars. A *hôpital général* housed individuals who had voluntarily sought refuge and persons brought there against their will. (The proportions could of course vary: in Caen, 23 percent of the inmates were confined involuntarily in the 1720s, compared to 58 percent in Bayeux.)[7] Nor was it clear exactly why indigents and beggars were being shunted into a *hôpital général:* to be punished for violating the laws against begging? To be deterred from future offenses? To be trained for work? To have their souls saved by the supervision of the sisters? Or simply to be kept off the streets and out of sight for a time?

By the 1760s the monarchy recognized that the *hôpitaux généraux* could not serve the multiple and contradictory roles thrust upon them. This time, as the government prepared a new sweep against the perceived hordes of beggars and rural vagrants, it created its own institution to confine them. These new *dépôts de mendicité,* one in each of the realm's thirty-six *généralités* under the authority of the royal intendants, were paid for in part by royal funds, and were supplied with inmates by the *maréchaussée,* the 3,500-man royal mounted constabulary. Believing *mendicité* to be an intolerable moral and social scourge, the state for the first time intervened directly to remove beggars from society.

Alongside the *Hôtel Dieu,* the *hôpital général,* and the new *dépôt de mendicité,* parish home relief had long existed in both town and country. In contrast to casual almsgiving or the public distribution of alms on a first-come, first-served basis (said to be the besetting error of monasteries in the Catholic world), parish relief could be targeted to those who seemed most deserving. Thus, as the historian Olwen Hufton has observed, in a society built on privilege, the privileged could be found among the poor as well. In the countryside, the parish poor received food at the back doors of designated homes in a routine orchestrated by the curé among his better-off parishio- ners—the only problem being that in so much of France, the needy far outnumbered the fortunate during hard times. In the towns, parish charity bureaus and confraternities distributed aid, sometimes supplemented by citywide organizations, such as the Miséricorde in Montpellier and in Aix, and the remarkably ineffective Grand Bureau des Pauvres in Paris. Charity bureaus distributed bread, clothing, and fuel, along with soup or meat for the sick, to people certified by their priest as both needy and worthy. Of the beggars arrested in Paris during the eighteenth century, however, perhaps only 15 to 20 percent could have qualified for such assistance by having resided in a neighborhood for at least two years.[8]

In the eyes of most historians, parish relief served as much to exercise a moral and religious surveillance as to aid the needy, in effect creating "a veritable class of parish poor known for their religious sentiments and piety."[9] The charity bureaus busied themselves especially with the so-called *pauvres honteux,* the antithesis of the beggars who so offended enlightened opinion by flaunting their misery or intimidating the citizenry into given them alms. The *pauvres honteux,* usually people of higher station who had fallen on hard times, concealed their need behind masks of stoic pride and confided it only to the curé and his aides, on the understanding that assistance would be offered discreetly. Parish relief therefore went disproportionately to relieve a type of genteel poverty that was certainly worthy of consideration but hardly more so than the destitution threatening the laboring poor as they aged, fell ill, suffered underemployment, or brought into the world too many children to support.

Charitable institutions derived most of their income from endowments—the legacies bestowed over the decades by Christians seeking salvation, status in the community, or a reputation for good works. In the North these bequests typically involved real property, while in the South they were more likely to comprise *rentes,* annuities on public or semi-public bodies such as a local guild, provincial estates, or the monarchy itself, which yielded an annual return in exchange for the original loan of capital to the borrower. During the eighteenth century the hospitals and *hôpitaux généraux* increasingly issued their own *rentes* to meet their deficits; that is, they borrowed capital from individuals seeking a modest but secure return on their money, paying these individuals 4 or 5 percent interest annually. (In the 1750s some 788 citizens held *rentes* on the Hôpital de La Charité of Aix-en-Provence, including numerous artisans and widows.) As more *rentes* were issued, however, these interest payments could eat up the institution's funds and throw its budget permanently out of kilter.[10]

Medical hospitals and *hôpitaux généraux* (hereafter commonly referred to as *hôpitaux*) encountered financial difficulty bordering on crisis because progressive opinion in the later eighteenth century grew disenchanted with the institutional approach to poor relief, or *hospicisme,* as it came to be called. The belief spread that financial resources could be stretched further and the poor aided more humanely if they remained in their own homes rather than being uprooted to enter a *hôpital* with its harsh if not unspeakable conditions, where

overhead costs devoured much of the budget. Sagely administered home
relief *(secours à domicile)* seemed preferable to putting the needy into an
institution if at all possible. In any event, donations and bequests dropped
off or at best remained flat by not increasing with inflation or population
growth. In Aix, 70 percent of the wills filed in the first half of the century
had contained charitable bequests, but only 30 percent of the wills did so in
the 1770s. Similarly, contributions to the annual appeal of the Hôpital de La
Charité declined after the 1720s from 3,000 or 4,000 livres annually to 1,000
or 2,000. The institutions made up the difference by marketing *rentes,* but also
by curtailing admissions. (The population of La Charité, which averaged
around 350 during the 1740s and 1750s, fell to about 100 in 1780.) A similar
decline occurred in the Montpellier region: in 1740–41, 45 percent of all wills
had charitable bequests, but in 1785–86, only 24 percent. True, in nominal
terms the total amount of the bequests and the average size of each rose, but
in real terms they declined.[11]

The charity of the urban elites was growing less consistent and more
discriminating, reflecting a dissatisfaction in some quarters over the religious
preoccupations, inefficiency, and demoralization of the large institutions.
With the financing and the very concept of the *hôpitaux* in doubt, the time
was ripe for changes in poor relief well before 1789. Since the countryside
entirely lacked adequate provision for assistance—the historic accretions of
charity having had little relation to the incidence of need—most writing on
the subject pointed to the royal government as the agency that could coordinate resources, plan projects, and (within limits) provide funds. More fundamentally, poverty and indigence, which the Counter-Reformation had viewed
in religious and moral terms, were now being considered in their socioeconomic context as well. It was not enough for the royal government to
provide occasional disaster relief in response to floods, hail, and the like. Nor
would confining beggars and vagrants suffice, even if it could actually be
accomplished. As Turgot argued when he was intendant of Limoges and then
comptroller-general in Paris in the 1770s, the provision of work to the
able-bodied—public works *(ateliers de secours)* such as highway and canal
building, draining and clearing wasteland, repairing roads, or textile manufacturing—logically took precedence over repression.[12]

REVOLUTIONARY VIEWS OF BIENFAISANCE

If a new sense of poor relief or *bienfaisance* took shape before 1789, the
Revolution offered the great moment of opportunity. Its concepts of national
sovereignty and integration reinforced the will to rationalize and reconstitute

bienfaisance. The administrative revolution—the new departments, districts, and communes, self-governing to some extent but linked hierarchically to each other and ultimately subordinate to the national government—created the channels by which this national will could be exercised. Finally, the ideals of equality and fraternity made it possible to conceive of *bienfaisance* as a kind of right or civic responsibility and thus to challenge the traditional if long-criticized sway of religiously inspired charity. The persistence of numerous old-regime assumptions and practices should not obscure the fact that the revolutionaries' approach to the needy constituted a new synthesis, though hardly a stable one. Its contours and fortunes oscillated sharply with shifts in revolutionary ideology itself, with new priorities which imposed themselves, and above all with the state's fiscal capacities, which (not to put too fine a point on it) seemed adequate in 1793 but virtually non-existent by 1795.

Headed by the aristocratic philanthropist LaRochefoucauld-Liancourt, the National Assembly's assiduous Committee on Mendicity distributed detailed questionnaires to the new district administrations in 1790, and in analyzing their responses achieved the most exhaustive investigation of poverty in France ever undertaken to date. After producing a dozen reports, however, the committee failed to enact any significant legislation before its mandate expired in September 1791.[13] The only substantive decree sponsored by the committee that the National Assembly adopted alloted 15 million livres for emergency public-works employment relief, in response to the desperate circumstances created by the subsistence crisis and deep economic recession that coincided with the political upheavals of 1789.

The government selected proposals submitted by the departments on a competitive basis; most involved surfacing roads, digging ditches for road drainage, and projects such as the Burgundy Canal, which won 600,000 livres for the Yonne department, the largest non-Parisian grant. With tens of thousands of desperate workers flocking into Paris from the depressed and resource-starved hinterland, however, the capital manifestly had the most pressing needs. By 1791, public works employed over 30,000 men in the Paris region at a cost of 900,000 livres a month. Not only did such outlays soon appear to be insupportable, but the lack of adequate planning and supervision, combined with the great confluence of restive workers, made the projects seem a dangerous breeding ground for disorder. Such public works were simply emergency measures in any case, and with a new harvest year offering better prospects, the Paris Commune and the Assembly phased out these projects and, with a clear conscience, sent "foreigners" home. (Smaller projects, such as the spinning workshops where over five thousand Parisian women and children turned out yarn in 1791, survived until 1795 despite persistent complaints about their rowdy and insubordinate atmosphere.) [14]

With all members of the National Assembly excluded from the next legislature by the self-denying ordinance, an entirely new committee in the Legislative Assembly inherited the mass of material assembled by LaRochefoucauld. But it was no more able than its celebrated predecessor to translate its agenda into law, since the fall of the monarchy in August 1792 cut short its own tenure. Before that event, however, one member of the committee did present an overview running well over 100 printed pages on "The General Organization of Public Assistance and the Destruction of Mendicity." [15] The report, by Bernard d'Airy, a lawyer from the Yonne, synthesized three years of revolutionary discourse on the transformation of *bienfaisance*. It is an apt starting point not only for its comprehensive if rambling sweep, but because it actually bridged the preparatory work of LaRochefoucauld's Comité de Mendicité and the policies ultimately enacted by the National Convention in 1793–94.

Bernard's report could not be debated by deputies preoccupied in 1792 with the war and the king, and thus made little impact at the time, but the Convention's Committee on Public Assistance resurrected the report when it began to map its own strategy the following year. The *rapporteur* of the first major presentation on the subject to the Convention acknowledged Bernard's paternity, saluted him for his "sublime language of *bienfaisance*," and suggested that all the deputies should read it, though only if they had "three hours to spare for sensibility at a time when the Republic demands laws from you." [16] Bernard's compendium of durable assumptions and new departures, his evocation of long-standing dilemmas and ambivalence, is the most direct portal into the revolutionary mind-set on *bienfaisance*.

The author began on a note shortly to be incorporated into the Jacobins' 1793 version of the Declaration of the Rights of Man. Since inequality inheres in civilization, Bernard observed, society must protect all its members. Therefore at the head of its code the French nation should declare: "Every man has the right to subsistence through work, if he is able-bodied; and to free assistance if he is unable to work." Heretofore society had erroneously regarded assistance "as a favor rather than a duty"; now assistance to the needy must be a "national responsibility," uniform in its reach across the entire realm.

The discourse on *bienfaisance* had always revealed a tension between enthusiastic, positive attitudes on the one hand (generosity of spirit or, now, a concept of rights) and punitive skepticism on the other (the fear of giving benefits to undeserving people, of fostering idleness). Bernard and the founding fathers of revolutionary *bienfaisance* wished only to guarantee the bare subsistence of their fellow citizens, and (with rare exceptions) little beyond that margin of survival. The formula for allotting *bienfaisance* should be calculated "with severity . . . nothing beyond the necessities of life [so as to preclude] that the person being aided will find his situation equal to that of the worker." This commonplace notion applied even to the treatment of the aged indigent, who were after all entirely beyond helping themselves. For *bienfaisance* involved a reckoning based on past, present, and future. An excessive provision of relief to the aged indigent would create a disincentive among current working people to save for their own old age. Along with work, according to Bernard, thrift *(prévoyance)* was the only path to security for the poor. Nothing must be allowed to undercut the play of individual initiative and responsibility for one's future. [17]

Bernard had much to say about abandoned infants and orphans, the most hapless victims of poverty. The institutional care and rural wetnursing arranged by old-regime *hôpitaux* amounted to a death sentence for most foundlings, and the revolutionaries naturally believed that they could do better. But it was more important to alleviate the desperation that led parents to abandon their own children to charity in the first place. Besides promising new kinds of refuge for foundlings and orphans, Bernard therefore advocated "home relief for the children of poor citizens." In other words, the state should help families support the burden of their "excess" offspring rather than waiting for these infants to be abandoned to hospitals. Subsistence aid for the children of poor working families would become the most fundamental component of revolutionary *bienfaisance*. [18]

Traditional charity had long been criticized for two contradictory deficiencies. The public distribution of alms, whether by individuals, groups, or institutions, was thought to be indiscriminate and thus counterproductive. Conversely, parish home relief and access to hospices were said to be allotted on too subjective a basis, with too much favoritism and attention to religious criteria. To counter both kinds of error, Bernard argued that *bienfaisance* should be as impersonal as possible (a stance similar to the Revolution's preference in criminal justice for fixed or determinate sentencing). In any case a more formulaic approach was incumbent if, as the Comité de Mendicité had insisted, assistance should be made uniform across the country, leveling out the wasted resources in some localities and the utter dearth elsewhere. Bernard therefore proposed that in assessing local and regional needs, the state should use an objective standard such as the number of citizens in a department who paid less than ten *journées de travail* in taxes. Secondly, he urged that hospital revenues be amalgamated and redeployed, though he did not insist that their properties (already classified as *biens nationaux*) be sold off forthwith. The nationalization or municipalization of the hospitals could serve the larger purpose of redirecting some of their resources to home relief. For the revolutionaries shared the Enlightenment bias against institutional relief with its heavy overhead, inefficient management, somber atmosphere, and discrimination in behalf of urban citizens, not to mention the religious ministrations that seemed to be the staffs' veritable purpose. Bernard advocated a real choice for the sick and the aged between home relief and entry into these grim institutions.

The great challenge was to fashion a system of home relief that could support the spectrum of legitimate needs. Salaried administrators or bureaucrats were a waste of money, Bernard argued, yet municipal officials were already overburdened. In a suggestion followed vainly by subsequent regimes, he proposed that each canton choose an unsalaried *agence de secours* to organize home relief in town and country. Progressive thinking in the eighteenth century had stressed the need to provide employment for ablebodied workers during the off season, and the *agence de secours* should also try to organize public works for the unemployed and urge private employers to expand their work force.[19]

If work was the mainspring of the "social pact," its opposite, begging *(mendicité)*, remained the obsession of governments before and after 1789. Philosophically, it is true, revolutionary liberalism seemed disarmed before the specter of begging. Can the law "impose on any individual an obligation to prefer work to rest?" Bernard inquired. Can the law presume to stop a generous person from extending aid to a beggar? Simple equity would seem to dictate that the poor person as well as the rich had the right to be inactive. The honest liberal also had to pause before the cliché that *mendicité* was the antechamber to crime, for it did not follow "that potential crimes should be taken as already committed, and penalties be applied to those which have not yet occurred under the vain pretext that they might some day." Having thus sanctioned *mendicité* in theory, however, Bernard readily found more powerful considerations opposed to its consequences. In the end, social utility must prevail over philosophical abstraction. The social and moral consequences of *mendicité* were simply intolerable; beggars formed a class which, by refusing to work, consumed without producing and "thus devoured the subsistence of the laboring individual." Unlike the rich person, who himself (or whose ancestors) had worked, and who now still relied on himself, the beggar depended on others, whose generosity he would eventually exhaust: "fatigued by the importunities of the undeserving poor, and unable any longer to recognize the deserving, citizens will refuse the latter as well." *Mendicité* is "subversive of all social spirit . . . and against the interest of productive activity."[20]

Liberal attitudes about work, however, ruled out simple repressive measures like the great confinements of the 1720s and 1770s. The disorderly and lethal *dépôts de mendicité* must be replaced by veritable workhouses, according to Bernard, so that "the offer of work and the refusal to accept it will precede the application of punishment." Without offering the able-bodied a genuine choice between work or punishment, they cannot be legitimately confined, since work is "the only punishment that can reasonably be inflicted on the lazy." Conversely, Bernard did not wish to stifle generous instincts, "that sublime penchant" of the possessing classes. Voluntary contributions and subscriptions to welfare agencies should be welcomed and encouraged.[21]

REVOLUTIONARY POLICY AND PRACTICE

In the first report by the Convention's Comité des Secours—which did little more than distill the essentials of Bernard's rambling presentation—Jean-Baptiste Bô divided the needy into three categories: the wilfully idle; the young, aged, and infirm; and the able-bodied temporarily deprived of work. As for the third category, the hasty, large-scale public works of 1790–91 had left a sour taste in official circles. The managerial details and conceptual dilemmas of such programs (their impact on private-sector labor markets, for example, or how to set wages) had clearly not been mastered. By 1793, however, this was not an urgent concern, since the war alleviated unemployment and even caused labor shortages in some regions. Public works remained on the agenda but held a low priority. When the economy collapsed in 1795 and the need for unemployment relief became acute once again, the situation had changed completely. This time the state was bankrupt of funds, plans, and will. Thus, despite all the emphasis on job provision in their thinking, the revolutionaries failed to advance, let alone institutionalize, Turgot's vision of public works for unemployment relief.

Broader planning for public assistance, however, moved forward. In the law of March 1793 the Convention established its direction of intent: a national commitment and a local framework for *bienfaisance*. Annual sums would be allotted to each department based on its relative number of non-taxpaying citizens and on the level of the prevailing standard wage *(journée de travail)*. (The higher that wage, the higher the cost of living, and the greater the department's needs for its indigent citizens were likely to be.) This law also slated the endowments and property of charitable institutions for sale as *biens nationaux* but, prudently, not until "the complete and definitive organization of public assistance is in full activity." Following Bernard's plan, it called for an unsalaried *agence de secours* in each canton to organize public assistance in the form of work relief for the able-bodied unemployed, home relief for the aged and disabled, and *maisons de santé* for the ill who could not be treated at home. The law also sketched the rudiments of a public health service.[22]

The real innovation came three months later, when the law of 28 June 1793 spelled out the categories and forms of home relief that the national treasury would support. This landmark in the Revolution's attempt to enlarge and standardize the horizon of public assistance had three notable features. First, it created objective criteria for entitlement to aid. Second, it placed special emphasis on working parents trying to raise families "at the moment it is arithmetically proven that the means of the father are not in proportion to his [family's] needs." Finally, the new law pledged annual monetary pensions rather than weekly distributions in kind, the nearly universal means of home relief before 1789.

In brief, the law of 28 June 1793 pledged pensions to aged and inform indigents, and to "mothers and fathers who have no resources other than the product of their labor, whenever the product of their labor is no longer commensurate with the needs of their family." This would be determined by weighing their income level (reflected in tax liability) as against the size of the family. With three children under the age of twelve (including a third-trimester pregnancy), a couple would qualify if they paid no tax at all; with four young children, a family would be eligible if it paid 5 livres or less; and with five children, if it paid between 5 and 10 livres. The qualifying child and any additional ones over that number would entitle the parents to an annual pension of 80 livres.

The law also covered widows with young children (promising a pension of up to 120 livres for her, in addition to 80 for each young child); orphans living as foster children with needy families; and *filles-mères* who were raising their illegitimate children. To be sure, the proposed pensions were extremely modest, reflecting the chronic ambivalence about *bienfaisance* which the *rapporteur* did not conceal: they constituted "assistance at once the most complete, comforting, and moral but the least costly . . . [and only] what is strictly necessary"; they struck a middle path between excessive generosity that saps individual initiative and a "criminal parsimony."[23] The law certainly did not cover every category of need. The populous district of Hazebrouck (Nord), for example, complained that "some people who currently support themselves by their work but who will require assistance at the least infirmity are not included. It is imperative to increase the general total of assistance." But as the returns for that district and others show, the pensions were meant for needy children above all. In Hazebrouck, the roll included 8,188 children, 871 infirm, and 1,974 aged.[24]

The landmark law of 28 June 1793 established a program on paper, but the Convention did not appropriate any funds until seven months later. On 1 February 1794 (13 pluviôse II) its public assistance committee finally proposed an appropriation of 5 million livres for a first installment. The Convention not only agreed but doubled the amount, and the Executive Commission on Public Assistance (formerly part of the Ministry of the Interior) took pains to create an efficient pipeline for the disbursement of these funds. A special desk to answer procedural questions made it easier for perplexed local officials to get useful advice. This was a dry run for a hugely complicated effort to identify the intended beneficiaries and to get the money, even a token amount, into their hands. Municipal officials aided by local clubs or committees were to interview citizens, check documentation, compile lists, and submit them to the districts, which would scrutinize, certify, and forward the lists to Paris. The money would then be allocated to the districts, which would pass it on to the communes.[25]

In Paris, forty-eight sectional welfare committees alerted citizens by crier, posters, and other means, and assisted applicants in securing documents such as birth certificates and tax records. Compiling these lists proved to be an exhausting task at which some committees worked "night and day." When the lists were ready, the commission promptly transferred the city's share of 250,000 livres to the committees, which just as promptly paid the citizens.[26] Naturally all did not go as smoothly in the provinces. Some districts never completed their returns properly, and most had trouble prodding some of their communes into action. This trial run was certainly not an unqualified success, but it did prove that it was possible to identify the neediest citizens with relative objectivity.

Surviving lists from five Paris sections evoke in detail the kinds of people targeted by this shrewdly crafted policy—typically a father employed in the overcrowded artisanal trades and a mother who worked irregularly in "the economy of the makeshift." Like Balande, aged forty, a journeyman carpenter and his wife Marie, aged twenty-eight, a laundress; assessed at 8 livres in taxes, they had filed for an exemption, and supported four children (three months, three, six, and eight years of age), as well as Marie's mother. Or Bornet, a journeyman shoemaker, aged twenty-eight, apparently the second husband of Marie Tapin, aged thirty-three, a vegetable peddler; they paid no taxes at all and had four children (aged two, four, seven, and twelve), with another on the way. Could the four children of Citizen Fermier, a forty-one-year-old water carrier, and Françoise l'Archer, a forty-two-year-old cleaning woman, have survived without help? The pensions also went to elderly people who had not managed to save for their old age, especially the numerous widows, and workers racked by disabilities like failing eyesight, eking out a living as best they could in a losing battle. As his sectional committee said of Charrier, a seventy-one-year-old *ancien garçon marbier:* "He does what he can, but his advanced age prevents him from earning his full subsistence. He needs to be helped."[27]

Yet it might have been better had the law of 28 June 1793 been inscribed on paper and forgotten. When the Convention paid this first installment on the promised pensions, it must have aroused great expectations all over France as needy citizens came forward for interviews and saw their names entered on the rolls. Having set in motion the mechanisms for dispensing these entitlements, however, the Convention made no further appropriations. Other priorities, other initiatives, other crises intervened. As one departmental administration laconically observed in its annual report for the Year IV (1796), under the heading "Children, the Elderly and Indigent to Whom the Law of 28 June 1793 Accords Assistance": "The administration has not been credited with any funds at all for that kind of expense." The law remained on the books until the legislature quietly repealed it in late 1796, but it was never implemented again.[28]

THIS IS NOT to say that the Jacobin Convention simply forgot the needy. Rather, it modified its priorities and put its commitment behind an overlapping law with a different thrust. As he stepped to the rostrum to introduce this proposal on 11 May 1794 (22 floréal II)—at the height of the Terror— Bertrand Barère must have savored the moment. For once this spokesman for the Committee of Public Safety was not about to denounce a new conspiracy and justify its repression; he was not demanding further sacrifice by citizens or added emergency powers for the government. Barère would now demonstrate that if the revolutionary government had to curtail liberty and take lives, it could also bestow recompense. His remarkable speech bristled with egalitarian sentiment. The rich had had their day; this was the moment for the poor. Unlike any previous address on *bienfaisance,* Barère's heralded a new sense of social reciprocity and fraternity, a redressing by the state of traditional inequities in civil society: "We must put an end to the servitude of the most basic needs, the slavery of misery, that most hideous of inequalities."[29]

The usual ambivalence about *bienfaisance* for once vanished before a vigorous commitment toward the most desperate of the poor moldering in rural isolation: aged farm workers and rural artisans at the end of their strength; indigent mothers and widows desolate in their rural hovels. These, Barère contended, were the most hardworking and useful but least rewarded citizens. When their strength finally expired, their employers habitually abandoned them to their misery. But this was the propitious moment to end all that. Public fortune was at its height, Barère declared somewhat obscurely: "The billions on which the rich count for the counter-revolution the Republic will devote to ameliorating the lot of the least fortunate citizens." Without any tactical need to aid them—aged, incapacitated farm workers were scarcely visible, nor did they actively contribute any longer to the republic's well-being—the Convention would now assist precisely such deserving but forgotten people.

Indeed, Barère posited their moral equivalency with the most honored of all citizens, the republic's soldiers: "Let the public treasury open at once to the defender and the nourisher of the fatherland." *Agriculteurs invalides,* he suggested, were on a moral plane with men incapacitated by war, the *militaires invalides* whom the Convention had already treated with generosity. As a circular to the districts later put it, "this law is the recompense for work rather than a gift to misfortune."[30] What is more, Barère proposed that their entitlement be solemnly recorded in a *"Grand Livre de la Bienfaisance Nationale."* After all, he observed, "the wealthy have already obtained a *grand livre* for the registration of their riches and credits"—a reference to the registry for the French national debt.

On the assumption that need was most desperate in the countryside, the law of 22 floréal allocated pensions exclusively to communities below 3,000 population. "It is to the cottages that this law will bring the *bienfaisance* that honors and comforts." The Convention urged local officials to scour rural habitations to locate aged and infirm citizens too weak to come forward. But unlike the law of 28 June 1793, this was not an open-ended program. In each of four categories the program established a fixed number of pensions for each department (with increments where the rural population numbered more than 100,000).[31]

Table VIII-1
Pensions per Department on the Grand Livre de Bienfaisance Nationale

Indigent farm workers over the age of sixty or infirm	400 pensions	@ 160 livres
Indigent rural artisans	200 pensions	@ 120 livres
Mothers and widows with small children	350 pensions	@ 60 livres + 20 livres per child
Indigent widows of farm workers and artisans	150 pensions	@ 60 livres

Specific sums allocated in the law to fund each category of pensions totaled around 12.6 million livres annually. And this was one law that the Convention implemented immediately. The funds soon began to flow from the Executive Commission on Public Assistance and continued throughout the Year III as districts submitted their returns. District and municipal officials took to heart this onerous task of identifying and documenting rural indigents. [32] Four fifths of the rural communes in the Hérault responded, for example, and the neediest districts received most of the pensions. In St. Pol (Pas-de-Calais), there were two applicants for every pension allotted. District officials in the Mayenne and the Orne likewise nominated almost twice as many citizens as could be funded; ultimately only about 2,500 received pensions in districts of those departments with a total rural population estimated at 178,000. [33] Though far from sufficient, the pensions on the *Grand Livre de Bienfaisance Nationale* aimed in the right direction and were beginning to reach the intended recipients.

The most dramatic expansion of *bienfaisance* grew directly from the militarization of the Revolution. As citizens were mobilized for war, their sacrifices, and the hardships imposed on their families, became top priorities. Even before the war, when the National Assembly had opted for a relatively small, professional armed force, it had shown unprecedented liberality toward the soldiers and officers who grew old or disabled in service. In a model of progressive policy, the National Assembly offered retired and disabled veterans a choice between institutional sanctuary (residence in a reformed Hôtel des Invalides) or a pension according to rank. [34] At that time no one had foreseen a wartime transformation of the army with waves of short-term volunteering, a sweeping draft, massive casualties, and war widows. The Convention rose to the occasion by fashioning a remarkably egalitarian veterans' policy. After June 1793, common soldiers who lost an arm or leg in combat ("who left their limbs on the battlefield," after the ministrations of the military surgeons) or who suffered a comparable incapacitating wound left the army as honorary lieutenants with commensurate pensions or benefits in the Invalides. [35] Under a law of May 1794, the needy widows of *militaires* who died in combat received the same generous pensions regardless of their husbands' rank, with increments only for seniority. In unprecedented fashion, the equality of civic virtue now overshadowed the traditional weight of military rank in calculating recompense. [36]

The Convention was just as quick to recognize that citizens mobilized into the army often left behind aging parents or wives and children who had relied on the men as their principal breadwinner. In November 1792 the deputies pledged aid to "fathers and mothers, wives and children whose only means of subsistence was the work of the volunteer." In 1793 they extended this to new draftees, and raised the levels of support to 100 livres each for most dependents. [37] Moreover the Convention used the full weight of the revolutionary government to deliver on this promise. If funds were slow in coming through regular channels, municipal officials could demand advances on those sums from their commune's largest taxpayers. "This measure is just," they were told. "The law calls the rich to the aid of the poor. Citizens! The law has thus put at your disposal a plenitude of means to satisfy all legitimate claims without delay. As organs of the nation's *bienfaisance,* fulfill your task with the fervor of patriotism." While revolutionary committees and sectional assemblies had otherwise lost the right to impose revolutionary taxes and forced loans on their own, the Convention specifically authorized municipal officials to do so for this type of "patriotic assistance." Reflecting this priority, the welfare commission in Toulouse had a civil section and a military section, each with its own secretary; the former employed one clerk, while the military section needed three. [38]

Table VIII-2
Expenditures by the Commission des Secours Publics

	Hôpitaux Civils	Hôpitaux Militaires	Objets Divers
AN II			
Floréal	3,131,000	11,760,000	5,109,000
Prairial	2,457,000	10,592,000	6,951,000
Thermidor	1,339,000	5,006,000	13,655,000
Fructidor	634,000	14,358,000	5,008,000
AN III			
Vendémiaire	1,657,000	9,117,000	4,018,000
Brumaire	488,000	8,497,000	1,005,000
Frimaire	577,000	7,793,000	1,617,000
Nivôse	2,859,000	11,548,000	5,518,000
Pluviôse	3,990,000	11,929,000	9,062,000
Ventôse	4,478,000	18,366,000	7,145,000
Germinal	1,765,000	9,894,000	3,305,000
Floréal	17,567,000	71,825,000	20,372,000
Prairial	8,796,000	34,808,000	6,381,000
Messidor	18,472,000	53,084,000	18,389,000
Thermidor	25,889,000	50,442,000	3,638,000
Fructidor	14,320,000	27,799,000	5,171,000

Source: A.N. F[15]* 9-11: Journal des Dépenses.

Meanwhile sick and convalescing soldiers swamped the nation's hospital facilities. Combat units frequently left 25 or 30 percent of their troops behind suffering from fevers, skin ailments, and venereal disease, as well as wounds.[39] Whether in special military hospitals or by invading civilian hospitals, these military convalescents drained the resources of the Commission on Public Assistance. About 62 percent of its total funding between floréal Year II and the end of the Year III paid for medical services to *militaires* back in France (see Table VIII-2). Moreover, one third of the Commission's non-hospital expenditures went for "patriotic assistance" to the needy dependents of *militaires*.[40] Obviously plans to make the national government responsible for *bienfaisance* were being diverted and distorted by the side effects of military mobilization in a democratic society. Barère's initiative in behalf of aging and destitute rural workers seems all the more remarkable in the light of these huge commitments to veterans, convalescing soldiers, and military dependents. When he compared *agriculteurs invalides* to *militaires invalides,* Barère paid them the highest tribute and made the strongest claim for social reciprocity. By the same token, when funds became scarce, needy veterans would remain the state's favored wards to the detriment of other deserving poor.

Bienfaisance in Revolutionary Paris

Barère was certainly right to target relief pensions to the hovels of aged rural workers and widows. Few rural cantons managed to establish *agences de secours* in anything but name, whereas urban communities stood a better chance of organizing to aid the needy. Most towns established *bureaux de bienfaisance,* either by transforming parish institutions or creating new ones, and none could compare to the welfare system of revolutionary Paris. Though its methods seem largely traditional, they were now secularized, standardized, and linked to the new political ideal of fraternity.

Before that system took shape in 1793, the capital had seen several overlapping attempts to provide home relief since the fall of the Bastille. During the awful winter of 1788–89, most of the capital's fifty-two parish charity bureaus had reacted energetically to the scarcities and miseries of their parishioners; expenditures that year surpassed any in recent experience. But the mobilization of citizens in the capital's sixty electoral districts for the elections to the Estates General spawned a vigorous new style of local activism. The district assemblies continued to meet after the elections and arrogated a variety of functions to themselves, including relief efforts in their neighborhoods that rivaled those of the parishes. With no mandate but their own, the districts established welfare committees that set to work immediately. From these districts or sections (the National Assembly reorganized the sixty districts into forty-eight sections in May 1790) a plan gradually emerged for a veritable municipal system of poor relief. Each section would choose a delegate to a central commission that would manage a citywide municipal poor-relief endowment, apportioning funds to each section according to its number of indigents. Each section would also elect an unsalaried *comité de bienfaisance* to identify the needy in its neighborhood, disburse aid, resolve any questions that arose, and collect funds to supplement municipal allotments.

The National Assembly met this demand only in part with a decree expropriating the multitude of parish poor relief endowments in the capital in order to create "a common center of *bienfaisance*" that would level out "the almost infinite inequalities of ancient origin in home relief caused by the diversity of local foundations." Instead of turning the income from this new municipal endowment over to the sections, however, the Paris Commune took direct control and appointed poor relief commissions headed by the curé in each of the thirty-three new parishes created under the Civil Constitution of the Clergy in 1791. At that juncture the Commune wished to bolster the new ecclesiastical establishment and to challenge the political pretensions of the sections. This hybrid system was therefore controversial from its inception and eventually succumbed to attacks on several grounds: that poor relief should be aligned with the municipal map of sectional organization; that committees should be elected directly by citizens in the sections rather than appointed; that clerical influence should entirely cease; and that an independent commission should manage the endowment, with the Commune limited to oversight. In March 1793 the critics won a decree from the Convention establishing sectional control over *bienfaisance* in Paris.[41]

Neighborhood activists faced an immense task and did great service to the capital's civic order with their tireless activity. The number of indigents fluctuated between 85,000 and 110,000 in a city of roughly 600,000 inhabitants, and of course varied greatly among the 48 sections, from a low of around 200 in several wealthy sections to about 5,000 in Finistère in the faubourg Saint-Marcel and 6,600 in Quinze-Vingts in the faubourg Saint-Antoine, with their heavy concentrations of marginal journeymen. The median was about 1,000 and the average per section about 1,500. Each section's general assembly elected a welfare committee ranging in size from sixteen to twenty-four members. In traditional fashion each committee divided its section into wards of one or several streets. Two commissioners were assigned to each and did most of their work out on those streets, identifying the needy, distributing aid after the committee's approval, and soliciting contributions; in addition, two commissioners were on call daily in each section to deal with emergencies.

The frequency and duration of committee meetings increased steadily. One year after their election, the welfare commissioners were among the most overworked officials in the city, despite their unpaid status. A cross section of older *"sans-culotte* bourgeois," at an average age of fifty-two, many welfare commissioners were retired businessmen or artisans. They usually enlisted the aid of female auxiliaries. At once compassionate and unflinching, these women proved especially helpful in dealing with the sick, pregnant women, and nursing mothers, and in repairing used clothing.[42]

The by-laws *(règlements)* drafted for the committees by the Paris Commune divided the indigent into three categories: the elderly and infirm, who could no longer provide for their basic needs; pregnant women and nursing mothers; and citizens "responsible for the support of a family, or whose misfortune is only temporary"—i.e., the working poor with dependent children, or those with or without children who had fallen ill but wished to avoid a hospital. The committees therefore had considerable latitude in determining who required public assistance. As the Central Commission, which managed the capital's new poor relief endowment, explained, the *comités de bienfaisance* could assist "workers and artisans of all types, the laborers and the women whose entire income consists of the modest product of their labor, which scarcely suffices for their own subsistence and that of their children and who, in hard times or in case of illness of temporary indisposition, require assistance proportional to their needs." The relatively flexible Parisian system thus accommodated a larger spectrum of circumstantial need than the Convention's necessarily formulaic national entitlements.[43]

The welfare committees' method of supplying assistance was also different, which is to say, more traditional. Reflecting the received opinion that assistance should be given in kind rather than in cash (both for moral reasons and to stretch the resources), Parisian welfare committees were enjoined in their *règlement* to provide aid in kind, cash to be granted only "in the most exceptional and scrupulously justified cases." With subsistence supplies uncertain and caseloads unpredictable, the *règlement* prudently made no specific pledges for the amount of aid, but in practice all citizens on the rolls received a weekly bread ration, provided through delegated bakers in exchange for coupons, and a measure of rice supplied to the committees in bulk by the Commune. As best they could the committees distributed meat or meat-based soup to pregnant women and to the sick, and milk and cereal to nursing mothers. Each committee adjusted these distributions to circumstances, such as failing meat supplies in 1794 and scarcity of flour in 1795. The committees also provided used clothing, linen, bedding, layettes, candles, and in the winter coal or wood. Some sections retained the dispensaries run by the Sisters of Charity under the parish bureaus to provide soup and medicine to the poor, but others closed down those facilities, sold off their property, and relied on individual distributions without the overhead or mediation of the sisters.

The sectional welfare committees in Paris had no authority over the hospitals but could scarcely be indifferent to them. They took up complaints by citizens of their sections, and arranged placements or transfers from one institution to another. The Central Commission urged each committee "to see to it that one of its members accompanies the ill or infirm of both sexes to the hospitals, and that he does not leave them until they are placed in their bed in a humane manner. In addition the committees should designate members to visit the *malades* of their section in the hospitals at least once a month to assure their good treatment." The committees did their best to fill this ombudsman function, further crowding a full agenda. In addition, they were asked periodically to carry out legislation by the Convention in behalf of the poor, such as certifying recipients for the first installment of the Convention's poor relief pensions, and preparing lists of "indigent patriots" who were supposed to benefit from the property confiscated by the state from convicted political suspects under the abortive Ventôse Laws of 1794.[44]

As public responsibility for the needy became an axiom of the republic's civic order, organized private philanthropy fell into disrepute as inappropriate. Yet voluntarism, channeled through public committees, persisted in the Parisian welfare system as it did elsewhere. Indeed, the welfare committees relied on contributions "from citizens whose wealth invites them to come to the aid of their needy brothers" to supplement their income from the municipal endowment. The Parisian *sans-culottes* balanced proportionality and uniformity with local activism and initiative in their system of *bienfaisance,* avoiding an impersonal, bureaucratic model of public assistance. Private donations favored sections with small numbers of indigents and relatively large numbers of wealthy citizens, but committees in less favored sections worked strenuously to prod contributions from their own citizens. In the hardpressed Quinze-Vingts, the results were meager: proceeds from collections at the conclusion of each meeting of the section's general assembly averaged little more than 10 livres. Finistère's committee, however, did better as it solicited door to door, enrolled subscribers for regular monthly donations, and occasionally announced a large contribution. The committee in Indivisibilité campaigned aggressively with letters to a thousand well-heeled citizens of the section; small contributions trickled in steadily, along with larger ones of 300 or even 600 livres. During the Year II (1793–94) the forty-eight committees disbursed assistance worth 960,000 livres in stabilized *assignats,* of which only 430,000 flowed from the municipal endowment. The remainder, more than half, came from contributions "given by citizens of the sections in fraternal solicitude." [45]

Far from attacking the Christian idea of giving, the sections assimilated it into the ethos of civic virtue, as Bernard d'Airy had urged in 1792. What the poor received could no longer be called "charity"; Finistère's committee was entirely sincere when it obliterated the inscription *Maison de Charité* from an old-regime soup kitchen it had taken over. But citizens of substantial or even modest means were still expected to donate to the needy through their local welfare committees. Indeed, the Jacobin ideology of civic virtue, social harmony, and symbolic egalitarianism demanded such tangible gestures of fraternity.

THE COLLAPSE OF 1795 AND ITS AFTERMATH

Meanwhile, what was happening to the charity hospitals, hospices, and *hôpitaux généraux*—that massive legacy of old-regime philanthropy? Though the popular classes viewed most of these urban institutions with loathing and dread, they remained refuges of last resort for the sick, disabled, and destitute where one was at least unlikely to starve or freeze to death. Financial support of the *hôpitaux* by old-regime elites had been weakening, as we have seen, and criticism of their wasteful overhead abounded, but there was no question of closing them down. The revolutionaries simply wished to deemphasize their role by offering the indigent a choice between home relief and confinement. Successive legislatures also eyed the *hôpitaux*'s substantial endowments covetously. From the start the Comité de Mendicité anticipated in 1790 that this property would eventually be nationalized as the state assumed financial responsibility and administrative oversight of *bienfaisance.*

To the extent that *hôpitaux* depended on income from feudal dues, tithes, *octrois,* or *rentes* on privileged corporate bodies, the Revolution brought immediate financial losses. When guilds, provincial estates, or ecclesiastical corporations were dissolved, for example, hospitals holding their *rentes* could not collect their interest. The government was supposed to compensate for such losses with state grants, but its allocations were always in arrears and rarely took account of real needs, inflation, or previous debts. Disruption also occurred in the way hospitals were run. Revolutionary municipalities often replaced trustees who had given years of dedicated service (and who customarily made interest-free advances out of pocket) with revolving-door appointees new to their tasks and relatively uncommitted. And if one could justify ousting overpaid priests serving as chaplains, the same could not be said of the overworked nursing sisters whom the government forced out as well after October 1793, when stratagems to spare them finally failed. To make matters worse many civilian hospitals were effectively militarized, inundated by wounded convalescents and sick soldiers. Absorbing scarce facilities and supplies, their disorderly ways made life miserable for civilian inmates and staffs alike. [46]

The most devastating blow, however, was yet to come. For extraneous fiscal reasons, the Convention reversed its own prudent stipulation in the law of March 1793 that charitable properties would be nationalized only "after the complete and definitive organization of public assistance is in full activity." On 11 July 1794 (23 messidor II) the deputies decreed that all charitable property and endowments (save the hospital buildings themselves) should be sold off as *biens nationaux* as soon as possible—just as they had done a year earlier with the endowments of the nation's *collèges.* The government did not reverse this rash policy until October 1796, when it halted the sales, and did not return unsold property to the institutions until 1797. For three years the *hôpitaux* depended almost entirely on government grants, precisely when such support became highly problematic. For these disruptions could not have come at a worse time. By 1795, thermidorian economic deregulation had provoked a surge of hyperinflation coincident with some of the worst crop failures in living memory. Just after government commitments to public assistance reached their peak—with the takeover of hospital funding and the pledge of pensions on the *Grand Livre de Bienfaisance Nationale*—the nation's currency collapsed.

We have already seen the havoc in educational programs caused by this conjuncture: the Convention's supreme effort to establish state-financed primary schooling disintegrated as the stipends promised to *instituteurs publics* by the Lakanal Law lost almost all value. The instruments of revolutionary *bienfaisance* foundered as well. Pensions had seemed a dignified way of sustaining the aged farm workers, artisans, and widows inscribed on the *Grand Livre de Bienfaisance Nationale,* but the hyperinflation of 1795–96 destroyed the value of those pensions completely. Installments of 207,000 livres in *assignats* scrupulously disbursed to some twenty departments in September 1795, for example, were scarcely worth a few thousand livres by that time. Likewise the "patriotic assistance" that the government continued paying to the dependents of *militaires* became nearly worthless, "not having been augmented at all relative to the discredit of the paper money." [47] Even the most successful municipal welfare systems had enormous difficulties in rendering home relief. After the nationalization of their municipal endowment in July 1794, the Parisian welfare committees faced endless delays in drawing their monthly allotments from the treasury, even as those allotments plummeted in value with each passing day. When the newly installed Directory pumped 600,000 livres of emergency funds into the Paris welfare system in December 1795, the actual purchasing power was a derisory 4,000 livres. [48]

A closer look at that episode reveals just how desperate things had become. Since precise accountability down to the last sou continued no matter how pointless, the Paris Central Commission drafted a twenty-five-page report to explain how this money had been used. The sectional welfare committees split over how to stretch their paltry emergency grants. Twenty-eight, despite the bias against offering aid in cash, doled it out directly in *assignats,* "because of the excessive price of commodities . . . the difficulties of procuring such items . . . and the meagerness of the sums allocated." Quinze-Vingts was caught in the middle. Hoping to buy food with its share, the committee changed its 25,000 livres of *assignats* into specie in order to bargain more effectively with vendors for scarce goods. The transaction produced 168 livres in hard cash. A commissioner took the money into the country looking for potatoes, but "their scarcity and excessive price made the trip useless." Next day the committee reluctantly changed the 168 livres back into *assignats* for direct distribution to the poor. So rapid was the inflation that it brought 28,750 livres of paper money in return! Committees that managed to acquire food scarcely did much better. Twenty sections purchased potatoes or beans for distribution, "wishing to come to the indigents' aid more directly . . . to economize for them," but their provisions did not go very far. Halle-au-Blé could distribute only one and a half pounds of potatoes each to about four hundred individuals, while in Homme Armée a litre of beans went to each family and half a litre to single persons. The Amis de la Patrie committee acquired six and a half *septiers* of potatoes for about 1,500 indigents, so that "individuals will end up getting perhaps four potatoes each." [49]

Ordinarily *hôpitaux* would be the last resort under such circumstances, but as the historian Alan Forrest puts it, "the Jacobins left to their successors a hospital service stripped of its independent resources and closely tied to the will and prosperity of the state." Now the state had neither the will nor the resources to make good. Sporadic grants from Paris were entirely insufficient, always late, and meant for current needs rather than payment of huge accumulated debts to insistent tradesmen and creditors. Lesser institutions closed down altogether. In the Hérault department, nineteen of forty-three *hôpitaux* shut their doors during this crisis, at least twelve of the smaller ones permanently. Others had to scale down their admissions just when demand increased. Inside the walls, conditions became unspeakable; inmates in Toulouse's major hospital lay shivering in their own filth since the institution could not afford to buy blankets or linens. In Rouen's *hôpitaux,* mortality rates hit alarming new highs. [50]

Out of this debacle the foremost casualty was the belief that the state could actually organize and support such services as primary education and *bienfaisance.* Where the nation's resources had once seemed abundant (thanks to nationalized church lands and printing presses), the treasury was now bare, revenues uncertain, and budgets swollen by military priorities. Thermidorian political leaders adapted quickly to this new climate of austerity, and rationalized it ideologically by attacking the Convention's ambitious plans for education and public assistance as chimerical, "a mania for leveling." "The time has not yet come to establish let alone realize the theory of public assistance," concluded the deputy C.-F. Lebrun. Ignoring the voluntarism that supplemented public funds under the Jacobins, thermidorians now argued that state control discouraged or even excluded private charitable acts: "If the government involves itself, the citizen dozes. . . . What does it matter whether aid is a product of *bienfaisance* or vanity?" More plausibly they concluded that *hôpitaux* needed reliable, locally controlled income. Nationalization precluded future bequests, caused local administrators to overstate their needs, and multiplied paperwork and delays horrendously. If *hôpitaux* had their own resources, they could collect income more efficiently and secure loans with their property as collateral. [51]

The Directory gradually renounced the republic's commitments. In October 1796 it halted sale of the *hôpitaux*'s unsold properties and vaguely pledged to make good eventually on those already sold, though it did nothing to compensate for the lost *rentes* on which southern institutions had depended. Shedding state responsibility, the government abdicated control to the municipalities, which were to appoint five-man hospital boards to manage the finances. At the same time (law of 7 frimaire V) the legislature formally repealed most of the public assistance laws of 1793–94, including all pension entitlements except those for veterans and war widows. Finally, in 1799, after a painstaking debate that lasted two years, the directorial legislature scaled back those veterans' pensions, and modified the criteria for awards with more consideration given to rank and seniority as against type of disability. Further retrenchment under the Consulate in 1803 lowered the scale of most veterans' pensions further and redefined categories of eligibility, generally to the detriment of rank-and-file soldiers. Traditional professional criteria for recompense had recovered their ascendancy over the egalitarian impulses of 1793 in meeting the nation's "sacred debt" to its veterans. [52]

WITH AN EYE to Paris, whose efficient system was still reeling from the disruptions caused by the transfer of its municipal endowment to the treasury in July 1794, the Directory sought to produce additional funds for home relief by levying a 10 percent tax on the price of admission for "spectacles, balls, concerts, races, etc. for the benefit of the indigent"—an expedient that had been used at times under the old regime. In the capital this entertainment tax produced about 10,000 livres per *décade*, roughly 350,000 livres a year earmarked for home relief. Though the money was difficult to collect and chronically in arrears, the surtax did produce a steady flow of revenue: when business at Parisian theaters fell off during the summer, outdoor entertainments such as the Bal de Tivoli compensated.[53] Elsewhere the results were negligible, and outside the big cities entirely nil. In the department of the Eure, for example, "the tax is scarcely a resource at all. Only Evreux has obtained a few feeble benefits from entertainments during the winter." In Bourg, *chef-lieu* of the Ain, the tax generated a mere 192 livres in 1804; in Châteauroux (Indre), 647 livres in the Years VIII–IX; and in Toulouse, no more than 12,000 livres in a typical year. During the Empire, the middle-sized city of Amiens (Somme) generated only between 1,200 to 2,400 livres annually from this source.[54]

In October 1798 the legislature authorized a more significant form of public funding for Paris, the *octroi municipal et de bienfaisance,* which the Consulate made obligatory for most other towns in March 1800. An excise tax on alcoholic beverages, tobacco, meat, and other consumer goods passing through urban portals, the *octroi* had been a staple and much-detested exaction of old-regime fiscality, which the National Assembly had quickly abolished. Now urban consumers again paid this regressive tax to underwrite municipal expenses and *bienfaisance,* with the latter component to be shared by *hôpitaux* and home relief. Along with further restitutions made by the Napoleonic regime for lost properties and *rentes,* the *octrois de bienfaisance* finally put the *hôpitaux* back on a relatively even keel. In a budget of about 106,000 livres, for example, the *Hôpital Général* of Montpellier received 63,000 livres from the *octroi,* and Lodève's an even higher proportion. The hospitals, however, generally derived far more benefit than the home relief agencies, which complained endlessly over not receiving a fair share.[55]

Exactly opposite to the revolutionary program of 1793–94, these methods of providing revenue set apart country from town more decisively than ever. Neither the urban entertainment tax nor the municipal *octroi* impacted on the tax-bearing capacity of rural property owners, the chief concern (as we have seen) of every regime. By the same token the two taxes provided no funds for relief in the countryside. Urban *bienfaisance* had a chance to recover, but in the bourgs and villages public assistance scarcely existed. Rural society lacked both mechanisms and funds to provide public assistance to the needy, but while the state tried to create a new framework for *bienfaisance,* it failed to redress deficiencies in funding.

"In the Year X one of my predecessors ordered the creation of a *comité de bienfaisance* in each canton in conformity with the law of the Year V," reported the prefect of the Aisne. "Their members were named and installed. . . . But up to this moment [1806] these useful establishments have remained inactive." Communes that did have endowments for the poor did not wish to see any of those funds submerged in a common pool for the needy of the canton, where the government believed they could be used more efficiently.[56] Similarly, commissioners from various communes sometimes proved unwilling to assemble at the canton's *chef-lieu.* Prefects appointed cantonal bureaus but readily admitted that they functioned only on paper, and could only hope that private almsgiving would revive "without involvement of the public administration." The situation in the Haute-Vienne was probably typical: "There was recently established a *bureau de bienfaisance* in each canton. . . . But that new institution has generally been thwarted by the custom of each individual to tender alms in his own way."[57]

In contrast, most cities did salvage a minimal form of public assistance—a hybrid of traditional practices, local subventions, and public management. In a relatively prosperous department like the Indre, the prefect knew of thirteen functioning *bureaux de bienfaisance.* Issoudun's, with revenue of 8,100 livres, assisted 700 persons, and Châteauroux's aided 483 indigents on a budget of 6,336 livres. (With incomes of between 2,000 and 480 livres, however, the other bureaus served only 100 or fewer individuals each.) In Amiens, the "public assistance budget" showed revenues in 1813 consisting of:

3,500 livres from annuities and rentes,
2,400 from the entertainment tax,
10,000 from donations solicited in homes and churches,
60,000 granted by the municipality from its *octroi.*

With these resources it aided 5,887 indigents in a population of about 45,000, many no doubt textile workers thrown out of work by a crisis in that industry: 665 households (2,660 individuals) on permanent relief, and 700 households (2,800 individuals) which received help only during the winter. In addition the bureau assisted 430 aged and infirm indigents who could not care for themselves (half of whom, it claimed, should have been housed in an *hospice des incurables* which the city did not have), and eighty *pauvres honteux* who received small stipends.[58]

What made urban *bienfaisance* "public"? Did it really differ in any way from pre-revolutionary parochial or municipal charity? It is hard to sort out this melange of traditional practices and new accretions, but the answer is a qualified yes. The *bureaux de bienfaisance* of the Empire and Restoration depended more on local public funds and were subject to greater scrutiny by public officials than their old-regime predecessors. They also dispensed aid in a more rationalized fashion. A self-congratulatory report by the prefect of Deux-Sèvres illustrates these points. Niort (population about 16,000), he wrote in 1807, had been free of beggars for the past six years. This happy state of affairs came in part from the abundant employment opportunities said to exist in the town: "It is not a question of creating jobs, but of forcing the lazy to work," claimed the prefect—which was fortunate since neither local nor national governments ever had much sucess in generating employment. In any case Niort's municipality showed no tolerance for begging, and threw any offenders into the *hôpital général*. But this policy in turn depended on enforcing a long-standing prohibition against offering alms in public: "The distribution of alms at the door was prohibited, and charitable people were invited to deposit their gifts in the treasury of the *bureau de bienfaisance.*" For nothing could be accomplished "as long as the misguided charity of individuals offered the lazy an encouragement." This ban on private alms left the town of Niort responsible for the dependent and for parents who could not support their families on their wages. For this the *bureau de bienfaisance* had a budget of 20,000 livres—4,000 from donations and 16,000 allocated by the town council from its *octroi.*[59]

In traditional fashion the bureau's members checked carefully on every recipient of home relief in Niort's four wards. They were not looking for piety, but to see "whether the father's wages sufficed for his [family's] needs; if the bureau notes a deficit, it fills it. If work is lacking, it procures it. The assistance is modest and always presupposes an income from work. The bureau is a constant surveillant over the indigent class, and inevitably leads it to virtue through work." Ample employment opportunities may have made Niort unusual, but this approach to public assistance became commonplace in urban France. Assistance came primarily in the form of a weekly bread ration—*pain de second qualité,* but carefully monitored for that quality by the bureau. During the winter the bureau added a supplement of 5 centimes in cash for each kilogram of bread. The bureau provided the sick with medication, meat, and soup, and encouraged mothers to nurse their infants if they could do so without impairing their ability to work; if not, "the newborn babies are put out to nurse at the bureau's expense." The welfare bureau also arranged for primary schooling and then for apprenticeships. (By 1806, it claimed, 325 youths had already completed their training.) Altogether the number of able-bodied recipients of aid in 1806 averaged 349 families per month (1,396 individuals) in addition to 61 *infirmes*—almost one tenth of the town's population.[60]

The moralizing paternalism of Niort's *bureau de bienfaisance* may have been insufferable, but its efficient distribution system kept families with dependent children from falling irrevocably across the line between poverty and indigence. Using municipal funds and private donations, this public agency assured the subsistence of working-class parents and busied itself with the welfare of their children. Capitalizing on the Revolution's clearing operations, the bureau modestly fulfilled the rationalizing vision of the National Assembly's Comité de Mendicité and its Enlightenment forbears. The system owed nothing, however, to the abortive entitlements initiated by the Convention which, with due allowance for their limitations, would have extended the reach of *bienfaisance* further than had ever been considered before.

DURABLE THEMES

THE REPRESSION OF BEGGING; PHILANTHROPY AND SELF-HELP

An Eighteenth-Century Obsession: "The Extinction of Mendicity"

Few towns could boast with Niort that they had eliminated begging, a problem which festered on the streets and in the public mind of the new regimes as it had for much of the eighteenth century. That obsession is apparent in pamphlets of the 1790s and 1800s on the subject of poverty, which usually bore such titles as "The Means to Extinguish Mendicity," as if they were still responding to a famous essay contest of the Châlons Academy in 1774.[1] In the cities, beggars offended and disgusted; on isolated rural byways, they threatened security and property. Begging and vagrancy were not merely the most visible excrescences of indigence but embodied its elusive causality, an uncertain amalgam of defective labor markets and individual moral failings. When someone begged in the streets, it was either because physical disability or lack of employment left no other recourse for survival, or because he or she found begging more congenial than working a twelve-hour day at subsistence wages. This enigma posed a daunting challenge to public policy, but no regime priding itself on a rational and humane civic order could ignore the problem indefinitely.

For almost a century the monarchy had encouraged sporadic attempts to get beggars off the streets into the *hôpitaux généraux,* while it threatened undomiciled vagrants with even harsher criminal sanctions such as a term in the galleys. As noted above, the government tried something new in the 1760s by establishing a new royal institution called the *dépôt de mendicité.* The

prospect of arrest by the *maréchaussée* (mounted constabulary) was supposed
to act as a deterrent, but it proved to have little impact. The depots quickly
became holding facilities of uncertain character, neither prisons nor refuges.
Still, the depots did facilitate stepped-up policing. One near Caen, for example, filled with inmates apprehended upon denunciation by ordinary citizens
for vagabondage and petty crime. A bounty system for the *cavaliers,* however,
also encouraged more indiscriminate sweeps of hapless individuals who did
not really threaten public order.

In any case a paucity of appropriate sites, inept administrators, limited
funds, and greedy provisioners drove the living standards in the depots
below the minimal levels specified in government regulations. Expressing a
common reaction, one prominent officials in 1774 found them to be "hideous . . . more horrible than criminal prisons." Turgot attempted to redirect
royal resources into work relief programs and hoped to shut all but a handful
of the noisome depots, but his fall in 1776 aborted that shift. Then in the
1780s the director of the Soissons *dépôt* tried to create a model institution
where beggars could be rehabilitated by discipline and work. Inmates at
Soissons had to show a willingness to work before they received food, and
diligent workers were rewarded with higher earnings. But elsewhere the
atmosphere in the depots tended to be callously cruel or appallingly lax. Local
officials used the depots to confine other difficult types such as prostitutes
infected with venereal disease, abandoned children, and the insane. Escapes
were common and death rates notoriously high, perhaps approaching 20
percent. These harsh, disorderly, and costly places offended enlightened
sensibility, yet without noticeably reducing mendicity. As dumping grounds
for social misfits, however, the depots were too convenient to eliminate. The
dépôts de mendicité, in short, seemed at once insupportable and indispensable.[2]

For the Convention, too, they proved enticing. The Jacobins instinctively
drew a distinction between "the reprehensible miserable and the blessed
poor." The former—lazy, scabrous, lacking all necessities—constituted a
calamitous social wound that had to be cauterized. Conversely, the republic
honored the laboring poor for their productivity, "honest mediocrity," and
the austerity of their lives. The Jacobins intended to meet the basic needs of
the laboring poor (and to mute the offensive display of opulence by the rich),
but with even greater urgency than the monarchy they wished to quarantine
the irredeemable.[3] As it had under the old regime, the act of begging
symbolized that line. Therefore, instead of closing down the depots, the
Jacobin Convention resuscitated them, albeit under a new name and a revised
strategy.

In his report to the Convention on "The Extinction of Mendicity,"
Jean-Baptiste Bô distinguished between occasional begging by unemployed

workers who stayed in the their own cantons and did not trouble public order as against the *"mendiants d'habitude,"* the vagabonds who wandered and menaced. Both must be provided with work, he declared: the former by means of local work relief projects during the dead agricultural season (which cantonal welfare bureaus were enjoined to organize), and the latter through confinement in the depots. The Convention forthrightly renamed the depots "houses of repression" *(maisons de répression)* and integrated them into the system of correctional justice. To begin with, the law of 22 vendémiaire II (13 October 1793) reiterated an earlier decree by the National Assembly, reminiscent of the English Poor Laws, that ordered localities to send beggars back to their native domiciles at public expense. Repeat offenders, however, were to be incarcerated in the depot for a year, along with vagrants and others caught begging under aggravating circumstances, who were to be sentenced immediately.

On paper, the Jacobins shifted the emphasis of the depots from simple repression (getting people off the streets) back to the concept of rehabilitation by work. Obliged to work at tasks appropriate to their "strength, age, and sex," inmates would be paid one third of their weekly earnings; the remainder would contribute to their upkeep with any surplus held for them until their release. The depots were supposed to be salubrious, removed from the temptations of the big cities, and strictly regimented "without degrading human nature."[4]

In practice, however, this program "for the extinction of mendicity" through work discipline languished in neglect. The government did not upgrade the thirty-four existing *dépôts de mendicité* or align them with these new principles, and could not provide the financing or administrative skills to create daily routines by which these institutions could actually offer useful work for their inmates. The depots simply remained dumping grounds for the deviant and miserable people who could not be handled by ordinary health care, penal, or welfare institutions. Thus ninety-two of one hundred female inmates in Bordeaux's depot in the Year III were prostitutes suffering from venereal disease. In the small depot at Riom (Puy-de-Dôme), the number of able-bodied poor confined for rehabilitation did not increase as intended but declined from thirty-two in 1790 to ten in the summer of 1796 and to only four three years later.[5]

The existence of these "houses of repression" did make it easier, however, to execute a triage among the beggars whose presence in the capital of the Revolution embarrassed and exasperated the revolutionary government. In the belief that one could distinguish between those who deserved *bienfaisance* and those who merited confinement, the Committee of Public Safety ordered the Parisian welfare committees to make a detailed census of habitual beggars in their neighborhoods. Then in May 1794 it decreed that disabled beggars *(mendiants invalides)* be given monthly stipends of 25 sours per day if married and 15 a day if single to obviate their recourse to begging. Thereafter begging could be strenuously prosecuted with a clear conscience, and able-bodied beggars in particular would face the certainty of arrest. In this way the revolutionary government believed that it was finally "extinguishing mendicity" on the streets and plazas of the capital. The *ci-devant mendiant* became a distinctive if bizarre category of the needy, who almost alone (along with the blind) received monthly cash allotments from their sectional welfare committees. [6]

Nor was this a mere token gesture. The lists of disabled beggars, expeditiously compiled by the forty-eight committees, contained about one thousand names. Some sections had a mere handful—Fontaine de Grenelle, Fraternité, and Tuileries registered only one *mendiant invalide* each for this program—but others had large concentrations, including République with 81, Panthéon with 88, and Cité with 139. Over half were women, which usually meant widows. And the money was paid! The Convention channeled monthly installments to the welfare committees as supplements to their own hardpressed budgets, and the committees in turn paid their wards with only rare interruptions. True, the hyperinflation of 1795–96 devalued the stipends brutally, but as soon as possible the committees arranged to pay the recipients in hard money. [7]

Until 1797, when the program was apparently terminated along with the Convention's other pension plans, the ex-beggars who so offended republican sensibilities in Paris paradoxically became the most cosseted civilian recipients of public assistance. The point being that the Jacobins found begging intolerable, but realized that indiscriminate confinement was unjust, as undesirable in its way as indiscriminate almsgiving. By careful classification and, it should be stressed, an unprecedented liberality, the Convention hoped to remove disabled beggars from the streets by inducement and then to clear out the unworthy able-bodied by arrest.

Ultimately the program of subventions to get *mendiants invalides* off the streets of Paris constitutes a lost footnote in the history of *bienfaisance*. Though it made punitive sanctions against able-bodied beggars more plausible, it did not set a precedent for any sustained action. The collapse of national finances and governmental will within the year aborted any chance for its extension, although the stipends continued to be paid in the capital for several years. Indeed, the withdrawal of the national government from active involvement in *bienfaisance* brought the entire campaign against mendicity to a halt. The depots moldered in neglect, evolved into prisons and insane asylums, or closed their doors altogether. Of the original 34 *dépôts de mendicité,* 29 still existed by 1807, but their 6,900 inmates were more likely to be accused criminals awaiting trial, convicted criminals from overflowing jails, the insane, prostitutes, or abandoned children, rather than vagabonds and beggars. Although the prefect of the Orne reported that twenty thousand people "habitually beg, most of them no longer able to work," the department's depot was being used as a criminal detention facility since the regular prisons lacked sufficient capacity. Even if he wished to have beggars arrested, the prefect had no place to send them.[8]

YET THE DÉPÔT *de mendicité* was a concept that would not expire no matter how often it failed to live up to expectations or was diverted to other uses. Within the Empire's councils the resolve gathered to resurrect the depots and indeed to establish one in every department. At the height of its powers, the imperial regime believed that it could succeed with a carefully crafted institutional attack on mendicity where others had failed. In preparing his new initiative, the minister of the interior consulted some of the leading Parisian philanthropists with long involvement in the problems of poverty, whose advice suggests how little the Revolution had altered the obsession with mendicity. To LaRochefoucauld-Liancourt—former chairman of the National Assembly's Comité de Mendicité—"almost all beggars beg out of laziness and habit" rather than from necessity. Since their attitude toward work constitutes the heart of the matter, "work alone is the means by which individual indigence can be helped."

Given its causality and its social effects (beggars were still a scandal and a menace), the government must treat such people severely. But repression only made sense if it involved a term of confinement "long enough so that they can be accustomed to work . . . and under a regimen severe enough to inspire them with a fear of returning." The banker and philanthropist Benjamin Delessert took a similar but more nuanced approach. Absent aggravating circumstances, a beggar could be regarded as a worker without a job who has nonetheless broken the law. Society must therefore rehabilitate him. "Until now the *dépôts* were merely refuges for the lazy. . . . No one tried to reform their morality by means of work and the habits of an orderly life." The new depots must be rigorously organized around work with several regimens varying in severity, so that recidivists or rebellious inmates could be placed in the harshest conditions and forced to work longer in order to earn a sum permitting their release. As to the work itself, "everything having to do with clothing the indigent" was appropriate, such as producing rough yarn and cloth.[9]

The law of July 1808 reviving the *dépôts* introduced a new classification scheme that essentially reversed the Jacobins' stillborn approach. In 1793, the "houses of repression" were intended for vagabonds, coercive beggars, and recidivists. In 1808, such *"mendiants vagabonds"* were to be shunted into the penal system immediately (as once they had been consigned to the galleys). The Empire reserved its *dépôts de mendicité* for "ordinary beggars." Hardened vagabonds would no longer be thrown among women and children or "the unfortunate whom old age, infirmities, or the temporary absence of work" had driven to begging. But how could one decide in which category an able-bodied male beggar belonged? Since most are begging "out of a slothful and idle spirit," observed the minister of the interior, "rigorous principles would justly require that they be treated as vagabonds." They cannot be excused on the pretext that work is lacking at a time when cultivators are hard put to find labor. Yet, he continued, "I believe that when the able-bodied poor do not remove themselves completely from the surveillance of the local authorities in their domicile, they should not be treated as severely as those who try to escape it."

As had been the case in the old regime, those who posed a less severe threat to public order belonged in a depot rather than a prison. Accordingly, the following types of beggars would be treated as *"mendiants non-vagabonds"* and confined in the depots: women and children under sixteen, whatever their domicile; those infirm or over sixty who could no longer work; and "able-bodied poor who have not left the arrondissement in which they are domiciled, unless there are aggravating circumstances which can place them in the category of *mendiants vagabonds.*" The last, to be shunted straight into prison, included beggars from outside the arrondissement; those demanding alms with insolence; making use of forged passports or certificates; acting in groups of four or more (not including children); and those caught with arms. The depots were no longer meant for the uprooted and incorrigible but were reserved for people who had slipped by circumstance or temporary weakness of character into the path of begging. [10]

While each prefect planned for the depot in his department, the ministry laid down a general *règlement* for the whole country. The official regimen fell short of the most punitive views, such as the belief by an official in Toulouse that a depot should be more like a prison than a hospice, with "visible signs of indignity . . . and coarse foods sufficient in quantity only to sustain life, so that his needs will force him to work." Rather, it resembled a well-ordered *hôpital général* of the late seventeenth century. The sexes were of course separated and all inmates sequestered from the outside world. They were to rise at 4:00 or 5:00 A.M. (6:00 or 7:00 in winter) and to retire at 8:00 or 9:00 P.M. (6:00 or 7:00 in winter), and no card playing or gambling would be tolerated. The regular diet was supposed to include meat twice a week, but

for those who refused to work or became insubordinate, the *règlement* prescribed short rations of bread and water. As the new British Poor Law of
1834 would later put it, the workhouse (or *dépôt*) must be "less eligible": the
inmates must not be given "a situation more favorable than free workers."[11]

Inspectors of the new depots found that "the diet is inferior to the one
followed in hospices for the aged, but it is so close to it that the beggars in
the *dépôts* are generally content." In the inherent paradox of the depot,
however, that very contentment created a potential problem: "One can even
fear," added the inspector, "that the generosity of this regime may serve as
an encouragement to mendicity." What a fascinating and perpetual dilemma!
If the living standard became too abysmal (as it had under the old regime),
then mortality would increase and right-thinking officials would balk. But if
the regimen was even tolerable, notwithstanding the depot's constraints, the
institution might become a magnet for the destitute, who would fill it to
capacity. The prefects of the Hérault and the Gard therefore warned against
permitting voluntary admissions, lest "the poor regard them as a refuge and
the veritable *mendiants* can no longer be confined there"; lest "everyone
consider the *dépôt* as a refuge which is supposed to serve as an endowment
for the beggar's calling."[12]

The question of admissions was linked to the vexing problem of finances.
Prefects had to produce local subventions to keep the depots going once the
state had borne its share of the start-up costs. Provisioning and overhead
cost between 220 and 250 francs a year per inmate, so one way to contain
costs was simply to keep down the number of inmates. While each depot had
a stated capacity, few accommodated those quotas. (In 1818, the 22 surviving
depots were supposed to hold roughly 8,000 individuals, but they only
housed about 5,000.) Worse yet, prefects could not resist using the depots
once again as convenient dumping grounds for troublesome social problems.
In 1813, 23 percent of the inmates in Montpellier suffered from skin diseases,
11 percent from venereal disease, and 8 percent were prostitutes. In Paris in
1812, only 195 inmates were able to work, while 537 could not; in Toulouse
in 1818, only 60 of the 200 inmates could work.[13]

In its annual report to the legislature on the state of the nation at the end
of 1810, the imperial regime had boasted of its new depots and suggested
that "the great task of repressing mendicity" was gaining momentum. Sixty-
five depots were in the planning stage, including thirty-six already operating
or about to open: "A few more years and mendicity will have entirely
disappeared." This was of course absurdly naive. Only thirty-seven depots
went into operation on French soil under this program, scarcely more than
the number existing in 1789. Twenty-two other departments completed the

laborious preliminary work of locating an appropriate site and preparing specifications for renovations, but never brought the projects to fruition.[14] And even if professional administrators continued to praise the concept after the Restoration, their voices scarcely harmonized. The director of the Bouches-du-Rhône *dépôt,* for example, saw the depots as a refuge for the relatively able-bodied and deserving poor (who could pay their way by work, more or less), as well as abandoned children, orphans, and "the poor created by misfortune." A former director of depots in Rennes, on the other hand, visualized the institution's mission as training young workers, and opposed "voluntary admissions [which] everywhere transform the *dépôts* into *hôpitaux."* Unabashedly, he advised the authorities "to seize the children of the poor in order to populate the *dépôts,"* thus turning them into "a seedbed for future workers."[15]

Most *conseils généraux des départements* of the Restoration, on the other hand, regarded the depots with distaste, although the institution's lineage was as much Bourbon as Napoleonic. These local elites complained most about the costs that had to be borne by departmental budgets, but they also noted the failure of the depots to curb, let alone eradicate, mendicity. Between 1814 and 1818, prefects officially closed at least twenty-five depots, some before they ever opened their doors, leaving twenty-two actually operating and another eight in the planning stage whose future remained uncertain. (Surprisingly, there was no regional pattern in the suppression of depots after 1814. The twenty-two survivors were scattered across all regions, including four in the South where the concept had always encountered opposition: Ariège, Bouches-du-Rhône, Gard, Hérault.) The government ceded the facilities of the closed depots (usually former abbeys, monasteries, or châteaux) to other purposes: eight became prisons or detention facilities, while seven were put to some military use (with another two, in the Meuse and Moselle, serving as hospitals for the occupying Allied forces). Local hospices or *hôpitaux* took over five, and three reverted to their original use as Catholic seminaries.[16]

But it was not simply competing local interests or tight-fisted departmental watchdogs who repudiated the depots. In his annual report for 1818, the minister of the interior himself expressed skepticism. He denied their aptness for the aged and disabled, who would be better off in a hospice or on home relief, and he questioned their usefulness in dealing with the idle able-bodied *(oisifs)* who, he believed, were quite willing to spend a term in the depot at taxpayer expense without changing their dissolute ways. As a refuge for the deserving poor, the depots were too expensive; as a deterrent or means of rehabilitation, they had manifestly failed.[17]

· · ·

WAS THE "EXTINCTION of mendicity" by institutional confinement losing its allure at last—the more so since certain Catholic traditionalists openly defended the virtue of almsgiving after the Restoration? The "extinction of mendicity," argued Houssart, one such commentator, was as chimerical as the Revolution's penchant for the leveling of fortunes. Begging was actually a transaction by which the wealthy could fulfill their obligation to the poor. "It is the hatred of religion which has led to its proscription." Moreover, he claimed, with the poor shut away, the rich will become even greater egoists. Conversely, begging is a right for an impoverished person who cannot find work; it would be cruel and unjust to confront such people with a choice between giving up their freedom or starving to death.[18] Restoration liberals, however, remained obsessed with begging and considered this to be retrograde thinking. Almsgiving may be good for the soul but it was bad social policy. As one professional reformer retorted: "Our gilded lackeys would no longer cut a figure if the populace did not throng around our coach to ask for alms." Liberals continued to advocate the repression of begging and the aptness of well-ordered depots, but during the Restoration they looked to philanthropy rather than government to demonstrate their utility. Private or quasi-public experiments would create new tactics for the "extinction of mendicity." According to the publicist and reformer Bernard Appert, theory and practice were about to culminate in the prototype of a new "Maison centrale de morale et de travail" being organized in the capital.[19]

The House of Work *(Maison de Travail)* was the brainchild of such philanthropists as Cochin (mayor of the 12th arrondissement in Paris and a founder of charity schools) and LaRochefoucauld-Liancourt. Though officially sanctioned by the minister of the interior and by DeBelleyme, a sympathetic prefect of police, the House of Work was not publicly funded or chartered. Yet its sponsors enlisted over 11,700 individual subscribers who pledged 700,000 francs toward a goal of 1 million; as of 1829, more than half the pledges had already been paid, and a suitable building had been leased with an option to buy.[20]

The sponsors believed that no institutions founded thus far had succeeded because their objectives were always confused and their systems of classification faulty. In Napoleon's *dépôts de mendicité*, for example, "the infirm was called to reside next to the lazy; poverty was confounded with begging. The *dépôts* found themselves overburdened with the obligation to feed a great number of persons deprived of their freedom." But this criticism had been leveled many times, by traditionalists like Houssart as well as liberals. What new tactics against beggars could these energetic philanthropists propose?

Before depriving them of their liberty or leaving them to their indolence, the essential point is to examine their position, to evaluate their resources, and to determine their degree of culpability. . . . The disorderliness of begging will scarcely be able to resist this determined investigation. . . . Factitious poverty will fear discovery and punishment, and mendicity will disappear.

The point was to isolate and take charge of the most problematic types among the poor, the able-bodied beggars *(mendiant valides),* who constituted "a class apart." Such people must not be simply incarcerated and forgotten, but must be offered assistance in the form of "moral support and the habit of free and directed work." At all costs the indiscriminate admissions of the former depots must be avoided: "If the refuge becomes at once a prison, hospice, workhouse, and general hotel for mendicity and distress, it will be impossible to limit the expenses or the abuses. . . . The act of public begging should be the sole cause of admission."[21]

The House of Work, with its carefully regulated work projects, was meant to complement two existing Parisian institutions: the *dépôt* at Villers-Cotterets for the infirm and aged, and the *dépôt* at Saint-Denis for condemned and imprisoned vagabonds. The *Maison de Travail* would be reserved exclusively for "able-bodied beggars who are curable by submission to a regimen of regeneration"—beggars whom the prefect of police agreed to remand to the *Maison.* We seem to be witnessing the birth of social work, as the *Maison*'s "investigating bureau" prepared to determine into which category an arrested beggar fell. The new institution would be based on meticulous classification, and the beggar would either be rehabilitated or identified as incorrigible and turned over to the penal system, doubtless for a term in the punitive Saint-Denis *dépôt.* In law all beggars were subject to that sanction, but the sponsors of the *Maison de Travail* viewed their institution as "a place of grace and exception" from the strictures of the penal code. If the absence of personal dignity leads the needy individual to beg, the law will arrest him but the intervention of the *Maison* will give him a one-time opportunity "to purge that state of reprobation."[22]

Philanthropists evidently found this project hard to resist. Meticulous, quasi-scientific classification and moral rehabilitation through work discipline reached their most exalted formulation. But alas, a shift in the political winds brought an unsympathetic prefect of police to power in the summer of 1829, who refused to authorize the transfer of arrested beggars to the *Maison.*[23] The project ground to a halt, despite the protests of its well-connected sponsors, thus postponing the inevitable disappointment. The Revolution of 1830 resuscitated the project, but in the records of the Assistance Publique we read that the *Maison de Travail* lasted only three years, giving way in 1832 to an orphan asylum.[24] Yet another campaign for "the extinction of mendicity" by institutional means had failed.

THE REVIVAL OF CHARITY AND PHILANTHROPY

After the rash experiment of 1794 nationalizing charitable endowments, most hospital administrators would have agreed that "humanitarian establishments ought to be endowed with properties and stable revenues, independent of the public treasury." Besides badgering Paris to restore their confiscated properties and annuities, hospital boards hoped to receive new bequests of cash and property to rebuild their endowments.[25] The Consulate authorized such bequests, but required that any charitable legacy over 300F be approved by the Council of State. This procedure enabled the government to protect the interests of family members against immoderate generosity by their relatives. According to a report on "legal charity" in the early nineteenth century, "the action of the Council of State tends . . . to moderate the exaggerated zeal of the benefactors and to restore to the dispossessed family the portion which seems beneficial for its needs."[26] In 1819, for example, the government approved bequests totalling 3,042,000F, but "rejected or reduced several important legacies to the benefit of the natural heirs. Altogether the reductions amounted to between 500,000F and 600,000F that year."[27]

Because of this statist regulation, we are unusually well informed about major charitable bequests after 1800. To begin with, the donors constituted a very small group, for only once did the Council of State approve more than 1,000 legacies in any year between 1800 and 1830. During the period 1814–35, 12,530 bequests were recorded for an average of 570 per year in all of France, with only modest growth in the number of donors over time. To some extent this is consonant with research in the notarial archives of Montpellier by Colin Jones, who found a long-term decline in charitable bequests across the eighteenth century which the Revolution accentuated. In wills of the 1740s, 45 percent of Montpellier's testators left charitable bequests, compared to 24 percent in the 1780s and only 17 percent in 1808–09. (The trend is even more pronounced considering that one quarter of the female testators still left such bequests under the Empire as opposed to only one male in ten.) But this research does not extend into the Restoration, when the decline probably halted.[28]

The amount of wealth donated to charity, in any case, assuredly grew. Under the Empire the annual total averaged around 1.5 million francs, but under the Restoration the typical annual amount more than doubled to about 3.5 million (see Figure IX-1). (Occasional sharp fluctuations upward were undoubtedly caused by one or two unusually large bequests; thus "the enormous increase in the year 1821 is explained by the liberalities of M. de Monthyon, whose value alone was nearly 4 million.")[29] Across the period the bequests comprised a traditional mix of assets: over half the value came in cash, about one quarter in real property, and the rest in *rentes* and other assets. But unlike the sample of legacies in the Hérault (where only 40 percent in 1808–09 went to Montpellier's two major *hôpitaux*), the bulk of all bequests—about 60 percent of the total value—went to the *hôpitaux*, while *bureaux de bienfaisance* and other home relief organizations received only 40 percent (see Table IX-1).[30] The durable attraction of the *hôpitaux*, after half a century of negative polemics about the defects of institutional relief, suggests that charitable benefactors came largely from the most traditional social elites.

Beside the fact that the property, *rentes*, and cash bequeathed to charitable

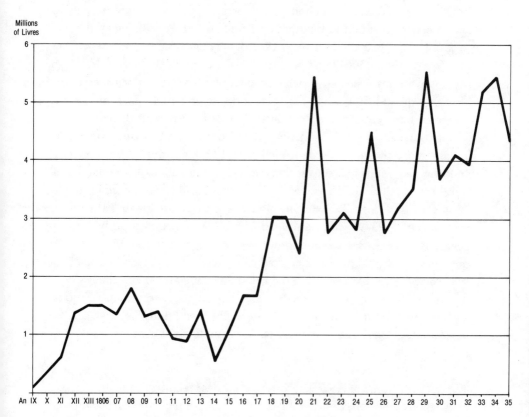

Figure IX-1: *Major Charitable Bequests, 1800–35*

Table IX-1
Value of Charitable Bequests by Type, 1800–30

	Hôpitaux	Bureaux de Bienfaisauce	Totals
Napoleonic Era (1800–14)	8,979,000	5,942,000	14,921,000
Restoration	32,358,000	18,663,000	51,021,000
Totals	41,337,000	24,605,000	65,942,000

Sources: A.N. F[15] 3959 and F[15]* 45.

institutions went disproportionately to the *hôpitaux,* this largess had no relationship to need across the country. Six departments received about one quarter of all bequests from 1800 to 1845: the Seine accounted for 18.7 million francs, followed by the Rhône (4.4 million), the Nord (3.3 million), the Seine-et-Oise (3.2 million), the Haute-Garonne (3.1 million), and the Bouches-du-Rhône (2.9 million). The median for total contributions by department in that period was about 1.1 million francs. Bringing up the rear were Corsica (20,000), Finistère (174,000), Hautes-Alpes (222,000), Cher (297,000), Creuse (306,000), and Charente-Inférieure (312,000).[31] In rough geographic terms, relatively generous philanthropists were to be found in the North, Midi, and East, while the West and Center were laggard; but almost everywhere the countryside drew little if any of the benefit directly.

Of course charity did not derive solely from bequests. Institutions offering assistance to the needy depended after 1796 on a mix of income from endowments, municipal subventions, individual donations, and collections. Local agencies like the Paris *comités de bienfaisance* had always relied on donations throughout the Revolution. Only the Convention's national pension programs of 1793–95 were conceived without reference to contributions by generous citizens. But national programs no longer existed after 1796, and the concept of public assistance gradually gave way to *"charité publique"*—a bastardized term that expressed the prevailing reality quite accurately. More than ever, assistance to the needy depended on collections, subscriptions, and donations channeled through quasi-public institutions *(hôpitaux* and *bureaux de bienfaisance)* under scrutiny by local public authority.

THE ERA OF *charité publique* also brought a new lease on life to the private associations whose new-style philanthropy had seemed so promising in the 1780s.[32] These associations had targeted the aged, the blind, the disabled,

needy pregnant women, and mothers of newborn infants for carefully calculated home relief and moral support. The most renowned group, the very
model of philanthropic activism, had been the Société Philanthropique,
founded in 1780. After sharp drops in its upper-class membership and funds
as the Revolution progressed, the society's directors appealed to the Convention for subsidies to continue its good works.[33] The deputies voted a
subvention in January 1793, but they refused a second request in September
and rebuffed another in May 1794 in emphatic terms, which seemed to
repudiate the very notion of organized private philanthropy:

> The French Nation has undertaken to aid the indigent; the goal of
> extinguishing mendicity will not be realized if funds destined for the relief
> of the poor are given over to private organizations. It is the Nation alone
> to which the suffering citizen has the right to make his claim. . . . At this
> moment, anyone who is unable to meet his basic needs will find resources
> in the generosity of the Nation, without having to resort to individual
> assistance which is too demeaning for French citizens.

The society understood the signal, dissolved itself, and turned its remaining
assets over to the Convention, with an immoderate self-deprecation bordering on sarcasm:

> The sublime right to aid the indigent among our patriotic brethren, our
> respectable *sans-culottes*, is a right that belongs to the public authority, the
> depository of the rights of all, and not to some feeble and powerless
> association of private men. The Société Philanthropique is merely an
> instrument of individual bienfaisance [while] you have organized *bienfai-
> sance publique* on a grand scale.[34]

The Société Maternelle also took the message and suspended its operations. In the 1780s that association had provided prenatal and neonatal
assistance to expectant mothers, with a particular emphasis on subsidizing
them to breastfeed their newborn infants. Despite its elitist patina, surviving
activists had cooperated effectively with the sectional *comités de bienfaisance* in
reaching pregnant and nursing women among the poor well into 1794, but
they could not withstand the Convention's sudden impatience with private
philanthropy.[35]

After Brumaire, the two associations reconstituted themselves. The four
or five hundred members of the Société Philanthropique paid 30 francs per
subscription, but the society also received an annual subsidy of 12,000 to
15,000 francs from the Napoleonic and Bourbon governments. Ever recep-

tive to the latest thinking on *bienfaisance,* the society now concentrated on establishing medical dispensaries for the poor and soup kitchens modeled on Count Rumford's prototype, but only after screening the recipients of such aid before giving them the required coupons. [36]

Rumford, a cosmopolitan Anglo-Saxon who held a high position in the Bavarian monarchy, had organized a workhouse and a meticulously planned soup kitchen in Munich. To economize on fuel consumption, Rumford designed a new kind of oven, and to assure a nutritious meal he formulated a standard recipe for soup built around barley and peas. Munich's indigents received daily meal tickets from public officials or charitable organizations, while working people could purchase the soup at a modest price. As a total package, Rumford's model gave a quasi-scientific aura to an old idea—its appeal as a novel form of mass production for *bienfaisance* resembled the allure of the Lancastrian or mutual method of primary schooling a decade later. The Société Philanthropique embraced this cause at the behest of the banker Delessert, who opened the first prototype in Paris in 1800 and published several articles extolling the virtues of *soupes de Rumford,* or *soupes économiques,* as they came to be called. Under the society's aegis twenty ovens operated in the capital by 1802, and the idea was taken up in at least nineteen departments. [37]

Initial popular reaction to this new-fangled concoction remote from the usual dietary staples was bound to be hostile. But the society did not flinch from this resistance and kept up its propaganda, eventually winning over the minister of the interior, who forwarded the society's annual reports to his prefects and urged them to spread the new gospel. "The indigent class in Paris was prejudiced in principle against the *soupes économiques,"* admitted a correspondent of the ministry in 1806, but this distaste had been overcome, he claimed, and the people of Paris now accepted that *soupes économiques* "are a food as agreeable as they are healthy." In the Drôme, a prefect similarly reported: "From the start I had to combat many prejudices. At first public opinion did not support me, but I persevered. Each winter the soups gained ground. Now they have prevailed, not everywhere . . . but enough to leave no doubt that they are here to stay." [38]

When the worst subsistence crisis of the Empire erupted in 1811–12, the government provided millions of francs for public works, grain purchases, and distributions of bread, but also for that new weapon in the arsenal of emergency relief, *soupes économiques.* [39] A decree of March 1812 proposed that 2 million rations be provided daily across the country, with the treasury to advance funds to local authorities for that purpose. Where the ground had not been prepared, and especially in rural communes, popular resistance ran high despite the desperation of ordinary working people. Not only were the vegetables hard to come by in some regions, but local populations resisted deviations from the accustomed subsistence diet. The "pronounced disgust," the "prejudices," the "antipathy of the inhabitants for any kind of innovation" stymied dozens of officials and philanthropists promoting wholesale relief by means of *soupes économiques.* In many towns, on the other hand, they apparently succeeded, as in Evreux (Eure), where "the indigent eagerly flocked toward this new resource." [40]

Paris was one place where the crash program to provide Rumford soups assuredly worked. Over forty ovens operated in the capital during that crisis year, distributing 24,000 rations a day. But even in good years the Société Philanthropique found a steady clientele of Parisian indigents (screened by its own members and local *bureaux de bienfaisance* for free meal tickets), as well as working people ready to pay a nominal price for the soup. In 1819, for example, its nine ovens served 240,000 rations, half of which were sold and half given free to coupon holders. Between its revival in 1800 and 1820, according to a contemporary account of *bienfaisance,* the society distributed over 15,700,000 portions of *soupe économique.* [41]

The estimable Société Maternelle also revived after Brumaire, bringing the latest precepts on prenatal and neonatal care back into the slums of Paris and other cities. Like the Société Philanthropique, its previous reputation won the organization an annual subvention from the minister of the interior of 12,000 to 15,000 francs. Between 1801 and 1810, it supported 4,113 newborn Parisian babies (of whom a respectable 78 percent survived to fifteen months) with a cumulative expenditure of 467,000 francs. By that time the society had affiliates in thirty-five departments as well, though its ambitious program was running at a deficit. [42]

With national programs for health care and welfare pensions a fading memory, and with local assistance bureaus operating on minimal budgets, private initiative had to fill the vacuum during the Empire. Official recognition and subsidies sometimes helped a private organization in raising funds and extending its reach; occasionally high officials or members of the imperial family lent their names and support to private charitable associations. But this was not a high priority for Napoleon, whose regime had no interest in the argument put forth by one pamphleteer that only the government could "open all the hearts and pocketbooks to compassion and pity with a law on *bienfaisance* regulating their rallying point." [43] Napoleon did not nominate men to the Legion of Honor for notable philanthropic work, and he certainly did not create a parallel "Legion of *Bienfaisance,*" as one writer had urged. [44] Only during the subsistence crisis of 1811–12 did the regime show a belated interest in local good works, when it demanded from prefects information about "persons who have distinguished themselves by their *bienfaisance* and those who have shown a lack of interest during [the crisis of] 1812." The resultant honor roll suggested the thinness and unevenness of serious philanthropy in imperial France. In the incomplete returns, at least fifteen prefects admitted with embarrassment that "individual charity has not had occasion to manifest itself."[45]

PHILANTHROPY AND RELIGION

Even before the Restoration produced a lurch in that direction, traditional religious preoccupations reasserted themselves in the domain of *bienfaisance* once the government again countenanced private charity. To be sure, the Neo-Jacobins had argued that voluntarism did not necessarily entail surrendering to religious values. The former agent of the Committee of Public Safety Marc-Antoine Jullien, for example, sketched a plan for local volunteer committees to collect funds from the wealthy under public auspices which, he hoped, would deprive the clergy of leverage.[46] But *charité publique* after Brumaire was bound to attract the Catholic laity and clergy back to the arena of good works as much as it drew the secular philanthropists.[47] In 1804, for example, the ex-bishop of Mende founded an *Asile des Vieillards et Orphelins de la Providence,* and an association of subscribers to support it, with the endorsement of the Paris Hospital Council, the Ministry of the Interior, and members of the imperial family; after 1814, the Bourbons and some of the "ancient families of the court" were even more active in their patronage. The organization's refuge for the aged started with twenty-four places (half free, half at a modest charge) and reached sixty, while its expanding operations included a charity workshop employing over one hundred people, and several charity schools.[48]

The society also branched out into home relief in collaboration with two parish charity bureaus, which had in turn been seconding the *bureaux de bienfaisance* of their neighborhoods by offering aid to the sick and needy, as well as schooling and job placement for the young. The Société de la Providence even distributed coupons for *soupes économiques* to its clients. In most respects, the activities of this society seem indistinguishable from secular philanthropy. Yet there was a difference. Catholic benefactors did more than aid the needy or train their children for work. In collaboration with the society, the parish charity bureau of Saint-Roche announced its principal aim as "contributing to the glory of God." Before offering aid, the parish commissioners gathered information from prospective clients, with their statements to be counter-signed by their confessors. The investigator was to determine, among other things, whether a couple had been married in church, and whether their children had been baptized and catechized. [49]

The imperial regime supported the *Asile de la Providence,* the Saint-Roche parish charity bureau, and such organizations as the Dames du Refuge de Saint-Michel (run by the Sisters of Charity) whose rescue mission for fallen women was supposed to "return them to good morals, Christian virtues, and the love of a working life." [50] Yet the government did not necessarily approve of religious tests being used by municipal welfare committees or major philanthropic organizations. That, at any rate, is the import of a revealing letter from an officer of the Société Maternelle to the Ministry of the Interior in December 1812, denying an allegation that a woman had been refused aid by the society because her marriage had not been religiously consecrated. At least one hundred cases of clients with only civil marriages could be cited, she asserted, and women of all religions had been admitted to their rolls. "Poverty and good conduct are the only rules." [51]

The social and religious ramifications of *charité publique* surfaced during a complex debate in the last years of the Empire over the organization of home relief in Paris. The ministry and the Hospital Council criticized the system's performance—a result, among other things, of overlaying a bureau in each of the forty-eight sections (dating from 1793) with an oversight committee in each of the city's twelve arrondissements (dating from 1796)—but were uncertain over how to increase its clout. They wanted parish priests on the committees, yet hesitated to name them as standing members "lest they have too great an influence." They wished to recruit socially prominent individuals—"to bring into these bureaus persons who have kept themselves away until now"—but wondered how to appeal to the vanity of such people when "the multiplicity of positions precluded the kind of consideration which ought to surround them." [52]

What a far cry from the spirit in which the *sans-culotte* bourgeoisie had shouldered the burden during the heady days of 1793 and the economic disasters of 1795! Even the Consulate's leading expert had paid tribute to those pioneers who had paved the way for the future "by developing the true principles of assistance": "A large number of men who devoted themselves to relieving the indigent in obscurity . . . without any hope of renown, without calling the attention of the government or the public to themselves." [53] The atmosphere had changed dramatically since those days of democratic civic virtue. Charity, religion, and social prestige formed a very different amalgam.

The evocative question of what to call these relief committees reflected this trend. Revolutionary nomenclature still had resonance. By 1813, the ministry prepared to change the name of the committees from *bureaux de bienfaisance* to *bureaux de charité*. Certain members of the Hospital Council reasonably objected that this change would "make them to some extent a religious institution." But such misgivings yielded to the regime's goal of attracting "the persons most worthy of occupying such positions, who might have been put off until now by an appellation that recalls times and circumstances which should be effaced from memory." After much deliberation, the ministry wished to streamline the system's organization, add the clergy as standing members, and change the name to "charity bureaus." As was true with almost any domestic initiative in 1813, however, "ensuing circumstances [of war] made it impossible to implement the new organization."[54]

With fewer misgivings, the Bourbons made such changes in 1816, and it is likely that some *bureaux de charité* became battlegrounds between secular-minded members and those who advocated religious criteria to evaluate requests for home relief. This is not to imply that the system as a whole became captive of religious forces. Only that an undercurrent of tensions persisted, causing the publicist Appert for one to worry early in 1830 that, "thanks to certain influences in the composition of these committees, assistance will be distributed to the poor more in relation to their docility and assiduousness in attending religious services than in proportion to their needs."[55]

The Revolution of 1830 shook the equilibrium of the capital's welfare establishment and reopened several questions. Liberal charity commissioners attacked the Hospital Council's stewardship, claiming that under its aegis *l'hospicisme* had reigned since 1800. In one sense this simply revived a long-standing feud over the respective merits of institutional and home relief. The welfare commissioners vainly hoped to gain parity or even independence from the sway of the Hospital Council. In their view the *hôpitaux,* with their large endowments and disproportionate share of the *octrois,* absorbed a grossly excessive share of resources, whereas such institutions were appropriate only for idiots and epileptics, "nature's rejects." *Secours à domicile* had one tenth the budget of the hospitals for about the same number of clients, they asserted; "the poor person, who receives less than 4 centimes by staying in his own home, costs nearly 8 sours a day in the *hôpital.* "

But the argument cut deeper, for the commissioners resurrected as their benchmark the blueprint of March 1793, which had favored home relief over institutions. It was under Napoleon that the emphasis had shifted back to the *hôpitaux*, consistent with that regime's despotic spirit, they claimed. "He saw in the poor only a class of men whom he must regiment. . . . A hospital was virtually a barracks . . . while the poor in his own home was reduced to gathering a few crumbs left over from the great feast of the *hôpitaux*. . . . In countries where despotism reigns . . . one helps the poor only by degrading them; they are humiliated in order to dominate them better." The Restoration, they contended, exacerbated the humiliation of the needy when it transformed the welfare committees into *bureaux de charité*.[56] There had been different nuances in the practice of *bienfaisance* across the past four decades that these liberals found worth remembering.

SELF-HELP: THE MONT DE PIÉTÉ

Public assistance pensions and charity, public works and *dépôts de mendicité*, *hôpitaux* and home relief did not exhaust the possibilities for aiding the needy. Enlightened thinking also encouraged self-help, and we must examine the fate of two old-regime vehicles for that ideal, the *Mont de Piété* and the mutual aid society. The *Mont de Piété*, or communal pawnshop, holds a curious place in the history of French *bienfaisance*. Though common in Northern Italy, Flanders, and a few areas of Southern France, not until 1777 was one founded in the capital. Yet in less than a decade the institution played a vital role in the domestic economy of many, perhaps most, Parisians. The *Mont de Piété* served both the laboring poor and petits bourgeois in straitened circumstances. Indeed, it is hard to imagine how the city's population survived without it. During periods of unemployment or illness, workers pawned clothing, linens, or household goods (provided their value was at least 3 livres), at the cost of a nominal transaction fee. When and if the situation improved, they could redeem the pledge upon payment of the principal plus 10 percent annual interest pro-rated monthly. The average duration of a loan was six to seven months. Of the *Mont de Piété*'s seven bureaus, five handled used clothing and the like, while two received articles made of precious metal, watches, jewelry, and shop merchandise. Timely loans from the *Mont de Piété* undoubtedly reduced the number of bankruptcies occasioned by bad debts among small artisans and gave shopkeepers the flexibility to convert unneeded inventories into cash; some "send their winter merchandise during the summer and their summer goods in the winter."[57]

The *Mont de Piété* thus had two faces. If we consider the total number of transactions, over 500,000 annually before the Revolution, the great majority came at the low end of the scale, between 3 and 12 livres. If we look at proportions of the money loaned out, on the other hand, fewer but more substantial borrowers naturally accounted for a considerable share. The balance between the two types of loans underlay the institution's viability. From the profits on transactions in gold, silver, jewelry, and merchandise, the *Mont de Piété* could carry hundreds of thousands of small borrowers "who bring it virtually nothing, since the benefits that it draws from the large loans permit it to lend to others at a loss." [58] Whatever the institution's value to small businessmen or to the genteel poor reduced to pawning their valuables, the *Mont de Piété* was of most use to the laboring poor.

When a borrower did not redeem his pledge after one year or failed to renew it (upon payment of the interest due), the pledge would be sold off by the assessors *(huissiers priseurs),* with the proceeds minus the interest due going to the owner. The *huissier* earned a commission on any profit from the sale, which was likely since he made his loans at four fifths the estimated value for gold and silver items, and two thirds for other articles. In fact, only between 5 to 8 percent of pledges had to be sold, since people rarely turned to the *Mont de Piété* with the intention of alienating their possessions for good. Finding that in the 1830s 60 percent of the pledges were redeemed on time, 35 percent renewed, and only 5 percent sold off, the minister of the interior reasonably concluded that "the poor classes attach just as much value as the others to the conservation of their possessions." [59]

Despite this supremely useful service to the poor, the *Mont de Piété* stood vulnerable to attack after 1789. Money-at-interest was always a delicate issue. True, the institution kept needy people from the clutches of unscrupulous usurers, while its net profits, after deductions for the staff of two hundred, went to the *hôpital général* (some 2 million livres altogether between 1777 and 1792). Yet the house did charge 10 percent interest, did pay 5 percent interest to individuals who placed their capital there, and did sell off a portion of the pledges at a profit for the *huissier.* It could appear, then, that there was something exploitative about the *Mont de Piété.* At the least a revolutionary militant like Concedieu, the comptroller of the *Mont de Piété* in 1791, advocated lowering the charges and "even lending up to a certain sum without charges," though how this might be financed he did not say. [60]

The *Mont de Piété* served most usefully during prolonged hard times, yet that was just when individuals might lose the capacity to redeem their possessions. In 1789, Louis XVI offered 300,000 livres in subsidies to help needy Parisians redeem pledges valued at under 24 livres. Could the Convention do any less during the subsistence crisis of the Year II? With the *assignats* throwing the economy of the *Mont de Piété* out of kilter already, the Convention on 23 January 1794 authorized the free redemption (without payment of principal or interest) of "necessary objects" valued under 20 livres, or the first 20 livres of pledges worth between 20 and 50 livres.[61] A boon to the poor who had already borrowed from the *Mont de Piété,* this policy made it improbable that others would be able to do so in the future unless the institution was transformed. Concedieu now argued for a full-scale nationalization, with the treasury footing the bill.[62] But other voices thought this an opportune moment to abolish the *Mont de Piété* altogether. Why this should be so at the height of Jacobin ascendancy makes interesting reading.

The Executive Commission on Public Assistance drafted a report that had little good to say about the institution. The typical ambivalence in revolutionary views on *bienfaisance* found pointed expression here. The *Mont de Piété,* after all, was entirely unregulated. Other than checking the provenance of jewelry and precious metals that might have been stolen, no one asked any questions about why people were pawning their possessions or what they intended to do with the money. The *Mont de Piété* was therefore "a seductive apparatus, where people find the unfortunate facility to satisy their penchant for dissipation"—a view that can be found again and again down to the 1830s.

More specifically, these austere Jacobins saw in the *Mont de Piété* an instrument for the oppression of housewives at the hands of dissolute husbands, like those who drank up their wages in a tavern. The *Mont de Piété* was "an abyss that swallows up precious possessions and useful articles, sacrificed sometimes for momentary needs but more often pulled from the daily use of good mothers under that pretext by the guilty [male] hands of disorder and dissolution." At the same time its exorbitant interest charges and sales commissions constituted "usury covered with the mask of *bienfaisance.*" A republic had no place for such "an intolerable monstrosity," such a "temple of usury," they concluded. And besides, the new laws on public assistance "embrace the totality of needs . . . and indict the shameful loans made by usury to the indolent."[63]

The Executive Commission on Public Assistance never publicized this splenetic abolitionist polemic, and instead replaced it with a more conventional "reform project," which admitted that *bienfaisance nationale* could not actually cover all needs of the "sick worker, the unemployed artisan, the merchant compromised by the default of a payment." In its official report, the commission still worried that the institution offered "too easy a form of help where there is a risk of encouraging idleness and debauchery," but it did not wish to deprive prospective borrowers of this recourse. A nationalized *Mont de Piété,* transformed into a *Caisse de prêts de secours* and subsidized by the treasury, should lend with no commission fees on pledges valued under 25 livres. [64] By the time the government sorted this out, however, it had become academic. In the hyperinflation of 1795–96, the entire concept lost its plausibility. The *Mont de Piété* was immobilized, its capital eaten up, in part by speculators. "It is the *assignats* above all to which we must attribute the decline of the *Mont de Piété*," concluded a report of July 1796. "Since the loans and repayments were always being made at nominal value, the result was that in the final analysis 1 livre did not represent [even] 1 cent *(denier)*." The institution would have closed altogether but for the self-serving maneuvers of its pared-down staff. To all intent and purpose it ceased to function for the time being. [65]

Though difficult to operate, the *Mont de Piété* remained a potentially valuable public service for the poor. The Napoleonic regime soon put the Paris *Mont de Piété* back on its feet while encouraging the foundation of others in the departments. The resurrected *Mont de Piété* became a quasi-public corporation: "It will be operated, under the surveillance of the prefect and the authority of the Minister of the Interior, by an unpaid charitable board," with the prefect appointing the salaried director. The state did not provide funding, however. Instead, it sold shares to get the venture started, and invited investors to place their capital in return for interest. The hospital board was a key player, expected to provide seed money and to reap the profits as of old. [66] Napoleonic support gave the Paris *Mont de Piété* a new lease on life, despite a financial crisis which required a six-month suspension of interest payments to investors in 1813–14 and almost caused more drastic damage. [67]

Most departments did not follow the government's exhortations to establish communal pawnshops, but thirty towns had one by 1830, and another eighteen were founded under the July Monarchy. The scale of activity naturally varied among these forty-six institutions in twenty-six departments: the Paris *Mont de Piété* handled over 1 million transactions annually after 1817, while those in Bordeaux and Lyon hit the threshold of 100,000 in 1828 and 1830, respectively. Nineteen institutions made only 10,000 to 50,000 loans annually, and fifteen made fewer than 10,000. [68] Interest rates and charges stabilized under the Empire, declining from the grotesque levels of 30 and even 70 percent that had prevailed in Paris during the hyperinflation of 1795–96, and continued to trend downward. In Paris, they fell from 12 percent under the Empire and Restoration to 9 percent after 1830. (At the same time the interest paid *by* the *Mont de Piété* on funds deposited there fell from a range of 6 to 4 percent to a range of 5 to 2.5 percent.) Outside of Paris interest rates in the *Mont de Piété* clustered between 6 and 12 percent annually. [69]

The value of a typical transaction in Paris averaged about 17 francs in the

1820s and 1830s. An official report indicates that 880,000 loans out of 1,211,000 in 1836 were valued between 3 to 12 francs, on all of which the house claimed to lose money. Even more interesting are some figures from 1846, perhaps representative of earlier decades, breaking down the transactions by social class. An average 1,000 borrowers in Paris included 128 shopkeepers and merchants, 165 rentiers, professionals and the like, and 707 workers. The *Mont de Piété* remained extremely useful to the popular classes, though some argued that it would do even more good if it lowered the minimum value of a pledge to 1 franc, or if pledges could be redeemed piece by piece rather than in one lot.[70]

On the other hand, certain moralizing philanthropists still objected to the *Mont de Piété*. Though statistics showed that only about 5 percent of the pledges were sold off in the 1820s and 1830s, a study project by the influential Société des Etablissements Charitables in 1836 wondered whether the *Mont de Piété* worked against "the spirit of thrift, economy, work, and the taste for property and its conservation. . . . Don't loans made too easily, even at fairly low interest, always have grave drawbacks? And shouldn't we try to put off as much as possible those who would be tempted to take advantage of them?" The *Mont de Piété* was flawed, according to this view, because it did not exercise guidance or control over the poor, "by having the right to demand from the borrower an account of his position and to refuse the loan if it is not truly useful to him." These reformers concluded that an endowed charitable lending bank would be preferable, provided it were run "like other private charitable establishments, and conserved the right to examine and refuse the borrowers."[71] Here, alive and well, was a classic tradition of eighteenth-century philanthropy, which encouraged thrift institutions for workers, but insisted on scrutiny and control over their use.

SELF-HELP: MUTUALISM

If the *Mont de Piété* provided a margin of survival during adversity, mutual aid societies *(sociétés de secours mutuels)* offered a more purposeful way to prepare for hard times. Saving 1 or 2 sous a week systematically, members pooled their contributions to provide sick benefits, funerals, and in some cases assistance against unemployment. Jacobins, liberals, and royalists all regarded thrift *(prévoyance)* as the likeliest antidote to indigence and the necessary partner of *bienfaisance*. Surprisingly, however, the Revolution had proven thoroughly uncongenial to mutual associations. As Louis Blanc and other democrats implied in the 1830s and 1840s, economic cooperation had been a missing link in the Jacobinism of 1793, whose incorporation was likely to make the Jacobin tradition more appealing to contemporary workers.[72] But in the 1790s other preoccupations obscured that logic, among them a Rousseauist emphasis on individual independence, however modest; an anti-religious bias operating against confraternities, the old regime's most common form of artisans' associations; the LeChapelier Law, which individualized labor relations and effectively banned trade unions; and extremely unsettled economic conditions during most of the decade. That, at any rate, might explain the fact that mutualist association ground to a halt in the 1790s. Mutualism revived tentatively under the Empire, however, and accelerated after 1814. A census of 175 Parisian *sociétés de secours mutuels* in 1827 indicates at most fourteen dating back before 1800. In contrast, forty-three Parisian societies were established during the Consulate and Empire, and the rest between 1815 and 1826, with twenty founded in 1820, and twenty-five the following year.[73]

Officials and philanthropists undoubtedly felt more comfortable when a mutual aid society comprised members from diverse occupational groups; with this "abnegation of the corporate spirit," associations were less likely to operate clandestinely as workers' trade unions. But workers and artisans had a practical reason to opt for that course themselves, since an occupational mix might soften the blows to their treasury caused by setbacks or depressions in a particular trade. Generally, however, single-trade associations were more common, for reasons of social proximity and solidarity that are easy enough to understand. (Only 39 of the 175 Parisian mutual societies were noted as having "members of all professions or diverse occupations," the others being associated with a specific trade, though not always exclusively.) For all its suspicions about clandestine labor actions in single-trade mutual societies, the government did not prohibit or actively discourage such organizations after 1800.[74]

Moreover the Société Philanthropique propagated the cause of mutualism and took some of these associations under its wings. The Société des Amis de l'Humanité, with about two hundred members by 1808, a majority from the Parisian printing trades, became a particular favorite of these philanthropists, who extolled the association's scrupulous by-laws and publicized their successful management. The presence of six "benefactors and honorary members" among the *amis* undoubtedly provided a cushion that enhanced the association's solvency and allowed it to pay out higher benefits. Moral and material patronage of workers' mutual aid societies became a standard plank in the agenda of liberal philanthropy. Appert even argued that the government itself should subscribe to all of these societies.[75]

Elite patronage was of course futile without the resolve of the workers themselves. In Grenoble, for example, "the origin of these associations is owed to the zeal of several glove workers, encouraged by the local administration, which made them aware of all the advantages." That they had a timely push is not to take anything away from the *gantiers,* whose achievement knowledgeable grenoblois long recognized. As one observer later put it, administrative experience contributed to the success of mutualism, and "the *gantiers* purchased theirs at great cost"—a remark reminiscent of E. P. Thompson's comment on English Friendly Societies, whose failures and defaulting officers, without benefit of middle-class members or paternalistic supervision, constituted "(often heart-breaking) schools of experience."[76] In Grenoble, the *gantiers'* example and assistance inspired workers in the building trades to form a mutual association two years later in 1805, and six other societies followed subsequently. Timely aid from the elites continued to make a difference on occasion. The society of Grenoble's hemp carders, for example, barely survived an economic downturn in 1817, but wealthy honorary members helped restore its viability.[77]

Marseille's fifteen mutual societies likewise functioned under paternalistic scrutiny. They "exist under the direction of the administration of the Société de Bienfaisance, which oversees the distribution of the aid of which the syndics are the trustees," reported the prefect in 1813. The police commissioner of the *quartier* presided over the assemblies of each mutual society (as they did in Lyon), with a member of the Société de Bienfaisance in attendance as well.[78] Was this surveillance oppressive? Undoubtedly it was calculated to hold the associations to the limited goal of aiding the sick—a restraint that militant tanners, bakers, and hatters in those two cities evaded aggressively.[79] But in relation to the societies' ostensible objectives, municipal or philanthropic oversight made peculation or inefficient management of their funds less likely. Every member benefited if trustees handled their weekly contributions scrupulously and profitably.

Self-help societies raised no doubts about a hidden agenda in Toulouse and the Haute-Garonne, where the prefect complained of a different kind of problem. In that department it was not the Société Philanthropique that encouraged artisans and workers to form mutual societies but the clergy, apparently led by the local archbishop. This patronage, and the prominence of patron saints in the names and activities of the societies, was no mere window dressing. In 1812, the prefect and the mayor of Toulouse urged the societies to eliminate the manifestly religious elements of their by-laws, but they refused. "In effect the members claim that to separate the religious rules from the practice of *bienfaisance* would be to destroy the societies because the two are inseparable." Like other Napoleonic officials uneasy about the resurgence of religion in *bienfaisance,* the prefect distrusted "the priests who founded these religious companies, who draw frequent oblations from their assemblies, and who will not easily lose their domination." But the minister of the interior advised him to leave the societies free to pursue their useful activity in their preferred fashion. [80]

Thrift was an unexceptionable notion, but one more easily proposed than implemented. The dread of dying penniless in a *hôpital* no doubt created a strong compulsion among urban workers to save. But even with the will, and the requisite discretionary income every week, where could a worker, artisan, or clerk confidently place his precious sous? The dearth of popular savings banks left a wide field open to philanthropic entrepreneurs and outright mountebanks promoting "double tontines," "establishments of humanity," and "assured retreats for the unfortunate." [81] Generally the government distrusted private annuity schemes or retirement homes for the working classes, "whose duration and utility are not based on any kind of guarantee, and which most often, formed under the veil of *bienfaisance,* actually constitute an object of commerce or speculation contrary to humanitarianism." In 1806 the government attempted to impose greater scrutiny on such schemes, which did not offer "a sufficient guarantee of their duration . . . and expose a multitude of families to seeing themselves deceived." [82] In mutual associations, fraud was rarely an issue, but the guarantee of solvency into the distant future assuredly was.

In the resurgence of mutualism, elite paternalism played a minor but perceptible role alongside the action of disciplined artisans and workers. Mutualism required government sufferance, and liberal philanthropists helped secure a supportive policy, despite the knowledge that mutual aid societies could easily screen illegal labor movements. The most ambitious philanthropists put greater effort into founding popular savings banks, and managed to do so in Paris, Bordeaux, Lyon, and Metz. The Paris *Caisse d'épargne,* established in 1818, accepted deposits of as little as 1 franc, and within two years had taken in over 1 million francs. [83] But small-scale mutual societies with fifty, one hundred, or two hundred members were far easier to launch and nurture. In the long run, it is true, these associations loom most importantly for their role in promoting working-class consciousness and solidarity, both within and beyond their ostensible purpose. William Sewell has thus argued that mutual aid societies often fronted for journeymen's corporations and clandestine labor action, particularly after 1830, although most of the associations founded between 1800 and 1830 probably adhered to the limited aims expressed in their government-approved regulations. [84] In any case, during the Empire and the Restoration, when municipal authorities and philanthropists saw mutual associations as a form of enlightened *bienfai-*

sance, paternalistic surveillance may have been a reasonable price to endure for an added margin of solvency.

FOUR DECADES OF *BIENFAISANCE:* A BALANCE SHEET

The French people had once aided the needy by the simple expedient of handing out alms to the hungry lined up at the gates of a monastery or to beggars importuning them in the street. Progressive thinkers in the eighteenth century stigmatized such indiscriminate almsgiving as a cardinal error that rewarded indolence and perpetuated indigence. Nor were they sanguine about the seventeenth-century innovation of confining the needy in *hôpitaux*. As perpetual monuments to private philanthropy, those institutions were popular with traditional elites who sought more purposeful channels for their benevolence. But to critics before and after 1789, *hospicisme* created a wasteful as well as demoralizing way to deal with the indigent. Enlightened circles by far preferred carefully administered home relief. Before the Revolution, however, priests and parish activists with a religious frame of reference dominated the distribution of *secours à domicile*. To the progressive mind, their religious criteria in assessing worthiness for assistance created a needless distraction.

The Revolution offered an opportunity to deemphasize the *hôpitaux,* secularize and systematize home relief, and make assistance to the needy relatively uniform across the nation. The Convention codified these long-standing objectives in the law of March 1793, which was simply a rough sketch of what a national system of *bienfaisance* might look like. Even so, the gesture was not insignificant. Almost four decades later the embattled charity commissioners of Paris looked back on it as a benchmark, as they called for new laws on public assistance and education to revive the Revolution's activism. "Louis Philippe can do no less for the people of 1830," they declared, "than the Convention did for those of 1793." [85]

Within months the Convention has passed beyond such generalities to break genuinely new ground. Proclaiming a national responsibility for certain categories of need, the deputies decreed that funds would pass from the treasury by way of the district administrations to the individuals in question. These entitlements (as we would call them today) for needy working parents with several children (law of 28 June 1793) and for aged agricultural workers, rural artisans, and rural widows (law of 22 floréal II) committed the national state directly to public assistance for the poor regardless of which region in France they inhabited. Alongside these programs the Convention also fashioned a package of "patriotic assistance," which promised subsistence pensions to the needy dependents of volunteers and draftees, as well as more substantial compensatory pensions for wounded veterans.

Ultimately (except for the veterans) successive governments forgot or renounced these promises. But the fact that implementation of *all* had begun, despite the monumental administrative and civic labors required, suggests that these measures constituted fundamental expressions of the "second" or republican revolution. If only up to a point, *bienfaisance* took on new conceptual dimensions in resonance with the ideology of equality and fraternity, or what might better be called civic reciprocity. Anticipating that spirit, when section Fontaine de Grenelle agitated for elected sectional welfare committees in late 1791, it conjured up this sentimental image: "Our fellow citizens will no longer be embarrassed to have a few moments of distress in front of someone who, perhaps the next day, will need to have recourse to the same *bienfaisance* himself."[86] No doubt rather fanciful, this invocation of fraternity seems, as far as one can judge, eminently sincere. After 1800, such language would have been unthinkable.

Notwithstanding the remarkable if ultimately abortive innovations by the Convention, continuity in *bienfaisance* from the 1770s to the 1820s makes equally strong claims on our attention, above all in the obsession with begging that framed so much of the discourse and practice of *bienfaisance*. This affront to social order and morality neither liberals, Jacobins, nor conservatives (with the interesting exceptions we have seen) could abide. In the 1790s, when revolutionaries did not hesitate to judge the moral character or patriotic intentions of their fellow citizens, it is no wonder that *mendicité* became a red flag. It seemed imperative to classify the needy into the deserving and undeserving, and by definition begging was an unworthy and socially destructive form of behavior. The offense did not automatically warrant punishment, but rather an effort at rehabilitation. The "extinction of mendicity" depended on social policies that would separate out the worthy (for example, by giving disabled beggars in Paris stipends to obviate their need to beg), offer employment and moral discipline to the able-bodied (if necessary by confinement in a *dépôt*), and remove the wilfully idle from society by criminal sanctions. With such aims in mind, royal officials, revolutionary legislators, imperial functionaries, and Restoration philanthropists alike carried on a recurrent but foredoomed search for the veritable principles of classification and institutional confinement.

This obsession with *mendicité* fed on their deep ambivalence toward the needy—a benign view on the one hand (whether based on Christian charity, simple humanitarianism, or some sense of revolutionary fraternity), and on the other hand a skepticism and distrust, a conviction that the indigent were lazy, improvident, and dissolute; that they would take advantage of any generosity and squander resources they had not earned. The antidote was first to keep assistance to a bare subsistence minimum (requisite too out of simple equity toward those who did work to support themselves), and second to scrutinize closely the recipients of aid. Even a service like the *Mont de Piété* could seem too permissive to some moral reformers because, in effect, it provided its services as indiscriminately as monasteries had once offered alms to the first in line. This ambivalence played itself out in revolutionary policy, not always with consistency. But after 1795 it was essentially resolved. Minimal state responsibility, nearly exclusive reliance on ad hoc local efforts, and an intrusive paternalistic philanthropy became the order of the day.

If we are to judge merely by outcome rather than attitudes, intentions, or promises, the conclusion is inescapable that the revolutionary decade unfolded harshly if not castrophically for most of the needy. But this was not a necessary result of the new approach to *bienfaisance,* where a morally rigorous public secularism replaced the traditional parochialism, paternalism (and laxism?) of the old regime. On their own terms, the Convention's entitlements and institutional reforms would have made a better provision for the poor than existed before. In the event, the demands of the war (which also produced a remarkable extension of *bienfaisance* in new directions), and the hyperinflation of 1795–96 left *bienfaisance* in ruins. Jacobin policy, however, directly caused the devastation that befell the *hôpitaux,* whose crisis culminated with the rash nationalization or expropriation of their property and endowments in July 1794. Yet by the 1820s, between the income from the new municipal *octrois* and the renewal of bequests, most of the larger *hôpitaux* had recovered.[87] In contrast, public home relief was left with grossly insufficient resources in most towns and was all but non-existent in the countryside, with no national pension entitlements surviving after 1796 to make up the difference.

In large cities the revival of private philanthropic organizations and religious charities, especially after the Restoration, undoubtedly compensated. The Société Philanthropique—propagating home relief, dispensaries, Rumford soups, and mutual societies—set the model for purposeful, paternalistic *bienfaisance* which, like mutual education, could be organized wholesale. Soon a philanthropic network developed with such focal points as Appert's *Journal des Prisons, hospices, écoles primaires et bienfaisance* and the non-denominational Société de la Morale Chrétienne.[88] The remnants of official "public charity" combined with the undertakings of organized philanthropists and Catholic charities probably left the needy in certain cities no worse or even better off than they had been. But disparities between city and country deepened. The Revolution had promised to redress this imbalance and had begun to do so impressively; it had not ascribed to urban citizens alone the right to public assistance. The failed revolution in *bienfaisance,* however, left the countryside to itself once again.

X

CIVIL JUSTICE
TRIBUNALS AND MAGISTRATES

Next to collecting taxes and fighting wars, French royal power asserted itself most tangibly in the administration of justice. True, the reach of the old-regime state petered out at the village level where seigneurs still held sway over petty justice. Serving a countryside without a public infrastructure at the local level, seigneurial justice could also be an abusive prerogative that gave lords and their bailiffs undue leverage in minor legal disputes with their own peasants. But the seigneurs had long since lost control over the judicial process when it came to more substantial cases. In that domain, even if it could never sweep away the historic diversity of provincial legal traditions, the French monarchy rationalized and homogenized wherever it could. Among the monuments of Louis XIV's reign stood two landmarks of legal codification: the uniform code of civil procedure of 1667; and the criminal ordinance of 1670, a combination of penology and procedure.

At the summit of France's judicial system stood the thirteen high courts, or *parlements,* in addition to a handful of tribunals with similar status specializing in fiscal affairs, such as the *Cour des Comptes.* Premiere among these institutions in every respect, the Parlement of Paris had as its *ressort* or bailiwick about one third of the nation's territory, including the Lyonnais, since France's second city did not have a parlement of its own. Outside of the royal palace itself no group of men had such prestige, power, and pretensions. Meanwhile the other parlements became bastions of regional pride, notably the parlements of Rennes (Brittany), Toulouse (Languedoc), Aix (Provence), and Bordeaux (Guyenne), which nurtured local traditions of civil jurisprudence, and in the case of Brittany aggressively defended provincial political privileges. The parlements served as courts of original jurisdiction for important civil and criminal cases, and also as courts of appeal within their *ressorts* for rulings by the approximately four hundred lower royal tribunals, known as the *bailliage* courts. By the seventeenth century the monarchy elevated about eighty of these lower courts into a higher tier of jurisdiction, known as *présidial* courts, which stood between ordinary *bailliage* courts and the parlements. That innovation aroused resentment among magistrates both above and below, and caused much dispute over whether an additional layer of appeals facilitated or encumbered the course of justice.[1]

Positions in all these tribunals—august parlements, *présidials,* and *bailliage* courts—were venal offices created and sold by the monarchy, which continued to collect large fees whenever a position changed hands. Though servitors of the crown charged with upholding royal law, each court in practice formed a quasi-autonomous corporation that effectively coopted new members when vacancies occurred. Like all venal officeholders, the judges owned their positions as a kind of property, held them for life, and were essentially irremovable. In social composition, however, the courts varied significantly. Though a small percentage of nobles sat on the lower court bench, most *bailliage* and *présidial* magistrates were commoners who could not gain ennoblement by virtue of ascent to their positions, nor reasonably aspire to elevation to the parlements. In contrast, the magistrates of the parlements were most definitely part of the nobility. Starting in the 1670s, appointment to a parlement brought the prospect of hereditary nobility. By the end of the eighteenth century the parlementaires enjoyed such high status that the large majority of newcomers were already nobles when they ascended to the bench (some by virtue of being the sons of parlementaires), and almost all were extremely wealthy. Ties of kinship and social status barred the way to all but the most exceptional commoners. But if the parlementaires could be described as privileged, wealthy, and exclusive, they were also fiercely proud of their professional dedication and sense of public responsibility.[2] The elite barristers who practiced before the parlements—though cut off socially from the magistrates—proudly basked in the latter's aura.[3] The parlementaires in short constituted an establishment and formed a veritable aristocracy.

Long after the Revolution consigned this old-regime magistracy to oblivion, and long after Napoleon—for all his hostility to revolutionary innovations—ratified the creation of a less exalted judicial order, admirers of that bygone era recalled the virtues of this vanquished aristocracy. "Why was the old Magistracy held in such high esteem?" asked the lawyer Dupin in 1814, when citizens regained the opportunity to express themselves on such subjects. Their prestige, he answered, resulted from their dedication to the public good; their science and knowledge; and their eminent birth and great wealth, which made them inaccessible to the seductions of fortune. Above reproach in private lives lived among their own kind, in public they appeared dignified, paternalistic, and majestic. Another Restoration critic of the "decadence" of the magistracy since 1789 similarly extolled the independence and breeding of the old-regime parlementaires with their status, wealth, power, knowledge, and renown. Compared to them, current judges were puny figures, "most being without patrimony and of scarcely distinguished birth," mere salaried employees dependent on the state's benign regard.[4] The Revolution had indeed created a new judicial universe. Why had it done so? Toward what ends and by what means? And how did its innovations fare?

"Destroy in Order to Reconstruct Anew"

The greatest political convulsions in eighteenth-century France had pitted the king's ministers against the parlements. The magistrates' power to exercise a kind of legislative veto by refusing to register royal edicts of questionable wisdom or legality, coupled with their extensive regulatory and police powers, thwarted the royal will periodically on fiscal, economic, and religious issues, such as the status of Jesuits and Jansenists. At times the monarchy backed down; occasionally it won over or intimidated the parlements. But in 1771 minister Maupeou resolved to settle this ongoing conflict decisively. Not only did he exile the magistrates (a traditional royal tactic, analogous to the parlementaires' occasional resort to a judicial strike). In what the public generally saw as a coup d'état, Maupeou replaced the parlements altogether with new upper courts whose members would not be independent venal officeholders but loyalists appointed by the crown. In the process he effected other changes such as allocating the new courts on a more proportionate geographic basis and paying regular salaries to the judges who normally derived income from fees.

Maupeou's reforms, however, went no further since his primary interest was political. He did nothing about the venality, jurisdictions, or procedures of the lower courts, the contours of the criminal justice system, or the numbing complexities that enveloped civil litigation. The fundamental result of Maupeou's "revolution" was to eliminate at a stroke the political pretensions of the parlements, their claim to "represent" the nation and to stand as a bulwark against absolutism. With exceptions like Voltaire, public opinion—stirred by an adroit parlementaire propaganda machine—roundly condemned Maupeou's despotic act, but for the duration of his tenure he persevered.[5]

When Louis XVI ascended the throne in 1774, the young monarch sought to establish his goodwill and popularity by dismissing Maupeou and recalling the parlements. Though chastened by this experience, the magistrates by no means abandoned their traditional political pretensions, and in 1776 the Parlement of Paris helped thwart the controversial reformist program of Turgot. Finally, during the pre-revolutionary crisis of 1787–88, the parlements used their leverage to push the monarchy into a corner where its only recourse lay in convening the Estates General. In a final show of will in May 1788, the crown lashed back and again exiled the magistrates as a prelude to abolishing the parlements altogether. But this time an outcry of public opinion obliged the government to relent almost immediately. The parlementaires returned in triumph from their brief exile, unaware that this victory would be their swan song.[6]

Within two years the Revolution entirely extruded this mighty elite from the civic order, with barely a murmur from public opinion and little more than astringent protests from a handful of parlements. After the summer of 1789 revolutionary ideology could not accommodate these unique institutions. Their historic amalgam of political, administrative, and judicial authority forced the parlements to the top of the National Assembly's agenda. One of the first systematic expositions of revolutionary ideology, the Report on the Judiciary presented by the otherwise conservative Nicolas Bergasse in the name of the Assembly's Committee on the Constitution on August 17, 1789, prefigured their fate. The magistracy had been effective in resisting royal despotism, he acknowledged, but now that despotism no longer threatened, the parlements' institutional power could itself become dangerous to liberty. "It is thus indispensable that a complete revolution be carried out in the system of our tribunals. . . . It is not possible simply to ameliorate; [we must] destroy in order to reconstruct anew."[7]

The legitimacy of existing judicial institutions had already been challenged by the August 4 decree, which condemned feudalism, venality of office, and regional particularism. Much dispute ensued about what constituted feudalism, but everyone agreed that seigneurial justice had to be eliminated promptly. The parlements, meanwhile, stood as exemplars of provincial identity and privilege, weighty impediments to the prospect of national unity. And, with the exception of the barristers, all elements of the judicial order— bailliage judges, parlementaires, attorneys, bailiffs, and notaries—were venal officeholders. New attitudes thus gave added weight to critiques of French civil and criminal justice that had been gathering force in books, pamphlets, and academic essay contests, and that spilled over in the *cahiers* of 1789.

The most resounding pre-revolutionary critiques, by such writers as Voltaire or the crusading Bordeaux parlementaire Dupaty, attacked the arbitrary procedures and harsh punishments of French criminal justice, matters that will be considered in Chapter XII. Complaints about civil justice centered on its costliness, complexities, and endless delays; on the lack of ready judicial redress exacerbated by the "cascade" of overlapping jurisdictions, multiple appeals, and arcane procedures that overwhelmed litigants. The National Assembly hoped to eliminate the "abyss" facing civil litigants by reconfiguring and redistributing the nation's tribunals, and by curbing the parasitic auxiliaries of the judicial system such as bailiffs and attorneys.[8]

The law quickly became the Revolution's transcendent deity. Judges, however, would no longer be its high priests, a "despotism of legists and a themistic aristocracy" (in the words of one deputy)[9]—a caste that had turned the law into an arcane science and a personal patrimony. Law would be made and, if need be, interpreted by the representatives of the people, the legislature. Judges—independent from the other branches of government, but deriving their mandate from the people—would simply uphold and apply the law as salaried employees of the state rather than as a caste or corporation within society. As it shaped a constitutional framework for the judicial system and filled in the particulars with a succession of organic laws, the National Assembly followed Bergasse's prescription for the total destruction of the old judiciary and the construction of an entirely new one.

As soon as the nationalization of Church property created new financial resources for the state, the Assembly liquidated the entire range of venal judicial and municipal offices. It respected property rights by offering compensation payments in *assignats* that could be used, if the recipient wished, to purchase national lands. To determine the value of these offices, the Assembly could have used the original price when the office was created or the price at the most recent turnover, but it chose the most expeditious method by using the valuations filed by all venal corporations in order to assess (which is to say, minimize) a new royal surtax in 1771. The Assembly was anxious to complete this operation quickly since the officeholders' acceptance of compensation would lend legitimacy to its reforms. Some corporations, particularly the notaries and the attorneys *(procureurs),* had ludicrously undervalued their offices in 1771. The judges, however, fared well since their evaluations had been more realistic.[10] In any case, the elimination of all venal offices cleared the ground for a complete reconstruction of the judicial order.

The *constituants* faced a delicate task: in expediting the resolution of civil disputes and the execution of contracts—in facilitating legal recourse for the people—they had also to assure the integrity of personal and property rights as defined by law. Though some spoke in such terms, the Assembly resisted the temptation of shifting wholesale to an ad hoc, non-professional system of civil justice. The law, with its inherent complexities, could not be regarded as entirely self-evident or "transparent," either before or after legal codification. The *constituants'* remarkable innovations fall roughly into four categories: creating new kinds of tribunals staffed by new kinds of judges; providing for conciliation, arbitration, and informal hearings outside the courtroom whenever possible; modifying the roles and prerogatives of lawyers; and reshaping the contours of criminal justice.

New Courts and New Judges

The Assembly sent the parlements on indefinite adjournment in November 1789. Most went meekly, although the magistrates in Toulouse and Rennes bitterly denounced the Assembly's pretensions. (Disaffection, or an inability to come to terms with the new regime, spread profoundly in this milieu. Of approximately 1,200 parlementaires whose fate can be traced, about 400 eventually emigrated, and at least 140 who did not were condemned to death during the Terror.)[11] But the ghosts of the parlements lingered in the Assembly's mind—a fear lest any semblance of judicial corporatism emerge in the new order. The ex-parlementaire Adrien Duport argued emphatically that the magistracy ought not to be "a metier fitting only for a small number of men"; a judgeship was not a lifetime occupation, still less a family patrimony. On this point the Assembly fully agreed, and on its corollary as well, that the status of the judiciary (as opposed to the law itself) must not be unduly exalted.[12] Duport indeed proposed to strip the magistracy's power to the bones by using lay juries in civil law. This would in turn foreclose most appellate jurisdiction, since a jury's finding must be definitive in substance. In Duport's plan the judges themselves, moreover, would not have been comfortably sedentary but would ride circuit in American or English style.

This minimalist concept proved too drastic for the Assembly. While the criminal jury received passionate endorsement (as we shall see), legislative debate sank the notion of a civil jury. Jacques-Guillaume Thouret, an ex-barrister from Rouen and *rapporteur* of the Constitutional Committee, convinced his colleagues that in civil law it was impossible to separate questions of fact and law—this distinction being the raison d'être of a jury system. Since one could as soon separate bricks from cement in a building as fact from law in a civil suit, he argued, there could be no meaningful division of labor between judges and juries. The rejection of juries in civil court required in turn some provision by which citizens could appeal the findings of a tribunal. Nor would the Assembly accept the prospect of ambulatory judges as an antidote to judicial corporatism. That contrivance seemed too cumbersome and was not the only way to bring justice closer to the people.

The Assembly did not hesitate to establish permanent courts, so long as they were numerous, modest in stature, and limited in scope. The fear of some legislators that such paltry institutions would not attract capable candidates, or that so many courts would strain the intellectual resources of the nation, were swept aside. Separating criminal from civil justice, the Assembly established a criminal court in each department but implanted far more civil courts by authorizing one in each of the nation's approximately six hundred districts. District tribunals would be manned by only five judges and a number of alternates (the latter to be paid when and if they served). The Assembly's treatment of Paris illustrated its attitude. To replace the Châtelet—the court of first resort in Paris and a mighty judicial company with prestige second only to the Parlement's—the Assembly installed six ordinary district courts in the capital rather than one unified court that could divide itself into sections as the Châtelet had. The wary legislators even refused to allow all six courts to share the spacious precincts of the Palais de Justice. Only one could locate there, the rest being scattered to generally makeshift quarters in other parts of the city. [13]

Rejecting proposals by Sieyès and others for a separate tier of appeals courts, however, the Assembly simply made each district court into a potential appeals court as well. That is, a litigant wishing to appeal a verdict could seek redress in any of the seven district courts closest to the original tribunal—the specific one to be decided by a process of elimination between the two parties to the suit. This idea of a revolving appellate jurisdiction repudiated traditional concepts of judicial hierarchy. Even more dramatic was the new procedure for naming judges. Almost without dissent the Assembly accepted Thouret's call for the election of judges by the district electoral assemblies. Some deputies still favored lifetime tenure (a better guarantee, they assumed, of judicial independence), but consensus emerged for a six-year term, with the possibility of reelection. Traditionalists prevailed, however, in requiring five years of judicial experience in bar, bench, or seigneurial court as a prerequisite for eligibility.

Should the nation's new judges, then, be subordinate in some fashion to the king, the head of state? Royalists took their stand here, insisting that electors should merely nominate two candidates for presentation to the king, who would designate and install the judges. By the narrow margin of 503 to 450 the Assembly rejected this scheme, thus depriving the king of any say in the matter. [14] Finally, the Assembly created a *Tribunal de Cassation,* a high court of review in Paris with forty-two magistrates, one to be elected alternately from each department. Its mandate was strictly limited to appeals motivated by alleged procedural irregularities in either criminal or civil trials; a panel of judges could either deny those allegations and uphold the verdict or affirm that irregularities had occurred, quash the verdict, and send the case back to another court for retrial.[15]

Elections to the new district courts were held before the National Assembly promulgated the new constitution and dissolved itself in September 1791. At that time, it will be recalled, the deputies would not be eligible to succeed themselves in the new legislature. The electoral assembly of Paris anticipated that situation by choosing distinguished members of the National Assembly for ten of the capital's thirty district court judgeships. (Three others were elected but declined.) Heading the list was Emmanuel Fréteau, an ex-parlementaire with anti-absolutist credentials before the Revolution and the brother-in-law of Dupaty, the legendary crusader for criminal justice reform. Though most former members of the Parisian Order of Barristers were disaffected by these judicial reforms (as we shall see), sixteen barristers won election and accepted judgeships on the new courts, while another seventeen were chosen as substitutes, most of whom took seats on the courts because of subsequent vacancies. When the six Parisian courts eventually organized themselves and chose their respective presidents, the list was remarkable: Duport, Fréteau, Thouret, J. B. Treilhard, A. J. B. Target, and Merlin de Douai—all influential deputies in the Assembly with distinguished careers as old-regime judges or lawyers. That such notable figures agreed to staff these mundane tribunals clearly helped establish their legitimacy.[16]

Elections in the provinces produced far less glamorous results. For every celebrity such as Robespierre (who almost immediately resigned his judgeship in Versailles to take a position in Paris), dozens of obscure ex-*bailliage* magistrates, seigneurial judges, or local lawyers won election, depending on circumstances. In contests for the 16 district courts in Burgundy, for example, 118 former *bailliage* magistrates were eligible for the 80 positions, but electors chose only 27. Roughly similar results occurred in Poitou: 24 out of 90 eligible ex-*bailliage* magistrates elected for 90 positions, as electors systematically bypassed former royal judges in several districts. Former magistrates were most likely to put themselves forward and win approval when the level of factional conflict in a district was low, according to the historian Philip Dawson; in districts where partisan controversy had already heated up, small-town lawyers were more likely to win at their expense. In the Breton department of the Morbihan, on the other hand, partisanship evidently did not figure much in these elections. Thirty percent of the new magistrates were ex-seigneurial judges, 20 percent ex-royal judges, and the rest legal practitioners of various kinds chosen in the main for their presumed capacity rather than political notoriety. Citizens who maintained local confidence subsequently passed back and forth between administrative and judicial office in successive elections.[17]

After the fall of the monarchy in 1792, all judicial offices except the *Tribunal de Cassation* were renewed by election under the liberalized franchise of the moment, and without the necessity of any courtroom experience for eligibility. Little is known about this electoral renewal, but the results (outside of supercharged Paris) do not seem to have been very dramatic. The Morbihan's electors returned over 50 percent of the sitting magistrates, and most of the new judges had similar backgrounds, though the evidence from Burgundy and Poitou suggests that most former *bailliage* magistrates elected in 1791 were retired either voluntarily or involuntarily at this point. Turnover and instability became far more pronounced in 1793–94 in the wake of the federalist revolt, when judges were (or were suspected of being) sympathetic to that heresy. In departments tainted by federalism, representatives-on-mission purged the district courts wholesale. This time veritable outsiders did find themselves on the civil bench, such as the score of notaries designated by Prieur de la Marne in the Morbihan, along with a smattering of merchants, teachers, and the like, chosen for their presumed patriotism, character, and modicum of experience in revolutionary politics.[18] Jacobin deputies extolled the amateurs whom they elevated to the bench, such as Citizen Labernade, a shoemaker in Blaye (Gironde), "in whom natural genius is combined with firmness of character."[19]

In fact such artisan-judges were rare exceptions, more a symbolic gesture than a studied policy. Still, the rhetoric about everyman-a-judge ran strong in the Year II. Thus on July 2, 1794, an official in the ministry circularized judges about the procedures for filling temporary vacancies on the bench when a quorum of regular judges or elected substitutes was lacking. The National Assembly had stipulated that the sitting judges were to designate local holders of law degrees (*graduées*) for this temporary function, and since the decree had never been modified, the courts still followed that practice. To which this good Jacobin objected: "Is it not a monument to that privilege accorded to a class of citizens who no longer have any political existence?" He advised the judges that according to the Convention's committee on legislation, "all French citizens of recognized probity and patriotism should be called to exercise judicial functions when a [temporary] replacement is needed."[20]

This interregnum of egalitarian amateurism lasted only a few months. Many of the magistrates ousted in the Year II were quietly returned to the courts in the Year III by thermidorian representatives-on-mission. All told the disruptions could be dramatic, many courts remained undermanned, and backlogs of civil cases grew. But a real breakdown never occurred. A decree by the Convention in April 1794 ordered district court judges to terminate all suits on their dockets within three months, "upon pain of dismissal," and there is evidence that they took this seriously.[21] A determined litigant could usually get his day in court even in the Year II.

Another shift came with the Directory, whose architects wanted fewer and more substantial civil courts. With the districts already scrapped as administrative units, the regime simply established one civil court in each department, to be manned by twenty elected judges. Electors were free to choose any taxpaying citizen. To require legal or judicial experience for eligibility at this juncture, it was argued, would have been futile given the political upheavals of the past four years, when most old-regime professionals had shown hostility or indifference toward the republic. Politics intruded nonetheless, getting this new judicial system off to an extremely shaky start. When it came to the legislature (as we have seen), the two-thirds decree ensured continuity between the Convention and the Directory at the expense of free choice for the voters. But no such constraints seemed to weigh on elections to the courts. Citizens believed themselves free to elect any judges they wished, and the rightist-royalist backlash had full play in those contests. In the end, however, the Directory proved unwilling to accept results that conferred judicial positions "into hands whose connections have inspired suspicions . . . into feeble hands."

The government ousted some judges-elect under the law of 3 brumaire Year IV, which barred the relatives of émigrés from administrative and judicial office, and it compelled others to resign by imposing an oath pledging "eternal hatred of royalty," which conscience forbade them to take. In the Vaucluse, the only departmental civil tribunal that has been studied, eight of the twenty elected judges resigned, and four more were barred by the law of 3 brumaire.[22] A preliminary tally by the Ministry of Justice showed 167 resignations, and 123 ousters under that exclusionary law. Furthermore, some departmental electoral assemblies could not complete the balloting for civil court judges within the allotted ten days. There is scarcely a court in the nation, concluded the ministry, "which does not have numerous forced departures or voluntary resignations," all of which disrupted and even jeopardized the course of civil justice.[23] But like most other difficulties in launching the Directory regime, the problem abated. Interim appointments by the executive and regular elections in 1798 and 1799 eventually filled the vacant positions. Most of these courts undoubtedly had at least a few able magistrates and even one or two *"jurisconsultes profondes,"* like Collet in the Vaucluse, who could set the tone and guide their fellow judges.[24] If experts later concluded that one court per department did not suffice after all, that was another matter.

MEDIATION AND CONCILIATION: THE JUSTICE OF THE PEACE

The district courts constituted merely one element of the National Assembly's new judicial order, and in some ways a secondary one. According to the preamble of the judiciary law of August 1790, "The most reasonable means for terminating disputes between citizens" was extra-judicial arbitration. The Constitution of 1791 pledged that this avenue of recourse would always remain open to citizens and, as we shall see, arbitration later became mandatory in certain instances. The law also stipulated that before any suit could be heard by a district court, the parties must take their case to a justice of the peace for a preliminary attempt at conciliation. As one deputy put it: "Rendering justice is only the second obligation of society. Preventing lawsuits is the first. Society must say to the parties: before arriving at the temple of justice pass first through that of concord."

Arbitration and conciliation—two forms of informal mediation outside the courtroom—held pride of place in the new system of civil justice. Of even greater immediacy, mediation was desirable for resolving the multitude of petty disputes among citizens, where modest monetary stakes could have substantial material and moral significance to the parties. As Thouret argued, it was indispensable "to procure for the inhabitants of the countryside a prompt, simple, and domestic justice, so to speak, which does not require the apparatus of a ruinous procedure and which demands no other laws than the indications of common sense." The linchpin in this effort would be the justice of the peace. [25]

Seigneurial judges had traditionally helped resolve minor disputes, but their intervention was hit or miss, effective in some regions but spotty in others where seigneurialism had weakened. Besides, in less than scrupulous hands their services came dearly and could amount to a racket. In any case, seigneurial justice was dead in the water after August 4. Into the vacuum the Assembly placed the justice of the peace *(juge de paix)*, a figure who embodied the very essence of revolutionary ideology. There would be one such elected magistrate in each of the approximately 5,500 cantons, with proportionate numbers in the cities. (Paris, for example, had forty-eight, one in each section.) To be eligible, a citizen need only be thirty years of age and meet the same property qualification as electors or candidates for district and departmental office. No legal background of any kind was required. The JPs were to be assisted by four unpaid *assessors* elected from among the canton's active citizens. With their two-year term (subject to reelection), and their modest pay (800 livres in the countryside, with gradations for urban localities up to 1,600 for the largest cities) the JPs were supposed to be amateurs.[26] The function was incompatible with the position of registered attorney, mayor, or public employee, and after October 1793, with the post of notary as well.

This was an ill-considered rule, since rural voters might well feel comfortable with notaries who in turn could earn a decent living from the two functions which neither might provide alone.[27] In the first election, notaries were indeed chosen, along with various kinds of legal practitioners (especially in the towns), proprietors, and a smattering of doctors and the like. Socioprofessional background, however, likely counted for less in this eminently local office than personal qualities: a candidate's reputation for being smart, assiduous, and upright, or alternately his capacity to enlist a clientele of voters on one basis or another.[28] A few prominent revolutionary careers began as justices of the peace, including the director François de Neufchâteau, the physician and Montagnard deputy Duhem, and Faure, a member of Napoleon's Council of State. Forty-seven of the first JPs were soon thereafter elected to the Legislative Assembly. The post also became a retreat for some who had held high revolutionary office: ex-*conventionnel* Roger Ducos, for example, served as a justice of the peace in 1797–99 before his reelection to the legislature, where he helped engineer the Brumaire coup. More typically, a member of the *présidial* court of Bourg in 1783, elected to the district court of that city in 1791, later served as JP in the canton of Mermieux between 1793 and 1800.[29]

The justices of the peace could not be insulated from revolutionary politics, despite the intentions of the *constituants*. JPs in the West were among the favorite targets of the chouans, while in the Midi these magistrates became avid or reluctant accomplices in the Counter-Terror against the Jacobins after Thermidor. In Paris, a caldron of partisan politics after the fall of the monarchy, only seven of the forty-eight JPs won reelection in the renewal of all judicial personnel in late 1792, and another eighteen men assumed the office after political purges in 1793–95. The socioprofessional character of the Parisian JPs changed in the process. Local activists of diverse backgrounds wrested the post from the legal professionals who had won during the first elections in the capital. Artisans, tradesmen, and merchants now accounted for eighteen of the capital's forty-eight JPs, and their representation was even greater among the elected *assesseurs* who assisted the magistrates.[30]

The mutation in personnel was probably less drastic in the provinces than in the sharply politicized capital; in Saintes (Charente), for example, five of nine justices were reelected in 1792 and only one was clearly defeated on political grounds. Moreover turnovers in the post did not necessarily occur because of politics; the incumbent might have wished to step down, or his constituents might simply have preferred someone else. Rotation of incumbents, after all, was scarcely inconsistent with the conceptual underpinnings of this office. In the rural canton of Fontaine-Française (Côte d'Or), voters named three men to the post during the revolutionary decade: Louis Tiquet, a "royal bailiff," won the first election; in late 1792 he was succeeded by his own clerk, Jean Claudon, a proprietor; and in late 1795 that young man was replaced in an almost uncontested election (94 out of 101 votes cast) by an older man, also a "proprietor" named Claudon, perhaps a relative. This canton thus exemplified the local amateurism envisioned by the legislators.[31]

Except under unusual circumstances, however, politics would not have impinged on the routine tasks of the JP. In the first place, he was a police magistrate. While urban JPs were assisted by police commissioners, rural JPs were more or less on their own as law enforcement officers at ground level. Crimes were reported to the JP, who was responsible for the preliminary investigation and identification of the suspected culprits. For petty crimes involving small fines or prison terms of a few days, the JP heard cases himself, and his verdict was final. These magistrates also staffed urban police courts and district correctional courts that tried misdemeanors.

Above all, the JP resolved minor civil disputes that did not involve real property. In cases where the monetary stakes were less than 50 livres (later raised to 100), he decided cases definitively; in cases of 50 to 100 livres (later raised to 200), his decisions were subject to appeal in a district court. It would be interesting to know how often citizens launched such appeals, but the fragmentary evidence is inconclusive. Cases in the departmental tribunal of the Vaucluse during the Directory were said to have "often" originated as appeals from a JP's decision, but Jean Bart's researchers in the Côte d'Or convinced him that "appeals brought against the judgments of the JPs were extremely rare." (Summaries of caseloads in the Napoleonic courts rarely referred to this, but of the 1,902 cases that came before the Indre's four tribunals in the last quarter of 1810, only 27 came on appeal.)[32] JPs heard cases without procedural formalities or written submissions, and attorneys were barred from the hearing room. The paperwork and associated costs remained minimal, usually nothing more than a summons to assure that both parties appeared, and a record of the verdict. The magistrates did not have to explain the reasons for their decision by citing a particular statute as the district courts did. Consequently cases tried before a JP could not be appealed on procedural grounds to the *Tribunal de Cassation*. In effect, while he was expected to rule according to law, the JP was free to rule in equity.[33]

Through mediation or their own decision, these magistrates settled conflicts involving contracts and small debts; disputes between workers and employers over wages; damages claimed for verbal injuries or defamation; damage to rented buildings; rural disputes over damage to crops, fields, or animals; infringement of field boundaries or illegal pasturing. When necessary, the magistrate could appoint "experts" acceptable to the parties to assess the alleged damage impartially, and he was free to go to the scene of the dispute himself.[34] The JP could scarcely anticipate the endless variety of conflicts that arose in the countryside. One day he might deal with a steer injured by the dog of the communal shepherd to whom it had been entrusted. At the next session he might have to calm the passions of peasants like Antonin and Barnabé in Pagnol's *The Baker's Wife,* that timeless evocation of village life in Southern France. When Antonin demands that his neighbor trim the shade trees that have cast a deep shadow on Antonin's garden, thereby ruining his giant spinach plants, the two men loudly assert their respective rights, hurl insults at each other, and finally decide that they must go the justice of the peace for redress—a step obviated later when the two become reconciled in a drunken revelry.

Like their counterparts on the district courts, JPs not only settled disputes but also offered what were called benevolent services *(jurisdiction gracieuse)*. They helped orphans acquire guardians or trustees, certified the emancipation of minor orphans when they reached their majority, protected the rights of absentees and disabled people, and were in charge of placing seals on property and lifting such seals. (Emigration and conscription each in its way made heavy demands for such intervention.) Finally, unmarried mothers who wished to establish paternity filed their *déclarations de grossesse* before the justice.[35]

In the case of major lawsuits, as already noted, litigants headed for the civil courts were obliged to make a preliminary effort to settle their dispute with the assistance of the JP. (When the two parties came from different cantons they went before the *bureau de conciliation* in a district capital, consisting of six unpaid citizens chosen by the municipal council, at least two of whom were lawyers. This institution disappeared with the abolition of the districts in 1796, leaving the burden entirely on the JP in the initiator's canton.) No lawsuit could be inscribed on a court's docket without a certificate attesting that a JP or *bureau de conciliation* had failed, "having vainly made every effort to conciliate the parties." Though a successful conciliation was not enforceable as a court sentence, it could be formalized by a notarial act as a contract. Again, attorneys were barred from these conciliation sessions, the assumption being that their personal interest lay in the failure of informal mediation.

The evidence on how this obligatory system of preliminary conciliation actually worked is difficult to evaluate. A durable professional journal, the *Gazette des Tribunaux,* considered the JPs effective weapons in the battle against legal chicanery: "The *bureaux de paix* hamper the greedy practitioners and disconcert their projects." A Third Republic historian, whose short book is a pean to these revolutionary magistrates, claimed that they succeeded admirably and adduced impressionistic evidence from the department of the Manche. In the canton of Coutances, he concluded, few cases were brought to the courts after the ministrations of the JPs. Ministry of Justice notations on the magistrates spoke of one JP in the department as "judging often, conciliating rarely," but most comments were positive: "conciliates often" or "indefatigable conciliator." In the Breton canton of Pont Scorff (Morbihan), Debauve found that 103 out of 257 attempts at conciliation in 1791–94 succeeded. The precious statistics from Clère's study of Haute-Marne, on the other hand, suggest initial success but subsequent decline in the rate of cases settled by conciliation. Most of the records have not survived in the canton of Fontaine-Française in Burgundy studied by Jean Bart, except for the Year VIII when twenty-six out of thirty-two attempts failed, and at one point the clerk, in a calculated slip, referred to the "bureau of non-conciliation." But Bart's sampling of other cantons in the Côte d'Or yielded more positive results; indeed in Mirabeau, what must have been an exceptionally able magistrate mediated twenty-three out of twenty-eight potential lawsuits in a five-month period of 1794–95.[36]

Several newly installed Napoleonic judges made a point of acknowledging how effective the JPs were in easing their own caseloads. "The Revolution has extinguished the seeds of many lawsuits and the bureaus of conciliation have settled many at their inception," observed the court in Langres (Haute-Marne) in 1800.[37] When prefects compiled printed handbooks about their departments, some paid homage to "those conciliating magistrates" who were settling civil cases without the intercession of lawyers. Few, however, provided hard data, and when they did, their categories were vague and inconsistent. In the Nord, excluding criminal cases, the justices of the peace dealt with a total of 156,000 matters during 1791–1802, which the author extrapolates to 180,000 to make up for lacunae in the documentation. Some 56,000 cases (or 61,000 extrapolated) were conciliated, or one out of three, while the magistrates decided another 71,000 on their own authority. But the figures on conciliations clearly include disputes brought directly to the JP for adjudication as well as major suits headed for civil court, and thus do not tell us specifically about the preliminary conciliation system.[38]

Detailed statistics for the Indre in Central France do offer an appearance of precision on this question. As best one can judge from the compiler's categories, during the eleven years 1791–1801 litigants presented about 19,000 major lawsuits to the department's forty-eight justices of the peace for the preliminary attempt at conciliation, of which they settled seven thousand amicably through their offices, though at a greater rate in the first few years than afterward.[39] The verdict on this technique of mediation would seem to be positive, though as we shall see judicial professionals later derided it.

THE RISE AND FALL OF ARBITRATION

In their constitutions and organic laws, the revolutionaries gave pride of place to conciliation and arbitration as against formal litigation directed by lawyers and decided by judges. The parties to any kind of civil dispute were encouraged to designate arbitrators of their own choice, thereby avoiding the need for a court trial. Even if such arbitrators were likely to be men with legal expertise, they would not be bound by procedural formalities and would be free to decide matters according to equity. Arbitrators might charge handsome fees for their services, but they could cut through red tape and minimize delays. The costs in time and money were therefore likely to be less burdensome than going to court. As a safeguard, if citizens chose to go to arbitration, the results could be appealed in court provided that both parties agreed on that option beforehand.

In 1793 the Convention became so mesmerized by this ideal that it seemed ready to adopt it as the prevailing modality of civil justice. The Jacobin Constitution of June 1793 implied (the language being exceedingly vague) that permanent courts and judges could be eliminated altogether, making arbitration not merely a possibility but a requirement. After encouraging citizens to use "arbiters of their own choice to pass upon their differences," the constitution simply added that "there shall be public arbiters elected [annually] by the electoral assemblies . . . with cognizance of disputes not definitively terminated by private arbiters or by the justices of the peace." Since the Convention shelved this constitution to make way for a temporary "revolutionary govenrment," *arbitres publics* were never actually instituted. The Convention remained free, however, to legislate provisionally in this area, and as an alternative to deprofessionalizing civil justice completely, several deputies revived Duport's notion of the civil jury. A speech advocating civil juries by the moderate deputy and future Napoleonic chancellor Jean-Jacques Cambacérès makes strange reading, unless one interprets it as a strategy for heading off the more drastic possibility of abolishing the district courts altogether and instituting binding arbitration. "It has been advocated that the tribunals be adorned with *sans-culottes,"* Cambacérès observed. "But isn't associating juries with the judges the veritable way to achieve that goal?" In the end Robespierre and other cooler heads sidetracked the proposal. The Convention adopted neither compulsory arbitration nor civil juries, and the district courts emerged more or less intact from this brief debate.[40]

In the area of domestic relations, however, compulsory arbitration had already become routine for French citizens since 1791. The *constituants* had embodied their notion of accessible, expeditive justice in an institution called the *tribunal de famille* or family court, which dealt with matrimonial disputes, conflicts among parents and children, and certain disputes over inheritance. Two subsequent revolutionary innovations heightened the importance of this novel concept. With the legalization of divorce for the first time in French history in September 1792, contested requests for divorce would be decided (as petitions for separation already were) by a family court, along with monetary awards and custody questions. Then in January 1794 the Convention passed its equal inheritance law, ordered that it operate retroactively to July 1789, and stipulated that any disputes were to be settled by a family court without possibility of appeal to the district courts.

The idea of the *tribunal de famille* was simple: when conflicts erupted within the family—between father and son, husband and wife, brother and sister— it was preferable to settle them as quickly and privately as possible. Each side in the dispute was required to name as arbitrators two relatives or, in their absence, "friends or neighbors." (Liberal interpretations of this provision by the Ministry of Justice assured that a lack of confidence in one's relatives was acceptable as a "default of relatives," while "friends and neighbors" could effectively mean anybody.) Should the four designated arbitrators deadlock, they would in turn name a fifth to break the tie, though this rarely came to pass. The arbitrators were not expected to contribute their services free of charge, but they could still settle the dispute close at hand, more expeditiously, and without the notoriety of a hearing in open court. Not being bound by legal formalities, their findings could be more flexible than those of ordinary courts.[41]

If the *constituants* truly expected these ad hoc forums to be composed of relatives exercising a kind of benevolent surveillance in the cause of family solidarity, then the experiment was a failure. A number of local studies make it clear that parties to these disputes generally went outside the family to find arbitrators and designated worldly men, often with legal experience. To be sure the records of the family courts show plenty of peasants, urban workers, and artisans participating, when parties to the dispute were of those social classes. But jurists, lawyers, legal clerks, notaries, and bailiffs served as arbitrators in at least 30 percent of the family courts hearing divorce cases during 1792–96 in Rouen, with their proportion increasing to 50 percent over time, just as the proportion of actual relatives declined to about 13 percent. Eleven Rouennais with legal training acted as arbitrators six or more times; Robert Philippe—a veritable specialist in divorce—appeared in twenty-three cases, in eight by appointment of the district court when one party in the dispute had failed to designate their own. [42] In the district of Angoulême, the proportion of arbitrators with legal expertise (in all types of family court cases and not just divorce) was comparable, and in Laon it reached over 50 percent. The number of relatives chosen as arbitrators, in contrast, was minuscule: 13 out 402 in Laon and 66 out of 1291 in Angoulême. [43]

Many parties to these disputes came before a *tribunal de famille* with legal counsel who submitted written memos. Even when no member of the panel had a legal background, sessions might be held in a lawyer's office. Veritable amateurism clearly did not appeal to citizens putting their domestic interests on the line. Yet apart from the selection of outside arbitrators, and the concomitant heftiness of their fees, the concept worked pretty much as anticipated. Each side got a full and fair hearing, and the process usually moved quickly, although some cases involved numerous witnesses and arbitrators had ample opportunity to cause delays if they chose to. A meticulous examination of the evidence for divorce proceedings in Rouen indicates that the panels disposed of about half the cases in one sitting, and another 33 percent within a month. [44]

Though the Convention rejected compulsory arbitration as a panacea for clogged courtrooms and legal chicanery, it did extend that practice in one other area as a byproduct of its anti-feudal crusade. In the law of 10 June 1793 the Montagnards responded to peasant agitation over the disposition of communal lands by authorizing communes to divide these properties provided that one third of the inhabitants voted to do so; the division would be along strictly egalitarian lines, with every village family receiving an equal share. But what of communal land that had been "usurped by feudal power" in the past? Earlier legislation had voided the most blatant and recent seigneurial appropriations, but most such claims had to be litigated in the courts where, according to one deputy, they became "the unrivaled resource of the greedy practitioner. Voluminous memoires, multiple consultations, useless petitions—nothing is spared to prolong the proceedings." The law of June 1793 made it much easier for communes to reclaim such land by placing a weighty burden of proof on the alleged seigneurial usurper, even when the land in question was ecclesiastical or émigré property that had become national property. The law also stipulated that all such claims—including intercommunal disputes—now had to be settled by arbitration, the decisions to be executed without the right of appeal. These provisions became retroactive to all disputes over communal property already in litigation. With this extremely important category of lawsuits given over to compulsory arbitration, the communes could expedite the resolution of their claims.[45]

The effects were dramatic, at least in the North. During the mere twelve months that this law held sway, at least sixty-nine suits in the Oise department went to arbitration, involving a total of 119 communes or hamlets, about one in seven of the department's communes. In the Haute-Marne, ninety-nine cases have been uncovered. The communes, as well as the defendants, generally chose lawyers, surveyors, or local officials, rather than peasants, as their arbitrators. This law was not a license for class war, but a simple process for carrying out the Convention's social policy. The communes by no means won all their cases, nor by definition could that happen in intercommunal disputes. But when the peasants challenged a *ci-devant* seigneur directly (perhaps half the cases), they were very likely to win. Tens of thousands of acres of forest and pasturelands reverted to village control.[46]

In sum, the Montagnard Convention did not embrace compulsory arbitration as a universal method for resolving civil conflicts, but it did mandate the practice in two important types of cases. Moreover in both instances—the equal inheritance law of January 1794 and the law of 10 June 1793 on communal property claims—arbitral sentences could not be appealed, and the laws were made retroactive to 1789. A backlash was not long in coming. In the political atmosphere after Thermidor, with its ostensible concern for legal propriety and property rights, compulsory arbitration began to look pernicious. The attack started over the issue of communal property, as the thermidorian Convention quickly suspended any further division of common land. Frenzied rhetoric about leveling and the "agrarian law"—shorthand for the expropriation and redistribution of all land—flowed from the rostrum. The deputies wished to preclude continuing attacks on alleged usurpations of common lands, for they believed that such expanding claims would eventually threaten legitimate property rights as well, not to mention the state's interest in its *biens nationaux*. At a minimum these cases ought to be subject to ordinary channels of judicial appeal, they argued, and so began the rolling back of compulsory arbitration.[47]

The Convention also grew uneasy over the possible tyranny of compulsory arbitration in domestic relations, especially the multitude of disputes that arose over retroactive application of the law on equal inheritance. Gradually the deputies reversed field and agreed that forced arbitration deprived citizens of the right to seek redress in duly constituted official courtrooms. This reversal did not come easily, however. Not until 9 ventôse IV (28 February 1796) did the directorial legislature finally and explicitly abolish any kind of compulsory arbitration in the future. Nor did it ever retroactively nullify the arbitrators' findings of 1793–94. But another law a few months later permitted appeals to the *Tribunal de Cassation* of prior arbitral sentences on procedural grounds. In subsequent years numerous arbitral judgments in favor of the communes were reversed either on appeal in the regular courts or in the *Tribunal de Cassation*. In a rare instance of judicial activism, the latter used every inch of latitude it could muster to favor defendants against the communes' claims, effectively reversing the Convention's manifest intentions on proof to title. As Dalloz's authoritative judicial handbook put it many years later, "The Cour de Cassation wished thereby to repair the countless injustices committed by the arbitrators either out of ignorance, a hatred of feudalism, or the blind desire to favor the communes at any price."[48]

The odium against compulsory arbitration undermined the *tribunal de famille* as well. The thermidorians' Constitution of the Year III said nothing one way or the other about this institution. In response to a flood of inquiries to the Ministry of Justice about the status of the family courts, Merlin de Douai replied evasively but in effect indicated that the constitution no longer authorized them. As the legislature debated and resolved the matter, the new conventional wisdom of judicial traditionalism took shape. Later Dalloz would exaggerate this revised view of the *tribunal de famille* in these terms: "Pleading without cost [sic] was an attraction; being alternately judge and party . . . was an object of commerce. Suits multiplied endlessly, chicanery knew no limits. . . . France became one large arena of pleaders." Critics alleged that experience had revealed fatal flaws in the family courts: the selection of lawyers rather than relatives, excessive charges, endless delays. Beyond that, the legislature now espoused a distinctive interpretation of liberty: "that no citizen should be forced to submit his dispute to judges other than those sitting on officially recognized courts." A right of appeal from family court arbitrators was not enough. Henceforth the regular courts would hear most of these cases.[49] Only divorce by mutual consent or on the grounds of incompatibility, as well as certain issues involving minor children, would still be handled by informal panels of relatives or friends known as "family assemblies."[50]

Voluntary arbitration of any dispute between individuals of course remained an option, but no longer the official preference. The backlash against the dramatic measures of 1793—retroactive, compulsory arbitration without appeal on inheritance disputes and communal property claims—rekindled respect for traditional judicial mechanisms. The idealized belief in informal arbitration faded into an official distaste for "the justice of the cabaret" and the intervention of interested parties. In 1806, the Napoleonic Code of Civil

Procedure hemmed in even voluntary arbitration with restrictive guidelines. Arbitrators were enjoined to find according to law, not equity, and verdicts could be appealed to the regular courts unless both parties had expressly ruled out such appeals beforehand. [51]

THE JPS UNDER FIRE

Even more than arbitration and family courts, the justice of the peace had symbolized the Revolution's commitment to a new style of civil justice. True, as early as July 1792, Minister of Justice Joly reported that his correspondence from the provinces indicated the need for "a general reform" of the JPs. Their composition, he claimed, reflected "a lack of experience and often of worldly intelligence; some are too rigid, others too indolent." He complained too that the assessors, the magistrate's indispensable (and unpaid) auxiliaries, were often unavailable or were negligent in performing their duties, thus paralyzing the JP's service, since the latter had no power to replace the assessors elected with him. The minister vaguely suggested that there should be more stringent conditions of eligibility and higher pay for the JPs in order to attract better candidates, as well as some compensation for the assessors and mechanisms for replacing those who defaulted. [52] Nothing came of this proposal, nor did subsequent regimes modify the recruitment or roles of the JPs, except for cutting back somewhat on their responsibilities in criminal justice. Neither the upheavals of the Convention nor the malaise of the Directory shook the standing of these magistrates in the new civic order.

Criticism was accumulating, however, and after Brumaire it came to a head. The Consulate's spokesmen declared that the National Assembly had given undue consideration to the special pleading of local interests in fixing cantonal seats and had therefore authorized an excessive number of JPs. The surest way to eliminate incompetent or lazy magistrates was to reduce their number sharply, upgrade the status and remuneration of the office, and thereby attract better candidates. The Directory too had proposed a drastic reduction in the number of cantons, but its concern was the incapacity and expense of the *administration municipale* in each canton rather than the JPs. With the cantonal administrations now gone altogether, forty departmental advisory councils *(conseils généraux de département)*, at their inaugural meetings in 1800, called for cutting the number of JPs. The Council of State agreed, and in January 1801 submitted a bill to enlarge the cantons and halve the number of JPs.

As it considered this legislation, the Tribunate was really debating what the nation ought to expect from this quintessential revolutionary creation.[53] The primary rationale for cutting the number of local magistrates almost in half was Joly's old complaint: a sufficient number of able, dignified, and educated men to serve in this post were simply not available in rural areas. The bill's opponents responded that the proposed reduction would inevitably give the institution an urban inflection; more lawyers would be elected and hearings would become more procedural and expensive. The justice's office, warned tribune Andrieux, would turn into a *cabinet de chicane*. But another tribune countered that he would prefer an enlightened legal scholar from a town to a well meaning but ignorant countryman. Moreover, people were more likely to respect officials whom they did not know personally, he claimed, adding that some of the rural JPs acted like petty tyrants in their small bailiwicks.

A more cynical kind of argument echoed the critique of family court arbitration: when access to judicial redress is too easy, it encourages lawsuits. Cutting the number of magistrates and enlarging their arrondissements would strike a blow at the habitual litigants *(plaideurs d'habitude)* who harassed their fellow citizens, argued tribune Bézard. "The distance and expenses will cause many of these small disputes to be settled amicably." Greater distance from the seat of justice would mean more time to cool off and more incentive to settle a dispute. As another tribune admitted, this reform would increase the travel expenses of citizens seeking the JP's services, but the costs would be borne by litigants rather than the taxpayers and it would be an incentive to settle disputes privately. (A suggestion that if the number of magistrates was reduced the remaining ones should at least ride circuit in their cantons was simply ignored.) In sum, the government maintained that fewer magistrates would mean higher-quality magistrates, and greater distances to the JPs' offices would benefit ordinary citizens by extinguishing petty disputes before they ever came to the magistrate. Citizens would be likelier to keep away from the JP's office to begin with, but if they did end up there they would receive more effective redress, whether in preliminary conciliations or in the disposition of cases.

Opponents of the bill took a diametrically opposite view, closer to the original imagery of Thouret and the *constituants* of simple, expeditious conflict resolution in the countryside. Far from diminishing the number of these local magistrates, argued tribune Benjamin Constant, the government should be multiplying them. With reduced rather than enlarged districts the magistrates could in fact serve without salary, thus answering the state's ever present concern to cut expenses. An effective mediator must have a knowledge of his locality; preferably he should know his constituents personally, for impartiality is not the key attribute of a local mediator but rather knowledge of what drives the parties to a dispute. Constant wanted the justices of the peace to evolve into unsalaried, paternalistic village notables distributed broadcast across the realm. Cutting the number of magistrates and establishing them in larger districts would be exactly the wrong approach, he vainly contended. The bill reducing the ranks of JPs was endorsed by the Tribunate and ratified by the Corps Léglislatif, 218 to 41.[54]

A few months later the government proposed to eliminate the assessors, who assisted the JPs without salary and had by all accounts proven unreliable. As a *rapporteur* pointed out, the Constitution of the Year VIII had carefully omitted any mention of the assessors even as it reaffirmed the role of the JPs, on the assumption that the assessors were a flawed component of the original concept. The new law simply abolished them, and provided as well that there would be two substitutes elected with each JP (namely, those who came in second and third in the balloting), who could immediately replace a magistrate when necessary. This constructive change came at a price. The required participation of assessors had indeed complicated or delayed conciliation sessions and hearings. But the assessors had also helped the JPs in dealing with petty rural disputes, where they could make preliminary evaluations at the scene of alleged damages. As Duchesne argued unavailingly in the Tribunate, if the assessors were suppressed, the testimony of paid experts would be required more often and the *practiciens* would have another foot in the door.[55]

Withal, the justice of the peace remained a special figure in the civic order. Even Napoleon's electoral system—if such we can call those convoluted charades for cooption—initially treated these magistrates uniquely. In 1800 they were the only officials to be elected by direct balloting in cantonal assemblies. Napoleon seems to have been irritated by the interest that these contests aroused, however, and he soon ordered a change in the rules. That anomaly therefore did not survive past the Year X, when the term of the JP increased from three years to ten, with one fifth of the magistrates to be renewed every two years. Each time a cantonal assembly was convened, it was to designate two candidates for the office, with the appointment to be made by the head of state. The list of possible designees grew each time new names were added, including incumbents who had to be nominated again in order to remain eligible. The rules on who could vote kept changing as well, but that did not necessarily affect the turnout. The historian Yves Coppolani has found participation of eligible voters as low as 6 percent and as high as 96 percent, the latter occurring during bitter contests waged by notables with large clienteles.[56] One way or another, however, the procedures for selecting a JP seemed to recognize that this official required the confidence of his constituents more than a mayor or a member of the legislature, whose appointments in the Napoleonic era did not derive even symbolically from the votes of their fellow citizens.

Despite Napoleonic revisions, imperial judges questioned one of the JPs' principal roles. The chance to vent their disdain for these amateurs came when the Council of State solicited comments from the appellate courts on a preliminary draft of the new Code of Civil Procedure in 1805. A torrent of judicial opinion condemned the preliminary attempt at conciliation before a JP that was incumbent on every civil litigant. Most of the appellate judges believed that the JPs simply could not do the job, since they lacked the skill and respect which an effective mediator required. It was a useless charade, declared the magistrates in Agen, Douai, Orléans, Metz, and Montpellier among others, simply one more time-consuming hurdle for litigants, which put them at least 15 francs more out of pocket. The appellate court in Caen considered preliminary conciliation "a vain and ridiculous formality . . . on questions which are almost always beyond the capacity of the JP." In Colmar, the judges deemed it a sublime theory that proved useless in practice, with a favorable result in perhaps two out of one hundred cases; their colleagues in Lyon offered a more grudging (and preposterous) estimate of one success in a thousand! Besançon's appeals court hoped "that the attempt at conciliation before the JP will be entirely suppressed. . . . It almost never succeeds; it wastes time, delays the course of the affairs, enlarges the procedure, and multiplies the costs. . . . Often the transaction is poorly recorded, which gives rise to new suits." The Besançon bench added that regular judges could themselves provide the parties with an opportunity for "amiable negotiation" or mediation when appropriate. [57]

In the end the Council of State withstood the onslaught, no doubt aware that disdainful imperial magistrates exaggerated the futility of the preliminary attempt at conciliation, although government spokesmen admitted that the process had enjoyed only a "feeble success." [58] Preliminary conciliation before the JPs remained obligatory in the Napoleonic Code of Civil Procedure. But the new code did jettison one dogma of the Revolution, despite objections by a number of appeals court judges, when it permitted attorneys to appear with their clients at these sessions. A government spokesman justified this to the Tribunate by arguing that if the attorneys appeared openly instead of acting behind the scenes, "it ought to be less difficult for the JPs to succeed at conciliation." [59] This was a dramatic turnabout, since in their passion for mediation the revolutionaries had hoped to minimize the intervention of lawyers. The role of attorneys can indeed by taken as a crucial test in any effort to facilitate the course of civil justice.

XI

THE LEGAL
PROFESSIONS IN
QUESTION

THE REVOLUTION AND THE LAWYERS

In old-regime France, as in England, litigants in civil court required two kinds of counsel. The French bar comprised two distinct professions differing not only in function but in training, traditions, organization, and image. The equivalent of English barristers, French *avocats* constituted the bar's prestigious upper branch. Graduates of the university law faculties, barristers were trained by rote methods in a rigid classical curriculum, with a high premium on erudition and eloquence. As experts on the substance of law, they had the exclusive right to plead orally in court and to prepare briefs arguing points of law. Like English solicitors, their less learned colleagues, the attorneys or *procureurs,* trained primarily by apprenticeship. Their function was known as the *instruction* of cases or postulation. Each party to a civil lawsuit was obliged to enlist a *procureur;* because they had such official standing these attorneys were known as *officiers ministériels.* Although not permitted to plead orally, they managed the paperwork and steered their clients through the tortuous procedures of French civil justice. *Procureurs* filed motions and petitions; prepared procedural briefs and factual outlines of the case; collected, copied, and authenticated documents; and gathered the written testimony of witnesses or experts. The *procureur* was the "maître de la cause," the surrogate of the litigant in the management of his case.[1]

At first glance the position of the barristers must have appeared secure in 1789. Over one hundred fifty sat as deputies in the Estates General, compared to only two *procureurs* and fourteen notaries. Pre-revolutionary pamphlets and *cahiers* denouncing the exorbitant costs and delays of civil justice targeted the attorneys more than the *avocats*. And since their profession did not entail purchase of an office, the barristers were not vulnerable to the attack on venality unleashed on August 4. Though anyone could become an *avocat* by earning the appropriate university degree, however, not all graduates were admitted to practice before the august parlements. Access was regulated not by the courts themselves but by the Orders of Barristers in parlementaire cities and other judicial centers.

True, many graduating barristers sought the title only to embellish a gentlemanly life style and never intended to practice for a living at all. But the exclusivism of their established colleagues frustrated at least some younger aspirants, especially in Paris where the Order of Barristers, some six hundred strong, kept tight rein over admission to its ranks. To be accepted by the order candidates had to undergo a long probationary period, show evidence of a certain financial status, and gain the approbation of the order's leading members. Depending on how one looked at it, the order's control over the roster of barristers and professional discipline amounted to an extreme form of corporate privilege or a model of the self-regulating profession. In the atmosphere of 1789, not surprisingly, corporate identity took on the appearance of privilege.[2]

Equally important, the *avocats'* calling foundered on the National Assembly's discovery of the natural right of citizens to defend themselves in court the best way they saw fit. The major repercussion of this awakening came in the domain of criminal law: for the first time criminal defendants gained an unrestricted right to counsel. In that sense the barrister's expertise was about to gain a wider arena. But at the same time the barristers' traditional monopoly on substantive briefs and oral argument in civil court began to look dubious and unwholesome, limiting the precious natural right of citizens to defend themselves in court.[3] The first report on the judiciary by Bergasse (in August) blasted the barristers' monopoly on pleading, and attacked their right to form an exclusive order. A second report, more favorable to the profession, proposed merely to end its monopoly, but did not question the right of barristers to form an association to uphold professional standards. As the Assembly's debates on other subjects continued, however, the animus against corporations and privileges of any kind became an obsession.

With scant debate, and the acquiescence of its prominent barrister members, the Assembly ultimately dissolved the learned Orders of Barristers and decreed that anyone could plead for a defendant in court. The defendant could do so himself, call upon a relative or friend, or enlist anyone in the community inspiring his trust, including his attorney.[4] Such people were to be known as *défenseurs officieux*. Somewhat fancifully, the Assembly deemed their service a benevolent civic function rather than a vocation.[5] Consistent with all this, counsel could no longer appear in the courtroom garbed in special costume. The very profession of *avocat,* with its traditional pattern of study, discipline, ethics, and attire, seemed marked for extinction. Enrollments in the Paris Law Faculty accordingly fell from an average of 646 before the Revolution to 376 in the spring of 1790, 184 that fall, and only 47 by April 1792; trends in the provincial universities were similar. When the Convention closed down the universities in 1793, it merely sealed their earlier demise.[6]

What, then, was to become of the thousands of *avocats?* For many the Revolution created new opportunities, since ex-barristers became candidates par excellence for the elective administrative posts and judgeships opening up across the land. In at least two judicial centers that have been studied in detail, however, revolutionary policy confused and even dismayed most barristers. Already alienated by the Assembly's harsh treatment of the parlements to which their own status had been linked, the barristers of Paris and Toulouse proved more likely to oppose the Revolution than to support or profit from it. Of the three hundred or so Parisian barristers who had actually practiced in the Parlement before the Revolution, only about fifty would plead in the new judicial system while a comparable number took positions as judges or JPs, but most boycotted the new institutions and went into internal exile biding their time. In Toulouse—the second city in the old-regime judicial firmament—about 80 percent of the parlement's 276 barristers shunned the new system, while only one fifth held any administrative or judicial office during the revolutionary decade or practiced before the new tribunals. Conversely, seventy ex-barristers of Toulouse put their names to a counter-revolutionary petition instigated by the ousted parlementaires. Thus the image of barristers as a revolutionary vanguard does not hold true for the ordinary members of that profession in at least two of its centers, where alienation rather than patriotic élan apparently took hold.[7]

When the Assembly considered the other branch of the bar, the *procureurs* were not likely to survive unscathed. These experts on procedure were lightning rods for the sense of victimization that citizens suffered when they fell into the "abyss" of the French legal system. The outside world regarded attorneys as parasites, practitioners of chicanery—the bad faith and manipulation that led to endless delays and escalating costs in the progress of a lawsuit. After all, their fees—regulated by an official tariff, monitored by the courts, and legally collectible—were directly proportional to the multiplication of paperwork and procedural complexities. For the time being, reforming the procedural code itself, the royal ordinance of 1667, was a task beyond the Assembly's capacity. At present reformers could merely strike at the privileged monopoly that had historically exploited that code.

The *procureurs* were immediately vulnerable because they constituted corporations with fixed numbers of members practicing before specific parlements or lower courts, who purchased their positions. Defending their privileges in utilitarian terms, the *procureurs* argued that their investments in a venal office guaranteed their integrity and accountability to clients who entrusted them with important documents. The corporate system with its fixed complement of *procureurs* at each tribunal, they argued, assured that attorneys were acquainted with one another and with the judges, facilitated the flow of procedure, and provided a forum for professional discipline. [8] The Assembly, buying none of this, annihilated these snug corporate establishments. Having abolished the offices of the royal magistrates, the Assembly did not hesitate to abolish the offices of the *procureurs*.

To compensate them the Assembly, it will be recalled, utilized the self-assessments filed by all venal corporations in 1771 as a basis for calculating a new royal surtax. To minimize this surtax, the corporations of notaries and of *procureurs* had ludicrously undervalued their offices in 1771 and would now pay dearly for that tactic. Moreover when a notary or *procureur* had purchased his position, he paid the previous owner for his practice as well as the formal *charge* or price of the office, but the Assembly's redemption procedures made little allowance for that component of the transaction. Frantic lobbying by the attorneys won only minor concessions on this point. The example of the senior *procureur* in Marseille illustrates the final settlement. He had purchased his office in 1761 for 40,000 livres and had seen its value rise to about 60,000 (the average of the three most recent turnovers in Marseille before 1790). The 1771 valuation, however, was a mere 10,000 livres! His indemnity consisted of the assessed valuation of his office in 1771, one quarter of his actual purchase price, and 5,000 livres for his prorated share of his corporation's debts. It totaled only 25,000 livres. *Procureurs* clamored that such compensation amounted to sheer expropriation, but the Assembly would not budge any further. [9]

Though the Assembly abolished the corporate monopoly and venal offices of the *procureurs,* it kept the attorney's function obligatory for the management or *instruction* of civil suits. Unlike the barristers, the profession was not meant to disappear. Attorneys would henceforth be called *avoués*. Where the *avocat*'s function had been thrown open to any citizen, the new *avoués* had to be bona fide legal practitioners of some sort. After rejecting the notion of electing *avoués* (as officers of the court) or of restricting the post for the time being to ex-*procureurs,* the Assembly decreed that all current members of the legal world were eligible to be inscribed as *avoués:* ex-*procureurs,* ex-royal judges, ex-*avocats* (relatively few of whom took the opportunity), and men with five years or more experience as head clerk for a *procureur.* In the future there would be an examination *(concours)* for admission to practice after five years of clerkship. *Avoués* had to register before a specific district court, to which their practice was restricted, but there was no limit on their numbers. Judges retained the power to scrutinize the fees and expenses of the attorneys, but the Assembly reduced the official rate scale to three quarters of the pre-revolutionary *tarif.*[10]

When the Assembly abolished the orders of *avocats* and corporations of *procureurs,* the old distinction between barristers and attorneys, between pleading and procedure, ostensibly fell as well. Naturally it survived on both sides of the old divide in the minds of traditionalists from each profession. Ex-*procureurs* whose clients permitted them to plead were derided by ex-*avocats* for their manifest lack of talent: "insipid, monotonous readers," charged one professional journal, mocking men "limited until now to functions which by their very nature are the death of talent." Older attorneys retained their professional pride as well. About two hundred former *procureurs* of the Châtelet in Paris banded together in a Société d'hommes de loi to expedite the cases they handled as *avoués,* and "to maintain by reciprocal surveillance the sentiments of honor and probity."[11]

The future also promised new opportunities and styles of legal practice and a new measure of flexibility for litigants. Competition *(émulation)* became the ideological watchword of the intended transformation. In the area of criminal law, citizens had an almost unlimited right to self-defense; most were likely to seek experienced *avocats,* but the latter had no monopoly on this function. In civil litigation, the Revolution created a free marketplace of registered attorneys in which competition would presumably serve the public interest as it was supposed to in other fields of endeavor. All this threw the legal world, once the epitome of traditionalism, into a state of flux. *Avoués,* inscribed for civil practice before a district tribunal, remained the only lawyers with a formal status. Individuals of any background who now specialized in oral defense usually called themselves *défenseurs officieux* on their shingles. Ex-barristers who served as legal consultants *(jurisconsultes),* whether or not they entered a courtroom, were known as *hommes de loi,* and were considered akin to *hommes de lettres.* Only the *avoué* engaged in a recognized metier unambiguously subject to payment of the *patente,* the new business license tax. Increasingly he became the visible prototype of the lawyer, similar to the new general practitioner of medicine, the *officier de santé.*[12]

The end of professional monopolies, and the competition that came with liberty, did not eliminate a fundamental problem. Whatever they were called, attorneys might still be prone to "chicanery." The Assembly revealed its residual distrust of the *avoués* it had created by barring these practitioners from hearings before the justices of the peace. But in the district courts, where the ordinance on civil procedure of 1667 still prevailed, the old ways continued. In July 1792 the minister of justice denounced

> the avidity of the *officiers ministériels*. Their chicanery and fraud were supposed to have been crushed in the debris of the old regime. But numerous complaints . . . testify only too well that they have known how to reproduce themselves in the new judicial order, and that the *avoués,* clerks, and bailiffs still know how to set traps against good faith and levy a tax on the simplicity of the litigants. [13]

For the moment this warning went unattended, since political crises left little time to deal with the role of lawyers, but dissatisfaction festered.

By 1793, however, the substantial ranks of the *avoués* had thinned considerably. In Paris, an estimated four or five hundred in 1791 fell to about 150 in the fall of 1793. The minister of justice told the Convention that "a large number of these officers have ceased exercising their functions and litigants have no one to turn to." At Auray (Morbihan), only three attorneys were practicing by 1793. One then became secretary to the district administration and another joined the army. Later that year the remaining *avoué* was arrested as a suspect! Some attorneys doubtless dropped out because they could not attract enough clients to earn a living. Others took positions as clerks to the justices of the peace, which by law were incompatible with the post of *avoué*. Nor could the posts of *avoué* and notary be held concurrently, and anyone who had hoped to combine the two practices was likely to opt for the notariat. Finally, a number of *avoués* had trouble securing the *certificat de civisme* or attestation of patriotism required of all public officials after January 1793.

With the resulting slowdown in the course of civil justice, some courts demanded relief. The tribunal at Lorient (Morbihan) asked the ministry to allow four local notaries to practice as *avoués;* in a neighboring district the judges wished to accept clerks without the requisite five years of experience. The tribunal at Auch (Gers) went further. It proposed to curb procedural formalities and eliminate the need for *avoués* altogether—as the suspended Constitution of 1793 promised to do some day. [14] The Convention referred these petitions to committee. A few weeks later a bill was reported and passed virtually without debate on 3 brumaire II (24 October 1793). Without explicitly abrogating the ordinance of 1667, it reduced the formalities of civil procedure by requiring only oral arguments or "simple memoirs," and it eliminated the requirement for *avoués* in the *instruction* of civil suits. Citizens could of course avail themselves of counsel, but henceforth their lawyers would be "simples fondés de pouvoir" without official standing in the court. [15]

DEREGULATION

The law of October 1793 was surely one of the Convention's more radical and utopian measures, though it has never found its way into general accounts of the Revolution. Like so many Jacobin policies, it was launched with an unguarded spirit of optimism. In a report summarizing the intentions of the Convention, the minister of justice sketched his hope for the future:

> The principal object of the law of 3 brumaire was to deliver justice from the unfortunate abuses, from the excessive ascendancy of formalities, which have long been denounced by public opinion. . . . The functions of the *avoués* have too often degenerated into guile and have shown themselves to be sordidly artificial. . . . The Legislature wants the avenues of justice to be unencumbered, free of charge, and easily accessible to all persons obliged to litigate. . . . [Judges] will discern the equity of the claims more easily through the straightforward presentation by an ordinary person unaccustomed to sophistic subtleties. [16]

The reformers of 1790 had shared the desire to make justice simple, direct, and inexpensive, but they had confronted the centuries-old procedural complexities of French civil law gingerly, no doubt believing that formal procedure protected the rights of litigants and made for an orderly presentation of information to the judges. Now, pushed by circumstances, the Convention seemed to will these complexities away in the belief that it could drastically reduce "chicanery." The most direct consequence of this policy was to abolish the organized bar completely. Legal assistance of any kind—defense in criminal trials and counsel in civil suits—could now be provided by any citizen who obtained a *certificat de civisme.*

While certain ex-attorneys and ex-barristers simply carried on, using their experience to advantage, others could not meet the increasingly stringent criteria of local revolutionary committees or municipalities for a *certificat de civisme.* Since this political bill of good health was now necessary for any appearance in court (as a *défenseur officieux* or *fondé de pouvoir*), they abandoned the practice of law, and even so some were arrested as suspects. The memoirs of legal notables as well as secondary works on the French legal profession have always treated this period of self-exile and persecution as constituting a total degradation of the bar. [17] But there was another side to the story. Complete deregulation made it possible for newcomers to set themselves up in legal practice: law clerks, bailiffs, ex-priests, teachers, functionaries, or

veterans coming out of the armies.[18] Citizen Loubix of Pau (Basses-Pyrénées), a law clerk before 1789, was representative of the new men who
combined a legal practice with public service during the revolutionary decade: clerk to a justice of the peace, *avoué* after 1791, elected judge in a district
court, *défenseur officieux,* and municipal officer. By 1799 he was one of the
more active lawyers in town, involved in forty-five of the approximately five
hundred cases on the civil court docket. Longpretz—an ex-priest from
Valenciennes (Nord) who left the clergy in 1792, married, and had a family—
served as a municipal officer, treasurer of the department's military hospitals,
secretary of the district, and judge on the departmental tribunal, after which
he consecrated himself "to the honorable function of *défenseur officieux.*"
Accepting deregulation at face value, men like Loubix and Longpretz moved
into legal practice as they had into public administration, assuming both to
be accessible to educated citizens of any background.[19]

Deregulation also facilitated new kinds of legal practice in which counsel
could be offered and fees earned without necessarily carrying litigation to
court. Notaries, for example, were now free to offer legal counsel, and certain
rural notaries undoubtedly combined the two vocations.[20] Experiments in
group practice promised new forms of legal service. A "Council of Jurisprudence" in Paris offered consultations for modest fees on family, commercial,
judicial, or administrative problems that citizens might face. It offered as well
to provide arbitrators "who can avoid all the delays and methods of chicanery." In Metz (Moselle), four men of republican convictions founded an
"Agency of Public Counselors" to aid citizens facing litigation, criminal
charges, or administrative problems. They hoped that timely advice and
support might spare their clients "the expensive and even ruinous costs of
complicated legal proceedings."[21]

These potential gains—professional opportunity, free competition, more
flexible types of service—were offset by the downside of deregulation. All
semblance of peer discipline and official control over legal practitioners
ceased. Experienced lawyers were demoralized not merely by the menacing
political climate but by the incompetence and sharp practices of their new
competitors. Some of the newcomers were undoubtedly the "charlatans,
solicitors, and intriguers," "the empirics or quacks" that their detractors
claimed. According to one later critic, "men who have made a career of
assisting the bailiffs as witnesses, all the former clerks who have the least
knowledge of affairs, have made themselves into lawyers." As the *conventionnel*
Antoine Thibaudeau later recalled, "the *défenseurs officieux, jurisconsultes* or
hommes de loi were agents and brokers; they pursued profit and scorned glory
. . . they exploited legal proceedings as if they were a branch of commerce."
Some of the new *défenseurs officieux* (the most common generic term for

lawyers in this period) allegedly solicited cases on a kind of contingency-fee basis.[22] Liberated from organized peer pressure or judicial control, lawyers could be late for court, insulting toward their colleagues, or drunk. Even if this happened only rarely, such assaults on the dignity of the courtroom must have been appalling to traditionalists.[23]

Nor had the law of October 1793, with its emphasis on oral argument, put an end to stalling tactics. A lawyer intent on delaying the proceedings could still raise new points or call for additional witnesses. "The slightest incident sometimes necessitates a hearing," one critic claimed. Moreover deregulation of the bar put citizens at the mercy of unprincipled lawyers because the judges lost the power to scrutinize the fees for which attorneys billed their clients. Some lawyers (new and old) allegedly demanded extortionate sums for their expenses and honoraria. In the Ain, victorious litigants complained that their lawyers charged more than the amounts they had won in court. Though these bills were no longer legally collectible through the offices of the court, unscrupulous practitioners could hold key documents in their charge for ransom.[24]

By 1797—when the directorial legislature finally had a chance to consider the matter—consensus reigned that something had to be done about unscrupulous and incompetent practitioners at the bar. Observers invoked the analogy with medical charlatans: just as malpractice threatened life in medicine, it threatened property in the handling of litigation.[25] Yet the deputies divided sharply over the prescribed remedy. Contrary to later claims by chroniclers of the bar, they were not prepared to rush headlong back to the system of 1791, let alone the corporatism of the old regime. Libertarian beliefs in an unfettered right to self-defense and in professional competition, which had helped bring about the disestablishment of the *avoués* in October 1793, endured. Free and thorough parliamentary debate in fact produced no agreement at all.

Some legislators still believed that the formal *instruction* of lawsuits inherently invited abuse. "The métier of the *avoué* is vicious in and of itself," declared one deputy. "How can one wish chicanery to disappear, if it can be made into a lucrative profession?" But as another suggested, properly handled, procedure was integral to justice: "It is by forms that you contain judicial power within just limits."[26] Almost all speakers agreed on the need to reestablish some professional standards by having a roster of trained lawyers available to the public. But should their services again be obligatory in civil litigation? And should the number of licensed practitioners at each tribunal be fixed? The most thoughtful speakers in this exhaustive legislative debate divided completely on such basic questions.[27]

One view held that since attorneys were not merely useful but indispensable to the course of civil justice, litigants *must* be represented by an *avoué*. According to C.-J. Mallarmé, reestablishing *avoués* without making their ministry obligatory was "contradictory and inadmissible." Although litigants should remain free to defend their own cause in court, the handling of documents and the use of procedure must be uniform. Traditional *instruction* was a "reciprocal guarantee" between litigants; both sides needed confidence in the authentication and transmission of relevant documents. Parties to a suit had to be represented during their absence from the departmental capitals where the civil tribunals were now located. Peasants living in the countryside were said to be the foremost victims of the prevailing "anarchy."

Certain speakers also insisted that the number of *avoués* at each tribunal must be fixed. Only then could attorneys and judges know each other and develop a mutual respect which would facilitate their work. Besides, claimed the veteran legislator Oudot, an excessive number of lawyers vying for a limited amount of business encouraged rapacity and sharp practices. Indeed, the strongest argument for limiting the number of *avoués* had less to do with efficiency than with the career prospects of attorneys. For that reason Mallarmé—a staunch advocate of the *avoué*'s obligatory role—argued *against* limiting their number, righteously asserting that the legislature should "never consider individual interests."

A return to traditionalism by making the *avoués'* ministry obligatory or fixing their numbers ran headlong into the new tradition of revolutionary liberalism. A.-F. Pison duGalland, once a member of the National Assembly, considered attorneys comparable to doctors, whose ranks were not restricted. "Competition should increase emulation," he argued. Both the free marketplace of talent and the unlimited right of self-defense would be served best simply by certifying a roster of trained lawyers without either limiting their number, making their role obligatory in a lawsuit, or obliging them to pay a discriminatory surety bond. After the Council of Five Hundred debated and rejected several draft decrees, Pison's view finally prevailed.

His proposal—which did not even resurrect the title of *avoué*—provided that a board of three judges and three legal scholars in each department would examine and certify candidates for a roster of *hommes de loi*. There would be no limit on their numbers, and parties to a lawsuit would be free to use their services or not. On the other hand, judges would regain the right to scrutinize and adjust the bills tendered by attorneys to their clients, and could discipline wayward or obstructive practitioners.[28] In sociological terms, the Council of Five Hundred proposed a return to "definitional" rather than "restrictive" licensing; the bill retreated from the "radical free field" of revolutionary deregulation, but only to a "modified free field" rather than to strict corporate or bureaucratic regulation.[29] Uncertified practitioners could still compete for business, while citizens gained access to certified counsel but were still free to arrange their affair as they wished.

This minimalist bill, however, did not resolve the matter, for the Council of Elders voted it down. The *rapporteur* objected primarily to its provisions for judicial discipline, which he considered too arbitrary. But the debate in the upper house also revived the argument over how much latitude uncertified individuals might still have to offer legal counsel. By refusing to make a certified lawyer's ministry obligatory, it was argued, the bill opened a back door to men rejected by the certification board to continue practicing. The Elders returned Pison's libertarian bill to the lower house for reconsideration. There it languished amidst more pressing issues, one more problem awaiting either a new consensus or a firm hand.[30]

THE REVOLUTION AND THE NOTARIAT

A propertied citizen of France might pass a lifetime without requiring an attorney or barrister, but he was bound to consult a notary at some point. Notaries gave proper form and legality to domestic, property, and monetary transactions. In 1579 the monarchy codified the regulations by which notaries drafted, certified, and retained such documents, stipulating procedures for the signatures of principals and witnesses and the requirements for establishing engrossed copies. Royal notaries shared these functions with ecclesiastical and seigneurial notaries. While rural notaries were likely to have a modest practice, urban notaries employing several clerks could earn substantial fees. Like the *procureurs,* royal notaries in the cities were organized into chartered companies, their positions being venal and hereditary. When such a notary's practice and archive of documents *(étude)* did not pass to his son, it could be sold to a senior clerk in his or another's office. At the summit of this profession stood the Company of Notaries in Paris, whose 113 members (a number fixed at the end of the sixteenth century and unchanging since then) could practice throughout the entire realm. Their well-endowed corporate treasury defended the company's prerogatives and slaked the recurrent demands of royal fiscality. So well connected were these men that voters chose 43 of the 113 as electors in the 400-man Paris electoral assembly of 1789.[31]

A good notary was a man with special attributes, a man, one might say, projecting an exaggerated image of bourgeois rectitude. Well educated in grammar and points of law, he could of course draft documents with exactitude and clarity. But more than a mere a redactor of contracts, he advised his clients of the ramifications and possible flaws in their proposed arrangements. The quality most valued in a notary was probity. Notaries had to inspire trust and confidence since they were privy to the best kept financial secrets of French families, and frequently held large sums of their money in short- or long-term escrow. The notary's investment in his office was supposed to guarantee his integrity with such funds, as well as his care of the original documents permanently lodged with him for safekeeping.[32]

The types of transactions that notaries handled both before and after the Revolution are suggested in an accounting from the Indre in the Year VII (1798–99)—a typical year in a typical northern department—where the 8,450 notarial acts executed by about 100 notaries break down as follows:[33]

3,544 sales of property
1,502 debt instruments
1,217 farm leases
  756 marriage contracts
  454 divisions or renunciations of inheritance
  334 transactions stemming from lawsuits
  264 rental leases
  238 divisions or renunciations of matrimonial property
  142 annuity contracts

These proportions were roughly similar during the 1780s and the 1790s, except that inheritance transactions and sales of property increased substantially from pre-revolutionary levels. Even with the nationalization of Church property, the end of seigneurialism, and the equal inheritance laws, notaries remained as busy as ever after 1789.

Though it was not the most pressing issue, the organization of the notariat had of course to be brought into harmony with the new regime. Ecclesiastical and seigneurial notaries obviously had no place in the future. The excessive number of incompetent practitioners in the countryside had to be reduced while a rationalized distribution of qualified notaries assured better service for rural citizens. Like those of the *procureurs,* the corporate privileges and exclusivism of the notarial "companies" had to be terminated, and their venal offices abolished with compensation. But it was not so simple. Venality and the concomitant right to dispose of these offices as property to one's heir or chosen successor was more functional in the case of the notaries. The notary's office encompassed not simply his venal *charge* and his clientele but his archive of documents *(étude),* a valuable form of property albeit one held as a public trust. The notarial calling placed a premium on continuity, training, and personal relations. Nor could the profession accommodate an unlimited number of practitioners; it could not be "opened up" on the model of the *avoués.* The notariat could not easily be incorporated into the bureaucracy or converted into a liberal profession. Yet revolutionary principles demanded careers opened to talent, competition, and an end to hereditary privileges. The Assembly faced a real dilemma.[34]

One solution would have been simply to abolish the very role of the notary, as had been done with the barristers. A flurry of denunciations by disgruntled citizens against the ultra-privileged corporation of Parisian notaries—for speculating with their clients' funds, overcharging, battening off public loans—made them a particular target. One Jacobin pamphleteer of 1790 argued for an entirely new set of arrangements that would eliminate the notary's profession. The drafting of contracts and agreements should be a competitive and unregulated vocation, without being linked to the legalization or deposit of documents. For Paris he proposed that the clerks of the forty-eight sections become the "certifiers of agreements" *(légalisateurs des conventions),* and that the clerks of the six district courts should maintain the deposit of legalized documents and provide engrossed copies to the public ("dépositaires et expéditonnaires publics de titres légalisés"). For their part the elected JPs' assessors could be available to the public as redactors of contracts, without monopolizing that function.[35]

This scheme for a public depository system drew little support. The argument of the notaries of Saumur that "a clerk will never have that religious concern for the safeguard of the documents shown by a proprietor" evidently had wide currency. "The court clerks have no interest in the surveillance of these archives," claimed the notaries of Grenoble, besides which, if the courts became public depositories, "all the practitioners would trample around the clerk's office and secrecy would no longer be preserved."[36] No revolutionary regime proposed to eliminate the unique role of the notary as both an adviser to clients and a public official whose ministrations legalized a document and then assured its permanent safekeeping. The reform in 1790 of the registry bureaus, where citizens recorded property deeds for a hefty fee to the state, did not obviate the notary's more extensive archive of contracts and agreements.

The question remained, then, of how to liquidate old-regime privileges engrafted onto the position, reorganize the notariat, and assure the future recruitment of notaries in keeping with professional imperatives, the public interest, and the libertarian principle of careers open to talent. Under the law of 6 October 1791, all existing notarial positions were abolished, to be replaced by *notaires publics.* The legislature would eventually fix the number of notaries in each department upon the recommendation of departmental authorities; each notary was required to reside in the place of his appointment, but was free to practice throughout his department. In this way, it was hoped, all localities could be served in proportion to their needs. In the interim, however, royal notaries were permitted to continue in place, with subsequent quotas to be reached by attrition.[37]

When it came to liquidating the royal offices and compensating the incumbents, the professional self-evaluations of 1771 returned to haunt the notaries, since they had assessed only the title or *finance* of their post and not the value of their practice. In Toulouse and Rennes, for example, the notaries' assessment of 1771 was 2,000 livres while the market price of the office in 1789 had reached 10,000; in Moulins, it was 1,000 livres compared to current estimates of 6,600. But the stakes in Paris were higher still. The Company of the Châtelet had assessed the office at 40,000 livres in 1771 when it was actually selling for 150,000; by 1789, it had almost doubled. While the Assembly voted to indemnify provincial notaries with only the self-assessed value of their office in 1771, it handled Paris as a special case—provoking an outcry from provincial notaries who demanded to be treated in the same way. The Assembly must have worried that purchase prices in the capital ranging between 200,000 and 300,000 livres in the last two decades were typically financed by loans from numerous individuals who might be ruined if the notaries defaulted on repayments. Compensation in Paris would therefore be based on the average price paid in the seventy most recent turnovers, less deduction for *recouvrements* (accounts payable on the notary's books) as well as a deduction based on the notary's degree of seniority.

Under the law of October 1791 all *notaires publics* had to pay a *cautionnement*, or surety bond, which varied according to the notary's residence. Notaries protested that they were the only judicial personnel required to do so, but the provincial notaries were particularly upset. At the top of the scale, the 40,000 livres bond required of Parisian notaries was much less than the compensation payments due them, but in cities like Bordeaux (15,000 livres) or Grenoble (4,000), notaries might end up with a net loss, and rural notaries, with their surety bond of 2,000 livres, assuredly would. The cries of foul were doubly shrill since, unlike tax receivers who could pledge real property for their surety bonds, the notaries were supposed to pay in cash, which would never earn them a sou of interest.[38]

Among the last officeholders to be dealt with, the notaries never did receive their compensation or pay their surety bonds before the Convention changed the rules of the game. Finance Minister Cambon, looking for ways to save money, told the Convention that the notaries who retained their positions had no right to be reimbursed for their full value, and that the evaluation of 1771 was the proper sum for their indemnity. The Convention so voted on 7 pluviôse II (26 January 1794), but also agreed to eliminate the *cautionnement*—now seeing it as an undemocratic measure detrimental to citizens without the ability to raise such a capital outlay. The government duly paid the reduced indemnities in the form of promissory notes that were severely devalued over the next few years. Recent purchasers of the office in Paris, who styled themselves "the young notaries," were especially hard hit and remonstrated to no avail that the notaries from whom they bought their offices should at least share in the loss by refunding part of the purchase price.[39] As one anonymous pamphleteer responded, "The Nation suppressed the office. It received only the price of the office [to begin with] and it reimburses only the office. . . . The notaries are compensated for their *finance,* they retain their calling, and have already long since profited from it."[40]

Apart from compensation, the most contentious issue in 1791 was how new notaries would be designated in the future. Professionals advocated a period of training as a clerk (a *stage*), preference for incumbent head clerks, and the right of a sitting notary to choose his successor. This was the tenor of the proposal made by the notary-deputy Nicolas Frochot to the Assembly, with the proviso that there be a departmental examination to establish the eligibility of all future candidates. Critics countered with the notion of a veritable *concours*—an open competitive examination with a rank list of preference. The law of 1791 produced a contorted compromise. Each department would appoint a panel to hold an annual examination, open to candidates who had spent at least four years under the tutelage of a notary in that department. (Lawyers were eligible to take the exam without this *stage.*) The rank list of the *concours* would determine the order for filling future vacancies, however, meaning that incumbents would not have the right simply to choose their son or head clerk as their successor for this public position. Yet the Assembly gave back with one hand what it had taken away with the other. What if the top candidate could not come to an agreement or afford to buy out the practice of a deceased or retiring incumbent? In a bow to professional interests, the Assembly nullified the pristine notion of a ranked *concours* and brought venality in by the back door. After heated debate, it stipulated that before a notary could receive his public commission, he had to prove "that he has reimbursed his predecessor or his heirs for the amount of the latter's surety bond and accounts payable or that he has made arrangements in regard to them." Furthermore, the incumbent retained the right to dispose of his archive to any notary of his choice.[41]

These ground rules too fell by the wayside when the Convention added a new, overriding requirement in November 1792: like the *avoués,* all notaries must secure a *certificat de civisme* from their municipalities. In Dijon, only twelve of the eighteen notaries received their certificates and continued to practice.[42] But the new requirements hit hardest in Paris after the onset of the Terror. Almost all of the capital's notaries had secured their certificates early in 1793, but in September the Convention ordered that they must appear again before the revolutionary committees of their sections. By this time the Parisian notariat suffered from a severe stigma, for they were suspect as the protectors of aristocrats and émigrés. In some sections the committees stalled, making it impossible for the notary to continue in practice. Others refused outright to award the certificate. Some practitioners, fearing that they would be rebuffed and knowing that this was grounds for arrest as a suspect, resigned as the only way to avoid prison. In the event, almost half the positions in Paris became vacant. Nine notaries had died, five were suspended, twenty-nine dismissed, and fifteen resigned under duress. [43]

Back in May 1793 the Convention had authorized departmental administrations to fill notarial vacancies provisionally in any way they saw fit. Amidst this turmoil the concept of a *concours* received its first trial in the capital. In ventôse Year II the department of Paris appointed a nine-man jury (including three of its administrators, three notaries, and three judges), which organized an examination to fill some of these vacancies. Thirty-two candidates registered, and twenty-six actually turned up for the examination, all notary's clerks. The jury passed twenty-two and rejected four. [44] Politics assuredly influenced the screening since *civisme* now loomed as relevant as talent and probity. The notary, after all, was a public official who stood at an extremely sensitive juncture between citizens and the laws.

Accordingly the board rejected L'Aîné on the grounds of poor citizenship. The jury was alerted to this possibility when "it noticed with surprise that the patriotic contribution as well as the taxes of citizen L'Aîné, paid only a few days before the opening of the *concours,* were excessively modest and did not correspond to the faculties that one might assume for the head clerk of a notary." It therefore ordered further scrutiny of his background and decided from what it learned "that the *civisme* of citizen L'Aîné does not appear sufficiently pronounced for us to feel confident in conferring public functions on him, especially when a host of former incumbents are justly being deprived of their positions because of *incivisme.*" (L'Aîné later protested that the jury was intimidated by Momoro, a notorious ultra-revolutionary who was a member of the panel. But the jury indignantly rejected this contention: Momoro had put in only one appearance during the entire *concours,* and had not been present when it rejected L'Aîné.) [45]

The issue of *civisme* no doubt made other clerks unwilling even to appear for the *concours.* The atmosphere which had produced so many vacancies in the first place "presided similarly over the ulterior arrangements," one disgruntled aspirant complained later. "The same system of terror turned aside from the *concours* a large number of knowledgeable individuals who have consumed their youth in the study of the notary's functions." This was an important point because after Thermidor the Convention both confirmed the status of the twenty-two new notaries admitted after the *concours,* and reintegrated the surviving notaries who had been dismissed or resigned under duress in the Year II. The clerks deterred by considerations of *civisme* from taking the examination during the Terror, however, were left out in the cold.[46]

THE DIRECTORY REGIME inherited the Convention's improvisations, in effect leaving it up to each department to deal with notarial vacancies as it saw fit, until such time as the legislature could draft a comprehensive revision of the law of October 1791. Meanwhile, few departments had managed even to set the number and distribution of notaries for approval by the legislature. Some did arrange a *concours* to fill vacancies, though they were not required to. In the Côte d'Or, a three-man jury examined and weighed the testimonials of five candidates to fill a vacancy in 1797. It looked for competence, *civisme,* and experience, though the *stage* was no longer a formal requirement. In Paris, two *concours* produced thirty-three new nominations between Years VI and VIII. In the countryside, however, the situation remained unstable. The ministry received complaints about an excess of notaries in unseemly competition, making the rounds of fairs and inns to drum up business; many were said to be unqualified, sowing the seeds of future lawsuits by their incompetence. Some notaries moved to towns in defiance of the residence requirements that still stood. Yet when vacancies in legitimate rural practices occurred, departmental administrations could not always find candidates to fill them.[47]

In sum, the notarial calling suffered from a degree of disorder and instability less drastic than the bar's but troubling because of the profession's centrality to the lives of ordinary citizens. The cycle was familiar: a sweeping reform by the National Assembly never put to the test of experience before the Convention grafted new and in some respects contradictory innovations onto the original project. This left an uncertain status quo under the Directory and the need for a new policy and a second round of comprehensive legislation to reorganize the notariat.

As they showed during their probing debate over the *avoués,* directorial legislators were less willing than might be supposed to desert revolutionary principles and simply return to traditional professional standards. To be sure, everyone wished to assure the competence of notaries, but when the Council of Five Hundred finally passed a bill in 1799, the traditional *stage* for future notaries was gone and the new *concours* reigned supreme. A clerkship require-

ment would revive the old exclusivism and corporate mentality of the notariat, argued the *rapporteur*. To limit someone in the means by which he gains
his professional knowledge would "circumscribe natural liberty," as well as
condemn individuals "to vegetate" in a notary's employ. For if an apprenticeship in Paris might be a "fecund source of enlightenment," the same could
not be said of the provinces. Clerks should have no built-in advantage,
though of course the jury would reward those clerks who were truly deserving. The *concours* proposed in 1799 was to be a two-part affair: first a qualifying examination for the purpose of certifying prospective candidates, and a
second examination for each specific vacancy. At that time the board would
of course weigh the morality and *civisme* of the candidates as well as their
talent. The proposal explicitly rejected the idea of resignation *in favorem*. [48]
Since this bill dealt with a multitude of technical issues, it was rejected the
first time around by the Council of Elders. But after several minor modifications, and with these major provisions in tact, the Council of Five Hundred
passed it a second time and sent it on to the Elders for reconsideration. [49]

Several notaries weighed in with pamphlets attacking the draft bill as
demoralizing and demeaning to their professional dignity. A clerkship "does
not limit talents but rather assures their existence," they argued. The proposal
made it unlikely that families would support children through the long
periods of clerkship that were the best preparation for this calling. Conversely an open, politically oriented *concours* would make the notariat a refuge
of failed lawyers and of citizens who lost positions as judges, court clerks,
administrators, or directorial commissioners. With unusual candor, the notary Bonnomet thus exposed a real weakness in the civic culture of the
republic:

> One cannot help thinking that this bill would open a wide door to all
> those who, constituting a Republic within the Republic, and regarding
> such positions as their patrimony, cry out against injustice when they are
> forced to abandon one position without being able to expect another.
> They count knowledge and morality for nothing, and *civic language* as
> everything; they decry heredity as anathema but reserve for themselves its
> substitute. [50]

Whether such arguments would have induced the Elders to reject the bill
again, we cannot know. Timing doomed it in any case. The Elders' committee made a favorable recommendation on 13 brumaire Year VIII, but before
debate could be concluded, Brumaire brought it to a halt.

PROFESSIONALISM REESTABLISHED

Napoleon's Council of State swept away the well-founded ambivalence of directorial legislators about the position of judges, lawyers, and notaries in the republic. With only modest concessions to revolutionary concepts, the regime began with a complete reorganization of the court system—the third within a decade. Scrapping the Directory's ninety-odd departmental civil tribunals as insufficient, the Consulate established about three hundred courts of primary jurisdiction *(tribunaux de première instance)*—one in each arrondissement, a jurisdiction roughly akin to the old districts but less numerous—usually three or four per department instead of five or six. The Directory had created comparable circumscriptions for its grand juries and correctional tribunals—courts manned by JPs and rotating civil court judges to hear misdemeanor cases. Quite logically the new *tribunaux de première instance* took on that function as well. Sitting above these 300-odd tribunals, a new tier of appeals courts *(tribunaux d'appel)* in twenty-seven cities would each serve three or four departments, thus ending the system of revolving appeals through the regular courts. Judges on both kinds of tribunals were to be named by the head of state with lifetime appointments. [51] The *constituants'* fears of permanent judicial corporations and entrenched professionalism had dissipated. The regime now viewed the magistracy as a vocation. Later it created training positions for probationary judges *(auditeurs)*, which among other things reinforced a tendency toward nepotism. [52]

Not that the Napoleonic magistrates could be considered an aristocracy of the robe. Lacking distinctive social status, collecting relatively modest pay, and beholden to the executive for patronage and advancement, the judges were simply state functionaries. True, lifetime appointments insulated judges from the need to face the voters every few years and from the vicissitudes of high politics—or so it seemed until 1808, when Napoleon purged the magistracy, or 1815, when the Bourbons imitated his example. But as the legal historian A.-J. Arnaud shrewdly observes, even in granting them ostensible lifetime tenure, Bonaparte enclosed his magistrates in a ghetto; their autonomy was actually a kind of quarantine, limiting their powers to nonpolitical questions. In that sense the spirit of 1789 still reigned, ruling out judicial activism. [53]

With the new courts came a restoration of the *avoués.* All the proposals legislators had beaten back in the debate of 1799 prevailed under the Consulate. Judges on each new court were to fix a quota of *avoués* and nominate men to fill those posts, subject to approval and official certification by the Ministry of Justice. These attorneys once again became officers of the court, whose services were mandatory in the *instruction* of a civil suit, though for the time being the law preserved the right of self-defense or counsel of one's choosing for oral pleading. Each attorney was to pay a surety bond *(cautionnement)* to the government, averaging between 600 to 900 francs in most lower courts (with a high of 2,700F in Paris) and between 1,800 and 4,500 francs in the appeals courts—money which the regime eagerly anticipated. The attorneys in each town were to form professional associations called *chambres des avoués* for purposes of discipline. As a logical corollary, the regime reinstated the ordinance on civil procedure of 1667, pending promulgation of a new code, completed in 1806. [54]

The Ministry of Justice understood that it was supervising a delicate operation. On the one hand it told the judges to promote the professional integrity of lawyers by curbing cutthroat competition: "The purpose of the law is to eliminate that multitude which harms itself by excessive competition and which, not being able to find sufficient resources in its profession, may be tempted to compensate by methods . . . that always victimize the public." Yet the people required ample access to counsel: "It could not be our intention not to conserve a sufficient number of upright, educated, and patriotic lawyers who have made a particular study of the law for many years." In theory the two goals were mutually compatible, but in practice there was an obvious tension, which the government perhaps resolved in its own mind by virtue of the fiscal motive for taking control of the bar: "one cannot hide the fact that the *cautionnement* of the *avoués* ought to provide the Government with resources that circumstances render precious." [55]

To carry out this new policy, the judges on each tribunal opened a register in which practitioners who wished to become *avoués* inscribed their names and vitae. The judges then fixed the quota for their court and nominated individuals for appointment by the ministry. In brief, they operated a triage on participants in the deregulated bar. In a sample of fifty-five courts of first instance that reported the size of their quota as against the number of applicants, the ratios distribute into contrasting situations. Twelve courts rejected proportionately large numbers of applicants, including Paris where 375 men sought 240 positions, and fifteen tribunals shut out a significant number. In sixteen courts there was—by coincidence or design—a close or exact fit between the number of applicants and the quota set by the judges. Twelve other tribunals could not fill their quotas. Notwithstanding a few courts with real shortages of *avoués,* the reorganization of 1800 officially proclaimed an oversupply of lawyers and presumably of aspirants to the bar in years to come. [56] Gone was all talk of competition and emulation. The

Napoleonic state closed down the free marketplace of legal counsel and gave full sway to an older guild mentality.

This triage produced numerous human casualties among men whose experience and career aspirations dated from the reforms of 1791 or the deregulation of 1793. Some judges explained their selections in 1800 simply by noting the insufficiency of places to accommodate all qualified applicants, or that the qualifications of some were inferior to their rivals for reasons of training or character. It all sounded very matter-of-fact, until one looks at the protests filed by excluded men. These angry or desperate petitions convey the losers' sense of victimization and futility as the official machinery ground them down. They also allege instances of conspiracies by ex-*procureurs,* the old insiders seeking to reestablish a professional dominance that they had lost in the Revolution's free marketplace. [57]

In Pau (Basses-Pyrénées), where twenty-four men applied, the judges fixed the quota of *avoués* at seventeen. Among the excluded was Loubix, whose successful career in the deregulated bar we noted earlier. Bewailing the ruin that he now faced, Loubix complained that the judges' choices had been made in collusion with the town's ex-*procureurs.* When three of the court's nominees did not take up their posts, the new *chambre des avoués* lobbied to have Pau's quota reduced to fourteen, astutely offering to pay the government its surety bonds for the three vacant places. Pierre Bozut similarly became embroiled with the tribunal of Autun (Saône-et-Loire). Bozut claimed that the designated *avoués* were generally ex-*procureurs* who had not practiced during the Revolution, whereas he had practiced as an *avoué* in the district court of Autun and had then served the republic in several capacities, including a term on the department's criminal tribunal. Bozut implied that past politics had influenced the judges; but more emphatically, he denounced a cabal of ex-*procureurs.* Five of the designated *avoués* did not take up their posts, from which he concluded that they had applied in connivance with the others "in order thereby to exclude candidates who did not please certain personages." [58]

The casualties were no less real when the judges faced an honest dilemma in choosing from an abundance of qualified or experienced applicants. In Cahors (Lot), the court reluctantly debarred promising young men such as Serre, "who was destined to shine at the bar," along with long-established practitioners, as the magistrates sifted out a quota of ten from a pool of twenty-four applicants. Some courts bent over backward to accommodate ex-*procureurs* and other long-time practitioners even when it meant enlarging their quotas beyond what seemed indicated. In Chalon (Saône-et-Loire), the court determined that twelve *avoués* would suffice, but with eighteen appli-

cants, almost all of whom had devoted years to the law and depended on it
for their living, "it seemed too harsh to pronounce an exclusion against
several men who merit the confidence of their fellow citizens, and thereby
become the instrument of their ruin . . . and hamper the citizens in their
choice of defenders." Hence the judges accepted fifteen instead of twelve.[59]

But this solicitude rarely extended to outsiders—men from varied backgrounds who had become *défenseurs officieux* after the deregulation of 1793.
Thus one of the excluded applicants in Chalon was Louis Dubois, like
Longpretz—rejected in Valenciennes—a married ex-priest. While serving
the republic as a district administrator, secretary to the municipality, and the
Directory's commissioner to the city, Dubois had developed a practice as a
défenseur officieux before the department's tribunals. Now he vainly aspired "to
the modest profession of *avoué.*" But like other ex-priests or educators,
Dubois was excluded from the reorganized bar.[60]

Having survived the triage, the new *avoués* did not necessarily reap a
bonanza. Their fees, again subject to regulation by the courts, generally
followed scales dating from 1791, which had reduced the pre-revolutionary
tarif by a quarter. This seemed to the attorneys entirely too low after a decade
of punishing inflation. For several years the *chambres des avoués* complained
bitterly of inadequate fees and high out-of-pocket expenses that came on top
of paying their surety bonds. While the government procrastinated on revising these fees, the attorneys moaned over their prospects. "It is impossible
for us to provide for our needs even with the greatest economy," complained
the *avoués* of Rodez (Aveyron). In Béziers (Hérault)—where the court had
accepted all fifteen applicants in 1800—the *chambre* claimed in 1802 that the
profession was doomed. "Today we see no one, not even our children,
embarking on this career. . . . The fear of not finding the means for making
a living leaves our profession in a state of abandon."[61]

The situation eased in 1806, when the government finally established new
and higher *tarifs* for the *avoués* in various judicial districts. After that, young
men assuredly did prepare for this career, even if it did not promise great
wealth. Aspirants now had to meet several qualifications, including one year
of study in the newly recreated law faculties; a period of clerkship; a certificate of good morals from the local *chambre des avoués;* and proof of having
satisfied the conscription laws—most often accomplished by drawing a high
number in the draft lottery, winning a dispensation for physical unfitness, or
hiring a replacement.[62] The Ministry of Justice and its judges, however, now
stood as the gatekeepers of the legal profession, not simply setting qualifications (a reasonable role) but adjusting quotas and making invidious selections
among qualified applicants. In effect the triage continued.

In the venerable southern judicial center of Toulouse—where the *chambre des avoués* had complained in 1801 that "We cannot make a living today from our emoluments"—things looked quite different by 1807, when each new vacancy attracted at least two candidates. When the *avoué* Chirac died, for example, the court submitted two names to Paris, indicating that it favored Auguières rather than the deceased's brother who regarded the post as his patrimony. Perhaps the court felt free to ignore this claim because, as Chirac *cadet* pointed out, Auguières happened to be the son-in-law of one of the judges. In any case, each man was qualified to become an *avoué*. The liberal, open-ended system of 1791 would have readily accommodated both without further ado. In Napoleonic France, they were forced into an undignified scramble for preferment. [63]

Informally, the position of *avoué* was becoming venal. Frustrated aspirants complained of a trafficking in vacant positions, and the dossiers show that the great majority of subsequent nominees had indeed purchased the practice of a retiring *avoué*. Yet this was not official or automatic. At any time the ministry could prefer another candidate, or simply reduce the quota of a particular court altogether. [64] Thus the imperial procurator in Toulouse agreed to the ministry's suggestion in 1812 that "We can, without inconvenience, suspend nominations for the posts of *avoué* vacant by virtue of resignations. The *avoués* currently practicing suffice to assure the service." Without inconvenience—except for the expectant applicants, who were devastated by this news and claimed to face "total ruin"! [65]

In Rouen, the same tightening occurred. The court originally set a generous quota, and new attorneys filtered in as deaths and retirements opened new slots. But in 1812 the situation began to change. With twenty-two *avoués* currently practicing, and three vacancies attracting several aspirants, the ministry proposed cutting the quota to twenty in order to ease competition. Prospective candidates became extremely nervous. One wrote in panic, imploring the ministry to approve his nomination. A graduate of the Paris law faculty, who had clerked for nearly ten years, he had borrowed heavily to purchase for 5,000 francs the practice of a Rouen *avoué* who had resigned in his favor, to rent a house on a nine-year lease, and to furnish it. This candidate squeaked through. But the blade fell in 1813 when the ministry finally insisted that twenty attorneys sufficed for the conduct of business in Rouen, as opposed to twenty-four or even twenty-one, and "would not approve the nomination of Sieur Chrétien for a place." [66] In Paris the process was even more brutal, as the ministry ordered a second triage among the *avoués* of the *tribunal de première instance* in 1808, slashing the number to 150, largely according to seniority. The majority of the 112 ousted *avoués* made soft landings with compensation or new posts, but some were distraught at losing their vocation. [67]

To be sure, most established attorneys approved of such slashes and indeed demanded them. Once the ministry had the right to limit entry into the profession, certain *chambres* naturally sought even further insulation from competition. This certainly must have been the case in Paris. In Saint-Gauden (Haute-Garonne), complained the *chambre*, "the number of *avoués* in this tribunal exceeds the fair proportion of work available. Several are virtually without work and cannot find the honorable means of existence in their profession." The *chambre* in Auxerre (Yonne) documented this common contention, as it urged the court not to certify any additional *avoués* should vacancies occur. A total of 320 civil cases filled the court's docket in 1813 (most requiring the services of lawyers on two sides). Auxerre's ten *avoués* shared these cases as follows: 149, 122, 77, 45, 45, 44, 43, 35, 26, 20. Only the top two or three could have prospered under these circumstances.[68] More disinterested imperial officials made the same point. The procurator at Beaune (Côte d'Or) observed that with three or four exceptions the *avoués* in his court had "only mediocre employment" and the profession was "scarcely lucrative." But these officials pushed the argument one step further than the *chambres* could. The lawyers on the bottom, he continued, "were tempted to degrade their profession . . . and vex their clients with procedures that are often useless and always expensive." Excessive competition encouraged "chicanery."[69]

Yet if new aspirants were blocked for the sake of limiting competition, it would become much harder to profit from the transmission of one's practice upon death or retirement. The Bourbons eased this problem for the attorneys by strengthening the older guild model even more. Restoration policy made official what the Napoleonic system had permitted only informally. Having just raised the *cautionnement* in order to produce new revenue, the regime placated the *avoués* in 1816 by effectively making their position venal or hereditary: "Every incumbent who has paid the surety bond shall in the future have the right to propose his successor." To protect the incomes and ethics of attorneys, however, the ministry continued to cut certain quotas, making it necessary in Paris, Bordeaux, and elsewhere after 1820 for an aspirant to purchase the vacated practices of two *avoués* in order to be commissioned.[70]

THE NAPOLEONIC REGIME reorganized the notariat along much the same lines as the civil bar. No doubt for fiscal reasons it immediately revived the 1791 requirement for a *cautionnement*, which had been dropped by the Convention as undemocratic before it was ever collected. After some finetuning, it established eight gradations depending on the notary's place of residence, ranging from 500 francs in the countryside to 12,000 francs in Paris, altogether a substantial infusion of revenue for the government. Where the National Assembly had permitted all notaries to practice within the entire extent of their department, regardless of background or qualification, the regime now divided the notariat into three classes: those in cities with an appeals court, whose *ressort* was as extensive as the court's; those in ordinary judicial seats, whose practice was limited to that arrondissement; and rural notaries, who could practice only within their canton. (The Parisian notaries, who reorganized themselves immediately after Brumaire with the approval of prefect Frochot, a former notary, were as grasping as ever. They lobbied for a fourth class comprising notaries residing in the seat of the *Tribunal de Cassation,* i.e., Paris, who could practice in the entire realm. This privilege the regime would not grant.) One pre-revolutionary kind of regulation was not resurrected: the regime did not impose a standard schedule of fees on the notariat.[71]

How to recruit future notaries had always been the most contentious issue. On this score the traditional view advocated in vain by the notariat since 1791 finally prevailed, as the Napoleonic regime scrapped the *concours* in any form. The official obituary for this quintessential revolutionary concept appeared in a handbook for notaries published under the aegis of the Ministry of Justice in 1805: "The *concours* was one of those brilliant ideas that can be cherished when one is dreaming about theory, but which is recognized in practice as unjust and ineffective. Instead of the exact evaluation that it promised, it yields only a vague and very uncertain probability." The author rationalized his opposition by claiming that the sample act which candidates had been called on to draft could never be long or challenging enough, never a complex liquidation or *partage,* for example.[72]

Dropping the *concours* entirely, the Empire now recognized the *stage*—apprenticeship as a notary's clerk—as the route to a practice, its length depending on the location of the vacancy. Aspirants also had to obtain a "certificate of capacity" from the local *chambre de discipline* of notaries, a group of senior notaries in each city similar to the *chambre des avoués.* The *chambre's* recommendation to the government was crucial for a candidate's prospects. Like the *avoué,* the notary's actual appointment came from the head of state, and the new law did not explicitly permit resignations *in favorem.* But that practice was entirely consonant with the screening power of the notarial *chambres,* which according to one observer used it complacently, "admitting too easily those who presented themselves." Or as one historian has put it, "the Chambers of discipline always designated the candidate with an agreement in his pocket."[73] In 1816, just as they did with the *avoués,* the Bourbons explicitly sanctioned the practice of venality, "rendering obligatory what had previously been only optional. . . . Notaries, their heirs, and their widows were authorized to nominate a successor to their office."[74]

THE REVIVAL OF LEGAL EDUCATION

The deregulation of 1793 had grievously offended former barristers as well as ex-*procureurs*. Already alienated by the downfall of the parlements and the loss of their monopolies and professional organizations in 1790, the ex-*avocats* viewed the law of October 1793 as the final degradation of the bar, while the abolition of the law faculties effectively proclaimed that France did not require trained legal experts. Such talents as eloquence, erudition, a mastery of precedent, and professional decorum were officially devalued, just as masters of the old procedural forms had seen their skills derided as "chicanery." After Brumaire the attorneys quickly regained the ground lost in 1793 and then some, for the restoration of the *avoués* in 1800 brought them closer to their pre-1789 corporate existence than the reform of 1791 had allowed. The barristers, however, had a slower and rougher passage back to the old ways. The indispensable first step was a resumption of traditional legal education, without which there could be no revival of their profession.

The republic had not turned its back completely on teaching law to the young, but its approach had been novel and halfhearted. Every *école centrale* (the state-sponsored secondary day school in each department) was supposed to hire four professors to offer courses for the senior students, aged sixteen to eighteen, in general grammar, belles-lettres, history, and legislation, the professors to be chosen by a departmental *juri d'instruction*. In most *écoles centrales,* legislation was the least popular course and enrolled only a handful of students. A ministerial survey in the Year VII (1799) found only 506 enrollments in legislation out of a total of 19,321 for all courses, though this particular course was known to attract unregistered auditors as well.[75] Some schools did not bother to fill the position at all, and most professors of legislation were "mediocre jurists and poor pedagogues," according to the most recent study. Their courses varied from school to school: some offered the same course every year, others employed a two- or three-year cycle; some taught two hours a day, some only an inadequate one hour. In a handful of former judicial centers, however, the professors of legislation made the most of their latitude in choosing subject matter and approach. These able professors attracted both regular students and auditors of more advanced age with specific vocational objectives.[76]

In 1799, the minister of the interior reminded professors of the Convention's original intention when it established this component of the curriculum in 1795: "The legislation course is not designed to form profound *jurisconsultes* . . . but to impart to young men the sound principles of private and public morality, with enough development to make them into virtuous citizens enlightened on their own interests and their country's."[77] Most professors duly offered a smattering of natural law, public law, and constitutional doctrine, thus giving a new inflection to legal studies. But others interpreted "legislation" more traditionally and concentrated more or less exclusively on civil law or *droit privée*. In the Hérault, for example, the professor of legislation at the *école centrale* conceived of his course vocationally, hoping that "in the future one can only become a notary or lawyer after having attended the legislation course." The professor in the Jura limited his lectures to civil jurisprudence at the behest of his students, while the two most distinguished legal professionals holding these posts, Lanjuinais in Rennes and Berriat Saint-Prix in Grenoble, did not take up moral or philosophical issues at all but dealt primarily with civil law.[78]

The best of these "legislation" courses, then, did not fulfill the Directory's civic intentions but did introduce aspiring lawyers to the intricacies of civil law. When the Consulate in 1800 signaled that it favored a retreat from the deregulation of 1793, enrollments for the course in a handful of schools increased to respectable levels.[79] Similarly, two private academies founded in Paris under the aegis of former barristers enjoyed increasing popularity— institutions which formed the veritable bridge of continuity between the traditions of the past and the reconstituted bar of the future.[80]

The Napoleonic regime definitively repudiated deregulation with the law of 22 ventôse XII (13 March 1804) reestablishing state law schools, to be phased in within the next two years. (Independent at first, they were absorbed as faculties of the Napoleonic University after 1808.) This same law gave official recognition to the function of the barrister *(avocat)* for the first time since 1790, and without exactly saying so put an end to the era of the *défenseur officieux*. Starting in 1808, no one could plead in court or be appointed as a judge without holding the *licence* from a law school (a degree awarded after three years of study and passage of four examinations.) The regime effected the transition, however, in a generous fashion. Bona fide ex-*avocats* who held degrees from old-regime law faculties naturally received pride of place in this legislation. But the new rules also recognized most current practitioners regardless of their background. All current members of the judiciary, for example, received a blanket dispensation from this requirement. *Défenseurs officieux* currently pleading before the tribunals who had done so without interruption for at least three years, as well as *avoués* who had been pleading before assuming their new positions in 1800, thereby won title to certification. Other practitioners were obliged to stand for examinations in the law schools and in effect earn an equivalency degree if they wished to continue pleading at the bar. [81]

Aspirants received full equivalency credit for any years of study in the legislation course of an *école centrale* or in the two private law academies in Paris. After 1806–07, by which time the central schools and the private academies had closed, the profession of barrister was fully reestablished on the basis of a three-year university degree, just as it had been before 1789. *Avoués,* in contrast, were required to pass only one year in law school, where they studied procedure, though most took the two-year bachelor's degree. But the government did not fully reestablish the rigid division between barristers and attorneys. Any *avoué* with the *licence* (including the long-time *avoués* who automatically gained equivalency) could "plead and draw up briefs in all kinds of affairs with which they are involved, concurrently or contradictorily with the *avocats.*" In the future certain *avoués* thus enjoyed greater professional parity with *avocats,* even if they never won the latter's historic cachet. [82]

The new law schools were shaped by the state more than the profession. Most had five professors, appointed of course by the head of state. Government control extended also into the curriculum, pedagogical techniques, and examinations. "General direction from a common center" precluded any relapse into local traditions of jurisprudence. Courses included procedure, criminal law, Roman law (the only course still taught in Latin), and public law, but the Napoleonic Civil Code dominated the entire curriculum. In all three years of the program, the principles of the new civil code formed the major subject of study, even in the course on procedure ostensibly devoted to technique. [83] During the Restoration's brief liberal interlude of 1819 this exclusive emphasis on the civil code loosened, as the monarchy established new chairs in natural law, public law, political economy, and the philosophy and history of law. But the government suppressed those chairs in 1822, again leaving the curriculum focused almost entirely on civil law. [84]

In establishing only twelve law schools, the Napoleonic regime limited their orbit to "somewhat distinguished towns and to fairly well off people." [85] The rationale for this policy was well understood by its critics, such as the imperial procurator at Nancy, which had an appeals court but no law school. The effect of this policy, he argued, was "to remove the means of instruction and thereby force a large number of young men to renounce a profession which is too costly to undertake with no assurance of success." (The costs of a legal education he estimated at a minimum of 4,000F; there were no scholarships, even for the matriculation fees that amounted to about 860F for the three-year course.) Yet if "the goal was to turn away from the bar those without fortune, so that the magistracy will be sought only by wealthy people," he continued, then the policy will fail, since "the study of jurisprudence is laborious and repelling, and it is very rare to see the well-to-do embrace the profession of barrister." In his opinion, the high cost of legal training as presently organized would not attract enough talented youths to produce the necessary flow of able barristers and judges.[86] But the opposite and more traditional view prevailed, as expressed by the Grand Master of the University in justifying a further rise in tuition fees in 1812:

> Is it really necessary and politic that such a large number of young men throw themselves heedlessly into the career of the Law, without having sufficient resources to sustain themselves there honorably? The professions to which the study of jurisprudence lead require, in order to be exercised with dignity, not only extensive knowledge but also those elevated sentiments that can scarcely be derived anywhere but through a liberal education and the habits and examples of a life of financial ease.[87]

As they had been before the Revolution, bench and bar, magistrates and barristers, were generally regarded as genteel vocations for citizens already financially secure, even if the reality fell somewhat short of that ideal. In any case, most of the schools did well. At their peak in 1812, Paris had 1,600 students, Toulouse almost 500, Brussels 300, Dijon, Poitiers, and Grenoble over 200 each, and Rennes, Aix, and Caen about 150 each.[88]

Eager to reestablish professionalism at the bar by requiring university training and certification, the Empire was slower to reconstitute the self-regulating associations of *avocats* that had been the touchstone of their professional identity under the old regime. General Bonaparte was contemptuous of the barristers' traditions and self-importance, and wary of their ethic of independence from the state. When well-known barristers put up a vigorous and successful defense of Bonaparte's rival General Moreau at a treason trial in 1804, his animus against the barristers' pretensions hardened. This brought him into conflict with the legal professionals in his inner councils, who had strong sympathies for the barristers' tradition of ethical independence and self-discipline. There followed an unusually long-running conflict within the regime over a relatively minor matter. Ten years passed before the government permitted Orders of Barristers to be reconstituted alongside the *chambres* of attorneys and of notaries.

In the process, the barristers lost a good measure of their vaunted autonomy. The official rosters of barristers were to be formed not by groups of senior barristers alone, but in concert with the president of each court and its imperial procurator, subject to approval by the Ministry of Justice. The head of each order would be selected by the government from among members of its elected council. In matters of discipline and disbarment, the orders lost the absolute authority they had wielded under the old regime, sharing it now in a process of appeal to governmental bodies. The full membership of an order could convene but once a year, and was strictly prohibited from discussing any political questions. With good reason, an historian of the Parisian barristers calls the reestablishment of their corporate identity in 1811 "a hollow victory" by the standards of survivors from the days of the parlements. This minority of veritable traditionalists, however, had managed to maintain the profession's lore and ideals through the years of revolutionary innovation, internal exile, and Napoleonic disdain. Even if their revived orders could no longer claim true autonomy, those personal standards once again shaped the profession's self-image.[89]

CONCLUSION: THE HALFWAY REVOLUTION IN CIVIL JUSTICE

The deputies of 1789 performed radical surgery at the two extremes of the old-regime judicial order, as they abolished forever the regional parlements with their independent pretensions and intimidating professionalism, and eliminated the unreliable ministrations of seigneurial justice. The National Assembly's most inspired creation, the justice of the peace, survived every ideological shift and recurrent wave of skepticism, and except for the electoral principle endured with only minor finetuning. The most ambitious JPs no doubt chafed at their low status and negligible official standing. Theirs was a dishonorable vocation, complained one rural magistrate in 1828: "poorly paid; revocable at will; deprived of all hope for advancement; unnoticed by the superior authorities; the very last in the municipal cortege at public ceremonies."[90] But such pleas for greater recognition missed the point. The JPs were intended to be and remained local amateurs. Yet they were not simply relegated to a jurisdictional ghetto labeled "petty disputes," important as that role was. All litigants had to pass through their portals for a preliminary attempt at conciliation before they could see the inside of a civil courtroom.

While most Napoleonic appellate judges considered this a useless charade that wasted everyone's time, the evidence does not support that grudging view. Even if their success was "feeble" (as the jurist and counselor of state Treilhard conceded in 1806), even if the JPs settled no more than 15 percent of cases and bound over a like proportion to arbitrators (as a recent case study of the nineteenth century has found),[91] this can scarcely be considered negligible. Indeed, this alternative route to settlement short of a trial in civil court became all the more important precisely because the revolutionaries finally lost their battle to free those courts from "chicanery."

It hardly needs to be said that the litigious impulses of the French people existed independently of judicial institutions or the fine points of civil law. In the Nord, according to a Napoleonic gazetteer, the more rural an area the less litigious it was, the implication being that townspeople were more susceptible to the promises of "chicanery." But in the civil tribunal of the Vaucluse during the Directory, the great preponderance of lawsuits originated in the countryside, and agriculturalists appear more disputatious than urbanites. The prefect of Aveyron echoed this belief, considering his department to be extremely litigious *(bien processif)* because of the great subdivision of real property and the independent spirit of rural inhabitants.[92]

The resort to litigation varied geographically, according to the published statistics of the mid-nineteenth century, with the *esprit processif* distinctly higher in Normandy, the Paris region eastward, and a large ellipse in the center reaching to the Southeast. Citizens of Brittany, the North, and most of the Mediterranean hinterland, proportionate to their populations, gave less business to the courts. Ruling out political trends, religious sociology, or urbanization as explanatory factors for these variations, Bernard Schnapper concludes—somewhat reductively it might seem—that regional variations in *mentalité judiciaire* constituted an independent variable, whose roots are probably traceable in part to the difference between Roman law regions (high litigiosity) and customary law regions.[93] On such inbred propensities the Revolution could scarcely have had much impact. But legal practitioners served or preyed on these passions, and here the Revolution could certainly have made a difference.

The fulcrum of any veritable revolution in civil justice was the system of procedure and the role of attorneys. Deregulation, the abolition of the *avoués,* and an official preference for simplified civil procedure in 1793 constituted a formidable assault on the traditional leverage by which attorneys exploited their clients. True, as the Convention carried liberal ideology to new extremes, deregulation in the courtroom raised as many new problems as it solved. But the ensuing lack of discipline and standards did not dictate the unabashed return to traditionalism instigated by Napoleon's policymakers. Even when the radical political moment had passed, republican legislators had not felt compelled to reimpose professional qualifications on candidates for elective judgeships, or to abandon the vision of a simplified, more "transparent" civil justice freed from the vexing arcana of old-regime civil procedure. Pison duGalland's bill on legal counsel adopted by the Council of Five Hundred in 1799 fashioned a plausible compromise between state control and individual freedom, between order at the bar and procedural informality; it kept the battle against "chicanery" high on the republic's agenda.

Napoleon's legal counselors almost completely abandoned that honorable struggle, dismissing it as a "mania for reform" and "immoderate thirst for perfectibility."[94] Reestablishing the *avoués* under tight state control and, after some delay, revising the *tarif* of their regulated fees upward, the regime capped this policy with its new Code of Civil Procedure in 1806. While eliminating some of the most abusive practices and stalling tactics of old, the code left a capacious field of procedural maneuvering open to the *avoués*.[95] To its advocates, this reaffirmation of procedural formalism ensured that judges could render justice more easily and confidently—"forms in law are like formulas in mathematics designed to help find the solution to problems with greater facility," claimed Siméon; for Treilhard, they were guarantees against errors and unwelcome surprises.[96] But the trade-off placed litigants back into the hands of lawyers with a built-in conflict of interest to maximize their fees.

Certain appellate judges futilely opposed a restoration of the most complex technique of traditional civil procedure: attack and response by the filing and exchanging of documents between attorneys, over and above preliminary statements of the case and oral argument at a hearing. "A trial by means of written documents is rarely anything more than an immense nourishment offered to the voracity of the *instruction,*" declared the judges at Bourges. "Thus it is in vain that one has bewailed and cried out against that abuse. Will the [Napoleonic] eye that probes all the afflictions of the state thus shut itself here?" Echoing the language of 1793, these judges argued in vain that "a brief *instruction* and pleading suffice for almost all cases. . . . Formal written filings (*l'instruction par écrit sur appointement*) are scarcely useful except to the officers of the court [i.e., the *avoués*]." To the judges in Orléans, *instruction écrite* was generally superfluous; "it will not throw new light on the case . . . and can bring confusion to the discussion."[97] Imperial procurators later confirmed the resurgence of "chicanery" in their courtrooms, but the most famous indictment came from a young man who had clerked in an *avoué*'s chambers before escaping to a more creative life. "In the provinces," wrote Honoré de Balzac, "the *avoués* cultivate that horde of small actions which pile up the paperwork and expenses. . . . They are married to petty passions; they conduct niggardly affairs; they live by generating expenses; they abuse the procedural code."[98]

The restored *avoués* also produced a substantial flow of revenue into the state's coffers. In presenting the new Code of Civil Procedure, Treilhard recalled that deregulation had permitted novel forms of extortion by unscrupulous practitioners, making justice dearer than ever, and he added that "the portion of fees from procedural acts, which the public treasury ought to have acquired, turned entirely to the profit of the attorney."[99] Now the *avoué* again became a middleman in collecting user fees for the state from his clients, above and beyond what he could legally charge for his own time, labor, and paperwork. There were the *droits d'enregistrement* (the principal documents of a case, procedural acts, and judgments had to be officially registered upon payment of fees); stamped paper (all judicial acts had to be rendered on stamped paper); and the *droits de greffe* (fees paid to the court clerk, most of which went to the state rather than the clerk himself, for the transcription of acts and their expedition). Both the state and the attorney therefore profited from the prolongation and complexity of a case, whether legitimate or artificial.

A text from 1847 with examples of the expenses occasioned by various kinds of civil suits indicates that, excluding honoraria for *avocats,* simple cases without hearings for witnesses or experts ranged between 170 and 276 francs in costs to a litigant, while cases with those additional degrees of complexity could cost between 480 and 590 francs (two thirds the annual income of a skilled worker). Over 40 percent of these costs went as fees to the state.[100] This income had the virtue of making civil justice more or less self-supporting without burdening the taxpayers. Moreover these user fees could be defended as a deterrent against a casual resort to litigation. But this would be of little comfort to the countless parties whose cases arose from necessity over which they had little or no control, such as those trying to collect a debt. The prefect of the Drôme believed, for example, that "three fifths of the civil trials have as their cause the default in payment of recognized debts, which indicates not so much a litigious spirit as a lack of wealth. The remainder of the civil cases turn on equivocal clauses in contracts, on disputes over divisions [of estates]. . . . If all the notaries were honest and skilled, the number of cases would diminish appreciably."[101]

If, thanks to Napoleonic revisions, the Revolution had little long-term impact on the procedures and costs of civil trials, did it at least reduce the volume of litigation? This obvious question is probably impossible to answer definitively. No uniform national statistics were published before the 1830s, and short of such a global view comparisons are treacherous. Judicial *ressorts* changed several times between the 1780s and the 1820s, especially across the divide of 1790. Moreover local statistics are almost never unambiguous or readily comparable. Some refer to the volume of cases entered on court dockets each quarter or year, others to judgments rendered; most statistics do not distinguish between litigation and petitions by individuals for a tribunal's *jurisdiction gracieuse.* Clearly, the collapse of the *assignats* generated a tangled mass of lawsuits that swelled court dockets in 1794–97, but impressionistic evidence suggests that once that problem receded, the Revolution was responsible for a net reduction in the caseloads of the nation's civil courts. When the Consulate's judges set relatively low quotas of *avoués* for their courts in 1800, they often rationalized that course by noting that the Revolution had "extinguished" whole categories of litigation, that the JPs were expeditiously settling many cases, and that procedure had become less complicated after 1793. [102] Although procedural complexity soon returned, complaints by the *chambres des avoués* under the Empire and Restoration that business was too scarce might be taken as the ultimate tribute to the Revolution's positive effect.

XII

TRIAL BY JURY

T
he lurid excesses of French criminal justice in the eighteenth century, the "theater of punishment" in sensational cases, made good copy. Damiens, the would-be assassin of Louis XV, was not simply executed but endured hours of excruciating torture in public before being drawn and quartered. The ordeal of Protestant Jean Calas was as bad. After his scandalously improbable conviction for murdering his own son, lest the young man convert to Catholicism, Calas was put to death on the wheel, his bones systematically broken before he could receive the coup de grâce. Royal courts reached such verdicts and meted out such punishments after largely secret trials without intervention of defense counsel; in the case of vagrants, capital punishment could be inflicted by lower courts in summary fashion and without appeal. In hindsight it now appears that the tracts of Beccaria, Voltaire, and other criminal justice reformers created something of a "black legend" by dwelling on such deficiencies while ignoring the scruples of old-regime magistrates in dealing with most criminal defendants.[1]

Moreover the system had itself generated certain reforms. Early in the century, for example, investigating magistrates subjected persons accused of capital crimes to interrogation by torture when these judges lacked a basis for certainty such as two eyewitnesses; if they had only "partial proof" of guilt, such as one witness or material evidence, judges could order torture to elicit a verifiable confession that would resolve the issue. Well before 1789, however, French magistrates generally abandoned this technique, since they had begun sentencing serious offenders to such punishments as a long term in the galleys rather than death. When the need for "legal certainty" as a basis for capital punishment thus diminished, judges no longer required confessions induced by torture. A royal decree of May 1788 renounced the practice of pre-trial torture altogether. [2]

Such reform within the system itself did not suffice to deter a frontal assault after 1789. To begin with, the existing structures of criminal justice, centered on the thirteen parlements and the approximately 400 *bailliage* or lower royal courts, could not survive the creation of departments. Criminal justice had to be realigned with the new civic geography, the archaic jurisdictional boundaries of the existing courts replaced by a uniform and coherent distribution of tribunals. The abolition of venality-in-office made any compromise with existing institutions all the more difficult. Under revolutionary standards, judicial offices could no longer be sold. But that was only the beginning. Far from being at the periphery of early revolutionary ideology, criminal justice stood at its core. For what greater form of liberty could there be than securing a citizen's right to a fair trial and protecting the innocent? [3]

THE REVOLUTION IN CRIMINAL PROCEDURE

The real revolution in criminal justice did not occur in the realm of penology. True, the penal code of 1791 dramatically modified the spectrum of punishments for certain crimes. Favoring imprisonment or hard labor (for a maximum of twenty-four years, never for life), the revolutionaries eliminated altogether such common punishments as banishment, whipping, and branding, while decriminalizing such offenses as sorcery and blasphemy. And where the royal ordinance of 1670 (which governed criminal justice until the Revolution) gave discretion to judges in meting out punishment, the penal code of 1791 introduced mandatory sentencing, exact uniformity of punishment for each category of crime.

In most other respects, however, the new penology had strong roots in the past. Though it removed the possibility of a death sentence for such crimes as domestic theft (a servant stealing from the master), highway robbery, and breaking-and-entering, the new penal code maintained a host of such "aggravating circumstances," which automatically elevated a robbery of even insignificant items into a very serious offense. Above all, after a spirited debate the *constituants* maintained the death penalty for an array of crimes, including premeditated murder or attempted murder, murder in the course of a robbery, arson, infanticide, and various forms of sedition or conspiracy against the state. It is arguable whether all this actually made for a less draconian penology, even if it appeared more rational. In defining crimes and prescribing punishment for the guilty, revolutionary penology could fairly be described as severe and inexorable.[4]

At the same time, revolutionary legislators transformed criminal procedure to the advantage of the accused and, as a consequence, to the detriment of state control. The fulcrum of this revolution in criminal justice, "the palladium of liberty," was trial by jury. Power devolved from the professional magistrates of the old regime into the hands of ordinary citizens. Those judges had deployed their authority in camera and largely through the medium of written depositions. Henceforth trials would be conducted in public and orally. Trial juries would not be bound by lengthy and fossilized written statements but would weigh all the nuances of direct oral testimony and active cross-examination. Further diluting the control that magistrates once had over their courtrooms, the accused now had the right to counsel, a right explicitly denied by the criminal ordinance of 1670 in the belief that lawyers would hinder the quest for truth.

Led by former magistrates and barristers, the National Assembly repudiated professional doctrines that had guided old-regime criminal procedure for over a century. It intended to separate the judgment of guilt or innocence by juries from the application of law to the guilty by judges, in theory leaving each to do their duty without prejudice or compunction. In place of the old regime's standards of "legal proofs" and "indices" of guilt, the jury system would introduce "the reliable illumination of common sense" into the criminal tribunals. For, as one jurist later claimed, the old-regime standard of legal proofs often led judges "to condemnations which repelled their consciences." In the words of *rapporteur* Adrien Duport, the former magistrate of the Paris Parlement, "One of the great advantages of juries is to substitute *moral* proof for what is called *legal* proof. . . . [Jurors] unlike judges are not obliged . . . to decide as they are *supposed* to see things rather than as they *actually* see them; to go against their conscience and instead follow the false and absurd rules of probability."[5]

The denunciation or discovery of a crime set off a complex chain of procedures whose first link was by far the weakest, reflecting the deficiency of law enforcement both before and after 1789. Urban police magistrates or newly elected rural justices of the peace (at once civil and police magistrates) conducted the preliminary investigation.[6] On their own, the justices of the peace resolved petty offenses carrying maximum penalties of a small fine or three days in jail. For more serious offenses, the new system bifurcated into two tracks, dealing respectively with what might be called misdemeanors and felonies, or what the French termed "correctional" and "criminal" offenses. Whether the gravity of the alleged crime made it a correctional or a criminal

offense was determined in the first instance by the investigating magistrate—a district civil court judge who served on a rotating basis for six
months as the director of the grand jury in the district capital.

Lesser offenses, which carried a maximum prison term of two years, were
heard by a correctional tribunal. After the legislature modified its form in
1796, the *tribunal de police correctionnel* consisted of the civil court judge serving
his term as the director of the grand jury and two justices of the peace. Each
department had three to eight correctional tribunals, corresponding roughly
to the old districts; in 1800, they were replaced by the Consulate's *tribunaux
de première instance,* in more or less the same locations, which tried both civil
and correctional cases. Among the more common correctional offenses were
simple assault, theft without aggravating circumstances, verbal attacks and
defamation, outrages to public authority, damaging crops in the countryside,
and morals offenses.[7] The volume of correctional cases probably ranged
between three to five times the typical fifty to one hundred felony cases tried
annually in a department's criminal tribunal, which also heard occasional
appeals from the correctional tribunals.

Correctional courts in departments with large tracts of national forests
were also inundated with violators of the forest code, brought to justice by
a special force of national forest guards. The correctional tribunal in Chaumont (Haute-Marne), for example, tried 1,276 of these contentious *délits
forestiers* in 1812, compared to only 147 other misdemeanors, while the
Moselle department saw an even higher ratio.[8] (Indeed, in all of France in
1829 out of a total of 176,000 citizens accused of misdemeanors, a staggering
110,000 were being prosecuted for *délits forestiers*.)[9] Legislators understood
that juries would be loath to convict perpetrators of such victimless crimes
who acted on their belief in traditional rights to wood.

Judges in the correctional courts heard cases publicly and with defense
lawyers, but without juries and with very little constraint on how they
disposed of these cases. They were free to mix fines and short prison terms,
or merely to require a gesture of contrition, as in a case of slander. In Lorient
(Morbihan), the correctional court imaginatively sentenced an apprentice
butcher and a soap manufacturer to short terms of detention at night, since
it deemed their work by day too useful to interrupt.[10]

Proceedings against alleged felonies unfolded very differently, their hallmark being trial by jury. If detained after preliminary investigation for a
serious crime (one carrying "peines infamantes ou afflictives," with a possible
prison term of two years or more), the accused was bound over to the
investigating magistrate in the district capital. After interrogating witnesses
and the accused in private, if he decided not to dismiss the charges, the
magistrate prepared a bill of indictment giving a concise summary of the

allegations for presentation to a grand jury *(jury d'accusation)*, whose convocation he supervised. The magistrate had virtually unchecked power up to this point, but once he completed his presentation (at which the accused was not present), the grand jury decided whether or not to indict. Loosely borrowed from across the English Channel, the grand jury was intended as a barrier against false accusations or abusive police activity. This panel of eight citizens need not determine guilt or innocence but simply whether there existed probable cause, "a strong presumption and the beginning of proof." If a majority of at least five believed this to be so, it voted "that there is cause" for the bill of indictment *(acte d'accusation)*. The defendant was then sent for trial to the departmental criminal tribunal.[11]

The *tribunal criminel* stood at the apex of the criminal justice pyramid, where it embodied the majesty and authority of the new regime, and provided a highly visible demonstration of justice at work. It was not always easy to establish this institution in appropriate physical surroundings; the ex-seminary in Vannes which officials of the Morbihan found for the department's tribunal lacked all amenities and exposed the participants to bitter cold during the winter. Venerable judicial seats such as Toulouse, Nancy, or Dijon naturally had a great advantage. "We have prepared all that the law requires . . . the courtroom is one of the most splendid in France," reported the departmental administration of the Côte d'Or. "There are rooms for counsel, for the jurors, and for the clerk. The ballot boxes are ready. . . ."[12] (See Figure XII-1). The criminal court consisted of a presiding judge and a public prosecutor, each elected for six-year terms by the departmental electoral assembly, and three other judges assigned from the district civil courts on a rotating basis. These positions were filled by men with legal experience in the old regime and government service of some sort in the new, and they were often stepping stones to national office.[13] But the real star was the twelve-man *jury de jugement*. As the trial began, the jurors' oath set the tone: "I swear to render my decision . . . following my conscience and my intimate and profound conviction, with the impartiality and constancy of a free man."[14]

Unlike grand jury hearings, criminal trials relied exclusively on oral testimony. Juries heard all testimony from witnesses and the accused in their own words, complete with hesitations and facial expressions, and all arguments by the prosecutor and defense lawyers. Jurors could even participate in the proceedings by posing their own questions through the presiding judge. While the president and the prosecutor studied the depositions taken by the *directeur du jury* in order to organize the trial, once it began the written pre-trial record became irrelevant, except that the president could point out glaring inconsistencies in testimony if they occurred. Even when important wit-

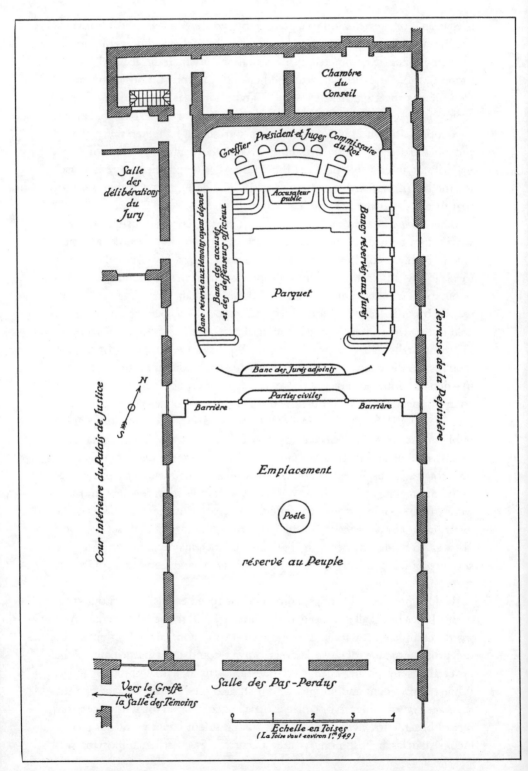

FIGURE XII-1: *Plan for the Criminal Tribunal in the Meurthe, 1792*

nesses failed to turn up at the trial, their previous depositions were inadmissible.[15] The National Assembly did not deem written statements to be consistent with forming a direct, "intimate conviction" about the case. The juror "must be seized by the presence and the words of the accused and the witnesses; his opinion must be formed less by reasoning than by sentiment." In some of the first jury trials in Paris, defending counsel apparently did not grasp this point. As one professional journal complained, defense lawyers should "absorb the text and spirit of the new law somewhat better. One is astonished to have heard several make a display of erudition consisting of citations from ancient jurisprudence . . . while everyone knows that the jury cannot and should not reach its decision except through its intimate conviction."[16] The lawyers would soon learn.

Once the jury retired to deliberate, it enjoyed complete sovereignty, unlike its English counterpart, which remained subject to suasion by judges.[17] Jurors voted on a series of standardized questions posed by the presiding judge: Did the stated crime occur? Was the accused guilty of its commission? Was the crime willful or involuntary (the famous *question intentionnelle*)? Were there aggravating circumstances (e.g., was a robbery committed with violence or at night)? Juries had to answer each question separately, and in cases with several defendants the total could become daunting. In one complex case in the Vienne department, for example, jurors had to answer 210 different questions.[18] In a more typical case, here is how a Parisian jury of 1795 handled its task:

> The verdict of the trial jury held: that a wallet was taken from citizen Costey at the door of a café; that Joseph Maubert is convicted of having taken it; that he took it with evil intent *(méchamment)* and for the purpose of stealing it; that the theft was committed by several persons; that the theft was committed at night; that Antoine Magnant is convicted of having aided and abetted the author of said theft both in the events that prepared and facilitated its execution and in the act which consummated it; that he did this with evil intent and for the purpose of crime.[19]

The jurors did not have to explain how they arrived at their verdict, and there was no appeal from their decision, although convicted defendants could appeal on procedural grounds to the *Tribunal de Cassation* in Paris. Under the law of 1791 three jurors out of twelve sufficed to acquit, and a majority of ten to convict. If the judges disagreed with a conviction by a split jury, however, they could add three alternates *(adjoints)* to the panel and require the fifteen to deliberate and vote again, with four white balls sufficing to acquit. The use of alternates was rarely necessary, but judges did bring

them in from time to time, as in the case cited above, where the verdict did
not differ the second time around.[20] Ideally, of course, jury verdicts would
be unanimous. In 1797, a new law required that the jury spend twenty-four
hours seeking such accord, failing which balloting would take place with a
majority sufficient to convict, or six to acquit. Scattered evidence suggests
that juries achieved the desired unanimity in the overwhelming majority of
cases. In the criminal tribunal of the Seine, for example, only 21 verdicts out
of about 1,800 in the Years VI–X failed to carry unanimously.[21]

Trial juries decided the facts of a case and its moral gravity, but the
separation of indictment and judgment blunted the inquisitorial style of
old-regime criminal justice. A trial was strictly bound by the specifications of
the indictment. A poorly drawn information resulting in an inexact indictment (more likely because the *directeur du jury* rotated every six months) might
bring an acquittal after the case unfolded in trial court, even if the accused
was obviously guilty of a somewhat different crime than the one specified.[22]
Once the jury rendered its verdict, the judges had virtually no latitude in
applying the punishments mandated by the penal code. In one of its first
homicide cases in the Var, for example, the jury found that the crime had
occurred, that the accused had committed it, that he had not acted in
self-defense, but because it was the outcome of a drunken brawl he had acted
involuntarily. The sentence in these circumstances was six months of detention.

A case in the Nord promised a different kind of outcome: "It was
expected that the question of premeditation would be decided against Mar-
coul. For it was difficult to imagine a man without premeditation inflicting
fifteen knife wounds on another, throwing him into a ditch, and depriving
him of life by smashing his head with large stones. But one of the witnesses
spoke of a brawl and that circumstance served the defendant in the eyes of
several jurors." The jury's qualified verdict obliged the judges to sentence the
defendant to twenty years' hard labor rather than death.[23] The *question
intentionnelle* caused no end of contention, yet it could not be avoided—it was
the very essence of judgment by common sense or "intimate conviction." It
also served to liberate judges from any twinge of ambivalence. As the
minister of justice told the presiding judges in 1793, with juries handling the
question intentionnelle, judges could apply the dictates of the penal code to the
guilty without hesitation, almost as passive instruments of the law.[24]

Sheer novelty posed numerous questions as judges empaneled the first
juries in March 1792. (No one had specified, for example, whether a particular panel should hear only one case or the full docket of cases for that
monthly session; and it was difficult to replace jurors excluded by the defendant, who was entitled to twenty preemptory challenges.)[25] But early indica-

tions were encouraging. The first juries took their responsibility with utmost seriousness, and if their verdicts occasionally seemed bizarre, they did not shake official enthusiasm for the new system:

> The jury system is in full gear in this department [reported the presiding judge in Bouches-du-Rhône]. In four different sessions it has had the best effect. . . . These types of assemblies have all the interest of a great drama; we have had sessions lasting fifteen hours through the night and into the morning, and the public never left. If there is an institution capable of propagating public spirit and allowing a man to sense his full dignity, it is the juries.[26]

In the Tarn, jury trials also went on from eight in the morning until midnight, but "the proceedings were extremely interesting and the public flocked to them in throngs." Before long, conscientious citizens could purchase C.-N. Osselin's *Almanach du juré français* to prepare them for this civic duty.[27]

Grand jurors in each district, and trial jurors for the whole department, were selected by lot from quarterly lists of thirty and two hundred, respectively. Who were the new jurors and how were they designated? Having established a property qualification for the eligibility of citizens as electors, the National Assembly readily extended it to jury service, though not without opposition. Robespierre among others carried his fight against the electoral *cens* to the issue of jury selection. Was it truly judgment by one's peers, he questioned, if three quarters of the citizens were ineligible for service? Robespierre also objected to the departmental executive officer (procurator syndic) selecting the two hundred names from the rosters at his disposal as an inappropriate political power. For the moment the Assembly overrode such objections, although the imbrication of the jury system with restrictive voting rights could be embarrassing, as when the mayor of Valenciennes was excluded from a jury list because he owned no real property and rented quarters below the requisite assessed value.[28]

Qualified citizens were enjoined to register for jury selection upon pain of losing their eligibility to vote. The registers were available, however, only in the *chef-lieu* of each district, and rural citizens showed little inclination to make a special trip for that purpose. Numerous departmental administrations deplored this obstacle to compliance and urged that inscription be permitted locally. Moreover, since qualified citizens could vote only if they had registered for jury service, officials feared that voter turnout would decline as a result.[29] This procedural squabble momentarily obscured the veritable problem, which would continue long after district registration was eliminated: the reluctance of citizens to serve on juries, especially rural inhabitants facing a long trip to the departmental *chef-lieu*. Penalties for evading a jury summons included a fine of 25 to 50 livres. But not signing up in the first place, or securing a phony medical certificate if called, could eliminate that threat. The initial jury lists were thus top heavy with the urban middle classes. In the Hérault in the third quarter of 1792, for example, the identifiable occupations of the two hundred listed citizens included seventy-seven bourgeois, merchants, and entrepreneurs; twenty-eight elected officeholders; seventeen lawyers; twelve other professionals; six artisans; and five government employees.[30]

In fact the original censitary requirement for jury service lasted only a year, as the Convention swept away the "monstrous and fatal distinction" between active and passive citizens after the fall of the monarchy, along with the requirement for registration in the district capital. After months of improvisation the Convention authorized a new method of jury selection in December 1793. Jury lists with one name per thousand inhabitants were to be compiled by the *agent national* in each district, "based on his personal knowledge and information given to him by the *agents nationaux* of the communes."[31] The *directeurs du jury* and public prosecutors then drew their grand and trial juries from these rosters. In the Year II (1793–94), district agents increasingly bowed to Jacobin perspectives in compiling their jury lists. As a district official in the Hérault explained, "I have consulted with the popular society of St. Pons in order to designate the most capable people for jury service." Meanwhile, the Convention voted an indemnity to all jurors of 3 livres per day, and 15 sous per mile of traveling, which made it marginally easier for good *sans-culottes* to serve—just as electors received such subsidies in 1792–93 for the same reason.[32]

JURIES AND REVOLUTIONARY POLITICS

Despite the auspicious start of the criminal juries, counter-revolution and Jacobin radicalism threatened to submerge this novel institution in partisan passions. Cases involving refractory priests, émigrés, and collective violence, which began to crowd the dockets of criminal courts in late 1792, exposed jurors to severe and unanticipated pressures. In March 1793, however, the Convention deflected these pressures by creating new options for dealing with politically defined offenses against the republic. First came the Revolutionary Tribunal in Paris and local revolutionary tribunals or extraordinary "commissions" established later by representatives-on-mission implementing the Terror in such places as Lyon, Marseille, Nantes, Bordeaux, Orange, and Nîmes. Ostensibly, the Revolutionary Tribunal utilized jurors to render verdicts of guilty or innocent, thus in the eyes of some tainting the "palladium of liberty" ever after. In fact, these "jurors" differed little from functionaries of the revolutionary government, being a permanent corps of citizens appointed directly by the Convention. [33]

In addition, the Convention authorized prosecutions of political offenses *"à forme révolutionnaire"* in the regular criminal tribunals. Public prosecutors could draw up indictments and try these cases directly before the judges of a criminal tribunal without resort to juries and (as later interpreted) without the intervention of defense lawyers. Sentences were to be carried out within twenty-four hours and without appeal. Ordinary juries seemed inappropriate as well as unreliable for expediting "revolutionary justice." Cases involving refractory priests, rebellion, and riot swamped the criminal tribunal of Morbihan in Brittany, for example, where in 1793–95 judges without juries convicted and sentenced to death about fifty defendants, compared to about fifteen death sentences following jury verdicts for ordinary crimes. In the southern department of the Hérault, though juries had been firm as disorder mounted early in 1793, jury trials for political offenses ceased in April, when the court began to try such cases *à forme révolutionnaire,* though not always with the severity desired by Paris. [34]

Overly scrupulous judges, however, could be purged by representatives-on-mission to encourage convictions. In the Haute-Garonne, a revolving door to the criminal bench brought in four different presiding judges and five public prosecutors (all, it should be said, qualified and competent men) between July 1793 and October 1795. And if new personnel did not suffice to assure convictions in the criminal courts, political defendants could be shunted to the revolutionary tribunals. In the Basses-Pyrénées (a restive war zone on the Spanish border), deputies-on-mission established two "extraordinary commissions" in the spring of 1794, having tired of the leniency shown by the criminal court bench, "composed entirely of lawyers who are almost always imbued with forms instead of principles." [35]

Putting criminal tribunals into a "revolutionary mode" without juries was a tempting alternative even for non-political offenses. The presiding judge in the Vosges department, for example, informed the minister of justice that several "offenses against the free circulation of food supplies" (i.e., food riots) were soon to be tried. He was sure, however, that the juries would not convict despite the manifest guilt of the accused, because "the death penalty frightens them, seems to them too severe, and they prefer to leave the offense unpunished than to give an affirmative verdict that entails capital punishment." The judge sagely proposed that the penalties should be made less severe and graduated according to circumstances, but the Jacobin minister disagreed. There were few things more important than provisioning the marketplace, he argued, and the rigor of this law upheld that purpose. He therefore proposed "eliminating the juries for this kind of judgment and turning the criminal tribunals into revolutionary tribunals in these cases as they are in several other kinds." But the Committee of Public Safety vetoed this advice, counseling instead that officials should enlighten jurors about their duties, and that the *agents nationaux* should exercise greater care in designating citizens for jury service. Since they were already doing this, it was hardly much of an answer, but it did block the minister's opportunistic proposal. [36]

The thermidorian reaction put even greater strain on the jury system, as most political crimes reverted to the ordinary jurisdiction of the criminal courts. Encouraged in some departments by reactionary judges, particularly in the South, juries were in a position to settle past accounts. Former Jacobins under indictment in 1795, whether on trumped-up charges or for veritable abuses of power, could expect harsh treatment rather than leniency or even fairness in such departments. And when vengeful citizens took the law into their own hands by assaulting or murdering former terrorists, they were likely to enjoy complete impunity. Anti-Jacobin retribution in the embattled Midi seems to have unfolded under the umbrella of a "judicial reaction" after Thermidor, which reached from top to bottom of the criminal justice system and took a profound toll on its integrity. Most justices of the peace either sympathized with communal anti-Jacobinism or were too intimidated to flout it. But even when they did act on a denunciation against a violent "counter-terrorist," the grand jury, led by a complicitous *directeur du jury*, was likely to dismiss the charges. And if a display of determination by republican officials did produce an indictment, the personnel of the criminal court might push to win the defendant's release. [37]

In these local dramas, the jury of course had a starring role, often cheered on by a partisan or menacing audience. At the extreme, men clearly identified as knife-wielding assassins in anti-Jacobin prison massacres in Marseille and elsewhere won acquittal on the *question intentionnelle*. But the problem did not end there. Throughout the Directory years, juries were prone to dismiss a spectrum of offenses and assaults inspired by hostility to the republic or to its current officials. This was extremely damaging to a regime that ostensibly wished to govern by law and to avoid extra-legal terrorism, although, as we have seen, the Directory's adherence to legality was anything but scrupulous in its struggle for political power. [38]

With the return of a propertied franchise in 1796, jury service was again limited to citizens eligible to serve as electors, but that scarcely mattered. Juries in 1798 probably differed little in social composition from those of 1793. After the anti-royalist Fructidor coup in 1797, the Directory scrapped current jury lists in about half the departments, having been particularly scandalized by a roster from the Mayenne in Western France that included five notorious *chouans*—an oversight which the ousted departmental administration blamed on a clerk who had merely copied the names submitted by several disloyal municipal administrations.[39] In a familiar refrain, the minister of justice hoped that a more careful selection of jurors might halt "the solemn impunity that juries have accorded to the most culpable enemies of the Republic." But juries continued to condone anti-republican outrages. Far from the torments of Western and Southeastern France, the Directory's commissioners in such departments as the Vosges and the Indre complained in almost identical words that juries "accord scandalous absolution to the enemies of the *patrie.* . . . This sublime institution has been corrupted, erected into a system of impunity." Again in June 1799 the minister of justice circularized the courts to urge greater care in forming jury panels and to deplore "the frightening number of biased, vicious, absurd, and contradictory jury verdicts."[40]

As Brumaire approached, then, "the murderous indulgence or ineptitude" of trial juries, especially their abuse of the *question intentionnelle,* exasperated republican officials. Yet, unlike the elected judiciary or departmental administrations, the jury system survived the constitutional revisions of Brumaire. Juries were often "an instrument of intolerance or reaction, of fury or vengeance," observed the *rapporteur* of a new law on jury selection in March 1800, "but even if mutilated by so many afflictions, the institution of the juries remains standing amidst all the ruins." In the future juries were to be drawn from the (stillborn) electoral confidence lists of the Consulate: the grand juries from the communal eligibility lists and trial juries from the more exclusive departmental lists. In the interim (a very long interim, as it turned out), justices of the peace were to submit the names of "educated and upright men" to the subprefects, who would then sift these local lists "with a sensible severity" and compile official rosters. With this emendation, the "sublime institution" endured into the Napoleonic era.[41]

JUDGING THE JURIES

The Napoleonic legal establishment—appointed judges, prosecutors, members of the Council of State, officials in the Ministry of Justice—proved to be divided over trial by jury. For many, the behavior of juries during the Terror and the reaction had a permanently souring effect, though most recognized that the political passion of those years was a distorting force likely to recede in the future. They acknowledged that the bias of jurors, the blatant favoritism or hostility in cases tinged with political overtones, should probably be discounted. "An excess of partisan spirit still marks the juries," reported the prefect of Haute-Garonne after his first tour of the department. "Every day that fine institution is degraded by verdicts that reason and the law reprove. Jurors all seem to embrace a jurisprudence under which they condemn or absolve according to opinion rather than the facts." Still, he believed, "peace and forgetting all about the past can bring the jury back to its veritable character."[42]

But what was the "veritable character" of the jury system? In the Year XII (1803–04), the minister of justice canvassed the presiding judges of the criminal courts, presumably the most knowledgeable individuals. A few months later, hoping to find support for his animus against juries, the tribune Carrion-Nisas carried out his own inquiry among these same judges and elicited a variety of frank opinions.[43] Like the Council of State—in a debate that unfolded sporadically over the next four years—these jurists split almost evenly between those who hoped to abolish the juries and those who wished to maintain and reform them. Although they often mentioned the politicization of juries from 1793 to 1800, that was not the issue. Nor was the ludicrous argument over whether or not such an English institution suited the French national character. The real debate hinged on whether or not juries in criminal cases were likely to arrive at a sound verdict. Specifically: were juries reluctant or unlikely to convict the guilty?

Few of the presiding judges bothered to assemble comprehensive statistics on the disposition of cases in their courts, but the numbers provided by the presiding judge in Aveyron must have been alarming: only 311 convictions as against 249 acquittals across the entire period of the Years II–XI, an acquittal rate of 45 percent.[44] Other figures compiled by historians reinforce that stark image. In the Aisne, juries in 1792–Year IV acquitted at a provocative 64 percent rate (269 acquittals out of 420 cases); in the Meurthe in 1792–Year VII, they acquitted at a 40 percent rate (271 acquittals out of 673 cases); and in the Marne in 1792–Year IX, at a 45.5 percent rate (329 acquittals out of 722 cases).[45] In the most thorough local study, Robert Allen has found that juries in the Côte d'Or disposed of 1,316 cases in 1792–1811 as follows: 565 acquittals (43 percent); 520 convictions (39.5 percent); and 231 convictions on reduced charges (17.5 percent), where the juries rejected aggravating circumstances alleged in the original indictment.[46]

On the other hand jury leniency clearly peaked around the Year IV, after which conviction rates gradually increased under the Directory and after Brumaire. L. J. Wigoder found that acquittal rates in the Haute-Marne in 1791–95 of 45 percent declined to 36 percent in 1796–1800, and 28 percent in 1801–05. A similar decline during the Napoleonic years is discernible in the neighboring Marne department. And in the Côte d'Or, after juries acquitted a staggering 73 percent of all defendants in the Year III, the Directory years saw acquittals drop to 41 percent; in 1800–1811, only 34 percent of the defendants in Côte d'Or won acquittals.[47] Bourguignon, a judge in Paris and strong partisan of juries, cited a different kind of statistic against the thesis of undue leniency. In Years X–XI, 981 criminal defendants stood trial in the capital: 788 by the regular criminal court and 193 by special courts operating without juries against certain types of offenders such as vagabonds and brigands. The juries acquitted only one quarter of their defendants, while the special courts absolved one third. Virtually the same contrasting proportions in the two types of courts may be found in the Sarthe.[48]

But the argument against juries was not simply statistical. Opponents of the institution denounced the fickleness of jurors, their softness, "false humanity," and "misdirected pity" in specific cases. Jurors seemed easily intimidated by friends and relatives of the accused or swayed by defense lawyers, especially when they encountered these interested parties at the inns of the smaller departmental capitals. As the historian Elisabeth Claverie has suggested for the 1820s, between sessions in the courtroom jurors might be participants in an informal, "subterranean" trial running parallel to the official proceedings.[49] A criminal trial was not a disembodied process to them but part of the social continuum, where ordinary values—honor, pity, or personal rights—might take precedence over the abstractions of the penal code.

Judges especially condemned the jurors' habit of weighing the mandatory punishments for various crimes, which they were supposed to ignore completely while deciding questions of fact. "Too often they calculate the consequences of their verdicts, which the lawyers never fail to make them aware of," wrote one judge. This was of course most evident in trials involving capital crimes. The judges did not imply that popular opinion categorically opposed capital punishment. Rather, they noted a reluctance to see it applied, a sense that execution was appropriate only under the most extreme circumstances—whereas the penal code automatically required that ultimate penalty for a number of crimes. Short of outright acquittals, juries could ignore manifestly aggravating circumstances and turn murder into manslaughter or breaking and entering into simple theft.[50] Abuse of the *question intentionnelle* could also spare someone who had clearly committed a felony in the eyes of the penal code. A distinguished authority on criminal justice cited a glaring example of this tactic in a case of bearing false witness: "They wish to save the accused. Therefore after answering the first question: 'it is a fact that Lambert had made a false deposition,' they declared on the second question that 'it is not a fact that he acted with a culpable intent.' These two responses were necessarily contradictory, since a criminal intent is inseparable from a false testimony." [51]

Hostile magistrates also believed that juries treated entire categories of offenses indulgently—what might be called crimes against public authority and morals offenses. "Juries regard as criminal only acts that harm private interest, never those which compromise or trouble the general order," claimed the presiding judge in the Nord. Violence directed against gendarmes, bailiffs, and other agents of public order was allegedly taken much too lightly by juries in the Basses-Pyrénées, Haute-Saône, Isère, and elsewhere. This is a fundamental question that merits further research; the magistrates may have been exaggerating, but they undoubtedly had reason to complain. Prosecutors in some departments clearly had trouble gaining convictions for infanticide (guilty verdicts in over half the cases in Haute-Marne, but only one conviction in fourteen cases in the Indre), and for rape or attempted rape. As the judge in Haute-Garonne complained: "How often have they not acquitted those accused of rape or of bigamy by stating that the punishment of such offenses is of concern only to God . . . ? We might as well strike from the penal code a host of crimes such as infanticide, murder resulting from a provocation, bigamy, rape of a person past puberty; fraud, when it merely involves passports or birth certificates . . . rebellion against the execution of judgments." [52]

One vehement opponent of juries, the presiding judge in the Saône-et-Loire, documented his negative opinion with an inventory of selected cases. Formerly a public prosecutor, he claimed to have had many discussions with jurors after they rendered their verdicts, in which "they did not hide that the question of punishment was their justification." His conclusion was certainly plausible: "they concern themselves with penal law above all, contrary to the purpose of the institution." Here are highlights from his mordant tableau of "absurd" acquittals: [53]

Murder: To juries in the Saône-et-Loire, cold-blooded murders seem rarely to have been premeditated or even voluntary. In one case, "the jury believed that there was not an intention to kill when someone fires a gun shot into a person's head." In a second case, "He shot at another citizen. The fact being proven, the accused wished to justify it as self-defense." The jury accepted this, though as the judge acidly observed, "there was not an absolute necessity to defend himself since the accused fired on the deceased from the door of his own house." One jury spared a man from a murder conviction who had brawled with a wagoner at an inn, laid in wait for his antagonist to resume his journey, and then stabbed him.

Another panel deemed a likely case of fratricide to be accidental, though this meant that "his brother had fallen on his open knife and thus killed himself."

Poisoning: Interesting cases to prosecute, no doubt, but evidently difficult to sell to a jury. One man tried twice to poison his father, but since the victim survived, the jury concluded that no crime had been committed. A steamy case of wife-poisoning, complete with amorous servant girl, featured some impressive forensic pathology by medical witnesses that apparently left the jury unmoved. Despite an impressive circumstantial case containing motive, means, and opportunity, it acquitted.

Infanticide: Five acquittals based on the jury's belief that there was no premeditation—despite defendants' efforts to conceal the pregnancy, and in one case an attempt to secure an abortion.

Arson: No doubt under the sway of defense lawyers, juries spared three accused arsonists on the equivalent of an insanity defense. "Convinced of his guilt, the jury believed that the man was in a state of madness, in order to spare him from execution."

Offenses against law enforcement: "The jury declared that the gendarmes were not acting in their official capacity" when they were attacked. "This absurdity is common in verdicts on all affairs of this kind."

Bigamy: Unable to deny the facts in such cases, "the jury supposes that the accused must have been ignorant of the need to dissolve the first tie," or, "the jury allowed itself to believe that the first marriage was illegal."

Breaking and entering: Because a theft involved only a dozen fowl, the jury ignored the manifest evidence of forced entry through a locked door and thereby saved the defendant from a much heavier prison term.

Domestic theft: In three instances of this aggravated offense, the juries embraced another outright falsehood: "in order to spare her from the penalty, the jury let itself believe that she was not a hired servant! That is the tactic used to save the guilty in that type of offense, considering the difference of punishments in the penal code."

Could advocates of the jury system also find support in experience? Carrion-Nisas must have been dismayed by the number of affirmative replies to his inquiry. The starting point for all positive arguments (and one conceded by most opponents) was that juries almost never condemned innocent defendants. Conversely, a few claimed, juries could be more rigorous than old-regime magistrates bound by rigid rules of formal jurisprudence. Juries showed compassion for "the impetuosity of an unthinking movement but were inexorable toward murderers and thieves . . . often striking those whom *legal proofs* would not reach," argued the presiding judge in Cantal. His colleague in Vendée agreed: "Verdicts by juries strike more scoundrels and return to society more innocent people than judgments based on *legal proof.*" Juries of course abused the latitude that they enjoyed, but often to good purpose: to the judge in Maine-et-Loire some verdicts "seem to imply contradictions, but when you have followed the proceedings you recognize the motives of the jurors."[54]

Supporters of the jury system acknowledged that juries anticipated the punishments for serious offenses and were often "prevaricators out of humanity"—contrary to their ostensible duty simply to determine the facts of the case. But these judges drew an entirely different implication than the critics. To remedy this abuse, alter the penal code rather than abolish the jury system. If judges had more latitude in sentencing and a milder array of punishments to draw from, juries would more readily convict, argued the chief judge in Vienne. His colleague in the Manche offered shrewd insights on the collective psychology of juries:

> In general, theft and all other crimes that originate in baseness are punished when they are well proven. It is otherwise with those produced by the rapid movement of a spirit agitated by a violent passion. In such cases the guilty have found indulgence from jurors who believe themselves capable of the same crime in the same circumstances.

He then drew the logical conclusion: knowing "the inflexibility of the penal laws . . . knowing that their decision binds the judge, they prefer to be too soft." The prosecutor in the Bas-Rhin likewise conceded that juries sometimes went against their own reading of the case's facts and responded negatively to the question of aggravating circumstances:

> [They thereby] come to the aid of the judges, so to speak, to whom the law leaves no latitude to apportion the punishment. Lacking the power to graduate punishments according to the degree of wickedness or excusability of the deed, one is sometimes not sorry to find in the declarations of the trial juries an equitable remedy for the imperfection of our criminal legislation.[55]

The chief magistrate in Seine-et-Oise eloquently justified the juries' discrimination and improvisation in the face of a rigid penal code. True, every monthly session usually brought an acquittal that astonished the court. But

> most often juries are prompted to indulgence for motives which, even if they are not in strict conformity with the rules of justice, are with those of equity. The weakness of age, gender, incapacity, hunger, extreme

poverty, drunkenness; a voluntary confession or the negligible profit derived from the crime; the rigor of the penalty; and above all the good reputation of the accused before the crime are often motives to the jurors for absolution. . . . When it is proven that the accused is a *mauvais sujet*, the juries are severe; if his conduct is that of a scoundrel, they are inexorable and very easy to convince. A man without morals, lazy, vagabond, without domicile, is accused of theft; his condemnation is virtually certain. Another is accused of murder. If he has previously escaped from similar charges, his condemnation is assured. We can all recall the adroit, well-defended scoundrels accused of serious crimes whom the former courts would not have dared to condemn . . . because judicial proof was lacking; but the juries are convinced.[56]

This seems a more nuanced evaluation than the bald claim by the judge in Haute-Garonne that "the institution of the jury is designed to punish the poor and acquit the rich."

The closest thing to an objective evaluation of jury trials in one department came from the chief judge in the Loiret, a department near Paris with average rates of criminality in the nineteenth century. He reported on 167 cases (mainly in five categories) heard between Year VI through XII, in which 54 defendants were acquitted, 18 sentenced to death, and 95 to other punishments (see Table XII-1).

The magistrate commented on all 167 cases, taking exception to only 14 verdicts, all acquittals except for one complex case of fraud. Only two of the acquittals for homicide drew his censure, and in only four acquittals for theft

Table XII-1

Selected Jury Verdicts in the Loiret, Years VI–XII

	Acquitted	*Death Penalty**	*Other Penalty*
Homicide, etc.	12	8	4
Infanticide	3	2	—
Arson	4	2	1
Fraud, etc.	11	—	11
Theft (all kinds)	18	3	70

*The three other death sentences involved two convictions for bearing false witness in a capital case, and the trial of Jouannau, condemned for "provocation to the dissolution of the government," whose sentence was later commuted to deportation.

Source: A.N. BB[30] 526: Relevé de plusieurs jugements rendus avec jurés par le Tribunal Criminel du Loiret.

did he see "indulgence" or "feebleness." The great majority of cases drew notations of "good" or (for acquittals) "no proof." In a few instances, including a capital theft case, he characterized the verdict as "severe but just." Most striking is this observation about three different capital convictions: "The accused denied the charge. There were no material proofs. [But] the jury well grasped the indications resulting from the testimony. On the day of the execution the condemned man confessed."[57]

THE PROBLEM OF recruiting jurors naturally weighed on this long-running debate. Advocates and opponents alike knew how difficult it was to find jurors both willing and able to serve. Some believed that citizens regarded jury service as a *corvée*, a damning image indeed of forced labor.[58] With the exception of Robert Allen's study of the Côte d'Or, however, very little is known about the actual composition of French juries or the reactions of citizens toward jury service. A group of surviving jury lists from 1800 is of scant help, except to suggest that by this time a reasonable balance seemed to exist between urban and rural jurors. The occupational concentrations varied widely from department to department: seventy-six lawyers and notaries in the Haute-Saône, for example, but only seventeen in the Loir-et-Cher and ten in the Landes; a preponderance of peasants *(laboureurs* and *cultivateurs)* in the Ille-et-Vilaine and the Landes, but only thirty-eight identified as such in Loir-et-Cher and forty-three in Haute-Saône; fifty-nine *négociants* in the Gard compared to twenty-three in Haute-Sâone and only seven in Loir-et-Cher; thirty-two artisans and shopkeepers in Loir-et-Cher as against sixteen in Haute-Saône.[59]

These printed quarterly lists of two hundred names, in any case, were only the beginning. Many citizens notified that they had been designated to serve scrambled to get themselves excused, and the well heeled or well connected had the advantage. "The wealthiest are the least disposed to sacrifice their leisure," claimed an official in Saône-et-Loire, echoing a common sentiment. They knew the ropes and could usually find a complacent *officier de santé* to sign a certificate attesting to some vague malady. It was even alleged that, reversing ordinary expectations, prospective jurors who found themselves empaneled might bribe the accused's lawyer to dismiss them in their quota of challenges. Moreover mayors and their deputies, in their role as *officiers de police judiciaire,* enjoyed automatic exemption, thus depriving the pool wholesale of likely candidates.

Observers claimed that the panels were weighted down with unqualified jurors. Half the listed jurors, "always the soundest part," generally failed to show up, according to the presiding judge of the Lot department. "The remaining half consists only of timid inhabitants of the countryside, who are less familiar with the ways of eluding the law's dispositions." In the Drôme, "one sees only pitiful peasants and miserable workers who are not able to recognize a proven fact when they see it." According to the presiding judge of the Haute-Garonne, the situation was hopeless. Jurors showed up on the 15th of the month, "almost all in a bad humor." If the session dragged on, they did not conceal "their impatience, their distracted and preoccupied air"; if a court officer pointed out that they were doing something incorrectly, they retorted "that it was wrong to call them." [60]

AN HISTORIC COMPROMISE

For years the Council of State debated whether to retain or abolish trial by jury, as Napoleon (whose personal distaste for the jury system was no secret) kept wavering. In the interim, several changes whittled away at the institution's scope. Mounting public disorder by draft evaders, vagrants, and brigands prompted the first inroads. While gendarmes pursued marauders as best they could, even when apprehended, "these scoundrels taken with arms in their hands have been acquitted" because juries facing such defendants were allegedly craven. Despite fierce opposition in the Tribunate, the Council of State pushed through a law in February 1801 creating special tribunals without juries to deal with vagabonds and brigands. A few days earlier, legislators had enacted a new code of preliminary procedure that enhanced the police powers of the state and diminished the role of the grand jury. Justices of the peace now reported to a deputy public prosecutor, a kind of state's attorney at the arrondissement or subprefectorial level. During preliminary investigation of a crime the rights of the accused shrank, and at the indictment stage the *directeur du jury* gained new leverage since his presentation to the grand jury was henceforth to be based exclusively on prior written depositions. The accused himself had never appeared before a grand jury, but now the witnesses were not to testify directly either. The link between oral testimony and citizen-jurors was severed at the indictment stage to the advantage of law enforcement officials. [61]

This proved to be a signpost toward an historic compromise. In 1808 the Council of State finally resolved to reprofessionalize criminal justice completely at the indictment stage by abolishing the grand jury altogether, but to retain the trial jury. The inquest of the Year XII had depicted grand juries as the shakiest element of the revolutionary model. True, a few judges (from Aisne, Lot, and Orne, among other places) had endorsed the grand jury and attacked the trial jury, arguing that "jurors more willingly determine to

prosecute than to condemn." But that remained a decidedly minority opinion. In Carrion-Nisas's survey, twenty-four presiding judges defended the
jury system in general and twenty-three opposed it, but ten other partisans
of the trial jury called for the abolition of grand juries.

The argument against the *jury d'accusation* was simple. At this stage—where
it was a question of strong likelihood and "the beginning of proof" rather
than either mere suspicion or certainty of guilt—the investigators could best
decide. Under the grand jury system, five out of eight jurors "suffice to
procure for the accused a certificate of innocence," whatever the prosecutor
and investigating magistrate believed. Jurors purportedly abused their power
to absolve; several judges used a striking phrase about "arrogating the right
to pardon" *(faire grâce)*. To make matters worse, the reform of 1801 required
grand jurors to weigh long written statements, though many could not read
or understand what was read to them. "Very often the grand jurors are
perplexed and bored by a long reading that makes no sense to them and that
they do not understand at all; then they take the side which a misguided
humanity suggests, namely, to discharge the accused."[62]

The Code of Criminal Procedure of 1808 dispensed with the grand juries,
leaving indictment in the hands of professional magistrates at the arrondissement level. These proceedings were to be secret, written, and weighted
toward the prosecution. A defendant indicted for a serious crime was then
remanded to the criminal assizes (the new name for the departmental criminal tribunal), headed by an appeals court judge on circuit. There, as if passing
from night to day, everything became public and oral for the benefit of the
jury (though the prior depositions of witnesses who failed to appear could
now be introduced), and defendants had full right to counsel. As trial by jury
and oral procedure prevailed so, inevitably, did the doctrine of moral proof
or "intimate conviction." Whatever the strengths or weaknesses of the evidence introduced, jurors by a majority vote could acquit or convict as they
saw fit. (If the judges unanimously agreed that a guilty verdict was erroneous,
however, they could order a new trial at the next session.) As recommended
by many judges, the government also simplified the questions posed to the
jury with the hope of downplaying the *question intentionnelle*. "They are called
upon only to decide whether or not the accused is guilty of the crime
attributed to him," explained a new handbook for jurors. But the *question
intentionnelle* reappeared immediately as if by the back door. "When the
accused will have proposed as an excuse a fact admitted as such by the law,"
the handbook continued, "the question to the jury will be posed as follows:
'is that fact established?' " Juries also retained the prerogative to affirm or
reject aggravating circumstances alleged in the indictment.[63]

Along with the new procedural code, the imperial government altered the mode of jury selection. Critics had argued that the process produced jurors who simply lacked the required capacity. Ideally they wanted an educated elite, wealthy enough to take as much as two weeks away from their work without qualms.[64] In practice it was easy to set property qualifications, but how could one assure literacy or mental capacity without complicating matters immeasurably and excluding propertied citizens who could otherwise be tapped? In the end the pool of jurors, like the regime's concept of *notables* in general, was defined primarily by wealth with only a nod in the direction of *capacité*. In this social bloc, uneducated peasant proprietors could still be called. Each prefect was to prepare lists of sixty names for each session from the following categories of citizens over the age of thirty in his department: members of the permanent electoral college; the three hundred largest taxpayers; functionaries nominated by the government; holders of doctor's and master's degrees from the University; notaries; businessmen paying the two highest categories of the *patente;* and administrative employees earning over 4,000 francs. Failure to answer a jury summons or secure a valid excuse brought a huge fine of 500 francs the first time and 1,000 francs for repeaters.[65]

This policy produced a more or less permanent corps of jurors considerably different from the panels envisaged in 1791. Yet the behavior of the jurors does not seem to have changed significantly. This rarefied amalgam of citizens apparently acted much like the more representative juries of 1792 or 1800. Through the Empire, Restoration, and July Monarchy judges still complained endlessly of "scandalous acquittals" and quixotic verdicts, such as the case in the Pyrénées-Orientales in 1845 where the jury accepted the claim of self-defense by a man who killed an old woman in the belief that she had cast a spell on him.[66] The annual criminal justice statistics published by the government starting in 1826 suggest that acquittal rates averaged around 40 percent in the early 1830s.[67] As before, a jury's severity or indulgence was likely to be influenced to a degree by the character and circumstances of the defendants (as the chief judge of the Seine-et-Oise had observed in the Year XII), and by the type of crime. Juries showed slight leniency toward middle-class defendants (presumably of good reputation) and toward women, especially in crimes of passion or infanticide, while they continued to be hardest on vagabonds and the destitute. The conviction rates of peasants and workers, however, show no bias one way or the other.[68]

SUCCESSIVE REGIMES DEPLORED "scandalous acquittals" and bizarre verdicts by juries, yet none saw fit to suppress this "palladium of liberty." The National Assembly introduced the jury system as the core of a truly liberal revolution in criminal procedure that contrasted to the relative traditionalism of its new penal code. The Assembly's code of criminal procedure sought to protect individual liberty by means of publicity, oral testimony, the right to counsel, and trial by jury. Only public trial enjoyed universal approval, however; Napoleonic judges who wished to eliminate juries usually claimed that defendants would be sufficiently protected by having their trials in public. But the other elements of the Assembly's plan logically reinforced each other. Indeed, the shaky image of the jury system was undoubtedly compounded by the disreputable stratagems of some criminal lawyers. These *défenseurs officieux* appeared to the judges as unscrupulous practitioners, who fed upon the gullibility of jurors and who violated the spirit of the law by dwelling on the fearsome punishments awaiting their clients if convicted, a consideration which juries were emphatically supposed to disregard. But the natural right to unrestricted defense withstood all criticism and endured in the fabric of French criminal justice along with trial by jury. Both worked to the potential advantage of many defendants.

Even discounting the refractory behavior of anti-republican juries under the Directory, officials had reason to be disenchanted with the jury system as they pondered its fate after 1800. The propensity of jurors to weigh prospective punishments, to acquit despite the evidence, or to disregard manifest aggravating circumstances was well documented. Notwithstanding the sympathetic insights of certain professional magistrates into the behavior of juries, the indictment against them seemed substantial. Yet the original mystique surrounding this "sublime institution" prevailed and the system survived.

In resolving this issue, the Council of State perpetuated an ambivalence built into the founding acts of the National Assembly. In their desire to protect property, society, and the state from assault, the *constituants* mandated severe punishment—long stretches of hard labor and even death—for a host of offenses long stigmatized as serious in old-regime jurisprudence. Apart from implementing the fashionable prescription for uniform penalties, thus putting an end to the discretion of judges in sentencing, the revolutionaries parted with old-regime penal traditions only in matters of detail. A harsh fate awaited most convicted felons. At the same time, the *constituants* placed defendants in a much more favorable position. It was as if the Assembly was saying: We will do everything to protect the innocent. We will tolerate obfuscation by manipulative defense lawyers in our courtrooms, and we will risk credulity, misplaced humanitarianism, and indulgence by jurors. Then, after a fair trial, if the common sense of the jurors returns a guilty verdict, the law will strike with severity.

It is thus not hard to understand why the jury system survived the derogations of the Terror, the abusive prejudices of the thermidorian reaction, and even Napoleon's negative attitude. The more perplexing question is, why did rigid determinate sentencing, that equivocal legacy of Beccaria, survive for so long alongside a jury system whose operations it severely deformed? The new criminal justice system undoubtedly adjusted to this contradiction in some measure by the informal "correctionalization" of offenses. In a kind of ad hoc plea bargaining, prosecutors or judges could at various points steer a case into the correctional courts, where the punishments would be much lighter but judgment by professionals without juries was assured. [69] Before 1830, however, no government would budge in its adherence to heavy fixed sentences for felonies.

As to the juries themselves, such changes in their social composition as might have occurred before 1808 (about which we know little) do not seem to have affected their behavior very much. The greatest official disappointment in this institution, apart from the willfulness of anti-republican juries after Thermidor, derived from the evident reluctance of citizens to serve. Logically, the criteria for jury service changed with the modifications of voting rights and eligibility in the succession of post-1789 regimes. But these vicissitudes in the process of jury selection surely undercut the routinization of jury service that remained its best hope. Naturally, the menacing political climate of the Terror and the reaction did not help in advancing this novel experiment. But even in more normal times citizens balked—whether propertied peasants in the countryside who had more urgent things to do, or urban *notables* who preferred to use their time for other pursuits.

Though successive regimes embraced this "palladium of liberty," they had few illusions and relied from the beginning on the threat of sanctions. Fines for evading a jury summons were substantial in 1792, grew higher from time to time, and reached confiscatory levels in 1808. At the outset, the very right to vote could depend on registering in the district capital for jury service; and again in 1808, the new categories of eligible citizens were told that they would "not be admitted to any administrative or judicial positions" if they failed to answer a jury summons. [70] Citizens had to be educated into this role, inured to performing it despite the inconvenience, tedium, or anxiety it might produce. A dramatic novelty had eventually to become a habit. Like paying taxes, voting, or repairing local roads, like every responsibility that came with the new civic order, jury service provoked evasion or resistance. But the state persevered, and trial by jury of criminal offenses established itself both as a right of defendants and an obligation of citizens.

XIII

CONSCRIPTION

I n 1790 the National Assembly pledged itself to the cause of world peace, renouncing the secret diplomacy of princes and wars of conquest. A mass conscript army had no place on this visionary agenda. In the abstract, no doubt, revolutionary opinion paid hommage to Rousseau's dictum that every citizen ought to be a soldier, and every soldier a citizen, but in practice the Assembly opted for a comparatively small professional army of volunteers. Then the war changed the situation completely. Massive mobilization became the key to the Revolution's survival, and military recruitment the cornerstone of its evolving civic order. As the war raged on from 1792 to 1814 with only brief pauses, Republic and Empire alike embraced the practice of conscription—a demand on their citizens as relentless as direct taxation had become centuries earlier.

By 1789 the French people were long since inured to paying those taxes, but military conscription brought an even sharper intrusion of the state into their lives, and created nearly as much contention as the Revolution's religious policies and political upheavals. Unlike the latter however, the demand on young men for military service not only persisted but intensified. With Napoleon, conscription became the decisive battle of wills between families and local communities on the one hand and a distant impersonal state on the other. It was a contest more fundamental in its way than the clash of opposing armies at the front.

From the Royal Army to the Mass Levy of 1793

Even before the disorders of 1789 corroded its discipline and coherence, the French army suffered from a crisis of confidence. Arguably Europe's strongest army since the time of Louis XIV, it had been sullied by one stalemate or defeat after another in the eighteenth century, a record scarcely balanced by crucial French support of America's war for independence against Britain. To the sharpest eyes in its own ranks, the royal army did not measure up professionally in either leadership or organization. Drastic, mutually conflicting prescriptions for reform jostled for attention in the royal councils during the 1770s and 1780s, but with limited results.

As an institution central to the historic mission of the monarchy, the army no longer sat comfortably astride French society. France's contentious elites increasingly eyed the officer corps with a mix of ambition and recrimination. Notwithstanding exceptions numbering about 10 percent, the army was officered by nobles, but almost all commissions for captain and colonel had to be purchased.[1] To some military reformers, this venality rather than social privilege formed the impediment to effective professionalism. Aristocrats from families with an established military tradition indubitably made the best and most dedicated officers, in this view, but a system of purchase favoring social-climbing nouveaux-riches hampered their access. The Ségur Ordinance of 1781, which limited future military commissions to men who could show four quarterings of nobility, ostensibly secured military rank for this historic constituency against the competition of monied, non-noble, or recently ennobled families.[2] Appointments as generals in any case devolved almost exclusively on well-connected aristocrats, who were doubly rewarded by the unregulated largesse of royal pensions. Among the junior grades, meanwhile, double complements of idle officers had become commonplace in most regiments—yet another practice precluding the "pure and tough" army sought by royal military reformers.

In the era of Louis XIV the rank-and-file of France's large standing army had appeared to most French people as an alien, even menacing body, recruited at the margins of society. By the late eighteenth century the army's social composition had changed enough to soften the edges of that image without nullifying it altogether. Recruited by voluntary or high-pressure enlistment for eight-year terms, largely from a cross section of ordinary working Frenchmen, the army still tilted heavily toward a traditional recruiting zone of frontier regions and towns, and still enrolled outcasts from the mainstream. For peasants in much of the country, therefore, the army remained a remote presence. Worse yet, the monarchy had introduced a compulsory militia lottery in the late seventeenth century to supplement the army's permanent core in wartime with about 100,000 extra men. This supremely unpopular innovation became permanent in 1726. With its numerous exemptions, the burden of the lottery for this *milice* fell almost exclusively on the non-privileged residents of rural communities. Much like a serf in Russia, the young peasant coerced into drawing the short straw in his community could be written off. Resentment was universal and resistance widespread. In the parish *cahiers* of 1789, rural Frenchmen denounced the *milice* with passion. [3]

But how did the political elites regard the army? One conventional attitude, prominent among *philosophes* who had little contact with military life, viewed standing armies as tools of despotism. That the French army contained a number of "foreign regiments" and relatively small but prominent contingents of foreign soldiers no doubt lent this image a certain plausibility. (In the capital, for example, while the French Guards crossed over to the popular cause decisively in July 1789, German-speaking cavalry from the Royal Allemand Regiment rode down crowds of Parisians until finally withdrawn by their officers.) [4] If a standing army served as a ready tool of despotism, then a nation in the throes of a revolution must obviously forestall that alliance. Like other props of absolutism, the army had to be transformed into a truly national institution. Some deputies professed to believe that a standing, professional army could be eliminated altogether—inspired perhaps by Rousseau's prescription in the *Social Contract* that "every citizen should be a soldier by duty, none by trade." An armed force of citizen-soldiers would be appropriate for a nation about to renounce aggressive wars and repudiate the secret diplomacy of princes. The nation's armed force need not be a society apart but could be replaced by some sort of universalized militia or, more plausibly, by a system of general conscription. [5]

Despite its enthusiasm for the image of the citizen-soldier, however, the National Assembly finally retreated from introducing conscription and accepted the need for a professional standing army. At the same time, while quickly abolishing the *milice* in deference to peasant opinion, the Assembly authorized the formation of a permanent militia or national guard in the nation's towns and bourgs—urban middle-class patriots having armed themselves to form such units spontaneously in the summer of 1789. But the Assembly understood that the national guard could not replace or duplicate the line army; on its own, this amateur, untrained, and part-time force could not defend the country's borders or put down major internal disturbances. Those tasks would be left to a reformed professional army of long-term volunteers, scaled down in 1790 to 150,000 men for the era of peace anticipated by the deputies. The Assembly asserted its control over the line army while leaving the king as its titular head; but in a decree of symbolic importance, it directed that historic regimental designations be replaced by numbers.[6]

The August 4 decree had already condemned the venal and privileged routes of access to officers commissions as adjuncts of feudalism. Instead, the Assembly made military office and promotion into a model of the career open to talent, or more precisely to a mix of talent (demonstrated aptitude on examination or in performance) and of merit (a term generally referring to seniority). Since no serving officer was to be expropriated, the Assembly assumed that turnover in the officer corps would be gradual. But when royalist officers began resigning and emigrating in large numbers, junior officers won rapid promotions, while NCOs of the royal army, who in the old regime could never have aspired to officers rank, found themselves wearing epaulets.[7]

The rank-and-file experienced an equally dramatic turnover and renewal for different reasons. Discontent over material privation, grievances over harsh discipline and the disposition of regimental funds, political agitation, and a general distrust of aristocratic officers led to widespread insubordination, desertion, and disciplinary discharges in the royal army in 1789–90. At one point the army's effective strength plummeted to about 130,000. But improved pay, reforms in military justice, new recruiting procedures, and sign-up bonuses allowed the line army to replenish its ranks from a cross section of ordinary French citizens in 1791, and again in 1792, when 70,000 new men enrolled. Thus, the line army of 1792 differed substantially from the royal army of 1789—its ranks were younger (65 percent under twenty-five), less experienced, more socially heterogeneous, and no doubt more attuned to the new patriotism. Many of the regulars, in other words, understood that they too were citizens.[8]

These changes occurred gradually, and in 1791 society at large might still plausibly have regarded the white-uniformed regulars as a distinctive and unappealing subculture. At any rate, what such young men chose to do with their lives was their own business. Soon, however, the deteriorating political situation brought military needs onto center stage. First, the king's flight to Varennes in June 1791 set off a war panic, leading the Assembly to bolster the line army with 100,000 volunteers from "active citizens" of the national guard who were asked to sign up for one campaign or one year. Recruited, organized, and equipped by local civilian authorities (and at a higher rate of pay than the line army), volunteers quickly came forward, especially in most frontier departments. A lively sense of patriotism, a short enlistment, higher pay, opportunity for achieving rank by election, and the prospect of less rigorous discipline than in the line army brought men into the armed forces as volunteers who might otherwise have shunned military life.[9]

After the war began, the sphere of recruitment widened much further. In July 1792, the Legislative Assembly called for an additional 100,000 short-term volunteers, this time assigning quotas to each department, eliminating height requirements, and opening the rosters to men who had not qualified as taxpaying "active citizens" in 1791. Enrollment bonuses provided by departments or municipalities helped attract poor workingmen, often married with children—"money given to volunteers as an expression of solidarity rather than evidence that they were trafficking in patriotism," according to the historian Jean-Paul Bertaud. The volunteer levy of 1792 reached deeper into rural society than previous recruitment drives: in 1791, only 15 percent of the volunteers came from the villages, but 69 percent of the volunteers in 1792 were rural. Again most frontier departments filled their battalions quickly, and a spectacular response in Paris enrolled 15,000 volunteers in the first week; but recruitment in this moment of national peril also went well in remoter regions of Central France that had not come forward the year before.[10]

By March 1793 it was clear that a faltering French army desperately needed yet more troops. Recognizing that volunteering had probably reached its limits, the Convention called for 300,000 new recruits, and assigned each department a quota to be filled with men between the ages of eighteen and forty in any manner chosen by individual communes. Fair-minded officials blanched before the alternatives. Many communes resorted to some form of "election," often as a way of shifting the burden to politically unpopular families—disruptively ardent patriots or notorious counter-revolutionaries, depending on circumstances—or to filling their quota with the marginal and powerless, thereby sparing able-bodied cultivators or workers necessary to the local economy. The alternative was a lottery of some sort, ostensibly fairer yet unpopular as being arbitrary in its outcome and reminiscent of the hated *milice*.

In either case, designated men could hire replacements, which seemed to insulate the wealthy and place the obligation essentially on families of modest circumstances. This levy of 300,000 men is best remembered for igniting the Vendée rebellion in Western France, but almost everywhere it stirred up protest and recrimination. The levy was an improvised and poorly planned muddle, a no-man's-land between genuine volunteering (either long- or short-term) and genuine conscription whose universality and inherent fairness might win grudging acceptance. In practice, the uncertain modalities of the March 1793 levy could not help but appear inequitable or arbitrary. Despite the presence of representatives-on-mission to oversee the process in each department, the levy raised only 150,000 men by the summer. The next move to recruit troops would be conceived in a different and more egalitarian spirit. [11]

Against the mounting threats of a five-front war and rebellions at home, the Convention on 23 August 1793 enacted an unprecedented *levée en masse*. As initially demanded by popular societies and *sans-culotte* militants, the mass levy conjured up the image of an entire nation in arms, throwing itself at its enemies and intimidating them by sheer mass and determination. "Eight days of enthusiasm can do more than eight years of combat," claimed one pamphleteer. The Montagnard Convention brushed aside such literal and magnificently anarchic versions of this notion and instead decreed that "All French persons are placed in permanent requisition for the service of the armies. Young men will go off to battle; married men will forge arms and transport provisions; women will make tents and clothing and serve in the hospitals." Specifically, unmarried, able-bodied men between eighteen and twenty-five were immediately "requisitioned" for military service. The men were accordingly known as *réquisitionnaires* or *réquis* (draftees). [12] There was no implication here that subsequent cohorts of young men would face induction into the army as part of their civic obligations. On the contrary, in October the Convention passed to the order of the day on the question of what to do about men who turned eighteen after 23 August 1793, "since the law [on the *levée en masse*] concerns only those who have attained the age of eighteen years at the time it was promulgated." [13]

The mass levy was a desperate, once-only emergency mobilization whose massive dislocations of the labor force the Convention expected to be brief. In keeping with its pragmatic approach, the decree exempted married men. It was bad enough to call up the sons on whom parents depended for labor in the fields and workshops; it would have been worse to disrupt married households, leaving behind abandoned wives and infants. By the same token, if the mass levy had been intended to inaugurate a system of conscription in the future, the exemption of married men would have opened a wholesale avenue for draft avoidance. The Convention initially intended that employees of the military transport service, government ministries, and local administrations should "remain at their posts," so as not to disorganize the state's military and administrative infrastructures. But those exemptions caused a backlash of resentment, and the Convention revoked some of them in September, although local exceptions remained possible. [14]

To enroll the *réquis*, departmental directorates or representatives-on-mission designated "levy agents," usually reliable *sans-culottes* or military veterans, who traveled through rural areas to consult birth records, assemble the men, and arrange for medical reviews to weed out the unfit. (The law indicated no minimum height, but 5 feet seemed to be an effective minimum, with the average height of *réquis* estimated at 5 feet 4 inches.) Intent on projecting a sense of fairness, the agents made much of the fact that the Convention prohibited the hiring of replacements. Yet even the notion of a universal obligation could be construed as inegalitarian because it might cause disproportionate hardship for needy families. After all, when a prosperous family lost a son or a farm servant to the army, it could hire other labor to work the fields, bring in the crops, or tend its livestock. Poor farmers or sharecroppers could not afford to hire replacements for the missing labor of their children and faced serious material losses. Having already taken up collections and subscriptions for the wives, children, and parents of needy volunteers, municipalities now tried to compensate for such hardships by doing the same for the dependents of the draftees, sometimes offering to provide labor for them as well. Over and above such morale-raising local efforts, as we have seen, the Convention pledged subsistence pensions to the needy dependents of the *réquis,* and placed the highest priority on the provision of this "patriotic assistance."[15]

The very different levies of March and August 1793 brought military service to the doorstep of most families across France. Many were no doubt dumfounded by this demand, no matter how great the peril on the frontiers. It was their business to bring in the crops and to feed their families, not to fight enemy armies. The insistent pressure from political activists and officials, the high-pitched patriotism of the moment, and various policing sanctions ultimately induced some 300,000 families to give up their young men to the republic in 1793–94, but perhaps 200,000 of the anticipated draftees evaded service—either hiding out immediately, escaping en route to the front, or deserting after reaching their units. Some draftees turned out in good faith but, demoralized by long delays at the departmental depot as they waited for their companies to form or for uniforms and equipment to be issued, they quietly returned home.

Which, then, was more notable: the success of the mass levy or its deficiencies? Considering that the mass levy followed several waves of voluntary enlistment that had already absorbed most young men inclined to military service, it seems remarkable that so many Frenchmen complied. Militarily, the 300,000 or so new draftees ultimately incorporated into the republic's army not only turned the war's tide but laid the permanent foundation for a new type of military force in the future. On the other hand, the unpopularity of compulsory military service was manifest in 1793; widespread evasion and desertion constituted "a drain that has no end," in the words of a beleaguered official. Finally, one fact is particularly striking: only an estimated 16 percent of the incorporated draftees of 1793 came from the towns.[16] For the first itme in French history, men of rural origin predominated in the army in the same proportions as they did in civil society. In the army of the republic, the locus of recruitment shifted decisively to the populous countryside.

THE BEGINNINGS OF CONSCRIPTION

By the end of 1797, Spain, Prussia, and Austria had made peace, and France's frontiers seemed secure—indeed, the republic had expanded by annexing Belgium and the left bank of the Rhine and dividing those territories into new departments. Yet the continent was not really at peace. Large French occupation garrisons stretched far from home across the new sister republics in Italy and elsewhere, while the state of war continued with Britain, and the Habsburg monarchy prepared to resume hostilities at a propitious moment. The army defending France and its sister republics consisted of units called demi-brigades in which the old line army, the remaining volunteers, and the draftees of 1793 had been amalgamated. But from a high of about 750,000 men in 1794, the strength of the republican army had by now slipped below 400,000.

Back home, the levies of 1793 left deep scars and a tangle of problems. The deserters and *insoumis*—draftees who had fled from service—created a massive challenge to the laws of the republic. Where once refractory priests, *chouans,* and émigrés had preoccupied the authorities, now *insoumis* and brigands (often one and the same) constituted the state's chief policing problem, a huge outlaw population nestled in the interstices of French society. The young men who had complied, who lived within the law, also posed a problem for the government, or more accurately a dilemma. The mass levy—the "requisition" of able-bodied men between eighteen and twenty-five—had after all been intended as only a brief disruption of the economy and of individual lives. But the war and their service had now dragged on for two, then three, then four years with no end in sight.

Quietly, the requisition started to unravel. In the wake of French victories, draftees (whose numbers are unlikely ever to be known) returned home on furlough with *congés temporaires* in their pockets. Some were recuperating from light wounds, accidents, or illness; others went on the understanding that they could provide labor for their desperate families. Local authorities often acted to prolong these furloughs and in effect allowed such soldiers to return to civil society by default.[17] Alongside these undischarged soldiers were the few but conspicuous draftees who had legally avoided incorporation in the first place, either by special occupational or hardship exemptions or for temporary medical reasons. As the strength of the army declined by almost half between 1795 and 1797, the government stepped up efforts to flush out *insoumis,* while it also began to reexamine previous exemptions and *congés temporaires.* But this necessarily meant subjecting countless families to renewed economic hardship. As the Directory's general secretary expressed the conundrum in June 1796:

> The more the Directory steps up its efforts to come to the aid of neglected arts, agriculture, and commerce, as well as families without support, by letting them keep the soldiers they claim when the public interest permits it, the more it fears sowing discouragement in the armies and disorganizing their ranks by permitting soldiers on active duty to return to their families.[18]

In an extraordinary move, the Directory began to review every claim for prolongation of an exemption or renewal of a *congé temporaire,* with Director Carnot—the architect of the Convention's military strategy in the Year II—personally taking on most of the chore. Over time the directors revoked most furloughs and hardship dispensations, but at the price of havoc in the affairs of families, enterprises, and local institutions. Their dilemma is apparent in the case of the Ancelin family of Beauvais. According to the municipal administration, the family's cloth factory was long one of the largest local employers, with a reputation for producing the highest quality goods. Since 1793, however, the factory's activity had declined substantially because of the father's administrative functions and the loss of his eldest son to the army. That son had initially enrolled as a volunteer in 1792 but had returned because of illness and had secured a replacement for the remainder of his term. Then the mass levy of 1793 had "obliged him to leave for the army again," where he has served ever since, although "he is absolutely necessary to his father's [enterprise]."[19]

The dossiers reviewed by Carnot and colleagues in 1796–97 fill seventy-eight cartons in the National Archives. In a sample, well over half involved cultivators claiming that the family farm required their labor. The more dependents they had, the needier their parents, or the more serious their disabilities, the more likely they were to win approval. But without dramatic or unusual circumstances, the Directory rejected peasant applicants and ordered them back to their units. The same was true of draftees seeking continued furlough or permanent discharges on occupational grounds for war-related work, rare artisinal skills, or clerical responsibilities in local administrations otherwise devoid of such talents.[20]

In sum, the requisition of 1793 lingered on as a civic problem as well as a military phenomenon. The government's military recruitment policy in the years 1795–97 amounted to little more than rounding up the draftees of 1793 who were not in their units—by running to ground the *insoumis,* reexamining the small number of individual exemptions, and revoking the far more numerous *congés temporaires* with which furloughed soldiers had quietly passed back into civil society without benefit of a formal discharge. The mass citizens' army created in 1793, in other words, depended on the draftees of 1793 for the next five years. Obviously that situation could not continue indefinitely. As peace proved elusive, France was about to cross the threshold from a one-time emergency mobilization to a permanent system of military conscription—something very different, but for which the mass levy of 1793 had prepared the ground.

THE IDEA OF systematic conscription—proposed but rejected in the National Assembly's original debate on military recruitment in 1790—was taken up again in 1795 by the Montagnard deputy Oudot during the Convention's debates on the Constitution of the Year III. Oudot's speech extolled the social and civic benefits of compulsory military service in a republic more than its (arguable) advantages as a form of military recruitment. But stripped of the Jacobin-style rhetoric so utterly unfashionable in the thermidorian period (which no doubt led the constitutional committee to table Oudot's proposal summarily), his remarks may have reflected a consensus among republicans on the beneficial side effects of conscription. In Oudot's view, two years of compulsory military service for all young men would provide "practical lessons in equality," since conscription, "a truly republican institution . . . [would] unite young citizens under a common discipline . . . mingling all occupations, professions, and levels of education." Just as Jacobins advocated public primary schooling for providing "a common education," Oudot believed that universal military service would counteract social and regional particularism, even as it habituated young men to obeying "those who speak in the name of the law." Admitting that there might be easier ways to provide military manpower and spare agriculture and the arts, he still favored conscription as "an indispensable institution of public instruction, the complement of a virile civic education . . . a means to unify the different parts of the Republic into a single whole, indivisible in its spirit and its mores as it is in its system of government." [21]

When the issue came up again in 1798, the debate in the legislature descended to an entirely pragmatic level. Formulated by Jean-Baptiste Jourdan, a celebrated general in the army of the Year II, the draft proposal began with the commonplace axiom that in a republic citizens were soldiers, and soldiers citizens. A republic had to be wary of an army separate and apart, he cautioned; it must not "entrust the care of its defense to a bunch of mercenary men." The challenge was simply to find the most effective way to fill the army's manpower needs under that assumption: "The soldiers of the fatherland consist of all Frenchmen capable of bearing arms. It only remains for us to determine how to call to the colors those whose presence will be necessary. . . . Many will be subject to service, but few are likely actually to serve." Under the Jourdan Law of 21 fructidor Year VI (7 September 1798), men between the ages of twenty and twenty-five would thereafter be subject to conscription, but would actually be called to service by legislative decree only as needed. Each annual birth cohort formed a "class" of *conscripts* (a new term designating young men who became subject to conscription in a particular year rather than those actually inducted). Mobilization would begin with the class of twenty-year-olds, and would move forward as needed. If they were not called by the end of their twenty-fifth year, conscripts would be permanently discharged from the obligation. The Jourdan Law seemed to take particular aim at the propertied classes in refusing to conscripts actually called to service the prerogative of hiring replacements. [22]

The Jourdan Law had barely been published before the government invoked it. Peace had broken down in Italy, and the War of the Second Coalition was beginning with French armies in retreat. At the end of September the legislature called up the entire *première classe* of twenty-year-olds, in theory for a maximum of five years. Suddenly conscription became the top priority of local officials. Early signs seemed promising as departmental administrations hastened to inform Paris that "the levy is being executed in our department with the greatest success" (Aisne), "without the least opposition" (Indre-et-Loire), "with ease and without obstacle" (Aude); that the parents support "a law based on justice and equality" (Pas-de-Calais). Over fifty central administrations congratulated themselves for rapidly mustering conscripts and sending some on to their units within weeks of the levy. Deputies read these communications from the rostrum, voted them "the honors of the session," and printed them as pamphlets. [23]

But this initial whirlwind of optimism petered out as allusions to *insoumission* gradually intruded. The Directory recognized that enthusiastic reports of success papered over a deep-seated and active resistance to conscription in many regions, and that the actual results of the levy were woefully inadequate. With no time to waste, it therefore asked the legislature in April 1799 to mobilize men as needed from the second and third classes (twenty-one and twenty-two-year-olds) to compensate for the poor response of the first class, each department being given a quota to be formed from this aggregated pool of manpower. (Nine western, Vendée-region departments were prudently exempted.) Finally, on 28 June 1799 the government called the entire second and third classes to the colors and ordered them formed into "auxiliary battalions," to be armed, uniformed, and equipped by local authorities and sent on their way to the front.[24]

Reviewing the results of these moves ten weeks later, the Directory could take some comfort in the fact that twenty-one departments (mostly in the East) had effectively mobilized their conscripts, with another fifteen departments promising similar results. But elsewhere pervasive delays and resistance derailed the levies.[25] In Lot-et-Garonne, *insoumission* reached "alarming proportions"; in neighboring Haute-Garonne, it was "frightening." At least two thirds of the recruits deserted from the first auxiliary battalion of the Ariège, while in the Aisne, 1,500 out of 3,600 deserted en route with arms and equipment, their evident impunity in turn encouraging others to desert. In some departments, groups of *insoumis* began forming violent and potentially seditious bands.[26]

Material deficiencies also hampered mobilization of the auxiliary battalions even where the men turned out. With the best will in the world, "absolute privation"—the lack of departmental funds to pay them, food to feed them, uniforms to clothe them—demoralized the conscripts and caused many to take flight even in frontier regions where military service was familiar.[27] But at bottom resistance to conscription itself was the problem. The youth of many regions simply found military service "insupportable" and "repugnant," and their families backed them, unwilling to be deprived of the young men who were often their principal source of labor or sustenance. The yawning gap between its new claim on French youth for military service and its evident inability to make good that claim revealed the Directory's weakness. Napoleon could modify various policies, increasing pressure on citizens here and easing it there, but he of all leaders could scarcely be expected to eliminate this most burdensome of demands.

THE NEW RULES OF THE GAME

Building on the Jourdan Law, the initial Napoleonic conscription strategy emphasized local autonomy and flexibility. Prefects subdivided their departmental quotas into quotas for each commune, where each newly appointed mayor, assisted by his municipal council, became the linchpin. For the first three years of the Consulate—in a throwback to the levy of March 1793—communal quotas could be filled by lottery or by some kind of designation according to local wishes. General Daru, one of Napoleon's military advisers, specifically justified such latitude:

As for the actual selection, it is confided to the officials most immediately concerned with the interests of the people—those officials who are domiciled in the place where they exercise their temporary functions, and have more need than any other officials [i.e., the prefects] to conserve the esteem of their fellow citizens. . . . The sole means of softening the law's impact is to take into account local circumstances. For it is impossible to resolve the problem of complete justice and uniformity. . . . Scrutiny by the interested parties is a sufficient guarantee of equity. [28]

But the regime eventually abandoned this flexible approach, as it faced the notorious fact that mayors and municipal councils were the weak links of state administration. In the matter of conscription, their *"insouciance"* and incompetence became insupportable. "The paternal intentions that determined the Government to confer the right of designation on the municipal councils," concluded the prefect of the Meurthe, "have been very poorly fulfilled." Ignorance and local passions combined to bog down recruitment. Sometimes these officials were accused of personal favoritism. In the Aisne, the prefect believed that "the village councils are less concerned with filling the contingent than with removing from the levy their own children, relatives, and friends." More commonly, prefects denounced a general laxness and a tendency of mayors to worry more about their constituents than about the government's needs. [29]

Mayors tried to mollify villagers by appearing to increase their chances in the conscription lottery. They could, for example, include manifestly underheight or unfit men in the local contingent, even if they were subsequently rejected by the departmental recruiting officer in the *chef-lieu* or by the military unit to which the conscripts ultimately reported. The prefect of Isère observed that the conscripts themselves insisted on such ruses, for they could not bear to see the pool reduced and their chance of drawing a low number increased. [30] In the end, however, such practices obliged officials to return to their communities again and again to fill their quotas. As thirteen irate conscripts of the Year IX from the Somme complained, "having responded three consecutive times to a drawing of lots for the contingent of their class, because of the medical exemptions *(dispenses)* that those who were liable knew how to procure for themselves, they have been called for the fourth time to a drawing." [31]

Though it took several years to develop the optimum administrative formula, the government soon eliminated most local discretion. After the Year XII it allotted quotas to each canton rather than each commune (on the cantons, see pp. 114–27), and the subprefect supervised each cantonal lottery, before which he examined the conscripts for obvious physical deficiencies. The process was further streamlined in 1804 by convoking the conscripts for review and designation in the *sous-préfecture* (three to six per department).[32] Not that the mayors could be eliminated from the picture altogether. The commune or village remained the basic unit of French society, and only the mayor had direct access to the birth registers, the key to the whole process. No one else could draw up the local list for each year's class of conscripts, notify them, explain procedures to their families, and make sure they showed up where they had to. The mayors remained essential to the system, but after 1804 they had responsibility without much power—either to spare their constituents or to undermine the government's intentions, unless, of course, they were corrupt. The mayors were integrated into a bureaucratic routine whose annual repetition and detailed formalities left less room for error or ill-will.

By 1806, the policies, procedures, and timetables were in place for a routinized, bureaucratic conscription. Rather than any dramatic innovation, this was the real breakthrough of the Napoleonic regime, the ultimate form of state penetration. Approximately one month after the promulgation of a mobilization law for a given class (see Table XIII.1 for the dates and sizes of these levies), the cantonal lists of all conscripts belonging to that class were supposed to be ready—rosters fashioned by the subprefects from lists submitted by each mayor based on the *état civil* of his commune. The subprefect conflated, alphabetized, printed, and distributed the cantonal list back to each commune, where it was to be placarded for ten days, after which citizens had five days to raise objections to the information on the list.

Meanwhile the mayor was to notify each conscript in writing of his status and convoke the conscripts and their parents to review the laws, penalties for infractions, and timetables. On the appointed day, the mayor and his assistant would lead the commune's conscripts to the cantonal seat and then on the subprefecture in the *chef-lieu d'arrondissement,* there to meet the subprefect and the recruitment council. The subprefect first weeded out the manifestly unfit (especially those below the minimum height, which kept changing) and then supervised each cantonal contingent in drawing lots.[33]

At that point the recruitment council—a board consisting of the prefect, the military commander of the department, and a recruiting officer—took over. They had previously publicized their schedule of rounds to each subprefecture, so that cantonal conscripts would not have to spend more than a day or two away from home. With the aid of doctors, the recruitment council determined who would receive a *dispense* for physical reasons, and verified the preliminary exclusions for height or infirmities made by the subprefect earlier. The families of such excused conscripts *(réformés)* had to pay an indemnity for their dispensation, provided that they paid at least 50

Table XIII-1
The Napoleonic Levies

Date of Law or Senatus-Consulte	Affected Classes	Numbers Called	Remarks
Mar. 1800	An VIII	30,000	
May 1802	An IX–An X	120,000	Half were reserves that were eventually called up
May 1803	An XI–An XII	120,000	"
Dec. 1804	An XIII	60,000	"
Sept. 1805	An XIV	60,000	"
Aug. 1806	1806	80,000	All mobilized
Dec. 1806	1807	80,000	(30,000 reserves)
Apr. 1807	1808	80,000	(20,000 reserves)
Feb. 1808	1809	80,000	"
Sept. 1808	1806–09	80,000	No further calls for classes An VIII–XIV
Sept. 1808/Jan. 1809	1810	80,000	(20,000 reserves)
Apr. 1809	1806–09	10,000	
	1810	30,000	
Oct. 1809	1806–10	36,000	No further calls for classes 1806–10 pledged
Dec. 1810/Feb. 1811	1811	120,000	(40,000 reserves)
Dec. 1811/Feb. 1812	1812	120,000	(No reserves)
Sept. 1812	1813	150,000	
Jan. 1813	national guard	100,000*	Service within the Empire only
	1814	150,000	
	1809–12	100,000	
Apr. 1813	national guard	80,000	
	1814	90,000	
	any class	10,000	Mounted honor guard
Aug. 1813	1809–14	30,000	From 24 southern departments
Oct. 1813	1811–14	120,000	
	1815	160,000	
Nov. 1813	1803–14	150,000	
		150,000	(Reservists)

Source: Bulletin des Lois, passim.
*Organized into units in March 1812, awaiting mobilization.

livres in direct taxes. Proportionate to their tax payments, the indemnities could run as high as 1,500 livres and constituted a significant source of revenue. The council also certified conscripts who qualified for a status known as the *dépôt de droit* or *fin du dépôt*. While not definitively excused from conscription, these men automatically received the highest numbers and would be the last in their class called to service. This temporary deferment went to the sole sons of widows, the elder brothers of orphans, and the brothers of men already serving. Finally, the recruitment council passed on replacements—of which more below. Altogether each departmental recruitment council had two weeks to complete its circuit of subprefectures, after which the first batch of recruits was supposed to be sent on its way.

The artifacts of this process multiplied and made it more familiar to French citizens. In addition to printed *instructions* by the prefects to all mayors in their departments, enterprising individuals published handbooks for citizens to guide them through the procedural labyrinth and apprize them of their rights.[34] In some regions, and not simply in the eastern departments with long military traditions, routinization made conscription "a habit," an accepted way of life. The prefect of Seine-Inférieure, for example, acknowledged that the citizens of his prosperous department had no taste for military service. They resisted it, however, only by exhausting every legal avenue at their disposal—*ils chicannent* (they quibble). It was imperative that every rule and regulation be followed, he advised, since citizens knew them all. "They insist on legal formalities . . . because the thing that most arouses an inhabitant of this department is the thought that he has been refused justice, or that he has been judged without being heard." When all claims and appeals were finally exhausted, he concluded, they accepted their fate. The conscripts then took on an aura of youthful spirit and departed without incident.[35] Thus the end of local discretion or autonomy was not necessarily arbitrary or tyrannical. Occasional complaints still surfaced that only a village mayor was in a position to know that X was asthmatic or that Y was epileptic, which might not show up in a brief impersonal physical examination. Yet a consistent rule of law was in almost everyone's interest; at any rate an appearance of scrupulous legality could be an effective ally of sheer power.

Of course this new system did not guarantee success. In the early years the actual departure of troops, not to mention incorporation into their units, lagged far behind anticipated schedules. For the class of Year XIII, the mobilization law was promulgated in December 1804, but only in September 1805 were the 30,000 recruits en route. The first substantial departures had not occurred until April. There were simply too many medical exemptions, draft evaders who did not show up on departure day, and (about 4,000) recruits who had deserted en route. Each and every one had to be replaced by someone from the same canton with the next lowest lottery number, amidst a blizzard of recrimination and paperwork.[36]

Napoleon compounded this nerve-racking repetition with his concept of reserve forces. Until 1810, each department's quota comprised an active contingent for immediate mobilization and a so-called reserve contingent designated for call-up if necessary (see Table XIII-1). In fact these reserves were always mobilized, some within weeks, others in months or years. This meant that prefects were usually dealing with two conscription calls at once: the organization of that year's "class," and mobilization of reserves from previous classes. The reserve contingents decreased in size relative to the active contingent until Napoleon eliminated them altogether in 1810. But the emperor had already begun the more pernicious practice of "supplementary levies" on previous classes by calling for 80,000 additional conscripts from the classes of 1806–09 in September 1808. Believing themselves free and secure, as one prefect complained, conscripts who had drawn high lottery numbers had given themselves over to their private affairs, only to find as much as two years later that they could still be drafted. "They have been terrified by the unforeseen and extraordinary call which has forced them to renounce those private affairs."[37] Conscripts were exempt from supplementary levies only if they had married *after* the initial lottery and designation, since (contrary to a widespread misapprehension among historians) being married did not exempt anyone from induction during the principal levy for his class. Nor, once a supplementary levy was decreed, could a vulnerable conscript avoid induction by marrying at that point.

To make matters worse, the interval between levies fluctuated wildly with strategic and diplomatic circumstances. In an extreme situation, Napoleon called up the three classes of 1806, 1807, and 1808 successively within the space of nine months (see Table XIII-1), which meant among other things that nineteen-year-olds, who had not always reached full height, were being called up prematurely only to be rejected. All told, no sooner would departmental rosters for one conscription near completion than those for the next one had to be opened.[38] Citizens hated this, and so did the prefects, who recognized that "partial and successive levies wear out and oppress the citizens." Thus the prefect of Loir-et-Cher wrote in November 1805: "I thought it prudent to defer publication of the call for the entire reserve contingent until the complete execution of the conscription of Year XIV. . . . There is a fear of provoking despair in striking such blows so close together." Prefects who fell conspicuously behind, however, were badgered, reprimanded, and even dismissed. In 1804 the government removed Joseph Verneilh as prefect of Mont Blanc because he still "owed" 121 recruits six months after the start of that year's conscription. Notwithstanding the forbidding conditions of his mountainous department and the poor physical state of many conscripts to begin with, the Council of State concluded that "the results are not favorable for him. . . . His recall will produce a good effect on his colleagues." [39]

THE VEXING QUESTION OF REPLACEMENT

Conceptually and pragmatically, replacement remained the most nettlesome issue posed by military conscription. From the start, opinion pulled in opposite directions. In the levy of 300,000 (March 1793), men designated to fill departmental quotas could hire replacements, but the Convention's *levée en masse* five months later emphatically prohibited that avenue of escape. In its turn the Jourdan Law barred the hiring of replacements, and the *première classe* was called to the colors in September 1798 without that option. The panic provoked by *insoumission* and a worsening military situation, however, pushed the government into a dizzying series of reversals. When it ordered another levy in April 1799 on conscripts of the second and third classes to compensate for draft resistance among the first class, the legislature stipulated that the men so designated by lottery could hire replacements who need only meet the minimal qualifications of volunteers. Replacements could thus be sought among eighteen- or nineteen-year-olds, even though such young men might be subject to conscription themselves in one or two years. Three months later, the government canceled the provision for replacement when it called up the entire second and third classes. [40]

Napoleonic policymakers proved to be highly ambivalent about replacement, as well they might. In general they sanctioned the practice, but periodically expressed misgivings and attempted to limit replacement substantially. During the first Napoleonic debate, it is true, replacement encountered few opponents. The Jourdan Law tended to make the French into a warrior people, argued one speaker in the Tribunate, but the possibility of hiring replacements would at least permit "family projects" to proceed unimpeded. A designated conscript should be obliged to fill his place in the contingent, but not necessarily by serving personally. The option of replacement, claimed the tribune, will obviate drastic steps that men might take to avoid induction, such as self-mutilation, while the transactions will put money into the hands of poor families. Finally, lawmakers would be nurturing the arts and sciences by offering this alternative. [41]

In this spirit, the first Napoleonic conscription law (17 ventôse VIII/8 March 1800) authorized replacement for conscripts (and retroactively for prior draftees on *congé*) "who cannot sustain the fatigues of war or who are recognized as more useful to the state in continuing their work and their studies rather than in becoming part of the army." This problematic formulation offered a blanket invitation to anyone who could afford a replacement simply to claim that option on one of those pretexts. True, replacement did not become an unqualified right, but depended on the willingness of the subprefect to accept the claim; but under most circumstances they were likely to approve it at this juncture if the conscript presented a reasonably apt replacement, especially since the levy of 1800 called for only 30,000 men from the class of twenty-year-olds. Meanwhile indigent citizens were entitled to a dispensation without a replacement if they proved themselves "incapable of supporting the fatigues of war."

Perhaps the most important feature of this law was its latitude in defining who could qualify as a replacement or *suppléant:* he need only be a physically fit French citizen between the age of eighteen and forty, and at least 5 feet 1 inch tall, but could come from any part of the country. Thus in a group of 231 *suppléants* from the Pas-de-Calais in 1800, almost 50 percent were under twenty years of age, along with another 14 percent who were over thirty-five. The possibility of hiring pre-draft-age youths made replacement much easier than it might have been. Moreover, thirty-three of the replacements came from other departments. [42]

In all, the minimal restrictions of the first Napoleonic conscription law opened the door to widespread replacement. A preliminary tally in October 1800 by the War Ministry of the levies of 1799 and 1800 noted at least 11,000 *suppléants* among the 70,000 incorporated recruits. But if 16 percent was the average, in at least eleven departments the ratio ran to over 30 percent, the highest being Seine-Inférieure (167 out of 327), Pas-de-Calais (469 of 949), and Gard (250 out of 521). Departments that produced large numbers of replacements included four on which governments always relied for rapid mobilization of large, high-quality contingents: the Nord (866 of 1,879), Moselle (652 of 2,809), Somme (548 of 3,126), and Bas-Rhin (472 of 2,468). Replacement clearly helped oil the wheels of recruitment in this traditional military zone of the republic. [43]

Yet in its next recruitment law in 1802, suffering from bad conscience, the government restricted the practice drastically. Affirming the principle of universal military obligation, its spokesmen squirmed uncomfortably over the question of replacement, suggesting that such an option ought at most to be left implicit. "Is it dignified for a law proclaiming a call to the defense of the nation to anticipate the practice of replacement? To define the procedure? . . . The law ought to limit itself to not preventing it." [44] This position did not reflect Napoleon's personal opinion, since the First Consul himself had no problem with replacement. During discussion of conscription in the

Council of State in 1801, he is quoted by Thibaudeau as taking a permissive line: "On the question of substitutes [i.e., replacements], we must allow them. . . . Among a people whose existence is based on the inequality of wealth, it is essential to allow the rich to buy substitutes. All we need is to make sure that the substitutes are fit for service, and to secure a share of the money paid for them."[45]

One of Napoleon's foremost advisers on military administration, however, did not share this attitude. J. G. Lacuée—a career officer and military intellectual under the old regime, member of the Legislative Assembly and directorial legislature, and later Napoleon's minister of war administration and director general of conscription—took a dim view of replacement, and his position seems to have shaped the second Napoleonic conscription law in this matter. While permitting *substitutions* among conscripts of a particular class and locality at the time of the *tirage*—that is, an exchange of numbers arranged by conscripts within a local contingent that had just drawn lots—it effectively forbade any other kind of replacement. This distinction between substitution and replacement is not always clear in contemporary reports (indeed, it is blurred in Thibaudeau's recollections) or for that matter in historical works, but it was crucial. From 1802 onward the state always deemed "amicable substitutions" among conscripts a legitimate, even benign practice, whereas replacement by outsiders remained a contentious issue.[46]

When the law of 1802 barred such replacements altogether, protests from prefects poured into the Ministries of War and the Interior. Replacement helped the levies function more smoothly, they argued. The prohibition especially hurt married men, who did not make good soldiers and who should have a chance to find replacements even though they were not entitled to exemption. From the Isère, the prefect noted that "some married conscripts have secured replacements without regard to the conditions outlined in the [current] law, citing the law of 17 ventôse VIII." But the new law had to be enforced and he eventually annulled those transactions.[47] The subprefect of St. Jean d'Angely, writing to M.-L. Regnaud, an influential native son who sat on the Council of State, invoked a range of arguments in favor of replacement.

> Conscripts are refused permission to secure replacements. They are only allowed to arrange things among themselves [i.e., substitutions], and only within the circle of those from whom the contingent of each commune will be chosen. This measure throws families into despair; it procures bad soldiers for the Republic instead of the good ones it would have through replacement. It contributes to multiplying desertion. It deprives the countryside of useful cultivators while retaining the shiftless ones, men with-

out resources or families who seek their subsistence in fraud or brigandage, and who could usefully serve their country under military discipline.

   This infinitely impolitic prohibition alienates a great many hearts from
the government. . . . Preceding laws on conscription had permitted
replacement. Why, when those laws have not been abrogated, should
such a puzzling difference be introduced for the conscription of the Years
IX and X?[48]

Regnaud endorsed this letter and added his own terse postscript:

The son of one of my uncles—formerly an *avocat du roi* and currently a
judge at St. Jean d'Angeley—has been called up. His commune's quota
was twelve conscripts. Only five were fit to march. He could not find a
substitute for himself. The same thing has happened in many places.

   Under such pressure, the government relented somewhat. In its next
revision of the conscription law, in April 1803, it did authorize replacement,
but with two important qualifications. The *suppléants* must come from among
"the non-designated conscripts from previous years . . . born and domiciled
in the arrondissement [subprefecture]." In December 1804 the regime tight-
ened these constraints even further: "*suppléants* must be taken only from the
five previous conscription classes, and only from within the boundaries of
the canton alone." In other words, no *future* conscripts could be used as
replacements and only local men from the canton might qualify.[49]

   Compared to the blanket prohibition of 1802 these changes opened the
door to replacement once again, but they scarcely satisfied the demand of
influential citizens for a viable replacement option. In a report to the emperor
summarizing prefectorial opinion, the War Ministry noted that "in all cases
the prefects believe that conscripts should be permitted to hire replacements
among the citizens of the [entire] department, aged between eighteen and
thirty-five or even forty." Lacuée, on the other hand, opposed further
concessions. "Though a great many people are asking that replacement be
made easier, you will not see me asking you to change the law," he wrote to
Napoleon. If anything, he leaned the other way: "To disgust Frenchmen with
having themselves replaced is well within my principles, and I would adopt
such measures as bring me closer to that goal."[50]

   As the government moved to resolve this question once and for all,
Lacuée effectively lost the debate. The definitive conscription law of 8
fructidor XIV (26 August 1806) still barred pre-draft-age replacements, but
suppléants could be hired among uninducted conscripts from the previous five
classes, domiciled anywhere within the department rather than merely the

same canton. Other restrictions included a minimum height three inches taller for replacements than for ordinary recruits. Replaced conscripts had to pay a 100 franc indemnity to the state beyond their payment to the *suppléants,* and if his *suppléant* deserted within the first two years or if he was called up in a supplementary levy on his own class, the conscript was obliged to serve personally.[51] Even with this loosening of previous restrictions, then, the law of 1806 (which essentially stood until the end of the Empire) proved far more constraining than the virtually unlimited replacement options of March 1793 or 1800. At least 65 percent of the replacements of 1800 in the Pas-de-Calais mentioned above, for example, would have been ineligible. Indeed, the incidence of replacement after 1806 fell substantially from that peak. Moreover the regime attempted to prevent public trafficking in replacements, and strictly prohibited the use of paid intermediaries to secure *suppléants.* Naturally such profit-seeking operators could not be eliminated altogether, but the restrictions on the age and geographical provenance of replacements crimped their field of operations substantially.[52]

NATIONALLY, THE PROPORTION of replacements in the levies between 1806 and 1810 reached only 4.5 percent. About 25,000 conscripts out of a total of 556,000 paid 100 francs to the government as the indemnity for securing a *suppléant.*[53] This figure does not include substitutions, which did not require that payment and which official accounts rarely mentioned. On average, there might have been one substitution for every two replacements. Statistics from the Côte d'Or indicate relatively few substitutions in that eastern department. In the classes of 1806 and 1810 (with quotas of 1,243 and 1,286), substitutions accounted for only 2.5 and 1.4 percent of those contingents respectively, while 4.1 and 5.2 percent of the recruits hired replacements. The best figures are from the Haute-Saône, where the four original levies on the classes of 1811–14 saw 234 substitutions and 464 replacements, and from Maine-et-Loire, where J.-P. Bois counted 336 substitutions and 505 replacements in the years 1806–14. There seem to be no cumulative figures for replacements in the last years of the Empire, but the incidence probably increased. In the Haute-Saône, for example, the rate of 8.5 percent in 1806–10 rose to 11.5 percent in 1811–14.[54]

As draft calls swelled and the number of conscripts seeking replacements increased, the price of such transactions mounted as well. In the early years the costs had been substantial but relatively moderate, according to two case studies of notarized contracts across the period: In the department of Charente and in the city of Avignon, replacement contracts cost under 1,000 francs in the first year or two. Costs began to climb after that, but with substantial variation from region to region.[55] In the Var, the prefect reported that replacements cost 1,500 to 1,800 francs in the levies of the Years IX and X (he was referring, perforce, to substitutions), and around 3,000 francs in the Years XI and XII, while in the Somme they remained at the 1,500 to 1,800F level. For the levy of the Year XIII, contracts ranged between 1,500 and 2,000 francs in the Bouches-du-Rhône, but reached from 1,900 to 3,600 francs in the Côte d'Or.[56]

Local circumstances caused fluctuations, and prices did not always climb linearly, but the upward trend was pronounced (see Table XIII.2). By 1808 replacement contracts crossed the 4,000F threshold, and by 1812 that amount had easily become the national average, with maximums reaching 7,000 or 8,000 francs. Thus, in the Hérault, contracts ranged in 1811–12 between a low of 3,200 and a high of 8,000 francs; in the Ain, prices were somewhat lower: eighty-eight replacement contracts for the levy of 1812 ranged between 1,040 and 5,880 francs, averaging out at 4,227 francs.[57]

A price of 4,000 or 6,000 francs posed a terrible burden even for prosperous peasants or urban bourgeois. Who in fact used this increasingly expen-

Table XIII-2
The Cost of Hiring Replacements, 1800–14

Year of Levy	*Location*	*Average Cost or Estimated Range*
Years 9 and 10	Var	1,500 to 1,800 F
Years 11 and 12	Var	2,400 to 4,000
Years 11 and 12	Somme	1,500 to 1,800 average
Year 13	Bouches-du-Rhône	1,500 average
Year 13	Côte d'Or	1,900 to 3,600
1806	Côte d'Or	3,000 to 4,000
1808–14	Avignon	4,000 to 5,600
1807	Charente	3,600 average to 7,000
1807	Tarn	3,000 to 3,500
1812	Tarn	4,000 to 7,000
1811	Hérault	6,072 average
1812	Hérault	5,319 average
1812	Ain	4,227 average
1811–14	Calvados (four communes)	4,553, 4,764, 5,178, and 6,700 (averages)

Sources: see notes 55–57.

sive avenue of draft avoidance? The two or three local studies based on
notarial archives suggest a wide range of individuals, including artisans in
Avignon, but they do not measure their findings against any yardstick. For
a different perspective, we have a national sample of one socioprofessional
group: about 350 aspirants to the bar between 1808 and 1813. Applicants for
government appointments as certified attorneys or *avoués,* they were obliged
to prove that they had satisfied the conscription laws in order to qualify for
consideration. Fifteen percent of these would-be attorneys had purchased
replacements or substitutes—far more than the national average, and more
than double the mere 7 percent of those applicants who had actually served
in the army prior to 1813.[58]

But professionals and wealthy *notables* by no means dominated the ranks
of families hiring replacements. Peasant proprietors seem to have been the
most intent on sparing their sons from the draft, even at prohibitive cost. In
the Ain, according to the prefect, "almost all the replacements [in 1812] have
been presented by cultivators, several of whom have put up a very large part
of their assets." The prefect of Maine-et-Loire made the same point in 1808
in connection with a prominent local family whose son had previously drawn
a high number but was called in the supplementary levy of that year:

> At the moment when cultivators, who were called up as he was, are
> ruining themselves forever by hiring replacements, the Moulue family has
> decided to provide a useful example [by having him serve]. . . . Distin-
> guished families will serve if they can count on certain favors. As the
> wealthy or comfortable man loses the habit of having his children re-
> placed, the people will cease wishing to imitate that ruinous mania.[59]

Independent peasants had strong reasons to hold on to their sons for
work on the family farm, and could finance installment payments for a
replacement by mortgaging some of their fields, although the interest would
drive up the net cost. In any case the government considered the option of
replacement—even if restrictions made it difficult and raised the cost—a
necessary safety valve for neutralizing resistance to conscription among
propertied families anxious to keep their sons at home. It also had the
beneficial effect of redistributing considerable sums from the propertied to
the poor; even poor men who drew good numbers and married after the *tirage*
for their class, and who were thus safe from supplementary levies, might hire
out as replacements if the price was right.

Nonetheless, the practice of replacement had to damage the sense of
equity on which conscription at least in part depended. Resentment at this
recourse for the propertied must have made it easier psychologically for the

son of a struggling smallholder or tenant farmer when he headed for the hills instead of answering his call-up. At the same time, suspicion that wealthy families were bribing their way into freedom through fraudulent medical exemptions probably caused even more alienation.

THE FIT AND THE UNFIT

In April 1807, Claude Fayet, a fabricator of riverboat poles, stood before a correctional court in the Saône-et-Loire, accused of "swindles upon several conscripts." In exchange for large sums of money, the indictment charged, he had promised to obtain dispensations for conscripts who had turned to him for help, crediting him "with considerable influence." The prosecutor alleged that "he administered potions to individuals subject to induction in order to ruin their health and bring about their *réforme*. . . . At Mâcon, before they appeared in front of the recruitment council, he had the conscripts swallow drinks contaminated by harmful concoctions, who then became so incommoded and changed that they were subsequently excused."

In his defense—a common one in such cases—Fayet admitted that he had been paid (typically 300F or 400F each) but only for escorting rural conscripts to Mâcon to show them the ropes, without engaging in any illegal activity. He was there simply to assure that the conscript received all the consideration to which he was entitled, including the necessary documents upon disposition of his case. The fact that many of these conscripts were in fact excused proved nothing, although the prosecutor might claim that he had taken money from their parents under false pretenses. In one particular instance, Fayet pleaded that he had been paid a commission for holding a large sum of money to be used for hiring a replacement. Fayet's downfall was sealed, however, when disinterested witnesses, such as other travelers staying at the same inns, testified that he had indeed administered potions to conscripts and had boasted about his influence in procuring *réformes*. The judges sentenced Fayet to the maximum penalty of two years in prison, a 5,000 franc fine, and court costs.[60]

Conscription created an alien and threatening rite of passage for all families, particularly daunting to rural citizens unwise in the ways of the world. Uncertainty and credulity made them inviting targets for influence peddlers and confidence men. To be sure, not all intermediaries who offered their services to these families merit such labels. Some no doubt did little more than escort a young rural conscript through an utterly unfamiliar and dangerous experience at the subprefecture.[61] But the correctional courts also saw a procession of swindlers who had dangled two kinds of enticement before anxious parents. Some promised to get the conscript off by assuring that he drew a good number, implying that they had influence with the authorities or, in very rare cases, that they possessed occult powers. More commonly, they would engage to obtain a *réforme,* either through bribery or by inducing a feigned infirmity. Where the intermediary actually intervened in that fashion, the swindle was legitimate, so to speak, being aimed against the government and not the family paying the money. But most of these operators did little or nothing, simply impressing or frightening the parents, like the schoolmaster in Mondidier who is alleged to have warned one of his marks: "Yesterday I got six excused, but one young man who did not wish to deal with me has fallen [in the *tirage*]."[62]

If the conscript was actually inducted, the intermediary would not collect the full amount agreed to; sharp operators might in fact return all the money of those not excused in order to cultivate other dupes.[63] But when a conscript drew a good number or received a legitimate *dispense,* the swindler could claim to have exercised his influence, and credulous and grateful parents would be none the wiser. The authorities attempted to discover and prosecute the men and women who preyed on the families of conscripts in this way—these "dishonest pimps," as one prosecutor called them—but for every case of extortion or fraud that ended up in court, others surely never came to light, not least because the only witnesses were apt to be relatives fearful of forfeiting the conscript's *dispense* or of being prosecuted themselves if they came forward. Conscription fraud, as several prefects observed, "places an odious tax on the inhabitants of the countryside, and poisons at its source that most useful institution."[64]

The government itself had several different, even contradictory, interests to protect at the medical review. On the one hand the system had to render a just dispensation to the unfit while also preventing physically fit but well-connected conscripts from slipping through by virtue of negligence, favoritism, fraud, or corruption. On the other hand the army required a medical review rigorous enough to weed out men who would be of little military use. The units that received recruits of dubious physical fitness might well send them home (necessitating a new round of inductions in the conscripts' cantons), or else incorporate them only to find that they could not fulfill their duties effectively.

As one prefect complained, recruiting officers could be excessively rigorous—not in the sense of dismissing dubious claims for *dispenses* but on the contrary in rejecting recruits whose physical fitness seemed adequate to civilian eyes, especially to those of their fellow conscripts, but not to the exacting standards of the military.[65] To Lacuée, now director general of conscription, it was indeed better to weed out the unfit during the conscription process rather than later. "Despite my strong exhortations and reiterated instructions," he complained, "the conscription of 1806 has produced a very large number of *réformes* carried out by the military units. These *réformes* cause great harm, occasioning enormous expenses for the state and causing many men to lose valuable stretches of time."[66]

Yet one could err in the opposite direction as well. Vincent-Marie Vaublanc, the prefect of the Moselle after 1806, for example, became known for his hard line in mustering out any conscript who was not "strong and vigorous, in condition to become a good soldier in a short time." In most departments, Vaublanc claimed, "they send to the military units young men who are feeble and malingerers, as long as they do not have severe infirmities. . . . In those departments, *réformes* are less numerous. But if it is a vice to multiply *réformes* [as we do in the Moselle], it is not much better to send to the army these young men who lack the strength to sustain its strains."[67] Lacuée presumably would have approved, but a new director general of conscription faulted Vaublanc's excessive rigor, because it was unjust to the aggregate of conscripts to be so demanding, and because such elastic standards for a *réforme* opened the door to corruption or favoritism. Though insisting he was right, Vaublanc agreed to grant *réformes* less readily in 1811, and to follow new ministry guidelines by inducting "men with flat or unusual feet, provided they are not deformed; those blind in the left eye; those with reducible hernias or small goiters"—conditions which had once been grounds for a *réforme* in his department. As the official *instruction* now suggested, such men might not be able to serve in line infantry units, but they could be fitted to other roles.[68]

While this eminently functional question of military fitness exercised battalion officers and War Ministry officials, ordinary citizens were even more sensitive to the equity of the medical review. Perceptions of impropriety in granting physical dispensations dogged the conscription system from its inception. "Even a single dispensation attributed to favoritism" could stir up a storm, one public prosecutor observed, in recounting how the son of a prefectorial counselor had been forced to flee his commune and the wrath of his fellow conscripts. "Having seen him shoot down birds in flight with dexterity, and regarding him as more adept than themselves at childhood games, they were more than mildly surprised to see him excused because of an alleged myopia, and they screamed."[69] Occasional indictments for fraud or corruption fed public suspicions, but government efforts to uncover such practices lagged far behind public belief in their existence. More than the option of replacement, it seems, questions about the impartiality of the review process, of unmerited *dispenses,* could polarize rich and poor and alienate citizens.

In the Drôme, for example, the prefect publicly acknowledged rumors about infidelities in the review process, "rumors which have become so widespread as to take on the character of a public clamor." Although he declared much of this to be calumny, he recognized the need for public confidence in the process, and informed the citizens of the department that he had requested an investigation by the prosecuting attorney. In private he used blunter language with the minister of justice, warning of a general and profound loss of confidence in the integrity of the conscription process.[70] Around the same time the prefect of the Orne in Normandy attributed a serious draft riot at Sées not to conscription itself but "to more or less legitimate complaints against those who believe that they are entitled to claim exemptions [i.e., *réformes*] . . . that if he is rich, he will be exempt." An even more demoralizing suspicion took hold in the Oise that the government itself encouraged such corrupt practices. "Some people have spread the rumor that the Government is not exactly upset when it is fairly easy to obtain *réformes,* because the excused conscripts pay an indemnity and, being replaced in every case by other able-bodied conscripts, it has gained the men and the money at the same time."[71] Citizens indeed knew that the indemnities for *dispenses* formed a kind of surtax on those families able to pay, and they could draw their own conclusions. By 1810, the government had in fact levied 26 million francs in such indemnities and had already collected over 23 million francs— virtually covering all administrative expenses of conscription in those years.[72]

A petition by one Fremont, a merchant in Vinacourt (Somme), suggests just how resentment could build among the families of conscripts. For the levy of 1808 in his canton, 150 conscripts presented themselves to fill a quota of 32. When his son drew No. 89, Fremont thought he could breathe easily. But the medical review excused thirty-seven conscripts with lower numbers, raising the critical threshold for his son dramatically. "It is neither probable nor acceptable that more than half the young men should be found incapable of serving," Fremont complained. "Fraud [among the wealthy] is evident. . . . All the canton is saying so, certain that *réformes* are going for 100 *louis* each." The perception of corruption disgusted many families and provoked draft evasion, he continued, in turn bringing the critical number up to 86. Four months later, another call came to fill vacancies in the canton's quota. With the cut-off this time at No. 96, his son was inducted and ordered to march.[73]

Though perhaps assuaged by the flow of revenue from the indemnities, officials fretted about the high numbers of *dispenses.* Nationally during the Napoleonic years over one third of all conscripts received dispensations as physically unfit for military service. Everywhere insufficient height accounted for the largest percentage of *dispenses,* even among the generally taller and more robust populations of the Northeast. Although the government low-ered the minimum height several times, it offset this by advancing the levies so that conscripts were being called for review at age nineteen or even eighteen rather than twenty.[74] After rejections for inadequate height, the leading infirmities that could gain a *dispense* varied from place to place. In some departments, endemic diseases such as goiter and scrofula (tuberculo-sis) ravaged the young conscripts; in others, lameness and deformities headed the list. In the Ain, flat feet, "weak constitutions" marked by skeletal thin-ness, and tubercular ulcers were especially common. Hernias, fractures, and vision problems usually contributed significantly to the total as well.[75]

Since the government set draft quotas with reference to the total popula-tion of departments rather than the likely number of apt conscripts, conscrip-tion became especially onerous in rugged departments like the Puy-de-Dôme known for their teeming but sickly inhabitants.

> The population in this department is late in its growth. Instead of dealing with men, levies upon eighteen- and nineteen-year-olds encounter a horde of children that one can only defer *(ajourner)* for subsequent levies. Many of them do not develop any further at all, and at each conscription the number of *réformés* for lack of height reaches from a quarter to a third of the class. There are some cantons where half the population never attains a human stature. Tuberculosis, goiters, and flat feet, which deform a large part of that race and render it unfit for marching, carry off another third. Rheumatism and ulcerated legs infest the rest.[76]

Similarly in the Breton department of Ille-et-Vilaine, claimed its prefect, almost half the conscripts proved physically unfit to begin with, either underdeveloped or suffering from "scrofulitic humors that prevail in many families."[77]

Faced with sharp regional variations in the proportion of *réformés*, officials pondered whether they reflected differences of human morphology or envi-ronment, or whether they pointed to an underlying distortion in the adminis-tration of conscription—either laxity, corruption, or excessive rigor. Espe-cially troubling were disparities in contiguous departments where "the human types ought to be the same." Thus for the five conscription classes of 1808–11, the rates of *réformes* in the adjacent eastern departments of Meurthe and Moselle were 30 and 50 percent (the anomaly of Vaublanc's approach in the Moselle no doubt explaining this particular case); in Mayenne and Sarthe, 38 and 47 percent; in the Breton departments of Vendée and Deux-Sèvres, 27 and 54 percent; and in the two Alsatian departments of Haut-Rhin and Bas-Rhin, 21 and 39 percent.[78]

Inadequate height and manifest infirmities, such as lost or atrophied limbs, lameness, goiters, scrofula, and blindness, could be judged with relative objectivity. But the inherent subjectivity of other disabilities constituted an intractable administrative challenge. Even if they were patent, need such infirmities disqualify a conscript from service? Hernias, for example, varied in graveness and permanence, as did ulcerations, breathing problems, urinary ailments, nervous disorders, or vision problems. Myopia and "weak constitution" *(faible complexion)*, two of the most common grounds for *dispenses,* were also among the most subjective. By 1811, the director general of conscription issued standard regulations to help define the criteria for such *dispenses,* but acknowledged that vision problems, among others, posed "many difficulties" for the recruitment councils. His *Instruction* listed physical symptoms such as dilation to aid doctors in establishing their diagnoses, but the uncertain state of medical technique obviously impeded this quest for certainty.[79]

In a study of 372 candidates for the bar in about half the departments, a startling 42 percent had satisfied the conscription laws with *dispenses* for physical cause. Of the 111 of these 158 *réformés* about whom we have specific information, a suspiciously high 27 were excused for vision problems, mostly myopia—the equivalent of a lucky wound in combat, an infirmity grave enough to gain a *réforme* without incapacitating one's future life—while a dozen were freed because of *faible complexion.* To be sure, some of these aspirants to the bar won *dispenses* for grave and even horrific maladies, and others, even if they seemed vague, may well have been debilitating. Pierre Maurel of the Hérault, for example, certainly sounded devastated by his afflictions: "a great feebleness in the organs of respiration; suffered several attacks of hemophystie; his whole physical system indicates insufficient stamina to support the fatigues of war." But the future attorneys had relatively few *dispenses* for objective deficiencies such as lack of height, scrofula, goiter, or lameness, while garnering a substantial number for relatively mild or subjective infirmities—including one conscript from the Haute-Saône excused because he was "atteint d'affections hypocondriales héréditaires"! One cannot help suspecting that some of these aspiring bourgeois might have enjoyed a measure of special consideration during the medical review.[80]

FRAUD, NO LESS than favoritism, bedeviled the review process as well. Self-mutilation by cutting off an index finger remained the most venerable route to a fraudulent *dispense.* If the conscript could convince the recruitment council, with the complicitous testimony of his neighbors, that he had lost his finger in an accident, he might get away with it. On the other hand this was a familiar act and a well-defined crime, subject to serious punishment.

Recruitment councils in most departments usually flushed out a handful of such self-mutilators, automatically placing them at the head of their contingent.[81] Subtler tactics were undoubtedly more common. Application of caustic substances to cause ulcerated lesions; damage inflicted to the genital area or to the eyes; feigning of epilepsy; and, as we have seen, ingestion of potions to make a conscript violently ill—these were the stratagems favored by families bent on obtaining fraudulent *dispenses*.[82] The recruitment council in the Somme let it be known that because fraud abounded in claims of myopia, it would be especially severe in dealing with that malady. "Ulcers have multiplied so prodigiously in hatred of conscription," reported the prefect of Puy-de-Dôme, "because of the ease with which they can be prepared long in advance."[83]

In a typical medical fraud that landed in court, a conscript of 1813 was taken by his father six weeks before the *tirage* to consult a doctor named Poiret,

> to find out if this young man was going to qualify for a *dispense* on the grounds of an infirmity . . . consisting of the contraction of the fingers on the left hand as a result of a burn, which was evidently a sufficient cause for a *réforme*. . . . Poiret nevertheless instilled in Breilly *père* the fear that his son would be obliged to serve. He persuaded him that in order to have his son win a *réforme,* it was necessary to aggravate his affliction, and accordingly he applied a caustic patch [for which he charged 800F].[84]

Dishonest medical practitioners abetted these frauds and profited from the fears and credulity of desperate parents, and so did lay empirics and outright mountebanks, such as the itinerant hawker convicted of "having sold to a conscript drugs said to induce artificial infirmities," although the substance proved upon analysis to be harmless, or the woman denounced by several conscripts whom she had defrauded "by selling them a kind of bandage which was supposed to get them *réformé.*" More troubling was the farmer charged with taking in future conscripts under guise of employing them "in order to instruct them in how to feign maladies such as deafness, epilepsy, and others, and also with giving them potions to induce the appearance of those maladies."[85]

In 1806, the minister of justice launched an inquiry into the problem of conscription fraud, while exhorting public prosecutors to root out those "vile swindlers . . . [whose] purported influence is nothing more than the infamous art of corrupting minor officials . . . [or who] hold families to ransom for services that they do not render." Most such cases ended up in misdemeanor or correctional courts that sat without juries, but even so the minister feared leniency in the disposition of such cases, and he demanded that prosecutors file appeals in the appellate courts against unwarranted acquittals or light sentences. Most prosecutors assured the minister that they had the situation under control and that acquittals were no longer common, but they acknowledged that such crimes were extremely hard to uncover. The minister thanked his prosecutors for their zeal, but warned them to remain vigilant against this seemingly irrepressible variety of cupidity: "Make sure that the attraction of gain cedes to the fear of punishment."[86]

The inadequate height or genuine infirmities of so many conscripts consistently weighed down recruitment and raised the chances that a physically fit young man would draw a low number. But the problem of fraudulent *dispenses* probably abated with time. Increasing familiarity with such ruses, the winnowing out of incompetent or corrupt doctors hired for the medical reviews, improved procedures for conducting those reviews, and the cumulative effect of prosecutions for fraud or corruption likely enhanced the integrity of the medical reviews.

The Battle Against Draft Evasion

If medical dispensations and replacement offered legal means to avoid military service, able-bodied French youths who could not hire a *suppléant* or qualify for a *dispense* might free themselves from conscription simply by fleeing. Some conscripts refused to turn out for the draft lottery at all or, after complying with their summons in the hope of drawing a high number, did not show up on the designated day of departure if their number proved too low. Still others bade their families farewell and set out with their comrades, only to desert en route to their units. The prefect had to replace all these draft evaders *(réfractaires)* with other local conscripts in order to meet his departmental quota, and he then shared responsibility for apprehending them. From the perspective of public order, draft evaders and military deserters— soldiers incorporated into their units who subsequently deserted—posed a similar policing problem and were often subsumed under the common heading of *insoumission*. Indeed, when bands of *insoumis* went marauding through the countryside, it mattered little whether they were draft evaders, military deserters, or both. But deserters did not have the direct impact of draft evaders on conscription, since desertions did not count against departmental draft quotas.[87]

Avoiding the army by deserting en route seemed to be a favored resort of conscripts during the directorial levies of 1798–99; as War Minister Schérer complained, "after demonstrating civic zeal, the conscripts have

melted away in large numbers before arriving at their destination." Though
it might reflect willful resistance, such desertion en route was prompted as
well by material causes: "The manner in which conscripts have been treated
along several routes has provoked desertion," Schérer admitted. "They are
made to sleep in the open air and are lacking food." [88] Routinization and
careful planning by recruitment officers for this first traumatic contact between civilians and military life was likely to reduce such reactive flight. But
a general resistance to conscription remained the foremost domestic challenge to the Napoleonic state. Far from curbing *insoumission,* Brumaire was
likely to increase its incidence as annual draft levies became a permanent
feature of the civic order.

Draft resistance occurred almost everywhere, but certain regions proved
far more refractory to military conscription than others. In the five levies
between Years IX and XIII, for example, 72 percent of the designated
conscripts nationally actually reached their units for incorporation, while an
average of 28 percent fled. But most of the eighteen eastern departments had
considerably smaller percentages of draft evaders than the national average,
while sixteen of the twenty-four departments of the Midi had significantly
higher rates of *insoumission,* as did all twelve departments in the Massif
Central. [89] Officials in Paris and the provinces understood that draft evasion
was most likely in mountainous, forested, or marshy areas that provided
ready refuge, and they recognized that in regions like the Limousin and the
Auvergne with long-standing patterns of migratory labor, many conscripts
were likely to be away when the call came. [90] Yet its own imperatives
doubtless clouded the official mind in its grasp of the problem.

For as Alan Forrest suggests in his recent book on resistance to military
service during the Revolution and Empire, *insoumission* was so massive that
it cannot be regarded simply as a matter of individual decisions. Instead, it
bespoke a social environment in regions where the habit of soldiering had
never taken root, an environment which condoned draft evasion and the
impetus to resist the authority of the state. "In large measure," Forrest
convincingly argues, "those electing to desert or to avoid service did so in a
climate that favored their actions, where they could be assured of a degree
of support or at least of understanding from their own communities." [91]
From this perspective, the gendarmerie was not, as it must have believed,
pursuing criminals and deviants when it hunted down *réfractaires,* but was
engaged in a demoralizing struggle with entire rural communities.

On its side the state hardly lacked weapons, for it could deploy the full
armature of the new prefectorial system, a streamlined network of courts and
public prosecutors, and the policing apparatus of the gendarmerie and the
military. Strings of decisive military victories, cynical news management

papering over casualties, and control of a potentially oppositional Church reinforced the government's position. But the outcome of this long, grinding struggle between the state and its citizens remained in doubt. The profound rural resistance described by Forrest logically leads one to expect that the government would never succeed. Understandably skeptical about the reality of state power at the grass roots, Forrest scarcely prepares himself or his readers for the astonishing outcome. For after years of intense frustration, the Napoleonic regime did finally prevail, as we shall see. [92]

Initially, however, the government had to retreat. Faced by a staggering backlog of draft evaders and deserters from the levies of the Convention and Directory, the Consulate finally wiped the slate clean in May 1802 by proclaiming an amnesty. *Insoumis* from the levies of the 1790s who turned themselves in would be "excused from resuming service." An estimated 155,000 fugitives took advantage of this pardon, while about 17,000 *insoumis* from subsequent conscription classes surrendered as well, the majority being obliged to take up service. [93] Of course an amnesty might make future recruitment even more difficult, just as a debt repudiation can deter future lenders. The alternative of pursuing an impossibly long list of fugitives, however, had become an administrative and policing nightmare corrosive to stability and order. [94] But even if the amnesty of 1802 would not be the last offered by the regime, amnesties could scarcely serve as a routine instrument of policy. Alongside the routinization that gradually made conscription a "habit," coercion became the order of the day.

The Jourdan Law of 1798 had proposed "exheredition" as the primary "coercive means" to enforce conscription. Draft evaders would not only lose their rights of citizenship but would suffer civil death, "unable to dispose of their property, nor receive any inheritance, legacy, or donation." The legislature understood that this sanction could be effective only against propertied families: "This precious class is [thereby] irrevocably fixed to the colors," declared deputy Laveaux, while acknowledging that "the class of non-proprietors cannot be reached by this article." [95] Against ordinary citizens, routine policing would have to suffice. The Consulate, however, quickly dropped this convoluted tactic in favor of a straightforward assault on the purse of refractory families through an automatic fine of 1,500 livres. After the departmental recruitment council declared a conscript to be a *réfractaire*, the prefect was to draft a decree holding the conscript and his family "civily responsible" for the fine, and then submit it to the local civil court, which was to register the decree and officially notify both the gendarmerie and the departmental recorder *(enregistrement)*. The decree was not contestable in court, however. If a family felt that it had been victimized by circumstances, misunderstanding, or administrative error, it could only protest to the War

Ministry, which alone had the power to reverse a prefect's declaration on the latter's recommendation.[96] Fathers who claimed to have done everything possible to persuade recalcitrant sons to comply with the law emerge as the most interesting petitioners for redress, but officials tended to be skeptical of such claims. As the prefect of the Oise put it, for every father "who has the misfortune of having children who rebel against his counsel," ten others have been complicitous.[97]

Like the quixotic penalty of exheredition, however, a 1,500 franc fine truly threatened only wealthy families; those without property or assets could hardly be made to pay. The statistics underscore the futility of that sanction for the general population. As of January 1810, over 267 million francs worth of fines had been levied against the families of *réfractaires*, but less than 1 percent had been collected! Moreover Lacuée concluded that only about 10 million francs of the remainder could be considered recoverable at all.[98] And even if this pecuniary sanction did at least deter the propertied from resorting to draft evasion, their complicity with others contributed to the overall pattern. Apart from any general sense of communal solidarity—Forrest, for example, suggests that villagers generally tolerated the petty criminality of fugitive *insoumis*[99]—draft evaders formed a reservoir of cheap labor comparable to indentured servants. For while some *réfractaires* lived at the margins and readily turned to brigandage, the majority no doubt tried to reestablish the semblance of a normal routine. Draft evaders typically lived a twilight existence, accepting subsistence wages in exchange for being sheltered from the gendarmerie by employers in their own communities or elsewhere.[100]

Such employers risked arrest for harboring a draft evader, a misdemeanor typically punishable upon conviction by a year in prison and a 500 franc fine. But how great was the actual risk? The law, after all, stipulated that they must have acted "knowingly" *(d'avoir recelé sciemment)*. Naturally prosecutors placed the onus of proof on the accused; employers were supposed to scrutinize the papers of young men they hired, and take them to the mayor for an official verification of those papers. Moreover the law did not require that the employer house the fugitive or even employ him on a long-term contractual basis to be guilty of harboring.[101] But it was another matter to win a conviction in court. For one thing, the proliferation of forged papers among draft evaders hampered the determination of culpability. Acting either from sympathy or venality, hometown mayors often produced false birth certificates, attestations that conscripts had satisfied the conscription laws, or internal passports—documents which allowed a *réfractaire* to begin creating a new identity elsewhere.[102]

Judges on the correctional courts, and even on the criminal courts which heard cases on appeal, displayed a pronounced leniency in these cases, often acquitting when any circumstance called into question how "knowingly" the accused harborer had acted. They also placed an impossible burden on the gendarmes, who were told to produce meticulous *procès-verbaux* for offenses that seemed to them open and shut. "The courts have not yet had the courage to convict a large number of those harboring conscripts," complained the prosecutor in Saône-et-Loire. "They do not find the *procès-verbaux* of the gendarmerie adequate . . . but require that they be supported by the testimony of witnesses—for even the declaration of only one witness does not seem sufficient to them."[103] In fact the state won twice as many convictions for conscription fraud and extortion as it did for the presumably more common practice of harboring a fugitive conscript.[104] Interestingly, after the Restoration, the Bourbon regime continued to prosecute cases of fraud or corruption, but immediately released those awaiting trial for harboring deserters and draft evaders—a retrospective clue, no doubt, to the prevailing public mood on this matter.[105]

Fining the parents of *réfractaires* or prosecuting *receleurs* did relatively little, then, to halt the tide of *insoumission*. Nor could an undermanned, overworked gendarmerie hope to apprehend a significant number of fugitives on the ever-lengthening lists that came down from the prefectures. To increase the pressure on *réfractaires* to turn themselves in, the state could also send out *garnisaires*—soldiers, local veterans, or national guardsmen billeted on the houses of the fugitives' parents at the latter's expense. The monarchy had long used *garnisaires* to extract payments from recalcitrant taxpayers, and the republic sporadically tried them to enforce the levies of the 1798–99. Under the Empire this was a standard technique of intimidation, but it became problematic when poor parents lacked the resources to cover the daily pay of the *garnisaires* (usually four to a home), the key to the whole procedure. True, the authorities could seize the family's possessions to meet the costs, but that prerogative too was likely to be futile when the parents were indigent or quick enough to transfer their assets.[106]

Finally, under their emergency power of *haute police* (reason of state), prefects could authorize the imprisonment of parents suspected of abetting draft evasion, in the hope of inducing their sons to surrender. But under conflicting instructions to spare their constituents (and the economy) as much as possible, prefects evidently used this power only in extreme situations.[107] All these coercive means brought unpleasant, even dire pressure on the families and produced some results, but their inherent limitations precluded any real breakthrough. Above all, they did not touch the veritable pressure points of communal complicity.

In January 1806, the prefect of Saône-et-Loire wrote a remarkably frank report to the minister of the interior: "I had exhausted every legal means I

could think of within my power to arrest about three hundred draft evaders
and deserters who were hiding out in the arrondissement of Autun," and
whose presence compromised all future levies. The prefect described it as a
typical situation, where most of the fugitives' parents were "proletarians
. . . [but] the wealthiest citizens were no strangers to their flight." On the
verge of "declaring my impotence and resigning," the prefect decided to
make one last try, "using the most decisive measures to vanquish the resistance." He ordered *garnisaires* into the homes of the fugitives' parents; but
since they could not pay the billeting costs of the operation, he assessed the
twenty largest taxpayers of the district with the anticipated charges, though
recognizing that his decree "was not authorized by legislation." Their contributions would be collectible like ordinary taxes, meaning that their property
would be seized if they did not pay. As intended, "the obligation to pay these
advances interested those citizens in joining to arrest the deserters." Within
a month, 255 fugitives were apprehended. "My decree was illegal," he concluded, "but I have fulfilled my duty." And, he added, he believed that his
colleagues in several departments were doing the same thing. [108]

This was indeed the case. Prefects in at least twenty departments with
serious rates of *insoumission* had begun to use *garnisaires* against communities
rather than individuals, usually by assessing the wealthiest taxpayers in advance, leaving them to claim compensation from their communes. By most
testimony, these measures produced a double success: the arrest of large
numbers of fugitives, and smoother results in subsequent levies. But this was
also a policy of dubious legality. When the matter came before the Council
of State—perhaps by way of an outraged citizen of Autun who had been
billed 84 francs—it found such tactics improper. New guidelines went out
from Paris, "requiring measures that were much gentler and therefore less
efficacious." [109]

Now it was the prefects' turn to protest. With exceptions, they vehemently maintained that without these draconian procedures, draft resistance
would be "incurable" and recruitment "impossible." [110] After some soul-
searching, the government reversed itself. "I will not pretend that this measure does not deviate a bit from civil law," observed Lacuée, "but constant
experience has convinced me that it is chimerical to adhere to the law rigidly
(s'en tenir au droit rigoureux) in the matter of conscription." [111] By mid-1808 the
gloves came off again, and even the official handbook of civil administration
sanctioned the practice. Prefects now routinely expedited the payment of
garnisaires, either by assessing the largest taxpayers (who would then try to
recover from the commune) or, after certifying the cost, by instructing the
commune to pay it directly from municipal funds or by means of a special
proportional surtax. [112]

From time to time the government also unleashed a more dramatic form of intimidation: the mobile column. The ultimate response to serious internal disorder, mobile columns conducted small-scale military campaigns against domestic targets when the gendarmerie no longer sufficed. Used in the recent past against brigands and royalists, mobile columns comprised regular troops reinforced with local auxiliaries. Communities caught in their path detested this scourge, which could scarcely seem more benign to them than brigandage itself, and villagers were known to flee en masse with their livestock before the onslaught of a mobile column. As the prefect of the Nord once complained, "the pay and food of the mobile columns becomes in each commune the subject of vexation and ruinous measures, which paralyzes the collection of taxes." Astute prefects did what they could to keep them at bay, but when *insoumission* got out of hand in a department the government was prepared to order them in.[113]

In 1810–11 the regime made an all-out, multi-front assault on *insoumission*. First it proclaimed a limited amnesty in conjunction with Napoleon's marriage in March 1810. (21,000 *insoumis* out of the current total of 115,000 responded, of whom 12,000 were incorporated into the army and the remainder discharged.)[114] Then in February 1811 the order went out from Paris to form mobile columns against the backlog of draft evaders and deserters still infesting many departments. Between those two dates, about 15,000 additional *insoumis* had been arrested, leaving a total of 78,000 earlier fugitives (45,000 *réfractaires* and 33,000 deserters), who were joined in the course of the next year by a trickle of new draft evaders and a deluge of new deserters. On the heels of a stepped-up use of *garnisaires,* the mobile columns produced dramatic results in the course of 1811, apprehending or flushing out over 100,000 *insoumis,* new and old.[115]

The threat of mobile columns prompted some communities to take policing into their own hands. Thus in the Gers, an endemically refractory department that had had several brushes with mobile columns in the past, the number of fugitives reportedly fell sharply because of "the numerous arrests that the communes have brought about on all sides or because of the voluntary surrenders that they induced, in order to avoid the costs of the mobile column that was about to enter their territory." In the Tarn-et-Garonne, wealthy proprietors offered rewards of 100 francs to *insoumis* who turned themselves in or to citizens apprehending them, while in the Hautes-Alpes parents rushed to persuade their children to descend from hiding—all in order to keep the mobile columns out of their cantons.[116]

Not surprisingly, the campaign of 1811 had a differential impact on draft evasion and desertion. Where once they had been more or less on a par numerically, desertion continued to increase while the mobile columns were operating, whereas draft evasion fell dramatically. In 1811, the ministry recorded over 54,000 new desertions, but only 6,500 new cases of draft evasion, and far fewer if non-French departments are subtracted. By the time the last mobile columns disbanded in February 1812, only 9,000 *réfractaires* remained at large, many of them probably dead or permanently vanished.[117]

TRIUMPH AND COLLAPSE

Even before the big push of 1811, draft evasion had been abating for several years. Bureaucratic routine, propaganda, fines, arrests, and *garnisaires* had cumulatively cut into the will to resist. In his final report as director general of conscription, Lacuée observed in January 1810 that "the number of *réfractaires* formerly so considerable has undergone a progressive decline. The class of 1806 had 52 per 1,000 conscripts; the class of 1810 has only about 16 out of 1,000."[118] Now in 1811 this trend accelerated, thanks to the mobile columns. From department after department—especially from laggard ones notorious for draft evasion—word came of unusual ease and success in conscription. Precisely when one would expect draft resistance to stiffen in the face of more frequent and larger levies (see Table XIII-1), it waned dramatically. The unprecedented compliance of the "classes" of 1811 and 1812 was clearly more than a temporary response to *force majeure*. It reflected the cumulative impact of bureaucratic and coercive pressure, and it continued after the mobile columns disbanded. It should be viewed as a structural mutation—not in attitude, for conscription remained unpopular, but in behavior. An instinctive and by now traditional resistance to conscription was giving way to a grudging compliance.

In the Aveyron, one of the more refractory departments in the generally recalcitrant Midi, the prefect reported in 1811 that *garnisaires* and mobile columns had helped greatly: "They proved to the inhabitants that there is no way of eluding the law and that it is in everyone's interest to have the designated conscripts march." His remarks on the next year's contingent were equally upbeat: "The levy of 1812 has been carried out with a success that exceeds all we could hope for." In the levies of 1806–10, Aveyron had over 4,500 *réfractaires;* now, it seemed, "the aversion to military service has been overcome." Despite its high quotas, only a handful fled the levies for the classes of 1811 and 1812.[119] The prefect in neighboring Gard believed that "soon the department will be entirely free of *réfractaires*"—a remarkable shift from his excuses and apologies of earlier years. Ardèche experienced the same change. From 143 *réfractaires* in the class of 1810, the class of 1811 had under ten. In the notorious Tarn, a similar breakthrough occurred. The class of 1807, for example, had over 200 *réfractaires* against its quota of 616; in the class of 1811, however, only 31 conscripts fled, of whom some were quickly apprehended. The following year the prefect reported that "operations were carried out with the greatest ease," and at the beginning of 1813 he was just as sanguine: "at no time in the past have the levies been carried out with such calm and docility." Even the supremely refractory Ariège deparmtent conformed to the trend of declining draft resistance: in 1806, the department had an impossibly large 1,002 *réfractaires;* subsequent years saw a gradual decline but still substantial numbers: 783, 714, 618, and 492. Then, in 1811, the number fell to about twenty.[120]

In the Massif Central—a region par excellence of draft evasion—the government enjoyed similar success. "Repugnance for military service" seemed endemic in the Corrèze, where almost 4,000 *réfractaires* had been denounced in 1806–10, with 400 in the class of 1810. But in the class of 1811, only fourteen conscripts fled. In neighboring Lot, the story was much the same, while in Haute-Loire, where the norm had been at least two hundred *réfractaires* a year before 1810, only seven were reported in 1811. Examples could be multiplied from all regions. The populous Nord department, for one, had always contributed one of the largest contingents of soldiers while also coping with hordes of draft evaders—4,850 having been recorded during 1806–10. In 1811, the prefect reported that with only six *réfractaires,* "no other levy has operated with such satisfying success."[121] In almost all departments, the class of 1812 (called up in December 1811) and the class of 1813 (mobilized in September 1812) complied in similar fashion. Deserters continued to plague the armies, but three bumper crops of conscripts in a row offset them.[122]

Even the dismal military reversals of the winter of 1812–13 did not shatter the new pattern of compliance back home. Naturally, however, the debacle of the *Grande Armée* caused the minister of the interior anxiety. In December 1812, he added to the staggering burden of prefectorial paperwork by requesting confidential letters from the prefects about public spirit in their departments, especially about rumors—those outriders of sedition—and about the progress of conscription, the touchstone of administration. These letters were read, docketed, and summarized in periodic reports to the emperor, and one can well imagine their importance in helping Napoleon set his course. Here he was reassured that his rear was secure, at least in France itself. At exactly a time when the government had every reason to fear massive resistance and its attendant disorders, the great majority of prefects reported up to April or May 1813 that "the levies are operating everywhere without difficulty."[123]

Were his prefects simply telling the minister and the emperor what they wanted to hear? If so, that was a new twist, for in the past they had always emphasized how recalcitrant the inhabitants were despite their administration's best efforts. To tell Paris that all was going well with conscription if in fact it was not would have been a game of short duration and a sure prescription for eventually losing the government's confidence. If there had been serious draft evasion and trouble in filling contingents in the winter of 1812–13, prefects would surely have conveyed their frustration at the uncivic behavior of the citizens, just as they had been doing for years before 1810. Their positive confidential letters, which amplify government statistics and reports, should be considered reliable on this point.

These letters also made it clear that the French people yearned desperately for peace, and dreaded a cycle of defeats and renewed offensives. Before the victory at Lutzen in May 1813, citizens of the Indre-et-Loire feared yet another supplementary levy; but now, the prefect optimistically noted, those rumors had ceased and they looked forward to a respite of two years.[124] This was of course not to be. Confident of replenishing his manpower, Napoleon rebuffed the coalition's peace overtures and resumed the struggle, while ordering new levies of unprecedented size on the class of 1814 and on prior classes.[125] In response, the last vestiges of confidence and goodwill dissipated, and with them any possibility that quotas sent down from Paris could actually be implemented.

By grotesquely overtaxing the remarkable conscription machine that his administration had created, the emperor shattered it completely in the course of 1813. As the prefect of Bas-Rhin had drily warned earlier, difficulties were inevitable "when the number of men required exceeds the number available." During 1813, the dépôts de droit in most departments were stripped of men normally deferred because of their widowed mothers, orphaned siblings, or brothers already in the army. Recruitment councils called back for reexamination conscripts previously excused for insufficient height or infirmities.[126] In the Moselle, for example, Boudelois, a conscript of 1809 "réformé à cause de myopie reconnu absolue et incurable" was summoned for reexamination in 1809, although he had recently been appointed a junior magistrate on the Cour Impériale in Metz.[127] Accelerated, expanded, and repeated levies everywhere jolted the accustomed patterns of life, which had already adjusted themselves to the routines and rhythmns of the regime's normal conscription demands.

In the law faculties of the Imperial University, to take but one small corner of society, the conscriptional juggernaut of 1812–13 had devastating effects. "A sizable number of students have been forced to abandon their studies; all are fearful, all have endured a fatal discouragement," lamented the University's inspectors. Where prefects had once informally deferred third-year law students, they were no longer doing so. Not only did enrollments fall, but repeated military levies distracted the remaining students and "prevented many from following their courses with exactitude and giving themselves over to study with the ardor they once displayed. Fear and uneasiness have produced much discouragement."[128] Nor was the nation's military academy spared. An impressive program had evolved at Saint-Cyr in which upperclassmen helped initiate neophytes into the rigors of military life and the art of command. But in 1812 future officers were dispatched to the front before they could complete their own training, in turn disorganizing and demoralizing the class that entered in 1813.[129]

The only safety for conscripts who had drawn good numbers in the original levy for their class was to marry after the *tirage* and before they were convoked for a supplementary levy. Large numbers of young men scrambled to find that safe harbor, as they had in 1809, after supplementary levies first began. Now, conscripts felt even more desperate. In the town of Angoulême, for example, a fine-grained study shows that the marriage rate among men of conscription age from well-off families rose from 5 percent in 1811 to 19 percent in 1813. A subprefect in Bouches-du-Rhône reported in 1813 that 2035 out of 4143 remaining conscripts in the classes of Year XI–1808 were wed, while the prefect of the Gers estimated that about 4,000 conscripts of prior classes had married "in time." So numerous were marriages in the Jura that the prefect had to deliver supplementary pages for the marriage registers in many communes.[130] In some departments, officials sourly claimed that a substantial number of desperate conscripts were taking widows or spinsters as their brides in highly suspect weddings. "Some of them marry women fifty years and older," complained the prefect of the Tarn. "The civil act is the only thing that attests to these marriages. Otherwise, no marriage contract, no celebration, and no cohabitation at all between the spouses."[131] A few hard-nosed prefects challenged these factitious marriages and rejected them as grounds for exemption.[132] But even legitimate marriages brought no dispensation for mobilized national guardsmen.

ONE MUST PAUSE here to cast a look back at the national guard, since the progressive militarization of French society under the Empire went beyond the regular conscription levies to a resurrection and transformation of that institution. As a kind of urban militia, the national guard had entered an almost terminal decline starting in the Directory years and accelerating under the Empire. Property-owning urban citizens, still nominally obligated to serve periodically on patrol and guard duty in the towns, came to rely on a system of replacement where they effectively paid a permanent cadre of needy men to take over their functions. While Paris collected a general tax to cover this expense, in most towns the eligible guardsmen paid individually when their turn on the roster came. For artisans and others of modest circumstances who could not afford replacements, personal service remained an onerous *corvée*. [133]

Besides functioning as an auxiliary urban police force in the Revolution's early years, the national guard was intended as a potential military reserve—a role it had filled admirably in the spring of 1791, when its ranks provided 100,000 volunteers to the army for one year's service. Napoleon and his advisers hesitated over whether to rely on such civilian reserves untempered by military training and discipline, but by 1805 they accepted the need for a force that could take over garrison duty on the Empire's vulnerable coastline and internal fortifications in an emergency. Organized on paper into legions and cohorts (to distinguish them from the brigades and battalions of the line army), national guards were to receive comparable pay and benefits when mobilized, but it remained unclear how extensive their service might be. Henceforth, however, national guard units would be officered by professionals appointed by the government rather local people chosen through elections.

In November 1806, the emperor signed a decree reaffirming the obligation of Frenchmen between the ages of twenty and sixty to serve in the national guard, with those between the ages of twenty and forty eligible to be called either for internal policing duty or limited military service. He soon mobilized units in some departments to guard the Rhine passages and the English Channel. Then in 1809 during the emperor's absence abroad, Police Minister Joseph Fouché ordered 30,000 national guards in fifteen northern departments mobilized to reinforce French positions against the English invasion of Walchern Island and the threat to Antwerp. At first, Napoleon approved this call-up and censured more timid members of his cabinet who had opposed it. Later, however, the emperor changed his mind and broke with his minister. Uncomfortable with the atavistic revolutionary character of Fouché's move, he subsequently blamed him for spreading alarm among citizens all across the Empire. [134]

After this dramatic episode the regime reconsidered its options, uneasy over the disorganization, public reaction, and cost-effectiveness of mobilizing national guards, but cognizant of a need for greater potential depth in its military establishment. The Senate rationalized matters by dividing the national guard into two components. The *premier ban* comprised non-serving conscripts of the six most recent classes, roughly 600,000 young men between the ages of twenty and twenty-six, while the *second ban* included citizens between twenty-six and forty as well as those who had hired a replacement to take their place in the line army. Napoleon intended to ready about one seventh of the *premier ban* for future mobilization. In effect, this would constitute a supplementary levy on the classes of 1807 to 1812—albeit for duty within the borders of the Empire. His decree of 14 March 1812 established 88 cohorts of 888 men each (without cavalry but with a company of *cannoniers* each), to be organized and prepared for mobilization should the military situation require it. That call went out immediately in the wake of the Russian debacle, on 12 January 1813. Raising the number to a round 100,000, the government simply integrated these national guardsmen into twenty-two regiments of the line and rushed them to Italy and Germany. [135]

Then in April 1813 Napoleon demanded another 80,000 national guards to reinforce his regular units, and also called for the organization of departmental legions of cavalry from the national guard, to be manned by wealthier citizens or their paid replacements. While the mobilization of the *premier ban* in January 1813 proceeded with relative ease, the second call-up caused consternation, rumors that the entire *second ban* would be called, and rebellious discontent. Along with a massive requisition of horses, which in some areas proved more contentious than any government demand on manpower, and the seizure of *biens communaux* discussed in Chapter V, the mobilization of national guards seemed an open-ended threat to families across the nation. [136] Having already taken its own conscription system as far as it could go, the regime seemed to recognize no limits at all.

The dam burst completely with the desperate call of November 1813 for 300,000 men from the classes of 1803 to 1814 for the impending battle of France. A quota of 2,300 in Aveyron finally defeated all mechanisms of persuasion or coercion. With a similar quota in Ardèche, "the levy of 300,000 men presents difficulties that no other has ever yet offered. . . . It was a question of mobilizing men whose age means that they have a position, a fixed existence; one can no longer expect to find that ready obedience that exists among young men of nineteen who are without ties to society." In the Loire, despondency and "resignation" gave way to aggressive hostility by the end of 1813. Demoralization and defeatism spread not only in frontier departments like the Nord, where serious conscription riots erupted, but deep inside the country. In Vienne and elsewhere, handwritten posters attacked the emperor as a destroyer of France. [137]

The final breakdown can be observed in the normally reliable Haute-Saône, where April's levies had already discouraged the prefect. "The star of public spirit is beginning to dim in this department," he warned, although citizens were still making the requisite sacrifices. The prefect himself worked from seven in the morning until ten at night on conscription and requisitions, noting the rumor that his colleague in Pyrénées-Orientales had suffered a nervous breakdown. The toll was greater on society at large. "There is scarcely a family that is not oppressed by conscription. . . . All these levies will not leave an able-bodied bachelor in the department, and they also require the mobilization of many *pères de famille.*" The misery and abandon of retreating columns of wounded soldiers further blackened the atmosphere. By December, graffiti and posters attacking the emperor appeared; on the 15th of that month mass desertion dissolved a contingent of mobilized national guards.[138] In most of France, as in this staunch eastern department, manpower, public spirit, and military cohesion collapsed.

EPILOGUE

In a decade of research on the civic order after 1789, nothing proved more surprising than the triumph of the Napoleonic conscription machine over an endemic pattern of draft resistance, particularly the timing of that success. For one had reason to assume (given the lack of thorough scholarship on the subject) that resistance would metastasize in response to inordinate draft calls after 1809, when Napoleon's international ambitions lost all vestige of restraint. Yet documents from one formerly refractory department after another offer compelling evidence for this unanticipated success. After years of bureaucratic routine and coercion, the state finally prevailed over an instinctive resistance to conscription by civil society in many regions. As it gradually broke the back of draft resistance, the regime placated wealthy families without permitting them a wholesale or definitive escape from the obligation of military service. Ironically, the very efficiency of his conscription machine emboldened the emperor to pursue his suicidal course. If Napoleon had found it within himself seriously to negotiate peace at Dresden or Prague in 1813, we can reasonably speculate that he would have returned to a country shorn of its imperial satellites but as master in his own house. Instead he made impossible demands on his conscription machine and brought on its collapse, leaving the Bourbons to pick up the pieces.

Even before power finally slipped from his grasp, Napoleon's compliant legislature—whose authority over conscription had long since passed to the Senate—deplored his military policy in December 1813: "Conscription has become a dreadful scourge for all France because this measure has always been carried to extremes in its enforcement. . . . A barbarous and purposeless war has regularly swallowed up our young men who have thereby been taken away from education, farming, business, and the trades."[139] Napoleon suppressed this address, but he could not stop Louis XVIII from denouncing conscription and courting popularity by promising to end it. Until 1818, the

Bourbons in fact relied on voluntary enlistments to man their scaled-down army of 150,000 men. Once France regained a semblance of its great power status on the international scene, however, volunteering seemed inadequate and the Bourbons revived the draft, albeit with several crucial differences.

The procedures for the draft lottery that implemented Gouvion Saint-Cyr's recruitment law of 1818 owed almost everything to the Napoleonic experience. But the Bourbon regime claimed that it was not reviving Napoleonic conscription since the new law "immediately frees all the young men who were not designated by lot; once the levy is complete, those not inducted are no longer conscripts."[140] Draft calls, moreover, would be relatively modest since the legislature fixed the size of the army at 240,000, the annual levy at no more than 40,000, and the term of service at six years. If the army needed reserves, it would turn to its own veterans, who remained on call for a number of years after their discharge. Restoration prefects reported that citizens did not resist the demands of this compulsory military recruitment. As one put it with unusual candor, "The young men whom the conscription system had prepared *de longue main* have obeyed with docility and have accepted it as a duty . . . [which is administered with] the strictest impartiality." In particular, as the prefect of the Yonne noted, citizens were reassured by "the promise of not being called back in the future" after the *tirage* for their class.[141]

A one-time-only exposure, low quotas, and well-established, relatively fair procedures for classification and review no doubt made it easier to reimpose this detested obligation without provoking massive resistance. Equally important, the Bourbons provided an extremely liberal replacement option. During the legislative debate, some deputies had gone so far as to suggest that wealthier citizens should be permitted to buy their way out of military service routinely. "All those who do not wish to serve personally shall be excused upon payment of a sum determined by law," proposed the deputy Barthe-Labastide. "By this means well-off families will know in advance the extent of the sacrifices that they will have to make."[142] While the Chamber resisted this astounding formulation, it did remove almost all limitations on hiring replacements, including the Napoleonic ban on intermediaries. Securing replacements for those who could afford to pay quickly became an organized traffic, in effect a branch of the insurance business.[143] Alternatively, propertied families could pool funds in cantonal associations that would secure replacements for those whose sons drew low numbers.[144]

Resort to replacement varied widely by region and from year to year, with the the proportion of replacements nationally averaging about 15 percent of departmental contingents in the 1820s. The price of replacement contracts apparently hovered around the relatively low levels of the early Napoleonic years, while the quality of replacements ranged from robust, mature military veterans to the flotsam of urban society. While new guidelines excused an even larger proportion of conscripts from service for inadequate height or infirmities under the Bourbons than during the Empire, the number of draft evaders (now called *absents*) was far lower, except in historic regions of labor migration like the Cantal and the Creuse. [145] The annual conscription levy of the 1820s might on rare occasions touch off a local commotion, but on the whole it had become as routine as Easter communion, the harvest festival, and taxes.

REFLECTIONS

After the National Assembly proclaimed the sovereignty of the people in 1789, grasped the reins of power as the people's representatives, and asserted the supremacy of law over all other interests, it established a framework of authority that incorporated an unprecedented political participation into a new set of uniform governmental structures. The new civic geography created by the Assembly became the foundation of civic innovations in the future, although the contours of that geography were by no means self-evident and were settled only after sharp debate. While intermediate jurisdictions (districts, cantons, arrondissements) came and went, the departments at the top and the communes at the bottom survived as the locus of civic life. Although the French people could not settle on a stable constitutional framework for their collective existence after 1789, the articulated administrative state fashioned in the Revolution's first year did endure. The question then became: What would successive regimes seek to do with the power they commanded? What policies and institutions did they fashion to implement their priorities? How were their innovations received locally, and how did they fare in practice?

The distinctive scope of this book allows us to view those priorities or choices along parallel lines, as some rose and fell from one regime to another, while others developed incrementally and cumulatively. By examining a dozen or so thematic issues in some depth, and tracing them across the succession of regimes into the Restoration, we can better assess the profound but open-ended impact of 1789 on the civic order.

The *constituants* had provided for a degree of local autonomy alongside their design for national uniformity and governmental hierarchy, but the old-regime heritage of state tutelage over the villages ultimately reasserted itself more forcefully than ever. Apart from the ledgers of the *état civil* and the accumulating copies of the *Bulletin des Lois,* the most tangible artifacts of the new civic order at the village level were the annual communal budgets sent on by local officials for approval to the departmental capitals. State intervention brought new normative expectations to rural communes, including mandates to hire a *garde champêtre* and to maintain local roads. All subsequent governments treated those norms as a high priority, and provisions for a *garde champêtre*'s salary and for the repair of *chemins vicinaux,* funded if necessary by special communal surtaxes, eventually became standard practice in the villages. Those mundane actions stand as markers toward the integration of the countryside into a well-ordered commonwealth—a process fully realized only in the 1880s, as Eugen Weber has argued, but already under way more substantially after 1789 than one might have supposed.[1]

Civic innovations clustered dramatically during the "radical moment" of the National Convention. In the realm of political participation—before the Terror suspended all elections and extinguished free speech—the Convention abandoned the two-tiered censitary suffrage of 1791, committed the republic to the ideal of universal male suffrage, encouraged the formation of political clubs, and offered both electors and trial jurors expense allowances to facilitate participation in those roles for citizens who lacked independent income. When the Convention convoked the first national referendum ever in July 1793, it asked citizens not simply to vote up or down on its new constitution but to discuss the charter in their primary assemblies.

National commitments to primary education and to poor relief had been proposed earlier by deputies to the National and Legislative Assemblies such as Talleyrand and Condorcet, LaRochefoucauld-Liancourt and Bernard d'Airy. But only in 1793 did the Convention move from discourse to practice. The Bouquier Law authorized payment by the national treasury of tuition charges for elementary schooling, coupled with an insistence that parents send their children to school. Dissatisfied with the results of that formula, the Convention adopted the Lakanal Law in November 1794 and aggressively implemented this ambitious approach to universal public education for boys and girls, which provided for state-salaried teachers screened by officials in the districts. Between 1793 and 1794, the Convention also initiated national public assistance programs. The first authorized subventions to poor working families with children they could not support, but the deputies implemented this pledge with only one installment on the promised payments. Instead, the Convention shifted its focus to the elderly and infirm of the countryside, allocating them pensions inscribed on a *"Grand Livre de Bienfaisance Nationale."* In their zeal to rid the country of beggars, meanwhile, the deputies resurrected the old regime's repressive *dépôts de mendicité,* but also broke new ground by offering pensions to get disabled beggars off the streets of the capital.

Another dramatic gesture came in October 1793, when the Convention abruptly deregulated the organized bar completely, suppressed the official functions of the *avoués* in civil litigation, and abolished their very title (the barristers having lost their titles and professional monopolies on pleading back in 1790). In another move against the complexity, delays, and "chicanery" of civil procedure, the Convention mandated compulsory arbitration of divorce proceedings in informal "family tribunals," and adjudication of disputes over *biens communaux* by arbitration. With the *levée en masse* of August 1793, the Convention had earlier transformed the concept of military service. Mobilizing all able-bodied, young bachelors, without the possibility of anyone buying a replacement, the Convention followed through by pledging "patriotic assistance" to needy relatives deprived of the draftees' labor, and generous veterans' benefits to the wounded.

While democratic space contracted brutally in the political and religious spheres during the Terror, the Jacobin government of 1793–94 thus opened other kinds of democratic or egalitarian prospects. Whatever their conceptual weaknesses or practical shortcomings, most of the programs for free public schools, welfare entitlements, and procedural reforms in civil justice, as well as agrarian reforms not discussed here, were implemented by the revolutionary government with conviction. The *conventionnels* formulated this heady brew in haste, however, and did not have the opportunity to see it settle and stabilize. By mid-1795, hyperinflation destroyed the republic's ability to sustain the public schools of the Lakanal Law or the old-age pensions on the *Grand Livre de Bienfaisance Nationale.* An ascendant conservative brand of republicanism then denounced those programs as misguided utopianism, and renounced such ambitious commitments in favor of a far more passive approach to primary education and poor relief.

Still, the Convention's initiatives had implanted the concepts of *instruction publique* and *bienfaisance publique,* and even if their scope contracted drastically for the time being, they did not disappear altogether from the nation's civic agenda. We have seen the debates, policy shifts, and local reactions as successive governments confronted those issues and others like them: the conflicts over the role of private teachers and Catholicism in elementary education; the debate over professionalism versus simplification at the civil bar, and over the selection of notaries by *concours;* the intense criticism and the defense of criminal juries for their propensity toward leniency; the increasing dependence on private charity in the realm of poor relief. But even where the state retreated from previous innovations, residues usually remained, as in the commitment of the Bourbon Restoration to *instruction publique*—interpreted, to be sure, in its own fashion.

The Napoleonic episode (as French historians prefer to call it) simultaneously consolidated and reshaped the new civic order. Even today, the centralizing thrust of that regime seems remarkable. Most visibly, the prefectorial system decisively revised the synthesis of local autonomy and central authority that the National Assembly and the Directory had in turn established. The prefects conflated most functions of the elected departmental administrations and the Directory's appointed commissioners, who had coexisted uneasily under the Constitution of 1795. To be sure, Napoleon appended the *conseils généraux des départements,* which, like their counterparts at the communal level, symbolized an abiding element of local input on tax assessments and budgets that should not be dismissed altogether as an empty gesture. But in the final analysis the prefects monopolized the power to act either directly or through their appointed mayors. We have seen the interior minister and his prefects struggling to expand their influence, to gather effective authority over conscription and other matters they deemed crucial, such as rural policing and the upkeep of *chemins vicinaux.* The unleashing of coordinated mobile columns across the land to pursue *insoumis* in 1811; the plan to brigade the *gardes champêtres* under the gendarmerie in 1812; and the nationalization of *biens communaux* in 1813 stand out as unprecedented extensions of state intervention in local life, the most extreme manifestations of the Napoleonic governing ethos.

Yet Napoleon's centralizing drive was not absolute or comprehensive by any means. First (although historians have without exception overlooked this), the regime intended that the reorganization of local government would entail the merger of small communes. When the Consulate discarded the Directory's cantonal municipalities, it qualified the restoration of communal authority not only by the imposition of appointed mayors (whom it treated— quite fancifully, it turned out—as functionaries of the national government), but also by launching "general projects" in the prefectures to amalgamate the more sparsely populated, poorer, and least viable communes, which numbered in the thousands. Yet, as we have seen, this potential juggernaut of rural consolidation, which would have obliterated communal identity far more than the cantonal form of local government, stalled within a short time. While the *réunion des communes* ostensibly remained on the Empire's agenda, it did not go forward in the intended fashion, because of residual scruples in Paris and local opposition.

Another reservation about Napoleon's reputation for centralizing authority must be registered in connection with poor relief and primary education. Under the Consulate and Empire, the impetus from the center in those domains diminished to the most minimal level, to a kind of benign neglect. Although Napoleon's government did sustain at least the notions of *instruction publique* and *charité publique,* and stopped short of surrendering those functions completely to local voluntarism, its modesty of ambition seems entirely out of keeping with Napoleonic activism in other areas. The relative passivity of the Consulate and Empire toward primary schooling and public assistance was a matter of choice, which leads back, then, to the question of Napoleon's own priorities.

Napoleon created a new framework for lawmaking (by diluting legislative authority with executive initiative) and local authority (by instituting the prefectorial system). He liquidated the religious conflict by cementing anew Church-State relations, in the process trying to enlist the parish clergy as his "moral prefects." His Ministry of Justice restored a degree of corporate organization, professional traditionalism, and state tutelage to bar and bench, where the Revolution had deregulated relentlessly, although the criminal jury survived this process of revision.[2] The Napoleonic state also acted vigorously in the realm of secondary education and cultural production.

The project of legal codification, a central ambition of 1789 to begin with, assuredly stood as one of Napoleon's top commitments. Legal codification advanced prodigiously, not merely with the Civil Code (much of its content foreshadowed by the labors of such men as Cambacérès during the revolutionary decade), but also with the four other codes completed during the Empire: the Criminal Code, the Code of Criminal Procedure, the Code of Civil Procedure, and the Commercial Code—leaving only the elusive Rural Code unachieved. But above all, the Napoleonic state acted in the area of conscription, the door to which had been opened in 1793 without (it seems safe to say) any anticipation of what would follow. We must conclude with some speculation about that singular development.

FROM ONE PERSPECTIVE the French Revolution is a story of unintended consequences and ironic outcomes, as the liberalism of 1789 collapsed into the Terror and then into the Napoleonic dictatorship. Like the classic historians of the nineteenth century, recent scholars have been preoccupied with the problem of 1789/1793. The latest view on this question holds that the ideology or mind-set of the revolutionaries in 1789 was already flawed by a radical dogmatism and a latent illiberalism. When the *constituants* situated power in the unbounded space of popular sovereignty without strict limitations, they gave the representatives of the people—or those claiming to speak for the people—license to justify in the name of the people any policy that served their objectives. The Terror, in this view, was prefigured in 1789, and did not simply emerge from changing circumstances, an injection of violent counter-revolution and radical fanaticism, or the imperatives of "revolutionary necessity."[3] Whatever the merits or deficiencies of such interpretation, the Terror changed the destiny of France. Although in itself an episode of short duration, the Terror unleashed a cycle of recrimination, hatred, and endemic local conflict that made the future prospects of a democratic polity in France very dim. General Bonaparte represented one possible exit from that dilemma, or a cure worse than the malady, depending on one's point of view.

But is the sequence of 1789/1793, of liberalism and Terror, actually the greatest irony posed by the French Revolution? For all the eternal fascination of that enigma, the perspective of this book underlines another unintended outcome of the Revolution: the fact that the great military mobilization of 1793 led to the permanence and continuous expansion of compulsory military service under Napoleon. That the state power marshaled by the revolutionaries of 1789 should in the end have achieved its greatest impact with Napoleonic conscription looms as the cruelest of ironies. True, military conscription was not a prospect entirely alien to the mental universe of 1789, steeped as the revolutionaries were in a sentimentalized Rousseauism, one of whose casual precepts held that citizens should be soldiers and soldiers citizens. Apart from embracing the concept of a national guard, however, the *constituants* in the end rejected this view. When the Convention, out of dire necessity, moved in that direction with the *levée en masse,* it intended this mass mobilization as a one-time only, emergency measure.

The republic's unresolved military and diplomatic situation in 1798 forced the issue again, as the Jourdan Law for the first time established systematic military conscription. As the statistics show, however, it was Napoleon who pressed this civic obligation relentlessly, making it by far the top priority of the French state. Nor did this occur under the duress of possible invasion or civil war and the consequent imperatives of patriotism, but in the relatively tranquil environment of the Empire before the Russian campaign. The Napoleonic conscription machine (with its tightly controlled safety valves of replacement and medical dispensations) arguably produced the most disastrous result of the French Revolution by virtue of the mass slaughter it facilitated through the disease, privation, and battle casualties of the Empire's extravagant military campaigns.

A large segment of the French people assuredly regarded conscription as the most baneful of civic obligations. Initially, the contention it provoked was overshadowed by the religious question—a conflict touched off by the National Assembly's Civil Constitution of the Clergy, deepened by the dechristianization campaigns of the Year II, and perpetuated by the Directory's destructive crusade to implement the republican calendar's ten-day week. The Concordat of 1801 essentially liquidated the religious problem. Military conscription, however, became the one issue that truly threatened civic peace, that produced mass resistance of a sustained, endemic character. But when historians chronicle that resistance, they miss the point if they do not emphasize that in the end—against all odds—the Napoleonic state eventually broke the back of draft evasion and rendered it a largely futile response to the state's inexorable demands.

By Napoleon's choice, conscription constituted the ultimate frontier of state building, of the articulation of the administrative state projected by the Revolution. Our perspective makes it easier to appreciate the import of this outcome, by viewing the results of that commitment as against, say, the potentialities of state action in primary education. Decisions over such matters were not preordained. Under Napoleon, however, conscription became the state's obsession, the preoccupation of officials up and down the government's hierarchy, despite the dispiriting fact that year after year masses of citizens attempted to vote with their feet against it. Under the relentless pressures of the state, the most problematic demand imaginable before the Revolution became a cornerstone of the new civic order.

ACKNOWLEDGMENTS

During the decade of research and writing that went into this book, I enjoyed a sustained intellectual and personal comradeship with several individuals. In France Jean-Paul Bertaud's hospitality, profound knowledge, and keen interest in my project made him a veritable *frère et ami*. The pleasure of working frequently alongside Alan Forrest in the archives similarly enriched my periods of research in Paris. Back in New York, during his four years at Columbia's Heyman Center for the Humanities, I enjoyed countless hours of conversation with Richard Andrews, who shared his passion for French history and the fruits of his research on criminal justice. My long friendship with Mel Edelstein also helped sustain my labors, and in particular yielded a flow of valuable information about revolutionary elections. Finally, R. R. Palmer has never ceased to be a constructive critic as well as an inspiration. To these five *compagnons de route* I extend my deepest thanks.

Exchanges with Steve Clay, Philip Dawson, and Mike Fitzsimmons, while less frequent, proved decidedly stimulating. Closer to home, an unexpected fount of encouragement and insight has come from my son Alex, whose creative talents lie in another field but who has the true intellectual's broad curiosity. My wife Nancy and my son David have been supportive allies through all the frustrations and breakthroughs occasioned by this sort of project. Finally I owe a great debt to my editor and publisher Donald Lamm, as much a servitor of Clio as any history professor could ever be, who knows that historical studies should be readable as well as learned.

Beyond the assistance of Columbia University's faculty research grants, my work was supported by fellowships from the Institute for Advanced Study in Princeton (with particular thanks to Peter Paret), the Ecole des Hautes Etudes en Sciences Sociales in Paris (with thanks to my hosts François Furet and Louis Bergeron), the National Endowment for the Humanities (with gratitude to David Coder for disentangling red tape), the John Simon Guggenheim Foundation, and the American Council of Learned

Societies. I especially appreciate the efforts of my student research assistants Emily Sack, Charles Sullivan, Alan Potofsky, and Anthony Crubaugh. Earlier versions of some material in this book appeared in *Past and Present, The Journal of Modern History, French Historical Studies,* and a number of conference volumes generated by the bi-centennial of the French Revolution, all of which are mentioned in the Notes, and whose editors I thank.

New York City
October 1992

A NOTE ON SOURCES

While the notes that follow constitute in effect a bibliography for each thematic chapter, this section is intended as an overview of the documentary basis for the book. It provides an annotated, sequential listing of materials consulted at the Archives Nationales and other archives, and a brief comment about some of the printed sources. Readers can use this as a point of reference for the shorthand of archival citations in the notes that follow.

SOURCES IN THE ARCHIVES NATIONALES AND OTHER ARCHIVES

D III: *Convention: Comité de Législation:* cartons 321 (criminal tribunals), 371, 378 (notaries), 379.

F ^{1a}: *Documents concernant l'administration départementale et communale:* cartons 50, 408, 417, 422. Contains local *affiches* and circulars on a variety of subjects.

F ^{1c} I: *Esprit public:* cartons 11–13, 43. Includes reports on internal unrest and digests prepared especially for Napoleon.

F ^{1c} II: *Elections:* cartons 31–32 on Napoleonic elections.

F ^{1c} III: subseries *Comptes administratifs, classement départementale* (82 cartons consulted, covering 73 departments). Overall, the most informative source for this study. The series is largely nil for the period of the Convention, somewhat helpful for the Restoration, but fundamental for the Directory and the Empire. Includes weekly or monthly reports from the Directory's commissioners, and quarterly reports from the Napoleonic prefects, as well as correspondence to and from the Interior Ministry about particular matters, petitions, and departmental *comptes-rendus.* Commissioners and prefects were asked to report on about two dozen topics, including "public spirit" and economic matters, but also schooling, *bienfaisance,* communal governance, road repair, policing and conscription.

F² I: *Administration départementale: Objets généraux.* This rarely used series includes cartons 121/10–15: *affaires militaires;* 144; 379–80: *état civil;* 444–45 and 541: *limites des départements et cantons;* 835–36; 840–42: *limites des communes;* 1027: *chemins vicinaux;* and 1201–04: *police rurale* (with revealing inquests on the governance of the communes and the *gardes champêtres*).

F² II: *Délimitation et réunion des communes, série départementale* (33 cartons consulted). Judging by its pristine, dust-covered state, this series had almost never been consulted before, and is the indispensable source on the stalled drive to merge rural communes.

F³ I: *Administration Communale: Objets généraux:* carton 1.

F³ II: *Administration Communale, série départementale* (12 cartons consulted). Especially important for the nationalization of *biens communaux* in 1813.

F⁹: *Affaires Militaires: Recrutement* (32 cartons consulted), including 140–45, 262–63 on the levies; a sampling of 19 departments in the *correspondence générale, classement départementale* [150–261]; 286–87 on fraud; 288–89 on exemptions. Along with F^{1c} III, this series includes material on departmental conscription quotas, procedures, the incidence and pursuit of draft resisters, medical exemptions, fraud, and replacement. Other sources used for conscription include material from series X^s in the Archives of the War Ministry at Vincennes, and from AF IV and BB^{18}, discussed below.

F¹⁵: *Secours* (38 cartons consulted). Contains good material on the Commission des Secours Publics; the implementation of the Convention's welfare entitlements; the unique home relief system of the Paris municipality; the *dépôts de mendicité;* the *Mont de Piété;* mutualism; and the resurgence of charity and organized philanthropy after 1800. For the Paris welfare system, I have also used material from the Departmental Archives of the Seine, and especially from the Archives de l'Assistance Publique in Paris, which holds the surviving minutes of five sectional welfare committees, along with a variety of sources on other aspects of *bienfaisance.*

F¹⁷: *Education* (36 cartons consulted). Particularly rich on the implementation of the Lakanal Law and the *juris d'instruction* of the Year III (especially cartons 1344/35, 1347, 1350–53, 1360–62, 10138); the deteriorating condition of the *instituteurs* (especially 1337, 1344/32 and 33); the period of relative neglect under the Napoleonic regime (especially 1363–66, 10107, 10368–70); and the surge of activity after the Restoration (especially 1395, 9367–68, 10372, 10375–76). For the struggles between private and public schools during the Directory, however, one must also consult the reports in F^{1c} III.

AF III: *Directoire Exécutif:* carton 32 (Ministry of Justice); 101 (public assistance); 104–05 (cantons); 109 *(instruction publique);* 149–151B, 184 (War Ministry);

313/1 and 313/78 (a sampling of the *Demandes relatives à des réquistions, congés et exemptions de service, an V*).

AF IV: *Secrétairerie d'Etat Impériale:* cartons 1051–53 (local affairs); 1064 *(gardes d'honneur);* 1066–67 (poor relief); 1121–26, 1147, 1375 (conscription); 1238 (Interior); 1316 *(affaires diverses).*

BB[2]: *Justice: Affaires Civiles:* cartons 23–25, 28, 32 (containing Ministry of Justice circulars), and 97.

BB[9]: *Organisation Judiciaire et Personnel: Officiers Ministériels.* For the role of the attorneys, the centerpiece of Chapter XI, I have used cartons 163–65 on the restoration of the *avoués* in 1800, and 34 cartons covering 51 departments in the subseries 114–61 *(Avoués: remplacements, demandes de place, fixation de leur nombre)* for subsequent developments at the bar. This material was rounded out with BB[9] B 1 and BB[26]: *Frais de Justice: Avoués—tarifs,* cartons 1–3.

BB[18]: *Division Criminelle: Correspondence Générale:* 11 cartons covering 18 departments from the series *Délits relatifs à la conscription et au recrutement* [1–85] relating to prosecutions for abetting or sheltering draft evaders, conscription fraud, and corruption.

BB[20] 1: Organization of juries.

BB[30]: A miscellaneous repository, which yielded some extremely valuable material: cartons 29–32 (Ministry of Justice, correspondence and reports); 526 (Comments by the presiding judges of the criminal courts in the Year XI on the jury system); 528 (Comments by civil court judges on the proposed Code of Civil Procedure); 1155B (Ministry of Justice circulars on juries and other subjects).

PRINTED PRIMARY SOURCES

Legislative debates generated printed opinions formulated by deputies on all sides of various issues; draft proposals and committee reports during the National Assembly, the Convention, and the Directory; and legislative proposals and supporting arguments by spokesmen for the executive under Napoleon. These are available in the Bibliothèque Nationale, and often in the Maclure Collection at the University of Pennsylvania.

For the study of education, the exhaustive compilation edited by J. Guillaume, *Procès-verbaux du Comité d'Instruction Publique de la Convention Nationale* (6 vols., 1891–1907) is indispensable, and for *bienfaisance,* A. deWatteville, *Législation charitable ou recueil des lois, décrets, ordonnances royales* . . . (1843) is helpful. An extremely useful repository of pamphlets, organized thematically, is the *Series AD: Imprimés* in the Archives Nationales. Cartons consulted there include:

AD I 32–33, 61, 71–72 (local administration and elections)
AD II 33, 37–38, 42, 57 (civil justice)
AD III 46–47 (juries)
AD VI 81–82 (military recruitment)
AD XIV 6, 10, 12 (public assistance)
AD XVI 17, 22, 47, 56 (towns and provinces)

PROVINCIAL NEWSPAPERS WERE not as helpful as anticipated but did occasionally prove rewarding. Those consulted include the *Journal de Poitiers; Journal de la Haute-Garonne; Observateur de l'Yonne; Journal du départment de l'Oise; Journal du département de Seine-et-Oise; Journal du département de Maine-et-Loire; Journal de Rouen;* and *L'Ami de la Liberté: journal d'Angers.* The *Gazette des Tribunaux* and the *Journal des Tribunaux,* both aimed at legal professionals, were good sources for bar, bench, and juries, while Appert's *Journal des Prisons, hospices, écoles primaires et bienfaisance* was valuable for *bienfaisance* after the Restoration. The specialized press on education, however, proved of little help for the study of primary schooling.

INFORMATION ON LOCAL conditions and civic institutions can be culled from departmental almanacs, of which I have consulted about a dozen, especially for the transitional Year VIII, and from the annual *Comptes-Rendus* of their steward-ship by the departmental administrations of the Directory years (which often turn up in the series F^{1c} III). Departmental handbooks published under the auspices of Napoleonic prefects are a goldmine of descriptive and statistical information on demographic, economic, and civic matters. I have used those for the Ain, Ardennes, Aude, Aveyron, Côte d'Or, Dordogne, Eure, Gers, Indre, Indre-et-Loire, Isère, Jura, Meurthe, Moselle, Nord, Oise, Hautes-Pyrénées, Bas-Rhin, Vaucluse, Haute-Vienne, and Vosges. They have been republished on microfiche in the collection entitled *Statistical Sources on the History of France: Prefect Studies Under the Empire,* ed. J.-C. Perrot (Clearwater Press), which also includes the *Description topographique et statistique* by J. Peuchet and P.-G. Chanlaire (1810).

A VALUABLE COMPILATION on conditions in the departments during the Consul-ate is the *Analyse des procès-verbaux des Conseils Généraux des départements: Sessions de l'an VIII et de l'an IX,* edited by Minister of the Interior Chaptal. For conscrip-tion, a fundamental source for the early Napoleonic years is the *Compte Général de la Conscription [1798–1805] de A.-A. Hargenvilliers,* ed. G. Vallé (1937). Among the official and unofficial handbooks that proved illuminating were *Manuel des Agents Municipaux* (an VII); *Manuel des Maires et des adjoints* (an VIII); *Manuel des gardes nationales et des conscrits de l'Empire française* (1812); M. Fleurigeon, *Le Guide des Jurés* (1811); and E. Cassin, *Almanach Philanthropique ou tableau des sociétés et institutions de bienfaisance . . . de Paris* (1827).

NOTES

Unless otherwise indicated, all French materials were published in Paris.

ABBREVIATIONS USED IN THE NOTES

A.A.P.   Archives de l'Assistance Publique

Acad   Académie (territorial division of the Imperial University)

Adm Cent   Central Administration of the Department during the Directory

A.G.   Archives de la Guerre (Vincennes)

AHR   *American Historical Review*

AHRF   *Annales historiques de la Révolution française*

A.N.   Archives Nationales

A.P.   *Archives parlementaires,* 1st series, ed. Mavidal and Laurent (1868–1914 and 1962–)

B.N.   Bibliothèque Nationale

C.A.   Conseil des Anciens (upper legislative house during the Directory)

C500   Conseil des Cinq Cents (lower legislative house during the Directory)

C.I.P.   Comité de l'Instruction Publique of the Convention

j.i.   *juri d'instruction*

JMH   *The Journal of Modern History*

JPHB   *Journal des Prisons, hospices, écoles primaires et bienfaisance*

M.G.   Minister of War

M.I.   Minister of the Interior

M.J.   Minister of Justice

P.G.   Procureur-Général

Pref   Prefect

RF   *La Révolution française* (periodical)

RHMC   *Revue d'histoire moderne et contemporaine*

T.C.   Tribunal Criminel

PREFACE

1. The work was published in several editions in the 1850s, and the standard English translation by Stuart Gilbert dates from 1955. See also R. Herr, *Tocqueville and the Old Regime* (Princeton, 1962), and F. Furet, *Interpreting the French Revolution* (New York, 1981 transl.), 132–63. For the morphology of the term "old regime" during the Revolution, see D. Venturino, "La Naissance de l'"Ancien Régime'," in C. Lucas, ed., *The Political Culture of the French Revolution* (Oxford, 1988), 11–40.

2. Indirectly by E. Weber, *Peasants into Frenchmen: The Modernization of Rural France, 1870–1914* (Stanford, 1976), and explicitly by F. Furet, *La Révolution, de Turgot à Jules Ferry (1770–1880)* (1988).

3. For an innovative general history, see D. Sutherland, *France 1789–1815: Revolution and Counterrevolution* (New York, 1986).

4. *The Identity of France*, Vol. I: *History and Environment* (New York, 1988 transl.), 125–26.

CHAPTER I: LAWMAKING AND LOCAL AUTHORITY

1. See W. Doyle, *Origins of the French Revolution* (Oxford, 1980), chs. 3–10; G. Taylor, "Revolutionary and Non-Revolutionary Content in the Cahiers of 1789," *French Historical Studies*, VII (1972), 479–502; R. Chartier, "Culture, lumières, doléances: les cahiers de 1789," *RHMC*, XXVIII (1981), 68–93; G. Shapiro, "Les Demandes les Plus Répandues dans les Cahiers de Doléances," in M. Vovelle, ed., *L'Image de la Révolution française* (3 vols., 1989), I: 7–14.

2. E. Morgan, *Inventing the People: The Rise of Popular Sovereignty in England and America* (New York, 1988), ch. 2.

3. F. Furet, "La Monarchie et le règlement électoral de 1789," and R. Halévi, "La Monarchie et les élections: position des problèmes," both in K. Baker, ed., *The Political Culture of the Old Regime* (Oxford, 1987). On the elections for the First Estate, see T. Tackett, *Priest and Parish in Eighteenth-Century France* (Princeton, 1977), ch. 10.

4. K. Baker, "Representation," and L. Hunt, "The National Assembly," both in Baker, ed., *Political Culture of the Old Regime;* Baker, "Sovereignty," in F. Furet and M. Ozouf, eds., *A Critical Dictionary of the French Revolution* (Cambridge, Mass., 1989 transl.).

5. J. Godechot, *The Taking of the Bastille: July 14th 1789* (London, 1970 transl.); L. Hunt, "Committees and Communes: Local Politics and National

Revolution in 1789," *Comparative Studies in Society and History,* XVIII (1976), 321–46.

6. See especially M. Fitzsimmons, "Privilege and the Polity in France, 1786–1791," *AHR,* XCII (April 1987), 269–95.

7. A. DeBaecque, et al., *L'An I des Droits de l'homme* (1988); P. Raynaud, "La Déclaration des droits de l'homme," in Lucas, ed., *Political Culture of the French Revolution;* M. Gauchet, "Rights of Man," in *Critical Dictionary of the French Revolution.*

8. On the treatment of the king, compare F. Furet and R. Halévi, "L'Année 1789," *Annales: E.C.S.* (January 1989), 3–24; Halévi, "Monarchiens," in *Critical Dictionary of the French Revolution;* and the unpublished paper by Halévi, "Le Roi Citoyen" with R. R. Palmer, *The Age of the Democratic Revolution* (2 vols, Princeton, 1959–64), I: 489–500.

9. *Projet de décret sur le respect dû à la Loi, proposé par le Comité de Constitution* (1790), 4, in A.N. AD I 86.

10. The account here follows C. Berlet, *Les Provinces au XVIIIe siècle et leur division en départements: essai sur la formation de l'unité française* (1913), 174–245, and M.-V. Ozouf-Marignier, *La Formation des Départments: la représentation du territoire français à la fin du 18e siècle* (1989), part I.

11. Quoted by Ozouf-Marignier, *La Formation des Départements,* 105.

12. For graphic illustrations of the process and results of this territorial division, see D. Nordman and M.-V. Ozouf-Marignier, eds., *Atlas de la Révolution française,* IV: *Le Territoire* (1) (1989), chs. 4–5.

13. See G. Lefebvre, *Les Paysans du Nord Pendant la Révolution française* (2nd edn., 1959); P. Bois, *Paysans de l'Ouest* (1971 edn.), part II; C. Tilly, *The Vendée: A Sociological Analysis of the Counterrevolution of 1793* (Cambridge, Mass., 1964).

14. Ozouf-Marignier, *La Formation des Départments,* part II, and papers by Ted Margadant which predate that volume: "Urban Crisis, Bourgeois Ambition and Revolutionary Ideology in Provincial France, 1789–1790," *Society for French Historical Studies* (March 1982), and "The Rhetoric of Contention: Conflicts Between Towns during the French Revolution," *French Historical Studies,* XVI (Fall 1989), 284–308. This research is synthesized in Margadant's book, *Urban Rivalries During the French Revolution* (Princeton, 1992).

15. The Aisne is discussed by Margadant, drawing on R. Hennequin, *La Formation du Département de l'Aisne en 1790* (Soissons, 1911).

16. A.N. F^2 II Aveyron 1: Pref to M.I., 5 vendémiaire X.

17. See I. Woloch, "The State and the Villages in Revolutionary France," in A. Forrest and P. Jones, eds., *Reshaping France: Town, Country and Region During the French Revolution* (Manchester, 1991); A.N. F^2 II Indre-et-Loire 1: communal maps for Chenusson and St. Laurent-en-Gâtine; A.N. AF III 105: Plan topographique du canton d'Anthully et des différents communes et hameaux le composant.

18.   J. Peuchet and P.G. Chanlaire, *Description topographique et statistique de la France* (1810), reproduced on microfiche by Clearwater Publishing Co. in "Statistical Sources on the History of France: Prefect Studies Under the Empire," edited by J.-C. Perrot. Statistical tables on forty-three departments derived from this compendium—with figures on the agglomerated, dispersed, and urban population of each department; the number of rural communes; and the average population of rural communes—are set out in an appendix to my article "The State and the Villages," in *Reshaping France.*

19.   These examples come from Peuchet and Chanlaire, *Description topographique,* and from A.N. F² II Haute-Garonne 1: Pref. to M.I., 30 October 1810; F² II Corrèze 1: Compte administratif, 1806.

20.   M. Bordes, *L'Administration provinciale et municipale en France au XVIIIe siècle* (1972), 175–98.

21.   J.-P. Jessenne, *Pouvoir au Village et Révolution: Artois, 1760–1848* (Lille, 1987), 44–89.

22.   F. Fortunet, ed., *Pouvoir Municipal et communauté rurale à l'époque révolutionnaire en Côte d'Or, 1789–an IV* (Dijon, 1981), ch. "Le Conseil général: lieu de pouvoir." Cf. P. Jones, *The Peasantry in the French Revolution* (Cambridge, Engl., 1988), ch. 6; and local studies by P. d'Hollander, B. Pommaret, and M. Tandeau de Marsac in *Limousin en Révolution* (Actes du Colloque de Limoges, 1989), 149–82.

23.   L. Gauthier, "Les Municipalités cantonales et la tradition révolutionnaire," *RF,* LXIX (1916), 243–55. For the subsequent role of the cantons, see Chapter IV below.

24.   T. J. LeGoff and D. M. Sutherland, "Revolution and Rural Community in Brittany," *Past and Present* (February 1974), 96–119; P. Jones, *Politics and Rural Society: The Southern Massif Central c 1750–1880* (Cambridge, Engl., 1985), chs. 4–6.

25.   See, e.g., *Almanach du District de Cambrai pour l'année 1792; Almanach du District de Reims, Année 1793; Almanach Civique du Département des Vosges pour l'année 1793.*

26.   For overviews of local administration, see the relevant sections in J. Godechot, *Les Institutions de la France sous la Révolution et l'Empire* (2nd edn., 1968); A. Cobban, "Local Government During the French Revolution," in his *Aspects of the French Revolution* (New York, 1968); and A. Patrick, "French Revolutionary Local Government, 1789–1792," in *Political Culture of the French Revolution.*

27.   L. Hunt, *Politics, Culture, and Class in the French Revolution* (Berkeley, 1984), ch. 5, makes suggestive observations about political careers in the 1790s.

28.   The printed *comptes-rendus* of the departmental administrations during the Directory often turn up in A.N. F¹ᶜ III (série départementale), subseries "Comptes administratifs."

29.   C. J. Mitchell, *The French Legislative Assembly of 1791* (Leiden and New York, 1988), esp. chs. 12–14; also M. Reinhard, *La Chute de la Royauté* (1969).

30. Mitchell, *Legislative Assembly,* ch. 2, convincingly reassesses the political divisions in that body.

31. *Ibid.,* 37, n. 25, citing unpublished calculations by Alison Patrick. For the influence wielded by dominant committee members in the Constituent Assembly, see the biographies of such figures as Thouret, Merlin de Douai, and LaRochefoucauld-Liancourt. See also R. K. Gooch, *Parliamentary Government in France: Revolutionary Origins, 1789–1791* (New York, 1960).

32. Mitchell, *Legislative Assembly,* ch. 3. For a superficial yet interesting survey of all the Revolution's legislative bodies, see G. Dodu, *Le Parlementarisme et les parlementaires sous la Révolution (1789–1799)* (1911).

33. There is no general history of the Convention, but a good sense of its character is conveyed in A. Patrick, *The Men of the First Republic: Political Alignments in the National Convention of 1792* (Baltimore, 1972).

34. The most recent assessment is M. Walzer, "The King's Trial and the Political Culture of the Revolution," in Lucas, ed., *Political Culture of the Revolution.*

35. B. Gainot, ed., *Dictionnaire des membres du Comité de Salut Public* (1990), 28–29. With one exception, noted below, none of these committees has been treated in any depth, but there is a remarkable documentary collection on the Comité d'Instruction Publique edited by J. Guillaume.

36. On the Committee of Public Safety, see the classic work of R. R. Palmer, *Twelve Who Ruled: The Year of the Terror in the French Revolution* (Princeton, 1941), and L. Gershoy, *Bertrand Barère: A Reluctant Terrorist* (Princeton, 1962).

37. These speeches fill the vast Maclure Collection at the University of Pennsylvania, catalogued by Hardy, Jensen, and Wolfe: *The Maclure Collection of French Revolutionary Materials* (Philadelphia, 1966). On the routine legislative business that swelled the parliament's agenda see, e.g., the discussion of cantonal *chefs-lieux* in Chapter IV below. During the Year VII, the monthly number of committees drafting bills in the Council of Five Hundred ranged between 73 and 138: *C500: Tableaux des Commissions créées par arrêtés du Conseil des Cinq-Cents: nivôse an VII-brumaire an VIII,* cited by Dodu, *Parlementarisme sous la Révolution,* 365.

38. For the futile debate on political clubs in 1799, see I. Woloch, *Jacobin Legacy: The Democratic Movement Under the Directory* (Princeton, 1970), 386–94. On press freedom and responsibility, G. LePoittevin, *La Liberté de la presse depuis la Révolution* (1901), 85–105. Reform of the legal profession and funding for primary schools are discussed in later chapters.

39. Woloch, *Jacobin Legacy,* chs. 3, 9–10, 12; H. Mitchell, *The Underground War Against Revolutionary France* (Oxford, 1965); M. Sydenham, *The First French Republic 1792–1804* (London, 1974), part II.

40. See J.-P. Bertaud, *Bonaparte Prend le Pouvoir: La République meurt-elle assassinée?* (1987), and L. Hunt, D. Lansky, and P. Hanson, "The Failure of the Liberal Republic in France, 1795–1799: The Road to Brumaire," *JMH,* LI (December 1979), 734–59.

41.   L. Bergeron, *France Under Napoleon* (Princeton, 1981 transl.), part I; J. Tulard, *Napoléon* (2nd edn., 1977), 5–29; C. Durand, *Etudes sur le Conseil d'état napoléonien* (1949); *Le Conseil d'Etat: son histoire à travers les documents d'époque* (1974), Intro. and ch. II.

42.   See the valuable study by Irene Collins, *Napoleon and His Parliaments 1800–1815* (London, 1979), 8–27, 140–44.

43.   *Ibid.,* 28–46.

44.   *Ibid.,* 40–41. For an example of the kind of controversy the First Consul hated, see the debate on the justices of the peace in Chapter X below. Here, as so often, Benjamin Constant seemed to lead the opposition.

45.   Bergeron, *France Under Napoleon,* 88–90; Collins, *Napoleon and His Parliaments,* 56–74, 109–20.

46.   Unlike most other legislation, the five comprehensive Napoleonic legal codes were subject to extensive preliminary consultation beyond the precincts of the Council of State. The presiding judges of the criminal courts, for example, were asked to comment at length on drafts of the Code of Criminal Procedure, and (as James Munson shows in his recent Columbia dissertation) organizations representing the interests of merchants had considerable input on the Commercial Code, though their advice was often disregarded in the end.

47.   Collins, *Napoleon and His Parliaments,* 121–39.

48.   G. Bertier de Sauvigny, *The Bourbon Restoration* (Philadelphia, 1966 transl.), chs. 3–4.

49.   On these local conflicts, see B. Edmonds, "Federalism and the Urban Revolt in France in 1793," *JMH,* LV (1983), 22–53, and A. Forrest, "Federalism," in *Political Culture of the French Revolution.* For the Convention's response, Patrick, *Men of the First Republic,* ch. 2.

50.   Palmer, *Twelve Who Ruled,* ch. 5; C. Lucas, *The Structure of the Terror: The Example of Javogues and the Loire* (Oxford, 1973), chs. 4–8.

51.   Jessenne, *Pouvoir au Village,* 94–108; Jones, *Peasantry in the Revolution,* ch. 7; and several of the papers in *Limousin en Révolution.*

52.   R. C. Cobb, *Les Armées révolutionnaires: instrument de la terreur dans les départements, Avril 1793–floréal an II* (2 vols., 1963); Cobb, *The Police and the People: French Popular Protest, 1789–1820* (Oxford, 1970), 172–324.

53.   For the Directory's commissioners, the best local studies are M. Reinhard, *Le Département de la Sarthe sous le régime directorial* (St. Brieuc, 1935), and J. Brélot, *La Vie politique en Côte d'Or sous le Directoire* (Dijon, 1930).

54.   *C500: Rapport par Izus . . . Tarn; CA: Rapport par Ducos . . . Ardèche; C500: Opinion de Lacombe Saint Michel . . . Var* in A.N. AD I 61.

55.   The prefectorial system is best viewed through such local studies as R. Durand, *Le Département des Côtes-du-Nord sous le Consulat et l'Empire* (2 vols., 1925); P. Viard, *L'Administration préfectoriale dans le département de la Côte d'Or sous le Consulat et l'Empire* (Lille, 1914); and J.-F. Soulet, *Les Premiers Préfets des Hautes-Pyrénées (1800–1814)* (1965).

56. Bergeron, *France Under Napoleon,* 23–31.

57. A.N. F^{1c} III Moselle 8: Comptes analytiques des travaux du Conseil de Préfecture, 1808; F^{1c} III Loir-et-Cher 6: Comptes analytiques des travaux du Conseil de Préfecture, 1809; F^{1c} III Sarthe 6: Contentieux: Conseil de Préfecture, An XIV–1806. Local almanachs, such as the *Almanach du département de Maine-et-Loire* (an IX), outlined the services of the conseil de préfecture.

58. Godechot, *Les Institutions,* 590–92.

59. *Arrêté et instruction pour la convocation des Conseils généraux de département,* 16 ventôse IX (A.N. AD XV 17); A.N. F^{1c} III Var 6: Pref to Conseil Général, 15 germinal IX.

60. Chaptal, ed., *Comptes-rendus des sessions des Conseils généraux des départements* (an VIII and an IX).

61. *Journal du département de la Haute-Garonne,* no. 1: 1 germinal XII. Cf. *Journal de Rouen,* no. 513: 16 messidor VIII on the arrondissement council.

62. Soulet, *Hautes-Pyrénées,* 57–59; Viard, *Côte d'Or,* 112.

63. A.N. AF IV 1052: M.I. circular to Prefects, 18 January 1808; M.I. to Emperor, 20 January 1808.

64. Viard, *Côte d'Or,* 116–21, on the decline of the councils.

65. A.N. F^{1c} III Vienne 5: M.I. to Pref, 14 April 1820, on the role of the councils.

66. On the launching of the prefectorial system, see especially J. Tulard, "Les Préfets de Napoléon," in *Les Préfets en France: 1800–1940* (Geneva, 1978).

67. See E. Whitcomb, "Napoleon's Prefects," *AHR,* LXXIX (October 1974), 1089–118—taking issue with older studies by Savary and Regnier.

68. *Ibid.*

69. N. Richardson, *The French Prefectorial Corps 1814–1830* (Cambridge, Engl., 1966).

CHAPTER II: POLITICAL PARTICIPATION: THE FIRST WAVES

1. See, among recent works, M. Ozouf, *La Fête Révolutionnaire, 1789–1799* (1976); F. Furet, *Interpreting the French Revolution* (Cambridge, Mass., 1981 transl.), part I; J. Starobinski, *1789: Les Emblèmes de la Raison* (1979); E. Kennedy, *A Cultural History of the French Revolution* (New Haven, 1989); and especially L. Hunt, *Politics, Culture, and Class in the French Revolution* (Berkeley, 1984), part I: "The Poetics of Power."

2. *The Social Contract,* Book III, ch. 15.

3. *Extrait des décrets et instructions de l'Assemblée Nationale sur les Assemblées primaires* (1791) in A.N. AD I 71.

4. B. Pommaret, "La Vie Municipale à Rancon (7 Fevrier 1790–5 Novembre 1795)," in *Limousin en Révolution* (Actes du Colloque de Limoges, 1989), 164; J. Bourdon, *La Réforme judiciaire de l' an VIII* (Rodez, 1941), I: 197.

5. See T. Tackett, *Religion, Revolution, and Regional Culture in Eighteenth-Century France: The Ecclesiastical Oath of 1791* (Princeton, 1986).

6. I. Woloch, *The French Veteran from the Revolution to the Restoration* (Chapel Hill, 1979), ch. 3.

7. On the *juris d'instruction,* see Chapter VI.

8. R. Girardin, *Discours sur la nécessité de la ratification de la loi par la volonté générale* (1791), cited in A. Crubaugh, "Legitimacy and Expediency in the French Revolution: The Issue of the Plebiscite" (Master's thesis, Columbia University, 1988), 15–16.

9. *Ibid.,* 16–21.

10. For a comprehensive discussion of the franchise question, see P. Gueniffey, "La Révolution française et les Elections: suffrage, participation et élections pendant la période constitutionnelle (1790–1792)" (Thèse pour le Doctorat de l'Ecole des Hautes Etudes en Sciences Sociales, 1989), part I, and Gueniffey, "Suffrage," in *Critical Dictionary of the French Revolution.*

11. See D. G. Levy, H. B. Applewhite, and M.D. Johnson, eds., *Women in Revolutionary Paris, 1789–1795* (New York, 1979), 87–96, and R. Necheles, *The Abbé Grégoire 1787–1831: Odyssey of an Egalitarian* (Westport, 1971), 25–45.

12. A point underscored by W. Sewell, Jr., "Le Citoyen/la Citoyenne: Activity, Passivity, and the Revolutionary Concept of Citizenship," in Lucas, ed., *The Political Culture of the French Revolution,* 108–09, 113, 121.

13. Some of the evidence is reviewed in Gueniffey, "Elections," chs. 4, 6, and M. Edelstein, "Electoral Participation and Sociology of the Landes in 1790" (forthcoming), 5–7.

14. Gueniffey, "Elections," ch. 6 (unpaginated).

15. See Chapter XII below.

16. Edelstein, "Landes," 7–11.

17. *Ibid.,* 21–26, 37–40.

18. Gueniffey, "Elections," ch. 11.

19. R. Marx, *Recherches sur la vie politique d'Alsace prérévolutionnaire et révolutionnaire* (Strasbourg, 1966), 63–64. See also *Extrait des décrets et instructions de l'Assemblée Nationale sur les Assemblées primaires* (1791).

20. A point emphasized by Gueniffey.

21. Morgan, *Inventing the People: The Rise of Popular Sovereignty in England and America,* 246–52. Cf. J. T. Main, *The Sovereign States, 1775–1783* (New York, 1973).

22. Marx, *Vie politique d'Alsace,* 73–111: "La Propagande."

23. Gueniffey, "Elections," chs. 7–10, and Gueniffey, "La Démocratie révolutionnaire et les Elections," in R. Waldinger, P. Dawson, and I. Woloch, eds., *The French Revolution and the Meaning of Citizenship* (forthcoming).

24. Morgan, *Inventing the People,* ch. 8.

25. G. Fournier, "Les Incidents Electoraux dans la Haute-Garonne, l'Aude,

l'Hérault, pendant la Révolution," in *Les Pratiques politiques en province à l'époque de la Révolution française* (Actes du Colloque de Montpellier, 1988), 63–76.

26.   For example, Gueniffey found an extremely rare list of voters taking the civic oath in 1791, in the canton of Garancière (Seine-et-Oise), with a total of 170 names. But the number of ballots in each of the assembly's three rounds was only 138, 116, and 93. Electoral participation studies would normally have to take the highest of these figures, 138, as the level of participation. See Gueniffey, "Elections," ch. 7 (unpaginated).

27.   Statistics drawn from Edelstein, "Electoral Behavior During the Constitutional Monarchy (1790–91): A 'Community' Interpretation," in *The French Revolution and the Meaning of Citizenship.* See also G. Fournier, "La Participation Electorale en Haute-Garonne pendant la Révolution," *Annales du Midi,* CI (January 1989), 47–71, and O. Audevart, "Les Elections en Haute-Vienne pendant la Révolution," *Limousin en Révolution,* 129–38.

28.   Edelstein, "Landes," 13.

29.   M. Crook, "Aux Urnes, Citoyens! Urban and Rural Electoral Behavior During the French Revolution," in Forrest and Jones, eds., *Reshaping France: Town, Country and Region During the French Revolution,* 152–67. Also J. L. Ormières, "Les Scrutins de 1790 et de 1791 et le Soulèvement de 1793: interprétation du comportement électoral," in F. Lebrun and R. Dupuy, eds., *Les Résistances à la Révolution* (1987), 82–86; M. Edelstein, "L'Apprentissage de la Citoyenneté: participation électorale des campagnards et citadins (1789–93)," in M. Vovelle, ed., *L'Image de la Révolution française* (Oxford and Paris, 1989), I: 15–25; Edelstein, "Electoral Behavior."

30.   Marx, *Vie politique d'Alsace,* 56–72; M. Crook, "Les Français Devant le Vote: participation et pratique électorale à l'époque de la Révolution," *Les Pratiques politiques en province,* 27–37. Cf. P. McPhee, "Electoral Democracy and Direct Democracy in France, 1789–1851," *European History Quarterly* (1986), 77–91.

31.   R. M. Andrews, "Boundaries of Citizenship: The Penal Regulation of Speech in Revolutionary France," *French Politics and Society,* VII (Summer 1989), 93–99.

32.   C. Tilly, "Civil Constitution and Counterrevolution in Southern Anjou," *French Historical Studies,* I (1959), 179–99. On reactive anti-revolutionary movements, see R. Dupuy, *De la Révolution à la Chouannerie: paysans en Bretagne 1788–1794* (1988), and Dupuy's conclusion to the volume *Résistances à la Révolution,* 469–74.

33.   I have drawn extensively on J. Popkin, *Revolutionary News: The Press in France 1789–1799* (Durham, N.C., 1990); H. Gough, *The Newspaper Press in the French Revolution* (Chicago, 1988); and C. Labrosse and P. Rétat, *Naissance du Journal Révolutionnaire: 1789* (Lyon, 1989). See also R. Darnton and D. Roche, eds., *Revolution in Print: The Press in France 1775–1800* (Berkeley, 1989).

34. Labrosse and Rétat, *Naissance du Journal,* 17–25.

35. See especially Popkin, *Revolutionary News,* ch. 2.

36. M. Edelstein, *La Feuille Villageoise: communication et modernisation dans les régions rurales pendant la Révolution* (1977), 67–84.

37. M. Taillefer, "Les Journaux Toulousains au début de la Révolution 1789–1793," in *Pratiques politiques en province,* 163–66.

38. See Gough, *Newspaper Press,* 26–33, 65–77, 84–87, and especially Gough, "The Provincial Press in the French Revolution," in *Reshaping France,* 193–205. Among the local studies, E. Labadie, *La Presse à Bordeaux pendant la Révolution* (Bordeaux, 1910).

39. J. Censer, *Prelude to Power: The Parisian Radical Press, 1789–1791* (Baltimore, 1976). Also on Marat's style, Popkin, *Revolutionary News,* 116–17, 146–51.

40. J.-P. Bertaud, *Les Amis du Roi: Journaux et journalistes royalistes en France de 1789 à 1792* (1984), especially 53–57 and ch. 6, "L'Anarchie constituée." Also W. J. Murray, *The Right Wing Press in the French Revolution* (London, 1986).

41. See J.-P. Bertaud, "Histoire de la Presse et Révolution," *AHRF,* no. 285 (July 1991), 281–98, and J. Popkin, *The Right-Wing Press in France, 1792–1800* (Chapel Hill, 1980).

42. On Hébert's journalistic appeal, see the insights of Popkin, *Revolutionary News,* 151–68.

43. See M. Kennedy, *The Jacobin Club of Marseilles, 1790–1794* (Ithaca, 1973), chs. 2–3, and Kennedy, *The Jacobin Clubs in the French Revolution, vol. I: The First Years* (Princeton, 1982), chs. 1–2, 4; G. Maintenant, *Les Jacobins* (1984).

44. See the important article by J. Boutier and P. Boutry, "Les Sociétés politiques en France de 1789 à l'an III: 'Une Machine'?" *RHMC,* XXXVI (1983), 29–67.

45. Boutier and Boutry, "La Diffusion des sociétés politiques en France (1789–an III): une enquête nationale," *AHRF,* no. 266 (September 1986), 366–98. See also vol. VI of the *Atlas de la Révolution française* (1992).

46. Kennedy, *Jacobin Clubs,* I: 53–72, and appendices D and E; Kennedy, *The Jacobin Clubs in the French Revolution, II: The Middle Years* (Princeton, 1988), 175–95, and appendix E.

47. Although their methods and perspectives differ, the work of Boutier & Boutry and Kennedy converges around a view at variance with the influential argument of Augustin Cochin that the Jacobin clubs constituted a "machine" calibrated to produce unanimity, which imposed itself on civil society. For an approach closer to Cochin's, see F. Furet, "Augustin Cochin: The Theory of Jacobinism," *Interpreting the French Revolution;* P. Gueniffey and R. Halévi, "Clubs and Popular Societies," and Furet, "Jacobinism," in *Critical Dictionary of the French Revolution;* and L. Jaume, *Le Discours Jacobin et la démocratie* (1989).

48. Kennedy, *The Jacobin Clubs,* I: 260–96. See also J. Bernet, "Aux Sources de la sociabilité politique contemporaine: les clubs des Jacobins sous la Révolution française (l'exemple champenois et picard, 1789–1795)," *AHRF,* no. 266

(1986), 483–85; and L. Gershoy, *Bertrand Barère: A Reluctant Terrorist* (Princeton, 1962), ch. 5.

49. On the division of opinion, see Kennedy, *Jacobin Clubs,* II: 229–84, and M. Reinhard, *La Chute de la Royauté* (1969), 347–48, 545, 593.

50. Merlin de Douai, *Rapport sur les changemens que nécessitent . . . les lois emanées depuis le 10 Août 1792 . . .* (frimaire an II) in A.N. AD III 46.

51. See J.-P. Jessenne, *Pouvoir au Village et Révolution: Artois 1760–1848* (Lille, 1987), 86–89; Crook, "Les Français devant le Vote," *Pratiques politiques en province;* Crook, "Aux urnes Citoyens!", *Reshaping France,* 157–58; Gueniffey, "Elections," ch. 7; J. Girardot, *Le Département de la Haute-Saône pendant la Révolution* (Vesoul, 1973), I: 180–82; and evidence from local studies summarized by Edelstein, "L'Apprentissage de la Citoyenneté," 22–23.

52. Gueniffey, "Elections," ch. 13; Patrick, *The Men of the First Republic: Political Alignments in the National Convention of 1792,* 145–52.

53. Patrick, *Men of the Republic,* ch. 7.

54. *Ibid.,* 152–57. Also Kennedy, *Jacobin Clubs,* II: 287–91.

55. Patrick, *Men of the Republic,* 157–65, 175–84. But cf. Gueniffey, "Elections," ch. 15, for a more critical view.

56. Quoted in E. Ducoudray, "De la presse d'opinion aux groupes de pression: les clubs électoraux parisiens en 1791–1792," *Studies on Voltaire and the Eighteenth Century,* no. 287 (1991), 297.

57. *Ibid.,* 298–301, 304–07; Gueniffey, "La Démocratie révolutionnaire et les élections," 18–22.

58. E. Ducoudray, "Bourgeois Parisiens en Révolution 1790–1792," in M. Vovelle, ed., *Paris et la Révolution* (1989), 71–88.

59. I follow Gueniffey, "Elections," ch. 14; see also Patrick, *Men of the Republic,* 181–83.

60. Patrick, *Men of the Republic,* 186–95. For alternative views of the two groups, see M. Sydenham, *The Girondins* (London, 1961); the articles "Girondins" and "Montagnards" by M. Ozouf in *Critical Dictionary of the French Revolution;* the contributions to A. Soboul, ed., *Actes du Colloque Girondins et Montagnards* (1980); and Gershoy, *Barère,* chs. 7–9. P. Higonnet, "The Social and Cultural Antecedents of Revolutionary Discontinuity: Montagnards and Girondins," *English Historical Review* (July 1985), 513–44, makes a compelling case for their kindred character.

61. Kennedy, *Jacobin Clubs,* II: 327–28, 342–47.

62. *Ibid.,* II: 362–65 and appendix G; Kennedy, *Jacobin Club of Marseilles,* chs. 4–5.

63. See W. Scott, *Terror and Repression in Revolutionary Marseilles* (London, 1973), chs. 3–5, 10; M. Crook, "Federalism and the French Revolution: The Revolt in Toulon in 1793," *History,* LXV (1980); B. Edmunds, "Federalism and the Urban Revolution in France in 1793," *JMH,* LV (1983), 22–53; A. Forrest, "Federalism," in *Political Culture of the French Revolution.*

64.   Gershoy, *Barère*, 161–67; Edmunds, "Federalism." Cf. P. R. Hanson, *Provincial Politics in the French Revolution: Caen and Limoges, 1789–1794* (Baton Rouge, 1989), ch. 4.

65.   See the multi-part article by René Baticle, "Le Plébiscite sur la Constitution de 1793: La réunion des Assemblées primaries," *RF*, LVII (1909), 496–524, and LVIII (1910), 5–30; "Le Recensement et le Résultat," *RF*, LVIII (1910), 117–55. Totals are given in LVIII: 131–32.

66.   Baticle, LVII: 510–11. See also S. Aberdam, "Projet: Naissance du suffrage universel: 1793, le Referendum sur la République" (unpublished paper, January 1992), 3.

67.   Baticle, LVIII: 149–55.

68.   See the last three segments of Baticle's study, "Le Plébiscite sur la Constitution de 1793: Les Amendments," *RF*, LVIII (1910), 193–237, 327–41, 385–410.

69.   S. Aberdam, "Un Aspect du référendum de 1793: les envoyés du souverain face aux représentants du peuple" (Révolution et République: Colloque de l'Université de Paris I, 1992) (forthcoming).

70.   Boutier and Boutry, "La Diffusion des Sociétés politiques," 389–98; Boutier and Boutry, "Les Sociétés politiques," 36–41.

71.   Until the appearance of Michael Kennedy's third volume on the clubs of the Year II, see the discussion of the clubs' composition and activities in C. Brinton, *The Jacobins: An Essay in the New History* (New York, 1930). The best interpretive overview is Boutier and Boutry, "Les Sociétés politiques." For a recent local study, see Bernet, "Les Clubs des Jacobins: l'exemple champenois et picard," 485–95.

72.   R. C. Cobb, "Some Aspects of the Revolutionary Mentality (April 1793–Thermidor, Year II)," in J. Kaplow, ed., *New Perspectives on the French Revolution* (New York, 1965), 305–37 (the direct quotes are from pp. 312, 315); also Cobb, *The Police and the People: French Popular Protest 1789–1820* (Oxford, 1970), 172–324.

73.   Cobb, *The Police and the People*, 118–71; Cobb, *Reactions to the French Revolution* (Oxford, 1972), chs. 1–3; Cobb, *Paris and Its Provinces, 1792–1802* (Oxford, 1975), chs. 1–4; articles by O. Hufton, C. Lucas, and G. Lewis in Lucas and Lewis, eds., *Beyond the Terror: Essays in French Regional History, 1794–1815* (Cambridge, Engl., 1983), a festschrift for Richard Cobb. Also J. Skinner, "The Revolutionary and Royalist Traditions in Southern Village Society: The Vaucluse Comtadin, 1789–1851," in *Reshaping France*.

CHAPTER III: POLITICAL PARTICIPATION: THE DENOUEMENT

1.   *Montieur,* XXV: 83; A. Lajusan, "Le Plébiscite de l'an III," *RF,* LX (1911), 5–37, 106–32, 236–63. Cf. Fournier, "Participation électorale en Haute-Garonne," 61–65.

2.   *Rapport fait au nom de la Commission des Onze par Baudin sur le mode de la reélection des deux tiers des membres de la Convention* (13 fructidor III) in A.N. AD I 71; A. Aulard, *A Political History of the French Revolution* (London, 1910 transl.), III: 315–18.

3.   *Tableau du dépouillement et recensement du voeu des assemblées primaires sur la constitution . . . et sur les décrets de 5 et 13 fructidor, soumis à sa sanction* (vendémiaire IV); Aulard, *Political History,* III: 319–22.

4.   J. R. Suratteau, "Les Elections de l'an IV," *AHRF,* no. 124 (1951), 374–93, and no. 125 (1952), 32–62.

5.   M. Genty, *L'Apprentissage de la Citoyenneté: Paris 1789–1795* (1987), 265–66 on 1791, and *Département de la Seine: Assemblées primaires, An VII* (An VII) in A.N. AD I 72, for enfranchised citizens in Paris (excluding rural cantons).

6.   *Règles pour les élections dans les assemblées primaires, proposés par Oudot* (27 messidor III); *Opinion de Louvet sur le mode des élections* (25 messidor III); and *Opinion de Garran,* in A.N. AD I 71.

7.   *Instruction sur les assemblées primaires, communales et électorales du 5 ventôse V:* "Inscriptions des candidats" and "Mode de scrutin." For a retrospective evaluation, *C.A.: Rapport par Baudin . . . sur la résolution du 6 pluviôse relative aux élections* (25 pluviôse VI).

8.   *C500: Rapport par Pons sur la suppression du scrutin de rejet* (6 pluviôse VI), and *C.A.: Rapport par Lebreton sur la suppression des listes de candidats* (24 pluviôse VI) in AD I 72.

9.   C. Lucas, "The Rules of the Game in Local Politics Under the Directory," *French Historical Studies,* XVI (1989), 345–71. The quotation is from pp. 364 and 370.

10.   See H. Mitchell, *The Underground War Against Revolutionary France* (Oxford, 1965); Popkin, *The Right-Wing Press in France;* and R. Gerard, *Un Journal de province sous la Révolution: Le 'Journal de Marseille' de Ferréol Beaugeard (1781–1797)* (1965), part II.

11.   *C.A.: Rapport par Baudin . . . concernant la promesse de fidelité à la République, par les prochaines Assemblées électorales* (29 ventôse V), and the argument against requiring a promise: *C.A.: Opinion de Tronson-Ducoudray* (1 germinal V) in A.N. AD I 71.

12. *Instruction . . . Ventôse V:* "Police Intérieure."

13. For the scanty evidence on voter turnout under the Directory, see M. Lyons, *France Under the Directory* (Cambridge, Engl., 1975), ch. 15; Fournier, "Participation électorale en Haute-Garonne," 65–70; and Crook, "Aux Urnes, Citoyens!", 159–64.

14. The results are analyzed exhaustively by J. R. Suratteau, "Les Elections de l'an V aux Conseils du Directoire," *AHRF* (1958), 21–63.

15. For a critical view of the Fructidor coup, see M. Syndenham, *The First French Republic, 1792–1804* (London, 1974), part II.

16. *C500: Rapport par Roux . . . sur les opérations des deux assemblées se disant électorales pour le département du Lot* (24 frimaire IV), and *C.A.: Rapport par Paradis . . . sur les opérations de l'assemblée électorale du Lot* (10 pluviôse IV) in A.N. AD XVI 47.

17. *C.A.: Rapport par Crenière sur la résolution du C500 du 6 prairial V; C.A.: Opinion de Lacombe Saint Michel sur les élections du Lot* (24 prairial V); *C.A.: Opinion de Marbot contre la résolution qui déclare nulles. . . .* (24 prairial V).

18. Suratteau, "Elections de l'an V," 34–35.

19. Woloch, *Jacobin Legacy: The Democratic Movement Under the Directory,* part II; M. Reinhard, *Le Départment de la Sarthe sous le Régime directorial* (St. Brieuc, 1935), chs. 11–12; J. Beyssi, "Le Parti Jacobin à Toulouse sous le Directoire," *AHRF* (1950), 28–54 and 108–33; H. Gough, "The Provincial Jacobin Press During the Directory," *History of European Ideas,* X (1989), 443–54. Cf. J. Popkin, "Les Journaux républicains, 1795–1799," *RHMC* (1984), 143–57.

20. *Adresse au C.A. sur les inscriptions réquises pour être admis à voter dans les assemblées primaires* (Impr. Vatar, 27 pluviôse VI), A.N. AD I 72; *C.A.: Opinion de Lindet sur la résolution du 22 nivôse VI* (27 pluviôse VI); *C500: Instruction sur la tenue des Assemblées primaires* (12 ventôse VI). Cf. Woloch, *Jacobin Legacy,* 241–57.

21. See Woloch, *Jacobin Legacy,* 257–71, with particular attention to the constitutional circle of Moulins.

22. J. R. Suratteau, *Les Elections de l'an VI et le coup d'état du 22 floréal (11 Mai 1798)* (1971), part II; Woloch, *Jacobin Legacy,* chs. 10–11; Reinhard, *Sarthe,* ch. 13.

23. Goupil-Prefelne, *Juste étendue du pouvoir du Corps Législatif sur les nominations faites, tant par les Assemblées primaires que par les Assembées électorales* (floréal VI), A.N. AD I 72.

24. See Suratteau, *Elections de l'an VI,* part III.

25. On the campaign to impose the republican calendar, see I. Woloch, " 'Republican Institutions,' 1797–99," in Lucas, ed., *Political Culture of the French Revolution,* and M. Ozouf, "Passé, présent, avenir à travers les textes administratifs de l'époque révolutionnaire," *L'Ecole de la France; essais sur la Révolution, l'utopie, et l'enseignement* (1984). For popular reactions, see S. Desan, *Reclaiming the Sacred: Lay Religion and Popular Politics in Revolutionary France* (Ithaca, 1990), chs. 4–5.

26. *Observateur de l'Yonne,* 27 germinal VII.

27. A. Meynier, *Les Coups d'Etat du Directoire, II: Le 22 floréal et le 30 prairial* (1927), 186–201; Woloch, *Jacobin Legacy,* 363–65.

28. *C500: Projet de résolution au nom de la Commission des Onze* (6 messidor VII), and *C500: Rapport par Duplantier . . . suivi du projet de Code des droits politiques et des élections* (thermidor VII) in A.N. AD I 72.

29. C. Langlois, "Le Plébiscite de l'an VIII ou le coup d'Etat du 18 pluviôse an VIII," *AHRF* (1972), 43–65, 231–46, 391–415.

30. C. Langlois, "Napoleon Bonaparte Plébiscité?" in *L'Election du Chef de l'Etat en France, de Hugues Capet à Nos Jours* (1988), 87–93.

31. See J. Y. Coppolani, *Les Elections en France à l'époque napoléonienne* (1980), passim but especially part I, ch. 2.

32. A.N. F^{1c} III Seine-Inférieure 8: tableau de la situation du département pendant l'an 10.

33. Coppolani, *Elections napoléoniennes,* 176–79.

34. A.N. F^{1c} II 31/2: *Décisions donnés par le Ministre sur divers questions . . . sur les Assemblées cantonales et les Collèges électoraux* (January 1807); *Modele Général de Listes* (1807); and, on proper attire, M.I. to Prefects, circular 26 fructidor XII. In general, see Coppolani, *Elections napoléoniennes,* part II: "La Représentation de la Comédie Electorale Napoléonienne."

35. A.N. F^{1c} III Sarthe 6: Pref to M.I., 24 September 1813 (with good statistics); F^{1c} III Allier 6: 8 October 1813; F^{1c} III Haute-Vienne 7: 25 November 1813; F^{1c} III Vienne 5: 10 October 1813; F^{1c} III Finistère 3: 5 October 1813; F^{1c} III Ille-et-Vilaine 7: 20 August 1813; F^{1c} III Haute-Marne 5: 12 October 1813.

36. A.N. F^{1c} III Jura 8: Pref to M.I., 4 October 1813; F^{1c} III Indre-et-Loire 7: 24 September 1813; F^{1c} III Isère 6: 8 October 1813.

37. See G. Dupeux, *French Society Since 1789* (New York, 1977 transl.), ch. 2; E. and P. Anderson, *Political Institutions and Social Change in Continental Europe in the Nineteenth Century* (Berkeley, 1967), ch. 8.

CHAPTER IV: INTEGRATING THE VILLAGES

1. Cited in L. Gauthier, "Les Municipalités cantonales et la tradition révolutionnaire," *RF,* LXIX (1916), 249–53.

2. The debate may be followed in the *Moniteur* (réimpression), XXV (an III): 106, 173–76, 189–92, 195.

3. M. Bloch, *French Rural History: An Essay on Its Basic Characteristics* (Berkeley, 1966), 167–70.

4. *Moniteur,* XXV: 106.

5. See the *Manuel des Agents Municipaux* (an VII), B.N. F 39474, and its *Supplément* (published early in year VIII); J. Godechot, *Les Institutions de la France sous la Révolution et l'Empire* (1968 edn.), 472–76.

6. For criticism of this restriction, see, e.g., A.N. F¹ᵃ 422 (Meurthe): "Mémoire sur les inconvenients de l'art. XI de la loi du 12 vendémiaire IV qui détermine un mode pour l'envoi et la publication des loix," fructidor V; A.N. F¹ᵃ 408: Commissioner to the canton of Carlux (Dordogne), 30 vendémiaire V; Departmental Commissioner to Côtes-du-Nord to M.I., 28 germinal IV; A.N. F¹ᶜ III Yonne 7: Compte, nivôse VII.

7. Jessenne, *Pouvoir au Village et Révolution: Artois 1760–1848,* 109–13; Reinhard, *Le Département de la Sarthe sous le régime directorial,* 37–57 and 161–64; C. Bloch, "Le Recrutement du personnel municipal de l'an IV," *RF,* XLVI (1904), 153–68 on the Loiret; and L. Gauthier, "L'Organisation des municipalités cantonales dans le département de la Vienne," *RF,* LXVI (1914), 427–40.

8. Jessenne, *Artois,* 115.

9. *Compte moral de l'administration départementale de la Marne pour les ans 4 et 5ème* (Chalôns, Brumaire VI), 44–48; *Compte-reundu par l'administration centrale des Basses-Pyrénées, Brumaire an 4–Germinal an 5* (Pau, an V), 5–9; A.N. F¹ᶜ III Somme 7: Compte, messidor VI; F¹ᶜ III Nord 7: Comptes, germinal and fructidor VII; F¹ᶜ III Vosges 7: Comptes, brumaire and frimaire VII. F¹ᶜ III Haut-Rhin 7: Compte vendémiaire VIII. See also E. Desgranges, *La Centralisation Républicaine sous le Directoire: les municipalités de canton dans le département de la Vienne* (Poitiers, 1954), ch. I, especially 19–20.

10. A.N. F¹ᵃ 50: M.I. circular to departmental commissioners, 23 prairial VI; A.N. F¹ᶜ III Jura 7: departmental commissioner's circular to cantonal commissioners, 8 messidor VI. Similar circulars to the cantonal commissioners may be found in F¹ᶜ III Aude 5; F¹ᶜ III Calvados 8; F¹ᶜ III Gironde 5; F¹ᶜ III Lot-et-Garonne 7; Desgranges, *Vienne,* 17–19.

11. A.N. F¹ᶜ III Marne 6: messidor VI, with a printed model form: "Compte de la Situation morale et politique du canton d'_____ pendant le mois de _____." The rubrics included Esprit public (with special attention to observance of the *décadi*); Instruction publique; Police générale et champêtre; Police des cultes; Subsistances; Hospices et bienfaisance; Epidémies et épizooties; Maisons d'arrêt et prisons; Contributions et biens nationaux; Grandes routes et chemins vicinaux; Agriculture et plantations; Eaux et fôrets; Commerce et industrie; Force armée.

12. A.N. F¹ᶜ III Seine-et-Marne 6: Tableau politique des commissaires du Directoire près les administrations municipales, prairial-messidor VI. See also Reinhard, *Sarthe,* 57–63, 161–68, and 176–78, and Desgranges, *Vienne,* who concludes that for all their deficiencies, "les commissaires du Directoire furent bien supérieurs aux agents des cantons" (p. 47).

13. E.g., A.N. F¹ᶜ III Indre 4: Compte, germinal VII.

14. A.N. F¹ᶜ I 43: Bauvinay to Merlin, 3 frimaire VII.

15. E. Ackerman, *Village on the Seine: Tradition and Change in Bonnières, 1815–1914* (Ithaca, 1978), 19–36. On the distribution of periodic fairs and markets, see

D. Margairaz, *Foires et Marchés dans la France préindustrielle* (1988), part I, and maps 1–2, pp. 242–45.

16. W. Skinner, "Marketing and Social Structure in Rural China," *J. of Asian Studies,* XXIV (November 1964), 3–43.

17. P. Jones, *Politics and Rural Society: The Southern Massif Central, c. 1750–1880* (Cambridge, Engl., 1985), 187–90.

18. A.N. AF III 104, doss. 466: petition from inhabitants of Salès to C500, prairial VI; petition from Lentille to C500, vendémiaire VI; petition from Peyrus-sevieille (Gers), frimaire VII; F ^{2} II Loir-et-Cher 1: petition from Mur, brumaire VI. Some of the requests dealt with by the legislature are collected in A.N. AD I 61, including *C500: Rapport par Abolen, 4 pluviôse VI; Rapport par Thomas, 11 thermidor VI; Rapport par Pollart, 17 pluviôse VII; Rapport par Lafargue, 29 pluviôse VII.*

19. A.N. AF III 104, doss. 466: to C500, 24 vendémiaire VI. Also petitions from Paches and Marmont, nivôse VI.

20. A.N. AF III 105: Two of the most interesting cases involved rivalry between Autricourt and Belan in the Côte d'Or, and Perthe and Villiers in the Haute-Marne (see Figures IV-1 and IV-2). Also Les Républicains de St. Bonnet (Gard), 22 messidor VI versus Les Citoyens de Montfrin, chef-lieu du canton, 20 messidor VI.

21. *Ibid.:* Petition from Ufaix to Deptal Admin, pluviôse VI, and *Message du Directoire, 3 germinal VI.* A.N. AF III 104: *C.A.: Rapport fait par Gastin, 13 fructidor VII* (on Seranon); Deptal Admin of the Meurthe, 24 fructidor VI. Other cases include *C500: Rapport par Souilhé, 6 ventôse VII* on Cabrerits (Lot); *Rapport par Benard-Lagrave, 8 floréal VII* on Oppy (Pas-de-Calais); *Rapport par Guillard, 3 prairial VII* on St. Lubin (Eure-et-Loire); *C.A.: Rapport par Simon, 23 prairial VII* on Val Fleuru (Loire), in A.N. AD I 61.

22. A.N. AF III 105: Admin Municip de Candes, 20 floréal VI; plan topographique; and Deptal Admin, 17 messidor VII. AF III 104, doss. 466: petition from inhabitants of five communes in Montsauche to C500, 1 ven-démiaire VI. AF III 105: Admin Municip de Gault to C500, 13 frimaire VII; petitions from six communes in the canton; and *Message du Directoire, 28 thermidor VII.* See also Admin Municip de Meuvi (Haute-Marne), 29 brumaire IV, and Deptal Admin, 16 brumaire VI.

23. A.N. AF III 105: Admin Municip de St. Just, 23 pluviôse V, and *procès-verbaux* of its session of 27 messidor VI; Admin Municip d'Allene, 2 germinal VII.

24. *Ibid.:* Deptal Admin Manche, 13 prairial VII; Les citoyens d'Eperluques (Pas-de-Calais), ventôse VI (with four pages of signatures!). A.N. AD I 61: *C500: Rapport par Gourlay, 29 messidor VI* on Fressin (Pas-de-Calais). Also A.N. AF III 104, doss. 466: petition from inhabitants of Roussilon, 15 brumaire VI; petition from Manon (Bouches-du-Rhône), 26 frimaire VI.

25.   A.N. AF III 105: Deptal Admin Pas-de-Calais, 6 ventôse VII; Les Républicaines des communes de Metz-en-Couture to M.I. (an VII).

26.   *Ibid.:* Admin Municip de Frasne (Doubs), 15 pluviôse VII and other petitions against transferring the *chef-lieu* permanently to the more centrally located Dampierre. Frasne was said to be larger, to have better facilities, "et jamais n'a formée de Vendée comme Dampierre." Also Admin Municip de Bouisse (Aude), 7 ventôse VI, protest against shifting its *chef-lieu* to Lanet.

27.   A.N. F^{1a} 50: M.I. to Departmental Administrations, 7 frimaire VI. This view was publicly endorsed in the *Compte-Rendu par les administrateurs du Pas-de-Calais, floréal V–floréal VI* (Arras), 87–88.

28.   A.N. AF III 104, doss. 467: Rapport du M.I. au Directoire, fructidor VI. Some of the departmental responses are collected in A.N. F^2 I 541. The proposals from the Landes and the Indre-et-Loire included a plan to reduce the number of communes as well.

29.   Though instances of special pleading, these petitions make the case for the ecological and social viability of the smallish cantons. The most interesting petitions include: Les habitans du canton d'Ingviller (Bas-Rhin), vendémiaire VII (see Figure IV-3), emphasizing the location of its *chef-lieu;* Le Président de l'admin municip de Montrevault (Maine-et-Loire), vendémiaire VII, emphasizing its role as a market bourg and livestock exchange; and Les habitans du canton de Haroué (Meurthe), vendémiaire VII, stressing its facilities and public accommodations. (AF III 104, doss. 467. Other protest petitions in A.N. F^2 I 541.)

30.   *C500: Opinion de Duplantier sur le projet de réduction des Cantons, 2 frimaire VII; Opinion de Delbrel contre la réduction du nombre des cantons, 2 frimaire VII; Opinion de Vezu . . . 2 frimaire VII,* in A.N. AD I 61.

31.   *C500: Réponse par Bara . . . aux objections faites contre le projet . . . 3 frimaire VII; Opinion de Mourer . . . 4 frimaire VII; Opinion de Bremontier . . . 4 frimaire VII.*

32.   A.N. F^{1a} 408: Pref Côtes-du-Nord circular to mayors, 14 messidor VIII; Pref Dordogne circulars to mayors, 9 prairial and 14 messidor VIII; F^{1a} 422: Pref Haute-Marne circular, 9 prairial VIII.

33.   A.N. F^{1c} III Yonne: M.I. to Pref, July 1819; F^{1c} III Calvados 8: M.I. to Pref, 31 July 1819.

34.   A.N. F^3 II Côte d'Or 1: Pref to M.I., 12 vendémiaire IX; A.N. F^2 II Vienne 1: Pref to M.I., 14 September 1807. (In over 100 communes, he claimed, he was forced to retain incapable mayors, or, worse yet, "de mauvais sujets qui ont sur les autres l'avantage de savoir un peu lire et écrire"); F^2 II Moselle 1: Pref to M.I., 24 November 1807 and 17 July 1809. Also A.N. F^{1c} III Charente 7: Tournée de l'an XI; F^{1c} III Creuse 7: Tournée de 1806; F^{1c} III Pas-de-Calais 8: Rapport du Pref, 9 thermidor XIII: "un grand nombre de ces maires ne savent qu'a peine lire et figurer . . . le despote et trop souvent le fripon"; L. Texier-Olivier, *Statistique générale . . . Département de la Haute-Vienne* (1808), 208; J. Bourdon, "L'Administration communale sous le Consulat," *Revue des Etudes Napoléoniennes,* I (1914), 290–95; J.-F. Soulet, *Les Premiers Préfets des Hautes-Pyrénées*

(1800–1814) (1965), 57: "J'ai au moins deux cents maires illettrés . . . comment peuvent-ils exécuter et répondre?"

35. M. Agulhon, L. Girard, et al., *Les Maires en France du Consulat à nos jours* (1986), 7–17, 35–55, and tables 1, 10, 19–21, and 24.

36. *Ibid.,* tables 7 and 12.

37. A.N. AF IV 1052: Pref Bouches-du-Rhône to Bonaparte, 15 frimaire XII; Godechot, *Les Institutions,* 597; J.-L. Suissa, *Le Département de l'Eure sous le Consulat et l'Empire* (Evreux, 1983), 28. Cf. F^{1c} III Aisne 9: Compte Annuel, January 1806: 57 mayors resigned, 6 were removed, and 13 died.

38. A.N. F^2 II Dordogne 1: Pref to M.I., 26 prairial XI; F^2 II Drôme 1: Pref to M.I., 22 April 1808. Also A.N. F^{1a} 417: Pref Landes, 8 frimaire XII on Peyrisse and 12 nivôse XII on Saas, where "il ne se trouve pas un seule homme qui sache lire et écrire."

39. *Journal du Département de l'Oise,* 18 thermidor VIII: "Aux Maires et Adjoints," and 28 thermidor, "Fonctions des Maires." Cf. *Manuel des Maires et des Adjoints* (an VIII), B.N. F 39475. The two roles are discussed by the prefect of Finistère: A.N. F^{1c} III Finistère 3: Compte 1811.

40. But on the difficulties of disseminating the laws, see A.N. F^{1a} 408: Pref Côtes-du-Nord to M.I., 29 fructidor XI, complaining "que les prêtres seuls ont le droit de parler au peuple dans les églises; que les maires ne peuvent y prendre la parole et qu'ils doivent faire les publications des lois et des ordres soit à la porte extérieure de l'église, soit sur la place publique."

41. *Journal du Département de l'Oise,* vol. I (an VIII–IX), *passim,* with a "Résumé de toutes les attributions des Maires" in the last issue.

42. *Ibid.,* 8 thermidor VIII.

43. A.N. F^2 II Vienne 1: Pref to M.I., 14 September 1807: "Leur *non faire* nuit autant que leur *mal faire."* A.N. F^2 I 144: Pref Pas-de-Calais to M.I., 11 February 1808, and *Mémorial Administratif du Pas-de-Calais,* nos. 1–6.

44. A.N. F^2 II Dordogne 1: Pref to M.I., 1 ventôse IX; A.N. F^3 I 1: Administration communale (n.d.).

45. *Analyse des procès-verbaux des Conseils généraux de département: Session de l'an 8* (an IX), 63 and 214; *Session de l'an 9* (an X), 808.

46. A.N. F^{1a} 417: Pref Landes circular to mayors, 7 frimaire XI; Pref Loir-et-Cher circular to mayors, 16 thermidor XI; F^2 II Mayenne 1: Pref to M.I., 10 May 1806; A.N. F^2 II Haute-Garonne 1: Pref to M.I., 21 May 1809; F^2 II Vienne 1: Pref to M.I., 14 September 1807.

47. A.N. F^2 I 380: Pref Loiret to M.I., 16 June 1806; A.N. F^{1a} 50: M.I. circular, 27 August 1807; Responses from prefects in A.N. F^2 I 380 including Indre-et-Loire, Loir-et-Cher, Mayenne, Meuse, and Nord.

48. *Journal du Département de l'Oise,* 28 vendémiaire IX; Godechot, *Les Institutions,* 597–99.

49. A.N. F^2 II Seine-Inférieure 1: Pref to M.I., 24 April 1807; A.N. F^{1c} III Ille-et-Vilaine 7: Pref to M.I., 22 October 1813. On the composition of these

councils, see Suissa, *Eure,* 27. For the Restoration, see F[1c] III Hautes-Alpes 3: Analyse du Rapport de Mars 1820: "pour éviter tout responsabilité presque tous les maires se sont placés dans une dépendance absolue de leurs conseils municipaux." Also F[1c] III Calvados 8: Pref to M.I., 20 January 1818; F[1c] III Aube 3: Compte November 1819; F[1c] III Yonne 7: M.I. to Pref, July 1819.

50.   H. Forestier, *L'Yonne au XIXème siècle, première partie: 1800–1830* (Auxerre, 1959), 667 (17 July 1820). Also A.N. F[1c] III Allier 6: Rapport annuel 1819, where "les dix plus imposés, presque tous fermiers, votent souvent contre les lois et les intérêts locaux."

51.   *Analyse des procès-verbaux: Session de l'an 8,* 39–41, and *Session de l'an 9,* 808.

52.   A.N. F[2] I 1201: Responses to circular letter, an XI.

53.   A.N. F[2] II Drôme 1: Pref to M.I., 25 ventôse XI; F[2] II Indre-et-Loire 1: Pref to M.I., 14 ventôse X. Cf. *Analyse des procès-verbaux: Session de l'an 9,* 720 (Orne), and Soulet, *Hautes-Pyrénées,* 56–57.

54.   *C500 Rapport par Humbert, 21 frimaire VI* (Maine-et-Loire); *Rapport par Maugenest, 9 prairial VI* (Drôme); *Rapport par Richard, 12 thermidor VI* (Saône-et-Loire); *Rapport par Henrys-Marcilly, 7 pluviôse VII* (Oise) in A.N. AD I 61.

55.   A.N. F[1a] 50: M.I. circular, 22 prairial VIII, and A.N. F[2] II Saône-et-Loire 1. Chaptal's circular of 28 brumaire IX is referred to, e.g., in F[2] II Loir-et-Cher 1: Pref to M.I., 26 germinal XI.

56.   *Analyse des procès-verbaux: Session de l'an 9,* 668, 710–11, 714, 716, 722; Pref Vienne in A.N. F[2] I 1201.

57.   A.N. F[2] I 444: Rapport au Ministre: Observations relatives aux réunions des communes (n.d.), and Rapport demandé par le M.I., fructidor IX. Also A.N. F[2] II Oise 1: M.I. to Pref, 29 pluviôse IX. Jean Bourdon's article of 1914, "L'Administration communale sous le Consulat," raises the issue of the *réunion des communes* but sheds little light on it for want of the relevant sources (295–304).

58.   A.N. F[2] II Bas-Rhin 1: M.I. to Pref, 11 ventôse X and Pref to M.I., 30 pluviôse XII; F[2] II Haute-Saône 1: M.I. to Pref, 22 brumaire XI. Also F[2] II Calvados 1: Pref to M.I., 6 messidor XII and response, 20 messidor.

59.   A.N. F[2] II Haute-Garonne 1: Pref to M.I., 12 germinal X; M.I. to Pref, 26 germinal X; Prefectorial *arrêté* 10 floréal X; Petition from Mirepoix (an X); M.I. to Pref, 14 thermidor X; and Pref to M.I., 15 fructidor X.

60.   A.N. F[2] II Seine-Inférieure 1: Pref to M.I., 24 April 1807; F[2] II Indre-et-Loire 1: Pref to M.I., 14 ventôse X; F[2] II Haute-Garonne 1: Pref to M.I., 17 July 1811; F[2] II Pas-de-Calais 1: 10 July 1810: "On tenterait en vain de consulter les conseils municipaux. Ils sont toujours d'un avis contraire et voudront rester separés et indépendens."

61.   A.N. F[1c] I 43: "Vues sur l'administration publique" (n.d., 1813?); *Observateur de l'Yonne,* 5 thermidor VIII; A.N. F[1c] III Yonne 7: Compte June 1819.

62.   A.N. F[2] I 444: Rapport au Ministre: observations relatives aux réunions des communes (n.d.).

63. A.N. F^2 II Doubs 1: Pref to M.I., 7 frimaire IX; F^2 II Moselle 1: Pref to M.I., 24 November 1807.

64. *Analyse des procès-verbaux: Session de l'an 8,* 49 (Somme and Haute-Saône); *Session de l'an 9,* 713 (Gard), 723 (Deux-Sèvres). F^2 II Côtc d'Or 1: Pref to Regnaud, 21 fructidor IX; F^2 II Corrèze 1: Pref to M.I., 27 fructidor X.

65. See A.N. F^2 I 444: Cadastre—Délimitation des Communes (February 1806); A.N. F^2 II Mayenne 1: Pref to M.I., 10 May 1806, and response, 17 May; F^2 II Moselle 1: Pref to M.I., 29 October 1810.

66. A.N. F^2 II Calvados 1: Projet de Réunion des communes, ventôse VIII; F^2 II Haute-Saône 1: Tableau de proposition de réunions des communes, 13 fructidor IX; F^2 II Indre-et-Loire 1: Proposition de réunion des communes, 14 ventôse X; F^2 II Dordogne 1: Pref to M.I., 18 frimaire and 26 prairial XI and Table des réunions; F^2 II Drôme 1: Tableaux, ventôse XI; F^2 II Nièvre 1: Tableau des réunions . . . pour être soumis à l'approbation du Gouvernement, 21 nivôse XII; F^2 II Pas-de-Calais 1: Pref to M.I., 22 ventôse XII and Projet (30 germinal XII); F^2 II Mayenne 1: Pref to M.I., 10 May 1806; F^2 II Moselle 1: Etat, 24 November 1807.

67. Indre-et-Loire and Drôme, note 66.

68. A.N. F^2 II Aveyron 1: Procès-verbal du Conseil Général, 29 germinal IX; Pref to M.I., 5 vendémiaire X and to Regnault, 2 j.c. an IX; Rapport au Ministre, 22 prairial XII. For the local context of this unique episode, see Peter Jones's insightful *Southern Massif Central,* 186–95.

69. A.N. F^2 II Aveyron 1: Projet de Circonscription des communes, 28 March 1809; Rapport à l'Empereur, 8 June 1809.

70. *Ibid.:* Sous-Pref de Millau to Pref, 15 December 1808. See also the "Observations" of the subprefects in Villefranche and St. Affrique.

71. *Ibid.* especially the *procès-verbaux* of the municipal councils of Villevayre, Valhourlhes, Rieupeyroux, St. André, and Livinlac, all dated October 1808. Jones, *Southern Massif Central,* speculates that opposition to amalgamation (or for that matter, to the cantonal system) was probably strongest when a rural commune was annexed to a substantial bourg (p. 192), but he does not refer to this inquiry.

72. A.N. F^2 II Aveyron 1: e.g., Les habitans de la commune de Perrodil, and Les habitans de Capelle Bleys.

73. Suissa, *Eure,* 13; A.N. F^{1c} III Eure 8: Compte annuel 1818, and Rapport, 1819; F^{1c} III Hérault 9: Compte, May 1820; F^{1c} III Vienne 5: Rapport, October 1818.

74. A.N. F^2 II Seine-Inférieure 1: Conseil général, 1820; F^2 II Moselle 1: Pref to M.I., 29 July 1817. Some local protests to *réunions* repeating themes cited earlier are collected in A.N. F^2 I 835, especially doss. Vendée, Gers, Seine-Inférieure.

75. A.N. F^{1c} III Calvados 8: M.I. to Pref, 31 July 1819; A.N. F^2 II Haute-Garonne 1: M.I. to Pref, 14 May 1818. This attitude persisted after the

July Revolution: see F² II Seine-et-Oise 1: M.I. to Pref, 11 January 1833, counseling against *réunions forcées*. This whole question, he sagely added, "n'est pas susceptible d'être réglée d'une manière uniforme pour toute la France."

76.   A.N. F² I 842 [Nomenclature des communes]: Responses to M.I. circular of 1 July 1826. Wishing to update the "Tableau de toutes les communes" that was drawn up in 1820–21 (see F² I 840–841), the minister asked for information on all *réunions* effected since then. The largest numbers occurred in Gers, 117; Jura, 95; Oise, 32; Seine-Inférieure, 27(?); Pyrénées-Orientales, 20; Calvados, 19; Dordogne, 18; Pas-de-Calais, 15; Charente-Inférieure, 14; and Lot-et-Garonne, 12. Twelve departments had between five and nine mergers, and twenty-eight between one and four.

77.   A.N. F² I 835: Sous-Pref de Mirande (Gers), 6 December 1823. Cf. A.N. F² II Orne 1: noting the opposition of communes to proposed *réunions*, March 1821.

78.   A.N. F² I 842: Réunions de communes prononcés depuis 1821: Dordogne, Gers, Jura.

79.   See, among many such opinions, A.N. F² I 444: Dastorq (député) to M.I., 30 May 1811; Mandet de la Haute-Loire à l'Empereur (n.d.); A.N. F³ II Côte d'Or 1: Pref to M.I., 12 vendémiaire IX and Viard, *Côte d'Or,* 76, 137–38; A.N. F² II Oise 1: Mémoire sur la réduction de tous les mairies de village, March 1809; A.N. F¹ᶜ III Corrèze 2: Comptes 1806; A.N. F³ I 1: "De l'Administration communale en France: Observations d'un Préfet"; A.N. F¹ᶜ I 43: "Vues sur l'administration publique"; and F¹ᶜ III Loire 6: Rapport, February 1818.

CHAPTER V: STATE INTERVENTION IN VILLAGE LIFE

1.   A. Delaborde (député de la Seine), *Considérations relatives au projet de lois municipales et départementales* (1829), 28–29 and 32–33 in A.N. AD I 33. For the position of liberal reformers, see C. Pouthas, "Les Projets de réforme administrative sous la Restauration," *Revue d'histoire moderne,* I (1926), 321–67.

2.   On old-regime fiscality, see P. Goubert, *L'Ancien régime, vol. II: Les Pouvoirs* (1973), ch. 7, and J. B. Collins, *Fiscal Limits of Absolutism: Direct Taxation in Early Seventeenth-Century France* (Berkeley, 1988). On royal expenditures, see F. Braesch, *Finances et monnaie révolutionnaires, 2e fasicule: 1788–89* (1936).

3.   Godechot, *Les Institutions de la France sous la Révolution et l'Empire,* 507–15 and 639–47; Reinhard, *Le Département de la Sarthe sous le régime directorial,* 391–95; on *garnisaires,* E. Desgranges, *La Centralisation Républicaine sous le Directoire: les municipalités de canton dans le département de la Vienne* (Poitiers, 1954), 73. Also Durand, *Le Département des Côtes-du-Nord sous le Consulat et l'Empire,* II: 269–96; and Suissa, *Le Département de l'Eure sous le Consulat et l'Empire,* 54–58.

4.   Reinhard, *Sarthe,* 395–412. Cf. A.N. F¹ᶜ III Nord 8: Tournée, fructidor

IX: "Objets principaux des plaintes des administrés;" and F^{1c} III Yonne 7: Observations des envoyés [vendémiaire IX?].

5. A.N. F^{1c} III Orne 8: Compte, 20 vendémiaire VI; F^{1c} III Corrèze 2: Compte, 21 pluviôse VI; F^{1c} III Gers 7: Compte, thermidor VI; *Compte de la Gestion de l'Admin Cent du Haut-Rhin pendant l'an V* (Colmar, an VI), 11; *Compte Moral de l'Admin Cent de la Marne pour les ans 4 et 5ème* (Châlons, an VI); *Compte de Gestion par les administrateurs du département de l'Eure, floréal V-floréal VI* (Evreux, an VI), 20–21.

6. *Compte Rendu par l'Admin Cent de la Mayenne, an V* (Laval, an VI). These responsibilities were later shifted about in various ways. See the discussion of the law of 15 frimaire VI in Desgranges, *Vienne,* 53–58, especially note 7, and the law of frimaire VII. For the Consulate, see J. Cambry, *Description du département de l'Oise* (1803), 31–38.

7. *Compte Rendu . . . Mayenne, an V,* 5; F. M. Perrin-Dulac, *Description générale du département de l'Isère* (2 vols., Grenoble, 1806), II: 33–34.

8. *Compte de la Gestion de l'Admin Cent du Jura* (Lons, an VI), summarizing the law of 9 germinal V. Cf. A.N. F^{1c} III Seine-et-Oise 8: Tournée, fructidor VIII: "Quelques municipalités de canton se sont permis d'imposer de leur autorité des centimes accessoires au rôle principal et ces deniers illégalement perçus ont été abusivement employés."

9. A.N. F^{1a} 422: *Instruction du Préfet de la Meurthe aux Maires* (an XII): "Moyens de suppléer à l'insufisance des revenues"; also Perrin-Dulac, *Isère,* II: 49; L. Texier-Olivier, *Statistique générale . . . Département de la Haute-Vienne* (1808), 209; Durand, *Côtes du Nord,* 307–16; and *Archives Statistiques de la France* (an XII–XIII, [Perrot Collection]), I, 52–53, 184–85, 201. On the minuscule yield of fines, see A.N. F³ II Eure 1, Etat de distribution du produit des amendes de Police, année 1812; and F³ II Yonne 1, Amendes de Police Municipale et correctionnelle de 1820.

10. Law of 13 floréal X and subsequent annual budget laws.

11. *Analyse des procès-verbaux: Session de l'an 8,* table; A.N. F² I 1201: [Enquête de l'an XI], doss." Dépenses locales." A.N. F^{1c} III Seine-Inférieure 8: M.I. to Pref, 12 frimaire XI.

12. A.N. F^{1c} III Hautes-Alpes 3: Situation administrative, 1811.

13. A.N. F² II Haute-Garonne 1: Pref to M.I., 21 September 1805; also F² II Aveyron 1: Observations du sous-Pref de Villefranche, 1808; A.N. F² I 379: Pref Jura to M.I., 3 June 1807; Texier-Olivier, *Haute-Vienne,* 209.

14. A.N. F³ II Calvados 1: *Instruction du Préfet aux Maires et aux percepteurs à vie sur les fonctions de ces deniers* (Caen, 1804), and budgets of three communes, 1809–10. Cf. F.J.-B. Alphonse, *Mémoire statistique du département de l'Indre* (an XII), 144: "Tableau des Revenus et des Dépenses des Municipalités, pour l'an 9," with categories aggregated for the whole department.

15. *Instructions sur l'Arrêté des Consuls du 4 thermidor X, relatif à la comptabilité*

des communes in A.N. AD I 33. Cf. A.N. F^2 II Haut-Rhin 1: Commune de Sent, budget an XIII; A.N. F^{1c} III Aisne 9: Compte, January 1806: Administration communale.

16.   A.N. F^{1a} 50: Circular to prefects, 10 November 1821.

17.   H. Root, *Peasants and King in Burgundy: The Agrarian Foundations of the Absolute State* (Berkeley, 1987), demonstrates in detail the tutelage of the monarchy over the communal property of Burgundian villages.

18.   A.N. AD XVI 17: *Extraits du Registre des déliberations du Conseil d'Etat,* an X, and *Bulletin des Lois,* nos. 287–90, an XI.

19.   Delaborde, *Considérations,* 29–31.

20.   A.N. F^{1a} 50: Administration Communale, law of 20 March 1813. A.N. F^{1c} III Gard 7: Compte, 2ème trim. 1813; F^{1c} III Maine-et-Loire 7: Pref to M.I., 16 August 1813; F^{1c} III Ain 5: Pref to M.I., 10 June 1813; F^{1c} III Calvados 1: Tableau . . . des communes [1813–June 1815]; Viard, *L'Administration préfectoriale dans le département de la Côte d'Or,* 331; Soulet, *Les Premiers Préfets des Hautes-Pyrénées,* 204–06; A.N. F^{1c} I 12: Comptes: Résumé des Bruits, March 1813.

21.   A.N. F^3 II Nord 1: Pref to M.I., 15 December 1813 and 1 September 1815; F^3 II Nièvre 1: Pref to M.I., 5 September 1815; F^3 II Eure 1: Pref to M.I., 12 August 1815, and Tableau de la situation actuelle de la vente des biens communaux, July 1815. Also F^3 II Dordogne 1: Etat de situation.

22.   A.N. F^{1c} III Eure 8: Compte Annuel 1818; F^{1c} III Loire Inférieure 7: Compte 1818.

23.   A.N. F^3 II Bas-Rhin 1: Pref to M.I., 9 July 1821; A.N. F^{1c} III Jura 8: Compte 1819–20. Also F^3 I 1: Admin des communes: circular to prefects, 21 April 1823; F^3 II Calvados 1: Pref to M.I. 23 May 1818 and 5 April 1819.

24.   A.N. F^3 II Yonne 1: 1820. My assessment of Restoration procedures relies on *Rapports au Roi sur les impositions communales* (1818–30), in-4° B.N. Lf^{132} 25.

25.   A.N. F^3 II Calvados 1: Pref to M.I., 23 May 1818.

26.   *Ibid.;* and A.N. F^{1a} 50: Circular of 10 November 1821.

27.   This is a major point of C. Pouthas, "Les Projets de Réforme." Cf. M. Dumiral, *De la Nécessité urgent . . . de mettre le régime municipal et communal en harmonie avec la Charte constitutionnelle* (1827) in A.N. AD I 33.

28.   F. Fortunet, "Le Code Rural ou l'impossible codification," *AHRF,* no. 247 (1982), 95–112.

29.   *Loi relative à la police rurale et à l'établissement des gardes champêtres,* 6 October 1791.

30.   *Moniteur* (réimpression), 23 messidor III, 181. Octave Festy provides a thorough introduction to this question in *Les Délits ruraux et leur répression sous la Révolution et le Consulat* (1956). However, he ends his account in 1803, just when the subject is about to become most interesting.

31.   *Moniteur,* 23 messidor III, 182.

32.   A.N. F^2 I 1203: Pref Aveyron, 25 September 1812.

33.   Festy, *Délits ruraux,* 44–74; A.N. F^2 I 1203: Pref Deux-Sèvres, 3 September 1812.

34.   Festy, *Délits ruraux,* 35–43; *Analyse des procès-verbaux: Session de l'an 8,* 110–12; A.N. F^2 I 1202: doss. "Chasse."

35.   A.N. F^2 I 1202: Préfecture de Police: Ord. concernant la chasse, 9 fructidor XII; A.N. F^{1c} III Haute-Marne 5: Pref to M.I., 9 messidor XI; H. Forestier, *L'Yonne au XIXème siècle, première partie: 1800–1830* (Auxerre, 1959), 495; F^{1c} III Tarn 6: Compte 1807; F^{1c} III Corrèze 2: Compte, 3ème trim. 1806; A.N. F^2 I 144: *Mémorial Administratif du Pas-de-Calais,* no. 4, 29 January 1808; Napoleonic decree of 11 July 1810.

36.   A.N. F^{1c} III Dordogne 7: Compte, April 1811; F^{1c} III Eure-et-Loire 7: Comptes 1811–13; F^{1c} III Corrèze 3: Compte, 4ème trim. 1811; F^{1c} III Bouches-du-Rhône 7: Compte, 3ème trim. 1813; F^{1c} III Mayenne 6: Rapport, 4ème trim. 1817; F^{1c} III Côtes-du-Nord 10: Rapport, 24 September 1819.

37.   A.N. F^2 I 1203: Pref Côte d'Or, 1812; A.N. F^{1c} III Haut-Rhin 6: Compte, prairial VII.

38.   For the following two paragraphs, see Festy, *Délits ruraux,* part II, and the ministry survey of prefects in the Year XI: A.N. F^2 I 1201: doss. "Gardes champêtres" and doss. "Dépenses locales." Also A.N. F^{1c} III Isère 6: Compte, 2 nivôse VI; F^{1c} III Seine-et-Marne 6: Rapport, messidor VII; F^{1c} III Haute-Garonne 8: Tournée, frimaire IX.

39.   Alphonse, *Indre,* 176.

40.   A.N. F^{1c} III Seine-Inférieure 8: Comptes, brumaire-pluviôse VI; A.N. F^2 I 1203: Pref Eure, placard, 7 pluviôse X.

41.   *Ibid.:* Message des Consuls, 3 frimaire VIII; *Arrêté,* 24 fructidor IX; "Nominations" [sic] 29 nivôse XII; Festy, *Délits ruraux,* 174–76; A.N. F^2 I 1201: Responses to circular letter from Moselle, Marne, Charente, and Hérault.

42.   A.N. F^2 I 1201 (An XI): Doubs; F^2 I 1203 (1812): Loiret and Vosges. Cf. A.N. F^{1c} III Vosges 7: Compte, frimaire-prairial VII.

43.   A.N. F^2 I 1203: Rapport au Premier Consul, 29 nivôse XII; decree of 23 fructidor XIII. For the earlier impasse, see, e.g., A.N. F^{1c} III Nord 8: M.I. to Pref, 29 thermidor XI; A.N. F^3 II Calvados 1: Pref to M.I., 13 messidor XII and response 28 thermidor. For prefectorial initiatives after the decree, see, e.g., F^2 I 1203: *Préfecture du département de Seine-et-Oise: Gardes Champêtres* (Versailles, 1811), including a model printed form for the *rôle de répartition* (see Figure V.1); circulars from the prefects of the Drôme and the Meuse; and F^{1c} III Gard 7: Comptes 1812.

44.   A.N. AF IV 1053: Gouvion to Bonaparte, 18 and 30 nivôse XI.

45.   A.N. F^2 I 1203: M.I. circular, 30 June 1806. Comments by the prefects of the Nord and Isère were made in 1812.

46.   A.N. F^{1a} 50: M.I. circular, 17 August 1812. The responses, collected in

A.N. F^2 I 1203, constitute a singularly rich source. Earlier approximations of *embrigadement* occurred in the Pas-de-Calais and the Somme, and the idea was proposed in the Indre.

47.   A.N. F^2 I 1203: on the *garde champêtre* as a potential *fonctionnaire,* see especially Aveyron, Bouches-du-Rhône, Calvados, Côte d'Or, Doubs, Haute-Garonne, Haute-Marne, Pas-de-Calais, Bas-Rhin, Var, and Yonne.

48.   *Ibid.:* Haut-Rhin.

49.   *Ibid.:* Among the strongest opposing voices were the prefects of Allier, Cantal, Côtes-du-Nord, Landes, Manche, Meurthe, Meuse, Nord, Oise, Vaucluse, and Vosges.

50.   *Ibid.:* Rapport au Ministre, March 1818 (a key document). See also A.N. F^3 II Calvados 1: Pref to M.I., 20 January and 23 May 1818, M.I. to Pref, June 1818.

51.   A.N. F^{1c} III Vosges 7: Rapport annuel 1822, taking note of "la dernière loi des finances qui simplifie le mode à suivre pour le recouvrement du salaire de ces gardes." Cf. F^{1c} III Ardennes 5: Rapport 1819.

52.   A.N. F^2 I 1203: Avis du Conseil d'Etat, 5 January 1818; A.N. F^{1c} III Jura 8: Compte 1819/20; F^2 I 1203: Pref Lot to Minister of Police, 18 December 1820; F^3 II Calvados 1: Pref to M.I., 3 June 1824. For the persistence of old complaints about the guards, see Dumiral, *De la Nécessité,* 107–08, cited in note 27.

53.   Unfortunately, the splendid first volume of the *Atlas de la Révolution française: Routes et communications,* ed. G. Arbellot, B. Lepetit, and J. Bertrand (1988) has little to say about the *chemins vicinaux.*

54.   G. Bossi, *Statistique générale . . . Département de l'Ain* (1808), 702–03.

55.   *Analyse des procès-verbaux: Session de l'an 8,* 216; *Session de l'an 9,* 806; Perrin-Dulac, *Isère,* I:236–46; M. de Saint-Amand, *Mémoire statistique du département de l'Eure* (an XIII), 182–83. On the continuing problem of usurpation, see A.N. F^{1c} III Saône-et-Loire 8: Tournée de 1808.

56.   A.N. F^2 I 1202, doss. "Chemins Vicinaux" [an X?]: Calvados, Charente, Moselle; A.N. F^{1c} III Indre 4: Pref to M.I., 6 j.c. XI; F^{1c} III Seine-et-Oise 8: Tournée de fructidor VIII.

57.   A.N. F^2 I 1201 [Enquête de l'an XI], doss. "Chemins Vicinaux": Ardennes, Doubs, Gironde, Jura. See also A.N. F^3 II Marne 1: Pref Haute-Marne to M.I., 12 November 1808 [misfiled].

58.   A.N. F^3 II Nièvre 1: M.I. to Pref, 5 March 1807.

59.   A.N. F^3 I 1: Law of 16 frimaire II.

60.   *Analyse des procès-verbaux: Session de l'an 9,* 438. Cf. A.N. F^3 II Marne 1: Rapport au M.I., 5 brumaire IX, and M.I. to Pref, 16 brumaire IX.

61.   A.N. F^2 I 1202 passim; *Analyse des procès-verbaux: Session de l'an 9,* 806, 135–36.

62.   A.N. F^3 II Yonne 1: Pref to M.I., 24 frimaire XI; F^3 II Nièvre 1: for a "billet de convocation."

63. A.N. F^2 I 1201 [Enquête de l'an XI]: Ariège, Charente-Inférieure, Indres, Vosges; A.N. F^3 II Marne 1: Pref Haute-Marne, *Arrêté* 9 messidor XIII [misfiled]; F^3 II Calvados 1: Pref to M.I., 23 pluviôse XIII; A.N. F^2 I 1027: Rapports au M.I., 23 ventôse and 19 floréal XI (key documents).

64. Texier-Olivier, *Haute-Vienne,* 536; Perrin-Dulac, *Isère,* I:239–40; A.N. F^3 II Marne 1: Pref Haute-Marne to M.I., 12 November 1808 [misfiled]; F^3 II Nord 1: Pref to mayors, circular 21 germinal XII. Cf. A. Smith, *Village Life in China* (2nd edn., Boston, 1970), 20–23.

65. Alphonse, *Indre,* 10; *Journal du Département de l'Oise,* 8 pluviôse, 18 floréal, 8 prairial IX.

66. A.N. F^3 II Côte d'Or 1: Pref to M.I., 29 September 1807; A.N. F^{1c} III Sarthe 6: Compte 3ème trim 1808.

67. A.N. F^2 I 1027: Rapports au M.I., 23 ventôse and 19 floréal XI; A.N. F^3 II Calvados 1: Pref to M.I., 23 pluviôse and 24 ventôse XIII; F^3 II Côte d'Or 1: M.I. to Pref, 27 February 1812, on *affouages.*

68. A.N. F^3 II Bas-Rhin 1: Pref to M.I., 10 March 1808 on the subprefecture of Wissembourg; A.N. F^{1a} 422: *Instruction par le Préfet de la Meurthe . . . an XIII;* Soulet, *Hautes-Pyrénées,* 199–20; F^3 II Nièvre 1: Sous-Pref de Château-Chinon, "Travaux vicinaux exécutés depuis l'an 8 jusqu'à 1814"; A.N. F^{1c} III Gard 7: Comptes 1812; F^{1c} III Oise 6: Comptes 1811.

69. A.N. F^2 I 1027: M.I. circulars, 9 April 1817 and 22 May 1818. On the ensuing muddle, see, e.g., A.N. F^{1c} III Eure 8: Rapport, November 1817; F^{1c} III Seine-et-Marne 6: Rapport, May 1818; A.N. F^3 II Calvados 1: Pref to M.I., 23 May 1818.

70. A.N. F^{1c} III Eure 8: Compte Annuel 1818; F^{1c} III Cher 6: Compte Annuel 1819; F^{1c} III Vienne 5: Rapport, 28 October 1818; F^{1c} III Ardèche 7: Compte, November 1818; F^{1c} III Charente-Inférieure 9: Rapport, September 1818; F^{1c} III Ille-et-Vilaine 7: Mémoire par le conseil général, 5 May 1817; Pref to M.I., 18 February 1818; and Compte Annuel 1819. Also F^{1c} III Dordogne 7: Pref to M.I., 13 July 1819, stating that persuasion has accomplished virtually nothing; and F^{1c} III Jura 8: Compte Annuel 1819.

71. Baron Ramond, *Rapport sur les chemins vicinaux par le Conseil d'Agriculture* (1819), in-$4°$ B.N. Lf^{149} 1, 3–18.

72. B.M.F. LeVavasseur, *Mémoire sur les chemins vicinaux* (1819), 6–17; cf. M. Besson (Sous-Préf de l'Indre), *Moyens proposés pour l'amélioration et l'entretien des chemins vicinaux* (1821), B.N. Lf^{135} 4 and 5.

73. A.N. F^3 II Puy-de-Dôme 1: Pref to M.I. 22 April 1819 and printed model form.

74. *Loi relative aux chemins vicinaux, 28 Juillet 1824.* But the *notables* were still complaining in 1826. See A.N. F^2 I 1027, "Analyse des votes des conseils généraux relativement aux chemins vicinaux." In these years the use of departmental *commissaires-voyeurs* became widespread, but their powers were still limited and their remuneration uncertain; local cooperation remained the essen-

tial ingredient (*ibid.,* M.I. circular, 30 August 1828; Dumiral, *De la Nécessité,* 98, 104–05).

75.   See E. Weber, *Peasants into Frenchmen: The Modernization of Rural France, 1870–1914* (Stanford, 1976), ch. 12, for the breakthrough in local communications of the 1880s.

CHAPTER VI: PRIMARY EDUCATION: CREATING PUBLIC SCHOOLS

1.   The synthesis by R. Chartier, M.-M. Compère, and D. Julia, *L'Education en France du XVIe au XVIIIe siècle* (1976), is indispensable. Among local studies, see D. Julia, "L'enseignement primaire dans le diocèse de Reims à la fin de l'ancien régime," *AHRF* (April 1970), and M. Laget, "Petites écoles en Languedoc au XVIIIe siècle," *Annales E.S.C.* (November 1971). On a school in a largely Protestant village in the South, see T. Sheppard, *Lourmarin in the Eighteenth Century* (Baltimore, 1971), 66–70.

2.   Using advanced statistical techniques, F. Furet and J. Ozouf, *Lire et Ecrire: l'alphabétisation des français de Calvin à Jules Ferry* (2 vols., 1977), have traced and reinterpreted the history of literacy and schooling across three centuries. See also the pioneering article by M. Fleury and P. Valmary, "Les progrès de l'instruction élémentaire de Louis XIV à Napoléon III d'après l'enquête de Louis Maggiolo," *Population,* XII (January 1957), and M. Vovelle, "Y a-t-il eu une révolution culturelle au XVIIIe siècle? A propos de l'éducation populaire en Provence," *RHMC,* XXII (January 1975).

3.   On the advantages of towns, see J. Quéniart, *Culture et sociétés urbaines dans la France de l'Ouest au XVIIIe siècle* (2 vols.: Lille, 1977), and D. Julia, et al., eds., *Atlas de la Révolution française, vol. II: L'Enseignement 1760–1815* (1987), ch. 1.

4.   On the ambivalence of elite discourse on popular education before the Revolution, see H. Chisick, *The Limits of Reform in the Enlightenment: Attitudes Toward the Education of the Lower Classes in Eighteenth-Century France* (Princeton, 1981). For opinion in the *cahiers* that did discuss primary education, see M. Gontard, *L'Enseignement primaire en France de la Révolution à la loi Guizot, 1789–1833* (1959), 66–77.

5.   See the substantial introduction to B. Baczko, *Une Education pour la démocratie: textes et projets de l'époque révolutionnaire* (1982), and M. Ozouf, "La Révolution française et l'idée de l'homme nouveau," in *The Political Culture of the French Revolution.*

6.   For the succession of plans, projects, and laws through 1795, as well as excerpts from the debates and supporting documents, all historians have drawn on the monumental work of J. Guillaume, *Procès-verbaux du Comité d'Instruction Publique de la Convention Nationale* (6 vols., 1891–1907), as well as his preliminary volume on the Legislative Assembly (1889). Many of the texts are reproduced

integrally in Baczko's volume and in thematic sections by D. Julia, *Les Trois couleurs du tableau noir: La Révolution* (1981). For an excellent overview of all aspects of education during the revolutionary decade, see R. R. Palmer, *The Improvement of Humanity: Education and the French Revolution* (Princeton, 1985), which supersedes such older works as E. Allain, *L'Oeuvre scolaire de la Révolution* (1891) and H. C. Barnard, *Education and the French Revolution* (Cambridge, Engl., 1969).

7.   H. Labroue, *La Mission du Conventionnel Lakanal dans la Dordogne en l'an II* (1912), 218–32.

8.   See Baczko, 33–37 and 345–87; Julia, *Les Trois couleurs,* 92–111; Palmer, 138–46; and J. R. Vignery, *The French Revolution and the Schools: The Educational Policies of the Mountain, 1792–94* (Madison, 1965).

9.   See Gontard, 100–06 and 113–22; Baczko, 46–49 and 415–20; and Palmer, 179–83.

10.   A.N. BB^{30} 30 [Bureau de la surveillance de l'exécution des lois]: "Lois démocratiques" and A.N. F^{17} 1331B: "Instruction rédigée au nom du Comité d'Instruction Publique" (hereafter cited as C.I.P.), 26 pluviôse an II.

11.   Guillaume, *Procès-verbaux,* V: 142–51, 177–85, and 223–38. J. Gros, *Lakanal et l'éducation nationale* (1912), is utterly superficial.

12.   Cf. Julia, *Les Trois couleurs,* ch. 6: "Quels programmes pour l'école primaire?"

13.   Guillaume *Procès-verbaux,* V: 232–33; Bazcko, 427–37; M. de Certeau, D. Julia, and J. Revel, *Une Politique de la langue: La Révolution française et le patois* (1976).

14.   Guillaume, *Procès-verbaux,* V: 177–85, 223–38, and 244–46.

15.   A.N. F^{17} 1347 [Exécution de la loi du 27 brumaire III]: dossiers 1 and 2. A.N. F17 1344/35 [Papiers de Lakanal]: District de Castelsarrasin (Haute-Garonne), 6 ventôse III.

16.   A.N. F^{17} 1344/35: District de Mont-de-Marsan (Landes) to Lakanal, 19 prairial III, expressed confusion over the changing guidelines. Lakanal told them to proceed with their original plan in their department with its widely dispersed population. Also F^{17} 1347, d.1: District de Château-Thierry (Aisne), 8 floréal III; d. 2: District de Cérilly (Allier), 9 germinal III; A.N. F^{17} 10138: *Juri d'instruction* (hereafter cited as j.i.) de Dijon, 10 ventôse III.

17.   In St. Chély (Lozère), "no commune has submitted a request for the establishment of primary schools" (A.N. F17 1347, d.1: District de St. Chély to C.I.P., 16 ventôse III), while the District of Sancerre (Cher) wrote to Lakanal: "you have no idea of the insouciance of the people over the education of their children." (F^{17} 1344/35: 29 floréal III; also District de Condom [Gers] to Lakanal, 17 prairial III.)

18.   See A.N. F^{17} 1347: Demandes d'écoles primaires dans les communes dont la population ne s'élève pas à 1000 habitans; F^{17} 1344/35: District de Montmarsan: Tableau des [28] communes qui ont fait des demandes sur le placement des écoles primaires, prairial III; District de Cusset (Allier): Tableau,

prairial III; F¹⁷ 1347, d. 2: District de Narbonne (Aude), 21 pluviôse III; District de Chartres (Eure-et-Loire), 4 nivôse III.

19.   A.N. F¹⁷ 1344/35: District de Provins to Lakanal, 13 floréal III; District d'Albi to Lakanal, 19 prairial III; P.V. District de St. Girons, 6 nivôse III; P.V. District de Quillan (Aude), 4 pluviôse III; G. Clause, "L'Enseignement à Reims pendant la Révolution (1789–1800)," *Actes du 95ème Congrès national des sociétés savantes*, I: *Histoire de l'enseignement de 1610 à nos jours* (1974), 682.

20.   A.N. F¹⁷ 1347, d.3: District de Sens (Yonne), 14 nivôse and 19 ventôse III; d.2: District de la Neste (Hautes-Pyrénées), 4 nivôse III; d. 5: District de Verneuil (Eure), 3 germinal III; District de Poitiers (Vienne), 25 ventôse III; d. 2: District de Sarlat: "Tableau pour la formation des écoles primaires" [ventôse III]; F¹⁷ 1344/35: District de Montargis (Loiret), circular, 27 ventôse III.

21.   A.N. F¹⁷ 1347, d.4: District de St. Quentin (Aisne), Tableau, 3 prairial III; Agent national de Ramberviller (Vosges), pluviôse III; j.i. de Tarbes (Hautes-Pyrénées), 18 prairial III, describing a district "entrecoupée de torrents, ravins et rivières et hérissé de bois et de bruyères."

22.   A.N. F¹⁷ 1347, d.4: Réclamation faite par les habitans d'Oriemont (Seine-et-Oise), 30 frimaire III; La Société populaire d'Etaulle (Charente-Inférieure), 30 frimaire III; La Municipalité de Corcelle (Ain), ventôse III; La Commune de Gargilesse (Indre), nivôse III; Les habitans de Boutigny (Seine-et-Marne), n.d.; Les Citoyens de huit communes de campagne situées dans les Landes, floréal III; Les Citoyens de Bagé (Ain) réunis en société populaire, 30 nivôse III. In the district of Montmédy (Meuse), only five of the 73 communes had populations greater than 1,000; the 68 others had a combined population of 23,000, which meant that they were entitled to a maximum of 23 primary schools: "the distribution of twenty-three teachers will dissatisfy all the communes that will not have them" (L'Agent national de Montmédy, 26 nivôse III).

23.   A.N. F¹⁷ 1347, d.1: District de Château-Thierry (Aisne), 8 floréal III; d. 4: Les Citoyens de Fresne (Aisne) tenues en assemblée populaire, 7 nivôse III; and about twenty other petitions from the eastern departments. See also Albert, Envoyé par la Convention dans l'Aube et la Marne, to C.I.P., 3 prairial III, and G. Sangnier, *Le District de Saint-Pol de Thermidor à Brumaire* (2 vols., Lille, 1946), 783–85.

24.   A.N. F¹⁷ 10138: j.i. de Dijon to C.I.P. [ventôse III]. This complaint was virtually universal.

25.   Figures taken from the correspondence of the districts and *juris d'instruction,* most of which is cited elsewhere, include: Châteauneuf (Eure-et-Loire): 24 *instituteurs* certified as against 9 *institutrices;* Cérilly (Allier) 13/9; St. Girons (Ariège) 22/13; Reims (Marne) 24/14; Castelsarrasin (Haute-Garonne) 18/12; Montargis (Loiret) 38/12; Albi (Tarn) 29/8; Grandpré (Ardennes) 12/3; Bordeaux (Gironde) 40/5; Cadillac (Gironde) 24/3; Sarrebourg (Meurthe) 9/2; Morlaix (Finistère) 17/1; and Romans (Drôme) 12/0. The exceptional districts

with substantial complements of *institutrices* include Brive (Corrèze) with fifty-six men certified vs. forty-two women (F 17 1344/35: p.v. 10 floréal III), and Marseille, fifty-three vs. forty-five (M. Festa, "L'Enseignement primaire à Marseille sous les législations scolaires de l'An II, III, IV" [Mémoire de Maitrise: Aix-en-Provence, 1970], 60).

26. A.N. F^{17} 1351: District de Vézelise (Meurthe) to C.I.P., 6 germinal III: A.N. F^{17} 1360: Agent national de Pithiviers (Loiret), 11 pluviôse III; F^{17} 10138: j.i. de Bergues (Nord) to C.I.P., 16 ventôse III; F^{17} 1347: Agent national de Compiègne (Oise), 7 ventôse III.

27. A.N. F^{17} 1353: District de Sens (Yonne) to C.I.P., 1 floréal III; A.N. F^{17} 1347: District de Chartres (Eure-et-Loire), 1 ventôse III; District de St. Pol (Pas-de-Calais), 5 floréal III. The district d'Epinal (Vosges), 23 nivôse III, proposed "de multiplier les écoles primaires pour les petites communes, d'y réunir les deux sections, d'exiger que l'instituteur soit marié, et que son épouse donne aux filles des leçons de travail concernant leur sexe."

28. A.N. F^{17} 1350: Bailleul from Valognes, 25 floréal III; Jard-Painvillier from Beauvais, 23 floréal III. Cf. j.i. d'Angoulême (Charente) to Lakanal, 15 prairial III (F^{17} 1344/35).

29. On the paucity and inaptness of *instituteurs,* see, e.g., A.N. F^{17} 10138: j.i. de Bordeaux, 23 ventôse III; j.i. de Dijon, 10 ventôse III; j.i. de l'Aigle (Orne), 21 ventôse III; j.i. de Blois (Loir-et-Cher), 19 ventôse III; F^{17} 1344/35: j.i. d'Ardour (Hautes-Pyrénées), 11 prairial III; District de Cérilly (Allier), 9 prairial III; District de Montflanquin, 18 prairial III; F^{17} 1331B: Commune of Avalon (Yonne) to C.I.P., 26 floréal III.

30. Sangnier, *Saint-Pol,* 179n.

31. E.g., A.N. F^{17} 10138: j.i. de Bagnères (Hautes-Pyrénées) to C.I.P., 17 pluviôse III; F^{17} 1347, d.2: j.i. de Marmande (Lot-et-Garonne), nivôse III.

32. See the excellent article by J. Vassort, "L'Enseignment primaire en Vendômois a l'époque révolutionnaire," *RHMC,* XXV (October 1978), 639–40.

33. See Baczko, 471–83; Julia, *Les Trois couleurs,* 153–71; and Palmer, 209–20.

34. Letters from several former students of the Ecole Normale in A.N. F^{17} 1331A, vendémiaire IV and F^{17} 1353.

35. A.N. F^{17} 1353: Rapport par le Commission Exécutif d'Instruction Publique (hereafter cited as Comm. Exec. I.P.), germinal III; Les officiers municipaux de St. Priest-des-Champs (Puy-de-Dôme) to C.I.P., n.d.; District d'Adour, 23 pluviôse III; Le Conseil général de Plonevez Porzay (Finistère) to C.I.P., 26 pluviôse III; F^{17} 1347, d.1: j.i. de Rodez (Aveyron) to C.I.P., 25 ventôse III; District de Soissons (Aisne), 3 pluviôse III.

36. A.N. F^{17} 10138: j.i. de Bergues to C.I.P., 16 ventôse III; j.i. d'Ambert (Puy-de-Dôme) to C.I.P., 11 prairial III; F^{17} 1344/35: P.V. District de Brive, 10 floréal III ("Sans cet inconveniant [le prix des denrées] il ne serait pas difficile de trouver de bons sujets pour instituteurs"); j.i. de Libourne (Gironde), 22

prairial III; District de Cadillac (Gironde), 11 prairial III; District de Libreval (Cher), 29 floréal III; District d'Albi (Tarn), 19 prairial III. See also a mass of petitions from *instituteurs* in A.N. F[17] 1353, including Saignet, instituteur à Lazerte (Lot), 20 thermidor III, and LeNormand, instituteur à Rouen, 7 fructidor III, both "élèves de l'Ecole Normale."

37.   A.N. F[17] 1149: Comm. Exec. I.P. Rapport, 3 vendémiaire IV. Another copy in F[17] 1351, d.4.

38.   *Ibid.*. A.N. F[17] 1351: Petition from two *instituteurs* in Bourg-l'Egalité to C.I.P., n.d.; F[17] 1353: Petition from the *instituteurs* of Tours (Indre-et-Loire).

39.   Correspondence about the rectories and gardens in A.N. F[17] 1352. *Instituteurs* were still claiming arrearages under the Lakanal Law as late as September 1797, usually in vain. See A.N. F[17] 1362: petition by the *instituteurs* of Vesoul (Haute-Saône), fructidor V; F[17] 1362, d. Seine-Inférieure; F[17] 10138: petitions from *instituteurs* in Allier, Ardèche, and elsewhere.

40.   A.N. F[17] 1149: Comm. Exec. I.P. "Observations sur les Ecoles primaires," 4 vendémiaire IV (another copy in F[17] 1351, d. 4). The j.i. of Dijon had recommended a similar course much earlier, adding: "Osons donc le dire: l'égalité d'instruction est une chimère comme le nivellement des fortunes. . . ." (F[17] 10138, 10 ventôse III).

41.   Guillaume, *Procès-verbaux,* VI: 336–37, 580, 793–94, 869–70; Gontard, 151–55. Daunou's report and law are reprinted in Baczko, 499–523.

42.   A.N. F[17] 10138: Les instituteurs de Moissac (Lot) to C500, 11 floréal V; F[17] 1362, d. Haute-Saône: Jean Potey, *instituteur,* to Directory, 15 vendémiaire VI.

43.   See, e.g., Vassort, "Vendômois," 645–52; Sangnier, *Saint-Pol,* 190; M. Schnerb, "L'Enseignement primaire dans le Puy-de-Dôme pendant la Révolution," *AHRF,* XII (March 1935), 105–06; Reinhard, *Le Département de la Sarthe sous le régime directorial,* 450–51. Also A.N. F[1c] III Eure 8: *Compte de gestion par . . . le département: floréal V–floréal VI,* 88 (260 districts were created but only 60 were operating); F[1c] III Basses-Pyrénées 7: *Compte rendu par l'Administration Centrale* (Germinal V), 21 (426 districts but only 187 teachers).

44.   A.N. F[17] 10138: Departmental Administration (hereafter cited as Adm Cent) de l'Allier *Arrêté,* 25 frimaire IV; Adm Cent d'Aveyron, 29 frimaire V; F[17] 1362, d. Haute-Saône, *Arrêté,* 3 ventôse V; A.N. F[17] 1344/32: *Département du Cher: Instruction publique,* 27 prairial IV; Vassort, "Vendômois," 642; other *règlements* in A.N. AF III 109.

45.   A.N. F[17] 1344/32: *Département de l'Oise: Instruction publique,* 4 prairial IV; Adm Cent Eure-et-Loire, 9 messidor VI; Vassort, "Vendômois," 643&n; Schnerb, "Puy-de-Dôme," 106; and the important article by E. Kennedy and M.-L. Netter, "Les Ecoles primaires sous le Directoire," *AHRF,* no. 243 (January 1981), 30.

46.   A.N. F[1c] III Seine 20: Compte vendémiaire VII; F[1c] III Indre 4: circular to municipalities and *instituteurs,* 17 ventôse VI.

47.   A.N. F^{17} 1344/35: District de Sancerre to Lakanal, floréal III; District de Montargis to Lakanal, 7 prairial III; F^{17} 10138: j.i. de Blois to C.I.P., 19 ventôse III; also j.i. de Bourbonne-les-Bains (Haute-Marne) to C.I.P., 23 ventôse III; j.i. de Schlcstatt (Bas-Rhin) to Bailly en mission, 21 pluviôse III; j.i. de Morlaix (Finistère) to C.I.P., 21 prairial III; j.i. de Sarrebourg (Meurthe) to C.I.P., 29 ventôse III.

48.   A.N. F^{17} 1350: Bailleul from Valogncs, 25 floréal III; Jard-Painvillier from Beauvais, 23 floréal III; Dupuis from Troyes, 6 floréal and from Besançon, 23 floréal III.

49.   A.N. F^{17} 10138: Bonnefoi to M.I., 12 floréal V.

50.   Kennedy and Netter, 10–12; A.N. F^{1c} III Côtes-du-Nord 10: Compte vendémiaire VII; Reinhard, *Sarthe,* 458–60; F^{17} 1344/32: *Bulletin de l'instruction publique dans le Lot-et-Garonne,* 15 vendémiaire VII.

51.   A.N. AF III 109 (d. 494): Des Citoyens de Riom au Corps législatif, frimaire VI; also Thomas, instituteur à St. Sange (Nièvre) au C500, brumaire VII: "It is not uncommon in small towns today to see two or three teachers of differing sentiments; the youngsters fervently adhere to the principles of their respective masters, and two groups do not cross paths . . . without abusing each other or worse."

52.   Reinhard, *Sarthe,* 451–54; Schnerb, "Puy-de-Dôme," 109; and dozens of petitions from republican *instituteurs* in A.N. AF III 109.

53.   A.N. F^{1c} III Haut-Rhin 6: Comptes, n.d. [vend. VII?] and messidor VII; F^{1c} III Oise 6: Compte 20 ventôse VI (Nonetheless, "les prêtres fait entendre aux parens que la *nation* faisait enseigner un culte qui *damnait"*); F^{1c} III Jura 7: Compte messidor VI; F^{1c} III Vosges 7: Compte frimaire-prairial VII; *Observateur de l'Yonne,* 25 pluviôse VI; F^{1c} III Dordogne 7: Compte 29 nivôse VII; F^{1c} III Marne 6: *Compte de gestion de l'Adm Cent* (An VII), 24–25; F^{1c} III Ardèche 7: *Compte rendu par l'Adm Cent . . . An VI.*

54.   Kennedy and Netter, 12–18; A.N. F^{17} 1344/32: Lot-et-Garonne: *Arrêté de l'Adm Cent, 15 floréal VI;* Vassort, "Vendômois," 639.

55.   A.N. F^{1c} III Doubs 6: Compte vendémiaire VI; F^{1c} III Ardennes 5: Compte fructidor VI; F^{1c} III Isère 6: Compte nivôse VI; A.N. F^{17} 1344/32: *Bulletin de la situation de l'instruction publique dans le département de Lot-et-Garonne, 15 vendémiaire VII;* Adm Cent Pas-de-Calais, circular, 26 prairial VII.

56.   G. Brégail, *L'Instruction primaire dans le Gers pendant la période révolutionnaire* (Auch, 1899), 42–45. On Condorcet, see Julia, *Les trois couleurs,* ch. V, especially 195–203.

57.   J.-F. Chassaing, "Les Manuels de l'enseignement primaire de la Révolution et les idées révolutionnaires," in J. Morange and J.-F. Chassaing, eds., *Le Mouvement de réforme de l'enseignement en France, 1760–1798* (1974). Excerpts from LaChabeaussière's *Catéchisme* are reprinted in Palmer, 239–40. See also E. Kennedy, "The French Revolutionary Catechisms," *Studies on Voltaire and the Eighteenth Century,* 199 (1981), 353–62.

58.   Chassaing, "Les Manuels," 166–75.

59.   A.N. AF III 109: Masson, *instituteur* d'Armeau au C500, frimaire VII; Vassort, "Vendômois," 650–51. Also A.N. F^{1c} III Cher 6: Compte messidor VI; F^{1c} III Seine-Inférieure 8: Compte brumaire VII. Cf. Bodeau, *instituteur* à Vimontier (Orne) to M.I., 7 messidor VI (F^{17} 1344/33).

60.   On the campaign to impose the revolutionary calendar, see I. Woloch, " 'Republican Institutions,' 1797–99," in Lucas, ed., *The Political Culture of the French Revolution,* 371–87, and M. Ozouf, "Passé, présent, avenir à travers les textes administratifs de l'époque révolutionnaire," in *L'Ecole de la France: essais sur la Révolution, l'utopie, et l'enseignement* (1984).

61.   A.N. F^{17} 1337: Rapport au Directoire, nivôse VI.

62.   A.N. F^{1c} III Doubs 6: Compte brumaire VII. Cf. Gontard, 179.

63.   "Message du Directoire au C500," 3 brumaire VII in A.N. AF III 109.

64.   *C500: Rapport par Luminais sur le mode de surveillance à établir . . . 28 nivôse VI* (Impr. Nationale) and *C500: Rapport par Dulaure . . . 2 frimaire VII.* These proposals are critically dissected by Louis-Grimaud, *Histoire de la liberté d'enseignement en France* (new edn., 1944), II: 408–46.

65.   Reinhard, *Sarthe,* 461–65; Vassort, "Vendômois," 637; Brégail, *Gers,* 45–46; A.N. F^{1c} III Moselle 8: *Compte Rendu par l'Adm Cent . . . floréal VII,* 27; F^{1c} III Loiret 5: Compte 20 ventôse VI; F^{1c} III Haute-Garonne 8: Compte 6 brumaire VII; A.N. F^{17} 1344/33: Adm Cent Haute-Loire to M.I., 11 fructidor VI; Adm Cent Côte d'Or, an VII; Adm Cent Marne to M.I., 2 thermidor VI; Louis-Grimaud, II: 369–73; Gontard, 173–76.

66.   A.N. F^{17} 1344/32: Adm Cent Lot-et-Garonne: *Arrêté 15 floréal VI;* F^{17} 1344/33: Adm Cent Eure-et-Loire, 2 prairial VI; p.v.s. of *agents municipaux* in the Vosges, nivôse VII.

67.   C. Derobert-Ratel, *Institutions et vie municipale à Aix-en-Provence sous la Révolution* (Aix, 1981), 499; Vassort, "Vendômois," 651.

68.   E.g., A.N. F^{1c} III Loire 6: Compte 13 brumaire VII: "Quelques administrations municipales visitent les instituteurs de leur arrondissement, mais le plus grand nombre néglige cet objet important malgré nos exhortations."

69.   A.N. F^{17} 1344/33: correspondence among local and departmental authorities in the Manche and the M.I., floréal-messidor VI. The same complaint was raised by officials in the Dordogne, nivôse VII.

70.   A.N. F^{1c} III Seine-Inférieure 8: Compte pluviôse VII.

71.   A.N. F^{1c} III Allier 6: *Compte rendu de l'Adm Cent, fructidor V-prairial VI;* A.N. F^{17} 1337: Adm Cent Ain to M.I., 4 ventôse VI; F^{1c} III Pas-de-Calais 8: Compte messidor VI; F^{1c} III Aude 5: Compte messidor VI; F^{1c} III Ardennes 5: Compte fructidor VI. Cf. *Journal de la Côte d'Or,* 20 brumaire VIII, and *Observateur de l'Yonne,* 25 germinal VIII.

72.   A.N. AF III 109: Dupont, *instituteur* à St. Omer, 23 germinal VII. Also A.N. F^{17} 1344/32: Adm Cent Manche to M.I. 8 messidor VII in behalf of LeLièvre, *instituteur.*

73.   A.N. F^{1c} III Basses-Pyrénées 7: Compte 28 nivôse VII; F^{1c} III Loire 6: Compte 23 nivôse VII. A.N. AF III 109 (d. 503): Les Citoyens de Château Chenon (Nièvre) to C500, 20 pluviôse VI; Des Républicains du faubourg Antoine to C500, 2 frimaire VI; Les Citoyens de Béthune (Pas-de-Calais) to C500, pluviôse VI, demanding "une instruction égale et commune"; Les Citoyens de Versailles to C500, nivôse VI, invoking "la dette publique de l'instruction."

74.   A.N. F^{17} 1337: Commissioner to Côte d'Or: "Vues d'exécution sur l'organisation de l'Instruction publique" (n.d.); A.N. F^{1c} III Vosges 7: Compte nivôse VI; F^{1c} III Ardennes 5: Compte prairial VII; F^{1c} III Haut-Rhin 6: Compte messidor VII; F^{1c} III Eure-et-Loire 7: Compte messidor VI; F^{1c} III Isère 6: Compte nivôse VII.

75.   "Toutes les administrations centrales soupirent après une loi du Corps législatif qui puisse donner enfin aux écoles primaires le mouvement et la vie." A.N. F^{1c} I 12: Résumé des comptes, ventôse VII.

76.   *C500: Rapport par Roger Martin sur les écoles primaires, secondaires et centrales, 6 brumaire VII;* Palmer, 257–68; Gontard, 180–83.

77.   *C500: Rapport par Hertault-Lamerville sur les écoles primaires, 22 brumaire VII* and *C500: Nouvelle rédaction des projets sur l'instruction publique . . . écoles primaires par Hertault-Lamerville, pluviôse VII.*

78.   *C500: Opinion de Duplantier sur les écoles primaires, 24 nivôse VII; C500: Opinion de Boileau . . . 24 nivôse VII; C500: Discours de Hertault-Lamerville en réponse aux opinions émises à la tribune . . . 14 germinal VII*, 3.

79.   *C500: Opinion d'André sur les écoles primaires, 21 germinal VII; Discours d'Hertault-Lamerville, 14 germinal,* 24–25; *C500: Opinion de Challan . . . 28 nivôse VII; C500: Opinion de Bremontier . . . 28 nivôse VII.* Cf. A.N. F^{1c} III Yonne 7: Compte frimaire VI and F^{1c} III Orne 8: Compte 8 messidor VI on the problem of small isolated communes.

80.   *C500: Opinion d'Andrieux sur les écoles primaires, 1 floréal VII.*

81.   *Nouvelle rédaction des projets.*

CHAPTER VII: PRIMARY EDUCATION: RETREAT AND CONSOLIDATION

1.   For Napoleonic policy, see the thorough discussion in Gontard, *L'Enseignement primaire,* 191–235.

2.   *Ibid.,* 201–11. The perspectives of the *idéologues* are examined in Palmer, *Improvement of Humanity,* 268–78. But compare the strong concern expressed by many departmental advisory councils in the Year IX over the lack of schooling in rural communes, and especially their continued advocacy of public salaries for teachers as a remedy for this neglect: Chaptal, ed., *Analyse des procès-verbaux des Conseils généraux de département: Session de l'an 9* (an X), 572–83. Several councils proposed that the position of *instituteur public* and secretary of the *mairie* be linked.

3. On the rectories, see, e.g., Kennedy and Netter, "Les Ecoles primaires sous le Directoire," 16–17 and 23. Cf. Furet and Ozouf, *Lire et ecrire,* 287–89.

4. A.N. F^{1a} 422: *Instruction du Préfet de la Meurthe aux maires . . . an XII;* A.N. F^{17} 1366 d. Bas-Rhin: Fourcroy to M.I., 17 nivôse XIII and Rapport 27 nivôse XIII. Cf. Bossi, *Ain,* 376–77, and Alphonse, *Indre,* 105.

5. H. Forestier, ed., *L'Yonne au XIXème siècle, première partie 1800–1830* (Auxerre, 1959), 652; A.N. F^{1c} III Seine-Inférieure 8: Sous-préfet de Dieppe, an X; A.N. F^{17} 1366: Pref Seine-Inférieure, an XIII. (The problem here was that "les communes réunies ne veulent point envoyer leurs enfans au chef lieu et refusent par suite de venir contribuer au sort de l'instituteur.") F^{17} 1363: Pref Aube, 1808: "La portion de leur traitement provenant de la cotisation volontaire est très incertaine; elle leur est quelquefois disputée par la mauvaise foi et plus souvent par l'égoisme des célibataires et des familles privées d'enfans." For successful examples of voluntairism, see A.N. F^{17} 1365 d. Oise: Fourcroy to M.I., 6 ventôse XIII; F^{17} 1366: Pref Bas-Rhin to Fourcroy, 18 messidor XI.

6. A.N. F^{17} 1365 d. Moselle: Pref to Fourcroy, 15 frimaire XII, and "Observations du Maire de Metz sur les écoles primaires," 14 prairial XI; F^{17} 1364 d. Lot-et-Garonne an XI. On Brittany, Pref Finistère to Fourcroy, 17 floréal XI; F17 1366 d. Deux-Sèvres; A.N. F^{1c} III Ille-et-Vilaine 7: Renseignemens 15 nivôse IX. See also A.N. F^{17} 1363 Cantal; F^{17} 1364 Indre-et-Loire and Isère.

7. E.g., A.N. F^{17} 1363: Pref Aisne to Fourcroy, 11 thermidor XI; F^{17} 1365: Pref Moselle to Fourcroy, 2 frimaire XIII; Pref Oise, 2 frimaire XII; F^{17} 1366 d. Var, nivôse XII.

8. A.N. F^{17} 1364 d. Jura: Rapport au M.I., 25 March 1806 and Mayor of Poligny to M.I., 14 February 1806.

9. A.N. F^{17} 1363: Mayor of Marseille to M.I., 10 June 1807; Pref Eure-et-Loire to Fourcroy, 8 frimaire XIV; Rapport au M.I. 9 nivôse XIV, and Fourcroy to Pref, 10 January 1806; Pref Calvados to Fourcroy, 8 July 1806 and M.I. to Fourcroy, 11 September 1806; Pref Drôme to Fourcroy, 15 November 1806.

10. A.N. F^{17} 1365: Pref Nord to Fourcroy, 2 May 1807 and response 19 June; F^{17} 1363: Etat de toutes les écoles primaires de l'Aube, 1808; F^{17} 1365: Pref Oise to Fourcroy, 2 frimaire XII; F^{17} 1363: Mayor of Marseille to M.I., 10 June 1807; F^{17} 1364: Pref Ille-et-Vilaine: Arrêté 10 thermidor XII, and Pref Hérault: Arrêté pluviôse XII. On the Directory years, cf. Kennedy and Netter, 29–30. Seventeen *conseils généraux des départements* expressed their interest in schooling for girls (*Analyse des procès-verbaux: Session de l'an 9,* 582–83).

11. On the concept of the University, see Palmer, *Improvement of Humanity,* 306–20.

12. Gontard, *Enseignement primaire,* 236–53.

13. The Academy of Besançon seems to have been a minor exception. The rector reported in 1812 that out of 1,437 candidates examined, 38 were rejected

for *incapacité notoire* and 46 as *trop faible:* A.N. F[17] 9367: Rector to Grand-maître, 5 May 1812.

14.   The following paragraphs are based on the dossiers in A.N. F[17] 10107 [*clôtures*], which also contains several incomplete lists of closings.

15.   A.N. F[17] 10107: examples in Boisemault (Eure), Bienville (Aisne), Villiers (Seine-et-Oise), Coudreceau (Eure-et-Loire), St. Symphorien (Eure-et-Loire), Collobrières (Bouches-du-Rhône), Villers-en-Cauchie (Nord), and Carpentras (Vaucluse). See also Rector of Rouen Acad to Grand-maître, 20 August 1812; Rector of Aix Acad to Grand-maître, 15 June 1812; Inspector Cuvier to Grand-maître, 9 February 1813.

16.   *Ibid.:* Landrin to Grand-maître, 1812. Cf. d. Dubois in Crécy (Seine-et-Marne).

17.   *Ibid.:* d. Marcou in Villeneuve (Charente-Inférieure).

18.   *Ibid.:* Rector of Poitiers Acad to Grand-maître, 27 November 1812. In Fontenay-aux-Roses (Seine), which ostensibly could not support two teachers adequately, the incumbent was Bourguignon, a forty-nine-year-old tailor who could not make a living from his trade. Fairand, his thirty-seven-year-old challenger, was a pensioned war veteran, said to be intelligent and of good character—exactly the kind of new blood that one hoped for in an *instituteur* (*ibid.:* d. Bourguignon-Fairand.) See also the dossiers on Humberot in Etrechy (Seine-et-Oise), Varon in St. Ouen (Seine-et-Oise), Gaillard in Beaumont-sur-Oise (Seine-et-Oise), and Hubac in Langéac (Haute-Loire).

19.   A.N. F[17] 9360: Grand-maître to Archévêque d'Aix, 25 March 1809; A.N. F[17] 10107: d. Marquie (Ariège), d. Foucard (Seine-et-Marne); Cuvier to Grand-maître, 18 March 1812.

20.   *Ibid.:* P.V. 9 March 1813.

21.   Gontard, *Enseignement primaire,* 267–359, presents a detailed account of Restoration policy; the quotes are from pp. 269 and 272. Cf. A. Rendu, *Essai sur l'instruction publique et particulièrement sur l'instruction primaire* (3 vols., 1819). For politics and opinion after 1814, see G. Bertier de Sauvigny, *The Bourbon Restoration* (Philadelphia, 1966), part II and ch. 17.

22.   Opinions of the *conseils généraux des départements* on education are collected in A.N. F[17] 1395. For anti-*Université* sentiment, see, e.g., Lozère, Mayenne, Pas-de-Calais, Puy-de-Dôme, Haut-Rhin, and Saône-et-Loire.

23.   *Ibid.: conseils généraux* of Cher, Finistère, Haute-Garonne, Ille-et-Vilaine, Maine-et-Loire, Var, Vaucluse.

24.   A.N. F[17] 10372: Acad de Besançon, "Observations sur la mise en exécution. . . ."

25.   The Ultra interlude is chronicled in Bertier de Sauvigny, *Bourbon Restoration,* part IV. For its impact on education, see A. Prost, *L'Enseignement en France, 1800–1967* (1968), 155–68.

26.   For difficulties with the *comités cantonaux* and/or the curés, see the

reports submitted by the rectors to Paris: A.N. F^{17} 10372: Acad d'Aix; Acad d'Angers, 1817; Acad de Caen, 1817; Acad de Clermont, 1817; A.N. F^{17} 9368: Acad de Limoges, 1820; Acad de Montpellier, 1822; Acad de Strasbourg, 1822; A.N. F^{17} 10374: Acad de Limoges; Acad de Grenoble, 1817.

27.   A.N. F^{17} 10372: Acad d'Aix; Acad d'Angers, July 1817; F^{17} 10375: Acad de Rennes.

28.   A.N. F^{17} 9367: Commission Royale de l'Instruction Publique, 1817; J. Vidalenc, *Le Département de l'Eure sous la monarchie constitutionnelle* (1952), 579; A.N. F^{17} 10372: Acad de Cahors, 1817; Acad de Clermont, 1817. The Academy of Amiens was evidently an exception. While 100 candidates were rejected there for *mauvaises moeurs,* about 100 others were barred "pour incapacité manifeste."

29.   A.N. F^{17} 10375: Acad de Rouen, "Rapport sur l'instruction primaire," August 1817; A.N. F^{17} 10374: Acad de Limoges.

30.   A.N. F^{17} 10372: Acad d'Aix, 1817; A.N. F^{17} 10374: Acad de Grenoble, 1817; Acad de Montpellier.

31.   A.N. F^{17} 10372: Acad de Besançon. The proportions are taken from various rectors' reports.

32.   Furet and Ozouf, *Lire et Ecrire,* 118–37 and 167–69; Prost, *Enseignement,* 132–40. In the Academy of Nancy, 165 out of 185 *brevets* granted in 1821 were second degree (A.N. F^{17} 9368).

33.   A.N. F^{17} 10372: Acad de Caen, *Règlement provisoire pour les écoles primaires* (1816); Acad de Rouen, *Règlement* (1816), cited in Vidalenc, *Eure,* 578–79; A.N. F^{17} 9368: Acad de Montpellier, 1822.

34.   But see A.N. F^{17} 10374: "Notes sur l'instruction publique par le recteur de l'Acad de Nîmes," 26 April 1817, explaining that the prefect of the Gard ordered teachers to refrain from teaching religious principles in religiously mixed cantons which could not sustain separate schools.

35.   The treatment of mutual schools by Gontard, *Enseignement primaire* (273–96, 310–30, 372–81) is now superseded by the exhaustive dissertation of Raymond Tronchot, *L'Enseignement mutuel en France de 1815 à 1833: les luttes politiques et religieuses autour de la question scolaire* (3 vols., Lille, 1973). See also P. Leuilliot, *L'Alsace au début du XIXème siécle* (3 vols., 1959–60), III: 303–18.

36.   Tronchot, II: 426–30; A.N. F^{17} 10374: Acad de Grenoble, Juillet 1817; A.N. F^{17} 10372: Acad de Bourges, 1817; A.N. F^{17} 1395: *conseils généraux* Ardennes, Lot-et-Garonne, Lozère, 1816.

37.   Tronchot, II: 535; F. Buisson, ed., *Dictionnaire de Pédagogie* (2 vols., 1882), I(1): 1112.

38.   A.N. F^{17} 1395: Gironde, 1816.

39.   For comparisons, see Tronchot, II: 425 and 445–47, and III: 588–89.

40.   A.N. F^{17} 1395: *Conseil général* Loire-Inférieure; A.N. F^{1c} III Ille-et-Vilaine 7: January 1820; Tronchot, II: 448–50.

41.   Quoted in Leuilliot, *Alsace,* III: 308. See also Tronchot, III: 589–90, and II: 339–40.

42. Buisson, *Dictionnaire*, I(1): 500–02. Cf. A.N. F^{1c} III Dordogne 7, 1819; F^{1c} III Seine-et-Oise 8, 1819; F^{1c} III Vienne 5: Analyse du Compte annuel de 1819: "Plusieurs écoles d'enseignement mutuel se sont formées et prospèrent, malgré l'opposition constante du conseil général, qui à voté 6,000F pour la seule Ecole des Frères. . . ."

43. A.N. F^{17} 10372: Acad d'Amiens, 1817.

44. A.N. F^{17} 9368: Acad de Montpellier, 1822; A.N. F^{17} 10372: Acad d'Amiens, 1817.

45. Tronchot, II:448, 460–64 and 472. In Lyon, the order's headquarters, the Frères had seven schools with 2,700 students (A.N. F^{17} 10372: Acad de Lyon, October 1817).

46. Tronchot, II: 546–52, and III: 582–91; A.N. F^{17} 9368: Acad de Montpellier, 1822. Gérando is quoted in Leuilliot, *Alsace*, III: 309.

47. Furet & Ozouf, *Lire et Ecrire*, 155–59, 286–87, and computer-generated maps 30–38 (pp. 316–17).

48. A.N. F^{17} 9368: Acads of Strasbourg, Besançon, Montpellier, and Nancy (where 1,062 teachers used the simultaneous method and 759 the individual method in 1821).

49. There are statistics, which must be taken with caution, in Gontard, 354 and 358; Tronchot, II: 546; Prost, 108. For the situation on the eve of the Guizot Law of 1833, see Furet & Ozouf, *Lire et Ecrire*, map 1 (p. 308) and pp. 271–73. For a comprehensive analysis of the ensuing decades, see R. Grew and P. Harrigan, *School, State, and Society: The Growth of Elementary Schooling in Nineteenth-Century France. A Quantitative Analysis* (Ann Arbor, Mich., 1991).

50. A.N. F^{17} 9368: Acad de Montpellier, 1822; A.N. F^{17} 10372: Acad de Cahors, 1817; A.N. F^{17} 10374: Acad de Limoges.

51. A.N. F^{17} 10372: Acad d'Amiens, 1817; Acad de Clermont, 1817; Acad de Pau.

52. A.N. F^{17} 10372: Acad de Cahors, 1817; A.N. F^{17} 10374: Acad de Nîmes, 1817 (on the Ardèche); A.N. F^{17} 10375: Acad de Rouen.

53. A.N. F^{17} 10375: Acad de Rennes, 1817 and A.N. F^{1c} III Ille-et-Vilaine 7: Pref 1824; A.N. F^{17} 9368: Acad de Strasbourg, 1822; Acad de Limoges, 1820; A.N. F^{17} 10374: Acad de Nîmes, 1817 (on the Lozère).

54. In the Academy of Besançon in 1821, 70,000 children attended school in "winter" but only 17,000 in "summer" (A.N. F^{17} 9368). See also A.N. F^{17} 10375: Inspector of the Acad de Paris, September 1817; A.N. F^{17} 9368: Acad de Montpellier, 1822. On seasonal attendance, cf. Furet & Ozouf, *Lire et Ecrire*, 284–85, and maps 20–23 (pp. 312–13).

55. A.N. F^{1c} III Vienne 5: Analyse du Compte Annuel de 1819.

56. For the lack of subsidies by the *conseils municipaux* and the call for regular salaries, see, inter alia, Acad de Rouen (A.N. F^{17} 10375), Acad de Strasbourg (F17 9368), Acad de Caen (F^{17} 10372), Acad de Limoges (F^{17} 10374), and the undated report [1817] from the Commission Royale d'Instruction publique (F^{17}

9367), which emphasized the negative impact on schooling for the poor from the lack of local subsidies or fixed salaries for *instituteurs.* The same themes of course appear in the reports of the Napoleonic rectors.

57.   See especially pp. 39–42, 54–58, 80–81, 97, and 109–15.

58.   Most recently by B. Baczko, *Une Éducation pour la démocratie* (1982) and D. Julia, *Les trois couleurs du tableau noir* (1981).

59.   See J. Van Horn Melton, *Absolutism and the Eighteenth-century Origins of Compulsory Schooling in Prussia and Austria* (Cambridge, Engl., 1988), part III.

60.   A. LaVopa, *Prussian School Teachers: Profession and Office, 1763–1848* (Chapel Hill, 1980), ch.1. Cf. M. J. Maynes, "The Virtues of Archaism: The Political Economy of Schooling in Europe, 1750–1850," *Comparative Studies in Society and History,* XXI (October 1979), 611–25, based on research in Southern France and Baden.

61.   LaVopa, chs. 2–3.

CHAPTER VIII: REVOLUTIONARY *BIENFAISANCE*

1.   See the superb study by Olwen Hufton, *The Poor of Eighteenth-Century France* (Oxford, 1974), part I.

2.   *Ibid.,* ch. XII, and M. Garden, *Lyon et les lyonnais au XVIIIe siècle* (1975), ch. 2. Cf. R. Fuchs, *Abandoned Children: Foundlings and Child Welfare in Nineteenth-Century France* (Albany, 1984).

3.   C. Romon, "Le Monde des pauvres à Paris au XVIIIe siècle," *Annales E.S.C.,* XXXVII (July 1982), no. 4, 730–31 and 750.

4.   O. Hufton, "Begging, Vagrancy, Vagabondage and the Law: An Aspect of the Problem of Poverty in Eighteenth-Century France," *European Studies Review,* II (1972), no. 2, 97–123; R. Schwartz, *Policing the Poor in Eighteenth-Century France* (Chapel Hill, 1988), 187–95 on "Namur."

5.   J. P. Gutton, *La Société et les pauvres: l'exemple de la généralité de Lyon, 1534–1789* (1971); Hufton, *The Poor,* ch. V.

6.   J. Depauw, "Pauvres, pauvres mendiants, mendiants valides ou vaga-bonds? Les hésitations de la législation royale," *RHMC,* XXI (1974), 401–18.

7.   Schwartz, *Policing the Poor,* 95.

8.   Romon, "Pauvres à Paris," 753; Hufton, "Begging," 99; L. Cahen, *Le Grand Bureau des Pauvres de Paris au milieu du XVIIIe siècle* (1908); and especially C. Jones, *Charity and Bienfaisance: The Treatment of the Poor in the Montpellier Region, 1740–1815* (Cambridge, Engl., 1982), 49–56.

9.   C. Bloch, *L'Assistance et l'état en France à la veille de la Révolution* (1908), 127–30. Cf. E. Sol, "Les Bureaux de charité en Quercy à la fin de l'ancien régime," *Annales du Midi,* no. 237 (1948), 260–84.

10.   On the financing and administration of old-regime *hôpitaux,* see C.

Fairchilds, *Poverty and Charity in Aix-en-Provence, 1640–1789* (Baltimore, 1976), part I.

11. Fairchilds, *Aix-en-Provence,* ch. 6; Jones, *Montpellier,* ch. 4; and K. Norberg, *Rich and Poor in Grenoble, 1600–1814* (Berkeley, 1985), chs. 8 and 10.

12. D. Dakin, *Turgot and the Ancien Régime in France* (New York, 1939); Bloch, *L'Assistance et l'état,* passim; Hufton, *The Poor,* 182–93. For "progressive" economic thinking at the time of the Revolution, see R. DuBoff, "Economic Thought in Revolutionary France, 1789–92: The Question of Poverty and Unemployment," *French Historical Studies,* IV (1966), 434–51.

13. C. Bloch and A. Tuetey, eds., *Procès-verbaux et rapports du Comité de Mendicité de la Constituante* (1911), and Ferdinand-Dreyfus, *Un Philanthrope d'autrefois: LaRochefoucauld-Liancourt, 1747–1827* (1903), ch. IV.

14. A. Forrest, *The French Revolution and the Poor* (Oxford, 1981), ch. VI.

15. Bernard d'Airy, *Rapport sur l'organisation générale des secours publics, et sur la destruction de la mendicité* (13 June 1792), B.N. Le[33] 3y. Cf. Ferdinand-Dreyfus, *L'Assistance sous la Législative et la Convention* (1905), ch. I.

16. J.-B. Bô, *Rapport . . . sur les bases de l'organisation générale des secours publics* (1793), B.N. Le[38] 2327, p. 3. Bernard evidently circulated his report to the departmental administrations: see J. Adher, ed., *Recueil de documents sur l'assistance publique dans le District de Toulouse de 1789 à 1800* (Toulouse, 1918), 447.

17. Bernard, *Rapport,* 6–14, 65–66.

18. *Ibid.,* 57–63.

19. *Ibid.,* 16–50, 65.

20. *Ibid.,* 84–89.

21. *Ibid.,* 92–105.

22. Texts of major laws and decrees were published by A. deWatteville, *Législation charitable ou recueil des lois, décrets, ordonnances royales . . .* (1843): law of 19 March 1793 (pp. 17–18).

23. Maignet, *Rapport sur l'organisation des secours à accorder annuellement aux enfans et aux vieillards* (June 1793), B.N. Le[38] 316; Watteville, *Législation charitable,* 20–24; Ferdinand-Dreyfus, *L'Assistance,* 63–70.

24. A.N. F[15] 2589: Districts of Hazebrouck, Caen, Sablé, Riom, and Pont à Mousson.

25. *A.P.,* LXXXIV (1962), 165–66; A.N. F[15]* 8 [Exécution du décret du 13 pluviôse II], passim. Watteville did *not* include the decree of 13 pluviôse in his collection, which may explain why subsequent historians of *bienfaisance* never seemed to know about it.

26. Archives de l'Assistance Publique, Paris (hereafter cited as A.A.P.): surviving records of five *comités de bienfaisance* of the Paris sections for the year II: Finistère, 13 ventôse, 7 prairial II; Indivisibilité, 14 messidor, 19 thermidor; Poissonnière, 8 germinal. Also A.N. F[15] 2872 and 3590.

27. A.N. F[15] 2871: especially sections Fraternité, Tuileries, and Obser-

482 NOTES TO PP. 250–257

vatoire. Cf. R. Monnier, *Le Faubourg Saint-Antoine, 1789–1815* (1981), 90–101, 229–43; and A.N. AF IV 1051: Etat Général des Indigens de Paris, an XII.

28.   A.N. F^{1c} III Charente-Inférieure 9: *Compte Rendu de l'Adm Cent, an IV–germinal an V,* ch. III. Repeal occurred in the law of 7 frimaire V (Watteville, *Législation charitable,* 42). For the failure of the program in Grenoble, see Norberg, *Rich and Poor,* 275–78.

29.   Bertrand Barère, *Premier rapport au nom du Comité de Salut Public sur les moyens d'extirper la mendicité dans les campagnes* (22 floréal II). This address appeared in at least six editions, including one in pocket-size format.

30.   A.N. F^{15} 2589: circular from Commission des Secours Publics, early year III.

31.   *Ibid.*. For the text of the law, Watteville, *Législation charitable,* 29–32.

32.   A.N. F^{15}* 10 [Secours aux cultivateurs . . . loi du 22 floréal II] passim.

33.   Jones, *Montpellier,* 177–83; A. Lacoste, "Application dans les départements de la Mayenne et de l'Orne des décrets de la Convention concernant les grands mesures d'assistance collective" (unpublished D.E.S., Paris, May 1961) in A.A.P. Z-87. Many of the female recipients were textile workers, suggesting what a thin reed such manufacturing was for rural subsistence. See also G. Sangnier, *Le District de Saint Pol,* 153.

34.   Woloch, *The French Veteran from the Revolution to the Restoration,* ch. III.

35.   *Ibid.,* chs. IV–V.

36.   I. Woloch, "War-Widows Pensions: Social Policy in Revolutionary and Napoleonic France," *Societas,* VI (1976), 235–54.

37.   A.N. F^{15} 3334; *A.P.,* LXXXIV, 129–31, 503–05. For this question, see Forrest, *Revolution and the Poor,* ch. VIII.

38.   A.N. F^{15} 2834/35: M.I. to municipal officials, 3 ventôse II; also A.N. BB^{30} 30 [Bureau de la surveillance de l'exécution des lois], ventôse II; A.N. F^{15}* 9–11: Secours aux parens des militaires; Adher, *Toulouse,* 457.

39.   J.-P. Bertaud, *The Army of the French Revolution* (Princeton, 1988 transl.), 251–59.

40.   Figures have been distilled from Commission des Secours Publics: Journal des Dépenses (A.N. F^{15}* 9–11). On the militarization of hospitals, see also Forrest, *Revolution and the Poor,* and Jones, *Montpellier,* 172–73 and 191–92.

41.   I. Woloch, "From Charity to Welfare in Revolutionary Paris," *JMH,* LVIII (December 1986), 780–87.

42.   *Ibid.,* 788–94. The lists of members may be found in A.N. F^{15} 132.

43.   *Corps Municipal de Paris: Plan d'Organisation des 48 comités de bienfaisance . . . 25 juillet 1793* reprinted in A. Tuetey, ed., *L'Assistance publique à Paris pendant la Révolution* (4 vols., 1897), IV:453–57; A.N. F^{15} 2871: Commission Centrale de Bienfaisance [de Paris] to Commission des Secours Publics, thermidor II.

44.   For the ways in which the committees disbursed assistance, see Wo-

loch, "Charity to Welfare," 795–801, drawing on the minutes of five committees in A.A.P. (Brutus, Finistère, Indivisibilité, Poissonnière, and Quinze-Vingts).

45. *Ibid.,* 801–04. See especially A.N. F^{15} 2871: Commission Centrale de Bienfaisance [de Paris] to the Treasury, 14 frimaire III; the minute books of the five committees; and A.N. F^{15} 2872: comptes an IV: sections Brutus, Mail, Réunion, and Gravilliers.

46. For the *hôpitaux,* I have relied on Forrest, *Revolution and the Poor,* chs. III–IV; Colin Jones's study of Montpellier; J. Adher's collection of sources on Toulouse; Norberg, *Rich and Poor in Grenoble,* ch. 11; and an older monograph by E. Chaudron, *L'Assistance publique à Troyes à la fin de l'ancien régime et pendant la Révolution, 1770–1800* (1923). On hospital administration, see also D. Higgs, "Politics and Charity at Toulouse, 1750–1850," in J. F. Bosher, ed., *French Government and Society, 1500–1850: Essays in Memory of Alfred Cobban* (London, 1973).

47. A.N. F^{15}* 10–11: Journal des dépenses. On aid to the dependents of *militaires,* see A.N. F^{15} 2866: Etat des attributions de la 3ème section (2ème division) de l'Intérieure, an IV–V, and A.N. F^{15} 2834/35: M.I. to departmental administrations, 15 floréal IV and 30 frimaire V.

48. Woloch, "Charity to Welfare," 804–08.

49. A.N. F^{15} 2871: Commission Centrale de Bienfaisance [de Paris]: Rapport sur le secours extraordinaire de 23 frimaire IV.

50. Jones, *Montpellier,* 184–200; Forrest, *Revolution and the Poor,* ch. IV; Adher, *Toulouse,* passim, especially Compte Rendu par les administrateurs de l'Hospice de lHumanité, 23 messidor IV, cited on p. 137; and R. C. Cobb, "Disette et Mortalité: la crise de l'an III et de l'an IV à Rouen," in *Terreur et Subsistances, 1793–1795* (1965), 326–37.

51. The parliamentary retreat was led by the "Girondin" Delecloy: *Rapport sur la loi du 23 messidor* (10 thermidor III), and *Rapport sur l'organisation générale des secours publics* (12 vendémiaire IV), both in A.N. AD XIV 10, and *Réflexions par Delecloy sur l'organisation des hospices [an V?],* B.N. Le^{43} 485. Among other opinions on assistance and *hôpitaux* see *C.A.: Opinion de Larmagnac sur les hospices civils* (15 vendémiaire V); *C.A.: Opinion de Lebrun . . .* (15 vendémiaire V); and *C500: Rapport par Delaporte sur . . . l'organisation des secours publics* (13 messidor IV)— containing the canard that under the "vicious" pension laws of 1793–94, "la somme que reçoit le pauvre n'est pour lui que l'occasion de se livrer à la débauche."

52. Woloch, *French Veteran,* 90–109.

53. A.N. F^{15} 2868: *Compte au Bureau Général de Bienfaisance, an V;* Rapport au M.I., 7 thermidor VI; Etats de la recette des théatres, an V; A.N. F^{1c} III Seine 20: Tableau de la situation, vendémiaire VII.

54. A.N. F^{1c} III Eure 8: *Compte de gestion par . . . le département, floréal V–floréal VI,* 72–73; F^{1c} III Calvados 8: Dept. Comm. to M.I., nivôse VII; F.J.-B.

d'Alphonse, *Mémoire statistique du département de l'Indre* (an XII), 146; G. Bossi, *Statistique générale de la France . . . Département de l'Ain* (1808), 444; Adher, *Toulouse,* 233; A.N. F[15] 109: Budget de l'administration des secours publics de la ville d'Amiens, 1814.

55.   A.N. F[15] 2872: Bureau Central [de Paris] to M.I., 16 germinal VI; M.I. circular to *comités de bienfaisance,* 15 thermidor VI in Archives départementales de la Seine, VD* 6978. For the dominance of the *hôpitaux* over *secours à domicile,* see Florence Gresse (née Cassaigne), "Le Conseil Général des hospices civils de Paris et les secours publics, 1801–1830" (unpublished thèse de l'Ecole des Chartes, 1975) in A.A.P. On the Hérault, see Jones, *Montpellier,* 213–18. See also Baron Charles Dupin, *Histoire de l'Administration des Secours publics* (1821), 86–89.

56.   A.N. F[15] 106: Pref Aisne to M.I., 10 February 1806; G. Delfau, *Annuaire statistique du département de la Dordogne pour l'an XII* (Périgueux, an XII), 168.

57.   P. Laboulinière, *Annuaire statistique du département des Hautes-Pyrénées* (1807), 276; L. Texier-Olivier, *Statistique Générale de la France . . . Département de la Haute-Vienne* (1808), 242. See also A.N. F[1c] III Orne 8: Tournée An XIII, "Bureaux de bienfaisance"; and comments by the *conseils généraux des départements,* an IX (Chaptal, ed., *Comptes Rendus des Sessions*).

58.   Alphonse, *Indre,* 147; Chaudron, *L'Assistance à Troyes,* 327; A.N. F[15] 109: Budget des secours publics . . . Amiens.

59.   A.N. F[15] 107: Rapport sur l'extinction de la mendicité dans la ville de Niort, 15 November 1807.

60.   *Ibid.*

CHAPTER IX: DURABLE THEMES

1.   To locate such pamphlets I have used André Monglond's bibliography, *La France révolutionnaire et impériale, Annales de bibliographie méthodique et descriptive, 1789–1802* (6 vols., Grenoble, 1930–38), and the B.N.'s *Catalogue de l'Histoire de France* (12 vols., 1855–95).

2.   See T. Adams, "Turgot, mendicité et réforme hospitalière," *Actes du 99e Congrès national des Sociétés Savantes [Besançon, 1974]* (1976: vol. II); Adams, "Moeurs et Hygiène publique au XVIIIe siècle: quelques aspects des dépôts de mendicité," *Annales de Démographie historique* (1975), 93–105; Depauw, "Pauvres mendiants"; Hufton, *The Poor,* 227–44; and the recent case study of Lower Normandy by Schwartz, *Policing the Poor,* especially 176–78.

3.   J.-P. Gross, "L'Idée de la pauvreté dans la pensée sociale des Jacobins: origines et prolongements," *AHRF,* no. 248 (April 1982), 196–223.

4.   J.-B. Bô, *Rapport sur l'Extinction de la mendicité* (vendémiaire II), B.N. Le[38] 499, and the law of 22 vendémiaire II in Watteville, *Législation charitable,* 24–27.

5.   Forrest, *Revolution and the Poor,* 88–94; L. Accarias, *L'Assistance publique sous la Révolution dans le département du Puy-de-Dôme* (1933), 132–35.

6.   Woloch, "Charity to Welfare," 800–01.

7.   Sectional accounts and correspondence in A.N. F^{15} 2589, 2822, and 2870.

8.   A.N. F^{15} 107: Précis sur l'administration . . . 1807: dépôts de mendicité. Also F^{15} 105: fol. Mendicité, pluviôse XII; F^{15} 107: Pref Orne to Conseil d'Etat, 25 September 1807; Charles Dupin, *Histoire de l'administration des secours publics* (1821), 403.

9.   A.N. F^{15} 106: fol. Mendicité, 1806–07—an extremely important source. Also F^{15} 107: Copie d'une note à sa Majesté, 2 September 1807. Cf. A.N. F^{1c} III Seine-Inférieure 8: Tableau . . . an X: "Il est indispensable de ouvrir [au mendiants valides] non pas un azile mais une maison de correction sévère et dans laquelle ils soient insensiblement reconciliés avec le travail et relevés à la dignité."

10.   A.N. F^{15} 108: M.I. circular to Prefects, 19 December 1808.

11.   A.N. F^{15} 108: Règlement provisoire du Dépôt de Mendicité, October 1808. Cf. D. Higgs, "Le Dépôt de Mendicité de Toulouse," *Annales du Midi*, LXXXVI (October 1974), 406–07.

12.   A.N. F^{15} 108: Rapport au M.I., August 1810; A.N. F^{1c} III Gard 7: Compte, 1er trimèstre 1812; Jones, *Montpellier,* 247.

13.   L'Ainé, *Rapport au Roi sur la situation des hospices . . . de la mendicité et des prisons* (1818), 20–25 in A.N. AD XIV 10; A.N. F^{15} 109: Dépôts de Mendicité: Produit du travail, 1811; Jones, *Montpellier,* 248–50; Higgs, "Dépôt de Toulouse," 410. But compare A.N. F^{1c} III Ille-et-Vilaine 7: Compte 1812: "Le Dépôt a rapidement développé une grande industrie."

14.   A.N. F^{15} 108: Notice sur les actes dont il peut être fait mention dans l'Exposé sur la situation de l'Empire (fol. 1811); L'Ainé, *Rapport au Roi, 1818,* 56–61. A *tableau* dated March 1812 indicates forty *dépôts en activité* (with another thirty-three anticipated by January 1813), but the forty included at least ten in annexed non-French departments. (A.N. AF IV 1067, fol. 87–91.)

15.   M. J. LaForest (directeur du dépôt des Bouches-du-Rhône), *De l'Extinction de la Mendicité en France, au profit du pauvre et de l'état* (Aix, 1814), B.N. Rp10008; LaForest, *De l'Utilité et de l'économie qu'il y aurait à fondre les dépôts en trente Maisons centrales de bienfaisance* (Aix, 1814), Rp9433; M. Guinan-Lauoreins, *Des Dépôts de Mendicité, et de l'influence qu'ils peuvent avoir sur la prospérité publique* (1814), Bibl. Hist. de la Ville de Paris, no. 29063.

16.   Analysis based on tables in L'Ainé, *Rapport au Roi, 1818,* 56–61.

17.   *Ibid.,* 25–26.

18.   L.P.A.H. [Houssart], *Des Avantages de la Mendicité bien reglée dans l'économie sociale; des inconvéniens de sa suppression absolue* (1816), A.A.P. A-2142^5. Houssart identified himself as secretary-treasurer of the charity bureau in the 10th arrondissement of Paris.

19.   A key source for the Restoration is the *Journal des Prisons, hospices, écoles primaires et bienfaisance* (hereafter cited as *JPHB*), a monthly edited by Bernard Appert in 1825–31. Appert vigorously supported mutual schooling, publicized

major acts of philanthropy, inspected public institutions of all kinds, and denounced abusive conditions when he encountered them. See especially *JPHB,* 1826: "Des classes inférieures de la société et de quelques unes des causes qui s'opposent à leurs progrès" (229–39), and 1825: "De la Charité" (404–06). On the "laquais dorés," 1830, p. 18. On the *dépôts:* 1828, "Mendicité" (524–28); 1825, on the well-run *dépôt* in the Aisne (28), and an exposé of the "dépôt de corruption" of St. Denis (145–49).

20.   M. Cochin (Maire du XIIème arrond.), *De l'Extinction de la Mendicité: Rapports faits le 27 Mars et 29 Novembre 1829 par le conseil provisoire chargé des travaux préparatoires de la fondation d'une Maison de Refuge et de Travail* (1829), B.N. R 31906, pp. 51, 102–03.

21.   *Ibid.,* 13–16, 21.

22.   *Ibid.,* 17, 24–25, 29–31, 69–71.

23.   *JPHB* (1830), 17–30—a key gloss on Cochin's pamphlet.

24.   M. Fosseyeux, *Catalogue des Manuscrits des Archives de l'Assistance publique* (1913), 16.

25.   Gérard de Melcy (ex-administrateur des hospices civils), *Réflexions sur les établissemens de bienfaisance* (an VIII), B.N. R 37144, pp. 13–14, 19.

26.   A.N. F[15] 3959: De la Charité Légale en France depuis l'an 9 jusqu'au 31 Décembre 1845—Rapport à Mon. d'Arcy, sous-secrétaire d'Etat.

27.   A.N. F[15] 112 [Dons et Legs]: Notes pour le M.I., 3 March 1820.

28.   Gasparin (M.I.), *Rapport au Roi sur les Hôpitaux, les hospices et les services de bienfaisance* (1837), A.A.P. C-913, p. 27: "Tableaux des Legs et Donations faits aux établissements de bienfaisance, de 1814 à 1835"; Jones, *Montpellier,* 208–12.

29.   A.N. F[15] 112: Notes pour le M.I., 31 January 1822.

30.   A.N. F[15] 3959: De la Charité Légale; A.N. F[15]* 45: Statistique des libéralités faites aux établissements de bienfaisance et dont l'acceptation a été autorisé par le Gouvernement depuis 1800 jusqu'au 31 Décembre 1845.

31.   A.N. F[15] 3959: De la Charité Légale: Tableau . . . par départements.

32.   A comprehensive view of Parisian philanthropy from the Enlightenment to the 1840s is now available in Catherine Duprat's 2,200-page thesis, "Les temps des philanthropes. La philanthropie parisienne des Lumières à la monarchie de Juillet" (thèse pour le doctorat d'Etat, Université de Paris I, Juin 1991). The thesis appeared too late to be consulted for this book, but a precis ("Exposé de Thèse," *AHRF,* no. 285 [July 1991], 387–93) suggests that her study is extremely rich and far-reaching.

33.   See the society's annual report: *Maison Philanthropique de Paris établie en 1780: Année 1793* in B.N. R 21467 and A.N. AD XIV 12.

34.   Tuetey, ed., *L'Assistance publique à Paris,* IV: 519–21. Cf. Ferdinand-Dreyfus, *L'Assistance pendant la Convention,* 49–53.

35.   Woloch, "Charity to Welfare," 794 and n.

36.   A.N. F[15] 1962: Rapport par Micault-la Vieuville . . . Société Philanthropique, 4 ventôse XII; F[15] 1883: Etat des dépenses affectées sur . . . l'octroi

[1809?]; F^{15} 1885A: Pastoret to M.I., December 1815: "Depuis son existence le M.I. a accordé un secours annuel de 15,000F."

37. See F. Redlich, "Science and Charity: Count Rumford and His Followers," *International Review of Social History,* XVI (1971), 184–216.

38. A.N. F^{15} 106: fol. Société Philanthropique: Pastoret and DeCandolle to M.I. [n.d., 1806?]; Pref Drôme to M.I., 14 May 1806.

39. A.N. F^{15} 2772: Tableau des secours spéciaux accordés pour l'hyver de 1811–1812 sur le domaine extraordinaire . . . and A.N. AF IV 1067 (nos. 9–10): M.I. to Napoleon, 21 January 1812.

40. A.N. AF IV 1067 (nos. 98, 105, 108, 172–73): Comptes rendus par les préfets, generally reporting "succès dans les villes, difficultés dans les campagnes," and the detailed Compte Rendu à sa Majesté de la situation au 14 Avril sur l'exécution du décret du 24 Mars 1812.

41. *Ibid.* (nos. 39 and 79): 6 February and 1 April 1812, on Paris. On the Société Philanthropique, see Dupin, *Histoire des secours publics,* 431–35, and E. Cassin, *Almanach Philanthropique ou Tableau des sociétés et institutions de bienfaisance, d'éducation et d'utilité publique de la ville de Paris* (1827), B.N. R 03759.

42. A.N. AF IV 1066: Compte rendu par l'administration de la Charité Maternelle, 18 Janvier 1810; A.N. F^{15} 1962: *Compte rendu par l'ancien comité de la Société de Charité Maternelle . . . 25 Mai 1812;* AF IV 1067 (nos. 34–35): Société Maternelle to Napoleon, Feburary 1812, indicating overexpansion and financial difficulties. Cf. Cassin, *Almanach Philanthropique,* 85.

43. C.F. Jourdan (de l'Isère), *Réflexions sur les moyens de détruire entièrement la mendicité* (1805), B.N. R 39564, p. 13.

44. R. Delagrelaye, *Mémoire sur la mendicité* (n.d.), B.N. R 12926, p. 45; Jourdan, *Réflexions,* 34–36; A.N. F^{15} 138: Desnaudières to First Consul, thermidor an XI, urging him to designate the richest landowner in each canton as *premier bienfaiteur.* The *comité de bienfaisance* of section Mont Blanc in Paris asked in vain to be included on the list of *notables* (F^{15} 133: the committee to M.I., 17 brumaire IX).

45. A.N. F^{15} 109: fol. Secours aux indigents, 1812.

46. M. A. Jullien, *Note sur le mode d'extinction de la mendicité* (an IX), B.N. in-4° R Pièce 1009, p. 3.

47. Duprat's thesis discusses both the parallelism and rivalries of secular philanthropists and Catholic-royalists. ("Exposé de Thèse," 390).

48. A.N. F^{15} 1885A: Rapport au Roi sur l'Asile des Vieillards et Orphelins de la Providence . . . et sur la Société de secours de la Providence (1815); A.N. AD XIV 12: *Asile de la Providence: Comptes,* 1810–11 and 1828–29.

49. A.N. F^{15} 1885A: *Règlement pour l'Association de la charité formée en la Paroisse de Saint-Roche* (1809), and MS règlement, 4ème section (secours à domicile).

50. A.N. F^{15} 1939: fol. Dames du Refuge de Saint-Michel (an XIII).

51. A.N. F^{15} 1939: Vice-président du Société Impériale de la Charité Maternelle to M.I., 16 December 1812.

52. A.N. F^{15} 110: Rapport au M.I., 3 August 1813; Avis du Pref de la Seine, 12 July 1813. Cf. Higgs, "Politics and Charity at Toulouse."

53. Duquesnoy, *Rapports au Conseil Général des Hospices sur . . . les secours à domicile* (an XI), A.A.P. C-237, pp. 15–18.

54. A.N. F^{15} 110: *op.cit.,* and Rapport, June 1816.

55. *JPHB* (1830), 53–54.

56. *Rapport . . . par les commissaires des douze bureaux de charité de Paris* (Novembre 1830), passim, in A.N. AD XIV 6. This report was submitted to the Hospital Council, which interpolated long footnotes in the printed version to refute some of these contentions. This in turn prompted a bitter *Réponse des Bureaux de charité aux notes marginales ajoutées par l'administration des hospices . . .* (Février 1831). When the commissioners made their next report to the Hospital Council in 1833, however, there was scarcely a sign of these disputes. Catherine Duprat's study explores the role of key philanthropists in the transition from the Bourbon to the Orléanist regimes, and the impact of that change on philanthropy ("Exposé de Thèse," 389).

57. *Observations sur le Mont de Piété par les douze huissiers-priseurs* (1790?), B.N. Lf^{43} 26; Concedieu, *L'Intérêt public ou le Mont de Piété tel qu'il devrait être à Paris* (1790), B.N. Inv R 32147. On the Italian *monti,* see S. Woolf, "The Treatment of the Poor in Napoleonic Tuscany, 1808–1814," *Annuario dell'Instituto Storico Italiano per l'età moderna e contemporenea,* XXIII–IV (1971–72), 441–45.

58. *Observations sur le Mont de Piété* (1793), reprinted in Tuetey, ed., *Assistance Publique à Paris,* IV: 390–93.

59. *Observations . . . des huissiers-priseurs,* 10; Gasparin, *Rapport au Roi, 1837,* 159. Readers seeking greater detail on this subject should consult C. Danieri, *Credit Where Credit Is Due: The Mont-de-Piété of Paris, 1777–1851* (New York, 1991), which appeared after the research and writing of this section were finished.

60. Concedieu, *L'Intérêt public,* 113.

61. See E. Duval, *Le Mont de Piété de Paris: les opérations de dégagements gratuites* (1887).

62. Concedieu, *Mémoire Justificatif* (an II), B.N. Ln^{27} 4662; Watteville, *Législation charitable,* 28–29. For free redemptions in Metz, see A.N. F^{15} 2866/67: Etat des nantissements.

63. A.N. F^{15} 2866/67: Commission des Secours Publics to Committee of Public Safety, Messidor II (first draft).

64. *Ibid.,* Rapport (second draft).

65. On the collapse of the institution's finances, see Tuetey, ed., *Assistance Publique à Paris,* IV: 408, 412–13, 418, 423–24; A.N. F^{15} 134: M.I. to Directory, 12 thermidor IV ("les prêts ont été principalement dirigés sur les gens aisés. . . . Sur plus de 40 mille emprunteurs pendant les neuf derniers mois, il y en a au moins les trois quarts audessus de 3000 livres"). Cf. Fréron (employé du Ministère de l'Intérieur), *Réflexions sur les Hôpitaux . . . et le Mont de Piété* (an VIII), B.N. R Pièce 6768. Danieri's study sheds more light on this episode.

66.   A.N. AF IV 1051: *Mont de Piété,* an XI; ministerial circulars of 18 fructidor XII and 3 prairial XIII (Watteville, *Législation charitable,* 115–18 and 121–22), and the décret portant règlement of 8 thermidor XIII (*ibid.,* 123–28). Cf. Pastoret, *Rapport au Roi* (1816), 283.

67.   A.N. F[15] 1885A: 29 January 1814. The prefect rejected an alternative plan to "forcer la vente des effets dont ses magasins sont remplis, en suspendant pour un tems la faculté accordée aux emprunteurs de renouveler leurs engagemens."

68.   A.N. F[15] 2611: circular letters and responses from various prefects on the difficulties of establishing a *Mont de Piété.* For a helpful overview, see A. DeWatteville, *Situation administrative et financière des Monts de Piété en France* (1848), A.A.P. B-1572, especially his "Tableau récapitulatif . . . 1844."

69.   Watteville, *Situation des Monts de Piété,* 43–44; E. Duval, *Les Opérations du Mont-de-Piété de Paris depuis sa création* (Nancy, 1894), 21.

70.   Gasparin, *Rapport au Roi, 1837,* 156–59; Duval, *Les Opérations,* 4–5.

71.   A.A.P.: Liasse 708, no. 9, especially *"Mont de Piété*—Questions." Cf. *JPHB* (1830), 72–80: excerpts from A. Beugnot, *Des Banques publiques de prêt sur gage et de leurs inconveniens* (1829), making the same points.

72.   L. Loubère, "The Intellectual Origins of French Jacobin Socialism," *International Review of Social History,* IV (1959), 415–31.

73.   Cassin, *Almanach Philanthropique . . . de la ville de Paris.*

74.   For an overview as of 1812–13, the best source is A.N. F[15] 3618 and 3619, with prefectorial responses to the M.I. circular letter of 31 October 1812. See also E. Laurent, *Le Pauperisme et les associations de prévoyance* (2 vols., 1865). Some of these societies were founded by masters, or by masters and journeymen. But in Lille's 90 mutual societies, workers in the textile trades constituted over three fifths of the membership of 5,730 (F[15] 3619: Etat indicatif des professions des ouvriers composant les sociétés de bienfaisance de Lille).

75.   A.N. F[15] 1883: Rapport fait à la Société Philanthropique par M. Dupont de Nemours, au nom de la commission des sociétés de prévoyance, 6 pluviôse XIII; Contrôle des membres de la Société des Amis de l'Humanité, 1808, and other documents. *JPHB* (1825), 118–19, and 313 for Appert's views.

76.   A. E. Cerfberr, *Des Sociétés de bienfaisance mutuelle ou des moyens d'ameliorer le sort des classes ouvriers* (Grenoble, 1836), A.A.P. B-1573/14; E. P. Thompson, *The Making of the English Working Class* (New York, 1966 edn.), 421.

77.   A.N. AD XIV 12: printed *règlements* of seven grenoblois mutual societies; A.N. F[15] 3619: Renseignemens sur les associations (Isère), 6 December 1812; Cerfberr, *Sociétés de bienfaisance,* on the *peigneurs de chanvre.*

78.   A.N. F[15] 3618: Pref Bouches-du-Rhône to M.I., 10 July and 17 November 1813, and Tableau des associations; M.I. to Pref, 18 March 1813. F[15] 3619: Pref Rhône to M.I., October 1812.

79.   W. Sewell, *Work and Revolution in France: The Language of Labor from the Old Regime to 1848* (Cambridge, Engl., 1980), ch. 8.

80. A.N. F^{15} 3618: Pref Haute-Garonne to M.I., 2 December 1812; M.I. to Pref, 31 December 1812; Pref to M.I., 22 February 1813. Also *règlements* of several societies in A.N. AD XIV 12. The societies in the Tarn were quite similar: F^{15} 3619: Pref Tarn to M.I., 29 March 1813, and *règlements.*

81. A.N. F^{15} 138, for various projects seeking government endorsement. One that did receive patronage from the Bonaparte family was D'Hailla, *Institution de bienfaisance ou retraite assurée à l'infortune et au malheur* (an X)—a plan to provide food, clothing, cash allowances, and lodging to persons who had contributed between 1 and 2 francs a month over a period of years (A.N. AD XIV 12).

82. A.N. F^{15} 138: doss. Grouber de Groubental: M.I. to Prefects, 3 November 1806, and Avis du Conseil d'Etat, 17 January 1806.

83. Ferdinand-Dreyfus, *LaRochefoucauld-Liancourt,* 447–54.

84. Sewell, *Work and Revolution,* ch. 8. Evidence for the view that "mutual aid societies were associated with protest activity only exceptionally" is discussed in L. Hunt and G. Sheridan, "Corporatism, Association, and the Language of Labor in France, 1750–1850," *JMH,* LVIII (December 1986), 815–21.

85. *Rapport par les commissaires . . . Novembre 1830,* 29.

86. *Pétition individuelle des Citoyens de la section Fontaine de Grenelle* (Décembre 1791), B.N. Lb^{40} 1828.

87. Compare Dupin, *Histoire des secours publics,* 213 (total expenditures of about 24 million francs in 1820 for the *hospices*), and Gasparin, *Rapport au Roi, 1837,* 15 (total expenditures of about 49 million francs in 1836, reflecting a comparable rise in income).

88. For the full agenda and multiple interests of early nineteenth-century philanthropists, beyond the poor relief or primary education discussed here, see Duprat, "Exposé de Thèse," 391–92.

CHAPTER X: CIVIL JUSTICE

1. Fine introductions are provided by J. Royer, *La Société judiciaire depuis le XVIIIe siècle* (1979), part I, and P. Dawson, *Provincial Magistrates and Revolutionary Politics in France, 1789–1795* (Cambridge, Mass., 1972), chs. 2–3.

2. On the social clout of the parlementaires, see F. Bluche, *Les Magistrats du Parlement de Paris au XVIIIe siècle* (1960); J. Meyer, *La Noblesse Bretonne au XVIIIe siècle* (1972 edn.); R. Forster, *The Nobility of Toulouse in the 18th Century* (Baltimore, 1960); W. Doyle, *The Parlement of Bordeaux and the End of the Old Regime* (London, 1974); and J. Egret, "L'aristocratie parlementaire française à la fin de l'ancien régime," *Revue historique,* CCVIII (1952), 1–14.

3. L. Berlanstein, *The Barristers of Toulouse in the Eighteenth Century* (Baltimore, 1975); M. Gresset, *Gens de Justice à Besançon de la conquête par Louis XIV à la*

Révolution française (2 vols., 1978); M. Fitzsimmons, *The Parisian Order of Barristers and the French Revolution* (Cambridge, Mass., 1987), ch. 1.

4. A. M. J. J. Dupin, *Des Magistrats d'autrefois, des magistrats de la Révolution, des magistrats à venir* (1814), B.N. Lf^{110} 7a; *L'Etat actuel des tribunaux en France et de la décadence de la magistrature* (1814), B.N. Lf^{109} 17.

5. J. Egret, *Louis XV et l'opposition parlementaire, 1715–1774* (1970); J. Carey, *Judicial Reform in France Before the Revolution of 1789* (Cambridge, Mass., 1981), 93–127.

6. B. Stone, *The Parlement of Paris 1774–1789* (Chapel Hill, 1981); W. Doyle, "The Parlements of France and the Breakdown of the Old Regime," *French Historical Studies,* VI (1970), 415–58.

7. A.P., VIII: 449.

8. The standard works include A. Hiver, *Histoire critique des institutions judiciaires de la France de 1789 à 1848* (1848); E. Seligmann, *La Justice en France pendant la Révolution, 1789–1792* (1901); and R. Aubin, *L'Organisation judiciaire d'après les cahiers de 1789* (1928).

9. A.P., XII: 488 (Goupil de Préfeln).

10. Dawson, *Provincial Magistrates,* 255–74. Cf. Dinocheau, *Rapport . . . sur la liquidation des offices ministériels* (1790), B.N. Le^{29} 1163.

11. H. Carré, *La Fin des Parlements, 1788–1790* (1912), ch. 6, especially p. 260.

12. Duport in A.P., XII: 416–18.

13. For the legislative debate, see Royer, *La Société judiciaire,* 175–236, and Seligmann, *La Justice,* 280–328. The fundamental Law on the Judiciairy of 16–24 August 1790 is reprinted in J. H. Stewart, *A Documentary Survey of the French Revolution* (New York, 1951).

14. Royer, *La Société judiciaire,* 178–79, 186.

15. Seligmann, *La Justice,* 321–24, on the law of 27 November 1790. The Tribunal was mandated to report annually on its business. The first (*Etat des jugemens de Cassation, Avril 1792–31 Mars 1793,* B.N. Le^{38} 252) indicated that the "278 jugemens qui ont cassé des actes de procédure ou des jugemens," comprised 224 criminal cases and 54 civil cases. Later the proportions showed more balance, e.g., 190 *cassations civils* and 247 *criminels* in the year between germinal an III–ventôse an IV (*Journal de la Justice,* no.7). In general, see J.-L. Halperin, *Le Tribunal de Cassation sous la Révolution, 1790–1799* (1988).

16. *Journal des Tribunaux* (par une société des hommes de loi), 1791: nos. 1 and 2; Seligmann, *La Justice,* 339–56. Cf. Fitzsimmons, *Parisian Barristers,* 71.

17. Dawson, *Provincial Magistrates,* 243–55; J. L. Debauve, *La Justice révolutionnaire dans le Morbihan, 1790–1795* (1965), 57–58, 80–81, 99; Seligmann, *La Justice,* 357–59.

18. Dawson, *Provincial Magistrates,* 291–92; Debauve, *Morbihan,* 57, 70, 81, 87–88, 119.

19.   A.N. BB[30] 32: Minister of Justice [M.J.] to Committee of Public Safety, 1 nivôse II.

20.   A.N. BB[2] 24: La Commission des Administrations civils, police et tribunaux [the successor to the Ministry of Justice], circular, 14 messidor II.

21.   *Ibid.:* circular, 6 thermidor II on the implementation of the Convention's decree of 27 germinal.

22.   A.N. AF III 32, fol. 112: Tableau de l'état actuel du département de la Justice, frimaire IV; A. Vincenti, *Le Tribunal du département du Vaucluse, de l'an IV à l'an VIII* (Aix-en-Provence, 1928), 45–50. Cf. A.N. BB[30] 1155B: M.J. to his commissioners, 18 germinal IV.

23.   A.N. BB[2] 97: Tableau de l'organisation des tribunaux civils, an IV; AF III 32, Tableau de l'état. . . .

24.   Vincenti, *Vaucluse,* 61, 77, 80–81.

25.   A.P., XVI: 737–38.

26.   Law of 16/24 August 1790, Title III, and law of 18/26 October 1790, Title III. The best introduction to the JPs is the case study by Jean Bart, "La Justice de Paix du canton de Fontaine-française à l'époque révolutionnaire," *Mémoires de la Société pour l'histoire du droit et des institutions des anciens pays bourguignons, comtois et romans,* XXVI (1965), 193–216. On possible historical precedents, including practices at the Châtelet in Paris, see the remarks of M. Pertué, "Notices," *AHRF,* no. 208 (April 1972), 314.

27.   V. Jeanvrot, *Les Juges de Paix élus sous la Révolution* (1883), 79; Debauve, *Morbihan,* 286; E. J. Guérin, *Les Justices de paix de Saintes depuis 1790 jusqu'à nos jours* (La Rochelle, 1915), 11–12.

28.   Debauve, *Morbihan,* 277–82, 291–93.

29.   Jeanvrot, *Les Juges de Paix,* 74–77, and passim.

30.   R. M. Andrews, "The Justices of the Peace of Revolutionary Paris, September 1792–November 1794," *Past and Present,* 52 (August 1971), 65–72, 82.

31.   Guérin, *Saintes,* 18–19; Bart, "Fontaine-française," 195–99.

32.   Vincenti, *Vaucluse,* 120; Bart, "Fontaine-française," 209; A.N. F[1c] III Indre 4: Compte, 4ème trimestre 1810.

33.   J. Berriat Saint-Prix, *Cours de procédure civile fait à la faculté de droit de Paris [1810]* (1825 edn.), 370–72.

34.   Debauve, *Morbihan,* 303–06; Bart, "Fontaine-française," 201–08. Cf. C. Billion, *Des Juges de Paix en France, ce qu'ils sont—ce qu'ils devraient être* (Lyon, 1824), B.N. Lf[116] 6.

35.   Debauve, *Morbihan,* 295–303; Vincenti, *Vaucluse,* 85.

36.   *Gazette des Tribunaux,* VII (March 1793), 7; Jeanvrot, *Les Juges de Paix,* 82–95; Debauve, *Morbihan,* 311–12; J.-J. Clère, "L'Arbitrage révolutionnaire: apogée et déclin d'une institution, 1790–1806," *Revue de l'Arbitrage* (1981), 10–11 (in one canton, 115 cases were conciliated out of 379 attempts in 1791–1801); Bart, "Fontaine-française," 212–15.

37.   A.N. BB^9 164: Tribunal de Langres to M.J., an VIII; commissaire à Nantes to M.J., an VIII; BB^9 163: Tribunal de Dax (Landes), fructidor VIII; BB^9 165: Tribunal de Pointoise, an VIII.

38.   L. Texier-Olivier, *Statistique générale de la France: Département de la Haute-Vienne* (1808), 244–45; M. Seguin de Pazzis, *Mémoire statistique sur le département du Vaucluse* (Carpentras, 1808), 196–97; P. Laboulinière, *Annuaire statistique du département des Hautes-Pyrénées* (Tarbes, 1807), 429–30; C. Dieudonné, *Statistique du département du Nord* (Douai, an XII), III: 230–40.

39.   F.J.-B. d'Alphonse, *Mémoire statistique du département de l'Indre* (an XII), 122–23.

40.   See *Resultat des Opinions de Cambacérès, séances de 17 et 19 Juin 1793* (Impr. Nat.), and *Rapport à la Convention sur le juré civil par Hérault* (Impr. Nat.), arguing against the civil jury.

41.   See the excellent article by J. F. Traer, "The French Family Court," *History*, LIX (June 1974), 211–28. Also M. Ferret, *Les Tribunaux de famille dans Montpellier* (Montpellier, 1926), and J. Forcioli, *Une Institution révolutionnaire: le tribunal de famille de Caen* (Caen, 1932).

42.   R. Phillips, *Family Breakdown in Late Eighteenth-Century France: Divorces in Rouen, 1792–1803* (Oxford, 1980), 17–33.

43.   Traer, "Family Court," 215–17; Debauve, *Morbihan*, 361, 385. For a critique, see *Gazette des Tribunaux*, V, 472.

44.   Phillips, *Rouen*, 28–29.

45.   Quotes by Clère, "L'Arbitrage," 18–19. On the *biens communaux,* see G. Bourgin, *Le Partage des biens communaux* (1908), and F. Gauthier, *La Voie paysan dans la Révolution française: l'exemple de la Picardie* (1977).

46.   G.-R. Ikni, "La Loi du dix juin 1793 et la sentence arbitrale: une procédure d'expropriation révolutionnaire?" in *La Révolution et l'ordre juridique privé: rationalité ou scandale?* (Actes du Colloque d'Orléans, 1986: 2 vols., 1988), II: 421–23 on the Oise; Clère, "L'Arbitrage," 20–21 on the Haute-Marne.

47.   Ikni, "La Loi du dix juin," 423–25; Clère, "L'Arbitrage," 22–27—an important article buried in an obscure journal.

48.   Quoted by Clère, "L'Arbitrage," 25.

49.   Traer, "Family Court," 225–28; Dalloz (1845) cited by Clère, 26.

50.   See Phillips, *Rouen*, 34–42.

51.   Clère, "L'Arbitrage," 27–28.

52.   Dejoly, *Compte Rendu à l'Assemblée Nationale le 9 Juillet 1792, sur l'état actuel des tribunaux . . . ,* B.N. Lf^{107} 1 (in-4°), 2–3.

53.   The debate can be followed in *Archives Parlementaires*, 2nd series: II, 126–32, 160–67, 233–38 (21–28 January 1801).

54.   *Ibid.,* 238. The law was dated 8 pluviôse IX. According to G. Delfau, *Annuaire statistique du département de la Dordogne pour l'an XII* (Périgueux, an XII), this reduction bore fruit quickly, since the number of new cases brought to the department's civil courts fell from 2,134 in Year IX to 1,686 in Year X, and 1,253

in Year XI. "On ne verra plus un aussi grand nombre de procès maintenant que des magistrats éclairés sont les régulateurs des cantons" (pp. 18–19).

55.   *Archives Parlementaires*, 2nd series: II, 506, 585–89, 603–08. The law was dated 29 ventôse IX.

56.   J. Y. Coppolani, *Les Elections en France à l'époque napoléonienne* (1980), 56–59, 79–81, 213–34, 361–69. For an example of the ministry rejecting someone who was the voters' obvious choice, see Jeanvrot, *Les Juges de Paix*, 77–78.

57.   A.N. BB^{30} 528: memoirs in pamphlet form from the various courts of appeal entitled *Observations de la Cour d'Appel séant à . . . sur le projet de Code de Procédure Civile.* See especially Agen, Besançon, Caen, Douai, Lyon, Orléans, Metz, Montpellier. For evidence of conciliation by civil court judges, see A.N. F^{1c} III Dordogne 7: Compte trimestrial Avril 1811 and 1812, and F^{1c} III Corrèze 2: Compte 1806.

58.   A.N. AD II 57: *Code de Procédure Civile, Avril 1806: Exposés des motifs par les orateurs du Gouvernement,* 25.

59.   *Ibid.: Rapports et discours des orateurs du Tribunat,* 13 (Faure). Appellate courts that objected included Agen, Bordeaux, Orléans, and Rouen (BB^{30} 528: *Observations . . .*).

CHAPTER XI: THE LEGAL PROFESSIONS IN QUESTION

1.   Berriat Saint-Prix, *Cours de Procédure Civile fait à la Faculté de Droit de Paris [1808–10]* (5th edn., 1825), 67–69. For introductions to the old-regime bar, see P. Dawson, "The Bourgeoisie de Robe in 1789," *French Historical Studies,* IV (1965), 1–21, and R. Kagan, "Law Students and Legal Careers in Eighteenth-Century France," *Past and Present,* 68 (August 1975), 38–72, with special reference to Dijon.

2.   On the Parisian barristers, see *Souvenirs de M. Berryer, doyen des Avocats de Paris de 1774 à 1838* (2 vols., 1839), and M. Fitzsimmons, *The Parisian Order of Barristers and the French Revolution* (Cambridge, Mass., 1987). The best provincial study is L. Berlanstein, *The Barristers of Toulouse in the Eighteenth Century* (Baltimore, 1975). See also H. Chauvot, *Le Barreau de Bordeaux de 1775 à 1815* (1856). According to Kagan, "Law Students," p. 50, there were eighty-one orders or *collèges des avocats* in the kingdom before 1789. The 100-page pamphlet *Projet de création de charges d'avocats au Parlement non Tablotans* (Berlin [sic], 1789), B.N. Lf^{49} 66, argued paradoxically that liberty would be served if the position of *avocat* became a venal office, freeing individuals from the need to curry favor from the "inquisitorial and despotic" Parisian Order of Barristers. On the growing role of prominent barristers as "public advocates," see D. Bell, "Lawyers into Demagogues: Chancellor Maupeou and the Transformation of Legal Practice in France, 1771–1789," *Past and Present,* 130 (February 1991), 107–41.

3.   See, e.g., *Réplique d'un citoyen de Paris à la Réponse d'un avocat* (1789), B.N. Lb[39] 1520.

4.   The debate is analyzed by Fitzsimmons, *Parisian Barristers,* 41–64.

5.   Cf. *Gazette des Nouveaux Tribunaux,* III, 95: Letter from Agier, district judge in Paris: "La fonction de défenseur officieux n'étant point par elle-même un état, mais un service momentané, un service d'ami absolument libre."

6.   Fitzsimmons, *Parisian Barristers,* 69–70, 88, 103.

7.   *Ibid.,* 69–75; Berryer, *Souvenirs,* 117; Berlanstein, *Barristers of Toulouse,* 161–70, 174–76. J. L. Debauve, *La Justice révolutionnaire dans le Morbihan 1790–1795* (1965), 470–76, and A. Vincenti, *Le Tribunal du département du Vaucluse de l'an IV à l'an VIII* (Aix-en-Provence, 1928), 108, suggest that litigants and criminal defendants frequently used the services of ex-*avocats,* but H. Thomas, *Le Tribunal Criminel de la Meurthe sous la Révolution* (Nancy, 1937), 14ff, concludes that "la carrière d'avocat devenait compromettante et penible." Judging from Kagan's remarks about barristers in Dijon before 1789, it would be surprising if alienation from the Revolution ran as high in that judicial center as it did in Paris and Toulouse.

8.   *Opinion de Guillaume sur le Rapport fait par Dinocheau . . . au sujet des officiers ministériels* (1790), B.N. Le[29] 1164; *Pétition des Procureurs au Châtelet de Paris à l'Assemblée Nationale* (October 1790), B.N. Lf[42] 62.

9.   Dinocheau, *Rapport . . . sur la liquidation des offices ministériels* (1790), B.N. Le[29] 1163; *Opinion de Guillaume sur le Rapport fait par Dinocheau; Petition des procureurs au Chatelet;* A. Estrangin, *Les Procureurs et les avoués à Marseille* (Marseille, 1900), 139–42. See also C. Bataillard and E. Nusse, *Histoire des procureurs et des avoués, 1483–1816* (2 vols., 1882), II: 289–90, 301–10.

10.   Guillaume, *De la Nécessité d'avoir des avoués dans les nouveaux tribunaux et d'accorder la préférence pour ces places aux anciens officiers ministériels* (December 1790), B.N. Lf[120] 5; G.P***, avoué, *Projet d'une pétition à présenter à l'Assemblée nationale par les hommes de loi, avoués et tous ceux qui . . . se chargent d'exercer et de défendre les droits litigieux qui leur sont confiés* (1791), Lf[120] 6; Delandin, *De l'Utilité de la conservation des hommes de loi en titre d'office* (December 1790), B.N. Le[29] 1182.

11.   *Gazette des Nouveaux Tribunaux,* I, 420–24, 428–30; II, 7–9, 237–38. (With vol. IV this professional journal changed its title to *Gazette des Tribunaux*). See also *Journal des Tribunaux,* III, 63–64 (November 1791), and Nusse, *Histoire des avoués,* 321.

12.   *Gazette des Tribunaux,* V, 91–94 (June 1792); VII, 124–25 (April 1793); Berryer, *Souvenirs,* 155–56.

13.   Dejoly, *Compte rendu à l'Assemblée Nationale le 9 Juillet 1792 sur l'état actuel des tribunaux,* B.N. Lf[107] 1 (in-4°), 12. Among other things he wished to require a surety bond *(cautionnement)* from "the horde" of new practitioners who were "dishonoring" the bar.

14.   Correspondence in A.N. D III 371, summarized in A.P., LXXIV:

175–77; Laurent (homme de loi et j.p.), *Sur l'organisations des hommes de loi* (an VI), B.N. Lf[120] 7, 7; Nusse, *Histoire des avoués,* 315; Debauve, *Morbihan,* 478–79.

15. A.P., LXXIV: 478–79. "Art. 1: Les citations dans les tribunaux de district seront faites par un simple exploit, qui énoncera laconiquement l'objet, ainsi que les motifs de la demande, et désignera le tribunal, le jour et l'heure de la comparution. Art. 2: L'usage des requêtes est supprimé dans toutes les affaires . . . et il y sera supplée par un simple mémoire. . . . Art. 9: Il sera statué dans toutes les tribunaux et dans toutes les affaires, sans aucuns frais, sur défenses verbales, ou sur un simple mémoire, qui sera lu à l'audience par l'un des juges. . . . Art. 12: Les fonctions d'avoués sont supprimées, sauf aux parties à se faire repré-senter par de simples fondés de pouvoir, qui seront tenus de justifier de certificat de civisme. Ils ne pourront former aucune répétition pour leurs soins ou salaires contre les citoyens dont ils auront accepté la confiance. . . ."

16. A.N. BB[30] 32: 2ème Compte, nivôse an II. See also the ringing affir-mation of the court at Redon when it registered the decree: L. Legoux, *Les Tribunaux de district en Ille-et-Vilaine* (Rennes, 1912), 111–12. For comparably radical reform proposals across the Atlantic, see M. Bloomfield, "Antilawyer Sentiment in the Early Republic," in his *American Lawyers in a Changing Society, 1776–1876* (Cambridge, Mass., 1976).

17. Notably in the *Souvenirs* of Berryer; Jean Fournel, *Histoire des avocats au Parlement et du barreau de Paris* (2 vols., 1815); Nusse, *Histoire des avoués,* 335–55. See also Delon de Mézerac, "Le Barreau Libre," *Revue des Deux Mondes,* 1 August 1893, 572–90, and Legoux, *Ille-et-Vilaine.*

18. For returning war veterans, see A.N. BB[9] 163: Saint-Sever (Landes), Chatillon (Côte d'Or), Pontarlier (Doubs), Brest (Finistère); BB[9] 164: Painboeuf (Haute-Loire), Montargis (Loiret), Riom (Puy-de-Dôme). This invaluable source, which gives a snapshot of the deregulated bar on the eve of its demise in 1800, is discussed below, note 57.

19. A.N. BB[9] 165: Loubix to M.J., 28 thermidor VIII and 23 nivôse IX. BB[9] 164: Longpretz to M.J., 17 fructidor VIII.

20. A.N. BB[16] 453 (Haute-Marne): Pissot to M.J., 19 ventôse VIII and reply.

21. A.N. F[1c] I 43: *Conseil de Jurisprudence . . . à donner aux particuliers des consultations* (an IV); A.N. AF III 250/Moselle: *Conseil public et correspondance générale . . . établi à Metz* (an V).

22. Laurent, *Sur l'organisation; C500: Oudot: Nouveau Rapport sur les avoués* (13 brumaire VI), 10–11; *C500: Opinion de Riou sur le rétablissement des avoués* (5 brumaire VI), 2; Thibaudeau quoted by Fitzsimmons, *Parisian Barristers,* 116.

23. A.N. BB[30] 1155B: M.J. circular to Tribunaux civils, 24 prairial and 18 thermidor VI; *Observateur de l'Yonne,* 15 fructidor VII: *Journal de Seine-et-Oise,* no. 5 (20 brumaire VIII): "Tribunal Civil: Rentré."

24. C. Bloch and J. Hilaire, "Nouveauté et modernité du droit révolution-naire: la procédure civile," *Actes du Colloque d'Orléans* (1988), II: 472–76; Laurent,

Sur l'Organisation. On the persistence of older forms and delays at the discretion of the judges, see A.N. D III 379, pièce 25: "Mémoire sur la nécessité absolue d'ajouter des articles supplémentaires à la loi du 3 Brumaire II sur . . . la suppression des avoués"; and A.N. BB[30] 1155B: M.J. circular to Tribunaux civils, 12 brumaire VII.

25.   *C500: Opinion de Laujacq sur les avoués* (21 brumaire VI), 6.

26.   *C500: Opinion de Renault sur les avoués* (13 brumaire VI), 2–3; *Opinion de Laujacq,* 3.

27.   Of the twenty or so reports and speeches during a debate in the Council of Five Hundred that spanned seven months, the weightiest include *Projet de Résolution présenté par Ludot relativement aux avoués* (21 vendémiaire VI); *Opinion de Ludot sur les avoués* (19 frimaire VI); *Projet de Résolution sur les avoués présenté par Oudot au nom de la commission de la classification des lois* (3 brumaire VI); *Nouveau rapport fait par Oudot au nom de la commission* (13 brumaire VI); *Opinion de Mallarmé sur le rétablissement des avoués* (9 frimaire VI); *Opinion de Pison-Dugalland sur le projet d'établissement d'Avoués* (9 frimaire VI). They are all available in the Maclure Collection, University of Pennsylvania.

28.   *C500: Rapport fait par Pison-Dugalland sur la première formation du tableau des hommes de loi et les frais judiciaires* (27 nivôse VI). Cf. *Opinion de Riou.*

29.   See M. Ramsey, "The Politics of Professional Monopoly in Nineteenth-Century Medicine: The French Model and Its Rivals," in G. Geison, ed., *Professions and the French State, 1700–1900* (Philadelphia, 1984), 230–36.

30.   *C.A.: Rapport fait par Regnier sur la résolution relative à la défense des parties devant les tribunaux* (29 ventôse VI); *Opinion de Decomberousse sur la résolution . . .* (16 germinal VI); *Opinion de Delzons sur la résolution . . .* (16 germinal VI); *Observations par Regnier sur une opinion relative à la résolution* (18 germinal VI).

31.   J.-L. Magnan, *Le Notariat et la Révolution française* (Montauban, 1952), ch. 1; F. Foiret, *Une Corporation Parisienne pendant la Révolution: Les Notaires* (1912), chs. 1–2; and E. D. Berge, *Histoire du Notariat* (1815), B.N. Lf[41] 12, pt. I. Whenever the monarchy created new notarial positions in Paris, the company bought them up.

32.   Foiret, *Une Corporation,* 341–43. For detailed case studies of notarial practice across four centuries, see J.-P. Poisson, *Notaires et société: travaux d'histoire et de sociologie notariales* (1985).

33.   F.J.-B. d'Alphonse, *Mémoire statistique du département de l'Indre* (an XII), 125–27.

34.   E. Suleiman, *Private Power and Centralization in France: the Notaries and the State* (Princeton, 1987) is a luminous analysis of how successive regimes since Napoleon, particularly in the twentieth century, have struggled to rationalize this hybrid public-private institution.

35.   C. Metman, *Essai sur le Notariat lu à la Société des Amis de la Constitution* (1790), B.N. Lf[41] 6. Cf. M.F. (ancien notaire), *Le Notariat dévoilé* (n.d.), Lf[41] 7.

36.   Quoted in Magnan, *Le Notariat,* 39–40 and 61–62. Cf. *Mémoire pour le*

collège des notaires d'Aix-en-Provence, sur la vénalité des offices ministériels (Aix, [1790?]), B.N. Lf^{41} 16.

37.   The debates preceding the law of 6 October 1791 are analyzed at length in Magnan, *Le Notariat.*

38.   See the dozens of petitions from groups of provincial notaries protesting the terms of their compensation and the burden of the *cautionnement* in A.N. D III 378 [Comité de Législation: Notaires]. Some figures on the valuations of 1771 are given by Magnan, *Le Notariat,* 52.

39.   Lecointre (notaire), *Représentations à la Convention sur la liquidation des notaires de Paris* (nivôse an II), Lf^{41} 47; *Pétition des jeunes notaires de Paris à la Convention* (an II), Lf^{41} 50; *Réflexions des jeunes notaires sur la pétition à la Convention* (10 pluviôse II), Lf^{41} 51; also *Pétition des notaires de la Manche à la Convention* (5 ventôse II), Lf^{41} 22 (in-4°).

40.   *Réponse aux différens écrits publiés au nom des jeunes notaires* (an II), Lf^{41} 46 (in-4°).

41.   Foiret, *Une Corporation,* 49–57. The case for preferential treatment of head clerks was made in *Idées succinctes: Projet d'institution des notaires* (1791), Lf^{41} 8.

42.   M. Petitjean, "La Réorganisation du notariat à l'époque révolutionnaire dans le département de la Côte d'Or," *Actes du Colloque d'Orléans* (1988), I: 288–92.

43.   This persecution is treated in detail by Foiret, *Une Corporation*—see especially 95–114, 259. A good source are the petitions by the ousted notaries written soon after Thermidor, e.g., Réclamations de Chavet, notaire destitué injustement, 25 thermidor II, and petitions by Raguideau, Colin, and Monnot (A.N. D III 378).

44.   A.N. D III 378: Rapport fait au département [de Paris] le 5 floréal an 2 . . . par le citoyen Concedieu, administrateur.

45.   *Ibid.:* Petition from L'Aîné, 22 germinal II, and response from the *juri,* 22 floréal II. See also petition from Gayot, and Département de Paris: Rapport 25 vendémiaire III.

46.   *Ibid.:* "Observations sur le notariat" par Gilbert [an III].

47.   Petitjean, "Côte d'Or," 292–94; Magnan, *Les Notaires,* 139–40, 145; Foiret, *Une Corporation,* 371–75; A.N. F^{1c} III Loiret 5: *Compte Rendu de l'Administration Centrale, Brumaire VI–Vendémiaire VII* (an VII), 7–8; F^{1c} III Var 6: *Compte Rendu par l'Administration Centrale An VI,* 8.

48.   *C.A.: Rapport fait par Charles Cailly au nom d'une commission spéciale . . . relative à l'organisation du notariat* (12 prairial VII), especially 22–23. Cailly's committee recommended approval of the lower house's comprehensive bill, though he noted: "S'il est un regret que nous ayons à exprimer, c'est celui de n'y pas trouver [pour les notaires] la nécessité d'un cours de législation dans les écoles centrales" (p. 24).

49.   *C500: Rapport par Favard sur la réorganisation du Notariat* (13 thermidor

VII); *C.A.: Rapport par Goupil-Préfeln fils . . . relative à l'organisation du notariat* (13 brumaire VIII), recommending approval.

50. Bonnomet (notaire), *Réflexions sur les deux concours pour l'admission au notariat* (14 brumaire VIII), B.N. Lf[119] 7, especially 6–8; also *Observations sur la résolution du C500 sur l'organisation du Notariat* (n.d.), Lf[119] 5; Mathieu (notaire), *Un Mot sur la résolution du 6 vendémiaire an 8 relative au Notariat* (1 frimaire VIII), Lf[119] 9, comparing the proposal to a penal code which would cripple the notariat, among other ways "en y appelant les premiers venus."

51. See the magisterial thesis of Jean Bourdon, *La Réforme judiciaire de l'an VIII* (2 vols., Rodez, 1941).

52. J.-P. Royer, *La Société judiciaire depuis le XVIIIe siècle* (1979), 275–78.

53. *Ibid.,* 237–60, and part III; A. J. Arnaud, *Les Juristes face à la société du XIXe siècle à nos jours* (1975), 10–11.

54. Bourdon, *La Réforme,* 437–53 on the law of 27 ventôse VIII (18 March 1800).

55. A.N. BB[30] 1155B: M.J. circular, 16 messidor VIII.

56. Figures compiled from a sampling of reports by the courts in A.N. BB[9] 163–65.

57. My discussion draws on A.N. BB[9] 114–65 [Avoués], a rich and voluminous source, which has scarcely ever been used. Jean Bourdon sampled some material for Paris (cartons 153–55, 165), but this whole question was of distinctly secondary interest to him. The material in this series concerns first what I call the triage of 1800, and then dossiers on subsequent aspirants for membership in the bar. The series is arranged alphabetically by department. In a sample of 300 applicants in 1800 whose earlier professional positions were systematically reported by the judges (not always the case, unfortunately), 144 were ex-*procureurs;* 58, *hommes de loi* or *avoués;* 33, clerks; and 20, ex-*avocats.*

58. A.N. BB[9] 165: Loubix to M.J., 28 thermidor VIII and 23 nivôse IX; BB[9] 152: *Observations de Pierre Bozut . . .* (Autun, an IX).

59. BB[9] 164: Cahors; BB[9] 165: Chalon; similarly BB[9] 164: Clermont (Puy-de-Dôme).

60. BB[9] 165: Chalon: Dubois to M.J., 17 fructidor VIII; BB[9] 164: Valenciennes: Longpretz to M.J., 17 fructidor VIII. For the exclusion of other outsiders see, e.g., BB[9] 163: Bourgoin (Isère); Les Andeleys (Eure); Pontarlier (Doubs); Chartres (Eure-et-Loire); BB[9] 165: Oloron (Basses-Pyrénées).

61. A.N. BB[26] 1–3 [Avoués: Tarifs]: correspondence from and to Reims, Montluçon, Toulouse, Orange, Vouzières, Pamiers, Tarascon, Nîmes, and especially the *Chambres* of Rodez and Béziers, an XI.

62. I. Woloch, "La Bourgeoisie devant la conscription napoléonienne: l'exemple du barreau," in *La Bataille, l'armée, la gloire* (Colloque de Clermont-Ferrand, 1985), I: 183–92.

63. A.N. BB[9] 132: Tribunal de 1er instance de Toulouse, 5 and 26 June 1807; Proc Imp to M.J., 24 June. For more detail, see Woloch, "The Fall and

Resurrection of the Civil Bar, 1789–1820s," *French Historical Studies,* XV (Fall 1987), 256–57.

64. BB^9 132: Toulouse, 1807–09. For the unofficial sale of practices, see also BB^9 153: Paris, dossiers Levasseur, Hubert, Audibert, Daubantin, Drouet, Voiret-Marcilly, and BB^9 128: Doubs: Proc Imp to M.J., February 1807.

65. BB^9 132: Proc Imp Toulouse to M.J., 29 December 1812; Penavaire to M.J., April 1813; Barda to M.J., February 1813.

66. BB^9 156: Tribunal de 1er instance de Rouen: Nominations, 1806–11; Delie to M.J., 7 July 1812; Président du Trib to M.J., 26 December 1812; M.J. to Proc Imp, February 1812 [sic: 1813]. See also BB^9 126: Dijon, esp. Royer, avoué to M.J., 14 January 1813.

67. BB^9 154: Paris: "Tableau des Avoués [late 1808]." Of the 112 *avoués supprimés,* 30 were bought out by the *Chambre des avoués* after a great struggle within the association. Fifteen or 20 of the fortunate 150 subsequently sold their practices to men on the excluded list. The anguish and hardships caused by this purge are suggested in the pamphlets by Leloup, *A Son Excellence le Grand Juge,* and Arrault, *A Sa Majesté Impériale,* who denounced a conspiracy of insiders in the *Chambre.* See also Nusse, *Histoire des avoués,* 389–90.

68. BB^9 132: Chambre des avoués de St. Gauden to M.J., 21 May and 2 June 1811; BB^9 161: Etat de répartition entre les Avoués d'Auxerre, 1813.

69. BB^9 126: Proc Imp Beaune to M.J., 28 August 1810; BB^9 156: Proc Imp LeHavre to M.J., 29 August 1811; BB^9 128: Tribunal de Besançon, 21 March 1812; BB^9 120: Tribunal de Rodez, 25 April 1812.

70. A.N. BB^9 B 1: Chambres des avoués protesting new cuts as too harsh included Paris, Bordeaux, Vienne, Béziers, Castres, and Villefranche. Those requesting still lower quotas included Agen, Briançon, Provins, and St. Malo.

71. Foiret, *Une Corporation,* 373–76, 389–91. The law was dated 25 ventôse XI (16 March 1803), but the *cautionnement* was reimposed as early as 7 ventôse VIII.

72. P. Delepierre (employé au Ministère de la Justice), *Tableau des Notaires . . . et de toutes les instructions qui y sont relatives* (1805), B.N. Lf^{119} 1, 34–35.

73. Berge, *Histoire du Notariat,* 164; Foiret, *Une Corporation,* 396–97.

74. P.-T. Cormier, *Essai sur le Notariat* (1824), B.N. Lf^{41} 13, 30–31.

75. R. R. Palmer, "The Central Schools of the First French Republic: A Statistical Survey," in D. N. Baker and P. J. Harrigan, eds., *The Making of Frenchmen: Current Directions in the History of Education in France, 1679–1979* (the Summer 1980 issue of *Historical Reflections*), 243–47.

76. J. Imbert, "L'Enseignement du droit dans les écoles centrales sous la Révolution," *Actes du Colloque d'Orléans* (1988), I: 249–65.

77. A. Duruy, *L'Instruction publique et la Révolution* (1882), 439–44.

78. Imbert, "L'Enseignement du droit"; also H. Richard, "Les Professeurs de législation des écoles centrales, témoins du droit privé intermédiaire," *Actes du Colloque d'Orléans* (1988), I: 267–86. The professors in Grenoble and Poitiers

also tried to prepare future notaries in their courses (Petitjean, "Côte d'Or," p. 298, n. 27).

79. A.N. BB[1] 148: Grand-Juge to présidents des cours d'appel, 19 germinal XIII, with statistics or nominal lists of students enrolled in the legislation courses over the years. A slightly different reckoning is in A.N. F[17] 1958: Tableau nominatif des élèves qui ont suivis les cours de législation aux écoles centrales et des cours particuliers (an XIII). Courses that began to show a modest degree of success included those in the Doubs, Haute-Garonne, Isère, Maine-et-Loire, Meurthe, Puy-de-Dôme, Basses-Pyrénées, Rhône, and Vienne.

80. Fitzsimmons, *Parisian Barristers,* 135–47, 162–66. A private course run by Bellecour in Toulouse had almost one hundred students in Year XIII, but the ministry suspected that "il y a pu être accordé des inscriptions de complaisance ou même à prix d'argent" (BB[1] 148).

81. A.N. BB[1] 203: Etats des dispenses de Représentation de diplôme de licencié accordées [1805–06?], listing about 960 individuals. A retrospective report of 1815 indicates that 1,372 dispensations were granted.

82. The rules on when *avoués* could or could not plead kept changing over the years, but whenever a sufficient number of *avocats* was lacking, which was often the case in the provinces, attorneys were free to plead. A chronicler of the Bordeaux bar believed that the *avoués* had gained a kind of ascendancy: Before the Revolution, "c'était en général aux avocats que le public s'adressait, et les avocats designaient à leurs clients les avoués dont ils préferaient le concours. Aujourdhui . . . l'avoué, se faisant de plus en plus légiste . . . reussissait à meriter la confiance des clients et attirait vers lui la direction suprême de presque toutes les affaires"—H. Chauvot, *Le Barreau de Bordeaux de 1775 à 1815* (1856), 593. Likewise, the *avocat* Verger believed that—though *avoués* were professionally like "les ouvriers dont se sert l'architecte dans une contruction"—those who have gained the *licence* by dispensation or attendance at law school had an unfair advantage in being able to "cumuler les deux qualités," since the public prefers the convenience of a single practitioner—*A mes Concitoyens: Dissertation sur la distinction à faire entre l'avocat et l'avoué* (1822), B.N. Lf[125] 6.

83. A.N. F[17] 1958: *Instruction pour les écoles de droit, proposée par M.M. les inspecteurs généraux* (March 1807); Compte rendu par le Grand-maître, May 1812; and A.N. F[17] 2102: reports of the inspectors on Dijon and Toulouse, 1811; Rapport général par Chabot, 1810.

84. Arnaud, *Les Juristes,* 31–33.

85. A.N. F[17] 1958: Chef de division de l'Instruction publique, Rapport to Fourcroy, 15 January 1808.

86. *Ibid.:* Proc Gén à Nancy to Grand-maître, 10 May 1808.

87. *Ibid.:* Compte rendu par le Grand-maître, May 1812.

88. *Ibid..* Also F[17] 2102: reports by Chabot and Perreau on enrollments in Poitiers, Grenoble, Caen, Rennes, Aix, Dijon, and Toulouse.

89. Fitzsimmons, *Parisian Barristers,* ch. 7; Chauvot, *Barreau de Bordeaux,*

323–24. When the Bourbons returned, they immediately made the order master of its own roster, by stipulating that its council could refuse to admit an aspirant to the *stage* without having to explain its decision. But the *avocats'* initial ardor for the Bourbons soon cooled, as that regime began to show the same impatience as Napoleon with the barristers' independent professional ethic and occasional gestures of political defiance. The Restoration soon made it clear that the Order of Barristers was subject to control by the state. See J. Fabre, *Le Barreau de Paris 1810–1870* (1895). For a suggestive comparative survey, see M. Burrage, "Revolution and the Collective Action of the French, American, and English Legal Professions," *Law and Social Inquiry,* XIII (Spring 1988), 225–77.

90.   E. L. Guiet (J.P.), *Sur l'état actual des justices de paix rurales* (LeMans, 1828), 5–8.

91.   F. Fortunet, "L'Expérience d'une justice au quotidien: comment être juge (de paix) et conciliateur?" (unpublished paper), 7–13.

92.   C. Dieudonné, *Statistique du département du Nord* (an XII), III: 234–36; A. A. Monteil, *Description du département de l'Aveyron* (Rodez, an X), II: 243–44; Vincenti, *Tribunal du Vaucluse,* 98–101.

93.   B. Schnapper, "Pour une géographie des mentalités judiciaires: la litigiosité en France au XIXe siècle," *Annales E.S.C.,* (1979), no. 2, 399–419.

94.   A.N. AD II 57: *Code de Procédure Civile . . . Exposés des motifs par les Orateurs du Gouvernement:* Treilhard, 2.

95.   Berriat Saint-Prix, *Cours de Procédure Civile,* 135–36; Treilhard, *Motifs,* 29–33.

96.   Siméon, *Motifs,* 199–200.

97.   A.N. BB[30] 528: *Observations . . . ,* especially courts at Bourges, Orléans, Nancy, Colmar. A similar view on *instruction par écrit sur appointement* was expressed in M.J. Rapport aux Consuls (n.d.—Year IX?) in BB[26] 2. To be sure, the courts had some control over when this method could be used: see *Rapports et discours des Orateurs du Tribunat, Avril 1806* (AD II 57), Faure, 25–28. On civil procedure in the interlude of 1793–1800, as it varied from court to court, see Vincenti, *Vaucluse,* 163–74, 182; Debauve, *Morbihan,* 179–81; and Bloch and Hilaire, "Droit révolutionnaire."

98.   *Illusions perdues,* quoted in J. Marquiset, *Les Gens de Justice dans la littérature* (1967), 202.

99.   Treilhard, *Motifs,* 17.

100.   B. Schnapper, "Le cout des procès civils au milieu du XIXe siècle," *Revue historique de Droit français et étranger,* LIX (1981), 621–33.

101.   A.N. F[1c] III Drôme 7: Compte annuel 1810; F[1c] III Haute-Marne 5: Comptes 1811.

102.   A.N. BB[9] 164: Langres (Haute-Marne) and Nantes (Loire-Inférieure); BB[9] 163: Dax (Landes), an VIII.

CHAPTER XII: TRIAL BY JURY

1. See R. Andrews, "The Cunning of Imagery: Rhetoric and Ideology in Cesare Beccaria's *Treatise on Crimes and Punishments,"* in *Begetting Images: Studies in the Art and Science of Symbol Production* (New York, 1989).

2. See J. Langbein, *Torture and the Law of Proof* (Chicago, 1976), and J. Kaufman, "The Critique of Criminal Justice in Eighteenth-Century France" (Ph.D. dissertation, Harvard University, 1976).

3. For an overview, see A. Hiver, *Histoire critique des institutions judiciaires de la France de 1789 à 1848* (1848), and E. Seligmann, *La Justice en France pendant la Révolution* (2 vols., 1901–13).

4. Code Pénal (25 September 1791) in J. B. Duvergier, ed., *Collection complète des lois . . .* (24 vols., 1824), III: 403–19. Cf. M. Foucault, *Discipline and Punish: The Birth of the Prison* (New York, 1977), parts 1–2. For more thorough discussions of the new penal code, see R. Martinage, "Les Origines de la pénologie dans le code pénal de 1791," and R. Martucci, "Le 'parti de la réforme criminelle' à la Constituante," in *La Révolution et l'ordre juridique privé: rationalité ou scandale? Actes du Colloque d'Orléans,* vol. I (1988); N. Castan, "Les Alarmes du pénal: du sujet gibier de justice à l'Etat en proie à ses citoyens (1788–1792)," and P. Lascoumes and P. Poncela, "Classer et punir autrement: les incriminations sous l'Ancien Régime et sous la Constituante," in R. Badinter, ed., *Une Autre Justice, 1789–1799: contributions à l'histoire de la justice sous la Révolution française* (1989), 29–38, 73–104. I am especially indebted to Richard Andrews's view of old-regime criminal justice, to be set forth in his study of the Paris Châtelet: *Law, Magistracy and Crime in Old Regime Paris, 1735–1789* (Cambridge University Press, forthcoming).

5. A. Duport, *Moyens d'exécution par les jurés au criminel et au civil rédigés en articles* (1790) in A.N. AD III 47. For more detailed expositions, see A. Padoa-Schioppa, "Le Jury d'Adrien Duport," and J.-J. Clère, "Les Constituants et l'organisation de la procédure pénale," in *Colloque d'Orléans,* II: 609–22, 441–56. The standard work on French criminal procedure is A. Esmein, *A History of Criminal Procedure with Special Reference to France* (1882; transl. Boston, 1913)—see 408–26. On criminal justice between 1789 and the implementation of trial by jury, see A. Wills, *Crime and Punishment in Revolutionary Paris* (Westport, 1981).

6. Cf. R. Martinage, "Les Innovations des constituants en matière de répression," in *Une Autre Justice,* 105–26.

7. On the correctional courts, see J.-L. Debauve, *La Justice révolutionnaire dans le Morbihan, 1790–1795* (1965), 328–55, and for a subsequent period, M. Bouloiseau, *Délinquence et répression: le tribunal correctionnel de Nice, 1800–14* (1979).

8.   A.N. F^{1c} III Haute-Marne 5: Tribunal de Chaumont, 1812; F^{1c} III Moselle 8: Rapports, 3ème et 4ème trimèstres 1811 (1,586 *délits forestiers* vs 147 other offenses); *Annuaire du département de Bas Rhin* (an VIII), 176–79; A.N. BB^2 28: Réponses au circulaire du M.J. sur l'état des tribunaux criminels et correction- nels, 27 germinal IV, indicating that in numerous departments *délits forestiers* were by far the most common offenses.

9.   A. D'Angeville, *Essai sur la statistique de la population française* (Bourg, 1836; reissued with introduction by E. LeRoy Ladurie, 1969), 94.

10.   Debauve, *Morbihan,* 343, 352.

11.   See the invaluable article "Juré, Jury" in Merlin (de Douai), ed., *Répertoire universel et raisonné de jurisprudence* (4th edn., 1826), XVI: 289–351, and H. Thomas, *Le Tribunal Criminel de la Meurthe sous la Révolution (1792–1799)* (Nancy, 1937), 187–229: "Reconstitution d'une affaire jugée par le tribunal criminel de la Meur- the."

12.   A.N. F^{1a} 408: Deptal Admin Côte d'Or to M.I., 1 March 1792; De- bauve, *Morbihan,* 208–09; Thomas, *Meurthe,* 160–61.

13.   J.-M. Luc, "Le Tribunal criminel de la Haute-Garonne," *AHRF* (1965), 332–43; Thomas, *Meurthe,* 105–36; Debauve, *Morbihan,* 212–19; J. Vercier, *La Justice criminelle dans le département de l'Hérault pendant la Révolution, 1789–1800* (Montpellier, 1926), 233, 246.

14.   Merlin, *Répertoire,* 316; Thomas, *Meurthe,* 219.

15.   *Journal des Tribunaux,* IV, 190–92 (March 1792). A.N. D III 321, doss. 4: Pres. du T.C. [Tribunal Criminel] Bouches-du-Rhône, 29 April 1792; T. C. Loire-Inférieure, 10 June 1792.

16.   *Gazette des Tribunaux,* IV, 289–90 (1792).

17.   Cf. T. A. Green, *Verdict According to Conscience: Perspectives on the English Criminal Trial Jury, 1200–1800* (Chicago, 1985), and J. M. Beattie, *Crime and the Courts in England, 1660–1800* (Oxford, 1986).

18.   B. Schnapper, "Le Jury Criminel," in *Une Autre Justice,* 165–66.

19.   A.N. D III 264/5, doss. J. Maubert and A. Magnant, pluviôse III—a case sent for review to the Convention's committee on legislation.

20.   Changes in procedure may be traced in Esmein, in Merlin's *Répertoire,* and in Bourguignon, *Deuxième Mémoire sur les Jurés* (an XII), B.N. Lf^{113} 16, 69–77. For other examples of the use of *adjoints* and a second deliberation, see Vercier, *Hérault,* 159, and A. Richard, "Le Tribunal criminel des Basses-Pyrénées, d'après une étude récente," *AHRF* (1926), 60.

21.   Schnapper, "Jury Criminel," 169.

22.   *Gazette des Tribunaux,* V, 9–13; VII, 65–67.

23.   *Ibid.,* V, 162–68 and 9–13.

24.   A.N. BB^2 32: M.J. aux T.C.s, circular, 28 July 1793.

25.   A.N. D III 321, doss. 4: T.C. Var, 11 May 1792.

26.   *Ibid.,* Pres T.C. Bouches-du-Rhône, 26 April 1792; T. C. Tarn, 1er trimestre 1792.

27.   *Almanach du juré français pour l'année 1793,* B.N. Lc[22] 35, written originally in early 1792, with an updated preface.

28.   Robespierre, *Principes de l'organisation des jurés et réfutation du système proposé par M. Duport* (1790), B.N. Lf[113] 10. *Gazette des Tribunaux,* V, 5–7 (T.C. Nord, 15 June 1792).

29.   A.N. D III 321, doss. 4: departmental directorates of Pas-de-Calais, Seine-et-Oise, Seine-Inférieure, and Haute-Vienne, 1792; Vercier, *Hérault,* 152–53.

30.   Vercier, *Hérault,* 131. Cf. Debauve, *Morbihan,* 222, for the overwhelming preponderance of the urban middle classes on juries in 1793–94. The first serious research on the composition of French juries may be found in Robert Allen's Columbia University Ph.D. dissertation: "The Criminal Court of the Côte d'Or, 1792–1811" (1990), ch. 5.

31.   *Gazette des Tribunaux,* VII, 90–91; Merlin de Douai, *Rapport sur les changemens que nécessitent, dans la loi du 16 Septembre 1791 concernant les jurés et la procédure criminelle, les lois émanées depuis le 10 Août 1792 . . .* [frimaire an II] in A.N. AD III 46. Also BB[30] 32: M.J. Compte, 2ème décade ventôse II on the law of 2 nivôse II on jury selection.

32.   Vercier, *Hérault,* 188–89. An indemnity for jurors was first proposed in November 1792 (M.J. to Convention, D III 371), and was authorized by a decree of 16 August 1793. A law of 6 ventôse V eliminated the daily stipend, leaving only an indemnity for travel.

33.   See J. L. Godfrey, *Revolutionary Justice: A Study of the Organization, Personnel, and Procedure of the Paris Tribunal, 1793–95* (Chapel Hill, 1951); W. Scott, *Terror and Repression in Revolutionary Marseilles,* chs. 6, 12; and A.-M. Duport, "Deux tribunaux d'exception du Sud-Est: le tribunal révolutionnaire de Nîmes et la commission populaire d'Orange," in *Colloque d'Orléans,* II: 675–85. See also Seligmann, *La Justice en France,* vol. II passim.

34.   Debauve, *Morbihan,* 253–65; Vercier, *Hérault,* 155–87, 245–46; Thomas, *Meurthe,* 273–84; A. Combier, *La Justice criminelle à Laon pendant la Révolution, 1789–1800* (2 vols., 1882), I: 44–54, 100–344; B. Schnapper, "L'Activité du Tribunal criminel de la Vienne, 1792–1800," *Colloque d'Orléans,* II: 623–38.

35.   Luc, "Haute-Garonne," 332–43; Richard, "Basses-Pyrénées," 63–69.

36.   A.N. BB[30] 32: M.J. Compte décadaire, 1 ventôse II.

37.   C. Doyle, "The Judicial Reaction in South-Eastern France, 1794–1800" (D. Phil dissertation, Oxford University, 1986). Also R. C. Cobb, *Reactions to the French Revolution,* and Lucas and Lewis, eds., *Beyond the Terror: essays in French Regional and Social History, 1794–1815,* especially Lucas, "Themes in Southern Violence After 9 Thermidor."

38.   Cf. C. Lucas, "The First Directory and the Rule of Law," *French Historical Studies,* X (1977), 231–60.

39.   A.N. F[1c] III Mayenne 6: *Liste des jurés . . . de la Mayenne. Premier trimestre de l'an VI* (Laval); Extrait des Registres de l'Administration Centrale, 24 fructidor

V; Les Citoyens soussignés de Mayenne, au Directoire, 3 j.c. an V. The Directory's mode of jury selection was established by the law of 3 brumaire IV (see Esmein and Merlin).

40.   A.N. BB[30] 1155B: M.J. circulars: 29 brumaire and 16 ventôse VI, 11 messidor VII. (The minister under the Consulate made the same complaint: circular, 5 messidor VIII.) A.N. F[1c] III Indre 4: Deptal commissioner, circular, 19 pluviôse VI; F[1c] III Vosges 7: Compte, messidor-fructidor VII; F[1c] III Pas-de-Calais 8: Compte, messidor VI; F[1a] 422: Deptal Admin Meurthe, circular, 5 thermidor VII.

41.   A.N. AD III 46: *Tribunat: Rapport par Gillet sur . . . la formation des listes de jurés,* 4 germinal VIII; *Opinion de Mathieu; Opinion de Ludot; Opinion de Coste,* 4 germinal VIII. A.N. BB[20] 1: circulars to justices of the peace Ain, Nièvre, Pyrénées-Orientales; BB[30] 1156: M.J. circular, 25 brumaire IX.

42.   A.N. F[1c] III Haute-Garonne 8: Pref to M.I., 15 frimaire IX.

43.   A.N. BB[30] 526: Relevé des lettres et observations des membres composants les cours de justice criminelles sur l'institution des jurés [an XII]. This is an extremely rich source on which I have relied heavily. See also J. E. Bonnet, *Du juri en France* (an X), B.N. Lf[113] 14, and Bourguignon, *Divers mémoires sur le jury* (an X–1810), Lf[113] 16.

44.   Aveyron in BB[30] 526.

45.   Combier, *Laon,* 79–82; Thomas, *Meurthe,* 555; R. Demogue, "Un Tribunal criminel sous la Révolution: Le T.C. de la Marne," *Revue de Champagne,* XVIII (July 1911), 161–77; XIX (September 1911), 208–16; XX (November 1911), 225–40, especially 240. In the T.C. of the Seine, juries acquitted 310 out of 660 defendants (47 percent) during floréal-fructidor Year IV (*Journal de la Justice,* nos. 6, 9, 12; *Journal des Droits et Devoirs,* pp. 41 and 210).

46.   R. Allen, "The Criminal Court of the Côte d'Or," ch. 3 (Verdicts and Defendants) and ch. 6 (The Problem of Jury Leniency).

47.   L. J. Wigoder, "Justice and the Criminal in the Haute-Marne, 1780–1815" (D. Phil dissertation, Oxford University, 1979), 205–09; Allen, "Côte d'Or," ch. 3, tables; Demogue, "T.C. de la Marne," *Revue de Champagne,* XXIII (May 1912), 321–36.

48.   Bourguignon, *Deuxième Mémoire,* 70–74; Les membres de la Cour de Justice criminelle de la Sarthe, 4 fructidor XII in A.N. BB[30] 526.

49.   E. Claverie, "De la difficulté de faire un citoyen: les 'acquittements scandaleux' du jury dans la France provinciale du début du XIXe siècle," *Etudes Rurales,* 95–96 (1984), 143–65.

50.   A.N. BB[30] 526: especially the presiding judges of Allier, Hautes-Alpes, Charente-Inférieure, Gard, Haute-Garonne, Haute-Saône.

51.   Merlin, *Répertoire,* XVI: 348. See also *C500: Opinion de Chazal sur la composition des juris, la question intentionnelle . . .* 18 vendémiaire V in AD III 46; A.N. BB[30] 1155B: M.J. circular, 19 ventôse VI; *Journal de la Justice,* no. 7, and II, 182–88.

52. A.N. BB[30] 526: Nord, Haute-Garonne, Basses-Pyrénées, Haute-Saône, Isère.

53. *Ibid.:* Tableau de déliberations prises par les jurys de jugement de Saône-et-Loire . . . évidemment absurdes et injustes.

54. *Ibid.:* especially Cantal, Maine-et-Loire, Seine-Inférieure, Vendée.

55. *Ibid.:* Manche, Bas-Rhin, Oise, Vienne (Observations sur l'institution de la procédure par jurés), and Le Procureur-Général de Bas-Rhin to Carrion-Nisas, messidor XII.

56. *Ibid.:* Le Président de la Cour de Justice Criminelle à Versailles to Carrion-Nisas, 6 thermidor XII; Haute-Garonne.

57. *Ibid.:* Relevé de plusieurs jugemens rendus avec jurés par le T.C. du Loiret, germinal VI–messidor XII. See also Département de l'Indre: Relevé exact . . . de toutes les affaires criminelles soumises à la décision du jury depuis 1792. On the Loiret, see D'Angeville, *Essai sur la statistique,* 222–23.

58. A.N. BB[30] 526: e.g., Aude, Aveyron, Vienne.

59. A.N. BB[20] 1: printed quarterly lists from Ille-et-Vilaine, Gard, Landes, Loir-et-Cher, and Haute-Saône. But see Allen, "Côte d'Or," ch. 5 (The Jurors).

60. A.N. BB[30] 526: Cantal, Cher, Drôme, Eure-et-Loire, Haute-Garonne, Gironde, Lot, Oise, Saône-et-Loire.

61. These and other innovations are discussed by Esmein, *Criminal Procedure,* 437–61, who also recounts the episodic debate on juries in the Council of State, drawing extensively on Locré's compilation, *Législation civile, commerciale et criminelle de la France* (463–99). On the Tribunate's debate over special tribunals, see above, Chapter I.

62. A.N. BB[30] 526: especially Hautes-Alpes, Drôme, Eure-et-Loire, Haut-Rhin, Seine-et-Oise, Tarn, and Vienne. For an early critique of the *juri d'accusation,* see Millot, "Essai sur le perfectionnement de l'ordre judiciaire," *Gazette des Tribunaux,* V (1792), 442–45.

63. Esmein, *Criminal Procedure,* 511–17; M. Fleurigeon, *Le Guide des Jurés* (1811), B.N. F 34935, 8–10 and 101–08.

64. E.g., Gispert-Dulçat (premier juge de la cour criminelle des Pyrénées-Orientales), *Essai sur l'évidence . . . suivi d'observations sur les jurés* (Perpignan, an XII), AD III 47, 53–54.

65. Fleurigeon, *Guide des Jurés,* 81–87. Cf. N. J. B. Boyard, *Coup-d'oeil sur le Jury tel qu'il est, et tel qu'il pourrait être en France* (Nancy, 1819), B.N. Lf[113] 30. *Liste générale du Jury pour 1829: Département de la Moselle,* B.N. Lf[113] 3—giving the tax assessment of each juror, always 300 livres or more.

66. Claverie, "Acquittements scandaleux," 156–57.

67. D'Angeville, *Essai sur la statistique,* 338–39.

68. J. Donovan, "Justice Unblind: The Juries and the Criminal Classes in France, 1825–1914," *Journal of Social History,* XV (Fall 1981), 89–107.

69. On "correctionalization," see Vercier, *Hérault,* 134–35, and Claverie, 162–63.

70.   A.N. F^{1a} 408: printed form for a jury summons in the Dordogne, prairial VII; Fleurigeon, *Guide des Jurés,* 86–87.

CHAPTER XIII: CONSCRIPTION

1.   E. G. Léonard, *L'Armée et ses problêmes au XVIIIe siècle* (1958); L. Mention, *Le Comte de Saint-Germain et ses réformes, 1775–77* (1884).

2.   D. Bien, "The Army in the French Enlightenment," *Past and Present,* 85 (November 1979), 68–98; Bien, "La Réaction aristocratique avant 1789: l'exemple de l'armée," *Annales, E.S.C.* (1974), 23–48 and 505–34.

3.   A. Corvisier, *L'Armée française de la fin du XVIIe siècle au ministère de Choiseul: Le Soldat* (2 vols., 1964); Corvisier, "Le Recrutement et la promotion dans l'armée française du XVIIe siècle à nos jours," *Revue international d'histoire militaire,* XXXVII (1976), 23–41; A. Huyon, "L'Obligation militaire en France sous l'ancien régime," *Revue historique des armées,* 1982 (no. 2), 4–18.

4.   S. Scott, *The Response of the Royal Army to the French Revolution: The Role and Development of the Line Army, 1787–93* (Oxford, 1978), 54, 58.

5.   For an overview of military reform, see the magisterial volume of J.-P. Bertaud, *The Army of the French Revolution: From Citizen-Soldiers to Instrument of Power* (Princeton, 1988 transl.), chs. I–II.

6.   Scott, *Royal Army,* 151–68. Cf. Th. Jung, *L'Armée et la Révolution: Dubois-Crancé, 1747–1814* (1884).

7.   Scott, *Royal Army,* 97–107, 190–206.

8.   *Ibid.,* 70–97, 182–90.

9.   J.-P. Bertaud, *Valmy: la démocratie en armes* (1970), ch. 5/I; E. Déprez, *Les Volontaires nationaux, 1791–1793* (1908).

10.   Bertaud, *Valmy,* ch. 5/II, and Bertaud, "Les Volontaires de 1792," in Forrest and Jones, eds., *Reshaping France: Town, Country, and Region in the French Revolution,* 168–78.

11.   Bertaud, *Army of the French Revolution,* ch. IV; A. Forrest, *Conscripts and Deserters: The Army and French Society During the Revolution and Empire* (Oxford, 1989), 26–34; J. G. Gallaher, "Recruitment in the District of Poitiers, 1793," *French Historical Studies,* III (1963); J. Richard, "La Levée des 300,000 hommes et les troubles de Mars 1793 en Bourgogne," *Annales de Bourgogne,* CXXXII (1961).

12.   Bertaud, *Army of the French Revolution,* ch. V; A. Soboul, *Les Soldats de l'an II* (1959).

13.   A.N. AD XVI 81: Decree of 1 October 1793.

14.   *Ibid.:* Decrees of 4 and 13 May, 3 and 14 September 1793; Archives de la Guerre (Vincennes) [cited hereafter as A.G.], X^s 64.

15.   A. Crépin, "Soutenance de Thèse: Levées d'hommes et esprit public en Seine-et-Marne (1791–1815)," *AHRF,* no. 286 (October 1991), 563–64, emphasizes the salutary impact of communal subventions. See also Bertaud, *La Vie*

Quotidienne dans les armées de la Révolution (1985), 43–46; Bertaud, *Army of the French Revolution,* 119–24; Woloch, *The French Veteran from the Revolution to the Restoration,* 80–88; and Forrest, *The French Revolution and the Poor,* 151–52.

16.   Bertaud, *Army of the French Revolution,* 127–32.

17.   A.N. F^9 235, doss. 1: Deptal Comm Puy-de-Dôme to M.I., 16 fructidor V, citing a circular by the minister of 24 thermidor V warning cantonal commissioners against issuing proclamations "pour inviter ou autoriser les réquis et autres militaires à rester tranquillement dans leurs foyers pour aider leurs parens dans les travaux de l'agriculture." Same issue in F^9 236 Basses-Pyrénées.

18.   A.N. F^9 288: to M.I., 14 messidor IV.

19.   A.N. AF III 313/1: War Ministry Rapport au Directoire, 25 thermidor IV.

20.   A.N. AF III 313/1–78. I have gone through the first of these alphabetical cartons systematically. Hardly typical, but compelling, is the case of Abraham, a draftee who was never incorporated, having been allowed to serve as a schoolmaster for the last five years, and having subsequently married. Over one hundred parents from Charleville signed a petition in behalf of this *maître éclairé:* "Au milieu de la disette d'instruction la loi leur avait toujours conservé un instituteur qui mérite . . . la confiance publique." From Villefranche de Beluze, the municipal administration wrote in behalf of its young secretary, currently home on a convalescent furlough and now married: "La République ne manquera pas de défenseurs, mais sans le Citoyen Bargues (le seul du canton capable de remplir cette place) notre administration se trouve sans secrétaire et conséquement absolument paralisée" (A.N. F^9 288: to M.G., 7 brumaire VI). On the general attempt to tighten previous regulations on exemptions and exceptions, see A.G. X^s 64, arrêté du 4 ventôse IV.

21.   Oudot, *Motion tendante à faire décréter dans la Constitution que tous les jeunes citoyens . . . serviront pendant deux ans dans les armées de la République* (thermidor III) in A.N. AD XVI 81. See also Poultier, *De la force Armée: chapitre oublié dans le projet de la commission des onze.*

22.   *C500: Rapport par Jourdan sur le recrutement de l'armée de terre* (2 thermidor VI); *C500: Opinion de Porte* (1 fructidor) in A.N. AD XVI 81.

23.   Among the dozens of such addresses, see *C.A. Les Membres de l'Administration Centrale de l'Aisne au Conseil des Anciens* (17 brumaire VII) and *C500: Les Membres de l'Administration Centrale de l'Indre-et-Loire* (28 brumaire VII), collected in A.N. AD XVI 81. Communications from Loiret and Gironde, however, raised a note of alarm.

24.   *C500: Message du Directoire* (28 germinal VII); *C500: Rapport par Jourdan* (8 messidor VII).

25.   *C500: Message du Directoire* (2 vendémiaire VIII); A.N. F^{1c} I 12: Extraits de la correspondance, messidor-fructidor VII.

26.   A.N. AF III 151B, fol. 709: Progrès d'execution de la loi du 28 germinal VII, and Deuxième compte au Directoire sur la loi du 14 messidor VII. Also

A.N. F^{1c} III Aisne 9: Deptal Comm to M.I., 22 ventôse VIII; A.N. F^{1c} III Ariège 3: Admin Centrale, 7 frimaire VIII; A.N. F^{1c} III Seine-Inférieure 8: Deptal Comm to M.I., 8 prairial VII. On brigandage, see the superb pages by Forrest, *Conscripts and Deserters,* chs. 6–7.

27. *Journal de Rouen,* 6 vendémiaire VIII; *Journal de la Côte d'Or,* 20 vendémiaire VIII; A.N. F^{1c} III Jura 7: Deptal Comm to M.I., 3 brumaire VIII.

28. *Discours prononcé par Daru, orateur du Tribunat, sur la conscription militaire* (28 floréal X), 39–40 in B.N. Le^{50} 132.

29. A.N. F^9 262, fol. 3: Commanders of 1st and 16th military districts to M.G., 21 messidor VIII; F^9 142: Pref Meurthe to M.I., 2 pluviôse XI; Pref Aisne, 30 nivôse XI. Unless otherwise indicated, prefectorial correspondence is directed to the minister of the interior.

30. A.N. F^9 142: Pref Aube, 5, 28 pluviôse XI; Pref Ardennes, 7 pluviôse XI; F^9 207: Pref Lot, 1 pluviôse XI; F^9 196: Pref Isère, 30 nivôse XI.

31. A.N. BB^{18} 76 Somme: Petition to M.I., 8 vendémiaire XII.

32. See A.N. F^9 168: M.G. to M.I., 3 ventôse XI, for one of the first suggestions of this change. A.N. F^9 141, fol. 4: Observations sur le mode de levée des conscrits: rapport a l'Empereur, 27 messidor XII.

33. A.N. F^9 143, circular to prefects, 20 fructidor XIII; A.N. F^9 235, fol. 5: *Instructions du préfet de Puy-de-Dôme,* 23 germinal XIII, 11 vendémiaire XIV; A.N. F^9 141, fol. 4: Pref Haute-Saône, 21 October 1805. For an example of the procedures being applied, see the *procès-verbal* of the canton of Cabannes, ventôse XII, in L.-A. Dessat and C.-J. L'Estoile, *Origines des armées révolutionnaires et impériales d'après les archives départementales de l'Ariège* (1906), 36–39.

34. A.N. F^9 144, fol. 1: *Arrêté du préfet de la Haute-Marne, 31 décembre 1806; Instruction spéciale sur la conscription en ce qui intéresse les conscrits et leurs parens, par le préfet de Seine-et-Marne* (1809), B.N. F 36666; *Manuel des gardes nationales et des conscrits de l'Empire française* (1812), B.N. V 45783.

35. A.N. F^9 141, fol. 4: Pref Seine-Inférieure, Mémoire sur la conscription de l'an XIV. Also A.N. F^{1c} III Haute-Garonne 8: Mémoire analytique des actes de l'administration, 4ème trim 1809; A.N. F^{1c} III Loiret 6: Compte, January 1811; A.N. F^{1c} III Sarthe 6: Compte, July 1811; A.N. F^{1c} III Eure-et-Loire 7: Compte 2ème trim 1812.

36. A.N. AF IV 1122: Rapport fait à l'Empereur, levée de l'an XIII; A.N. F^9 163: Pref Bouches-du-Rhône, 18 October 1806 and subsequent letters.

37. A.N. F^{1c} III Sarthe 6: Compte 3ème trim 1808; also Compte 1er trim 1807.

38. Between the levies of Years VIII and XIV, the class or cohort comprised twenty-year-olds whose birthday fell between successive Septembers. With the transition from the revolutionary calendar back to the Gregorian calendar, the class of 1806 was a larger pool of those born between September 1785 and December 1786. It was also somewhat younger, for it encompassed youths who had not reached twenty years of age at the time they were called.

Thereafter a class corresponded to those born in a given calendar year. It was also in 1806 that the authority to order a call-up was shifted from the legislature to the more compliant Senate. See G. Vallée, *La Conscription dans le département de la Charente, 1798–1807* (1936), 536–40.

39.   A.N. F^9 202, fol. 5: Pref Loir-et-Cher, 16 frimaire, 15 brumaire XIV; A.N. F^9 168, fol. 6: Pref Cher, 15 brumaire and subsequent letters; A.N. AF IV 1121: Council of State to Napoleon, floréal XII. Cf. Verneilh, *Exposé des opérations relatives à la levée des conscrits des ans 11 et 12 à Mont Blanc* (germinal XII), B.N. LK^4 624.

40.   Laws of 28 germinal, 14 messidor VII in *Bulletin des Lois*.

41.   *Tribunat: Opinion de Delpierre sur la question . . . de les autoriser à se faire remplacer dans certain cas* (13 ventôse VIII) and *Opinion de Desmousseaux* (13 ventôse VIII) in A.N. AD XVI 81. Also A.N. AF IV 1121: Idées et faits sur l'état de recrutement de l'armée, frimaire VIII.

42.   A.N. F^9 232 Pas-de-Calais: Contrôle nominatif des conscrits partant d'Arras, germinal-fructidor VIII.

43.   A.N. AF IV 1121: Tableau de la situation de la levée des réquisition-naires et conscrits à l'époque du 5 brumaire an IX. For local confirmation see A.N. F^9 251bis Somme, 5 thermidor VIII; A.N. F^9 239 Bas-Rhin, 6 prairial VIII; A.N. F^9 215 Marne, 17 fructidor VIII.

44.   *Discours prononcé par Dessole, orateur du gouvernement* (28 floréal X), 2 in B.N. Le^{50} 131.

45.   A. C. Thibaudeau, *Bonaparte and the Consulate* (London, 1908), 88. His position was echoed by Daru in the Tribunate: "We will not be able to prevent the rich from enjoying the advantages that their wealth confers; if the law does not leave them the means, they will find it by way of corruption" (*Discours par Daru, 28 floréal X,* 42).

46.   Laws of 28 floréal, 18 thermidor X in *Bulletin des Lois*. Vallée, *Charente,* 377–78, is somewhat misleading on this point.

47.   A.N. AF IV 1121, Bureau de Recrutement: Rapport aux Consuls, 26 brumaire XI; A.N. F^9 143, fol. 2: Bureau de l'Ouest: Conscription de l'an IX et X; A.N. F^9 142 Aube, 5, 28 pluviôse XI; A.N. F^9 196 Isère, 30 nivôse XI.

48.   A.N. AF IV 1121, frimaire XI.

49.   Laws of 6 floréal XI and 8 nivôse XIII in *Bulletin des Lois*. Cf. *Tribunat: Rapport par Sahuc sur . . . la conscription de l'an XIII* (12 germinal XII).

50.   A.N. F^9 141, fol. 4: Observations sur le mode de levée des conscrits, 27 messidor XII; A.N. AF IV 1122: Council of State, Rapport sur les suppléants (par Lacuée), an XIII.

51.   See A.N. F^9 144: *Préfet de la Seine: avis aux conscrits* (September 1808); A.N. AF IV 1124: Etat des . . . ramplaçans qui ont deserté des corps, January 1810, which lists 701 deserters; A.G. X^s 65: Director General of Conscription to prefects, 18 July 1811: "Many replacements have been annulled by the effect of the supplementary and complementary levies on the classes of 1806 to 1810."

Also A.G. X^s 64: Comptes for 1811: "Restitution de sommes de 100F pour remplacemens annullés," mentioning 223 cases.

52. For the government's adamant stand on trafficking in replacements, see A.N. F^{1c} III Nord 8: Compte analytique du 1er trim de 1811; A.N. F^9 141, Dunkerque, 23 October 1813. But Cf. P. Viard, "La Désignation des conscrits appelés à marcher de 1800 à 1813 dans le département du Nord," *Revue du Nord* (1924), 196: "Ici se manifeste l'activité d'agences interlopes que les préfets foudraient en termes aussi véhements qu'inefficaces." However, Merlin de Douai, *Répertoire universel et raisonné de jurisprudence* (4th edn., 1826), art. "Conscription," suggests that intermediaries would have trouble using the courts to enforce their "conventions aléatoires." In the Hérault, peasants formed associations to which they each contributed a designated amount, the combined funds to be used to hire replacements should some of their sons be inducted. But Napoleon's supplementary levies strained this system severely: A.N. BB^{18} 32 Hérault: Gelly to M. J., January 1809. Most Jews, incidentally, were not permitted substitution or replacement: *Manuel des gardes nationales et des conscrits,* 114, 119.

53. A.N. AF IV 1124: Situation au 1er Janvier 1810 du recouvrement des sommes de 100F due pour des remplacemens (classes de 1806–10).

54. P. Viard, *L'Administration préfectoriale dans le départment de la Côte d'Or,* 152; A.N. F^{1c} III Haute-Saône 8: Levées de 1811–1814; J.-P. Bois, "Conscrits du Maine-et-Loire sous l'Empire," *Annales de Bretagne,* LXXXIII (1976), 490. Also A.N. F^{1c} III Tarn 6: Levée de 1813; A.N. F^{1c} III Nord 8: Conscriptions de 1811, 1812.

55. G. Vallée, "Le Remplacement militaire en Charente, 1798–1814," *RF,* LXXX (1927) and LXXXI (1928); A. Maureau, "Le Remplacement militaire de l'an VIII à 1814 d'après les registres de notaires d'Avignon," *Revue de l'Institut Napoléon* (1975).

56. A.N. F^{1c} III Bouches-du-Rhône 7: Compte 2ème trim an XIII; A.N. F^{1c} III Var 6: Situation 2ème trim an XIII and compte 2ème trim an XIII; A.N. F^9 251bis Somme: Etat numérique des actes de substitution . . . années 11 and 12; Viard, *Côte d'Or,* 153.

57. A.N. F^{1c} III Hérault 9: Correspondence for 1811–12; A.N. F^{1c} III Ain 5: Comptes 1812; A.N. F^{1c} III Tarn 6: Comptes 1807, 1809, 1812; A.N. F^{1c} III Bouches-du-Rhône 7: Compte 1812; G. Désert, "Le Remplacement dans le Calvados sous l'Empire et les monarchies censitaires," *Revue d'histoire économique et sociale,* XLIII (1965), 70–72, with information on four communes.

58. I. Woloch, "La Bourgeoisie devant la conscription napoléonienne: l'exemple du barreau," in *La Bataille, l'armée, la gloire: actes du colloque de Clermont-Ferrand, 1983* (2 vols., Clermont-Ferrand, 1985), I: 183–92.

59. A.N. F^{1c} III Ain 5: Compte 1812; A.N. F^2 I 121/13: Pref Maine-et-Loire, 26 October 1808.

60. A.N. BB^{18} 67 Saône-et-Loire: Extrait des registres du tribunal criminel à Charolles, 11 April 1807.

61. For the acquittal by a criminal court (on appeal from a correctional court) of a good faith intermediary, see A.N. BB[18] 32 Hérault: May 1808 on appeal from Béziers. On the purported nervousness of a conscript's family, see A.N. BB[18] 50 Moselle: doss. N. Richartz, 1808.

62. A.N. BB[18] 76 Somme: Jugement du tribunal civil de Mondidier jugéant correctionnellement, 18 September 1806.

63. A.N. BB[18] 76 Somme: Rapport au M.J., September 1808, for acquittal on a charge of fraudulent intervention, where the money was returned when the conscript was inducted.

64. A.N. BB[18] 71: Responses to a ministerial circular, from the public prosecutors (hereafter P.G. or *procureur-général*) of Ardèche, Eure, and Vaucluse; A.N. BB[18] 67 Saône-et-Loire: Pref to M.J., 4 ventôse XII; A.N. BB[18] 50 Moselle: Pref to Director General, 14 September 1806.

65. A.N. F[1c] III Saône-et-Loire 8: Mémoire du préfet, 4 nivôse XIII.

66. A.N. AF IV 1123: Lacuée to Napoleon, 29 January 1807.

67. A.N. BB[18] 50 Moselle: Director General to M.J., 25 November, 9 December 1808; A.N. F[1c] III Moselle 8: Rapport 3ème trim 1811; A.N. AF IV 1125: Dumas to Napoleon, 27 April 1811.

68. A.N. F[9] 223 Moselle: Tableau comparatif, 25 November 1812.

69. A.N. BB[18] 71: P.G. Haute-Saône, response to circular of 3 October 1806.

70. A.N. BB[18] 20 Drôme: Arrêté du Préfet (affiche: 19 pluviôse XII); Pref to M.J., 1 germinal XIII.

71. A.N. BB[18] 50 Orne: Jugement rendu contre les auteurs d'un mouvement séditieux qui a eu lieu à Sées relativement à la désignation des conscrits (an XII); A.N. BB[18] 55 Oise: Pref to M.I., 17 fructidor XIII, on other scandals in the Oise.

72. A.N. AF IV 1124: Situation du recouvrement des indemnités de réforme depuis l'an IX jusqu'à celle de 1810.

73. A.N. BB[18] 76 Somme: Frémont, marchand à Vinacourt, to M.J., 31 December 1807, 13 January 1808.

74. On the problem of height, see A.N. AF IV 1123: Lacuée to Napoleon, 21 January and 31 March 1807; A.N. F[9] 223: Pref Moselle, 19 May 1807.

75. E.g., A.N. F[9] 251bis (Somme): Etat des conscrits de l'an XI and XII . . . dispenses definitives; A.N. F[1c] III Nord 8: conscription de 1811; Texier-Olivier, *Haute-Vienne,* 89 (tableau de réformes, 1806); Bossi, *Ain,* 298.

76. A.N. F[9] 144: Pref Puy-de-Dôme, 25 November 1807.

77. A.N. F[1c] III Ille-et-Vilaine 7: Compte 1812.

78. A.N. AF IV 1125: Dumas to Napoleon, 27 April 1811.

79. *Instruction Générale de 1811:* Tableaux des infirmités qui rendent ceux qui en sont atteints impropres au service militaire. It is divided into two parts: Infirmités évidentes and Infirmités ou maladies reservés aux conseils de recrutement. See especially note C (pp. 3–4) on vision problems. For insight into the

state of medical practice, see M. Ramsey, "Conscription, Malingerers, and Popular Medicine in Napoleonic France," *Proceedings of the Consortium on Revolutionary Europe (1978)*.

80. Woloch, "La Bourgeoisie devant la conscription," 187–89.

81. See Forrest, *Conscripts and Deserters,* 136–37; A.N. AF IV 1126: Dumas to Napoleon, 6 March 1812.

82. For an overview, see Ramsey, "Conscription, Malingerers, and Popular Medicine."

83. A.N. BB[18] 76 Somme: Mémoire pour Trannoy, docteur en médicine, contre M. le P.G. (Amiens, 1808); A.N. F[9] 144: Pref Puy-de-Dôme, 14 March 1808; A.N. BB[18] 20 Drôme: P.G. to M.J., 8 May 1808 and 12 June 1809 on induced hernias and ailments.

84. A.N. BB[18] 76 Somme: Arrêté de la Cour Impériale d'Amiens, October 1814.

85. A.N. BB[18] 20 Doubs: Tribunal de 1er Instance de Besançon, 23 November 1808; A.N. BB[18] 39 Loire-Inférieure: Director General to M.G., 5 April 1808; A.N. BB[18] 47 Mayenne: P.G. to M.J., 3 June 1807.

86. A.N. BB[18] 71: circulars of 3 October 1806 and 1 May 1807, and responses by the procureurs-généraux.

87. Modern scholarly work on *insoumission* began with G. Vallée, *La Conscription dans le département de la Charente, 1798–1807* (1936), to whom all subsequent scholars are indebted. Other early efforts include R. Legrand, "Le Recrutement des armées et les désertions, 1791–1815," in *Aspects de la Révolution en Picardie* (Abbéville, 1957); J. Vidalenc, "La désertion dans le département du Calvados sous le Premier Empire," *RHMC,* VI (1959); J. Waquet, "Réflexions sur les émotions populaires et le recrutement militaire de 1799 à 1831," *Actes du 91e Congrès des Sociétés Savantes, 1966,* III (1969); Waquet, "La Société civile devant l'insoumission et la désertion à l'époque de la conscription militaire (1798–1814)," *Bibliothèque de l'Ecole des Chartes,* CXXXVI (1968), 187–222; and J.-P. Bertaud, "Aperçus sur l'insoumission et la désertion à l'époque révolutionnaire: étude des sources," *Bulletin d'histoire économique et sociale de la Révolution française, Année 1969* (1970), 17–48. In the 1980s, Alan Forrest began publishing articles on the subject, which culminated in his splendid synthesis, *Conscripts and Deserters,* a French version having first appeared in 1988. My own, somewhat different view of the subject was set forth in "Napoleonic Conscription: State Power and Civil Society," *Past and Present,* 111 (May 1986), 101–29.

88. A.N. F[9] 262, fol. 2: M.G. circular, 13 nivôse VII, and Levée des conscrits, an VII: Observations générales; A.N. F[1c] I 12: Bas-Rhin, pluviôse VIII.

89. *Compte Général de la Conscription, [1798–1805] de A.-A. Hargenvilliers,* ed. G. Vallée (1937), chs. V–VII and Table IV.

90. E.g., A.N. F[9] 144: Pref Puy-de-Dôme, 25 November 1807. See Forrest, "La Formation des attitudes villageoises envers le service militaire, 1792–1814,"

in *La Bataille, l'armée, la guerre,* I: 173–82, and A. Chatelain, "Resistance à la conscription et migrations temporaires," *AHRF,* no. 210 (November 1972), 606–25.

91. Forrest, *Conscripts and Deserters,* 97, and in general chs. 4–5.

92. The fact that Vallée's pioneering monograph on recruitment and *insoumission* unfortunately stopped in 1807 may have helped obscure, for scholars who followed in his wake, the significant change that occurred later.

93. A.N. AF IV 1121: Résultats de la loi du 24 floréal X sur l'amnistie.

94. *Ibid.:* Lacuée to Bonaparte [n.d., early Year XII?], and pluviôse XII; Council of State, 20 vendémiaire XII. For the continuing problem of *insoumission* see, e.g., A.N. F^9 232: Pref Pas-de-Calais to M.G., 5 floréal XII; A.N. F^9 236: Pref Basses-Pyrénées, 9 fructidor XIII, 3 frimaire XIV; A.N. F^9 207: Pref Lot, 10 and 13 floréal XIII.

95. *C500: Opinion de Porte* (1 fructidor VI); *C500: Opinion de Duplantier* (2 fructidor VI); *CA: Rapport par Laveaux* (19 fructidor VI) in A.N. AD XVI 81.

96. A.N. BB^{18} 32 Hérault: Tableau de jugemens rendus par le tribunal de 1er instance de Béziers contre les conscrits réfractaires, and Arrêtés du Préfet qui déclare réfractaires les conscrits appellés et non présentés, 5 fructidor XI. A.N. BB^{18} 20 Doubs: Comm. près le tribunal civil à Besançon to M.J., 23 frimaire XII; Pref Doubs to M.J., 27 germinal XII. A.N. BB^{18}76 Somme: Pref to M.J., 5 fructidor XII; M.J. to Finance Ministry, 20 fructidor XII. A.N. F^{1c} III Pas-de-Calais 8: Compte analytique des Arrêtés du préfecture, 1810. Under a decree of 8 fructidor XIII, the fine was to range from 500 to 1,500 francs, although it was usually levied at the maximum amount.

97. A.N. BB^{18} 55 Oise: *Préfecture de l'Oise: Conscription* (affiche, 3 February 1807). Cf. A.N. BB^{18} 67 Saône-et-Loire: Blondeau to M.J., 7 July 1809; Perrault to M.J., an XIII.

98. A.N. AF IV 1124: Situation du recouvrement des amendes prononcés ... January 1810; AF IV 1123: Lacuée to Napoleon, 16 June 1808; A.N. F^{1c} III Corrèze 3: Compte 1er trim 1808.

99. One of several important points in Forrest, *Conscripts and Deserters,* ch. 6, "Desertion and Criminality."

100. *Ibid.,* 109–17.

101. See Merlin de Douai, ed., *Répertoire Universel,* art. "Conscription," for some of the complexities in this matter. Cf. A.N. BB^{18} 76 Somme: Jugement du Tribunal de Mondidier, March 1808 (Barbier); A.N. BB^{18} 20 Drôme: Rapport au M.J., January 1808.

102. A.N. BB^{18} 18 Creuse, passim; A.N. BB^{18} 47 Mayenne: P.G. to M.J., 21 October 1808; A.N. BB^{18} 71: P.G. Saône-et-Loire to M.J., 1806; A.N. BB^{18} 20 Drôme: Rapport au M.J., 1807; A.N. BB^{18} 32 Hérault: P.G. to M.J., 1 March 1806; A.N. BB^{18} 55 Orne: P.G. to M.J., 30 December 1807, 18 January 1809. On the mayors, see Chapter IV above, and Forrest, *Conscripts and Deserters,* 223–27.

103.   A.N. BB[18] 67 Saône-et-Loire: Comm. près le Tribunal Criminel, 14 floréal XII; A.N. BB[18] 47 Mayenne: P.G. to M.J., 11 October 1808, 22 August 1809.

104.   A.N. AF IV 1124: Tableau par département des condamnations rendues publiques . . . prononcées pour délits graves en matière de conscription, January 1810: fraudes et escroqueries, 459; faux, 41; receleurs, 285.

105.   A.N. BB[18] 32 Hérault: P.G. Montpellier to M.J., 13 May 1814; A.N. BB[18] 47 Mayenne: note by M.J., 23 April 1814.

106.   A.N. F[1c] III Corrèze 2: Compte 2ème trim 1807; A.N. F[1c] III Pas-de-Calais 8: Compte analytique des Arrêtés du préfecture, 2ème sem 1809.

107.   A.N. BB[18] 47 Mayenne: P.G. to M.J., 25 March 1807; A.N. F[1c] III Pas-de-Calais 8: Compte analytique, 2ème sem 1809: Caboche and Veuve Boulard; Waquet, "La Société civile devant l'insoumission," 205 and note.

108.   A.N. F[2] I 121/12: 24 January 1806.

109.   A.N. F[9] 236 (Basses-Pyrénées): Lacuée to M.I., 8 July 1807; A.N. F[2] I 121/12: Burnet d'Autun to M.I., 4 nivôse XIV; A.N. BB[18] 76 Somme: Leclercq to M.J., 16 June 1807. A.N. F[2] I 121/11: Council of State, avis, 1 June 1807; Director General, circular to prefects, 18 August 1807, on the Council of State's ruling (A.N. AD XVI 82).

110.   A.N. AF IV 1123: Renseignemens sur l'emploi des garnisaires, June 1808. See also A.N. F[9] 144, fol. 6: Pref Lozère, 3 December 1807; Vidalenc, "Desertion dans le Calvados," 66–67. The prefect of Loire-Inférieure, however, preferred "gentleness and adjustments rather than measures of rigor and the neglect of proper forms": Waquet, "Réflexions sur les émotions populaires," 65–66.

111.   A.N. AF IV 1123: Lacuée to Napoleon, 16 June 1808; M.G. to Napoleon, 23 September 1808.

112.   M. Fleurigeon, *Code Administratif ou recueil de toutes les lois*. . . . (1809), III: 282–370. A.N. F[1c] III Pas-de-Calais 8: Compte Analytique des Arrêtés du préfecture, 1er sem 1810; Viard, *Côte d'Or,* 158.

113.   A.N. AF IV 1121: Pref Nord to M.G., 19 brumaire IX; A.N. F[1c] III Drôme 7: Compte 1811; A.N. F[1c] III Creuse 7: Pref to Director General, 3 September 1811; Forrest, *Conscripts and Deserters,* 211–13.

114.   A.N. AF IV 1126: Situation des départements sur les réfractaires et déserteurs . . . classes de 1806–10 (1811); A.G. X[s] 65: Compte . . . 1er trim 1811.

115.   A.N. AF IV 1126: Situation, 1811.

116.   A.N. F[1c] III Gers 7: Compte 3ème trim 1811; A.N. F[1c] III Hautes-Alpes 3: Situation administrative, 2ème trim 1811; Waquet, "Société civile et conscription," 206.

117.   A.N. AF IV 1126. The figures are discussed in detail my article "Napoleonic Conscription," 122.

118.   A.N. AF IV 1124: Compte générale, January 1810, Introduction. Also A.N. AF IV 1375: Tableau récapitulatif, an XIII–1808.

119.   A.N. F^{1c} III Aveyron 7: Comptes, 1811–13. Figures for previous numbers of *réfractaires* in these paragraphs are generally drawn from A.N. AF IV 1124 (no. 4): Situation sur les réfractaires.

120.   A.N. F^{1c} III Gard 7: Comptes, 1811–13; A.N. F^{1c} III Ardèche 7: Comptes, 1811–12; A.N. F^{1c} III Tarn 6: Comptes, 1807, 1809–13; A.N. F^{1c} III Ariège 3: Comptes, 1811.

121.   A.N. F^{1c} III Corrèze 3: Comptes, 1808, 1811; A.N. F^{1c} III Haute-Loire 5: Comptes, 1811; A.N. F^{1c} III Lot 7: Comptes, 1811–12; A.N. F^{1c} III Nord 8: 2ème compte 1811.

122.   See, e.g., A.N. F^{1c} III Loiret 6: Comptes, 1811; A.N. F^{1c} III Oise 6: Comptes, 1811; A.N. F^{1c} III Haut-Rhin 7: Rapports, 1811; A.N. F^{1c} III Isère 6: Rapports, 1811; A.N. F^{1c} III Ain 5: Comptes, 1812; A.N. F^{1c} III Eure-et-Loire 7: Comptes, 1811, 1812; A.N. F^{1c} III Jura 8: Comptes, 1812, 1813. Figures in a departmental table reproduced by J. Tulard, *La Vie Quotidienne des français sous Napoléon* (1978), 149–51, vary slightly from such prefects' reports. In any case, Tulard does not convey the significance of the numbers he reproduces.

123.   These summaries may be found in A.N. F^{1c} I 12: Comptes-résumés des bruits: December 1812–June 1813.

124.   A.N. F^{1c} III Indre-et-Loire 7: 10 June 1813.

125.   See Table XIII-1. In the Somme, for example, about 5,000 men had been called in the Years VIII–XIII, and 8,000 in 1806–10. Between December 1812 and February 1814, over 17,000 men were called (A.N. AF IV 1124 and A.N. F^9 251bis.) See also R. Darquenne, *La Conscription dans le département de Jemappes, 1798–1813* (Mons, 1970), 138–39.

126.   A.N. F^{1c} III Bas-Rhin 8: Situation morale, 1er sem 1813; A.N. F^9 239: Pref Bas-Rhin, 30 April 1813; A.N. F^{1c} III Maine-et-Loire 7: 8 March 1813; A.N. F^{1c} III Haute-Vienne 7: Pref of Vienne (misfiled), 15 June 1813; A.N. F^{1c} III Sarthe 6: Compte, 7 May 1813; A.N. F^{1c} III Corrèze 3: 8 September 1813; A.N. F^9 196 Isère: 10 June 1813; A.N. F^9 263: M.G. circular, 27 August 1813, and Situation, 19 November 1813; A.N. F^9 151 Aisne: 2 January 1814.

127.   A.N. BB^{18} 50 Moselle: Pres de la Cour Impériale de Metz to M.J. 17 October 1813.

128.   A.N. F^{17} 2102: Rapport sur Rennes et Caen [July] 1813, and Rapport par Chabot on Dijon, Grenoble, and Strasbourg, November 1813.

129.   Montalant-Bougleux, *Souvenirs sur l'école impériale militaire de Saint-Cyr* (Versailles, 1835), 11–13, 35.

130.   A.N. F^{1c} III Gers 7: Compte 4ème trim 1813; A.N. F^{1c} III Bouches-du-Rhône 7: Sous-Pref of Aix to M.I., 19 December 1813; A.N. F^{1c} III Eure-et-Loire 7: 9 May 1813; A.N. F^{1c} III Jura 8: 10 February 1813; A.N. F^{1c} III Sarthe 6: 3 April 1813; Forrest, *Conscripts and Deserters,* 53, citing research by Vallée on Angoulême; Viard, *Côte d'Or,* 320.

131.   On factitious or abusive marriages, A.N. F^{1c} I 12: April–May 1813 on the Tarn and Eure-et-Loire; Forrest, *Conscripts and Deserters,* 50–51.

132.   A.N. AF IV 1124: Pref Nord to Director General, 17 November 1809; Lacuée to Napoleon, 19 July and 21 November 1809; A.N. BB[18] 76 Somme: Director General to M.J., 19 August 1813.

133.   A.N. F[2] I 121/14: Rapport au M.I. on Rouen, 11 pluviôse XIII; Pref Meurthe to M.I., 28 April 1807; Pref Yonne, 11 November 1807; Pref Calvados, 11 December 1808; Pref Nièvre, 28 September 1811.

134.   G. Carrot, *Une Institution de la Nation: La Garde Nationale, 1789–1871* (Nice, 1979), ch. 2. See also *Les Quatres Ages de la Garde Nationale . . . jusqu'en 1818,* par un électeur de la Seine (1818), B.N. Lf[133] 1, and P. Devaux, *La Garde Nationale de Bourges et les gardes nationales mobilisées du Cher pendant le Consulat et l'Empire.*

135.   Carrot, *La Garde Nationale,* ch. 3.

136.   A.N. F[1c] I 12: Comptes-résumé des bruits; A.N. AF IV 1147: Rapport sur une levée extraordinaire de 80,000 hommes, 7 November 1813; A.N. F[1c] III Ain 5: 11 November 1813; A.N. F[1c] III Finistère 3: Bulletins, 1 July and 1–12 September 1813; A.N. F[1c] III Haute-Marne 5: 8 November 1813.

137.   A.N. F[1c] III Aveyron 7: Compte 4ème trim 1813; A.N. F[1c] III Ardèche 7: Compte 4ème trim 1813; A.N. F[1c] III Loire 6: Pref to M.I., 9 September, 4 and 7 October, 1 December 1813; A.N. F[1c] III Finistère 3: Bulletin 11–31 January 1814; A.N. F[1c] III Vienne 5: 4 February 1814; Waquet, "Réflexions sur les émotions populaires," 60–61, on the Nord.

138.   A.N. F[1c] III Haute-Saône 8: 9, 16, 23 April, 4 August, 30 October, 6, 15 December 1813.

139.   Quoted in Bertier de Sauvigny, *The Bourbon Restoration,* 10.

140.   *Discours à la Chambre des Députées par le M. de la Guerre sur le projet de loi du recrutement* (26 January 1818), 7, in A.N. AD XVI 82.

141.   A.N. F[1c] III Jura 8: Compte Annuel, 1819–20, Recrutement; A.N. F[1c] III Yonne 7: Compte Annuel, June 1819, Recrutement.

142.   *Opinion de M. Barthe-Labastide sur le recrutement de l'armée* (15 January 1818), 3.

143.   B. Schnapper, *Le Remplacement militaire en France: quelques aspects politiques, économiques et sociaux du recrutement au XIXe siècle* (1968). See also N. Sales de Bohigas, "Some Opinions on Exemption from Military Service in Nineteenth-Century Europe," *Comparative Studies in Society and History,* X (1967–68), 261–89.

144.   A.N. F[9] 156, doss. 10 (Ardèche): Pref to M.I., 12 August 1828.

145.   J.-P. Aron, P. Dumont, E. LeRoy Ladurie, *Anthropologie du conscrit français d'après les comptes numériques du recrutement de l'armée, 1819–1828* (1972), with statistical tables of contingents, *reformés, absents,* and replacements, by department. For comments on the quality of replacements and the problems they caused, see A.N. F[1c] III Eure 8: Rapport 1819 on recruitment; A.N. F[1c] III Ille-et-Vilaine 7: Rapport 1819.

REFLECTIONS

1. Weber, *Peasants into Frenchmen: The Modernization of Rural France, 1870–1914*. But cf. C. Tilly, "Did the Cake of Custom Break?" in J. Merriman, ed., *Consciousness and Class Experience in 19th and 20th Century Europe* (New York, 1980), 17–44. For a remarkably original study of the development of the modern French state, see P. Rosanvallon, *L'Etat en France de 1789 à nos jours* (1990).

2. Recent studies of the Napoleonic retreat from revolutionary liberalism and deregulation in other areas include C. Hesse, *Publishing and Cultural Politics in Revolutionary Paris, 1789–1810* (Berkeley, 1991), ch. 6; J. Munson, "Businessmen, Business Conduct, and the Civic Organization of Commercial Life Under the Directory and Napoleon" (Ph.D. dissertation, Columbia University, 1992); and A. Potofsky, "The Builders of Modern Paris: The Organization of Labor from Turgot to Napoleon" (Ph.D. dissertation, Columbia University, 1993), ch. 6.

3. This view is developed in Furet and Ozouf, eds., *A Critical Dictionary of the French Revolution*. For an assessment, see I. Woloch, "On the Latent Illiberalism of the French Revolution," *AHR*, XCV (December 1990), 1452–70.

INDEX